RISK MANAGEMENT IN BANKING

Risk Management in Banking

Joël Bessis

JOHN WILEY & SONS, LTD

Other Wiley Editorial Offices

John Wiley & Sons, Inc., 605 Third Avenue,
New York, NY 10158-0012, USA

WILEY-VCH Verlag GmbH, Pappelallee 3,
D-69469 Weinheim, Germany

John Wiley & Sons (Australia) Ltd, 33 Park Road, Milton,
Queensland 4064, Australia

John Wiley & Sons (Asia) Pte Ltd, 2 Clementi Loop #02-01,
Jin Xing Distripark, Singapore 129809

John Wiley & Sons (Canada) Ltd, 22 Worcester Road,
Rexdale, Ontario M9W 1L1, Canada

Library of Congress Cataloguing-in-Publication Data

Bessis, Joël.
    [Gestion des risques et gestion actif-passif des banques. English]
    Risk management in banking/Joël Bessis.—2nd ed.
       p. cm.
    Includes bibliographical references and index.
    ISBN 0-471-49977-3 (cloth)—ISBN 0-471-89336-6 (pbk.)
       1. Bank management. 2. Risk management. 3. Asset-liability management. I. Title.

HG1615 .B45713 2001
332.1'068'1—dc21
                                                                                    2001045562

British Library Cataloguing in Publication Data

A catalogue record for this book is available from the British Library

ISBN 0-471-49977-3   (Cloth)
ISBN 0-471-89336-6 (Paper)

Typeset in 10/12pt Times Roman by Laserwords Private Limited, Chennai, India.
Printed and bound in Great Britain by TJ International Ltd, Padstow, England.
This book is printed on acid-free paper responsibly manufactured from sustainable forestation, for which at
least two trees are planted for each one used for paper production.

Contents

Introduction

Risk management in banking designates the entire set of risk management processes and models allowing banks to implement risk-based policies and practices. They cover all techniques and management tools required for measuring, monitoring and controlling risks. The spectrum of models and processes extends to all risks: credit risk, market risk, interest rate risk, liquidity risk and operational risk, to mention only major areas. Broadly speaking, risk designates any uncertainty that might trigger losses. Risk-based policies and practices have a common goal: enhancing the risk–return profile of the bank portfolio. The innovation in this area is the gradual extension of new quantified risk measures to all categories of risks, providing new views on risks, in addition to qualitative indicators of risks.

Current risks are tomorrow's potential losses. Still, they are not as visible as tangible revenues and costs are. Risk measurement is a conceptual and a practical challenge, which probably explains why risk management suffered from a lack of credible measures. The recent period has seen the emergence of a number of models and of 'risk management tools' for quantifying and monitoring risks. Such tools enhance considerably the views on risks and provide the ability to control them. This book essentially presents the risk management 'toolbox', focusing on the underlying concepts and models, plus their practical implementation.

The move towards risk-based practices accelerated in recent years and now extends to the entire banking industry. The basic underlying reasons are: banks have major incentives to move rapidly in that direction; regulations developed guidelines for risk measurement and for defining risk-based capital (equity); the risk management 'toolbox' of models enriched considerably, for all types of risks, providing tools making risk measures instrumental and their integration into bank processes feasible.

THE RATIONALE FOR RISK-BASED PRACTICES

Why are visibility and sensitivity to risks so important for bank managemen because banks are 'risk machines': they take risks, they transform them, and them in banking products and services. Risk-based practices designate those practices using quantified risk measures. Their scope evidently extends to risk-taking decisions, under an 'ex ante' perspective, and risk monitoring, under an 'ex post' perspective, once risk decisions are made. There are powerful motives to implement risk-based practices: to provide a balanced view of risk and return from a management point of view; to develop competitive advantages, to comply with increasingly stringent regulations.

A representative example of 'new' risk-based practices is the implementation of risk-adjusted performance measures. In the financial universe, risk and return are two sides of the same coin. It is easy to lend and to obtain attractive revenues from risky borrowers. The price to pay is a risk that is higher than the prudent bank's risk. The prudent bank limits risks and, therefore, both future losses and expected revenues, by restricting business volume and screening out risky borrowers. The prudent bank avoids losses but it might suffer from lower market share and lower revenues. However, after a while, the risk-taker might find out that higher losses materialize, and obtain an ex post performance lower than the prudent lender performance. Who performs best? Unless assigning some measure of risk to income, it is impossible to compare policies driven by different risk appetites. Comparing performances without risk adjustment is like comparing apples and oranges. The rationale of risk adjustment is in making comparable different performances attached to different risk levels, and in general making comparable the risk–return profiles of transactions and portfolios.

Under a competitive perspective, screening borrowers and differentiating the prices accordingly, given the borrowers' standing and their contributions to the bank's portfolio risk–return profile, are key issues. Not doing so results in adverse economics for banks. Banks who do not differentiate risks lend to borrowers rejected by banks who better screen and differentiate risks. By overpricing good risks, they discourage good borrowers. By underpricing risks to risky customers, they attract them. By discouraging the relatively good ones and attracting the relatively bad ones, the less advanced banks face the risk of becoming riskier and poorer than banks adopting sound risk-based practices at an earlier stage. Those banking institutions that actively manage their risks have a competitive advantage. They take risks more consciously, they anticipate adverse changes, they protect themselves from unexpected events and they gain the expertise to price risks. The competitors who lack such abilities may gain business in the short-term. Nevertheless, they will lose ground with time, when those risks materialize into losses.

Under a management perspective, without a balanced view of expected return and risk, banks have a 'myopic' view of the consequences of their business policies in terms of future losses, because it is easier to measure income than to capture the underlying risks. Even though risks remain a critical factor to all banks, they suffer from the limitations of traditional risk indicators. The underlying major issue is to assign a value to risks in order to make them commensurable with income and fully address the risk–return trade-off.

Regulation guidelines and requirements have become more stringent on the development of risk measures. This single motive suffices for developing quantified risk-based practices. However, it is not the only incentive for structuring the risk management tools and processes. The above motivations inspired some banks who became pioneers in this field many years before the regulations set up guidelines that led the entire industry towards more 'risk-sensitive' practices. Both motivations and regulations make risk measurement a core building block of valuable risk-based practices. However, both face the same highly challenging risk measuring issue.

RISK QUANTIFICATION IS A MAJOR CHALLENGE

Since risks are so important in banking, it is surprising that risk quantification remained limited until recently. Quantitative finance addresses extensively risk in the capital markets. However, the extension to the various risks of financial institutions remained a challenge for multiple reasons. Risks are less tangible and visible than income. Academic models provided foundations for risk modelling, but did not provide instrumental tools helping decision-makers. Indeed, a large fraction of this book addresses the gap between conceptual models and banking risk management issues. Moreover, the regulators' focus on risks is still relatively recent. It dates from the early stages of the reregulation phase, when the Cooke ratio imposed a charge in terms of capital for any credit risk exposure. Risk-based practices suffered from real challenges: simple solutions do not help; risk measures require models; models not instrumental; quantitative finance aimed at financial markets more than at financial institutions. For such reasons, the prerequisites for making instrumental risk quantifications remained out of reach.

Visibility on Losses is Not Visibility on Risks

Risks remain intangible and invisible until they materialize into losses. Simple solutions do not really help to capture risks. For instance, a credit risk exposure from a loan is not the risk. The risk depends on the likelihood of losses and the magnitude of recoveries in addition to the size of the amount at risk. Observing and recording losses and their frequencies could help. Unfortunately, loss histories are insufficient. It is not simple to link observable losses and earning declines with specific sources of risks. Tracking credit losses does not tell whether they result from inadequate limits, underestimating credit risk, inadequate guarantees, or excessive risk concentration. Recording the fluctuations of the interest income is easy, but tracing back such changes to interest rates is less obvious. Without links to instrumental risk controls, earning and loss histories are of limited interest because they do not help in taking forward looking corrective actions. Visibility on losses is not visibility on risks.

Tracking Risks for Management Purposes Requires Models

Tracking risks for management purposes requires models for better capturing risks and relating them to instrumental controls. Intuitively, the only way to quantify invisible risks is to model them. Moreover, multiple risk indicators are not substitutes for quantified measures. Surveillance of risk typically includes such various items as exposure size, watch lists for credit risk, or value changes triggered by market movements for market instruments. These indicators capture the multiple dimensions of risk, but they do not add them up into a quantified measure. Finally, missing links between future losses from current risks and risk drivers, which are instrumental for controlling risk, make it unfeasible to timely monitor risks. The contribution of models addresses such issues. They provide quantified measures of risk or, in other words, they value the risk of banks. Moreover, they do so in a way that allows tracing back risks to management controls over risk exposures of financial institutions. Without such links, risk measures would 'float in the air', without providing management tools.

Financial Markets versus Financial Institutions

The abundance of models in quantitative finance did not address the issues that financial institutions face until recently, except in certain specific areas such as asset portfolio management. They undermined the foundations of risk management, without bridging the gap between models and the needs of financial institutions.

Quantitative finance became a huge field that took off long ago, with plenty of pioneering contributions, many of them making their authors Nobel Prize winners. In the market place, quantification is 'natural' because of the continuous observation of prices and market parameters (interest rates, equity indexes, etc.). For interest rate risk, modelling the term structure of interest rates is a classical field in market finance. The pioneering work of Sharpe linked stock prices to equity risk in the stock market. The Black–Scholes option model is the foundation for pricing derivative instruments, options and futures, which today are standard instruments for managing risks. The scientific literature also addressed credit risk a long time ago. The major contribution of Robert Merton on modelling default within an option framework, a pillar of current credit risk modelling, dates from 1974.

These contributions fostered major innovations, from pricing market instruments and derivatives (options) that serve for investing and hedging risks, to defining benchmarks and guidelines for the portfolios management of market instruments (stocks and bonds). They also helped financial institutions to develop their business through ever-changing product innovations. Innovation made it feasible to customize products for matching investors' needs with specific risk–return bundles. It also allowed both financial and corporate entities to hedge their risks with derivatives. The need for investors to take exposures and, for those taking exposures, to hedge them provided business for both risk-takers and risk-hedgers. However, these developments fell short of directly addressing the basic prerequisites of a risk management system in financial institutions.

Prerequisites for Risk Management in Financial Institutions

The basic prerequisites for deploying risk management in banks are:

- Risks measuring and valuation.
- Tracing risks back to risk drivers under the management control.

Jumping to market instruments for managing risks without prior knowledge of exposures to the various risks is evidently meaningless unless we know the magnitude of the risks to keep under control, and what they actually mean in terms of potential value lost. The risk valuation issue is not simple. It is much easier to address in the market universe.

However, interest rate risk requires other management models and tools. All banking business lines generate exposures to interest rate risks. However, linking interest income and rates requires modelling the balance sheet behaviour. Since the balance sheet generates both interest revenues and interest costs, they offset each other to a certain extent, depending on matches and mismatches between sizes of assets and liabilities and interest rate references. Capturing the extent of offsetting effects between assets and liabilities also requires dedicated models.

Credit risk remained a challenge until recently, even though it is the oldest of all banking risks. Bank practices rely on traditional indicators, such as credit risk exposures measured by outstanding balances of loans at risk with borrowers, or amounts at risk, and internal ratings measuring the 'quality' of risk. Banking institutions have always monitored credit risk actively, through a number of systems such as limits, delegations, internal ratings and watch lists. Ratings agencies monitor credit risk of public debt issues. However, credit risk assessment remained judgmental, a characteristic of the 'credit culture', focusing on 'fundamentals': all qualitative variables that drive the credit worthiness of a borrower. The 'fundamental' view on credit risk still prevails, and it will obviously remain relevant.

Credit risk benefits from diversification effects that limit the size of credit losses of a portfolio. Credit risk focus is more on transactions. When moving to the global portfolio view, we know that a large fraction of the risk of individual transactions is diversified away. A very simple question is: By how much? This question remained unanswered until portfolio models, specifically designed for that purpose, emerged in the nineties. It is easy to understand why. Credit risk is largely invisible. The simultaneous default of two large corporate firms, for whom the likelihood of default is small, is probably an unobservable event. Still, this is the issue underlying credit risk diversification. Because of the scarcity of data available, the diversification issue for credit risk remained beyond reach until new modelling techniques appeared. Portfolio models, which appeared only in the nineties, turned around the difficulty by modelling the likelihood of modelled defaults, rather than actual defaults.

This is where modelling risks contributes. It pushes further away the frontier between measurable risks and invisible–intangible risks and, moreover, it links risks to the sources of uncertainty that generate them.

PHASES OF DEVELOPMENT OF THE REGULATORY GUIDELINES

Banks have plenty of motives for developing risk-based practices and risk models. In addition, regulators made this development a major priority for the banking industry, because they focus on 'systemic risk', the risk of the entire banking industry made up of financial institutions whose fates are intertwined by the density of relationships within the financial system.

The risk environment has changed drastically. Banking failures have been numerous in the past. In recent periods their number has tended to decrease in most, although not all, of the Organization for Economic Coordination and Development (OECD) countries, but they became spectacular. Banking failures make risks material and convey the impression that the banking industry is never far away from major problems. Mutual lending–borrowing and trading create strong interdependencies between banks. An individual failure of a large bank might trigger the 'contagion' effect, through which other banks suffer unsustainable losses and eventually fail. From an industry perspective, 'systemic risk', the risk of a collapse of the entire industry because of dense mutual relations, is always in the background. Regulators have been very active in promoting pre-emptive policies for avoiding individual bank failures and for helping the industry absorb the shock of failures when they happen. To achieve these results, regulators have totally renovated the regulatory framework. They promoted and enforced new guidelines for measuring and controlling the risks of individual players.

Originally, regulations were traditional conservative rules, requiring 'prudence' from each player. The regulatory scheme was passive and tended to differentiate prudent rules for each major banking business line. Differentiated regulations segmented the market and limited competition because some players could do what others could not. Obvious examples of segmentation of the banking industry were commercial versus investment banking, or commercial banks versus savings institutions. Innovation made rules obsolete, because players found ways to bypass them and to compete directly with other segments of the banking industry. Obsolete barriers between the business lines of banks, plus failures, triggered a gradual deregulation wave, allowing players to move from their original business field to the entire spectrum of business lines of the financial industry. The corollary of deregulation is an increased competition between unequally experienced players, and the implication is increased risks. Failures followed, making the need for reregulation obvious. Reregulation gave birth to the current regulatory scheme, still evolving with new guidelines, the latest being the New Basel Accord of January 2001.

Under the new regulatory scheme, initiated with the Cooke ratio in 1988, 'risk-based capital' or, equivalently, 'capital adequacy' is a central concept. The philosophy of 'capital adequacy' is that capital should be capable of sustaining the future losses arising from current risks. Such a sound and simple principle is hardly debatable. The philosophy provides an elegant and simple solution to the difficult issue of setting up a 'pre-emptive', 'ex ante' regulatory policy. By contrast, older regulatory policies focused more on corrective actions, or 'after-the-fact' actions, once banks failed. Such corrective actions remain necessary. They were prompt when spectacular failures took place in the financial industry (LTCM, Baring Brothers). Nevertheless, avoiding 'contagion' when bank failures occur is not a substitute for pre-emptive actions aimed at avoiding them.

The practicality of doing so remains subject to adequate modelling. The trend towards more internal and external assessment on risks and returns emerged and took momentum in several areas. Through successive accords, regulators promoted the building up of information on all inputs necessary for risk quantification. Accounting standards evolved as well. The 'fair value' concept gained ground, raising hot debates on what is the 'right' value of bank assets and how to accrue earnings in traditional commercial banking activities. It implies that a loan providing a return not in line with its risk and cost of funding should appear at lower than face value.

The last New Basel Accord promotes the 'three pillars' foundation of supervision: new capital requirements for credit risk and operational risks; supervisory processes; disclosure of risk information by banks. Together, the three pillars allow external supervisors to audit the quality of the information, a basic condition for assessing the quality and reliability of risk measures in order to gain more autonomy in the assessment of capital requirements. Regulatory requirements for market, credit and operational risk, plus the closer supervision of interest rate risk, pave the way for a comprehensive modelling of banking risks, and a tight integration with risk management processes, leading to bank-wide risk management across all business lines and all major risks.

FROM RISK MODELS TO RISK MANAGEMENT

Risk models have two major contributions: measuring risks and relating these measures to management controls over risks. Banking risk models address both issues by embedding the specifics of each major risk. As a direct consequence, there is a wide spectrum of modelling building blocks, differing across and within risks. They share the risk-based capital and the 'Value at Risk' (VaR) concepts that are the basic foundations of the new views on risk modelling, risk controlling and risk regulations. Risk management requires an entire set of models and tools for linking risk management (business) issues with financial views on risks and profitability. Together, they make up the risk management toolbox, which provides the necessary inputs that feed and enrich the risk process, to finally close the gap between models and management processes.

Risk Models and Risks

Managing the banking exposure to interest rate risk and trading interest rate risk are different businesses. Both commercial activities and trading activities use up liquidity that financial institutions need to fund in the market. Risk management, in this case, relates to the structural posture that banks take because of asset and liability mismatches of volumes, maturity and interest rate references. Asset–Liability Management (ALM) is in charge of managing this exposure. ALM models developed gradually until they became standard references for managing the liquidity and interest rate risk of the banking portfolio.

For market risk, there is a large overlap between modelling market prices and measuring market risk exposures of financial institutions. This overlap covers most of the needs, except one: modelling the potential losses from trading activities. Market risk models appeared soon after the Basel guidelines started to address the issues of market risk. They appeared sufficiently reliable to allow internal usage by banks, under supervision of regulators, for defining their capital requirements.

For credit risk, the foundations exist for deploying instrumental tools fitting banks' requirements and, potentially, regulators' requirements. Scarce information on credit events remains a major obstacle. Nevertheless, the need for quantification increased over time, necessitating measuring the size of risk, the likelihood of losses, the magnitude of losses under default and the magnitude of diversification within banks' portfolios. Modelling the qualitative assessment of risk based on the fundamentals of borrowers has a long track record of statistical research, which rebounds today because of the regulators' emphasis on extending the credit risk data. Since the early nineties, portfolio models proposed measures of credit risk diversification within portfolios, offering new paths for quantifying risks and defining the capital capable of sustaining the various levels of portfolio losses.

Whether the banks should go along this path, however, is no longer a question since the New Basel Accord of January 2001 set up guidelines for credit risk-sensitive measures, therefore preparing the foundations for the full-blown modelling of the credit risk of banks' portfolios. Other major risks appeared when progressing in the knowledge of risks. Operational risk became a major priority, since January 2001, when the regulatory authorities formally announced the need to charge bank capital against this risk.

Capital and VaR

It has become impossible to discuss risk models without referring to economic capital and VaR. The 'capital adequacy' principle states that the bank's capital should match risks. Since capital is the most scarce and costly resource, the focus of risk monitoring and risk measurement follows. The central role of risk-based capital in regulations is a major incentive to the development of new tools and management techniques.

Undoubtedly a most important innovation of recent years in terms of the modelling 'toolbox' is the VaR concept for assessing capital requirements. The VaR concept is a foundation of risk-based capital or, equivalently, 'economic capital'. The VaR methodology aims at valuing potential losses resulting from current risks and relies on simple facts and principles. VaR recognizes that the loss over a portfolio of transactions could extend to the entire portfolio, but this is an event that has a zero probability given the effective portfolio diversification of banks. Therefore, measuring potential losses requires some rule for defining their magnitude for a diversified portfolio. VaR is the upper bound of losses that should not be exceeded in more than a small fraction of all future outcomes. Management and regulators define benchmarks for this small preset fraction, called the 'confidence level', measuring the appetite for risk of banks. Economic capital is VaR-based and crystallizes the quantified present value of potential future losses for making sure that banks have enough capital to sustain worst-case losses. Such risk valuation potentially extends to all main risks.

Regulators made the concept instrumental for VaR-based market risk models in 1996. Moreover, even though the New Accord of 2001 falls short of allowing usage of credit models for measuring credit risk capital, it ensures the development of reliable inputs for such models.

The Risk Management Toolbox

Risk-based practices require the deployment of multiple tools, or models, to meet the specifications of risk management within financial institutions. Risk models value risks and link them to their drivers and to the business universe. By performing these tasks, risk models contribute directly to risk processes. The goal of risk management is to enhance the risk–return profiles of transactions, of business lines' portfolios of transactions and of the entire bank's portfolio. Risk models provide these risk–return profiles. The risk management toolbox also addresses other major specifications. Since two risks of 1 add up to less than 2, unlike income and costs, we do not know how to divide a global risk into risk allocations for individual transactions, product families, market segments and business lines, unless we have some dedicated tools for performing this function. The Funds Transfer Pricing (FTP) system allocates income and the capital allocation system allocates risks. These tools provide a double link:

- The top-down/bottom-up link for risks and income.
- The transversal business-to-financial sphere linkage.

Without such links, between the financial and the business spheres and between global risks and individual transaction profiles, there would be no way to move back and forth from a business perspective to a financial perspective and along the chain from individual transactions to the entire bank's global portfolio.

Risk Management Processes

Risk management processes are evolving with the gradual emergence of new risk measures. Innovations relate to:

- The recognition of the need for quantification to develop risk-based practices and meet risk-based capital requirements.
- The willingness of bankers to adopt a more proactive view on risks.
- The gradual development of regulator guidelines for imposing risk-based techniques, enhanced disclosures on risks and ensuring a sounder and safer level playing field for the financial system.
- The emergence of new techniques of managing risks (credit derivatives, new securitizations that off-load credit risk from the banks' balance sheets) serving to reshape the risk–return profile of banks.
- The emergence of new organizational processes for better integrating these advances, such as loan portfolio management.

Without risk models, such innovations would remain limited. By valuing risks, models contribute to a more balanced view of income and risks and to a better control of risk drivers, upstream, before they materialize into losses. By linking the business and the risk views, the risk management 'toolbox' makes models instrumental for management. By feeding risk processes with adequate risk–return measures, they contribute to enriching them and leveraging them to new levels.

Figure 1 shows how models contribute to the 'vertical' top-down and bottom-up processes, and how they contribute as well to the 'horizontal' links between the risk and return views of the business dimensions (transactions, markets and products, business lines).

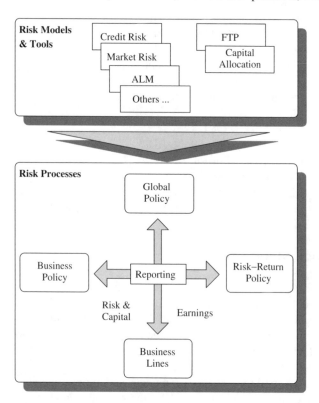

FIGURE I   Comprehensive and consistent set of models for bank-wide risk management

THE STRUCTURE OF THE BOOK

The structure of the book divides each topic into single modular pieces addressing the various issues above. The first section develops general issues, focusing on risks, risk measuring and risk management processes. The next major section addresses sequentially ALM, market risk and credit risk.

Book Outline

The structure of the book is in 17 sections, each divided into several chapters. This structure provides a very distinct division across topics, each chapter dedicated to a major single topic. The benefit is that it is possible to move across chapters without necessarily following a sequential process throughout the book. The drawback is that only a few chapters provide an overview of interrelated topics. These chapters provide a synthesis of subsequent specific topics, allowing the reader to get both a summary and an overview of a series of interrelated topics.

Section 1.	Banking Risks
Section 2.	Risk Regulations
Section 3.	Risk Management Processes
Section 4.	Risk Models
Section 5.	Asset–Liability Management
Section 6.	Asset–Liability Management Models
Section 7.	Options and Convexity Risk in Banking
Section 8.	Mark-to-Market Management in Banking
Section 9.	Funds Transfer Pricing
Section 10.	Portfolio Analysis: Correlations
Section 11.	Market Risk
Section 12.	Credit Risk Models
Section 13.	Credit Risk: 'Standalone Risk'
Section 14.	Credit Risk: 'Portfolio Risk'
Section 15.	Capital Allocation
Section 16.	Risk-adjusted Performance
Section 17.	Portfolio and Capital Management (Credit Risk)

Building Block Structure

The structure of the book follows from several choices. The starting point is a wide array of risk models and tools that complement each other and use sometimes similar, sometimes different techniques for achieving the same goals. This raises major structuring issues for ensuring a consistent coverage of the risk management toolbox. The book relies on a building block structure shared by models; some of them extending across many blocks, some belonging to one major block.

The structuring by building blocks of models and tools remedies the drawbacks of a sequential presentation of industry models; these bundle modelling techniques within each building block according to the model designers' assembling choices. By contrast, a building block structure lists issues separately, and allows us to discuss explicitly the various modelling options. To facilitate the understanding of vendors' models, some chapters provide an overview of all existing models, while detailed presentations provide an overview of all techniques applying to a single basic building block.

Moreover, since model differentiation across risks is strong, there is a need to organize the structure by nature of risk. The sections of the book dealing directly with risk modelling cross-tabulate the main risks with the main building blocks of models. The main risks are interest rate risk, market risk and credit risk. The basic structure, within each risk, addresses four major modules as shown in Figure 2.

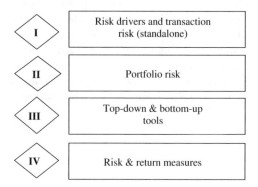

FIGURE 2   The building block structure of risk models

The basic blocks, I and II, are dedicated by source of risk. The two other blocks, III and IV, are transversal to all risks. The structure of the book follows from these principles.

Focus

The focus is on risk management issues for financial institutions rather than risk modelling applied to financial markets. There is an abundant literature on financial markets and financial derivatives. A basic understanding of what derivatives achieve in terms of hedging or structuring transactions is a prerequisite. However, sections on instruments are limited to the essentials of what hedging instruments are and their applications. Readers can obtain details on derivatives and pricing from other sources in the abundant literature.

We found that textbooks rarely address risk management in banking and in financial institutions in a comprehensive manner. Some focus on the technical aspects. Others focus on pure implementation issues to the detriment of technical substance. In other cases, the scope is unbalanced, with plenty of details on some risks (market risk notably) and fewer on others. We have tried to maintain a balance across the main risks without sacrificing scope.

The text focuses on the essential concepts underlying the risk analytics of existing models. It does detail the analytics without attempting to provide a comprehensive coverage of each existing model. This results in a more balanced view of all techniques for modelling banking risk. In addition, model vendors' documentation is available directly from sites dedicated to risk management modelling. There is simply no need to replicate such documents. When developing the analytics, we considered that providing a universal framework, allowing the contrast of various techniques based on their essential characteristics, was of greater help than replicating public documentation. Accordingly, we skipped some details available elsewhere and located some technicalities in appendices. However, readers will find the essentials, the basics for understanding the technicalities, and the examples for grasping their practical value added. In addition, the text develops many numerical examples, while restricting the analytics to the essential ingredients. A first motive is that simple examples help illustrate the essentials better than a detailed description. Of course, simple examples are no substitute for full-blown models.

The text is almost self-contained. It details the prerequisites for understanding full-blown models. It summarizes the technicalities of full-blown models and it substitutes examples and applications for further details. Still, it gathers enough substance to provide an analytical framework, developed sufficiently to make it easy to grasp details not expanded here and map them to the major building blocks of risk modelling.

Finally, there is a balance to strike between technicalities and applications. The goal of risk management is to use risk models and tools for instrumental purposes, for developing risk-based practices and enriching risk processes. Such an instrumental orientation strongly inspired this text.

*   *   *

The first edition of this book presented details on ALM and introduced major advances in market risk and credit risk modelling. This second edition expands considerably on credit risk and market risk models. In addition, it does so within a unified framework for capturing all major risks and deploying bank-wide risk management tools and processes. Accordingly, the volume has roughly doubled in size. This is illustrative of the fast and continuous development of the field of risk management in financial institutions.

SECTION I

Banking Risks

1

Banking Business Lines

The banking industry has a wide array of business lines. Risk management practices and techniques vary significantly between the main poles, such as retail banking, investment banking and trading, and within the main poles, between business lines. The differences across business lines appear so important, say between retail banking and trading for example, that considering using the same concepts and techniques for risk management purposes could appear hopeless. There is, indeed, a differentiation, but risk management tools, borrowing from the same core techniques, apply across the entire spectrum of banking activities generating financial risks. However, risks and risk management differ across business lines. This first chapter provides an overview of banking activities. It describes the main business poles, and within each pole the business lines. Regulations make a clear distinction between commercial banking and trading activities, with the common segmentation between 'banking book' and 'trading book'. In fact, there are major distinctions within business lines of lending activities, which extend from retail banking to specialized finance.

This chapter provides an overview of the banking business lines and of the essentials of financial statements.

BUSINESS POLES IN THE BANKING INDUSTRY

The banking industry has a wide array of business lines. Figure 1.1 maps these activities, grouping them into main poles: traditional commercial banking; investment banking, with specialized transactions; trading. Poles subdivide into various business lines.

Management practices are very different across and within the main poles. Retail banking tends to be mass oriented and 'industrial', because of the large number of transactions. Lending to individuals relies more on statistical techniques. Management reporting on such large numbers of transactions focuses on large subsets of transactions.

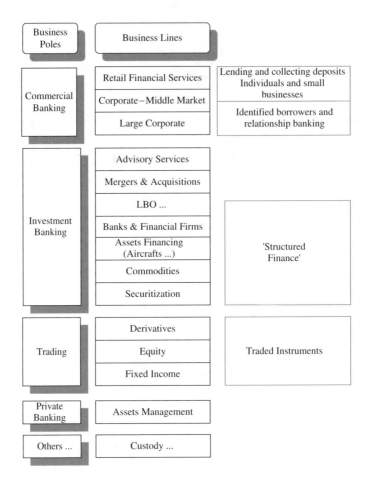

FIGURE 1.1   Breaking down the bank portfolio along organizational dimensions

Criteria for grouping the transactions include date of origination, type of customer, product family (consumer loans, credit cards, leasing).

For medium and large corporate borrowers, individual decisions require more judgment because mechanical rules are not sufficient to assess the actual credit standing of a corporation. For the middle market segment to large corporate businesses, 'relationship banking' prevails. The relation is stable, based on mutual confidence, and generates multiple services. Risk decisions necessitate individual evaluation of transactions. Obligors' reviews are periodical.

Investment banking is the domain of large transactions customized to the needs of big corporates or financial institutions. 'Specialized finance' extends from specific fields with standard practices, such as export and commodities financing, to 'structured financing', implying specific structuring and customization for making large and risky transactions feasible, such as project finance or corporate acquisitions. 'Structuring' designates the assembling of financial products and derivatives, plus contractual clauses for monitoring risk ('covenants'). Without such risk mitigants, transactions would not be feasible. This domain overlaps with traditional 'merchant' banking and market business lines. Trading involves traditional proprietary trading and trading for third parties. In the second case, traders interact with customers and other banking business units to bundle customized products for large borrowers, including 'professionals' of the finance industry, banks, insurance, brokers and funds. Other activities do not generate directly traditional banking risks, such as private banking, or asset management and advisory services. However, they generate other risks, such as operational risk, similarly to other business lines, as defined in the next chapter.

The view prevailing in this book is that all main business lines share the common goals of risk–expected return enhancement, which also drives the management of global bank portfolios. Therefore, it is preferable to differentiate business lines beyond the traditional distinctions between the banking portfolio and the trading portfolio. The matrix shown in Figure 1.2 is a convenient representation of all major lines across which practices differ. Subsequent chapters differentiate, whenever necessary, risk and profitability across the cells of the matrix, cross-tabulating main product lines and main market segments. Banking business lines differ depending on the specific organizations of banks and on their core businesses. Depending on the degree of specialization, along with geographical subdivisions, they may or may not combine one or several market segments and product families. Nevertheless, these two dimensions remain the basic foundations for differentiating risk management practices and designing 'risk models'.

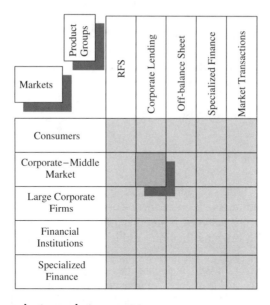

FIGURE 1.2 Main product–market segments
RFS refers to 'Retail Financial Services'.
LBO refers to 'Leveraged Buy-Out', a transaction allowing a major fraction of the equity of a company to be acquired using a significant debt (leverage).
Specialized finance refers to structured finance, project finance, LBO or assets financing.

Product lines vary within the above broad groups. For instance, standard lending transactions include overnight loans, short-term loans (less than 1 year), revolving facilities, term loans, committed lines of credit, or large corporate general loans. Retail financial services cover all lending activities, from credit card and consumer loans to mortgage loans. Off-balance sheet transactions are guarantees and backup lines of credit providing significant revenues to banks. Specialized finance includes project finance, commodities financing, asset financing (from real estate to aircraft) and trade financing. Market transactions cover all basic compartments, fixed income, equity and foreign exchange trading, including derivatives from standard swaps and options to exotic and customized products. Major market segments appear explicitly in the matrix. They also subdivide. Financial institutions include banks as well as insurance or brokers. Specialized finance includes various fields, including structured finance. The greyed cell represents a basic market–product couple. Risk management involves risk and expected return measuring, reporting and management for such transactions, for the bank portfolio as a whole and for such basic couples. The next section reverts to the basic distinction between banking book and trading book, which is essentially product-driven.

THE BANKING AND THE TRADING BOOKS

The 'banking book' groups and records all commercial banking activities. It includes all lending and borrowing, usually both for traditional commercial activities, and overlaps with investment banking operations. The 'trading book' groups all market transactions tradable in the market. The major difference between these two segments is that the 'buy and hold' philosophy prevails for the banking book, contrasting with the trading philosophy of capital markets. Accounting rules differ for the banking portfolio and the trading portfolio. Accounting rules use accrual accounting of revenues and costs, and rely on book values for assets and liabilities. Trading relies on market values (mark-to-market) of transactions and Profit and Loss (P&L), which are variations of the mark-to-market value of transactions between two dates. The rationale for separating these 'portfolios' results from such major characteristics.

The Banking Book

The banking portfolio follows traditional accounting rules of accrued interest income and costs. Customers are mainly non-financial corporations or individuals, although inter-banking transactions occur between professional financial institutions.

The banking portfolio generates liquidity and interest rate risks. All assets and liabilities generate accrued revenues and costs, of which a large fraction is interest rate-driven. Any maturity mismatch between assets and liabilities results in excesses or deficits of funds. Mismatch also exists between interest references, 'fixed' or 'variable, and results from customers' demand and the bank's business policy. In general, both mismatches exist in the 'banking book' balance sheet. For instance, there are excess funds when collection of deposits and savings is important, or a deficit of funds whenever the lending activity uses up more resources than the deposits from customers. Financial transactions (on the capital markets) serve to manage such mismatches between commercial assets and liabilities through either investment of excess funds or long-term debt by banks.

Asset–Liability Management (ALM) applies to the banking portfolio and focuses on interest rate and liquidity risks. The asset side of the banking portfolio also generates credit risk. The liability side contributes to interest rate risk, but does not generate credit risk, since the lenders or depositors are at risk with the bank. There is no market risk for the banking book.

The Trading Portfolio

The market transactions are not subject to the same management rules. The turnover of tradable positions is faster than that of the banking portfolio. Earnings are P&L equal to changes of the mark-to-market values of traded instruments.

Customers include corporations (corporate counterparties) or other financial players belonging to the banking industry (professional counterparties). The market portfolio generates market risk, defined broadly as the risk of adverse changes in market values over a liquidation period. It is also subject to market liquidity risk, the risk that the volume of transactions narrows so much that trades trigger price movements. The trading portfolio extends across geographical borders, just as capital markets do, whereas traditional commercial banking is more 'local'. Many market transactions use non-tradable instruments, or derivatives such as swaps and options traded over-the-counter. Such transactions might have a very long maturity. They trigger credit risk, the risk of a loss if the counterparty fails.

Off-balance Sheet Transactions

Off-balance sheet transactions are contingencies given and received. For banking transactions, contingencies include guarantees given to customers or to third parties, committed credit lines not yet drawn by customers, or backup lines of credit. Those are contractual commitments, which customers use at their initiative. A guarantee is the commitment of the bank to fulfil the obligations of the customer, contingent on some event such as failure to face payment obligations. For received contingencies, the beneficiary is the bank.

'Given contingencies' generate revenues, as either upfront and/or periodic fees, or interest spreads calculated as percentages of outstanding balances. They do not generate 'immediate' exposures since there is no outflow of funds at origination, but they do trigger credit risk because of the possible future usage of contingencies given. The outflows occur conditionally on what happens to the counterparty. If a borrower draws on a credit line previously unused, the resulting loan moves up on the balance sheet. 'Off-balance sheet' lines turn into 'on-balance sheet' exposures when exercised.

Derivatives are 'off-balance sheet' market transactions. They include swaps, futures contracts, foreign exchange contracts and options. As other contingencies, they are obligations to make contractual payments conditional upon occurrence of a specified event. Received contingencies create symmetrical obligations for counterparties who sold them to the bank.

BANKS' FINANCIAL STATEMENTS

There are several ways of grouping transactions. The balance sheet provides a snapshot view of all assets and liabilities at a given date. The income statement summarizes all revenues and costs to determine the income of a period.

Balance Sheet

In a simplified view (Table 1.1), the balance sheet includes four basic levels, in addition to the off-balance sheet, which divide it horizontally:

- Treasury and banking transactions.
- Intermediation (lending and collecting deposits).
- Financial assets (trading portfolio).
- Long-term assets and liabilities: fixed assets, investments in subsidiaries and equity plus long-term debt.

TABLE 1.1   Simplified balance sheet

Assets	Equity and liabilities
Cash	Short-term debt
Lending	Deposits
Financial assets	Financial assets
Fixed assets	Long-term debt
	Equity
Off-balance sheet (contingencies received)	Off-balance sheet (contingencies given)

The relative weights of the major compartments vary from one institution to another, depending on their core businesses. Equity is typically low in all banks' balance sheets. Lending and deposits are traditionally large in retail and commercial banking. Investment banking, including both specialized finance and trading, typically funds operations in the market. In European banks, 'universal banking' allows banking institutions to operate over the entire spectrum of business lines, contrasting with the separation between investment banking and commercial banking, which still prevails in the United States.

Income Statement and Valuation

The current national accounting standards use accrual measures of revenues and costs to determine the net income of the banking book. Under such standards, net income ignores any change of 'mark-to-market' value, except for securities traded in the market or considered as short-term holdings. International accounting standards progress towards 'fair value' accounting for the banking book, and notably for transactions hedging risk. Fair value is similar to mark-to-market[1], except that it extends to non-tradable assets such as loans.

There is a strong tendency towards generalizing the 'fair value' view of the balance sheet for all activities, which is subject to hot debates for the 'banking book'. Accounting standards are progressively evolving in that direction. The implications are major in terms of profitability, since gains and losses of the balance sheet 'value' between two

---

[1] See Chapter 8 for details on calculating 'mark-to-market' values on non-tradable transactions.

dates would count as profit and losses. A major driving force for looking at 'fair values' is the need to use risk-adjusted values in modelling risks. In what follows, because of the existing variations around the general concept of 'fair value', we designate such values equivalently as 'economic values', 'mark-to-market' or 'mark-to-model' values depending on the type of valuation technique used. Fair values have become so important, if only because of risk modelling, that we discuss them in detail in Chapter 8.

For the banking portfolio, the traditional accounting measures of earnings are contribution margins calculated at various levels of the income statement. They move from the 'interest income' of the bank, which is the difference between all interest revenues plus fees and all interest costs, down to net income. The total revenue cumulates the interest margin with all fees for the period. The interest income of commercial banking commonly serves as the main target for management policies of interest rate risk because it is entirely interest-driven. Another alternative target variable is the Net Present Value (NPV) of the balance sheet, measured as a Mark-to-Market (MTM) of assets minus that of liabilities. Commercial banks try to increase the fraction of revenues made up of fees for making the net income less interest rate-sensitive. Table 1.2 summarizes the main revenues and costs of the income statement.

TABLE 1.2 Income statement and earnings

Interest margin plus fees
Capital gains and losses
−Operating costs
=Operating income (EBTD)[a]
−Depreciation
−Provisions
−Tax
=Net income

[a]EBTD = Earnings Before Tax and Depreciation.

Provisions for loan losses deserve special attention. The provision policy should ideally be an indicator of the current credit risk of banking loans. However, provisions have to comply with accounting and fiscal rules and differ from economic provisions. Economic provisions are 'ex ante' provisions, rather than provisions resulting from the materialization of credit risk. They should anticipate the effective credit risk without the distortions due to legal and tax constraints. Economic provisioning is a debated topic, because unless new standards and rules emerge for implementation, it remains an internal risk management tool without impact on the income statement bottom line.

Performance Measures

Performance measures derive directly from the income statement. The ratio of net income to equity is the accounting Return On Equity (ROE). It often serves as a target profitability measure at the overall bank level. The accounting ROE ratio is not the market return on equity, which is a price return, or the ratio of the price variation between two dates of the bank's stock (ignoring dividends). Under some specific conditions[2], it might serve as a profitability benchmark. Both the ROE and the market return on equity should be in line with shareholders' expectations for a given level of risk of the bank's stock. A current order of magnitude for the target ROE is 15% after tax, or about 25% before tax. When considering banking transactions, the Return On Assets (ROA) is another measure of profitability for banking transactions. The most common calculation of ROA is the ratio of the current periodical income, interest income and current fees, divided by asset balance. The current ROA applies both to single individual transactions and to the total balance sheet.

The drawback of accounting ROE and ROA measures, and of the P&L of the trading portfolio, is that they do not include any risk adjustment. Hence, they are not comparable from one borrower to another, because their credit risk differs, from one trading transaction to another, and because the market risk varies across products. This drawback is the origin of the concept of risk-adjusted performance measures. This is an incentive for moving, at least in internal reports of risks and performances, to 'economic values', 'mark-to-market' or 'mark-to-model' values, because these are both risk- and revenue-adjusted[3].

---

[2] It can be shown that a target accounting ROE implies an identical value for the market return on the bank's equity under the theoretical condition that the Price–Earnings Ratio (PER) remains constant. See Chapter 53.

[3] See Chapter 8 to explain how mark-to-market values embed both risk and expected return.

2

Banking Risks

Risks are uncertainties resulting in adverse variations of profitability or in losses. In the banking universe, there are a large number of risks. Most are well known. However, there has been a significant extension of focus, from the traditional qualitative risk assessment towards the quantitative management of risks, due to both evolving risk practices and strong regulatory incentives. The different risks need careful definition to provide sound bases serving for quantitative measures of risk. As a result, risk definitions have gained precision over the years. The regulations, imposing capital charges against all risks, greatly helped the process. The underlying philosophy of capital requirement is to bring capital in line with risks. This philosophy implies modelling the value of risk. The foundation of such risk measures is in terms of potential losses. The capital charge is a quantitative value. Under regulatory treatment, it follows regulatory rules applying to all players. Under an economic view, it implies modelling potential losses from each source of risk, which turns out to be the 'economic' capital 'adequate' to risk. Most of the book explains how to assign economic values to risks. Therefore, the universal need to value risks, which are intangible and invisible, requires that risks be well-defined. Risk definitions serve as the starting point for both regulatory and economic treatments of risks.

This book focuses on three main risks: interest rate risk for the banking book; market risk for the trading book; credit risk. However, this chapter does provide a comprehensive overview of banking risks.

BANKING RISKS

Banking risks are defined as adverse impacts on profitability of several distinct sources of uncertainty (Figure 2.1). Risk measurement requires capturing the source of the uncertainty and the magnitude of its potential adverse effect on profitability. Profitability refers to both accounting and mark-to-market measures.

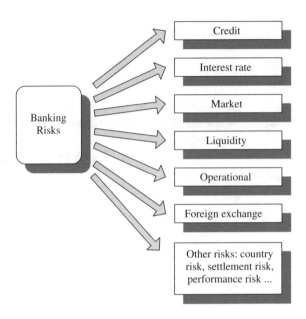

FIGURE 2.1   Main bank risks

This book focuses on financial risks, or risks related to the market movements or the economic changes of the environment. Market risk is relatively easy to quantify thanks to the large volume of price observations. Credit risk 'looked like' a 'commercial' risk because it is business-driven. Innovation changed this view. Since credit risk is a major risk, the regulators insisted on continuously improving its measurement in order to quantify the amount of capital that banks should hold. Credit risk and the principle of diversification are as old as banks are. It sounds like a paradox that major recent innovations focus on this old and well-known risk. Operational risk also attracts attention[1]. It covers all organizational malfunctioning, of which consequences can be highly important and, sometimes, fatal to an institution.

Following the regulators' focus on valuing risk as a capital charge, model designers developed risk models aimed at the quantification of potential losses arising from each source of risk. The central concept of such models is the well-known 'Value at Risk' (VaR). Briefly stated, a VaR is a potential loss due to a defined risk. The issue is how to define a potential loss, given that the loss can be as high as the current portfolio value. Of course, the probability of such an event is zero. In order to define the potential adverse deviation of value, or loss, a methodology is required to identify what could be a 'maximum' deviation. Under the VaR methodology, the worst-case loss is a 'maximum' bound not exceeded in more than a preset fraction (for instance 1%) of all possible states over a defined period. Models help to determine a market risk VaR and a credit risk VaR. The VaR concept also extends to other risks. Subsequent developments explain how to move from the following definitions of risk to VaR modelling and measuring.

---

[1] The New Basel Accord of January 2001 requires a capital charge against operational risk.

CREDIT RISK

Credit risk is the first of all risks in terms of importance. Default risk, a major source of loss, is the risk that customers default, meaning that they fail to comply with their obligations to service debt. Default triggers a total or partial loss of any amount lent to the counterparty. Credit risk is also the risk of a decline in the credit standing of an obligor of the issuer of a bond or stock. Such deterioration does not imply default, but it does imply that the probability of default increases. In the market universe, a deterioration of the credit standing of a borrower does materialize into a loss because it triggers an upward move of the required market yield to compensate the higher risk and triggers a value decline. 'Issuer' risk designates the obligors' credit risk, to make it distinct from the specific risk of a particular issue, among several of the same issuer, depending on the nature of the instrument and its credit mitigants (seniority level and guarantees). The view of credit risk differs for the banking portfolio and the trading portfolio.

Banking Portfolio

Credit risk is critical since the default of a small number of important customers can generate large losses, potentially leading to insolvency. There are various default events: delay in payment obligations; restructuring of debt obligations due to a major deterioration of the credit standing of the borrower; bankruptcies. Simple delinquencies, or payment delays, do not turn out as plain defaults, with a durable inability of lenders to face debt obligations. Many are resolved within a short period (say less than 3 months). Restructuring is very close to default because it results from the view that the borrower will not face payment obligations unless its funding structure changes. Plain defaults imply that the non-payment will be permanent. Bankruptcies, possibly liquidation of the firm or merging with an acquiring firm, are possible outcomes. They all trigger significant losses. Default means any situation other than a simple delinquency.

Credit risk is difficult to quantify on an 'ex ante' basis, since we need an assessment of the likelihood of a default event and of the recoveries under default, which are context-dependent[2]. In addition, banking portfolios benefit from diversification effects, which are much more difficult to capture because of the scarcity of data on interdependencies between default events of different borrowers are interdependent.

Trading Portfolio

Capital markets value the credit risk of issuers and borrowers in prices. Unlike loans, the credit risk of traded debts is also indicated by the agencies' ratings, assessing the quality of public debt issues, or through changes of the value of their stocks. Credit risk is also visible through credit spreads, the add-ons to the risk-free rate defining the required market risk yield on debts.

The capability of trading market assets mitigates the credit risk since there is no need to hold these securities until the deterioration of credit risk materializes into effective losses.

---

[2] Context refers to all factors influencing loss under default, such as the outstanding balance of debt at default, the existence of guarantees, or the policy of all stakeholders with respect to existing debt.

If the credit standing of the obligor declines, it is still possible to sell these instruments in the market at a lower value. The loss due to credit risk depends on the value of these instruments and their liquidity. If the default is unexpected, the loss is the difference between the pre- and post-default prices. The faculty of trading the assets limits the loss if sale occurs before default. The selling price depends on the market liquidity. Therefore, there is some interaction between credit risk and trading risk.

For over-the-counter instruments, such as derivatives (swaps and options), whose development has been spectacular in the recent period, sale is not readily feasible. The bank faces the risk of losing the value of such instruments when it is positive. Since this value varies constantly with the market parameters, credit risk changes with market movements during the entire residual life of the instrument. Credit risk and market risk interact because these values depend on the market moves.

Credit risk for traded instruments raises a number of conceptual and practical difficulties. What is the value subject to loss, or exposure, in future periods? Does the current price embed already the credit risk, since market prices normally anticipate future events, and to what extent? Will it be easy to sell these instruments when signs of deterioration get stronger, and at what discount from the current value since the market for such instruments might narrow when credit risk materializes? Will the bank hold these instruments longer than under normal conditions?

Measuring Credit Risk

Even though procedures for dealing with credit risk have existed since banks started lending, credit risk measurement raises several issues. The major credit risk components are exposure, likelihood of default, or of a deterioration of the credit standing, and the recoveries under default. Scarcity of data makes the assessment of these components a challenge.

Ratings are traditional measures of the credit quality of debts. Some major features of ratings systems are[3]:

- Ratings are ordinal or relative measures of risk rather than cardinal or absolute measures, such as default probability.
- External ratings are those of rating agencies, Moody's, Standard & Poor's (S&P) and Fitch, to name the global ones. They apply to debt issues rather than issuers because various debt issues from the same issuer have different risks depending on seniority level and guarantees. Detailed rating scales of agencies have 20 levels, ignoring the near default rating levels.
- By contrast, an issuer's rating characterizes only the default probability of the issuer.
- Banks use internal rating scales because most of their borrowers do not have publicly rated debt issues. Internal rating scales of banks are customized to banks' requirements, and usually characterize both borrower's risk and facility's risk.
- There are various types of ratings. Ratings characterize sovereign risk, the risk of country debt and the risk of the local currency. Ratings are also either short-term

---

[3] Chapters 35 and 36 detail further the specifications of rating systems.

or long-term. There are various types of country-related ratings: sovereign ratings of government sponsored borrowers; ratings of currencies; ratings of foreign currencies held locally; ratings of transfer risk, the risk of being unable to transfer cash out of the country.

- Because ratings are ordinal measures of credit risk, they are not sufficient to value credit risk.

Moreover, ratings apply only to individual debts of borrowers, and they do not address the bank's portfolio risk, which benefits from diversification effects. Portfolio models show that portfolio risk varies across banks depending on the number of borrowers, the discrepancies in size between exposures and the extent of diversification among types of borrowers, industries and countries. The portfolio credit risk is critical in terms of potential losses and, therefore, for finding out how much capital is required to absorb such losses.

Modelling default probability directly with credit risk models remained a major challenge, not addressed until recent years. A second challenge of credit risk measurement is capturing portfolio effects. Due to the scarcity of data in the case of credit risk, quantifying the diversification effect sounds like a formidable challenge. It requires assessing the joint likelihood of default for any pair of borrowers, which gets higher if their individual risks correlate. Given its importance for banks, it is not surprising that banks, regulators and model designers made a lot of effort to better identify the relevant inputs for valuing credit risk and model diversification effects with 'portfolio models'. Accordingly, a large fraction of this book addresses credit risk modelling.

COUNTRY AND PERFORMANCE RISKS

Credit risk is the risk of loss due to a deterioration of the credit standing of a borrower. Some risks are close to credit risk, but distinct, such as country risk and performance risk.

Country Risk

Country risk is, loosely speaking, the risk of a 'crisis' in a country. There are many risks related to local crises, including:

- Sovereign risk, which is the risk of default of sovereign issuers, such as central banks or government sponsored banks. The risk of default often refers to that of debt restructuring for countries.
- A deterioration of the economic conditions. This might lead to a deterioration of the credit standing of local obligors, beyond what it should be under normal conditions. Indeed, firms' default frequencies increase when economic conditions deteriorate.
- A deterioration of the value of the local foreign currency in terms of the bank's base currency.

- The impossibility of transferring funds from the country, either because there are legal restrictions imposed locally or because the currency is not convertible any more. Convertibility or transfer risks are common and restrictive definitions of country risks.
- A market crisis triggering large losses for those holding exposures in the local markets.

A common practice stipulates that country risk is a floor for the risk of a local borrower, or equivalently, that the country rating caps local borrowers' ratings. In general, country ratings serve as benchmarks for corporate and banking entities. The rationale is that, if transfers become impossible, the risk materializes for all corporates in the country. There are debates around such rules, since the intrinsic credit standing of a borrower is not necessarily lower than on that of the country.

Performance Risk

Performance risk exists when the transaction risk depends more on how the borrower performs for specific projects or operations than on its overall credit standing. Performance risk appears notably when dealing with commodities. As long as delivery of commodities occurs, what the borrower does has little importance. Performance risk is 'transactional' because it relates to a specific transaction. Moreover, commodities shift from one owner to another during transportation. The lender is at risk with each one of them sequentially. Risk remains more transaction-related than related to the various owners because the commodity value backs the transaction. Sometimes, oil is a major export, which becomes even more strategic in the event of an economic crisis, making the financing of the commodity immune to country risk. In fact, a country risk increase has the paradoxical effect of decreasing the risk of the transaction because exports improve the country credit standing.

LIQUIDITY RISK

Liquidity risk refers to multiple dimensions: inability to raise funds at normal cost; market liquidity risk; asset liquidity risk.

Funding risk depends on how risky the market perceives the issuer and its funding policy to be. An institution coming to the market with unexpected and frequent needs for funds sends negative signals, which might restrict the willingness to lend to this institution. The cost of funds also depends on the bank's credit standing. If the perception of the credit standing deteriorates, funding becomes more costly. The problem extends beyond pure liquidity issues. The cost of funding is a critical profitability driver. The credit standing of the bank influences this cost, making the rating a critical factor for a bank. In addition, the rating drives the ability to do business with other financial institutions and to attract investors because many follow some minimum rating guidelines to invest and lend.

The liquidity of the market relates to liquidity crunches because of lack of volume. Prices become highly volatile, sometimes embedding high discounts from par, when counterparties are unwilling to trade. Funding risk materializes as a much higher cost of funds, although the cause lies more with the market than the specific bank. Market liquidity risk materializes as an impaired ability to raise money at a reasonable cost.

Asset liquidity risk results from lack of liquidity related to the nature of assets rather than to the market liquidity. Holding a pool of liquid assets acts as a cushion against fluctuating market liquidity, because liquid assets allow meeting short-term obligations without recourse to external funding. This is the rationale for banks to hold a sufficient fraction of their balance sheet of liquid assets, which is a regulatory rule. The 'liquidity ratio' of banks makes it mandatory to hold more short-term assets than short-term liabilities, in order to meet short-run obligations. In order to fulfil this role, liquid assets should mature in the short-term because market prices of long-term assets are more volatile[4], possibly triggering substantial losses in the event of a sale. Moreover, some assets are less tradable than others, because their trading volume is narrow. Some stocks trade less than others do, and exotic products might not trade easily because of their high level of customization, possibly resulting in depressed prices. In such cases, any sale might trigger price declines, so that the proceeds from a one-shot or a progressive sale become uncertain and generate losses. To a certain extent, funding risk interacts with market liquidity and asset liquidity because the inability to face payment obligations triggers sales of assets, possibly at depressed prices.

Liquidity risk might become a major risk for the banking portfolio. Extreme lack of liquidity results in bankruptcy, making liquidity risk a fatal risk. However, extreme conditions are often the outcome of other risks. Important unexpected losses raise doubts with respect to the future of the organization and liquidity issues. When a commercial bank gets into trouble, depositors 'run' to get their money back. Lenders refrain from further lending to the troubled institution. Massive withdrawals of funds or the closing of credit lines by other institutions are direct outcomes of such situations. A brutal liquidity crisis follows, which might end up in bankruptcy.

In what follows, we adopt an Asset–Liability Management (ALM) view of the liquidity situation. This restricts liquidity risk to bank-specific factors other than the credit risk of the bank and the market liquidity. The time profiles of projected uses and sources of funds, and their 'gaps' or liquidity mismatches, capture the liquidity position of a bank. The purpose of debt management is to manage these future liquidity gaps within acceptable limits, given the market perception of the bank.

This perspective does not fully address liquidity risk, and the market risk definitions below address this only partially. Liquidity risk, in terms of market liquidity or asset liquidity, remains a major issue that current techniques do not address fully. Practices rely on empirical and continuous observations of market liquidity, while liquidity risk models remain too theoretical to allow instrumental applications. This is presumably a field necessitating increased modelling research and improvement of practices.

INTEREST RATE RISK

The interest rate risk is the risk of a decline in earnings due to the movements of interest rates.

---

[4] Long-term interest-bearing assets are more sensitive to interest rate movements. See the duration concept used for capturing the sensitivity of the mark-to-market value of the balance sheet in Chapter 22.

Most of the items of banks' balance sheets generate revenues and costs that are interest rate-driven. Since interest rates are unstable, so are earnings. Any one who lends or borrows is subject to interest rate risk. The lender earning a variable rate has the risk of seeing revenues reduced by a decline in interest rates. The borrower paying a variable rate bears higher costs when interest rates increase. Both positions are risky since they generate revenues or costs indexed to market rates. The other side of the coin is that interest rate exposure generates chances of gains as well.

There are various and complex indexations on market rates. Variable rate loans have rates periodically reset using some market rate references. In addition, any transaction reaching maturity and renewed will stick to the future and uncertain market conditions. Hence, fixed rates become variable at maturity for loan renewals and variable rates remain fixed between two reset dates. In addition, the period between two rate resets is not necessarily constant. For instance, the prime rate of banks remains fixed between two resets, over periods of varying lengths, even though market rates constantly move. The same happens for the rates of special savings deposits, when they are subject to legal and fiscal rules. This variety makes the measure of interest rate sensitivity of assets and liabilities to market rates more complex.

Implicit options in banking products are another source of interest rate risk. A well-known case is that of the prepayment of loans that carry a fixed rate. A person who borrows can always repay the loan and borrow at a new rate, a right that he or she will exercise when interest rates decline substantially. Deposits carry options as well, since deposit holders transfer funds to term deposits earning interest revenues when interest rates increase. Optional risks are 'indirect' interest rate risks. They do not arise directly and only from a change in interest rate. They also result from the behaviour of customers, such as geographic mobility or the sale of their homes to get back cash. Economically, fixed rate borrowers compare the benefits and the costs of exercising options embedded in banking products, and make a choice depending on market conditions.

Given the importance of those products in the balance sheets of banks, optional risk is far from negligible. Measuring the option risk is more difficult than measuring the usual risk which arises from simple indexation to market rates. Section 5 of this book details related techniques.

MARKET RISK

Market risk is the risk of adverse deviations of the mark-to-market value of the trading portfolio, due to market movements, during the period required to liquidate the transactions. The period of liquidation is critical to assess such adverse deviations. If it gets longer, so do the deviations from the current market value.

Earnings for the market portfolio are Profit and Loss (P&L) arising from transactions. The P&L between two dates is the variation of the market value. Any decline in value results in a market loss. The potential worst-case loss is higher when the holding period gets longer because market volatility tends to increase over longer horizons.

However, it is possible to liquidate tradable instruments or to hedge their future changes of value at any time. This is the rationale for limiting market risk to the liquidation period. In general, the liquidation period varies with the type of instruments. It could be short (1 day) for foreign exchange and much longer for 'exotic' derivatives. The regulators provide rules to set the liquidation period. They use as reference a 10-day liquidation period and impose a multiple over banks' internal measures of market value potential losses (see Chapter 3).

Liquidation involves asset and market liquidity risks. Price volatility is not the same in high-liquidity and poor-liquidity situations. When liquidity is high, the adverse deviations of prices are much lower than in a poor-liquidity environment, within a given horizon. 'Pure' market risk, generated by changes of market parameters (interest rates, equity indexes, exchange rates), differs from market liquidity risk. This interaction raises important issues. What is the 'normal' volatility of market parameters under fair liquidity situations? What could it become under poorer liquidity situations? How sensitive are the prices to liquidity crises? The liquidity issue becomes critical in emerging markets. Prices in emerging markets often diverge considerably from a theoretical 'fair value'.

Market risk does not refer to market losses due to causes other than market movements, loosely defined as inclusive of liquidity risk. Any deficiency in the monitoring of the market portfolio might result in market values deviating by any magnitude until liquidation finally occurs. In the meantime, the potential deviations can exceed by far any deviation that could occur within a short liquidation period. This risk is an operational risk, not a market risk[5].

In order to define the potential adverse deviation, a methodology is required to identify what could be a 'maximum' adverse deviation of the portfolio market value. This is the VaR methodology. The market risk VaR technique aims at capturing downside deviations of prices during a preset period for liquidating assets, considering the changes in the market parameters. Controlling market risk means keeping the variations of the value of a given portfolio within given boundary values through actions on limits, which are upper bounds imposed on risks, and hedging for isolating the portfolio from the uncontrollable market movements.

FOREIGN EXCHANGE RISK

The currency risk is that of incurring losses due to changes in the exchange rates. Variations in earnings result from the indexation of revenues and charges to exchange rates, or of changes of the values of assets and liabilities denominated in foreign currencies.

Foreign exchange risk is a classical field of international finance, so that we can rely on traditional techniques in this book, without expanding them. For the banking portfolio, foreign exchange risk relates to ALM. Multi-currency ALM uses similar techniques for each local currency. Classical hedging instruments accommodate both interest rate and exchange rate risk. For market transactions, foreign exchange rates are a subset of market parameters, so that techniques applying to other market parameters apply as well.

The conversion risk resuls from the need to convert all foreign currency-denominated transactions into a base reference currency. This risk does exist, beyond accounting conversion in a single currency, if the capital base that protects the bank from losses

---

[5] An example is the failure of Baring Brothers, due to deficiencies in the control of the risk positions (see Leeson, 1996).

is in local currency. A credit loss in a foreign country might result in magnified losses in local currency if the local currency depreciates relative to the currency of the foreign exposure.

SOLVENCY RISK

Solvency risk is the risk of being unable to absorb losses, generated by all types of risks, with the available capital. It differs from bankruptcy risk resulting from defaulting on debt obligations and inability to raise funds for meeting such obligations. Solvency risk is equivalent to the default risk of the bank.

Solvency is a joint outcome of available capital and of all risks. The basic principle of 'capital adequacy', promoted by regulators, is to define what level of capital allows a bank to sustain the potential losses arising from all current risks and complying with an acceptable solvency level. The capital adequacy principle follows the major orientations of risk management. The implementation of this principle requires:

- Valuing all risks to make them comparable to the capital base of a bank.
- Adjusting capital to a level matching the valuation of risks, which implies defining a 'tolerance' level for the risk that losses exceed this amount, a risk that should remain very low to be acceptable.

Meeting these specifications drives the regulators' philosophy and prudent rules. The VaR concept addresses these issues directly by providing potential loss values for various confidence levels (probability that actual losses exceed an upper bound).

OPERATIONAL RISK

Operational risks are those of malfunctions of the information system, reporting systems, internal risk-monitoring rules and internal procedures designed to take timely corrective actions, or the compliance with internal risk policy rules. The New Basel Accord of January 2001 defines operational risk as 'the risk of direct or indirect loss resulting from inadequate or failed internal processes, people and systems or from external events'.

In the absence of efficient tracking and reporting of risks, some important risks remain ignored, do not trigger any corrective action and can result in disastrous consequences. In essence, operational risk is an 'event risk'. There is a wide range of events potentially triggering losses[6]. The very first step for addressing operational risk is to set up a common classification of events that should serve as a receptacle for data gathering processes on event frequencies and costs. Such taxonomy is still flexible and industry standards will emerge in the future. What follows is a tentative classification. Operational risks appear at different levels:

---

[6] See Marshall (2001) for a comprehensive view of operational risk and how to handle it for assessing potential losses.

- People.
- Processes. ·
- Technical.
- Information technology.

'People' risk designates human errors, lack of expertise and fraud, including lack of compliance with existing procedures and policies.

Process risk scope includes:

- Inadequate procedures and controls for reporting, monitoring and decision-making.
- Inadequate procedures on processing information, such as errors in booking transactions and failure to scrutinize legal documentation.
- Organizational deficiencies.
- Risk surveillance and excess limits: management deficiencies in risk monitoring, such as not providing the right incentives to report risks, or not abiding by the procedures and policies in force.
- Errors in the recording process of transactions.
- The technical deficiencies of the information system or the risk measures.

Technical risks relate to model errors, implementation and the absence of adequate tools for measuring risks.

Technology risks relate to deficiencies of the information system and system failure.

For operational risks, there are sources of historical data on various incidents and their costs, which serve to measure the number of incidents and the direct losses attached to such incidents. Beyond external statistics, other proxy sources on operational events are expert judgments, questioning local managers on possible events and what would be their implications, pooling data from similar institutions and insurance costs that should relate to event frequencies and costs.

The general principle for addressing operational risk measurement is to assess the likelihood and cost of adverse events. The practical difficulties lie in agreeing on a common classification of events and on the data gathering process, with several potential sources of event frequencies and costs. The data gathering phase is the first stage, followed by data analysis and statistical techniques. They help in finding correlations and drivers of risks. For example, business volume might make some events more frequent, while others depend on different factors. The process ends up with some estimate of worst-case losses due to event risks.

MODEL RISK

Model risk is significant in the market universe, which traditionally makes relatively intensive usage of models for pricing purposes. Model risk is growing more important, with the extension of modelling techniques to other risks, notably credit risk, where scarcity of data remains a major obstacle for testing the reliability of inputs and models. This book details many modelling approaches, making model risk self-explanatory.

Model risk materializes, for instance, as gaps between predicted values of variables, such as the VaR, and actual values observed from experience. Pricing models used for market instruments predict prices, which are readily comparable to observed prices. Often, modelled prices do not track actual prices accurately. When P&L calculations for the trading portfolio rely on 'pricers', there are 'P&L leaks' due to models. Such 'P&L leaks' represent the dollar value of model risk for 'pricers'. Unfortunately, it is much easier to track gaps between predicted prices and actual prices than between modelled worst-case losses and actual large losses. The difficulty is even greater for credit risk, since major credit risk events remain too scarce.

The sources of model risk, however, relate to common sense. Models are subject to misspecifications, because they ignore some parameters for practical reasons. Model implementation suffers from errors of statistical techniques, lack of observable data for obtaining reliable fits (credit risk) and judgmental choices on dealing with 'outliers', those observations that models fail to capture with reasonable accuracy. Credit risk models of interdependencies between individual defaults of borrowers rely on inferring such relations from 'modelled' events rather than observable events, because default data remains scarce. Consequently, measuring errors is not yet feasible until credit risk data becomes more reliable than it is currently. This is an objective of the New Basel Accord, from January 2001 (Chapter 3), making the data gathering process a key element in implementing the advanced techniques for measuring credit risk capital.

SECTION 2

Risk Regulations

3

Banking Regulations

Regulations have several goals: improving the safety of the banking industry, by imposing capital requirements in line with banks' risks; levelling the competitive playing field of banks through setting common benchmarks for all players; promoting sound business and supervisory practices. Regulations have a decisive impact on risk management. The regulatory framework sets up the constraints and guidelines that inspire risk management practices, and stimulates the development and enhancement of the internal risk models and processes of banks. Regulations promote better definitions of risks, and create incentives for developing better methodologies for measuring risks. They impose recognition of the core concept of the capital adequacy principle and of 'risk-based capital', stating that banks' capital should be in line with risks, and that defining capital requirements implies a quantitative assessment of risks.

Regulations imposing capital charge against risks are a strong incentive to improve risk measures and controls. They set minimum standards for sound practices, while the banking industry works on improving the risk measures and internal models for meeting their own goals in terms of best practices of risk management.

Starting from crude estimates of capital charges, with the initial so-called 'Cooke ratio', the regulators evolved towards increasingly 'risk-sensitive' capital requirements. The Existing Accord on credit risk dates from 1988. The Accord Amendment for market risk (1996) and the New Basel Accord (2001) provide very significant enhancements of risk measures. The existing accord imposed capital charge against credit risk. The amendment provided a standardized approach for dealing with market risk, and offered the opportunity to use internal models, subject to validation by the supervisory bodies, allowing banks to use their own models for assessing the market risk capital. The new accord imposes a higher differentiation of credit risk based on additional risk inputs characterizing banks' facilities. By doing so, it paves the way towards internal credit risk modelling, already instrumental in major institutions.

Regulations are inspired by economic principles, expanded on in subsequent chapters. However, regulations tend to strike a compromise between moving towards economic measures while being practical enough to be applicable by all players. This chapter describes the main features of regulations, and discusses the underlying economic rationale, as a transition towards subsequent developments. It does not provide a comprehensive and detailed presentation of regulations. Details are easily available from public documents on the Bank of International Settlements (BIS) site, and there is no need to replicate them.

A number of dilemmas inspired the deregulation process in the eighties, followed by the reregulation wave. An ideal scheme would combine a minimal insurance mechanism without providing any incentive for taking more risk, and still foster competition among institutions. Old schemes failed to ensure system safety, as spectacular failures of the eighties demonstrate. New regulations make the 'capital adequacy' principle a central foundation, starting from the end of the eighties up to the current period. Regulatory requirements use minimum forfeit amounts of capital held against risks to ensure that capital is high enough to sustain future losses materializing from current risks.

The main issue is to assess potential losses arising from current measures. Regulations provide sets of forfeits and rules defining the capital base as a function of banks' exposures. The risk modelling approach addresses the same issue, but specifies all inputs and models necessary to obtain the best feasible economic estimates of the required capital. Regulations lag behind in sophistication because they need to set up rules that apply to all. As a result, regulatory capital does not coincide with modelled economic capital. The notable exception is market risk, since the 1996 Accord Amendment for market risk that allowed usage of internal models, subject to validation and supervision by the regulatory bodies. The New Accord of January 2001 progresses significantly towards more risk-sensitive measures of credit risk at the cost of an additional complexity. It proposes three approaches for defining capital requirements: the simplest is the 'standardized' approach, while the 'foundation' and the 'advanced' approach allow further refinements of capital requirements without, however, accepting internal models for credit risk. It has become obvious, when looking at regulatory accords, that the capital adequacy concept imposes continuous progress for quantifying potential losses, for measuring capital charges, making risk valuation a major goal and a major challenge for the industry.

The regulatory system has evolved through the years. The 1996 Accord Amendment refined market risk measures, allowed internal models and is still in force. Capital requirements still do not apply to interest rate risk, although periodical enhanced reports are mandatory and the regulatory bodies can impose corrective actions. The last stage of the process is the New Basel Accord, published in early 2001, focusing on capital requirement definition (Pillar 1), with major enhancements to credit risk measures, a first coverage of operational risk, disclosure, supervisory review process (Pillar 2) and market discipline (Pillar 3). Simultaneously, it enhances some features of the 1988 Existing Accord, currently under implementation. The New Basel Accord target implementation date is early 2004.

The first section discusses the basic issues and dilemmas that inspired the new regulation waves. The second section introduces the central concept of 'capital adequacy', which plays a pivotal role for regulations, quantitative risk analytics and risk management. The third section summarizes the rules of the Current Accord, which still applies, and the 1996 Amendment. Finally, the fourth section details the New Basel Accord in its January 2001 format, subject to revisions from banking industry feedback in mid-2001.

REGULATORY ISSUES

The source of regulations lies in the differences between the objectives of banks and those of the regulatory authorities. Expected profitability is a major incentive for taking risks. Individual banks' risks create 'systemic risk', the risk that the whole banking system fails. Systemic risk results from the high interrelations between banks through mutual lending and borrowing commitments. The failure of a single institution generates a risk of failure for all banks that have ongoing commitments with the defaulting bank. Systemic risk is a major challenge for the regulator. Individual institutions are more concerned with their own risk. The regulators tend to focus on major goals:

- The risk of the whole system, or 'systemic risk', leading to pre-emptive actions against bank failures by the regulators, all inspired by the most important capital adequacy to risk principle.
- Promoting a level playing field, without distortions in terms of unfair competitive advantages.
- Promoting sound practices, contributing to the financial system safety.

The regulators face several dilemmas when attempting to control risks. Regulation and competition conflict, since many regulations restrict the operations of banks. New rules may create unpredictable behaviour to turn around the associated constraints. For this reason, regulators avoid making brutal changes in the environment that would generate other uncertainties.

The Need for Regulation

Risk taking is a normal behaviour of financial institutions, given that risk and expected return are so tightly interrelated. Because of the protection of bank depositors that exists in most countries, banks also benefit from 'quasi-free' insurance, since depositors cannot impose a real market discipline on banks. The banking system is subject to 'moral hazard': enjoying risk protection is an incentive for taking more risks because of the absence of penalties.

Sometimes, adverse conditions are incentives to maximize risks. When banks face serious difficulties, the barriers that limit risks disappear. In such situations, and in the absence of aggressive behaviour, failure becomes almost unavoidable. By taking additional risks, banks maximize the chances of survival. The higher the risk, the wider the range of possible outcomes, including favourable ones. At the same time, the losses of shareholders and managers do not increase because of limited liability. In the absence of real downside risk, it becomes rational to increase risk. This is the classical attitude of a call option holder. He gets the upside of the bet with a limited downside. The potential for upside gain without the downside risk encourages risk taking because it maximizes the expected gains.

The Dilemmas of the Regulator

A number of factors helped stabilize the banking environment in the seventies. Strong and constraining regulations weighed heavily on the banks' management. Commercial banking meant essentially collecting resources and lending. Limited competition facilitated a fair and stable profitability. Concerns for the safety of the industry and the control of its money creation power were the main priorities for regulators. The rules limited the scope of the operations of the various credit institutions, and limited their risks as well. There were low incentives for change and competition.

The regulators faced a safety–competition trade-off in addition to the negative side effects of risk insurance. In the period preceding deregulation, too many regulations segmented the banking industry, restraining competition. Deregulation increased competition between players unprepared by their past experiences, thereby resulting in increasing risks for the system. Reregulation aimed at setting up a regulatory framework reconciling risk control and fair competition.

Regulation and Competition

Regulations limit the scope of operations of the various types of financial institutions, thereby interfering directly with free competition. Examples of inconsistency between competition and regulations have grown more and more numerous. A well-known example, in the United States in the early eighties, was the unfair competition between commercial banks, subject to regulation Q, imposing a ceiling on the interest paid on deposits, and investment bankers offering money market funds through interest-earning products. Similar difficulties appear whenever rules enforce the segmentation of industry between those who operate in financial markets and others, savings and banking institutions, etc. The unfair competition stimulated the disappearance of such rules and the barriers to competition were progressively lifted. This old dilemma led to the deregulation of the banking industry. The seventies and the eighties were the periods of the first drastic waves of change in the industry.

The disappearance of old rules created a vacancy. The regulators could not rely any longer on rules that segmented the industry as barriers to risk-taking behaviour. They started redefining new rules that could ensure the safety of the banking industry. The BIS (Bank for International Settlements) in Basel defined these new regulations, and national regulators relayed them for implementation within the national environments.

Deregulation drastically widened the range of products and services offered by banks. Most credit institutions diversified their operations out of their original businesses. Moreover, the pace of creation of new products remained constantly high, especially for those acting in the financial markets, such as derivatives or futures. The active research for new market opportunities and products stimulated the growth of fields other than intermediation. Value-added services, such as advisory, structured transactions, asset acquisition, Leveraged Buy-Out (LBO), project finance, securitization of mortgages and credit card debts, derivatives and off-balance sheet operations, developed at a rapid pace. The banks entered new business fields and faced new risks. The market share of bank lending decreased with the development of capital markets and the competition within existing market shares rose abruptly.

Those waves of change generated risks. Risks increased because of new competition, product innovations, a shift from commercial banking to capital markets, increased market volatility and the disappearance of old barriers. This was a radical change in the banking industry. Lifting existing constraints stimulates new competition and increases risks and failures for those players who are less ready to enter new businesses. Deregulation implies that players can freely enter new markets. The process necessitates an orderly and gradual progress to avoid bank management disruption. This is still an ongoing process, notably in the United States and Japan, where the Glass–Steagall Act and the Article 65 enforced a separation between commercial banking and the capital markets. For those countries where universal banking exists, the transition is less drastic, but leads to a significant restructuring of the industry. It is not surprising that risk management has emerged with such strong force at the time of these waves of transformations.

Risk Control versus Risk Insurance

Risk control is pre-emptive, while insurance is passive, after the fact. The regulatory framework aims at making it an obligation to have a capital level matching risks. This is a pre-emptive policy. However, after the fact, there is still a need to limit the consequences of failures. Losses of depositors are the old consequences of bank failures. The consequences of bank failures are that they potentially trigger systemic risk, because of banks' interdependencies, such as the recent LTCM collapse. Hence, there is a need for after-the-fact regulatory action. If such actions rely on an insurance-like scheme, such as the insurance deposit scheme, it can foster risk-taking behaviour. Until reregulation through capital changes came into force, old regulations created insurance-based incentives for taking risks.

Any rule that limits the adverse consequences of risk-taking behaviour is an incentive for risk taking rather than risk reduction. Regulators need to minimize adverse effects of failures for the whole system without at the same time encouraging the risk-taking behaviour. The ideal solution would be to control the risks without insuring them. In practice, there is no such ideal solution. The deposit insurance scheme protects depositors against bank failures. Nevertheless, it does generate the adverse side effect of encouraging risk taking. Theoretically, depositors should monitor the bank behaviour, just as any lender does. In practice, if depositors' money were at risk, the functioning of the banking system would greatly deteriorate. Any sign of increased risks would trigger withdrawals of funds that would maximize the difficulties, possibly leading to failures. Such an adverse effect alone is a good reason to insure depositors, at least largely, against bank failure.

The new regulation focuses on pre-emptive (ex ante) actions, while still enforcing after-the-fact (ex post) corrective actions.

CAPITAL ADEQUACY

A number of rules, aimed at limiting risks in a simple manner, have been in force for a long time. For instance, several ratios are subject to minimum values. The liquidity ratio imposes that short-term assets be greater than short-term liabilities. Individual exposures to single borrowers are subject to caps.

The main 'pillar' of the regulations is 'capital adequacy': by enforcing a capital level in line with risks, regulators focus on pre-emptive actions limiting the risk of failure. Guidelines are defined by a group of regulators meeting in Basel at the BIS, hence the name 'Basel' Accord. The process attempts to reach a consensus on the feasibility of implementing new complex guidelines by interacting with the industry. Basel guidelines are subject to some implementation variations from one country to another, according to the view of local supervisors.

The first implemented accord focused on credit risk, with the famous 'Cooke ratio'. The Cooke ratio sets up the minimum required capital as a fixed percentage of assets weighted according to their nature in 1988. The scope of regulations extended progressively later. The extension to market risk, with the 1996 Amendment, was a major step. The New Basel Accord of January 2001 considerably enhances the old credit risk regulations. The schedule of successive accords is as follows:

- 1988 Current Accord published.
- 1996 Market Risk Amendment allowing usage of internal models.
- 1999 First Consultative Package on the New Accord.
- January 2001 Second Consultative Package.
- End-May 2001 Deadline for comments.
- End-2001 Publication of the New Accord.
- 2004 Implementation of the New Basel Capital Accord.

The next subsections refer to the 1988 'Current Accord' plus the market risk capital regulations. The last section expands the 'New Accord' in its current 'consultative' form[1], which builds on the 'Existing Accord' on credit risk, while making capital requirements more risk-sensitive.

Risk-based Capital Regulations

The capital base is not limited to equity plus retained earnings. It includes any debt subordinated to other commitments by the bank. Equity represents at least 50% of the total capital base for credit risk. Equity is also the 'Tier 1' of capital or the 'core capital'.

---

[1] The consultation with industry expires by mid-2001, and a final version should follow.

The Cooke ratio stipulates that the capital base should be at least 8% of weighted assets. The weights depend on the credit quality of the borrowers, as described below. For market risk, the rules are more complex because the regulations aim at a greater accuracy in capturing the economics of market risk, taking advantage of the widely available information on market parameters and prices.

The 1996 Amendment for market risk opened the door to internal models that have the capability to value capital requirements with more accurate and sophisticated tools than simple forfeits. Regulations allow the usage of internal bank models for market risk only, subject to validation by supervisors. Market risk models provide 'Value at Risk' (VaR)-based measurements of economic capital, complying with specific guidelines for implementing models set by Basel, which substitute for regulatory forfeits. The New Accord of January 2001 paves the way for modelling credit risk, but recognizes that it is still of major importance to lay down more reliable foundations for inputs to credit risk models, rather than allowing banks to use model credit risk with unreliable inputs, mainly due to scarce information on credit risk.

The Implications of Capital Requirements

Before detailing the regulations, the implications of risk-based capital deserve attention. Traditionally, capital represents a very small fraction of total assets of banks, especially when comparing the minimum requirements to similar ratios of non-financial institutions. A capital percentage of 8% of assets is equivalent to a leverage ratio (debt/equity ratio) of $92/8 = 11.5$. This leverage ratio would be unsustainable with non-financial institutions, since borrowers would consider it as impairing too much the repayment ability and causing an increase in the bankruptcy risk beyond acceptable levels. The high leverage of banking institutions results from a number of factors. Economically, the discipline imposed by borrowers does not apply to depositors who benefit from deposit insurance programmes in all countries. Smooth operations of banks require easy and immediate access to financial markets, so that funding is not a problem, as long as the perceived risk by potential lenders remains acceptable. In addition, bank ratings by specialized agencies make risks visible and explicit.

The Function of Capital

The theoretical reason for holding capital is that it should provide protection against unexpected losses. Without capital, banks will fail at the first dollar of loss not covered by provisions. It is possible to compare regulatory forfeits to historical default rates for a first assessment of the magnitude of the safety cushion against losses embedded in regulatory capital. Default rates of corporate borrowers above 1% are speculative. Investment grade borrowers have yearly default rates between 0% and 0.1%. At the other extreme of the risk scale, corporate borrowers (small businesses) can have default rates ranging from 3% to 16% or more across the economic cycle.

The 8% ratio of capital to weighted assets seems too high if compared to average observed default rates under good conditions, and perhaps too low with portfolios of high-risk borrowers when a downturn in economic conditions occurs. However, the 8%

ratio does not aim at protecting banks against average losses. Provisions and reserves should, theoretically, take care of those. Rather, it aims at a protection against deviations from average. The ratio means that capital would cover deviations of losses, in excess of loan loss provisions, up to 8%, given the average portfolio structure of banks. However, without modelling potential portfolio losses, it is impossible to say whether this capital in excess of provisions is very or moderately conservative. Portfolio models provide 'loss distributions' for credit risk, the combinations of loss values plus the probability that losses hit each level, and allow us to see how likely various loss levels are, for each specific portfolio.

In addition, loss provisioning might not be conservative enough, so that capital should also be sufficient to absorb a fraction of average losses in addition to loss in excess of average. Legal reserves restrain banks from economic provisioning, as well as window dressing or the need to maximize retained earnings that feed into capital. Economic provisioning designates a system by which provisions follow ex ante estimates of what the future average losses could be, while actual provisions are more ex post, after the fact. Still, regulatory capital is not a substitute for provisions.

The Dilemma between Risk Controlling and Risk Taking

There is a trade-off between risk taking and risk controlling. Available capital puts a limit on risk taking which, in turn, limits the ability to develop business. This generates a conflict between business goals, in terms of volume and risks, and the limits resulting from available capital. The available capital might not suffice to sustain new business developments. Capital availability could result in tighter limits for account officers and traders, and for the volume of operations. On the other hand, flexible constraints allow banks to take more risks, which leads to an increase in risk for the whole system. Striking the right balance between too much risk control and not enough is not an easy task.

Risk-based Capital and Growth

The capital ratio sets the minimum value of capital, given the volume of operations and their risks. The constraint might require raising new equity, liquidation of assets or risk reduction actions. Raising additional capital requires that the profitability of shareholders is in line with their expectations. When funding capital growth through retained earnings only, the profitability should be high enough for the capital to grow in line with the requirements. These are two distinct constraints.

A common proxy for the minimum required return of shareholders is an accounting Return On Equity (ROE) of 15% after tax, or 25% before tax. When the target is funding capital, the minimum accounting ROE should be in line with this funding constraint. The higher the growth of the volume of operations, the higher the increase in required capital (if the 'average' risk level remains unchanged). Profitability limits the sustainable growth if outside sources of capital are not used. The ROE becomes equal to the growth rate of capital if no dividends are paid[2]. Therefore, any growth above ROE is not sustainable when funding through retained earnings only, under constant average risk. The first implication of capital requirements is that the ROE caps the growth of banks when they rely on retained earnings only. The second implication is that capital should provide the required market return to stockholders given the risk of the bank's stocks. Sometimes, the bank growth is too high to be sustainable given capital requirements. Sometimes, the required compensation to shareholders is the 'effective' constraint, while funding capital growth internally is not[3].

The only options available to escape the capital constraints are to liquidate assets or to reduce risks. Direct sales of assets or securitizations serve this purpose, among others. Direct loan sales become feasible through the emerging loan trading market. Chapter 60 discusses structured transactions as a tool for capital management.

THE 'CURRENT ACCORD' CAPITAL REGULATIONS

The regulation is quite detailed in order to cover all specific situations. Three sections covering credit risk, market risk and interest rate risk summarize the main orientations.

The Cooke Ratio and Credit Risk

The 1988 Accord requires internationally active banks in the G10 countries to hold capital equal to at least 8% of weighted assets. Banks should hold at least half of its measured capital in Tier 1 form. The Cooke ratio addresses credit risk. Tier 1 capital is subject to a minimum constraint of 3% of total assets. The calculation of the ratio uses asset weights for differentiating the capital load according to quality in terms of credit standing. The weight scale starts from zero, for commitments with public counterparties, up to 100% for private businesses. Other weights are: 20% for banks and municipalities within OECD countries; 50% for residential mortgage backed loans. Off-balance sheet outstanding balances are weighted at 50%, in combination with the above weights scale. The 1988 Accord requires a two-step approach whereby banks convert their off-balance sheet positions into a credit equivalent amount through a scale of conversion factors, which are then weighted according to the counterparty's risk weighting. The factor is 100% for direct credit substitutes such as guarantees and decreases for less stringent commitments.

---

[2] If the leverage is constant, capital being a fixed fraction of total liabilities, the growth rate of accounting capital is also the growth rate of the total liabilities. Leverage is the debt/equity ratio, or $L = D/E$ where D is debt, E is equity plus retained earnings and L is leverage. The ROE is the ratio of net income (NI) to equity and retained earnings, or $ROE = NI/E$. ROE is identical to the sustainable growth rate of capital since it is the ratio of potential additional capital (net income NI) to existing capital. Since L is constant, total liabilities are always equal to $(1 + L) \times E$. Hence, they grow at the same rate as E, which is identical to ROE under assumptions of no dividends and no outside capital.

[3] In fact, both constraints are equivalent when the growth rate is exactly 15%, if this figure is representative of both accounting return on equity and the required market return to shareholders.

The major strength of the Cooke ratio is its simplicity. Its major drawbacks are:

- The absence of differentiation between the different risks of private corporations. An 8% ratio applying for both a large corporation rated 'Aa' (an investment grade rating) and a small business does not make much sense economically. This is obvious when looking at the default rates associated with high and low ratings. The accord is not risk-sensitive enough.
- In addition, short facilities have zero weights, while long facilities have a full capital load, creating arbitrage opportunities to reduce the capital load. This unequal treatment leads to artificial arbitrage by banks, such as renewing short loans rather than lending long.
- There is no allowance for recoveries if a default occurs, even in cases where recoveries are likely, such as for cash or liquid securities collateral.
- Summing arithmetically capital charges of all transactions does not capture diversification effects. In fact, there is an embedded diversification effect in the 8% ratio since it recognizes that the likelihood of losses exceeding more than 8% of weighted assets is very low. However, the same ratio applies to all portfolios, whatever their degree of diversification.

The regulators recognized these facts and reviewed these issues, leading to the New Basel Accord detailed in a subsequent dedicated section.

Market Risk

A significant amendment was enacted in 1995–6, when the Committee introduced a measure whereby trading positions in bonds, equities, foreign exchange and commodities were removed from the credit risk framework and given explicit capital charges related to the bank's open position in each instrument. Capital requirements extended explicitly to market risk. The amendment made explicit the notions of banking book and trading book, defined capital charges for market risk and allowed banks to use Tier 3 capital in addition to the previous two tiers.

Scope

Market risk is the risk of losses in on- and off-balance sheet positions arising from movements in market prices. The risks subject to this requirement are:

- The risks pertaining to interest rate-related instruments and equities in the trading book.
- Foreign exchange risk and commodities risk throughout the bank.

The 1995 proposal introduced capital charges to be applied to the current market value of open positions (including derivative positions) in interest rate-related instruments and equities in banks' trading books, and to banks' total currency and commodities positions.

The extension to market risk provides two alternative techniques for assessing capital charges. The 'standardized approach' allows measurement of the four risks: interest rate, equity position, foreign exchange and commodity risks, using sets of forfeits. Under the standardized approach, there are specific forfeits and rules for defining to which base they apply, allowing some offsetting effects within portfolios of traded instruments. Offsetting effects reduce the base for calculating the capital charge by using a net exposure rather than gross exposures. Full netting effects apply only to positions subject to an identical underlying risk or, equivalently, a zero basis risk[4]. For instance, it is possible to offset opposite positions in the same stocks or the same interest rates.

The second method allows banks to use risk measures derived from their own internal risk management models, subject to a number of conditions, related to qualitative standards of models and processes.

The April 1995 proposal allowed banks to use new 'Tier 3' capital, essentially made up of short-term subordinated debt to meet their market risks. Tier 3 capital is subject to a number of conditions, such as being limited to market risk capital and being subject to a 'lock-in clause', stipulating that no such capital can be repaid if that payment results in a bank's overall capital being lower than a minimum capital requirement.

The Basel extension to market risk relies heavily on the principles of sound economic measures of risks, although the standardized approach falls short of such a target by looking at a feasible compromise between simplicity and complexities of implementation.

Underlying Economic Principles for Measuring Market Risks

The economics of market risk are relatively easy to grasp. Tradable assets have random variations of which distributions result from observable sensitivities of instruments and volatilities of market parameters. The standalone market risk of an instrument is a VaR (or maximum potential loss) resulting from Profit and Loss (P&L) distribution derived from the underlying market parameter variations. Things get more involved for portfolios because risks offset to some extent. The 'portfolio effect' reduces the portfolio risk, making it lower than the sum of all individual standalone risks.

For example, long and short exposures to the same instrument are exactly offset. Long and short exposures to similar instruments are also partially offset. The price movements of a 4-year bond and a 5-year bond correlate because the 4-year and 5-year interest rates do. However, the correlation is not perfect since a 1% change in the former does not mechanically trigger a 1% change in the latter. There is a case for offsetting exposures of long and short positions in similar instruments, but only to a certain extent. A mechanical offset would leave out of the picture the residual risk resulting from the mismatch of the instrument characteristics. This residual risk is a 'basis risk' resulting from the mismatch between the reference rates applying to each instrument.

Moving one step further, let us consider a common underlying flat rate across all maturities, with a maturity mismatch between opposing exposures in similar instruments. Any shift in the entire spectrum of interest rates by the same amount (a parallel shift of 1% for instance) does not result in the same price change for the two instruments because

---

[4] 'Basis risk' exists when the underlying sources of risk differ, even if only slightly.

their sensitivities differ. The magnitudes of the two price changes vary across instruments as sensitivities to common parameters do.

With different instruments, such as equity and bonds, a conservative view would consider that all prices move adversely simultaneously. This makes no sense because the market parameters—interest rates, foreign exchange rates and equity indexes—are interdependent. Some tend to move in the same direction, others in opposite directions. In addition, the strength of such 'associations' varies across pairs of market parameters. The statistical measure for such 'associations' is the correlation. Briefly stated, market parameters comply with a correlation structure, so that the assumption of simultaneous adverse co-movements is irrelevant. When trying to assess how prices change within a portfolio, the issue is: how to model co-movements of underlying parameters in conjunction with sensitivities differing across exposures.

This leads to the basic concepts of 'general' versus 'specific' risk. General risk is the risk dependent on market parameters driving all prices. This dependence generates price co-movements, or price correlations, because all prices depend, to some extent, on a common set of market parameters. The price volatility unrelated to market parameters is the specific risk. By definition, it designates price variations unrelated to market parameter variations. Statistically, specific risk is easy to isolate over a given period. It is sufficient to relate prices to market parameters statistically to get a direct measure of general risk. The remaining fraction of the price volatility is the specific risk.

The Basel Committee offer two approaches for market risk:

- The standardized approach relies on relatively simple rules and forfeits for defining capital charges, which avoids getting into the technicalities of modelling price changes.
- The proprietary model approach allows banks to use internal full-blown models for assessing market risk VaR, subject to qualifying conditions.

The critical inputs include:

- The current valuation of exposures.
- Their sensitivities to the underlying market parameter(s)[5].
- Rules governing offsetting effects between opposing exposures in 'similar' instruments and, eventually, across the entire range of instruments.

Full-blown models should capture all valuation, sensitivity and correlation effects. The 'standardized' approach for market risk uses forfeits and allows partial diversification effects, striking a balance between complexities and measurement accuracy.

The Standardized Approach

The standardized approach relies on forfeits for assessing capital charges as a percentage of current exposures, on grids for capturing the differences in sensitivities of various market instruments and on offsetting rules allowing netting of the risks within a portfolio

---

[5] Sensitivities are variations of values for a unit change in market parameter, as detailed in Chapter 6.

whenever there is no residual 'basis' risk. Forfeits capture conservatively the potential adverse deviations of instruments. Forfeits vary across market compartments and products, such as bonds of different maturities, because their sensitivity changes. For stocks, forfeits are 8% of the net balances, after allowed offsetting of long and short comparable exposures. For bonds, forfeits are also 8%, but various weights apply to this common ratio, based upon maturity buckets.

Adding the individual risks, without offsetting exposures, overestimates the portfolio risk because the underlying assumption is that all adverse deviations occur simultaneously. Within a given class of instruments, such as bonds, equity or foreign exchange, regulators allow offsetting risks to a certain extent. For instance, being long and short on the same stock results in zero risk, because the gain in the long leg offsets the loss in the short leg when the stock goes up, and vice versa. Offsetting is limited to exact matches of instrument characteristics. In other instances, regulators rely on the 'specific' versus 'general' risk distinction, following the principle of adding specific risk forfeits while allowing limiting offsetting effects for general risk. The rationale is that general risk refers to co-movements of prices, while specific risk is unrelated to underlying market parameters. Such conservative measures provide a strong incentive to move to the modelling approach that captures portfolio effects. These general rules differ by product family. What follows provides only an overview of the main product families. All forfeit values and grids are available from the BIS documents.

Interest Rate Instruments

For interest rate instruments, the capital charge adds individual transaction forfeits, varying from 0% (government) to 8% for maturities over 24 months. Offsetting specific risks is not feasible except for identical debt issues. The capital requirement for general market risk captures the risk of loss arising from changes in market interest rates. There are two principal methods for measuring general risk: a 'maturity' method and a 'duration' method.

The maturity method uses 13 time bands for assigning instruments. It aims at capturing the varying sensitivities across time bands of instruments. Offsetting long and short positions within time bands is possible, but there are additional residual capital charges applying because of intra-band maturity mismatches. Since interest rates across time bands correlate as well, partial offsets across time bands are possible. The procedure uses 'zones' of maturity buckets grouping the narrower time bands. Offsets decrease with the distance between the time bands. The accord sets percentages of exposures significantly lower than 1, to cap the exposures allowed to offset (100% implying a total offset of the entire exposure).

The duration method allows direct measurement of the sensitivities, skipping the time band complexity by using the continuous spectrum of durations. It is necessary to assign sensitivities to a duration-based 'ladder', and within each slot, the capital charge is a forfeit. Sensitivities in values should refer to preset changes of interest rates, whose values are within the 0.6% to 1.00% range. Offsetting is subject to a floor for residual risk (basis risk, since there are duration mismatches within bands).

Derivatives

Derivatives are combinations of underlying exposures, and each component is subject to the same treatments as above. For example, a swap is a combination of two exposures, the receiving leg and the paying leg. Therefore, forfeit values add unless the absence of any residual risk allows full offsets. There is no specific risk for derivatives. For options, there are special provisions based on sensitivities to the various factors that influence their prices, and their changes with these factors. For options, the accord proposes the scenario matrix analysis. Each cell of the matrix shows the portfolio value given a combination of scenarios of underlying asset price and volatility (stressed according to regulators' recommendations). The highest loss value in the matrix provides the capital charge for the entire portfolio of options.

Equity

The basic distinction between specific versus general risk applies to equity products. The capital charge for specific risk is 8%, unless the portfolio is both liquid and well diversified, in which case the charge is 4%. Offsetting long and short exposures is feasible for general risk, but not for specific risk. The general market risk charge is 8%. Equity derivatives should follow the same 'decomposition' rule as underlying exposures.

Foreign Exchange

Two processes serve for calculating the capital requirement for foreign exchange risk. The first is to measure the exposure in a single currency position. The second is to measure the risks inherent in a bank's mix of long and short positions in different currencies. Structural positions are exempt of capital charges. They refer to exposures protecting the bank from movements of exchange rates, such as assets and liabilities in foreign currencies remaining matched. The 'shorthand method' treats all currencies alike, and applies the forfeited 8% capital charge over the greatest netted exposure (either long or short).

Commodities

Commodity risk is more complex than market instrument risk because it combines a pure commodity price risk with other risks, such as basis risk (mismatch of prices of similar commodities), interest rate risk (for carrying cost of exposures) and forward price risk. In addition, there is directional risk in commodities prices. The principle is to assign transactions to maturity buckets, to allow offsetting of matched exposures, and to assign a higher capital charge for risk.

Proprietary Models of Market Risk VaR

The principles of the extension to proprietary market risk models are as follows:

- Market risk is the risk of loss during the minimum period required to liquidate transactions in the market.
- The potential loss is the 99th loss percentile[6] (one-tailed) for market risk models.
- This minimum period depends on the type of products, and on their sensitivities to a given variation of their underlying market parameters. However, a general 10-day period for liquidating position is the normal reference for measuring downside risk.
- Potential losses depend on market movements during this period, and the sensitivities of different assets.

Models should incorporate historical observation over at least 1 year. In addition, the capital charge is the higher of the previous day's VaR or three times the average daily VaR of the preceding 60 days. A multiplication factor applies to this modelled VaR. It accounts for potential weaknesses in the modelling process or exceptional circumstances. In addition, the regulators emphasize:

- Stress-testing, to see what happens under exceptional conditions. Stress-testing uses extreme scenarios maximizing losses to find out how large they can be.
- Back-testing of models to ensure that models capture the actual deviations of the portfolios. Back testing implies using the model with past data to check whether the modelled deviations of values are in line or not with the historical deviations of values, once known.

These additional requirements serve to modulate the capital charge, through the multiplier of VaR, according to the reliability of the model, in addition to fostering model improvements through time. Reliable models get a 'premium' in capital with a lower multiplier of VaR.

Derivatives and Credit Risk

Derivatives are over-the-counter instruments (interest rate swaps, currency swaps, options) not liquid as market instruments. Theoretically, banks hold these assets until maturity, and bear credit risk since they exchange flows of funds with counterparties subject to default risk. For derivatives, credit risk interacts with market risk in that the mark-to-market (liquidation) value depends on market movements. It is the present value of all future flows at market rates. Under a 'hold to maturity' view, the potential future values over their life is the credit risk exposure because they are the value of all future flows that the defaulted counterparty will not pay. Future liquidation values are random because they are market-driven. To address random exposures over a long-term period, it is necessary to model the time profile of liquidation values. The principle is to determine the time profile of upper bounds that future values will not exceed with more than a preset low probability (confidence level) (see Chapter 39).

From the regulatory standpoint, the issue is to define applicable rules as percentage forfeits of the notional of derivatives. The underlying principles for defining such forfeits are identical to those of models. The current credit risk exposure is the current liquidation value. There is the additional risk due to the potential upward deviations of liquidation

---

[6] A loss percentile is the loss value not exceeded in more than the given preset percentage, such as 99%. See Chapter 7.

value from the current value during the life of the instruments. Such drifts depend on the market parameter volatilities and on instrument sensitivities. It is feasible to calibrate forfeit values representative of such drifts on market observations.

The regulators provided forfeits for capturing these potential changes of exposures. The forfeit add-ons are percentages of notional depending on the underlying parameter and the maturity buckets. Underlying parameters are interest rate, foreign exchange, equity and commodities. The maturity buckets are up to 1 year, between 1 and 5 years and beyond 5 years. The capital charge adds arithmetically individual forfeits. Forfeit add-ons are proxies and adding them does not allow offsetting effects, thereby providing a strong incentive for modelling derivative exposures and their offsetting effects.

The G30 group, in 1993, defined the framework for monitoring derivative credit risk. The G30 report recommended techniques for assessing uncertain exposures, and for modelling the potential unexpected deviations of portfolios of derivatives over long periods. The methodology relies on internal models to capture worst-case deviations of values at preset confidence levels. In addition, it emphasized the need for enhanced reporting, management control and disclosure of risk between counterparties.

Interest Rate Risk (Banking Portfolio)

Interest rate risk, for the banking portfolio, has generated debate and controversy. The current regulation does not require capital to match interest rate risk. Nevertheless, regulators require periodical internal reports to be made available. Supervising authorities take corrective actions if they feel them required.

Measures of interest rate risk include the sensitivity of the interest income to shifts in interest rates and that of the net market value of assets and liabilities. The interest margin is adequate in the short-term. Market value sensitivities of both assets and liabilities capture the entire stream of future flows and provide a more long-term view. Regulators recommend using both. Subsequent chapters discuss the adequate models for such sensitivities, gaps and net present value of the balance sheet and its duration (see Chapters 21 and 22).

THE NEW BASEL ACCORD

The New Basel Accord is the set of consultative documents that describes recommended rules for enhancing credit risk measures, extending the scope of capital requirements to operational risk, providing various enhancements to the 'existing' accord and detailing the 'supervision' and 'market discipline' pillars. The accord allows for a 3-year transition period before full enforcement, with all requirements met by banks at the end of 2004. Table 3.1 describes the rationale of the New Accord.

The new package is very extensive. It provides a menu of options, extended coverage and more elaborate measures, in addition to descriptions of work in progress, with yet unsettled issues to be streamlined in the final package. The New Accord comprises three pillars:

• Pillar 1 Minimum Capital Requirements.

- Pillar 2 Supervisory Review Process.
- Pillar 3 Market Discipline.

TABLE 3.1   Rationale for a new accord: the need for more flexibility and risk sensitivity

Existing Accord	Proposed New Accord
Focuses on a single risk measure	More emphasis on banks' own internal methodologies, supervisory review and market discipline
One size fits all: only one option proposed to banks	Flexibility, menu of approaches, incentives: banks have several options
Broad brush structure (forfeits)	More credit risk sensitivity for better risk management

The Committee emphasizes the mutually reinforcing role of these three pillars—minimum capital requirements, supervisory review and market discipline. Taken together, the three pillars contribute to a higher level of safety and soundness in the financial system. Previous implementations of the regulations for credit and market risk, confirmed by VaR models for both risks, revealed that the banking book generates more risk than the trading book. Credit risk faces a double challenge. The measurement issues are more difficult to tackle for credit risk than for market risk and, in addition, the tolerance for errors should be lower because of the relative sizes of credit versus market risk.

Overview of the Economic Contributions of the New Accord

The economic contributions of the New Accord extend to supervisory processes and market discipline. Economically, the New Accord appears to be a major step forward.

On the quantitative side of risk measurements, the accord offers a choice between the 'standardized', the 'foundation' and the 'advanced' approaches, addresses and provides remedies for several critical issues that led banks to arbitrage the old capital requirements against more relevant economic measures. It remedies the major drawbacks of the former 'Cooke ratio', with a limited set of weights and a unique weight for all risky counterparties of 100%. Neither the definition of capital and Tier 1/Tier 2, nor the 8% coefficient change.

The new set of ratios (the 'McDonough ratios') corrects this deficiency. Risk weights define the capital charge for credit risk. Weights are based on credit risk 'components', allowing a much improved differentiation of risks. They apply to some specific cases where the old weights appeared inadequate, such as for credit enhancement notes issued for securitization which, by definition, concentrate a major fraction of the securitized assets[7]. Such distortions multiplied the discrepancies between economic risk-based policies and regulatory-based policies, leading banks to arbitrage the regulatory weights. In addition, banks relied on regulatory weights and forfeits not in line with risks, leading to distortion in risk assessment, prices, risk-adjusted measures of performance, etc.

---

[7] The mechanisms of securitizations are described in Chapter 34, and when detailing the economics of securitizations.

The New Accord provides a more 'risk-sensitive' framework that should considerably reduce such distortions. In addition, it makes clear that data gathering on all critical credit risk drivers of transactions is a major priority, providing a major incentive to solve the 'incompleteness' of credit risk data.

It also extends the scope of capital requirements to operational risk. Measures of operational risk remained in their 'infancy' for some time because of a lack of data, but the accord should stimulate rapid progress.

From an economic standpoint, the accord suffers from the inaccuracy limitations of forfeit-based measures, a limitation mitigated by the need to strike a balance between accuracy and practicality.

The accord does not go as far as authorizing the usage of credit risk VaR models, as it did for market risk. It mentions, as reasons for refraining from going that far, the difficulties of establishing the reliability of both inputs and outputs of such models. Finally, it still leaves aside interest rate risk for capital requirements and includes it in the supervision process (Pillar 2).

Pillar 1: Overall Minimum Capital Requirements

The primary changes to the minimum capital requirements set out in the 1988 Accord are the approaches to credit risk and the inclusion of explicit capital requirements for operational risk. The accord provides a range of 'risk-sensitive options' for addressing both types of risk. For credit risk, this range includes the standardized approach, with the simplest requirements, and extends to the 'foundation' and 'advanced' Internal Ratings-Based (IRB) approaches. Internal ratings are assessments of the relative credit risks of borrowers and/or facilities, assigned by banks[8].

The Committee desires to produce neither a net increase nor a net decrease—on average—in minimum regulatory capital. With respect to the IRB approaches, the Committee's ultimate goal is to improve regulatory capital adequacy for underlying credit risks and to provide capital incentives relative to the standardized approach through lower risk weights, on average, for the 'foundation' and the 'advanced' approaches.

Under the New Accord, the denominator of the minimum total capital ratio will consist of three parts: the sum of all risk-weighted assets for credit risk, plus 12.5 times the sum of the capital charges for market risk and operational risk. Assuming that a bank has $875 of risk-weighted assets, a market risk capital charge of $10 and an operational risk capital charge of $20, the denominator of the total capital ratio would equal $875 + [(10 + 20) \times 12.5]$ or $1250.

Risk Weights under Pillar 1

The New Accord strongly differentiates risk weights using a 'menu' of approaches designated as 'standardized', 'foundation' and 'advanced'.

---

[8] See Chapters 35 and 36 on rating systems and credit data by rating class available from rating agencies.

The Standardized Approach

In the standardized approach to credit risk, exposures to various types of counter-parties—sovereigns, banks and corporates—have risk weights based on assessments (ratings) by External Credit Assessment Institutions (ECAIs or rating agencies) or Export Credit Agencies (ECAs) for sovereign risks.

The risk-weighted assets in the standardized approach are the product of exposure amounts and supervisory determined risk weights. As in the current accord, the risk weights depend on the category of the borrower: sovereign, bank or corporate. Unlike in the current accord, there will be no distinction on the sovereign risk weighting depending on whether or not the sovereign is a member of the Organization for Economic Coordination and Development (OECD). Instead, the risk weights for exposures depend on external credit assessments. The treatment of off-balance sheet exposures remains largely unchanged, with a few exceptions.

To improve risk sensitivity while keeping the standardized approach simple, the Committee proposes to base risk weights on external credit assessments. The usage of the supervisory weights is the major difference from the IRB approach, which relies on internal ratings. The approach is more risk-sensitive than the existing accord, through the inclusion of an additional risk bucket (50%) for corporate exposures, plus a 150% risk weight for low rating exposures. Unrated exposures have a 100% weight, lower than the 150% weight. The higher risk bucket (150%) also serves for certain categories of assets. The standardized approach does not allow weights to vary with maturity, except in the case of short-term facilities with banking counterparties in the mid-range of ratings, where weights decrease from 50% to 20% and from 100% to 50%, depending on the rating[9].

The unrated class at 150% could trigger 'adverse selection' behaviour, by which low-rated entities give up their ratings to benefit from a risk weight of 100%, rather than 150%. On the other hand, the majority of corporates—and, in many countries, the majority of banks—do not need to acquire a rating in order to fund their activities. Therefore, the fact that a borrower has no rating does not generally signal low credit quality. The accord attempts to strike a compromise between these conflicting facts and stipulates that national supervisors have some flexibility in adjusting this weight. The 150% weight remains subject to consultation with the banking industry as of current date.

For sovereign risks, the external ratings are those of an ECAI or ECA. For banks, the risk weights scale is the same, but the rating assignment might follow either one of two processes. Either the sovereign rating is one notch lower than the sovereign ratings, or it is the intrinsic bank rating. In Tables 3.2 and 3.3 we provide the grids of risk weights for sovereign ratings and corporates. The grid for banks under the first option is identical to that of sovereign ratings.

TABLE 3.2   Risk weights of sovereigns

	AAA to AA−	A+ to A−	BBB+ to BBB−	BB+ to B−	Below B−	Unrated
Risk weights	0%	20%	50%	100%	150%	100%

---

[9] By contrast, the advanced IRB approach makes risk weights sensitive to maturity and ratings through the default probabilities.

TABLE 3.3   Risk weights of corporates

	AAA to AA−	A+ to A−	BBB+ to BB−	Below BB−	Unrated
Risk weights	20%	50%	100%	150%	100%

Source: Basel Committee, January 2001.

Internal Ratings-based Framework

The IRB approach lays down the principles for evaluating economically credit risk. It proposes a treatment similar to the standardized approach for corporate, bank and sovereign exposures, plus separate schemes for retail banking, project finance and equity exposures. There are two versions of the IRB approach: the 'foundation' and the 'advanced' approaches.

For each exposure class, the treatment uses three main elements called 'risk components'. A bank can use either its own estimates for each of them or standardized supervisory estimates, depending on the approach. A 'risk-weight function' converts the risk components into risk weights for calculating risk-weighted assets. The risk components are the probability of default (PD), the loss given default (Lgd) and the 'Exposure At Default' (EAD). The PD estimate must represent a conservative view of a long-run average PD, 'through the cycle', rather than a short-term assessment of risk. Risk weights are a function of PD and Lgd.

Maturity is a credit risk component that should influence risk weights, given the objective of increased risk sensitivity. However, the inclusion of maturity creates additional complexities and a disincentive for lending long-term. Hence, the accord provides alternative formulas for inclusion of maturity, which mitigate a simple mechanical effect on capital.

The BIS proposes the Benchmark Risk Weight (BRW) for including the maturity effect on credit risk and capital weights. The function depends on the default probability DP. The benchmark example refers to the specific case of a 3-year asset, with various default probabilities and an Lgd of 50%. Three representative points show the sensitivity of risk weights to the annualized default probability (Table 3.4).

TABLE 3.4   Sensitivity of risk weights with maturity: benchmark case (3-year asset, 50% Lgd)

DP (%)	0.03	0.7	20
BRW (%)	14	100	625

For DP = 0.7%, the BRW is 100% and the maximum risk weight, for DP = 20%, reaches 625%. This value is a cap for all maturities and all default probabilities. The weight profile with varying DP is more sensitive than the standardized approach weights, which vary in the range 20% to 150% for all maturities over 1 year. The weights increase less than proportionally with default probability until they reach the cap.

The New Accord suggests using a forfeit maturity of 3 years for all assets for the 'foundation' approach, but leaves the door open to the usage of effective maturity. Risk weights adjusted for effective maturity apply to the 'advanced' approach.

Retail Exposures

The Committee proposes a treatment of retail portfolios, based on the conceptual framework outlined above, modified to capture the specifics of retail exposures. Fixed rating scales and the assignment of borrower ratings are not standard practices for retail banking (see Chapters 37 and 38). Rather, banks commonly divide the portfolio into 'segments' made up of exposures with similar risk characteristics. The accord proposes to group retail exposures into segments. The assessment of risk components will be at the segment level rather than at the individual exposure level, as is the case for corporate exposures. In the case of retail exposures, the accord also proposes, as an alternative assessment of risk, to evaluate directly 'expected loss'. Expected loss is the product of DP and Lgd. This approach bypasses the separate assessment, for each segment, of the PD and Lgd. The maturity (M) of the exposure is not a risk input for retail banking capital.

Foundation Approach

The 'foundation' IRB approach allows banks meeting robust supervisory standards to input their own assessment of the PD associated with the obligor. Estimates of additional risk factors, such as loss incurred by the bank given a default (Lgd) and EAD, should follow standardized supervisory estimates. Exposures not secured by a recognized form of collateral will receive a fixed Lgd depending on whether the transaction is senior or subordinated. The minimum requirements for the foundation IRB approach relate to meaningful differentiation of credit risk with internal ratings, the comprehensiveness of the rating system, the criteria of the rating system and similar.

There are a variety of methodologies and data sources that banks may use to associate an estimate of PD with each of its internal grades. The three broad approaches are: use of data based on a bank's own default experience; mapping to external data such as those of 'ECA'; use of statistical default models. Hence, a bank can use the foundation approach as long as it maps, in a sound manner, its own assessment of ratings with default probabilities, including usage of external data.

Advanced Approach

A first difference with the 'foundation' approach is that the bank assesses the same risk components plus the Lgd parameter characterizing recoveries. The subsequent presentation of credit risk models demonstrates that capital is highly sensitive to this risk input. In general, banks have implemented ratings scales for some time, but they lack risk data on recoveries.

The treatment of maturity also differs from the 'foundation' approach, which refers to a single benchmark for all assets. BRWs depend on maturity in the 'advanced' approach. The cap of 625% still applies as in the forfeit 3 years to maturity. The maturity effect depends on an annualized default probability as in the 'foundation' approach, plus a term b in a BRW function of DP and maturity depending on the effective maturity of assets. This is a more comprehensive response to the need to make capital sensitive to the maturity effect. It strikes a compromise between 'risk sensitivity' and the practical requirement of avoiding heavy capital charges for long-term commitments that would discourage banks from entering into such transactions.

As a remark, credit risk models (see Chapter 42) capture maturity effects through revaluation of facilities according to their final risk class at a horizon often set at 1 year. The revaluation process at the horizon does depend on maturity since it discounts future cash flows from loans at risk-adjusted discount rates. Nevertheless, the relationship depends on the risk and excess return of the asset over market required yields, as explained in Chapter 8. Consequently, there is no simple relation between credit risk and maturity. Presumably, the BRW function combines contributions of empirical data of behaviour over time of historical default frequencies and relations between capital and maturity from models.

However, the Committee is stopping short of permitting banks to calculate their capital requirements based on their own portfolio credit risk models. Reasons are the current lack of reliability of inputs required by such models, plus the difficulty of demonstrating the reliability of model capital estimates. However, by imposing the build-up of risk data for the next 3 years, the New Accord paves the way for a later implementation.

Given the difficulty of assessing the implications of these approaches on capital requirements, the Committee imposes some conservative guidelines such as a floor on required capital. The Committee emphasizes the need for banks to anticipate regulatory requirements by performing stress testing and establishing additional capital cushions of their own (i.e. through Pillar 2) during periods of economic growth. In the longer run, the Committee encourages banks to consider the merits of building such stress considerations directly into their internal ratings framework.

Guarantees

The New Accord grants greater recognition of credit risk mitigation techniques, including collateral, guarantees and credit derivatives, and netting. The new proposals provide capital reductions for various forms of transactions that reduce risk. They also impose minimum operational standards because a poor management of operational risks—including legal risks—would raise doubts with respect to the actual value of such mitigants. Further, banks are required to hold capital against residual risks resulting from any mismatch between credit risk hedges and the corresponding exposure. Mismatches refer to differences in amounts or maturities. In both cases, capital requirements will apply to the residual risks.

Collateral

The Committee has adopted for the standardized approach a definition of eligible collateral that is broader than that in the 1988 Accord. In general, banks can recognize as collateral: cash; a restricted range of debt securities issued by sovereigns, public sector entities, banks, securities firms and corporates; certain equity securities traded on recognized exchanges; certain mutual fund holdings; gold.

For collateral, it is necessary to account for time changes of exposure and collateral values. 'Haircuts' define the required excess collateral over exposure to ensure effective credit risk protection, given time periods necessary for readjusting the collateral level (re-margining), recognizing the counterparty's failure to pay or to deliver margin and the bank's ability to liquidate collateral for cash. Two sets of haircuts have been developed for a comprehensive approach to collateral: those established by the Committee (i.e. standard supervisory haircuts); others based on banks' 'own estimates' of collateral volatility subject to minimum requirements (see Chapter 41).

There is a capital floor, denoted w, whose purpose is twofold: to encourage banks to focus on and monitor the credit quality of the borrower in collateralized transactions; to reflect the fact that, irrespective of the extent of over-collateralization, a collateralized transaction can never be totally without risk. A normal w value is 0.15.

Guarantees and Credit Derivatives

For a bank to obtain any capital relief from the receipt of credit derivatives or guarantees, the credit protection must be direct, explicit, irrevocable and unconditional. The Committee recognizes that banks only suffer losses in guaranteed transactions when both the obligor and the guarantor default. This 'double default' effect reduces the credit risk if there is a low correlation between the default probabilities of the obligor and the guarantor[10]. The Committee considers that it is difficult to assess this situation and does not grant recognition to the 'double default' effect. The 'substitution approach' provided in the 1988 Accord applies for guarantees and credit derivatives, although an additional capital floor, w, applies. The substitution approach simply substitutes the risk of the guarantor for that of the borrower subject to full recognition of the enforceability of the guarantee.

On-balance Sheet Netting

On-balance sheet netting in the banking book is possible subject to certain operational standards. Its scope will be limited to the netting of loans and deposits with the same single counterparty.

Portfolio Granularity

The Committee is proposing to make another extension of the 1988 Accord in that minimum capital requirements do not depend only on the characteristics of an individual exposure but also on the 'concentration risk' of the bank portfolio. Concentration designates the large sizes of exposures to single borrowers, or groups of closely related borrowers, potentially triggering large losses. The accord proposes a measure of granularity[11] and incorporates this risk factor into the IRB approach by means of a standard supervisory capital adjustment applied to all exposures, except those in the retail portfolio. This treatment does not include industry, geographic or forms of credit risk concentration other than size concentration. The 'granularity' adjustment applies to the total risk-weighted assets at the consolidated bank level, based on the comparison of a reference portfolio with known granularity.

---

[10] Chapter 41 provides details on the technique for assessing the default probability reduction resulting from 'double' or 'joint' default of the primary borrower and the guarantor.

[11] An example is the 'Herfindahl index' calculation, measuring size concentration, given in Chapters 55–57.

Other Specific Risks

The New Accord addresses various other risks: asset securitizations; project finance; equity exposures.

The accord considers that asset securitizations deserve a more stringent treatment. It assigns risk weights more in line with the risks of structured notes issued by such structures and, notably, the credit enhancement note, subject to the first loss risk. These notes concentrate a large fraction of the risk of the pool of securitized assets[12].

It also imposes the 'clean break' principle through which the non-recourse sale of assets should be unambiguous, limiting the temptation of banks to support sponsored structures for reputation motives (reputation risk[13]). Under the standardized approach, any invested amount in the credit enhancement note of securitization becomes deductible from capital. For banks investing in securitization notes, the Committee proposes to rely on ratings provided by an ECAI.

Other issues with securitizations relate to operational risk. Revolving securitizations with early amortization features, or liquidity lines provided to structures (commitments to provide liquidity for funding the structure under certain conditions), generate some residual risks. There is a forfeited capital loading for such residual risk.

The Committee considers that project finance requires a specific treatment. The accord also imposes risk-sensitive approaches for equity positions held in the banking book. The rationale is to remedy the possibility that banks could benefit from a lower capital charge when they hold the equity rather than the debt of an obligor.

Interest Rate Risk

The accord considers it more appropriate to treat interest rate risk in the banking book under Pillar 2, rather than defining capital requirements. This implies no capital load, but an enhanced supervisory process. The guidance on interest rate risk considers banks' internal systems as the main tool for the measurement of interest rate risk in the banking book and the supervisory response. To facilitate supervisors' monitoring of interest rate risk across institutions, banks should provide the results of their internal measurement systems using standardized interest rate shocks. If supervisors determine that a bank is not holding capital commensurate with the level of interest rate risk, they can require that the bank reduces its risk, holds an additional amount of capital or combines the two.

Operational Risk

The Committee adopted a standard industry definition of operational risk: 'the risk of direct or indirect loss resulting from inadequate or failed internal processes, people and systems or from external events'.

As a first approximation in developing minimum capital charges, the Committee estimates operational risk at 20% of minimum regulatory capital as measured under the 1988

---

[12] See details in subsequent descriptions of structures (Chapter 40).

[13] Reputation risk is the risk of adverse perception of the sponsoring bank if structure explicitly related to the bank suffers from credit risk deterioration or from a default event.

Accord. The Committee proposes a range of three increasingly sophisticated approaches to capital requirements for operational risk: basic indicator; standardized; internal measurement.

The 'basic indicator approach' links the capital charge for operational risk to a single indicator that serves as a proxy for the bank's overall risk exposure. For example, if gross income is the indicator, each bank should hold capital for operational risk equal to a fixed percentage ('alpha factor') of its gross income.

The 'standardized approach' builds on the basic indicator approach by dividing a bank's activities into a number of standardized business lines (e.g. corporate finance and retail banking). Within each business line, the capital charge is a selected indicator of operational risk times a fixed percentage ('beta factor'). Both the indicator and the beta factors may differ across business lines.

The 'internal measurement approach' allows individual banks to rely on internal data for regulatory capital purposes. The technique necessitates three inputs for a specified set of business lines and risk types: an operational risk exposure indicator; the probability that a loss event occurs; the losses given such events. Together, these components make up a loss distribution for operational risks. Nevertheless, the loss distribution might differ from the industry-wide loss distribution, thereby necessitating an adjustment, which is the 'gamma factor'.

Pillar 2: Supervisory Review Process

The second pillar of the new framework aims at ensuring that each bank has sound internal processes to assess the adequacy of its capital based on a thorough evaluation of its risks. Supervisors will be responsible for evaluating how well banks are assessing their capital needs relative to their risks. The Committee regards the market discipline through enhanced disclosure as a fundamental part of the New Accord. It considers that disclosure requirements and recommendations will allow market participants to assess key pieces of information for the application of the revised accord.

The risk-sensitive approaches developed by the New Accord rely extensively on banks' internal methodologies, giving banks more discretion in calculating their capital requirements. Hence, separate disclosure requirements become prerequisites for supervisory recognition of internal methodologies for credit risk, credit risk mitigation techniques and other areas of implementation.

The Committee formulated four basic principles that should inspire supervisors' policies:

- Banks should have a process for assessing their overall capital in relation to their risk profile and a strategy for maintaining their capital levels.
- Supervisors should review and evaluate banks' internal capital adequacy assessments and strategies, as well as their ability to monitor and ensure their compliance with regulatory capital ratios. Supervisors should take appropriate supervisory actions if they are not satisfied with the results of this process.
- Supervisors should expect banks to operate above the minimum regulatory capital ratios and should have the ability to require banks to hold capital in excess of this minimum.

- Supervisors should intervene at an early stage to prevent capital from falling below the minimum levels required to support the risk of a particular bank, and should require corrective actions if capital is not maintained or restored.

Pillar 3: Market Discipline

The third major element of the Committee's approach to capital adequacy is market discipline. The accord emphasizes the potential for market discipline to reinforce capital regulations and other supervisory efforts in promoting safety and soundness in banks and financial systems.

Given the influence of internal methodologies on the capital requirements established, it considers that comprehensive disclosure is important for market participants to understand the relationship between the risk profile and the capital of an institution. Accordingly, the usage of internal approaches is contingent upon a number of criteria, including appropriate disclosure.

For these reasons, the accord is setting out a number of disclosure proposals as requirements, some of them being prerequisites to supervisory approval. Core disclosures convey vital information for all institutions and are important for market discipline. Disclosures are subject to 'materiality'. Information is 'material' if its omission or misstatement could change or influence the assessment or decision of any user relying on that information. Supplementary disclosures may convey information of significance for market discipline actions with respect to a particular institution.

SECTION 3

Risk Management Processes

4

Risk Management Processes

The ultimate goal of risk management is to facilitate a consistent implementation of both risks and business policies. Classical risk practices consist of setting risk limits while ensuring that business remains profitable. Modern best practices consist of setting risk limits based on economic measures of risk while ensuring the best risk-adjusted performances. In both cases, the goal remains to enhance the risk–return profile of transactions and of the bank's portfolios. Nevertheless, new best practices are more 'risk-sensitive' through quantification of risks.

The key difference is the implementation of risk measures. Risks are invisible and intangible uncertainties, which might materialize into future losses, while earnings are a standard output of reporting systems complying with established accounting standards. Such differences create a bias towards an asymmetric view of risk and return, making it more difficult to strike the right balance between both. Characterizing the risk–return profile of transactions and of portfolios is key for implementing risk-driven processes. The innovation of new best practices consists of plugging new risk–return measures into risk management processes, enriching them and leveraging them with more balanced views of profitability and risks.

The purpose of this chapter is to show how quantified risk measures feed the risk management processes. It does not address the risk measuring issue and does not describe the contribution of risk models, for which inputs are critical to enrich risk processes. Because quantifying intangible risks is a difficult challenge, concentrating on risk measures leaves in the shadow the wider view of risk processes implementing such risk measures. Since the view on risk processes is wider than the view on risk measuring techniques, we move first from a global view of risk processes before getting to the narrower and more technical view of risk measuring.

The 'risk–return profiles' of transactions and portfolios are the centrepiece of the entire system and processes. For this reason, risk–return profiles are the interface between new risk models and risk processes. All risk models and measures converge to provide these profiles at the transaction, the business lines and the global portfolio levels. Risk models provide new risk measures as inputs for processes. Classical processes address risks without the full capability of providing adequate quantification of risks. Risk models provide new measures of return and risks, leveraging risk processes and extending them to areas that were previously beyond reach.

New risk measures interact with risk processes. Vertical processes address the relationship between global goals and business decisions. The bottom-up and top-down processes of risk management allow the 'top' level to set up global guidelines conveyed to business lines. Simultaneously, periodical reporting from the business levels to the top allows deviations from guidelines to be detected, such as excess limits, and corrective actions to be taken, while comparing projected versus actual achievements.

Transversal processes address risk and return management at 'horizontal' levels, such as the level of individual transactions, at the very bottom of the management 'pyramid', at the intermediate business line levels, as well as at the bank's top level, for comparing risk and return measures to profitability target and risk limits. There are three basic horizontal processes: setting up risk–return guidelines and benchmarks; risk–return decision-making ('ex ante perspective'); risk–return monitoring ('ex post perspective').

The first section provides an overview of the vertical and horizontal processes. The subsequent sections detail the three basic 'transversal' processes (benchmarks, decision-making, monitoring). The last section summarizes some general features of 'bank-wide risk management' processes.

THE BASIC BUILDING BLOCKS OF RISK MANAGEMENT PROCESSES

Processes cover all necessary management actions for taking decisions and monitoring operations that influence the risk and return profiles of transactions, subportfolios of business lines or the overall bank portfolio. They extend from the preparation of decisions, to decision-making and control. They include all procedures and policies required to organize these processes. Risk management combines top-down and bottom-up processes with 'horizontal' processes. The top-down and bottom-up views relate to the vertical dimension of management, from general management to individual transactions, and vice versa. The horizontal layers refer to individual transactions, business lines, product lines and market segments, in addition to the overall global level. They require to move back and forth from a risk–return view of the bank to a business view, whose main dimensions are the product families and the market segments.

Bottom-up and Top-down Processes

The top-down process starts with global target earnings and risk limits converted into signals to business units. These signals include target revenues, risk limits and guidelines applicable to business unit policies. They make it necessary to allocate income and risks to business units and transactions. Otherwise, the global targets remain disconnected from operations. The monitoring and reporting of risks is bottom-up oriented, starting with transactions and ending with consolidated risks, income and volumes of transactions. Aggregation is required for supervision purposes and to compare, at all levels where decision-making occurs, goals with actual operations.

In the end, the process involves the entire banking hierarchy from top to bottom, to turn global targets into signals to business units, and from bottom to top, to aggregate risks and profitability and monitor them. The pyramid image of Figure 4.1 illustrates the risk diversification effect obtained when moving up along the hierarchy. Each face of the pyramid represents a dimension of risk, such as credit risk or market risk. The overall risk is less than the simple arithmetic addition of all original risks generated by transactions (at the base of the pyramid) or subsets (subportfolios) of transactions. From bottom to top, risks diversify. This allows us to take more risks at the transaction level since risk aggregation diversifies away a large fraction of the sum of all individual transaction risks. Only post-diversification risk remains retained by the bank.

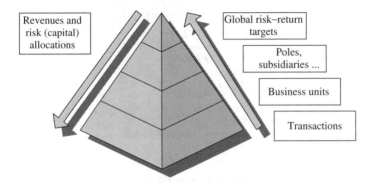

FIGURE 4.1   The pyramid of risk management

Risk models play a critical role in this 'vertical' process. Not only do they provide risk visibility at the transaction and business units level, but they also need to provide the right techniques for capturing risk diversification when moving up and down along the pyramid. Without quantification of the diversification effect, there are missing links between the sustainable risks, at the level of transactions, and the aggregated risk at the top of the pyramid that the bank capital should hedge. In other words, we do not know the overall risk when we have, say, two risks of 1 each, because the risk of the sum $(1 + 1)$ is lower than 2, the sum of risks. There are missing links as well between the sustainable post-diversification risk, the bank's capital and the risks tolerable at the bottom of the pyramid for individual transactions, business lines, market segments and product families. In other words, if a global post-diversification risk of 2 is sustainable at the top of the pyramid, it is compatible with a sum of individual risks larger than 2 at the bottom. How large can the sum of individual risks be (3, 4, 5 or more), compatible with an overall global risk limit of 2, remains unknown unless we have tools to allocate the global risk. The capital allocation system addresses these needs. This requires a unified risk management framework.

Transversal Process Building Blocks

Transversal processes apply to any horizontal level, such as business lines, product lines or market segments. The typical building transversal blocks of such processes (Figure 4.2) are:

1. Setting up risk limits, delegations and target returns.
2. Monitoring the compliance of risk–return profiles of transactions or subportfolios with guidelines, reporting and defining of corrective actions.
3. Risk and return decisions, both at the transaction and at the portfolio levels, such as lending, rebalancing the portfolio or hedging.

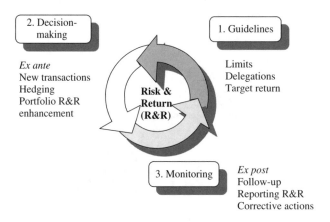

FIGURE 4.2   The three-block transversal processes

These are integrated processes, since there are feedback loops between guidelines, decisions and monitoring. Risk management becomes effective and successful only if it develops up to the stage where it facilitates decision-making and monitoring.

Overview of Processes

Putting together these two views could produce a chart as in Figure 4.3, which shows how vertical and transversal dimensions interact.

Risk Models and Risk Processes

Risk models contribute to all processes because they provide them with better and richer measures of risk, making them comparable to income, and because they allow banks to enrich the processes using new tools such as risk-adjusted performance or valuing the risk reduction effects of altering the portfolio structure. Figure 4.4 illustrates how models provide the risk–return measures feeding transversal and vertical processes.

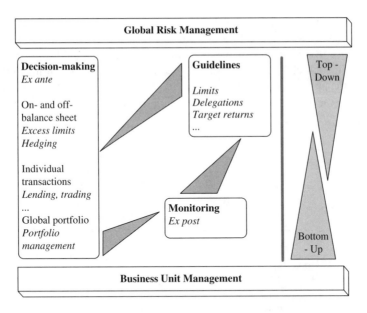

FIGURE 4.3   The three basic building blocks of risk management processes

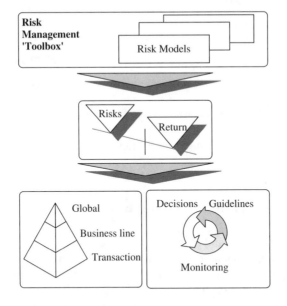

FIGURE 4.4   Overall views of risk processes and risk–return

Risk Processes and Business Policy

Business policy deals with dimensions other than risk and return. Attaching risk and returns to transactions and portfolios is not enough, if we cannot convert these views into the two basic dimensions of business policy: products and markets. This requires a third type of process reconciling the risk and return view with the product–market view. For business purposes, it is natural to segment the risk management process across business lines, products and markets. The product–market matrices provide a synthethic business view of the bank. Broad business lines and market segments could look like the matrix in Figure 4.5. In each cell, it is necessary to capture the risk and return profiles to make economically meaningful decisions. The chart illustrates the combinations of axes for reporting purposes, and the need for Information Technology (IT) to keep in line with such multidimensional reports and analyses.

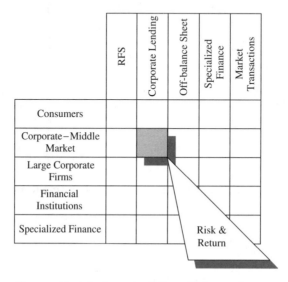

FIGURE 4.5   Reporting credit risk characteristics within product–market couples
RFS refers to 'Retail Financial Services'.
Specialized finance refers to structured finance, project finance, LBO or assets financing.

The next section discusses the three basic transversal processes: setting up guidelines; decision-making; monitoring.

PROCESS #1: SETTING UP RISK AND RETURN GUIDELINES

Guidelines include risk limits and delegations, and benchmarks for return. The purpose of limits is to set up an upper bound of exposures to risks so that an unexpected event cannot impair significantly the earnings and credit standing of the bank. Setting up benchmarks of return refers to the target profitability goals of the bank, and how they translate into pricing. When setting up such guidelines, banks face trade-offs in terms of business volume versus risk and business volume versus profitability.

Risk Benchmarks: Limits and Delegations

Traditional risk benchmarks are limits and delegations. For credit risk, limits set upper bounds to credit risk on obligors, markets and industries, or country risk. For market risk, limits set upper bounds to market risk sensitivity to the various market parameters.

Delegations serve to decentralize the decision-making process. They mean business lines do not need to refer always to the central functions to make risk decisions as long as the risk is not too large.

Classical procedures and policies have served to monitor credit risk for as long as banks have existed. Limit systems set caps on amounts at risk with any one customer, with a single industry or country. To set up limits, some basic rules are simple, such as: avoid any single loss endangering the bank; diversify the commitments across various dimensions such as customers, industries and regions; avoid lending to any borrower an amount that would increase debt beyond borrowing capacity. The equity of the borrower sets up some reasonable limit on debt given acceptable levels of debt/equity ratios and repayment ability. The capital of the bank sets up another limit to lending given the diversification requirements and/or the credit policy guidelines.

Credit officers and credit committees reach a minimal agreement before making a credit decision by examining in detail credit applications. Delegations, at various levels of the bank, stipulate who has permission to take credit commitments depending on their size. Typical criteria for delegations are size of commitments or risk classes.

Central reporting of the largest outstanding loans to customers serves to ensure that these amounts stay within reasonable limits, especially when several business units originate transactions with the same clients. This makes it necessary to have 'global limit' systems aggregating all risks on any single counterparty, no matter who initiates the risk. Finally, there are risk diversification rules across counterparties.

The rationale for risk limits potentially conflicts with the development of business volume. Banking foundations are about trust and relationships with customers. A continuous relationship allows business to be carried on. The business rationale aims at developing such relationships through new transactions. The risk rationale lies in limiting business volume because the latter implies risks. 'Name lending' applies to big corporations, with an excellent credit standing. Given the high quality of risk and the importance of business opportunities with big customers, it gets harder to limit volume. This is the opposite of a limit rationale. In addition, allowing large credit limits is necessary in other instances. For instance, banks need to develop business relationships with a small number of big players, for their own needs, such as setting up hedges for interest rate risk.

The same principles apply to controlling market risk. In these cases, to limit the potential loss of adverse markets moves, banks set upper bounds to sensitivities of instruments and portfolios. Sensitivities are changes in value due to forfeit shocks on market parameters such as interest rates, foreign exchange rates or equity indexes. Traders comply with such limits through trading and hedging their risks. Limits depend on expectations about market conditions and trading book exposures.

To control the interest rate risk of the banking portfolio, limits apply to the sensitivities of the interest income or the Net Present Value (NPV, the mark-to-market valuation of assets minus liabilities) to shocks on interest rates. By bounding these values, banks limit the adverse movements of these target variables.

Risk limits imply upper bounds on business volume, except when it is possible to hedge risks and avoid any excess exposure over limits. This is feasible for market transactions and for hedging interest rate risk, unless the cost of setting up the hedge is too high. For credit risk, there was no hedge until recently. Today, insurance, guarantees, credit derivatives and securitization offer a wide range of techniques for taking on more risk while still complying with risk limits.

Return Benchmarks

The target profitability of the bank provides signals to business units for making business. Classical profitability measures include interest income and fees for the banking portfolio, Return On Equity (ROE) for the bank and for individual transactions, using the former Cooke ratio to determine the capital loading of a transaction or a portfolio, and Return On Assets (ROA) relating income to the size of the exposure. For the trading book, the profitability is in Profit and Loss (P&L), independent of whether sales of assets occur or not. Such measures have existed for a long time. Nevertheless, such measures fall short of addressing the issue of the trade-off between risk and return.

However, only the risk and return profile of transactions or portfolios is relevant because it is easy to sacrifice or gain return by altering risk. Risk-based pricing refers to pricing differentiation based on risks. It implies that risks be defined at the transaction level, the subportfolio level and the entire bank portfolio level. Two systems are prerequisites for this process: the capital allocation system, which allocates risks; the funds transfer pricing system, which allocates income. The allocation of income and risks applies to transactions, business lines, market segments, customers or product lines. The specifications and roles of these two tools are expanded in Chapters 51 and 52 (capital allocation) and Chapters 26 and 27 (funds transfer pricing).

Pricing benchmarks are based on economic transfer prices in line with the cost of funds. The Funds Transfer Pricing (FTP) system defines such economic prices and to which internal exchanges of funds they apply. Benchmark transfer prices generally refer to market rates. With internal prices, the income allocation consists simply of calculating the income as the difference between interest revenues and these prices. The target overall profitability results in target mark-ups over these economic prices.

Risk allocation is similar to income allocation, except that it is less intuitive and more complex because risks do not add up arithmetically as income does. Capital allocation is a technique for allocating risks based on objective criteria. Risk allocations are capital allocations in monetary units. Capital refers to 'economic capital', or the amount of capital that matches the potential losses as measured by the 'Value at Risk' (VaR) methodology.

Both transfer pricing and capital allocation systems are unique devices that allow interactions between risk management and business lines in a consistent bank-wide risk management framework. If they do not have strong economic foundations, they put the entire credibility of the risk management at stake and fail to provide the bottom-up and top-down links between 'global' targets and limits and 'local' business targets and limits.

PROCESS #2: DECISION-MAKING (EX ANTE PERSPECTIVE)

The challenge for decision-making purposes is to capture risks upstream in the decision process, rather than downstream, once decisions are made. Helping the business decision process necessitates an 'ex ante' perspective, plus adequate tools for measuring and pricing risk consistently. Risk decisions refer to transactions or business line decisions, as well as portfolio decisions. New transactions, portfolio rebalancing and portfolio restructuring through securitizations (sales of bundled assets into the markets) are risk decisions. Hedging decisions effectively alter the risk–return profiles of transactions or of the entire portfolio. Decisions refer to both 'on-balance sheet', or business, decisions and 'off-balance sheet', or hedging, decisions. Without a balanced risk–return view, the policy gets 'myopic' in terms of risks, or ignores the effect on income of hedging transactions.

On-balance Sheet Actions

On-balance sheet actions relate to both new business and the existing portfolio of trans-actions. New business raises such basic questions as: Are the expected revenues in line with risks? What is the impact on the risk of the bank? Considering spreads and fees only is not enough. Lending to high-risk lenders makes it easy to generate margins, but at the expense of additional risks which might not be in line with income.

Without some risk–return measures, it is impossible to solve the dilemma between revenues and volume, other than on a judgmental basis. This is what banks have done, and still do, for lack of better measures of risks. Banks have experience and perception of risks. Nevertheless, risk measures, combined with judgmental expertise, provide benchmarks that are more objective and help solve dilemmas such as volume versus profitability. Risk measures facilitate these decisions because they shed new light on risks. A common fear of focusing on risks is the possibility of discouraging risk taking by making risks explicit. In fact, the purpose is just the opposite. Risk monitoring can encourage risk taking by providing explicit information on risks. With unknown risks, prudence might prevail and prevent risk-taking decisions even though the profitability could well be in line with risks. When volume is the priority, controlling risks might become a second-level priority unless risks become more explicit. In both cases, risk models provide information for taking known and calculated risks.

Similar questions arise ex post, once decisions are made. Since new business does not influence income and risks to an extent comparable to the existing portfolio, it is important to deal with the existing portfolio as well. Traditionally, periodical corrective actions, such as managing non-performing loans and providing incentives to existing customers to take advantage of new services, help to enhance the risk–return profile. Portfolio management extends this rationale further to new actions, such as securitizations that off-load risk in the market, syndications, loan trading or hedging credit risk, that were not feasible formerly. This is an emerging function for banks, which traditionally stick to the 'originate and hold' view of the existing portfolio, detailed further below.

Off-balance Sheet Actions

Off-balance sheet recommendations refer mainly to hedging transactions. Asset–Liability Management (ALM) is in charge of controlling the liquidity and interest rate risk of the banking portfolio and is responsible for hedging programmes. Traders pursue the same goals when using off-balance instruments to offset exposures whenever they need to. Now, loan portfolio management and hedging policies also take shape, through credit derivatives and insurance. Hedging makes extensive use of derivative instruments. Derivatives include interest rate swaps, currency swaps and options on interest rates, if we consider interest rate only. Credit derivatives are new instruments. All derivatives shape both risk and return since they generate costs, the cost of hedging, and income as well because they capture the underlying market parameters or asset returns. For instance, a swap receiving the variable rate and paying a fixed rate might reduce the interest exposure and, simultaneously, generate variable rate revenues. A total return swap exchanges the return of a reference debt against a fixed rate, thereby protecting the buyer from capital losses of the reference asset in exchange for a return giving up the asset capital gains. Setting up such hedges requires a comprehensive view on how they affect both risk and return dimensions.

Loan Portfolio Management

Even though banks have always followed well-known diversification principles, active management of the banking portfolio remained limited. Portfolio management is widely implemented with market transactions because diversification effects are obvious, hedging is feasible with financial instruments and market risk quantification is easy. This is not the case for the banking portfolio. The classical emphasis of credit analysis is at the transaction level, rather than the portfolio level, subject to limits defined by the credit department. Therefore, loan portfolio management is one of the newest fields of credit risk management.

Incentives for the Development of Loan Portfolio Management

There are many incentives for developing portfolio management for banking transactions:

- The willingness to make diversification (portfolio) effects more explicit and to quantify them.
- The belief that there is a significant potential to improve the risk–return trade-off through management of the banking portfolio as a whole, rather than focusing only on individual banking transactions.
- The growing usage of securitizations to off-load risk into the market, rather than the classical arbitrage between the on-balance sheet cost of funding versus the market cost of funds.
- The emergence of new instruments to manage credit risk: credit derivatives.
- The emergence of the loan trading market, where loans, usually illiquid, become tradable over an organized market.

Such new opportunities generate new tools. Portfolio management deals with the optimization of the risk–return profile by altering the portfolio structure. Classical portfolio management relies more on commercial guidelines, on a minimum diversification and/or aims at limiting possible risk concentrations in some industries or with some big customers. New portfolio management techniques focus on the potential for enhancing actively the profile of the portfolio and on the means to achieve such goals. For example, reallocating exposures across customers or industries can reduce risk without sacrificing profitability, or increase profitability without increasing risks. This is the familiar technique of manipulating the relative importance of individual exposures to improve the portfolio profile, a technique well known and developed for market portfolios.

The first major innovation in this area is the implementation of portfolio models providing measures of credit risk diversification. The second innovation is the new flexibility to shape the risk profile of portfolios through securitization, loan sales and usage of credit derivatives. Credit derivatives are instruments based on simple mechanisms. They include total return swaps, default options and credit spread swaps. Total return swaps exchange the return of any asset against some market index. Default options provide compensation in the event of default of a borrower, in exchange for the payment of a premium. Credit spread swaps exchange one market credit spread against another one. Such derivatives can be used, as other traditional derivatives, to hedge credit risk.

The Loan Portfolio Management Function

The potential gains of more active portfolio management are still subject to debate. Manipulating the 'weights' of commitments for some customers might look like pure theory, given the practice of relationship banking. Banks maintain continuous relationships with customers that they know well, and are willing to keep doing business with. Volumes are not so flexible. Hence, a debate emerged on the relative merits of portfolio management and relationship banking.

There might be an apparent conflict between stable relations and flexible portfolio management. What would be the benefit of trading loans if it adversely influenced 'relationship banking'? In fact, the opposite holds. The ability to sell loans improves the possibility of generating new ones and develops, rather than restricts, relationship banking.

Once we start to focus on portfolio management, the separation of origination from portfolio management appears a logical step, although this remains a major organizational and technical issue. The rationale of portfolio management is global risk–return enhancement. This implies moving away from the traditional 'buy and hold' policy and not sticking to the portfolio structure resulting from the origination business unit. Portfolio management requires degrees of freedom to be effective. They imply separation, to a certain extent, from origination. The related issues are numerous. What would be the actual role of a portfolio management unit? Should the transfer of transactions from origination to portfolio management be extensive or limited? What would be the internal transfer prices between both units? Can we actually trade intangible risk reductions, modelled rather than observed, against tangible revenues? Perhaps, once risk measures are explicit, the benefits of such trade-offs may become more visible and less debated.

Because of these challenges, the development of the emerging portfolio management function is gradual, going through various stages:

- Portfolio risk reporting.
- Portfolio risk modelling.
- A more intensive usage of classical techniques such as syndication or securitizations.
- New credit derivatives instruments and loan trading.
- Separation of portfolio management and origination, since both functions differ in their perspective and both can be profit centres.

PROCESS #3: RISK–RETURN MONITORING (EX POST PERSPECTIVE)

The monitoring and periodical reviews of risks are a standard piece of any controlling system. They result in corrective actions or confirmations of existing guidelines. For credit risk, the monitoring process has been in existence since banks started lending. Periodical reviews of risk serve to assess any significant event that might change the policy of the bank with respect to some counterparties, industries or countries. Monitoring systems extend to early warning systems triggering special reviews, including borrowers in a 'watch list', up to provisioning. Corrective actions avoid further deteriorations through restructuring of individual transactions. Research on industries and countries, plus periodical reviews result in confirmation of existing limits or adjustments. Reviews and corrective actions are also event-driven, for example by a sudden credit standing deterioration of a major counterparty. Analogous processes apply for market risk and ALM.

A prerequisite for risk–return monitoring is to have measures of risk and return at all relevant levels, global, business lines and transactions. Qualitative assessment of risk is insufficient. The challenge is to implement risk-based performance tools. These compare ex post revenues with the current risks or define ex ante which pricing would be in line with the overall target profitability, given risks. The standard tools for risk-adjusted performance, as well as risk-based pricing, are the RaRoC (Risk-adjusted Return on Capital) and SVA (Shareholders Value Added) measures detailed in Chapters 53 and 54. Risk-based performance allows:

- Monitoring risk–return profiles across business lines, market segments and customers, product families and individual transactions.
- Making explicit the possible mispricing of subportfolios or transactions compared to what risk-based pricing would be.
- Defining corrective or enhancement actions.

Defining target risk-adjusted profitability benchmarks does not imply that such pricing is effective. Competition might not allow charging risk-based prices without losing business. This does not imply that target prices are irrelevant. Mispricing is the gap between target prices and effective prices. Such gaps appear as RaRoC ratios or SVA values not in line with objectives. Monitoring ex post mispricing serves the purpose of determining ex post what contributes to the bank profitability on a risk-adjusted basis. Without mispricing reports, there would be no basis for taking corrective actions and revising guidelines.

BANK-WIDE RISK MANAGEMENT

The emergence of risk models allowed risk management to extend 'bank-wide'. 'Bank-wide' means across all business lines and risks. Bank-wide risk management implies using the entire set of techniques and models of the risk management 'toolbox'. Risk management practices traditionally differ across risks and business lines, so that a bank-wide scope requires a single unified and consistent framework.

Risk Management Differs across Risks

Risk management appears more fragmented than unified. This contrasts with the philosophy of 'bank-wide risk management', which suggests some common grounds and common frameworks for different risks. Risk practice differs across business lines. The market risk culture and the credit culture seem not to have much in common yet. Market culture is quantitative in nature and model-driven. By contrast, the credit culture focuses on the fundamentals of firms and on the relationship with borrowers to expand the scope of services. Moreover, the credit culture tends to ignore modelling because of the challenge of quantifying credit risk. In the capital markets universe, trading risks is continuous since there is a market for doing so. At the opposite end of the spectrum, the 'buy and hold' philosophy prevails in the banking portfolio.

ALM does not have much to do with credit and market risk management, in terms of goals as well as tools and processes. It needs dedicated tools and risk measures to define a proper funding and investment policy, and to control interest rate risk for the whole bank. Indeed, ALM remains very different from market and credit risk and expands over a number of sections in this book.

Indeed, risk models cannot yet pretend to address the issues of all business lines. Risk-adjusted performance is easier to implement in the middle market than with project finance or for Leveraged Buy-Outs (LBOs), which is unfortunate because risk-adjusted performances would certainly facilitate decision-making in these fields.

On the other hand, the foundations of risk measures seem robust enough to address most risks, with techniques based on the simple 'potential loss', or VaR, concept. Making the concept instrumental is quite a challenge, as illustrated by the current difficulties of building up data for credit risk and operational risk. But the concept is simple enough to provide visibility on which roads to follow to get better measures and understand why crude measures fail to provide sound bases for decision-making and influencing, in general, the risk management processes. Because of such limitations, new best practices will not apply to all activities in the near future, and will presumably extend gradually.

Different Risks Fit into a Single Framework

The view progressively expanded in this book is that risk management remains differentiated, but that all risks tend to fit in a common basic framework. The underlying intuition is that many borders between market and credit risk tend to progressively disappear, while common concepts, such as VaR and portfolio models, apply gradually to all risks. The changing views in credit risk illustrate the transformation:

- Credit risk hedges now exist with credit derivatives.
- The 'buy and hold' culture tends to recede and the credit risk management gets closer to the 'trading philosophy'.
- The portfolio view of credit risk gains ground because it brings some new ways of enhancing the risk–return profile of the banking portfolio.
- Accordingly, the 'model culture' is now entering the credit risk sphere and increasingly interacts with the credit culture.
- The building up of data has been productive for those banks that made it a priority.
- Regulations using quantitative measures of risk perceived as intangibles gained acceptance in the industry and stimulate progress.

FIGURE 4.6   Global integration of differentiated risks and risk management techniques

A preliminary conclusion is that there are now sufficient common grounds across risks to capture them within a common framework. This facilitates the presentation of concepts, methodologies, techniques and implementations, making it easier to wrap around a framework showing how tools and techniques capture differentiated risks and risk management processes in ways that facilitate their global and comprehensive integration (Figure 4.6).

5

Risk Management Organization

The development of bank-wide risk management organization is an ongoing process. The original traditional commercial bank organization tends to be dual, with the financial sphere versus the business sphere. The business lines tend to develop volume, sometimes at the expense of risks and profitability, while the financial sphere tends to focus on profitability, with dedicated credit and market risk monitoring units. This dual view is fading away with the emergence of new dedicated functions implemented bank-wide.

Bank-wide risk management has promoted the centralization of risk management and a clean break between risk-taking business lines and risk-supervising units. Technical and organizational necessities foster the process. Risk supervision requires separating the supervising units from the business units, since these need to take more risk to achieve their profitability targets. Risk centralization is also a byproduct of risk diversification. Only post-diversification risks are relevant for the entire bank's portfolio, and required capital, once the aggregation of individual risks diversified away a large fraction of them. The risk department emerged from the need for global oversight on credit risk, market risk and interest rate risk, now extending to operational risk.

Separating risk control from business, plus the need for global oversight, first gave birth to the dedicated Asset–Liability Management (ALM) function, for interest rate risk, and later on stimulated the emergence of risk departments, grouping former credit and market risk units. While risk measuring and monitoring developed, other central functions with different focuses, such as management control, accounting, compliance with regulations, reporting and auditing, differentiated. This chapter focuses on the risk management functions, and illustrates how they emerged and how they relate to other functions.

The modern risk management organization separates risk management units from business units. The banking portfolio generates interest rate risk, transferred from business lines, which have no control over interest rate movements, to the ALM unit which is in charge of managing it. The banking portfolio and ALM, when setting up hedges with derivatives, generate credit risk, supervised by the credit risk unit. The market risk unit supervises the trading portfolio. The portfolio management unit deals with the portfolio of loans as a whole, for risk control purposes and for a more active restructuring policy through actions such as direct sales or securitization. The emerging 'portfolio management' unit might necessitate a frontier with origination through loans management post-origination. It might be related to the risk department, or be a profit-making entity as well.

The first section maps risk origination with risk management units supervising. The second section provides an overview of central functions, and of the risk department. The third section details the ALM role. The fourth section focuses on risk oversight and supervision by the risk department entity. The fifth section details the emerging role of the 'loan portfolio management' unit. The last section emphasizes the critical role of Information Technology (IT) for dealing with a much wider range of models, risk data warehouses and risk measures than before.

MAPPING ORGANIZATION WITH RISK MANAGEMENT NECESSITIES

Figure 5.1 shows who originates what risks and which central functions supervise them. Various banks have various organizations. There is no unique way of organizing the

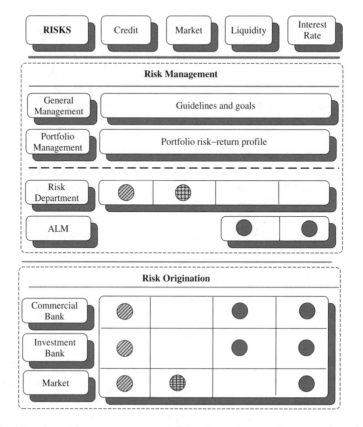

FIGURE 5.1   Mapping risk management with business lines and central functions

risk management processes. Available risk models and management tools and techniques influence organization schemes, as various stages of differentiation illustrate.

THE DIFFERENTIATION OF CENTRAL FUNCTIONS

The functions of the different central units tend to differentiate from each other when going further into the details of risk and income actions. Figure 5.2 illustrates the differentiation process of central functions according to their perimeter of responsibilities.

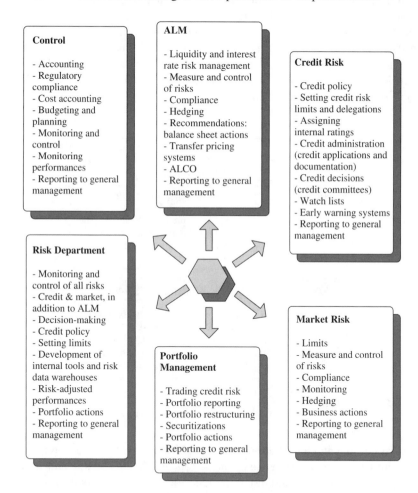

Control

- Accounting
- Regulatory compliance
- Cost accounting
- Budgeting and planning
- Monitoring and control
- Monitoring performances
- Reporting to general management

ALM

- Liquidity and interest rate risk management
- Measure and control of risks
- Compliance
- Hedging
- Recommendations: balance sheet actions
- Transfer pricing systems
- ALCO
- Reporting to general management

Credit Risk

- Credit policy
- Setting credit risk limits and delegations
- Assigning internal ratings
- Credit administration (credit applications and documentation)
- Credit decisions (credit committees)
- Watch lists
- Early warning systems
- Reporting to general management

Risk Department

- Monitoring and control of all risks
- Credit & market, in addition to ALM
- Decision-making
- Credit policy
- Setting limits
- Development of internal tools and risk data warehouses
- Risk-adjusted performances
- Portfolio actions
- Reporting to general management

Portfolio Management

- Trading credit risk
- Portfolio reporting
- Portfolio restructuring
- Securitizations
- Portfolio actions
- Reporting to general management

Market Risk

- Limits
- Measure and control of risks
- Compliance
- Monitoring
- Hedging
- Business actions
- Reporting to general management

FIGURE 5.2 Functions of central units and of the risk department

THE ALM FUNCTION

ALM is the unit in charge of managing the interest rate risk and liquidity of the bank. It focuses essentially on the commercial banking pole, although the market portfolio also generates liquidity requirements.

The ALM Committee (ALCO) is in charge of implementing ALM decisions, while the technical unit prepares all analyses necessary for taking decisions and runs the ALM models. The ALCO agenda includes 'global balance sheet management' and the guidelines for making the business lines policy consistent with the global policy.

ALM addresses the issue of defining adequate structures of the balance sheet and the hedging programmes for liquidity and interest rate risks. The very first mission of ALM is to provide relevant risk measures of these risks and to keep them under control given expectations of future interest rates. Liquidity and interest rate policies are interdependent since any projected liquidity gap requires future funding or investing at an unknown rate as of today, unless setting up hedges today.

ALM scope (Figure 5.3) varies across institutions, from a limited scope dedicated to balance sheet interest and liquidity risk management, to being a profit centre, in addition to its mission of hedging the interest rate and liquidity risks of the bank. In between, ALM extends beyond pure global balance sheet management functions towards a better integration and interaction with business policies.

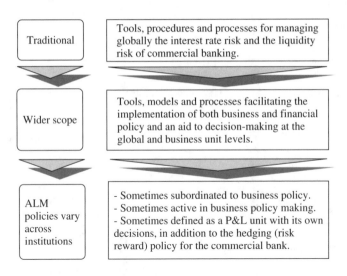

FIGURE 5.3   ALM scope

The ALCO is the implementation arm of ALM. It groups heads or business lines together with the general bank management, sets up the guidelines and policies with respect to interest rate risk and liquidity risk for the banking portfolio. The ALCO discusses financial options for hedging risks and makes recommendations with respect to business policies. Both financial and business policies should ensure a good balance between 'on-balance sheet' actions (business policy and development) and 'off-balance sheet' actions (hedging policies). Financial actions include funding, investing and hedging. Since these are market transactions, they always have an influence on the interest income, creating a trade-off between risk and interest income. Technical analyses underlie the recommendations, usually conducted by a technical unit which prepares ALCO meetings and recommendations.

Other units interact with ALM, such as a dedicated unit for funding, in charge of raising funds, or the treasury, which manages the day-to-day cash flows and derivatives, without setting the basic guidelines of interest rate risk management. Management control and accounting also interact with ALM to set the economic transfer prices, or because of the Profit and Loss (P&L) incidence of accounting standards for hedging operations. The transfer pricing system is in charge of allocating income between banking business units and transactions, and is traditionally under ALM control.

THE RISK DEPARTMENT AND OVERSIGHT ON RISKS

Dedicated units normally address credit risk and market risk, while ALM addresses the commercial banking side of interest rate risk and funding. Risk supervisors should be independent of business lines to ensure that risk control is not under the influence of business and profit-making policies. This separation principle repeatedly appears in guidelines. Separation should go as far as setting up limits that preclude business lines from developing new transactions because they would impair the bank's risk too much. The functions of the risk department include active participation in risk decision-making, with a veto power on transactions, plus the ability to impose restructuring of transactions to mitigate their risk. This empowers the risk-supervising unit to full control of risks, possibly at the cost of restricting risky business.

Getting an overview of risks is feasible with separate entities dedicated to each main risk. However, when reaching this stage, it sounds natural to integrate the risk supervision function into a risk department, while still preserving the differentiation of risk measures and management. There are several reasons for integration in a single department, some of them organizational and others technical.

From an organizational standpoint, integration facilitates the overview of all risks across all business lines. In theory, separate risk functions can do the same job. In practice, because of process harmonization, lack of interaction between information systems and lack of uniform reporting systems, it is worth placing the differentiated entities under the same control. Moreover, separate risk control entities, such as market and credit risk units, could possibly deal separately with business lines, to the detriment of the global policy. When transactions get sophisticated, separating functions could result in disruptions. A single transaction can trigger multiple risks, some of them not obvious at first sight. Market transactions and ALM hedges create credit risk. Investment banking activities or structured finance generate credit risk, interest rate risk and operational risk. Multiple views on risks might hurt the supervisory process, while a single picture of all risks is a simple practical way to have a broader view on all risks triggered by the same complex transactions.

For such reasons the risk department emerged in major institutions, preserving the differentiation of different risks, but guaranteeing the integration of risk monitoring, risk analyses and risk reporting. Under this scheme, the risk department manages and controls risks, while business lines generate risks (Figure 5.4). Each major business pole can have its own risk unit, interacting with the risk department.

Few banks set up a portfolio management unit, but many progress along such lines. The portfolio management unit is in charge of restructuring the portfolio, after origination, to enhance its risk–return profile. The first stages of portfolio management extend from

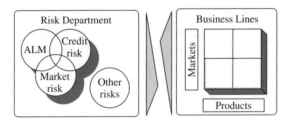

FIGURE 5.4   Risk department, risk units and business lines

reporting on risks and portfolio structure, to interaction with the limit setting process and the definitions of credit policy guidelines. At further stages, the portfolio management unit trades credit risk after origination through direct sales of loans, securitizations or credit risk hedging. Active portfolio management is a reality, with or without a dedicated unit, since all techniques and instruments allowing us to perform such tasks have been developed to a sufficient extent. The full recognition of the portfolio management unit would imply acting as a separate entity, with effective control over assets post-origination, and making it a profit centre. The goal is to enhance the risk–return profile of the entire portfolio. Transfers of assets from origination should not result in lost revenues by origination without compensation. The ultimate stage would imply full separation and transfer prices between origination and portfolio management, to effectively allocate income to each of these two poles.

The risk department currently plays a major role in the gradual development of portfolio management. It has an overview of the bank's portfolio and facilitates the innovation process of hedging credit risk. It has a unique neutral position for supervising rebalancing of the portfolio and altering of its risk–return profile. Nevertheless, the risk department cannot go as far as making profit, as a portfolio management unit should ultimately do, since this would negate its neutral posture with respect to risk. It acts as a facilitator during the transition period when risk management develops along these new dimensions.

INFORMATION TECHNOLOGY

Information technology plays a key role in banks in general, and particularly in risk management. There are several reasons for this:

- Risk data is continuously getting richer.
- New models, running at the bank-wide scale, produce new measures of risk.
- Bringing these measures to life necessitates dedicated front-ends for user decision-making.

Risk data extends from observable inputs, such as market prices, to new risk measures such as Value at Risk (VaR). New risk data warehouses are required to put together data and to organize the data gathering process, building up historical data on new inputs, such as those required by the 2001 Basel Accord.

VaR necessitates models that did not exist a few years ago, running at the entire bank scale to produce market risk and credit risk measures. IT scope extends to the implementation of these models, and to assembling their outputs in a usable form for end-users. Due to the scale of operations of bank systems, creating the required risk data warehouse with the inputs and outputs of these models, and providing links to front-ends and reporting modules for end-users, are major projects. Bringing the information to life is an IT challenge because it requires new generation tools capable of on-line queries and analyses embedded in front-ends and reporting. Without such aids, decision-makers might simply ignore the information because of lack of time. Since new risk measures are not intuitive, managers not yet familiar with them need tools to facilitate their usage.

'On-Line Analysis and Processing' (OLAP) systems are critical to forward relevant information to end-users whenever they need it. Multiple risk measures generate several new metrics for risks, which supplement the simple and traditional book exposures for credit risk, for example. The risk views now extend to expected and unexpected losses, capital and risk allocations, in addition to mark-to-market measures of loan exposures (the major building blocks of risk models are described in Chapter 9). Profitability measures also extend to new dimensions, from traditional earnings to risk-adjusted measures, ex ante and ex post, at all levels, transactions, subportfolios and the bank's portfolio. Simultaneously, business lines look at other dimensions, transactions, product families, market segments or business unit subportfolios.

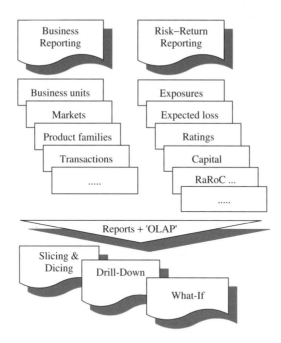

FIGURE 5.5 IT and portfolio reporting

Combining several risk dimensions with profitability dimensions and business dimensions has become a conceptual and practical challenge. Multidimensional views of the bank's portfolio have become more complex to handle. New generation IT systems can handle the task. However, IT still needs to design risk, profitability and business reports so that they integrate smoothly within the bank's processes. Multidimensional reporting requires a more extensive usage of new tools:

- Slicing and dicing the portfolio across any one of these dimensions, or combinations of them, such as reporting the risk-adjusted profitability by market segment, business unit or both.
- A drilling-down function to find out which transactions are the source of risk for subsets of transactions. The simplest example would be to find which transactions and obligors contribute most to the risk of a business unit, or simply understanding what transactions make a risk metric (exposure, expected loss, risk allocation) higher than expected.
- 'What if' simulation capabilities to find out the outcomes of various scenarios such as adding or withdrawing a transaction or a business line, conducting sensitivity analyses to find which risk drivers influence risk more, or when considering rebalancing the bank's subportfolios.

New risk softwares increasingly embed such functions for structuring and customizing reports. Figure 5.5 illustrates the multiple dimensions and related reporting challenges.

To avoid falling into the trap of managing reports rather than business, on-line customization is necessary to produce the relevant information on time. Front-end tools with 'what if' and simulation functions, producing risk–return reports both for the existing portfolio and new transactions, become important for both the credit universe and the market universe.

SECTION 4

Risk Models

6

Risk Measures

Risk management relies on quantitative measures of risks. There are various risk measures. All aim at capturing the variation of a given target variable, such as earnings, market value or losses due to default, generated by uncertainty. Quantitative indicators of risks fall into three types:

- Sensitivity, which captures the deviation of a target variable due to a unit movement of a single market parameter (for instance, an interest rate shift of 1%). Sensitivities are often market risk-related because they relate value changes to market parameters, which are value drivers. The interest rate gap is the sensitivity of the interest margin of the banking portfolio to a forfeit move of the yield curve. Sensitivities are variations due to forfeit moves of underlying parameters driving the value of target variables.
- Volatility, which captures the variations around the average of any random parameter or target variable, both upside and downside. Unlike forfeit movements, volatility characterizes the varying instability of any uncertain parameters, which forfeit changes ignore. Volatility measures the dispersion around its mean of any random parameter or of target variables, such as losses for credit risk.
- Downside measures of risk, which focus on adverse deviations only. They characterize the 'worst-case' deviations of a target variable, such as earnings, market values or credit losses, with probabilities for all potential values. Downside risk measures require modelling to have probability distributions of target variables. The 'Value at Risk' (VaR) is a downside risk measure. It is the adverse deviation of a target variable, such as the value of a transaction, not exceeded in more than a preset fraction of all possible future outcomes. Downside risk is the most 'comprehensive' measure of risk. It integrates sensitivity and volatility with the adverse effect of uncertainty (Figure 6.1).

This chapter details related techniques and provides examples of well-known risk measures. In spite of the wide usage of risk measures, risks remain intangible, making

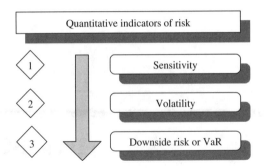

FIGURE 6.1   Risk measures

the distinction between risks and risk measures important. The first section draws a line between intangible risks and quantitative measures. The next sections provide examples of sensitivity and volatility measures. The final section discusses VaR and downside risk.

MEASURING UNCERTAINTY

Not all random factors that alter the environment and the financial markets—interest rates, exchange rates, stock indexes—are measurable. There are unexpected and exceptional events that radically and abruptly alter the general environment. Such unpredictable events might generate fatal risks and drive businesses to bankruptcy.

The direct way to deal with these types of risks is stress scenarios, or 'worst-case' scenarios, where all relevant parameters take extreme values. These values are unlikely, but they serve the purpose of illustrating the consequences of such extreme situations. Stress testing is a common practice to address highly unlikely events. For instance, rating agencies use stress scenarios to assess the risk of an industry or a transaction. Most bank capital markets units use stress scenarios to see how the market portfolio would behave. Extreme Value Theory (see Embrechts et al., 1997 plus the discussion on stress testing market VaR models) helps in modelling extreme events but remains subject to judgmental assessment. Quantitative risk measures do not capture all uncertainties. They depend on assumptions, which can underestimate some risks. Risks depend on qualitative factors and on intangible events, which quantification does not fully capture. Any due diligence of risks combines judgments and quantitative risk assessment.

Quantitative techniques address only measurable risks, without being substitutes for judgment. Still, the current trend is to focus on quantitative measures, enhancing them and extending their range throughout all types of risks. First, when data becomes available, risks are easier to measure and some otherwise intangible risks might become more prone to measurement. Second, when it is difficult to quantify a risk, it might be feasible to qualify it and rank comparable risks, as ratings agencies do. Finally, risk measures became more critical when regulators made it clear that they should provide the basis for capital requirements protecting the bank against unfavourable conditions. Quantitative measures gain feasibility and credibility for all these reasons. This chapter looks at the basic quantified risk measures, before tackling VaR in the next chapter.

SENSITIVITY

Sensitivities are ratios of the variation of a target variable, such as interest margin or change in mark-to-market values of instruments, to a forfeit shock of the underlying random parameter driving this change. This property makes them very convenient for measuring risks, because they link any target variable of interest to the underlying sources of uncertainty that influence these variables. Examples of underlying parameters are interest rates, exchange rates and stock prices. Market risk models use sensitivities widely, known as the 'Greek letters' relating various market instrument values to the underlying market parameters that influence them. Asset–Liability Management (ALM) uses gaps, which are sensitivities of the interest income of the banking portfolio to shifts of interest rates.

Sensitivities have well-known drawbacks. First, they refer to a given forfeit change of risk drivers (such as a 1% shift of interest rates), without considering that some parameters are quite unstable while others are not. Second, they depend on the prevailing conditions, the value of the market parameters and of assets, making them proxies of actual changes. This section provides definitions and examples.

Sensitivity Definitions and Implications

Percentage sensitivities are ratios of relative variations of values to the same forfeit shock on the underlying parameter. For instance, the sensitivity of a bond price with respect to a unit interest rate variation is equal to 5. This sensitivity means that a 1% interest rate variation generates a relative price variation of the bond of $5 \times 1\% = 5\%$. A 'value' sensitivity is the absolute value of the change in value of an instrument for a given change in the underlying parameters. If the bond price is 1000, its variation is $5\% \times 1000 = 50$. Let V be the market value of an instrument. This value depends on one or several market parameters, m, that can be prices (such as indexes) or percentages (such as interest rates). By definition:

$$s(\% \text{ change of value}) = (\Delta V / V) \times \Delta m$$

$$S(\text{value}) = (\Delta V / V) \times V \times \Delta m$$

Another formula is $s(\% \text{ change of value}) = (\Delta V / V) \times (\Delta m / m)$, if the sensitivity measures the 'return sensitivity', such as for stock return sensitivity to the index return. For example, if a stock return varies twice as much as the equity index, this last ratio equals 2.

A high sensitivity implies a higher risk than a low sensitivity. Moreover, the sensitivity quantifies the change. The sensitivity is only an approximation because it provides the change in value for a small variation of the underlying parameter. It is a 'local' measure because it depends on current values of both the asset and the market parameter. If they change, both S and s do[1].

---

[1] Formally, the sensitivity is the first derivative of the value with respect to m. The next order derivatives take care of the change in the first derivative.

Sensitivities and Risk Controlling

Most of the random factors that influence the earnings of a bank are not controllable by the bank. They are random market or environment changes, such as those that increase the default probabilities of borrowers. A bank does not have any influence on market or economic conditions. Hence, the sources of uncertainty are beyond control. By contrast, it is possible to control the 'exposure' or the 'sensitivities' to these outside sources of uncertainties. There are two ways to control risk: through risk exposures and through sensitivities.

Controlling exposures consists of limiting the size of the amount 'at risk'. For credit risk, banks cap individual exposures to any obligor, industry or country. In doing so, they bound losses per obligor, industry or country. However, the obvious drawback lies in limiting business volume. Therefore, it should be feasible to increase business volume without necessarily increasing credit risk. An alternative technique for controlling risk is by limiting the sensitivity of the bank earnings to external random factors that are beyond its control.

Controlling risk used to be easier for ALM and market risk, using derivatives. Derivatives allow banks to alter the sensitivities to interest rates and other market risks and keep them within limits. For market risk, hedging exposures helps to keep the various sensitivities (the 'Greeks') within stated limits (Chapter 30 reviews the main sensitivities). Short-selling bonds or stocks, for example, offsets the risk of long positions in stocks or bonds. For ALM, banks control the magnitude of 'gaps', which are the sensitivities of the interest margin to changes in interest rates.

Sensitivities have straightforward practical usages. For example, a positive variable interest rate gap of 1000 implies that the interest margin changes by $1000 \times 1\% = 10$ if there is a parallel upward shift of the yield curve.

The same techniques now apply with credit derivatives, which provide protection against both the deterioration of credit standing and the default of a borrower. Credit derivatives are insurances sold to lenders by sellers of these protections. The usage of credit derivatives extends at a fast pace because there was no way, until recently, to limit credit risk without limiting size, with a mechanical adverse effect on business volume. Other techniques, notably securitizations, expand at a very fast pace when players realize they could off-load risk and free credit lines for new business.

VOLATILITY

In order to avoid using a unique forfeit change in underlying parameters, independently of the stability or instability of such parameters, it is possible to combine sensitivities with measures of parameter instability. The volatility characterizes the stability or instability of any random variables. It is a very common statistical measure of the dispersion around the average of any random variable such as market parameters, earnings or mark-to-market values. Volatility is the standard deviation of the values of these variables. Standard deviation is the square root of the variance of a random variable (see Appendix).

Expectations, Variance and Volatility

The mean, or the expectation, is the average of the values of a variable weighted by the probabilities of such values. The variance is the sum of the squared deviations around the mean weighted by the probabilities of such deviations. The volatility is the square root of the variance[2]. When using time series of historical observations, the practice is to assign to each observation the same weight. The arithmetic mean is an estimator of the expectation. The arithmetic average of the squared deviations from this mean is the historical variance. Standard formulas apply to obtain these statistics. The appendix to this chapter illustrates basic calculations. Here, we concentrate on basic definitions and their relevance to volatility for risk measures.

Probability and Frequency Distributions

The curve plotting the frequencies of occurrences for each of the possible values of the uncertain variable is a frequency distribution. It approximates the actual probability distribution of the random variable. The x-axis gives the possible values of the parameter. The y-axis shows either the number of occurrences of this given value, or the percentage over the total number of observations. Such frequency distributions are historical or modelled distributions. The second class of distributions uses well-known curves that have attractive properties, simplifying considerably the calculation of statistics characterizing these distributions. Theoretical distributions are continuous, rather than discrete[3]. Continuous distributions often serve as good approximations of observed distributions of market values.

A probability distribution of a random variable is either a density or a cumulative distribution. The density is the probability of having a value within any very small band of values. The cumulative function is the probability of occurrence of values between the lowest and a preset upper bound. It cumulates all densities of values lower than this upper bound. 'pdf' and 'cdf' designate respectively the probability density function and the cumulative density function.

A very commonly used theoretical distribution is the normal curve, with its familiar bell shape (Figure 6.2). This theoretical distribution actually looks like many observed

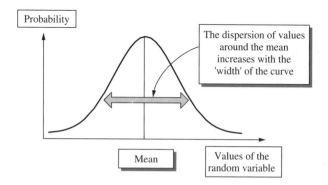

FIGURE 6.2   Mean and dispersion for a distribution curve

---

[2] Expectation and variance are also called the first two 'moments' of a probability distribution.

[3] An example of a simple discrete distribution is the distribution of loss under default risk. There are only two events: default or no default, with assigned probabilities such as 1% and 99%. There is a 1% chance that the lender suffers from the loss under default, while the loss remains zero under no default.

distributions of a large number of random phenomena. The two basic statistics, mean and standard deviation, are sufficient to fully determine the entire normal distribution.

The normal distribution $N(\mu, \sigma)$ has mean μ and standard deviation σ. The pdf of the normal distribution is:

$$Pr(\mathbf{X} = X) = (1/\sigma\sqrt{2\pi})\exp[-(X - \mu)^2/2\sigma^2]$$

Bold letters ($\mathbf{X}$) designate random variables and italic letters (X) a particular value of the random variable. The standardized normal distribution $N(0, 1)$ has a mean of 0 and a variance of 1. The variable $\mathbf{Z} = (\mathbf{X} - \mu)/\sigma$ follows a standardized normal distribution $N(0, 1)$, with probability density:

$$Pr(\mathbf{Z} = Z) = (1/\sqrt{2\pi})\exp[-Z^2/2]$$

The cumulative normal distribution is available from tables or easily calculated with proxy formulas. The cumulative standardized normal distribution is $\Phi(0, 1)$. The normal distribution is parametric, meaning that it is entirely defined by its expectation and variance.

The normal distribution applies notably to relative stock price return, or ratio of price variations to the initial price over small periods. However, the normal distribution implies potentially extreme negative values, which are inconsistent with observed market prices. It can be shown that the lognormal distribution, which does not allow negative values, is more consistent with the price behaviour. The lognormal distribution is such that the logarithm of the random variable follows a normal distribution. Analytically, $\ln(\mathbf{X})$ follows $N(\mu, \sigma)$, where ln is the Napierian logarithm and $N(\mu, \sigma)$ the pdf of the normal distribution. The lognormal distribution is asymmetric, unlike the normal curve, because it does not allow negatives at the lower end of values, and permits unlimited positive values[4]. Other asymmetric distributions have become popular when modelling credit risk. They are asymmetric because the frequency of small losses is much higher than the frequency of large losses within a portfolio of loans.

The moments of a distribution characterize its shape. The moments are the weighted averages of the deviations from the mean, elevated to power 2, 3, 4, etc., using the discrete probabilities of discrete values, or the probability densities as weights. The first moment is the expectation, or mean, of the function. The second moment is the variance. It characterizes dispersion around the mean. The square root of the variance is the standard deviation. It is identical to the 'volatility'. The third moment is skewness, which characterizes departure from symmetry. The fourth moment is kurtosis, which characterizes the flatness of the distribution.

Volatility

The volatility measures the dispersion of any random variable around its mean. It is feasible to calculate historical volatility using any set of historical data, whether or not they follow a normal distribution. It characterizes the dispersion of market parameters, such as that of interest rates, exchange rate and equity index, because the day-to-day observations are readily available.

Volatilities need constant updating when new observations are available. An alternative measure of volatility is the implicit volatility embedded in options prices. It derives

---

[4] When $\mathbf{X}$ takes extreme negative values, the logarithm tends towards zero but remains positive.

the value of volatility from the theoretical relationship (the Black–Scholes formula) of observed option prices with all underlying parameters, one of them being the volatility of the underlying. A benefit of implicit volatilities is that they are forward looking measures, as prices are. A drawback of this approach is that implicit volatilities are fairly volatile, more than historical volatility.

For other than market data, such as accounting earnings, the frequency of observations is more limited. It is always possible to calculate a standard deviation with any number of observations. Nevertheless, a limited number of observations might result in a distorted image of the dispersion. The calculation uses available observations, which are simply a sample from the entire distribution of values. If the sample size is large, statistics calculated over the sample are good proxies of the characteristics of the underlying distributions. When the sample size gets smaller, there is a 'sampling error'. Obviously, the sampling error might get very large when we have very few observations. The calculation remains feasible but becomes irrelevant.

The 'Earnings at Risk' (EaR) approach for estimating economic capital (Chapter 7) uses the observed volatility of earning values as the basis for calculating potential losses, hence the capital value capable of absorbing them. Hence, even though accounting data is scarcer than market data, the volatility of earnings might serve some useful purpose in measuring risk.

Historical Volatilities

The calculation of historical mean and volatility requires time series. Defining a time series requires defining the period of observation and the frequency of observations. For example, we can observe daily stock returns for an entire year, roughly 250 working days. The choice of frequency determines the nature of volatility. A daily volatility results from daily observations, a weekly volatility from weekly observations, and so on. We are simply sampling from an underlying distribution a variable number of daily observations.

When a distribution does not change over time, it is 'stationary'. Daily volatilities are easier to calculate since we have more information. Because the size of the sample varies greatly according to the length of the period, the sampling error—the difference between the unobservable 'real' value of volatility and that calculated—is presumably greater with short observation periods such as 1 or 3 months.

Convenient rules allow an easy conversion of daily volatilities into monthly or yearly volatilities. These simple rules rely on assumptions detailed in Chapter 30. In essence, they assume that the random process is stable through consecutive periods. For instance, for a random stock return, this would mean that the distribution of the stock return is exactly the same from one period to another.

Monthly volatilities are larger than daily volatilities because the changes over 1 month are likely to be larger than the daily changes. A practical rule states that the volatility over horizon T, σ_T, is equal to $\sigma_{1\text{day}}\sqrt{T}$, when T is in days. For example, the daily volatility of a stock return is 1%, measured from 252 daily observations over a 1-year period. The monthly volatility would be $\sigma_{1\text{month}} = \sigma_{1\text{day}}\sqrt{30} = 1\% \times 5.477 = 5.477\%$. The volatility increases with time, but less than proportionally[5]. According to this rule, the multiples used

---

[5] This formula $\sigma_t = \sigma_1\sqrt{t}$ applies when the possible values of a variable at t do not depend on the value at $t-1$.

TABLE 6.1   Time coefficients applicable to volatility

Period	1	2	3	4	5	6	7	8	9	10
Multiple	1.000	1.414	1.732	2.000	2.236	2.449	2.646	2.828	3.000	3.162

to convert a one-period (1 day, for instance) volatility into a multiple-period volatility (1 year, rounded to 250 days, for example) are as given in Table 6.1.

The formula is known as the 'square root of time rule'. It requires specifying the base period, whether 1 day or 1 year. For instance, the 1-year volatility when the yearly volatility is, say, 10% is 14.14%. The 'square root' rule is convenient but applies only under restrictive assumptions. Techniques for modelling volatilities as a function of time and across different periods have developed considerably. The basic findings are summarized in the market risk chapter (Chapter 30). Because the rule implies an ever-increasing volatility over time, it does not apply beyond the medium term to random parameters that tend to revert to a long-term value, such as interest rates.

VOLATILITY AND DOWNSIDE RISK

Risk materializes only when earnings deviate adversely, whereas volatility captures both upside and downside deviations. The purpose of downside risk measures is to capture loss, ignoring the gains.

Volatility and downside risk relate to each other, but are not equivalent. Volatility of earnings increases the chances of losses, and this is precisely why it is a risk measure. However, if downside changes are not possible, there is volatility but no downside risk at all. A case in point is options. The buyer of an option has an uncertain gain, but no loss risk, when looking forward, once he has paid the price for acquiring the option (the premium). A call option on stock provides the right to purchase the stock at 100. If the stock price goes up to 120, exercise generates a profit of $120 - 100 = 20$. The potential profit is random just as the stock price is. However, the downside risk is zero since the option holder does not exercise his option when the price falls below 100, and does not incur any loss (besides the upfront premium paid). However, the seller of the call option has a downside risk, since he needs to sell the stock to the buyer at 100, even when he has to pay a higher price to purchase the stock, unless he holds it already.

The downside risk actually has two components: potential losses and the probability of occurrence. The difficulty is to assess these probabilities. Worst-case scenarios serve to quantify extreme losses. However, the chances of observing the scenarios are subjective. If someone else has a different perception of the environment uncertainty, he or she might consider that another scenario is more relevant or more likely. The measure of risk changes with the perception of uncertainty. For these reasons, downside risk measures necessitate the prior modelling of the probability distributions of potential losses.

APPENDIX: STATISTICS

There are well-known standard formulas for calculating the mean, variance and standard deviation. Some definitions may appear complex at first sight. Actually, these statistics are easy to calculate, as shown in the examples below[6]. Let $\mathbf{X}$ be the random variable, with particular values X.

The formulas for calculating the mean and standard deviation of discrete observed values of a random variable, the usual case when using time series of observations, are given below. The random variable is $\mathbf{X}$, the mean is $E(\mathbf{X})$. With historical time series, probabilities are the frequencies of the observed values, eventually grouped in narrow bands. The assigned probability to a single value among n is $1/n$. The expectation becomes:

$$E(\mathbf{X}) = \left(\sum_i X_i \right) / n$$

The volatility, or standard deviation, is:

$$\sigma(\mathbf{X}) = (1/n) \sqrt{\sum_i [X_i - E(\mathbf{X})]^2}$$

In general, probabilities have to be assigned to values, for instance by assuming that the distribution curve is given. The corresponding formulas are given in any statistics textbook. The mean and the standard deviation depend on the probabilities p_i assigned to each value X_i of the random variable $\mathbf{X}$. The total of all probabilities is 100% since the distribution covers all feasible values. The mean is:

$$E(\mathbf{X}) = \left(\sum_i p_i X_i \right) / n$$

The variance is the weighted average by the probabilities of the squared deviations from the mean. The volatility is the square root of this value. The volatility is equal to:

$$\sigma(\mathbf{X}) = \sqrt{\sum_i p_i [X_i - E(\mathbf{X})]^2}$$

The variance $V(\mathbf{X})$ is identical to σ^2. With time series, all p_i are equal to $1/n$, which results in the simplified formulas above.

The example in Table 6.2 shows how to calculate a yearly volatility of earnings over a 12-year time series of earnings observations. The expectation is the mean of all observed values. The variance is the sum of squared deviations from the mean, and the standard deviation is the square root. The table gives a sample of calculations using these definitions. Monthly observations of accounting earnings are available for 1 year, or 12 observed values.

Volatilities are in the same unit as the random variable. If, for instance, the exchange rate of the euro against the dollar is 0.9 USD/EUR, the standard deviation of the exchange rate is also expressed in USD/EUR, for instance 0.09 USD/EUR. The percentage volatility is the ratio of the standard deviation to the current value of the variable. For instance, the above 0.09 USD/EUR volatility is also equal to 10% of the current exchange rate since

---

[6] Since the average algebraic deviation from the mean is zero by definition. Squared deviations do not cancel out. Dispersion should preferably be in the same unit as the random variable. This is the case with the standard deviation, making it directly comparable to the observed values of a random parameter.

TABLE 6.2 Calculation of mean and volatility with a time series of observed data: example

Dates	Earnings (dollars)	Deviations from mean	Squared deviations
1	15.00	12.08	146.01
2	12.00	9.08	82.51
3	8.00	5.08	25.84
4	7.00	4.08	16.67
5	2.00	−0.92	0.84
6	−3.00	−5.92	35.01
7	−7.00	−9.92	98.34
8	−10.00	−12.92	166.84
9	−5.00	−7.92	62.67
10	0.00	−2.92	8.51
11	5.00	2.08	4.34
12	11.00	8.08	65.34
Sum	35.00	**Sum**	712.92
		Statistics:[a]	
Mean	2.92	Variance	59.41
		Volatility	7.71

[a]The mean is the sum of observed values divided by the number of observations (12). The variance is the sum of squared deviations divided by 12. The volatility is the square root of variance.

$0.09/0.9 = 10\%$. For accounting earnings, the volatility could either be in dollars or as a percentage of current earnings. For interest rates, the volatility is a percentage, as the interest rate, or a percentage of the current level of the interest rate.

Continuous distributions are the extreme case when there is a probability that the variable takes a value within any band of values, no matter how small. Formally, when $\mathbf{X}$ is continuous, for each interval $[X, X + dX]$, there is a probability of observing values, which depends on $\mathbf{X}$. The probability density function provides this probability. There are many continuous distributions, which serve as proxies for representing actual phenomena, the most well known being the normal distribution. The pdf is such that all probabilities sum to 1, as with the frequency distribution above.

A useful property facilitating the calculation of the variance is that:

$$\sigma^2(\mathbf{X}) = E(\mathbf{X}^2) - [E(\mathbf{X})]^2$$

Another property of the variance is:

$$\sigma^2(a\mathbf{X}) = a^2 \times \sigma^2(\mathbf{X})$$

This also implies that $\sigma(a\mathbf{X}) = a \times \sigma(\mathbf{X})$.

7

VaR and Capital

The 'Value at Risk' (VaR) is a potential loss. 'Potential losses' can theoretically extend to the value of the entire portfolio, although everyone would agree that this is an exceptional event, with near-zero probability. To resolve this issue, the VaR is the 'maximum loss' at a preset confidence level. The confidence level is the probability that the loss exceeds this upper bound.

Determining the VaR requires modelling the distribution of values at some future time point, in order to define various 'loss percentiles', each one corresponding to a confidence level. VaR applies to all risks. Market risk is an adverse deviation of value during a certain liquidation period. Credit risk materializes through defaults of migrations across risk classes. Defaults trigger losses. Migrations trigger risk-adjusted value changes. VaR for credit risk is an adverse deviation of value, due to credit risk losses or migrations, at a preset confidence level. VaR applies as long as we can build up a distribution of future values of transactions or of losses.

The VaR methodology serves to define risk-based capital, or economic capital. Economic capital, or 'risk-based capital', is the capital required to absorb potential unexpected losses at the preset confidence level. The confidence level reflects the risk appetite of the bank. By definition, it is also the probability that the loss exceeds the capital, triggering bank insolvency. Hence, the confidence level is equivalent to the default probability of the bank.

The VaR concept shines for three major reasons: it provides a complete view of portfolio risk; it measures economic capital; it assigns fungible values to risks. Unlike intuition would suggest, the average loss is not sufficient to define portfolio risk because portfolio losses vary randomly around this average. Because VaR captures the downside risk, it is the basis for measuring economic capital, the ultimate safety cushion for absorbing losses. Finally, instead of capturing risks through multiple qualitative indicators (sensitivities, ratings, watch lists, excess limits, etc.), VaR assigns a dollar value to risk. Valuation makes all risks fungible, whatever the sources of uncertainty. By contrast, classical indicators do not add up as dollar values do.

'Earnings at Risk' (EaR) is a simple and practical version of VaR. EaR measures, at preset confidence levels, the potential adverse deviations of earnings. EaR is not VaR but shares the same underlying concept, and has the benefit of being relatively easy to measure. Although similar to VaR, EaR does not relate the adverse deviations of earnings to the underlying risks because EaR aggregates the effects of all risks.

By contrast, VaR requires linking losses to each risk. Relating risk measures to the sources of risk is a prerequisite for risk management, because the latter aims at controlling risk ex ante, rather than after its materialization into losses. VaR models the value of risk and relates it to the instrumental variables, allowing ex ante control of risk using such parameters as sensitivities to market risk, exposure limits, concentration for credit risk, and so on.

The first section describes the potential uses of VaR, and shows how VaR 'synthesizes' other traditional measures of risk. The second section details the different levels of potential losses of interest. They include: expected loss; unexpected and exceptional losses from loss distributions. The next sections detail the loss distribution and relate VaR to loss percentiles (or 'loss at a preset confidence level'), using the normal distribution as an example to introduce further developments. The last section discusses benefits and drawbacks of EaR.

VAR AND RISK MANAGEMENT

VaR is a powerful concept for risk management because of the range and importance of its applications. It is also the foundation of economic capital measures, which underlie all related tools, from risk-based performance to portfolio management.

The Contributions of VaR-based Measures

VaR provides the measure of economic capital defined as an upper bound of future potential losses. Once defined at the bank-wide level, the capital allocation system assigns capital, or a risk measure after diversification effect, to any subset of the bank's portfolio, which allows risk-adjusted performances to be defined, using both capital allocation and transfer pricing systems. Economic capital is a major advance because it addresses such issues as:

- Is capital adequate, given risks?
- Are the risks acceptable, given available capital?
- With given risks, any level of capital determines the confidence level, or the bank's default probability. Both risks and capital should adjust to meet a target confidence level which, in the end, determines the bank's risk and solvency.

VaR and Common Indicators of Risk

VaR has many benefits when compared to traditional measures of risk. It assigns a value to risk, it is synthetic and it is fungible. In addition, the VaR methodology serves to define risk-based capital. The progress is significant over other measures.

Figure 7.1 illustrates the qualitative gap between traditional risk measures and VaR. It describes the various indicators of risk serving various purposes for measuring or monitoring risks. Such indicators or quantified measures are not fungible, and it is not possible to convert them, except for market instrument sensitivities, into potential losses. By contrast, VaR synthesizes all of them and represents a loss, or a risk value. Because VaR is synthetic, it is not a replacement for such specific measures, but it summarizes them.

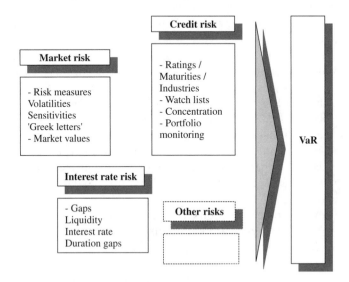

FIGURE 7.1 From traditional measures of risk to VaR

POTENTIAL LOSS

This section further details the VaR concept. There are several types of potential losses: Expected Loss (EL); Unexpected Loss (UL); exceptional losses. The unexpected loss is the upper bound of loss not exceeded in more than a limited given fraction of all outcomes. Such potential loss is also a loss percentile defined with the preset confidence level. Since the confidence level might take various values, it is necessary to be able to define all of them. Hence, modelling the unexpected loss requires modelling the loss distribution of the bank portfolio, which provides the frequencies of all various possible values of losses. Obtaining such loss distributions is the major challenge of risk models. VaR is the unexpected loss set by the confidence level. The exceptional loss, or extreme loss, is the loss in excess of unexpected loss. It ranges from the unexpected loss, as a lower bound, up to the entire portfolio value, but values within this upper range have extremely low probability of occurrence.

Expected Loss

The expected loss serves for credit risk. Market risk considers only deviations of values as losses, and ignores expected Profit and Loss (P&L) gains for being conservative. Expected loss represents a statistical loss over a portfolio of a large number of loans. The law of large numbers says that losses will sometimes be high or low. Intuition suggests that they revert to some long-term average.

This is the foundation for economic provisioning and 'expected loss risk management'. Intuition suggests that provisioning the expected loss should be enough to absorb losses. This might be true in the long-term. By definition, statistical losses average losses over a number of periods and yearly losses presumably tend to revert to some long-term mean. The intuition is misleading, however, because it ignores the transitory periods when losses exceed a long-term average. Lower than long-term average loss in good years could compensate, in theory, higher losses in bad years. There is no guarantee that losses will revert quickly to some long-run average. Deviations might last longer than expected. Therefore, economic provisioning will result in transitory excess losses over the long-term average. Unless there is capital to absorb such excesses, it cannot ensure bank solvency. The first loss above average would trigger default.

However, the choice of reference period for calculating the average loss counts. Starting in good years, we might have an optimistic reference value for expected loss and vice versa. Regulators insist on measuring 'through the cycle' to average these effects. This is a sound recommendation, so that economic provisions, if implemented, do not underestimate average losses in bad years because they refer to loss observed during the expansion phase of the economic cycle.

Statistical losses are more a portfolio concept rather than an individual transaction concept. For one single transaction, the customer may default or not. However, for a single exposure, the real loss is never equal to the average. On the other hand, for a portfolio, the expected loss is the mean of the distribution of losses. It makes sense to charge to each transaction this average, because each one should contribute to the overall required provision.

The more diversified a portfolio is, the lower is the loss volatility and the closer losses tend to be to the average value. However, this does not allow us to ignore the unexpected loss. One purpose of VaR models is to specify precisely both dimensions of risk, average level and chances/magnitudes of deviations from this average. Focusing on only one does not provide the risk profile of a portfolio. In fact, characterizing this profile requires the entire loss distribution to see how likely are large losses of various magnitudes.

The EL, as a long-term average, is a loss value that we will face it sooner or later. Therefore, it makes sense to deduct the EL from revenues, since it represents an overall averaged charge. If there were no random deviations around this average, there would be no need to add capital to economic provisions. This rationale implies that capital should be in excess of expected loss under economic provisioning.

Unexpected Loss and VaR

Unexpected losses are potential losses in excess of the expected value. The VaR approach defines potential losses as loss percentiles at given confidence levels. The loss percentile is the upper bound of loss not exceeded in more than a given fraction of all possible cases, this fraction being the confidence level. It is $L(\alpha)$, where α is the one-tailed[1] probability

---

[1] Only adverse deviations count as losses. Opposite deviations are gains and do not value risk.

of exceeding $L(\alpha)$. For example, $L(1\%) = 100$ means that the loss exceeds the value of 100 in no more than 1% of cases (one out of 100 possible scenarios, or two to three days within a year)[2]. The purpose of VaR models is to provide the loss distribution, or the probability of each loss value, to derive all loss percentiles for various confidence levels. The unexpected loss is the excess of the loss percentiles over the expected loss, $L(\alpha) - EL$. Economic capital is equal to unexpected loss measured as a loss percentile in excess of expected loss (under economic provisioning).

Exceptional Losses

Unexpected loss does not include exceptional losses beyond the loss percentile defined by a confidence level. Exceptional losses are in excess of the sum of the expected loss plus the unexpected loss, equal to the loss percentile $L(\alpha)$. Only stress scenarios, or extreme loss modelling when feasible, help in finding the order of magnitude of such losses. Nevertheless, the probability of such scenarios is likely to remain judgmental rather than subject to statistical benchmarks because of the difficulty of inferring extreme losses which, by definition, are almost unobservable.

MEASURING EXPECTED AND UNEXPECTED LOSSES

The two major ingredients for defining expected and unexpected losses are the loss distribution and the confidence level. The confidence level results from a management choice reflecting the risk appetite, or the tolerance for risk, of the management and the bank's policy with respect to its credit standing. Modelling loss distributions raises major technical challenges because the focus is on extreme deviations rather than on the central tendency. Since downside risk characterizes VaR and economic capital, loss volatility and the underlying loss distribution are critical.

Loss Distributions

In theory, historical loss distributions are observable historically. For market risk, loss distributions are simply the distributions of adverse price deviations of the instruments. Since there are approximately as many chances that values increase or decrease, such deviations tend to be bell-shaped, with some central tendency. Of course, the loss distribution is a distribution of negative earnings truncated at the zero level. The bell-shaped distribution facilitates modelling, especially when using the normal or the lognormal distributions as approximations.

Unfortunately, historical data is scarce for credit risk and does not necessarily reflect the current risk of banks. Therefore, it is necessary to model loss distributions. For credit risk, losses are not negative earnings. They result from defaults, or loss of asset value because of credit standing deterioration. Such distributions are highly skewed to the left, because the most frequent losses are very small. Both types of distributions are shown in Figure 7.2.

---

[2] An alternative notation is $L(99\%)$, where 99% represents the probability that the loss value does not exceed the same upper bound.

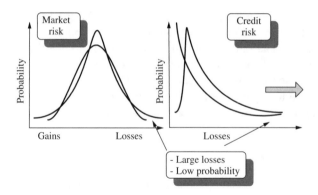

FIGURE 7.2   Fat tails and extreme losses

With distributions, the visual representation of losses is simple. In Figure 7.3, losses appear at the right-hand side of the zero level along the x-axis. The VaR at a given confidence level is such that the probability of exceeding the unexpected loss is equal to this confidence level. The area under the curve at the right of VaR represents this probability. The maximum total loss at the same confidence level is the sum of the expected loss plus unexpected loss (or VaR). Losses at the extreme right-hand side and beyond unexpected losses are 'exceptional'. The VaR represents the capital in excess of expected loss necessary for absorbing deviations from average losses.

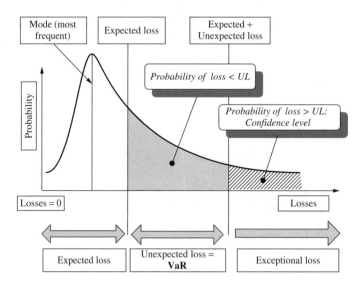

FIGURE 7.3   Unexpected loss and VaR

A well-known characteristic of loss distributions is that they have 'fat tails'. Fat tails are the extreme sections of the distribution, and indicate that large losses, although unlikely because their probabilities remain low, still have some likelihood to occur that is not negligible. The 'fatness' of the tail refers to the non-zero probabilities over the long end of the distributions.

The VaR is easy to determine under simplifying assumptions on the distribution curve of losses. With normal curves, the VaR is a multiple of loss volatility that depends on the confidence level. For example, the 2.5% one-tailed confidence level corresponds to a multiple of loss volatility of 1.96. Therefore, if the loss volatility is 100, the unexpected loss will not exceed the upper bound of 196 in more than two or three cases out of 100 scenarios. Unfortunately, such multiples do not apply when the distribution has a different shape, for instance for credit risk.

When implementing techniques based on confidence levels and loss percentiles, there is a need for common benchmarks, such as confidence levels, for all players. With a very tight confidence level, the VaR could be so high that business transactions would soon become limited by authorizations, or not feasible at all. If competitors use different VaR models or confidence levels, banks will not operate on equal grounds. Tighter confidence levels than competitors' levels would reduce the volume of business of the most prudent banks and allow competitors having more risk appetite to take advantage of an overly prudent policy.

LOSS PERCENTILES OF THE NORMAL DISTRIBUTION

The normal distribution is a proxy for market random P&L over a short period, but it cannot apply to credit risk, for which loss distributions are highly asymmetrical. In this section, we use the normal distribution to illustrate the VaR concept and the confidence levels.

The VaR at a confidence level α is the 'loss percentile' $L(\alpha)$. In Figure 7.4, the area under the curve, beyond the boundary value on the left-hand side, represents the probability that losses exceed this boundary value. Visually, a higher volatility means that the curve dispersion around its mean is wider. Hence, the chances that losses exceed a given boundary value grow larger. The confidence intervals are probabilities that losses exceed an upper bound (negative earnings, beyond the zero level). They are 'one-tailed' because only one-sided negative deviations materialize downside risk.

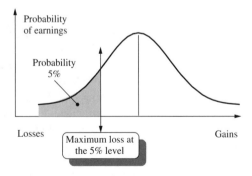

FIGURE 7.4   Volatility and downside risk

When both upside and downside deviations of the mean are considered, the confidence interval is 'two-tailed'. With a symmetric distribution, the two-tailed probability is twice the one-tailed probability. When the probability of losses exceeding a maximum value is

2.5%, the probability that losses exceed either the lower or the upper bounds is 5%. Unless otherwise stated, we will stick to the 'one-tailed' rule for specifying confidence intervals.

Confidence intervals are boundary values corresponding to a specified confidence level. In the case of the normal curve, confidence intervals are simply multiples of the volatility. Figure 7.5 shows their values. With the normal curve, the upper bounds of (negative) deviations corresponding to the confidence levels of 16%, 10%, 5%, 2.5% and all other values are in the normal distribution table. They correspond respectively to deviations from the mean of 1, 1.28, 1.65 and 1.96 times the standard deviation σ of the curve. Any other confidence interval corresponds to deviations expressed as multiples of volatilities for this distribution.

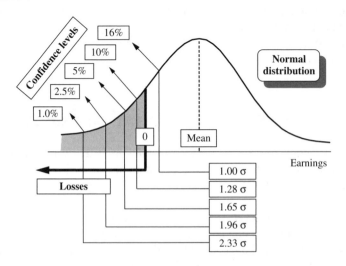

FIGURE 7.5   Confidence levels with the normal distribution

ISSUES AND ADVANCES IN MODELLING VAR AND PORTFOLIO RISKS

When we characterize an individual asset, independent of a portfolio context, we adopt a 'standalone' view and calculate a 'standalone' VaR. This serves only as an intermediate step for moving from 'standalone' loss distributions of individual assets to the portfolio loss distribution, which combines losses from all individual assets held in the portfolio. Standalone loss distributions list all possible values of losses for an asset with their probabilities. For instance, a loan whose value is outstanding balance under no default and zero under default has a loss distribution characterized by a 0% loss with probability of, say, 98% and a 100% loss with probability of 2%.

The obvious difficulty in VaR measures is the modelling of the loss distribution of a portfolio. The focus on high losses implies modelling the 'fat tail' of the distributions rather than looking at the central tendency. Even with market-driven P&L, the normal distribution does a poor job of modelling distribution tails. For credit risk, the issue is worse since the loss distributions are highly skewed. Loss distributions depend on portfolio structure, size discrepancies (concentration risk on big exposures) and the interdependencies between individual losses (the fact that a loss occurrence increases or decreases the likelihood of occurrence of other losses). In subsequent chapters, 'portfolio models' designate models providing the loss distribution of portfolios.

Diversification and granularity effects within a portfolio were recognized long ago but banks could not quantify them. What is new with portfolio models is that they provide the ability to quantify concentration and diversification effects on the portfolio risk. The added complexity is the price to pay for this single most important value added of the new portfolio models. 'Fat tails' of actual distributions make the quantification of extreme losses and their probability of occurrence hazardous. The main VaR modelling drawback is that they are highly demanding in terms of data. Because of the technicalities of modelling loss distribution for market and credit risk, several dedicated chapters address the various building blocks of such models: for market risk, see Chapter 32; for credit risk, see Chapters 44–50.

RISK-BASED CAPITAL

The VaR methodology applies to measure risk-based capital. The latter differs from regulatory capital or from available capital in that it measures actual risks. Regulatory capital uses forfeits falling short of measuring actual risks. Economic capital necessitates the VaR methodology, with the modelling of loss distribution, with all related complexities. The EaR concept is an alternative and simpler route to capital than VaR. For this reason, it is useful to detail the technique and to contrast the relative merits of EaR versus VaR.

The Limitations of Simple Approaches to Capital

The simplest way to define the required capital is to use regulatory capital. This is a common practice in the absence of any simple and convincing measure of capital. In addition, the regulatory capital is a requirement. At first sight, there seems to be no need to be more accurate than the regulators. However, regulatory capital has many limitations, even after the enhancements proposed by the New Accord.

Using regulatory capital as a surrogate for economic capital generates important distortions because of the divergence between the real risks and the forfeited risks of regulatory capital. For regulation purposes, credit risk is dependent on outstanding balances (book exposures) and on risk weights. Such forfeits are less risk-sensitive than economic measures. In addition, standardized regulatory approaches measure risk over a portfolio by a simple addition of individual risks for credit risk. This ignores the diversification effect and results in the same measure of risk for widely diversified portfolios and for highly concentrated portfolios.

The shortcomings of forfeit measures have implications for the entire risk management system. What follows applies to credit risk, since market models are allowed. Visibility on actual risks remains limited. Credit risk limits remain based on book exposures since regulatory capital depends on these. The target performance also uses forfeit measures of capital. The allocation of this capital across business units does not depend on their 'true' risks. Any risk-based policy for measuring risk-adjusted performances, or for risk-based pricing, suffers from such distortions. The most important benefit of economic capital is to correct such distortions.

Earnings at Risk

EaR is an important methodology for measuring capital. A simple way of approaching risk is to use the historical distributions of earnings. The wider the dispersion of time series of earnings, the higher the risk of the bank.

Principle

Several measures of earnings can be used to capture their instability over time: accounting earnings; interest margins; cash flows; market values, notably for the trading portfolio. The volatility is the adequate measure of such dispersion. It is the standard deviation of a series of observations. Such calculation always applies. For instance, even with few observations, it remains possible to calculate volatility. Of course, the larger the data set, the more relevant the measure will be. The concept applies to any subportfolio as well as to the entire bank portfolio. When adding the earning volatility across subportfolios, the total should exceed the loss volatility of the entire portfolio because of diversification.

Once earnings distributions are obtained, it is easy to use loss volatility as the unit for measuring capital. Deriving capital follows the same principle as VaR. It implies looking for some aggregated level of losses that is not likely to be exceeded in more than a given fraction of all outcomes.

Benefits

The major benefit of EaR is in providing a very easy overview of risks. This is the quicker approach to risk measurement. It is not time intensive, nor does it require much data. It relies on existing data since incomes are always available. EaR requires few Information Technology (IT) resources and does not imply major investments. There is no need to construct a risk data warehouse, since existing databases provide most of the required information and relate it easily to transactions. It is easy to track major variations of earnings to some specific events and to interpret them.

EaR provides a number of outputs: the earnings volatility, the changes of earnings volatility when the perimeter of aggregation increases, measuring the diversification effect. The level of capital is an amount that losses are not likely to exceed. This is a simple method of producing a number of outputs without too much effort. This is so true that EaR has attracted attention everywhere, since it is a simple matter to implement it.

Drawbacks

There are a number of drawbacks to this methodology. Some of them are purely technical. A volatility calculation raises technical issues, for instance when trends of time series increase volatility. In such cases, the volatility comes from the trend rather than instability. There is no need to detail further technical difficulties, since they are easy to identify. The technique requires assumptions, but the number of options remains tractable and easily managed. In general, the drawbacks of simplicity are that EaR provides only crude measures.

However, the major drawbacks relate to risk management. It is not possible to define the sources of the risk making the earnings volatile. Presumably, various types of risks materialize simultaneously and create adverse deviations of earnings. The contributions of these risks to the final volatility remain unknown. Unlike VaR models, EaR captures risks as an outcome of all risks, not at their source. Without links to the sources of risk, market, credit or interest rates, EaR serves to define aggregated capital, but it does not allow us to trace back risks to their sources.

A comprehensive and integrated risk management system links measures with specific sources of risk. The VaR for market risk and credit risk, and the ALM measures of interest rate, are specific to each risk. They fit better bank-wide risk management systems because they allow controlling each risk upstream, rather than after the fact. The EaR methodology does not meet such specifications. On the other hand, it is relatively easy to implement compared to full-blown systems. EaR appears to be an additional tool for risk management, but not a substitute.

8

Valuation

Under the traditional accounting framework applying to the banking portfolio, loans are valued at book value and earnings are interest income accrued over a period. Although traditional accounting has undisputed merits, it has economic drawbacks. Periodical measures of income ignore what happens in subsequent periods. The book value of a loan does not change when the revenues or the risks are higher or lower than average. Hence, book values are not revenue- or risk-adjusted, while 'economic values' are.

In essence, an 'economic value' is a form of mark-to-market measure. It is a discounted value of future contractual cash flows generated by assets, using appropriate discount rates. The discounting process embeds the revenues from the assets in the cash flows, and embeds the risk also in the discount rates. This explains the current case for 'fair value'. Marking-to-market does not imply that assets are actually tradable. The mark-to-market values of the trading portfolio are market prices. However, a loan has a mark-to-market value even though it is not tradable. Since the risk–return trade-off is universal in the banking universe, a major drawback of book values is that they are not faithful images of such risks and returns. Another drawback is that book values are not sensitive to the actual 'richness' or 'poorness' of transactions, and of their risks, which conflicts with the philosophy of a 'faithful' image.

Risk models also rely on mark-to-market valuations. 'Mark-to-model' valuations are similar to mark-to-market, but exclude some value drivers. For example, isolating the effect of credit risk on value does not require using continuously adjusted interest rates. 'Mark-to-future' is a 'mark-to-model' valuation at future time points, differentiated across scenarios characterizing the random outcomes from current date up to a future time point. Value at Risk (VaR) risk models use revaluations of assets at future dates for all sets of random outcomes, to provide the value distribution from which VaR derives. This makes the 'revaluation block' of models critical for understanding VaR.

However, moving to 'fair value' is a quantum leap because of the implication in terms of profitability. The relevant measure of profitability becomes Profit and Loss (P&L) rather than accrual income. Traditional measures of performance for the banking portfolio are interest income plus fees. For the market portfolio they are P&L or the change of mark-to-market values of assets traded between any two dates. Moving to fair values would imply P&L measures, and P&L volatility blurring the profitability view of the bank. The debate on accounting rules follows.

Whatever the outcome on accounting standards, economic values will be necessary for two main reasons: they value both risks and returns; valuation is a major building block of credit models because all VaR models need to define the distribution of future values over the entire range of their future risk states.

Because of the current growing emphasis on 'fair value', we review here valuation issues and introduce 'mark-to-model' techniques. The first section is a reminder of accounting standards. The next section details mark-to-market calculations and market yields. The third section summarizes why economic valuation is a building block of risk models. The fourth discusses the relative merits of book versus economic valuations. The fifth section introduces risk-adjusted performance measures, which allow separation of the risk and return components of economic value, rather than bundling them in a single fair value number.

ACCOUNTING STANDARDS

Accounting standards have evolved progressively following the guidelines of several boards. The Financial Accounting Standard Board (FASB) promotes the Generally Accepted Accounting Practices (GAAP) that apply to all financial institutions. The International Accounting Standard (IAS) Committee promotes guidelines to which international institutions, such as the multinational banks, abide. All committees and boards promote the 'fair value' concept, which is a mark-to-market value. 'Fair value' is identical to market prices for traded instruments. Otherwise, it is an economic value. It is risk-adjusted because it uses risky market yields for valuation. It is revenue-adjusted because it discounts all future cash flows. Economic values might be either above or below face value depending on the gap between asset returns and the market required yield applicable to assets of the same risk class.

The main implication of fair value accounting is that earnings would result from the fluctuations of values, generating volatile P&L. The sensitivity of value to market movements is much higher for interest-earning assets with fixed rates than with floating rates, as subsequent sections illustrate.

Fair value is implemented partially. The IAS rules recommended that all derivatives should be valued at mark-to-market prices. The rule applies to derivatives serving as hedges to bank exposures. The implication is that a pair made up of a banking exposure valued at book value matched with a derivative could generate a value fluctuating because of the valuation of the derivative while the book value remains insensitive to market movements. The pair would generate a fluctuating value and, accordingly, a volatile P&L due to the valuation of the derivative. This is inconsistent with the purpose of the hedge, which is to stabilize the earnings for the couple 'exposure plus hedge'. To correct the effect of the valuation mismatch, the rule allows valuation of both exposure and hedge at the fair value.

It is too early to assess all implications of fair values. Moreover, many risk models use mark-to-model valuation for better measuring risk, notably credit risk models that apply to the banking portfolio. Nevertheless, it is necessary to review fair value calculations in order to understand them. The subsequent sections develop gradually all concepts for determining mark-to-market 'fair values'.

MARK-TO-MARKET VALUATION

This section develops the basic mark-to-market model step-by-step. First, it explains the essentials of principles for discounting, the interpretation of the discounting process and the implication for selecting a relevant discount rate. Second, it introduces the identity between market interest rates, or yields, and required rates of return on market investments in assets providing interest revenues. Third, it explains the relationship between market prices and yield to maturity, and explains how this applies to non-marketable assets as well, such as loans. For the sake of clarity, we use a one-period example. Then, using the yield to maturity (Ytm) concept, we extend the same conclusions to a multiple-period framework with simple examples.

The Simple 'Discounted Cash Flow' Valuation and the 'Time Value of Money'

The familiar Discounted Cash Flow (DCF) model explains how to convert future values into present values and vice versa, using market transactions. Therefore, it explains which are the discount rates relevant for such actual time translations. It is also the foundation of mark-to-market approaches, although it is not a full mark-to-market because the plain DCF model does not embed factors embedded in actual mark-to-market values, such as the credit spreads specific to each asset. The present value of an asset is the discounted value of the stream of future flows that it generates. When using market rates as discount rates, the present value is a mark-to-market value. The present value of a stream of future flows F_t is:

$$V = \sum_t F_t / [1 + y(t)]^t$$

The market rates are rates applying to a single flow at date t, or the zero-coupon rates $y(t)$. The formula applies to any asset that generates a stream of contractual and certain flows. Cash flows include, in addition to interest and principal repayments, fees such as upfront flat fees, recurring fees and non-recurring fees (Figure 8.1).

With floaters, interest payments are indexed to market rates, and the present value is equal to the face value. For instance, an asset with a face value of 100 generates a flow over the next period that includes both the interest and the principal repayment. This final flow is equal to $100(1 + r)$, r also being the market rate that applies to the period. When this flow is discounted with these market rates, the present value is constant and equal to $100(1 + r)/(1 + r) = 100$. The same result applies when the horizon extends beyond one period with the same assumptions. Nevertheless, when the asset pays more than the discount rate, say $y + m$, with m being a constant percentage, while the discount rate is y, the one-period flow becomes $100(1 + y + m)$ with discounted value at y: $100(1 + y +$

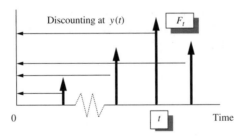

FIGURE 8.1 The present value of assets with the DCF model

$m)/(1 + y) = 100[1 + m/(1 + y)]$. The value becomes higher than face value, by a term proportional to $m/(1 + y)$, and sensitive to the yield y.

The relevant discount rates are those that allow flows to be transferred across time through borrowing and lending. This is why market rates are relevant. For instance, transferring a future flow of 1000 to today requires borrowing an amount equal to $1000/(1 + y_b)$, where y_b is the borrowing rate. Transferring a present flow of 1000 to a future date requires lending at the market rate y_l. The final flow is $1000(1 + y_l)$. Hence, market rates are relevant for the DCF model (Figure 8.2).

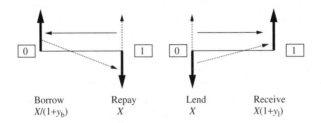

FIGURE 8.2 Discounting and borrowing or lending at market rates

The simple DCF model refers to borrowing and lending rates of an entity. The actual market values of traded assets use different discount rates, which are market rates given the risk of the asset. Full mark-to-market valuation implies using the DCF model with these rates.

Continuous and Discrete Compounding or Discounting

Pricing models use continuous compounding instead of discrete compounding, even though actual product valuation uses discrete compounding. Because some future examples use continuous calculations, we summarize the essentials here. The basic formulas for future and present values are very simple, with a discount rate y (continuous) and a horizon n:

$$FV_c(y, n) = \exp(yn) = e^{yn}$$

$$PV_c(y, n) = \exp(-yn) = e^{-yn}$$

The index c stands for continuous. Using discounted cash flow formulas to value the present value of a stream of cash flows, simply substitutes e^{-rt} in the discount factor

$1/(1+y)^t$. The formulas do not give the same numerical results, although there is a continuous rate that does. If the discrete rate is y, the discrete time and the continuous time formulas are respectively:

$$PV_c(y) = \sum_{t=1}^{n} CF_t/(1+y)^t$$

$$PV_c(y) = \sum_{t=1}^{n} CF_t \exp(-yt)$$

We provide details and, notably, the rule for finding continuous rates equivalent to discrete rates in the appendix to this chapter.

Market Required Rates and Asset Yields or Returns

The yield of a tradable asset is similar to a market interest rate. However, banking assets and liabilities generally do not provide or pay the market rates because of positive spreads over market rates for assets and costs of deposits lower than market rates on the liability side. Valuation depends on the spread between asset and market yields.

The asset fixed return is $r = 6\%$ and y is the required market yield for this asset. The market required yield depends on maturity and the risk of the asset. We assume both are given, and the corresponding y is 7%. We receive a contractual cash flow, 1 year from now, equal to $1 + r$ in 1 year, r being the interest payment. For instance, an asset of face value 1000 provides contractually 6% for 1 year, with a bullet repayment in 1 year. The contractual risk-free flow in 1 year is 1060. The 1-year return on the asset is 6%, if we pay the asset at face value 1000 since $r = (1060 - 1000)/1000 = 6\%$. If the market rate y is 7%, the investors want 7%. If they still pay 1000 for this asset, they get only 6%, which is lower. Therefore, they need to pay less, say a price P unknown. The price P is such that the return should be 7%: $(1060 - P)/P = 7\%$. This equation is identical to:

$$P = 1060/(1 + 7\%) = 990.65$$

If $y = 7\%$ is the 1-year market required rate, the present value, or mark-to-market value, of the future flow is $990.65 = 1060(1 + y) = 1000(1 + r)/(1 + y)$.

If we pay the face value, the 1-year return becomes equal to the market yield because $[(1 + y) - 1]/1 = y$. Hence, any market interest rate has the dimension of a return, or a yield. Getting $1 + y$, one period from now, from an investment of 1 means that its yield is y. Market rates are required returns from an investor perspective. Since the market provides y, a rate resulting from the forces of supply and demand for funds, any investor requires this return (Figure 8.3).

The implication is that the investor pays the price that provides the required market return whatever the actual contractual flows are. Paying 990.65 generates the required market return of 7%. This price is lower than the face value. If the market return is identical to the contractual asset rate of 6%, the investor actually gets exactly 6% by paying the face value 1000 since $(1060 - P)/P = 6\%$. If the market return is lower than the contractual asset rate of 6%, say 5%, the investor actually gets more than 5%

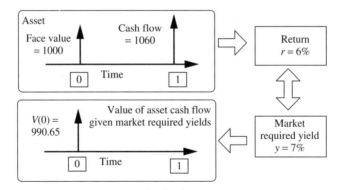

FIGURE 8.3   Asset return versus market required yield

by paying 1000 since $(1060 - P)/P = 6\%$. For the investor to get exactly 5%, he pays exactly $P = 1060/(1 + 5\%) = 1009.52$. The price becomes higher than the face value. The general conclusions are that the value is identical to the face value only when the asset return is in line with the required market return. Table 8.1 summarizes these basic conclusions.

TABLE 8.1   Asset return versus market required yield

Asset return r > market required return y	value > book value
Asset return r < market required return y	value > book value
Asset return r = market required return y	value = book value

Asset Return and Market Rate

Since the asset value is the discounted value of all future cash flows at market rates, there is an inverse relationship between interest rate and asset value and the market rate. This inverse relationship appears above when discounting at 6% and 7%. The asset value drops from 1000 to 990.65. The value–interest rate profile is a downward sloping curve. This relationship applies to fixed rate assets. It serves constantly when looking at the balance sheet economic value (Net Present Value, NPV) in Asset–Liability Management (ALM) (Figure 8.4).

The value of a floater providing interest revenues calculated at a rate equal to the discounting rate does not depend on prevailing rates. This is obvious in the case of a single period, since the asset provides $1 + r$ at the end of the period and this flow discounted at i has a present value of $(1 + r)/(1 + r) = 1$. Although this is not intuitive, the property extends to any type of floater, for instance, an amortizing asset generating revenue calculated with the same rate as the discount rate. This can be seen through examples. An amortizing loan of 1000, earning 10%, repaid in equal amounts of 200 for 5 years, provides the cash flow stream, splitting flows into capital and interest: $200 + 100, 200 + 80, 200 + 60, 200 + 40, 200 + 20$. The discounted value of these flows at 10% is equal to 1000. If the rate floats, and becomes 12% for instance, the cash flow stream then

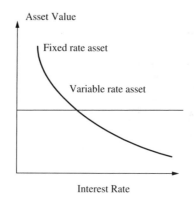

FIGURE 8.4   Fixed rate asset value and interest rate

becomes: $200 + 120, 200 + 96, 200 + 72, 200 + 48, 200 + 24^1$. Discounting these flows at 12% results in a present value of 1000 again.

When the asset yield is above the discount rates, there is an 'excess spread' in the cash flows. For example, if the asset provides 10.5% when rates are 10%, the spread is 0.5%. When rates are 12%, the spread also remains at 0.5% because the asset provides 12.5%. A floater is the sum of a zero-spread floater (at 12%) whose value remains equal to the face value whatever the rates, plus a smaller fixed rate asset providing a constant 0.5% of the outstanding balance, which is sensitive to rate changes. Since the amount is much smaller than the face value, the value change of such a variable rate asset is much smaller than that of a similar fixed rate asset.

Interest Rates and Yields to Maturity

These results extend to any number of periods through the yield to maturity concept. When considering various maturities, we have different market yields for each of them. The entire spectrum of yields across maturities is the 'yield curve', or the term structure of interest rates[2]. In practice, two different types of yields are used: zero-coupon yields and yields to maturity. The zero-coupon rates apply to each individual future flow. The yields to maturity are 'compounded averages' across all periods. We index current yields by the maturity t, the notation being $y(t)$. The date t is the end of period t. For instance, $y(1)$ is the yield at the end of period 1. If the period is 1 year, and if we are at date 0 today, $y(1)$ is the spot rate for 1 year, $y(2)$ the spot rate for 2 years, etc.

Using zero-coupon rates serves to price an asset starting from the contractual stream of cash flows and the market zero-coupon rates. Market prices of bonds are the discounted cash flows of various maturities using these yields. Instead of using these various rates, it is convenient to use a single discount rate, called the yield to maturity (or 'Ytm'). Using the Ytm addresses the issue of finding the return for an investor between now and

---

[1] The interest flows are 12% times the outstanding balance, starting at 1000 and amortized by 200 at each period.

[2] See Chapter 12 for details on the term structure of rates and zero-coupon rates.

maturity, given the contractual stream of cash flows and the price of the asset[3]. The Ytm is the unique discount rate making the present value of all future flows identical to the observed price.

Yield to Maturity and Asset Return

For a loan, there is also a yield to maturity. It is the discount rate making the borrowed amount, net of any fees, identical to the discounted contractual cash flows of the loan. The yield to maturity derives from the stream of contractual cash flows and the current price of a bond or of the net amount borrowed.

The following example illustrates the concept with a bullet bond (principal repayment is at maturity) generating coupons equal to 6% of face value, with a face value equal to 1000, and maturing in 3 years. The stream of cash flows is therefore 60, 60 and 1060, the last one including the principal repayment. In this example, we assume that cash flows are certain (risk-free) and use market yields to maturity applicable to the 3-year maturity. The asset rate is 6%. Discounting all flows at 6% provides exactly 1000, implying that the yield to maturity of the bond valued at 1000 is 6%. It is equal to its book return of 6%. This is a general property. When discounting at a rate equal to the asset contractual return $r = 6\%$, we always find the face value 1000 as long as the bond repays without any premium or discount to the principal borrowed. If the market yield to maturity for a 3-year asset rises to 7%, the value of the asset cash flow declines to 973.77. This is identical to what happens in our former example. If the required yield is above the book return of 6%, the value falls below par. Back to the 7% market yield to maturity, the asset mark-to-market value providing the required yield to maturity to investors has to be 973.77. An investor paying this value would have a 7% yield to maturity equal to the market required yield. The reverse would happen with a yield to maturity lower than 6%. The value would be above the book value of 1000. These conclusions are identical to those of the above example of a 1-year asset (Table 8.2).

TABLE 8.2 Value and yield to maturity

Date	0	1	2	3
Rate		6%	6%	6%
Cash flows		60	60	1060
Discounted cash flows		56.60	53.40	890.00
Current value	1000			
Rate		7%	7%	7%
Discounted cash flows		56.07	52.41	865.28
Current value	973.77			

[3] The second application relies on assumptions limiting the usage of the Ytm, which we ignore at this stage. It is easy to show that the Ytm is the effective yield obtained by the investor if he holds the asset to maturity and if all intermediate flows received, whatever their nature, interest or principal repayments, are reinvested in the market at the original yield to maturity. The second assumption is unrealistic since there is no way to guarantee that the future market rate prevailing will be in line with the original Ytm calculation, except by an extraordinary coincidence.

Value and Term Structure of Yields

When using different yields to maturity, the discounting calculations serve to determine the mark-to-market value of any asset, including loans, even though these are not traded in the market. In this latter case, the value is a theoretical mark-to-market, rather than an actual price in line with market rates. We can compare the theoretical price with actual prices for traded assets, which we cannot do for non-traded assets. Using the market zero-coupon yields of Table 8.3, we find that the discounted value of the bond flows is:

$$V = 60/(1 + 5.00\%) + 60/(1 + 6.00\%)^2 + 1060/(1 + 7.00\%)^3$$
$$V = 57.14 + 53.40 + 865.28 = 975.82$$

TABLE 8.3   Term structure of 'zero-coupon' market rates

End of period	1	2	3
Market rate, date t	5.00%	6.00%	7.00%

The value has no reason to be identical to 1000. It represents a mark-to-market valuation of a contractual and certain stream of cash flows. There is a yield to maturity making the value identical to the discounted value of cash flows, using it as a unique discount rate across all periods. It is such that:

$$975.82 = 60/(1 + y) + 60/(1 + y)^2 + 1060/(1 + y)^3$$

The value is $y = 6.920\%$[4]. It is higher than the 6% on the face value, because we acquire this asset at a value below par (975.82). The 6.92% yield is the 'averaged' return of an investor buying this asset at its market price, with these cash flows and holding it to maturity.

Risk-free versus Risky Yields

Some yields are risk-free because the investors are certain of getting the contractual flows of assets, whereas others are risky because there is a chance that the borrower will default on his obligations to pay debt. Risk-free debt is government debt. The risky yield and the risk-free yield at date t are y and y_f. The risky required yield has to be higher than the risk-free rate for the same maturity to compensate the investors for the additional risk borne by acquiring risky debt. For each maturity t, there is a risk-free yield $y_f(t)$ and a risky yield $y(t)$ for each risk class of debt. The market provides both yield curves, derived from observed bond prices. The difference is the credit spread. Risky yields are the sum of the risk-free yield plus a 'credit spread' corresponding to the risk class of the asset and the maturity. The credit spread is $cs(t) = y(t) - y_f(t)$. Both zero-coupon yields and

---

[4] It is easy to check that discounting all contractual flows at this rate, we actually find the 949.23 value. The rate y is the internal rate of return of the stream of flows when using 949.23 as initial value.

yields to maturity are such that $y(t) = y_f(t) + cs(t)$. When using full mark-to-market, the discount rates depend on both the maturity of flows and their credit risk[5] (Table 8.4).

Credit spreads vary with maturity and other factors. The spreads theoretically reflect the credit risk of assets under normal conditions. Since the prices of risky bonds might also depend on other factors such as product and market liquidity, spreads might not depend only on credit risk. Credit spreads are observable from yields and increase with credit risk, a relationship observed across rating classes.

TABLE 8.4 Term structure of risk-free and risky yields

End of period	1	2	3
Risky yield	5.00%	6.00%	7.00%
Risk-free yield	4.50%	5.00%	5.90%
Credit spreads	0.50%	1.00%	1.10%

There are two basic ways to discount future flows: using zero-coupon yields for each date, or using a unique yield to maturity. Zero-coupon yields embed credit spreads for each maturity. The yield to maturity embeds an average credit spread for risky debts. $V(0)$ is the current value of an asset at date 0. By definition of the risky yield to maturity, the mark-to-market value of the entire stream of contractual cash flows is:

$$V(0) = \sum_{t=1}^{T} F_t / (1 + y)^t$$

$$V(0) = \sum_{t=1}^{T} F_t / [1 + y_f(t) + cs(t)]^t$$

Risk and Relative Richness of Facilities

Marking-to-model differentiates facilities according to relative richness and credit risk irrespective of whether assets are traded or illiquid banking facilities. Rich facilities providing revenues higher than market have a value higher than book, and conversely with low revenue facilities. Richness results from both revenues and risk. The 'excess spread' concept characterizes richness. It is the spread between the asset return over the sum of the risk-free rate plus the credit spread corresponding to the risk class of the asset.

To make this explicit, let us consider a zero-coupon maturing at T, with a unit face value, providing the fixed yield r to the lender, and a risk such that the risky discount rate is y, including the credit spread:

$$V = (1 + r)^T / (1 + y)^T$$

It is obvious that $V > 1$ and $V \leq 1$ depending on whether $r > y$ or $r \leq y$. From the above, valuation is at par value (book value) when the excess spread is zero. Deviations

---

[5] There is an alternative valuation technique for risky debt using so-called risk-neutral probabilities of default. In addition, credit spreads provide information on these probabilities. The details are in Chapter 42 dedicated to the valuation of credit risk.

from par result from both revenues and risks. Mark-to-model valuation reflects risk and excess revenues compared to the market benchmark.

Figure 8.5 shows two cases, with fair value above and below book value, from these two return and risk adjustments. The risk adjustment results from discounting at a rate $y > y_f$, with a risk premium over the risk-free rate. The return adjustment corresponds to the excess return $r - y_f$ of the asset above the risk-free rate. The overall adjustment nets the two effects and results in the excess return of the asset over the risky discount rate, or $r - y$. If both adjustments compensate, implying $y = r$, the value remains at par.

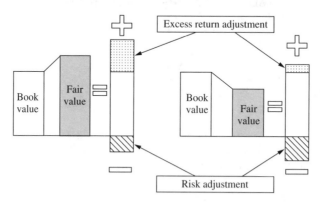

FIGURE 8.5   From book value to fair value: excess return and risk adjustments

The excess spread is $r - y$. The gap between r and y is the 'relative richness' of the asset, relative to the required market return. A rich asset provides a higher return than the market requires given risk. Its mark-to-market value is above book value. A poor asset pays less than the required market return y. Its value is below book value. These properties apply for all risky assets, except that, for each risk class, we need to refer to market rates corresponding to this specific risk class.

As an example, we assume that a risky asset provides a 6% yield, with a principal of 100 and a 1-year maturity. The market required risky yield is 5.5% and the risk-free y_f required yield is 5.5%. The excess spread is 6% $-5.5\% = 0.5\%$. The value of the asset at an excess spread of zero implies a zero excess spread, or an asset return of 5.5%. With this return, the market value of the asset is obviously the face value, or 1000. The value of risk is the difference between the value at the required risky rate and the value at the risk-free yield, or $1060/(1+5.5\%) - 1060/(1+5\%) = 1004.74 - 1009.52 = -4.78$. The value of the excess spread is the difference between the value of an asset providing exactly the required risky yield, or 100, and the value of the actual asset with a positive excess spread, or 1004.74, which is $+4.74$.

MARK-TO-MODEL VERSUS FULL MARK-TO-MARKET VALUATION

In many risk models, the valuation building block plays a critical role:

- For ALM models, the NPV of the balance sheet is the present value of assets minus the value of liabilities. It serves as a target variable of ALM models because it captures the entire stream of cash flows generated by assets and liabilities (see Chapter 22). Intuitively, if assets provide excess return over market yields, and liabilities cost less than market yields, assets are above par and liabilities below par value. The difference should capture the expected profitability of the balance sheet in terms of present value.

- For market risk VaR models, the loss percentile derives from the distribution of future values of all assets at a future time point. The future value is random because of market movements and the distribution implies revaluation of assets at the future time point as a function of random market moves.
- For credit risk models, the same principle applies, except that we focus on random credit risk events to find the distribution of uncertain values at a future horizon. The credit events include defaults and changes of credit standing, implying a value adjustment with market risky yields. The revaluation building block provides the spectrum of future values corresponding to all future credit states.

The valuation calculation depends on various options. Full mark-to-market valuation uses all parameters influencing prices to find out the distribution of random values at future time points. This is not so for ALM and credit risk.

The NPV of the balance sheet uses a single set of market rates differentiated by maturity, but not by risk class. The calculation differs from mark-to-market and fair value, in that it does not differentiate the discount rates according to the risk of each individual asset. The interpretation of the NPV is straightforward if we consider the bank as 'borrowing' from the market at its average cost of funding, which depends on its risk class. The bank could effectively bring back to present all future asset cash flows to present by borrowing against them. Borrowing 'against' them means borrowing the exact amount that would require future repayments, inclusive of interest, identical to the cash flows of all assets at this future date. This is a mark-to-model rather than a full mark-to-market.

Mark-to-model calculations eliminate some of the drawbacks of the full MTM. For instance, when isolating credit risk, day-to-day variations due to interest rate fluctuations are not necessarily relevant because the aim is to differentiate future values according to their future random credit states. One option is to price the credit risk using the current 'crystallized' rates allowing credit spreads only to vary according to the future credit states at the horizon. The process avoids generating unstable values due to interest rate risk, which NPV scenarios capture for ALM.

Mark-to-future refers to the forward valuation of the assets. It is different from mark-to-market because it addresses the issue of unknown future values using models to determine the possible future risk states of assets. The valuation block of VaR models uses both current valuation and mark-to-future to generate the value distribution at a future time point.

BENEFITS AND DRAWBACKS OF ECONOMIC VALUES

The theoretical answer to the problem of considering both revenues and risk in exposures is to mark-to-market transactions. Pure mark-to-market applies to market transactions only. Economic values, or 'fair values', are similar and apply to all assets, including banking portfolio loans. The economic values discount all future flows with rates that reflect the risk of each transaction.

The arguments for accounting standards for the banking book relate to stability of earnings. A major drawback of mark-to-market is that the P&L would change every day, as the market does, thereby generating earnings instability. This is more the case, however, with fixed rate assets than with floating rate assets. The latter have values closer to par when interest rates vary. Moreover, it is not possible to trade the assets and liabilities of the banking portfolio, so that marking them to market does not make much sense. Lack of liquidity could result in large discounts from the theoretical mark-to-market values.

In spite of their traditional strengths, accounting values suffer from a number of deficiencies. Accounting flows capture earnings over a given period. They do not give information about the long-term profitability of existing facilities. They ignore the market conditions, which serve as an economic benchmark for actual returns. For example, a fixed rate loan earning an historical interest rate has less value today if interest rates increased. It earns less than a similar loan based on current market conditions. Therefore, accounting measures of performance do not provide an image of profitability relative to current interest rates. In addition, different spreads apply to different credit risks. Hence, without risk adjustment, the interest incomes are not comparable from one transaction to another. Contractual interest income is not risk-adjusted. The same applies to book value. Whether a loan is profitable or not, it has the same accounting value. Whether it is risky or not, it also has the same value.

On the other hand, 'fair value' is economic and richer in terms of information. A faithful image should provide the 'true' value of a loan, considering its richness as well as its risk. Book values do not. Economic or fair values do. They have informational and reporting value added for both the bank and outside observers.

RISK-ADJUSTED PERFORMANCES AND ECONOMIC VALUES

Risk-adjusted performances are a compromise between accounting measures of performance and the necessity of adjusting income for risk. Although not going the full way to economic valuation, since they are accrual income-based measures, they do provide a risk adjustment. The popular risk-adjusted measures of accounting profitability are the Risk-adjusted Return on Capital (RaRoC) and the Shareholders Value Added (SVA)[6]. Both combine profitability and risk.

RaRoC nets expected losses from accrued revenues and divides them by the capital allocated to a transaction, using a capital (risk) allocation system. The RaRoC ratio should be above an appropriate hurdle rate representative of a minimum profitability. SVA nets both the expected loss from revenues and the cost of the required capital, valued with an appropriate price in line with shareholder's required return. A positive SVA implies creation of value, while a negative SVA implies destruction of value from the bank's shareholders' standpoint. The same principle applies for market transactions, except for expected loss. Capital results from either market risk or credit risk. It is either regulatory capital or economic capital, the latter being conceptually a better choice.

Both calculations use the accrued income flow of a period, instead of discounting to present all future flows. Economic valuation, or 'mark-to-market', is not a substitute for risk-adjusted performances because it combines both the revenue and the risk adjustments

---

[6] Both are detailed in Chapters 53 and 54. Here, we focus on the difference between such measures and valuation.

in a single figure. The excess spread, or spread between contractual return and the market required yield, also combines both adjustments. Instead of bundling these two adjustments in a single value, RaRoC or SVA make both revenues and risk adjustments explicit.

APPENDIX: DISCRETE TIME AND CONTINUOUS TIME COMPOUNDING

This appendix details the calculations of continuous time compounding and discounting and how to derive the continuous rate equivalent to a discrete time rate. Continuous time compounding serves for the pricing model literature.

Future Values

The future value $FV(y, n, 1)$ of an investment of 1 at y for n years, compounding only once per year, is $(1 + y)^n$. Dividing the year into k subperiods, we have $FV(y, n, k) = (1 + y/k)^{kn}$. For instance, at $y = 10\%$ per year, the future value is:

$$FV(10\%, 1, 1) = (1 + 10\%) = 1.1000 \quad \text{for one subperiod}$$

$$FV(10\%, 1, 2) = (1 + 10\%/2)^2 = 1.1025 \quad \text{for two subperiods}$$

$$FV(10\%, 1, 4) = (1 + 10\%/4)^4 = 1.1038 \quad \text{for four subperiods}$$

The limit when k tends towards infinity provides the 'continuous compounding' formula. When k increases, kn grows and y/k decreases. Mathematically, the limit becomes:

$$FV_c(y, n) = \exp(yn) = e^{yn}$$

The exponential function is $\exp(x) = e^x$. For $n = 1$ and $y = 10\%$, the limit is:

$$FV_c(10\%, 1) = \exp(10\% \times 1) = 1.1052$$

Present Values

The present value $PV_c(y, n, k)$ of a future flow in n years results from $FV_c(y, n, k)$. If $FV_c(n) = e^{yn}$, the present value of 1 dated n at the current date is:

$$PV_c(y, n) = \exp(-yn) = e^{-yn}$$

For one period:

$$PV(10\%, 1) = (1 + 10\%)^{-1} = 0.90909$$

$$PV_c(10\%, 1) = \exp(-10\% \times 1) = 0.90484$$

When the period n comprises k distinct subperiods, the present value formula uses the actual number of subperiods for n. If $n = 1$ year, the present value for one subperiod is $PV_c(10\%, 1)$ and becomes $PV_c(10\%, 0.5)$ if $k = 2$.

Equivalence between Continuous and Discrete Rates

There is a discrete rate y such that the future values are identical when compounding with discrete subperiods and continuously. It is such that the future value at the continuous rate y_c is identical to the future value at the discrete rate y_d. The equivalence results from:

$$(1 + y/k)^{kn} = \exp(y_c n)$$

This rate y does not depend on n: $(1 + y/k)^k = \exp(y_c)$. Hence, taking the Napierian logarithm (ln) of both sides:

$$y_c = k \ln(1 + y/k)$$

$$y = k[\exp(y_c/k) - 1]$$

As an example, $y = 10\%$ is equivalent for 1 year and $k = 1$ to a continuous rate such that:

$$10\% = \exp(y_c) - 1 \quad \text{or} \quad \exp(y_c) = 1 - 10\% = 0.9$$

It is equivalent to state that:

$$y_c = k \ln(1 + y/k) = \ln(1 + 10\%) = 9.531\%$$

This allows us to move back and forth from continuous to discrete rates.

9

Risk Model Building Blocks

The development of risk models for banks has been extremely fast and rich in the recent period, starting with Asset–Liability Management (ALM) models, followed by market Value at Risk (VaR) models for risk and the continuous development of credit risk models, to name the main trends only. The risk models to which we refer in this book are 'instrumental' models, which help in implementing better risk management measures and practices in banks. Looking at the universe of models—the variety of models, the risks they address and their techniques—raises real issues over how to structure a presentation of what they are, what they achieve and how they do it.

Looking closely at risk models reveals a common structure along major 'blocks', each of them addressing essential issues such as: What are the risk drivers of a transaction? How do we deal with risk diversification within portfolios? How do we obtain loss distributions necessary for calculating VaR? The purpose of this chapter is to define the basic 'building blocks' of risk models. The definition follows from a few basic principles:

- The primary goal of risk management is to enhance the risk–return profiles of transactions and portfolios. The risk–return profiles of transactions or portfolios are a centrepiece of risk management processes. Traditional accounting practices provide returns. By contrast, risks raise measurement challenges because they are intangible and invisible until they materialize.
- Risk–return measures appear as the ultimate goal of risk models. Their main innovation is in risk measurement. Models achieve this goal by assembling various techniques and tools that articulate to each other. Together, they make up the risk management 'toolbox'.
- Risk models differ along two main dimensions: the nature of the risk (interest rate risk, market, credit, etc.) that they address; whether they apply to isolated transactions or portfolios, because portfolios raise the issue of measuring diversification in addition

to measuring the standalone risk of transactions. Accordingly, techniques to address various risks for standalone transactions or portfolios differ.

Such principles suggest a common architecture for adopting a 'building block' structure of risk models. Summarizing, we find that risk models combine four main building blocks:

   I. Risk drivers and standalone risk of transactions. Risk drivers are all factors influencing risks, which are necessary inputs for measuring the risk of individual transactions. When considered in isolation, the intrinsic of a transaction is 'standalone'.
  II. Portfolio risk. Portfolio models aim to capture the diversification effect that makes the risk of a portfolio of transactions smaller than the sum of the risks of the individual transactions. They serve to measure the economic capital under the VaR methodology.
 III. Top-down and bottom-up links. These links relate global risk to individual transaction risks, or subportfolio risks. They convert global risk and return targets into risk limits and target profitability for business lines (top-down) and, conversely, for facilitating decision-making at the transaction level and for aggregating business line risks and returns for global reporting purposes (bottom-up).
  IV. Risk-adjusted performance measuring and reporting, for transactions and portfolios. Both risk–return profiles feed the basic risk processes: profitability and limit setting, providing guidelines for risk decisions and risk monitoring.

The detailed presentation uses these four main blocks as foundations for structuring the entire book. Each main block subdivides into smaller modules, dedicated to intermediate tasks, leading to nine basic blocks. The book presents blocks I and II for the three main risks: interest rate risk, market risk and credit risk. On the other hand, tools and techniques of blocks III and IV appear transversal to all risks and do not require a presentation differentiated by risk. After dealing with blocks I and II separately for each main risk, we revert to a transversal presentation of blocks III and IV.

   The first section focuses on the double role of risk–return profiles: as target variables of risk policies for decision-making; as a key interface between risk models and risk processes. The second section reviews the progressive development stages of risk models. The third section provides an overview of the main building blocks structure. The next sections detail each of the blocks. The last section provides a view of how sub-blocks assemble and how they map to different risks.

RISK MODELS AND RISK PROCESSES

Risk–return is the centrepiece of risk management processes. All bank systems provide common measures of income, such as accrual revenues, fees and interest income for the banking portfolio, and Profit and Loss (P&L) for the market portfolio. Measuring risk is a more difficult challenge. Without a balanced view on both risk and return, the management of banks is severely impaired since these two dimensions are intertwining in every process, setting guidelines, making risk decisions or monitoring performance. Therefore, the major contributions of models are to capture risks in all instances where it is necessary to set targets, make risk decisions, both at the transaction level and at the portfolio level.

There are multiple risk models. ALM models aims to model the interest rate risk of banks at the global balance sheet level. Market risk and credit risk models serve both to measure the risk of individual transactions (standalone risk) and to measure the portfolio risk. To reach this second goal, they need to address the intrinsic risk of individual transactions, independent of the portfolio context. This requires identifying all risk drivers and modelling how they alter the risk of transactions. When reaching the portfolio risk stage, complexities appear because of the diversification effect, making the risk of the portfolio—the risk of the sum of individual transactions—much less than the sum of all individual risks. The issue is to quantify such diversification effects that portfolio models address.

The applications of portfolio models are critical and numerous. They serve to determine the likelihood of various levels of potential losses of a portfolio. The global portfolio loss becomes the foundation for allocating risk to individual transactions, after diversification effects. Once this stage is reached, it becomes relatively simple to characterize the risk–return profile of the portfolio as well as those of transactions, since we have the global risk and the risk allocations, plus the income available from the accounting systems.

Moving to portfolio models is a quantum leap because they provide access to the risk post-diversification effect for any portfolio, the global portfolio or any subset of transactions. This is a major innovation, notably for credit risk. Measuring risks allows the risk–return view to be extended bank-wide, across business lines and from transactions to the entire bank portfolio. This faculty considerably leverages the efficiency of the bank processes that previously dealt with income without tangible measures of portfolio risks.

The building blocks of bank processes respond to common sense needs: setting guidelines, making decisions, monitoring risk and return, plus the 'vertical' processes of sending signals to business lines, complying with overall targets and obtaining a consolidated view of risk and return. Risk models provide risk, the otherwise 'missing' input to processes. Figure 9.1 summarizes the overview of interaction between risk models and risk processes.

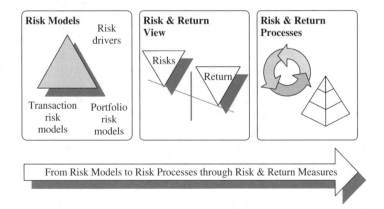

FIGURE 9.1   From risk models to risk processes through risk and return measures

GENERATIONS OF BANK RISK MODELS

There are a range of banking risk models differing in their purposes and techniques, and the risks that they address.

The ALM models were the first to appear. They aimed to capture the interest rate risk of the banking book of commercial banks. Later on, they developed into several building blocks, some of them addressing the interest rate risk of the interest income, others the interest rate risk of the mark-to-market value of the balance sheet, and others aiming to value embedded prepayment options in banking products.

Regulations focused on capital requirements and banks focused on economic capital. The capital adequacy principle led to the VaR concept and to VaR models for market risk and credit risk. Market risk models aim to capture the market portfolio risk and find the capital requirement adequate for making this risk sustainable. They address the behaviour of risk drivers, interest rates, foreign exchange rates and equity indexes and, from this first block, derive market risk for the portfolio as VaR.

There are several generations of risk models. The academic community looked at modelling the borrowers' risk, captured through ratings or observed default events, from observable characteristics such as financial variables a long time ago. There is renewed interest in such models because of the requirements of the New Basel Accord to provide better measures of credit risk drivers at the borrower and the transaction levels. The newest generation of models addresses both transaction risk and portfolio risk with new approaches. Risk drivers are exposures, default probabilities and recoveries. Modelling default probability became a priority. New models appeared relating observable attributes of firms to default and ratings, using new techniques, such as the neural network approach. The implementation of the conceptual view of default as an option held by stockholders[1] is a major advance that fostered much progress.

Various techniques address the portfolio diversification issue, trying to assess the likelihood of simultaneous adverse default or risk deterioration events depending on the portfolio structure. Modelling credit risk and finding the risk of portfolios remained a major challenge because of the scarcity of data, in contrast to market models, which use the considerable volume of market price information. Recent models share common modules: identifying and modelling risk drivers in order to model the standalone risk of individual transactions; modelling diversification effects within portfolios to derive the portfolio risk.

Other tools serve for linking risk measures with the business processes, by allocating income and risks to transactions and portfolios. Allocating income is not a pure accounting problem since it is necessary to define the financial cost matching the transaction revenues. Risks raise a more difficult challenge. The Funds Transfer Pricing (FTP) system and the capital—or risk—allocation system perform these two tasks. Once attached to risk models, they allow us to reach the ultimate stage of assigning a risk–return profile to any transaction or portfolio. Then, the bank processes can take over and use these risks–returns as inputs for management and business purposes.

---

[1] This is the Merton (1974) model, later implemented by the KMV Corporation to measure the 'expected default frequency' (Edf ©). The default option is the option held by stockholders to give up the assets of the firm if their value falls below that of debt. See Chapter 38.

RISK MODEL BUILDING BLOCKS

The risk management toolbox comprises four main building blocks that Figure 9.2 maps with nine basic risk modelling building blocks, each related to a specific issue. The four main blocks are:

I. Risk measurement of transactions on a standalone basis, or 'intrinsic risk', without considering the portfolio context that diversifies away a large fraction of the sum of individual risks.
II. Risk modelling of portfolios, addressing the issue of portfolio risk diversification and its measurement through basic characteristics such as expected (statistical) losses and potential losses.
III. Risk allocation and income allocation within portfolios. The risk allocation mechanisms should capture the diversification effect within the portfolio. The diversification effect results in a lower risk of the portfolio than the sum of the intrinsic risks of transactions. Since risks do not add arithmetically as income does, the mechanism is more complex than earnings allocations to subsets of the portfolio.
IV. Determination of the risk–return profiles of transactions, subsets of the bank portfolio, such as business lines, and the overall bank portfolio. The risk–return profile is the ultimate aim of modelling, which risk management attempts to enhance for individual transactions and portfolios.

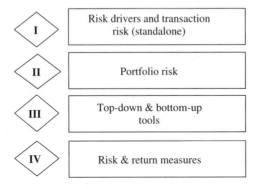

FIGURE 9.2   The main modelling building blocks

This basic structure applies to all risks. The contents of the first two blocks differ with risks, although all modelling techniques need similar inputs and produce similar outputs. The third and fourth blocks apply to all risk, and there is less need to differentiate them for credit and market risks, for instance.

When considering all risk models, it appears they share the same basic structure. The four main building blocks each differentiate into sub-blocks dedicated to specific tasks. Various specific 'modules' provide the necessary information to progress step-by-step towards the ultimate goal of assigning risk–return profiles to transactions and portfolios. Figure 9.3 breaks down these building blocks into modules addressing intermediate issues. The top section describes the main blocks. The bottom section illustrates the linkages between risk models and risk processes. All modules need to fit with each other, using

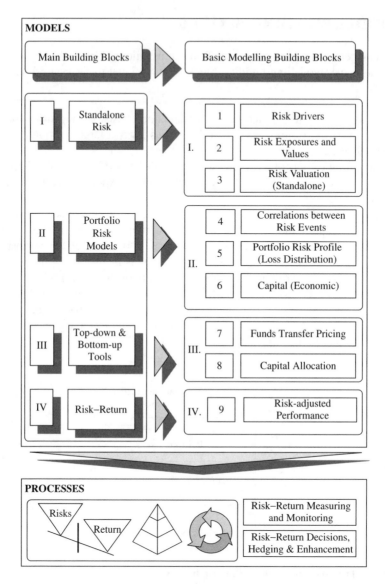

FIGURE 9.3   Main risk modelling building blocks

the inputs of the previous ones, and providing outputs that serve as inputs to the next ones. This structure conveniently organizes the presentation of various modelling contributions. Vendors' models bundle several modules together. Other modules serve to fill out gaps in inputs that other building blocks need to proceed further, such as the modelling of the market risk or the credit drivers of transactions.

This 'four/nine' block structures the entire presentation expanded in this book. The book expands this structure for each of the three risks: interest rate risk for ALM, market risk and credit risk.

What follows describes in detail the basic modelling blocks.

BLOCK I: STANDALONE RISK

Block I requires risk and transaction data to capture individual transaction risks.

Risk Drivers

Block I starts by identifying 'risk drivers', those parameters whose uncertainty alters values and revenues. These random risk drivers are identical to value drivers because measures of risk are variations of value. For ALM, the main risk drivers are the interest rates, which drive the interest income. For market risk, risk drivers are all the market parameters that trigger changes in value of the transactions. They differ across the market compartments: fixed income, foreign exchange or equity. The credit risk drivers are all parameters that influence the credit standing of counterparties and the loss for the bank if it deteriorates. They include exposure, recoveries under default, plus the likelihood of default, or default probability (DP) and its changes (migration risk) when time passes. Later on, we make a distinction between risk drivers and risk factors. Risk factors alter risk drivers, which then directly influence risk events, such as default or the change in value of transactions. The distinction is purely technical. In risk models, risk drivers relate directly to risk events, while risk factors serve for modelling these direct drivers. The distinction is expanded in Chapters 31 and 44 addressing correlation modelling with 'factor' models, hence the above distinction.

The basic distinction for controlling risk is between risk drivers, which are the sources of uncertainty, and the exposure and sensitivities of transaction values to such sources. Risk drivers remain beyond the control of the bank, while exposures and sensitivities to risk drivers result from the bank's decisions.

Exposures

Block I's second sub-block relates to exposure size and economic valuation. Book value, or notional amount (for derivatives), characterizes size. Economic valuation is the 'fair value', risk and revenue-adjusted. Economic valuation requires mapping exposures to the relevant risk drivers and deriving values from them. Because it is risk-adjusted, any change in the risk drivers materializes in a value change, favourable or unfavourable.

Exposure serves as a basis for calculating value changes. For market risk, exposures are mark-to-market and change continuously with market movements. Exposures for credit risk are at book values for commercial banking. Since book values do not change when the default probabilities change, economic values serve for full valuation of credit risk. Exposures data include, specifically, the expected size under a default event (Exposure At Default, EAD), plus the recoveries, which result in loss given default (Lgd) lower than exposure.

For ALM, exposures are the 'surfaces' serving to calculate interest revenues and costs. ALM uses both book values and economic values. Note that ALM's first stage is to consolidate all banking portfolio exposures by currency and type of interest rates, thereby capturing the entire balance sheet view from the very beginning. By contrast, credit and market risks modelling starts at the transaction level, to characterize the individual risk, and the global portfolio risk is dealt with in other blocks.

Standalone Risk and Mark-to-Future

Sub-block 3 is forward looking. It looks at future events materializing risks today for each individual transaction, or on a 'standalone' basis. Such events include deviations of interest rates for the banking portfolio, all market parameters for market risk and all factors influencing the credit standing of borrowers for credit risk. Sub-block 3 assesses risk as any downside deviation of value at a future time point. Since future values are uncertain, they follow a distribution at this horizon. Adverse deviations are the losses materializing risk. 'Marking-to-future' designates the technical processes of calculating potential values at a future date, and deriving losses from this distribution. The principle is the same for transactions and portfolios. The difference is the effect of diversification within a portfolio, which standalone risk ignores.

Obtaining the Risk Driver Inputs

Risk drivers and exposure are ingredients of risk models. Sometimes, it is possible to observe them, such as interest rates whose instability over time is readily observable. Sometimes, they are assigned a value because they result from a judgment on risk quality, such as ratings from rating agencies or from internal rating systems. A rating is simply a grade assigned to the creditworthiness combining a number of factors that influence the credit standing of borrowers.

Several models help in modelling the uncertainty of the risk drivers. For instance, interest rate models allow us to derive multiple scenarios of interest rates that are consistent with their observed behaviour. Rating models attempt to mimic ratings from agencies through some observable characteristics of firms, such as financial data. Default probability models, such as KMV's Credit Monitor or Moody's RiskCalc, provide modelled estimates of default probabilities.

BLOCK II: PORTFOLIO RISK

Block I focuses on a standalone view of risk, ignoring the portfolio context and the diversification effects. Block II's goal is to capture the risk profile of the portfolio rather than the risk of single transactions considered in isolation.

Diversification Effects

Diversification requires new inputs characterizing the portfolio risk, mainly the sizes of individual exposures and the correlations between risk events of individual transactions. The idea is intuitive. Should all transactions suffer losses simultaneously, the portfolio loss would be the sum of all simultaneous losses. Fortunately, not all losses materialize at the same time, and the portfolio loss varies according to the number and magnitude of individual losses occurring within a given period. Intuitively, a small number of losses are much more frequent than a simultaneous failure of many of them. This is the essence of diversification: not all risks materialize together. Which losses are going to materialize and how many will occur within the period are uncertain. This is the challenge of quantifying diversification effects, which requires 'portfolio models'.

The technical measure of association between transaction risks is the 'correlation'. For instance, the adverse deviations of interest income, a usual target variable for ALM policies, result from interest rate variations. The correlation between interest rates tends to reduce the diversification effect. All interest revenues and costs tend to move simultaneously in the same direction. Asset and liability exposures to interest rates are offset to the extent that they relate to the same interest rate references.

The adverse deviations of the market value of the trading portfolio correlate because they depend on a common set of market parameters, equity indexes, interest rates and foreign exchange rates. However, diversification effects are important because some of these risk drivers are highly correlated, but others are not, and sometimes they vary in opposite directions. Moreover, positions in opposite directions offset.

Credit defaults and migrations tend to correlate because they depend on the same general economic conditions, although with different sensitivities. Models demonstrated that portfolio risk is highly sensitive to such correlations. In spite of such positive correlations, diversification effects are very significant for credit risk. The opposite of 'diversification' is 'concentration'. If all firms in the same region tend to default together, there is a credit risk concentration in the portfolio because of the very high default correlation. A risk concentration also designates large sizes of exposures. A single exposure of 1000 might be riskier than 10 exposures of 100, even if borrowers' defaults correlate, because there is no diversification for this 1000, whereas there is some across 10 different firms. 'Granularity' designates risk concentration due to size effect. It is higher with a single exposure of 1000 than with 10 exposures of 100.

Correlation Modelling

Obtaining correlations requires modelling. Correlations between risk events of each individual transaction result from the correlation between their risk and value drivers. Correlations for market risk drivers, and for interest rates for ALM, are directly observable. Correlations between credit risk events, such as defaults, suffer from such a scarcity of data that it is difficult to infer correlations from available data on yearly defaults. In fact, credit risk remains largely 'invisible'. Credit risk models turn around the difficulty by inferring correlations between credit risk events from the correlations of observable risk factors that influence them. For all main risks, correlation modelling is critical because of the high sensitivity of portfolio risk to correlations and size discrepancies between exposures.

Portfolio Risk and VaR

Once correlations are obtained, the next step is to characterize the entire spectrum of outcomes for the portfolio, and its downside risk. Since a portfolio is subject to various levels of losses, the most comprehensive way of characterizing the risk profile is with the distribution of losses, assigning a probability to each level of portfolio loss.

Portfolio losses are declines in value triggered by various correlated risk events. From a risk perspective, the main risk statistics extracted from loss distributions are the expected loss, the loss volatility characterizing the dispersion around the mean and the loss percentiles at various confidence levels for measuring downside risk and VaR. The VaR is also the 'economic capital' at the same preset confidence level.

BLOCK III: REVENUE AND RISK ALLOCATION

Blocks I and II concentrate on individual and global risk measures. For the bank as a whole, only portfolio risk and overall return count. However, focusing only on these aggregated targets would not suffice to develop risk management practices within business lines and for decision-making purposes. Moving downwards to risk processes requires other tools. They are the top-down links, sending signals to business lines, and the bottom-up links, consolidating and reporting, making up block III. Two basic devices serve for linking global targets and business policy (Figure 9.4):

- The FTP system. The system allocates income to individual transactions and to business lines, or any other portfolio segment, such as product families or market segments.
- The capital allocation system, which allocates risks to any portfolio subset and down to individual transactions.

FIGURE 9.4   From global risk management to business lines

Funds Transfer Pricing

Transfer pricing systems exist in all institutions. Transfer prices, are internal references used to price financial resources across business units. Transfer pricing applies essentially to the banking book. The interest income allocated to any transaction is the difference between the customer rate and the internal reference rate, or 'transfer price', that applies for this transaction. Transfer rates also serve as a reference for setting customer rates. They should represent the economic cost of making the funds available. Without such references, there is no way to measure the income generated by transactions or business units (for commercial banking) and no basis for setting customer rates.

Transfer prices serve other interrelated purposes in a commercial bank. Chapters 26 and 27 detail the specifications making the income allocation process consistent with all risk and return processes.

Capital Allocation

Unlike revenues and costs, risks do not add arithmetically to portfolio risk because of diversification. Two risks of 1 each do not add up to 2, but add up in general to less than 2 because of the diversification effect, a basic pillar for the banking industry. Portfolio risk models characterize the portfolio risk as a distribution of loss values with a probability attached to each value. From this distribution, it is possible to derive all loss statistics of interest after diversification effects. This represents a major progress but, as such, it does not solve the issue of moving back to the risk retained by each individual transaction, after diversification effects.

Since we cannot rely on arithmetic summation for risks, there is no obvious way to allocate the overall risk to subportfolios or transactions. To perform this task, we need a capital (risk) allocation model. The capital allocation model assigns to any subset of a portfolio a fraction of the overall risk, called the 'risk contribution'. Risk contributions are much smaller than 'standalone' risk measures, or measures of the intrinsic risk of transactions considered in isolation, pre-diversification effects, because they measure only the fraction of risk retained by a transaction post-diversification. The capital allocation system performs this risk allocation and provides risk contributions for all individual transactions as well as for any portfolio subsets. The underlying principle is to turn the non-arithmetic properties of risks into additive risk contributions that sum up arithmetically to the overall bank's portfolio risk.

The capital allocation system allocates capital in proportion to the risk contributions provided by portfolio models. For example, using some adequate technique, we can define the standalone risk of three transactions, for example 20, 30 and 30. The sum is 80. However, the portfolio model shows that VaR is only 40. The capital allocation module tells us how much capital to assign to each of the three transactions, for example 10, 15 and 25. They sum up to the overall risk of 40. These figures are 'capital allocations', or 'risk contributions' to the portfolio risk.

The FTP and capital allocation systems provide the necessary links between the global portfolio management of the bank and the business decisions. Without these two pieces, there would be missing links between the global policy of the bank and the business lines. The two pieces complement each other for obtaining risk-adjusted performance measures. Block III leads directly to the ultimate stage of defining risk and return profiles and risk-based performance and pricing.

Aggregating VaR for Different Risks

Note that the overall portfolio management for the bank includes integrating all risks in a common unified framework. The VaR concept solves the issue by valuing risks in dollar value. Adding the VaR of different risks remains a problem, however, since the different main risks may correlate more or less, or be independent. A sample global report of a VaR implementation for a bank illustrates the overview (Table 9.1).

TABLE 9.1   Example of a VaR report

Risks	VaR capital	
Credit	260	65.0%
Market	50	12.5%
Interest rate (ALM)	50	12.5%
Operational risk	80	20.0%
Total	400	

In this example, total potential losses are valued at 40. The reports aggregate the VaR generated by different risks, which is a prudent rule. However, it is unlikely that unexpected losses will hit their upper bounds at the same time for credit risk, market risk and other risks. Therefore, the arithmetic total is an overestimate of aggregated VaR across risks.

BLOCK IV: RISK AND RETURN MANAGEMENT

Block IV achieves the ultimate result of providing the risk–return profiles of the overall bank portfolio, of transactions or subportfolios. It also allows breaking down aggregated risk and return into those of transactions or subportfolios. Reporting modules take over at this final stage for slicing risks and return along all relevant dimensions for management. The consistency of blocks I to IV ensures that any breakdown of risks and returns reconciles with the overall risk and return of the bank. At this stage, it becomes possible to plug the right measures into the basic risk management processes: guidelines-setting, decision-making and monitoring. In order to reach this final frontier with processes, it is necessary to add a risk-based performance 'module'.

The generic name of risk-adjusted profitability is RaRoC (Risk-adjusted Return on Capital). Risk-Adjusted Performance Measurement (RAPM) designates the risk adjustment of individual transactions that allows comparison of their profitability on the same basis. It is more an ex post measure of performance, once the decision of lending is made, that applies to existing transactions. Risk-Based Pricing (RBP) relates to ex ante decision-making, when we need to define the target price ensuring that the transaction profitability is in line with both risk and the overall target profitability of the bank. For reasons detailed later in Chapters 51 and 52, we differentiate the two concepts, and adopt this terminology. RBP serves to define ex ante the risk-based price. RAPM serves to compare the performance of existing transactions.

RAPM simply combines the outputs of the previous building blocks: the income allocation system, which is the FTP system, and the capital allocation system. Once both exist, the implementation is very simple. We illustrate the application for ex post RAPM. Transaction A has a capital allocation of 5 and its revenue, given the transfer price, is 0.5. Transaction B has a capital allocation of 3 and a revenue of 0.4. The RaRoC of transaction A is $0.5/5 = 10\%$ and that of transaction B is $0.4/3 = 13.33\%$. We see that the less risky transaction B has a better risk-adjusted profitability than the riskier transaction A, even though its revenue is lower.

THE RISK MANAGEMENT TOOLBOX: AN OVERVIEW

This section summarizes: the nature of risk and return decisions that models aim to facilitate; how the several building blocks assemble to provide such risk–return profiles; how they differentiate across the main risks, interest rate risk, credit risk and market risk.

Risk Modelling and Risk Decisions

All model blocks lead ultimately to risk and return profiles for transactions, subportfolios of business units, product families or market segments, plus the overall bank portfolio. The purpose of characterizing this risk–return profile is to provide essential inputs for decision-making. The spectrum of decisions includes:

- New transactions.
- Hedging, both individual transactions (micro-hedges) and subportfolios (macro-hedges).
- Risk–return enhancement of transactions, through restructuring for example.
- Portfolio management, which essentially consists of enhancing the portfolio risk–return profile.

Note that this spectrum includes both on-balance sheet and off-balance sheet decisions. On-balance sheet actions refer to any decisions altering the volume, pricing and risk of transactions, while off-balance sheet decisions refer more to hedging risk.

How Building Blocks Assemble

In this section, we review the building block structure of risk models and tools leading to the ultimate stage of modelling the risk–return profiles of transactions and portfolios. It is relatively easy to group together various sub-blocks to demonstrate how they integrate and fit comprehensively to converge towards risk and return profiles.

An alternative view is by nature of risk, interest rate risk for commercial banking (ALM), market risk or credit risk, plus other risks. The structure by building blocks proves robust across all risks because it distinguishes the basic modules that apply to all. The differences are that modules differ across risks. For instance, market risk uses extensively data-intensive techniques. Credit risk relies more on technical detours to remedy the scarcity of data. ALM focuses on the global balance sheet from the very start simply because the interest rate risk exposure does not raise a conceptual challenge, but rather an information technology challenge.

We provide below both views of the risk models:

- The building blocks view, across risks.
- The view by risk, with the three main risks 'view' developed in this text: interest rate risk in commercial banking (ALM), market risk and credit risk.

Figure 9.5 summarizes how basic blocks link together to move towards the final risk and return block. Making available this information allows the main risk management processes to operate. The figure uses symbols representative of the purpose of risk modelling blocks and of risk process blocks.

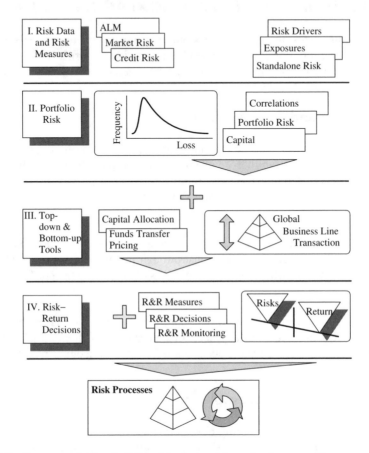

FIGURE 9.5   From modelling building blocks to risk and return profiles

How Building Blocks Map to the Main Risks

All building blocks map to different risks: interest rate risk, market risk and credit risk. The book uses this mapping as the foundation for structuring the outline of the subsequent detailed presentations.

   In practice, the organization by risk type applies essentially for building blocks I and II. The FTP system and the capital allocation system are 'standalone modules'. The ALM is in charge of the FTP module. The capital (or risk) allocation module applies to market and credit risk with the same basic rules. Finally, the 'risk–return' module uses all contributions of upper blocks. The book uses the matrix in Table 9.2, developing the modelling for each main risk. The book structure is shown by the cells of the table.

TABLE 9.2   Cross-tabulating model building blocks with main risks

	ALM	Market risk	Credit risk
I. Standalone risk of transactions			
II. Portfolio risk			
III. Top-down and bottom-up tools			
IV. Risk and return			

Figure 9.6 combines the risk view with the building block view, and shows how all blocks articulate to each other.

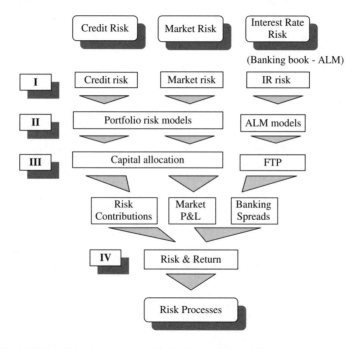

FIGURE 9.6   Building blocks view and risks view of the risk management toolbox

SECTION 5

Asset–Liability Management

10

ALM Overview

Asset–Liability Management (ALM) is the unit in charge of managing the Interest Rate Risk (IRR) and the liquidity of the bank. Therefore, it focuses essentially on the commercial banking pole.

ALM addresses two types of interest rate risks. The first risk is that of interest income shifts due to interest rate movements, given that all balance sheet assets and liabilities generate revenues and costs directly related to interest rate references. A second risk results from options embedded in banking products, such as the prepayment option of individual borrowers who can renegotiate the rate of their loans when the interest rates decline. The optional risk of ALM raises specific issues discussed in a second section. These two risks, although related, need different techniques.

ALM policies use two target variables: the interest income and the Net Present Value (NPV) of assets minus liabilities. Intuitively, the stream of future interest incomes varies in line with the NPV. The main difference is that NPV captures the entire stream of future cash flows generated by the portfolio, while the interest income relates to one or several periods. The NPV view necessitates specific techniques, discussed in different chapters from those relating to the interest income sensitivity to interest rates.

This chapter presents a general overview of the main building blocks of ALM. For ALM, the portfolio, or balance sheet, view dominates. It is easier to aggregate the exposures and the risk of individual transactions in the case of ALM than for other risks, because all exposures share interest rates as common risk drivers.

ALM BUILDING BLOCKS

In the case of ALM, the global view dominates because it is easier to aggregate the exposures and the risk of individual transactions than for other risks. Figure 10.1

summarizes the main characteristics of ALM building blocks using the common structure proposed for all risks.

The next sections detail blocks I: standalone risk and II: banking book—portfolio—risk.

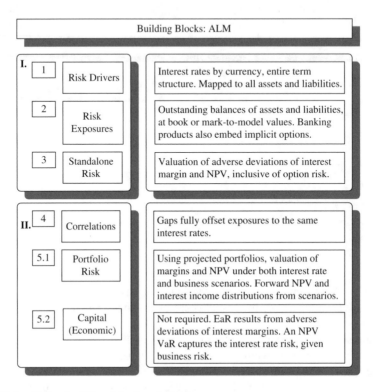

FIGURE 10.1   Major building blocks of ALM

BLOCK I: STANDALONE RISK

The risk drivers are all interest rates by currency. Exposures in the banking portfolio are the outstanding balances of all assets and liabilities, except equity, at book value. To capture the entire profile of cash flows generated by all assets and liabilities, the NPV of assets and liabilities is used at market rates.

Risk materializes by an adverse change of either one of these two targets. The standalone risk of any individual exposure results from the sensitivity to interest rate changes of the interest income or of its value. The downside risk is that of adverse variations of these two target variables due to interest rate moves. Hence, the valuation of losses results from revaluation at future dates of interest income or of the NPV for each scenario of interest rates.

There are two sources of interest rate exposure: liquidity flows and interest rate resets. Each liquidity flow creates an interest rate exposure. For a future inflow, for instance from a future new debt or a repayment of loans, the interest rate risk results from the unknown rate of the utilization of this inflow for lending or investing. Interest rate risk arises also from interest rate resets in the absence of liquidity flows. A floating rate long-term debt has several reset dates. For example, a 10-year bullet loan with a floating LIBOR 1-year rate has rate resets every year, while the main cash flow occurs at maturity.

Interest rate risk depends on the nature, fixed or variable, of interest rates attached to transactions. When a transaction earns a variable rate, rate resets influence interest revenues both positively and negatively. When it earns a fixed rate, the asset has less value if rates rise above its fixed rate, which makes sense since it generates revenues lower than the market does, and vice versa. When a debt pays a fixed rate above market rate, there is an economic cost resulting from borrowing at a rate higher than the rate. This is an 'opportunity cost', the cost of giving up more profitable opportunities. Interest rate variations trigger changes of either accounting revenues or costs, or opportunity (economic) costs.

The exposures are sensitive to the entire set of common interest rates. Each interest rate is a common index for several assets and liabilities. Since they are sensitive to the same rate, 'gaps' offset these exposures to obtain the net exposure for the balance sheet for each relevant rate.

ALM also deals with the 'indirect' interest rate risk resulting from options embedded in retail banking products. The options are mainly prepayment options that individuals hold, allowing them to renegotiate fixed rates when rates move down. These options have a significant value for all retail banking lines dealing with personal mortgage loans. Should he exercise his option, a borrower would borrow at a lower rate, thereby reducing interest revenues. Depositors also have options to shift their demand deposits to higher interest-earning liabilities, which they exercise when rates increase.

The value of options is particularly relevant for loans since banks can price them rather than give them away to customers. The expected value of options is their price. The potential risk of options for the lender is the potential upside of values during their life, depending on how rates behave. Dealing with optional risk addresses two questions: What is the value of the option for pricing it to customers? What is the downside risk of options given all possible time paths of rates until expiration? The techniques for addressing these questions differ from those of classical ALM models. They are identical to the valuation techniques for market options. The main difference with market risk is that the horizon is much longer. Technical details are given in Chapters 20 and 21.

BLOCK II: PORTFOLIO RISK

ALM exposures are global in nature. They result from mismatches of the volumes of assets and liabilities or from interest rate mismatches. The mismatch, or 'gap', is a central and simple concept for ALM. A liquidity gap is a difference between assets and liabilities, resulting in a deficit or an excess of funds. An interest rate gap is a mismatch between the size of assets and liabilities indexed to the same reference interest rate. The NPV is the mismatch between liability values and asset values. The sensitivity of the NPV to interest rate changes results from a mismatch of the variations of values of assets and liabilities. For these reasons, ALM addresses from the very beginning the aggregated and netted exposure of the entire balance sheet. Implicit options embedded in banking products add an additional complexity to ALM risk.

The interest rate risk of the balance sheet depends on correlations between interest rates. Often, these correlations are high, so that there is no need to differentiate the movements of similar interest rates, although this is only an approximation. In addition, only netted exposures are relevant for assets and liabilities indexed to the same, or to similar, interest rates. Treasurers manage netted cash flows, and ALM controls net exposures to interest rate risk.

Measuring risk consists of characterizing the downside variations of target variables under various scenarios. ALM uses the simulation methodology to obtain the risk–return profile of the balance sheet using several interest rate scenarios. The expected return is the probability weighted average of profitability across scenarios, measured by interest income or NPV. The downside risk is the volatility of the target variables, interest income or NPV, across scenarios, or their worst-case values. ALM models serve to revalue at future time points the target variables as a function of interest rate movements. To achieve this purpose, ALM models recalculate all interest revenues and costs, or all cash flows for NPV, for all scenarios. The process differs from the market risk and the credit risk techniques in several ways:

- The revaluation process focuses on interest income and NPV, instead of market values for market risk and credit risk-adjusted values at the horizon for credit risk.
- Since the ALM horizon is medium to long-term, ALM does not rely only on the existing portfolio as a 'crystallized' portfolio over a long time. Simulations also extend to projections of the portfolio, adding new assets and liabilities resulting from business scenarios. By contrast, market risk and credit models focus on the crystallized portfolio as of today.
- Because of business projections, ALM scenarios deal with business risk as well as interest rate risk, while the market risk and credit risk models ignore business risk.
- Because ALM discusses periodically the bank position with respect to interest and liquidity risk in conjunction with business activities, it often relies on a discrete number of scenarios, rather than attempting to cover the entire spectrum of outcomes as market and credit models do. In addition, it is much easier to define worst-case scenarios for ALM risk than it is for market risk and credit risk, because only interest rates influence the target variables in ways relatively easy to identify.
- Since there is no regulatory capital for ALM risk, there is no need to go as far as full-blown simulations to obtain a full distribution of the target variables at future horizons. However, simulations do allow us to derive an NPV 'Value at Risk' (VaR) for interest rate risk. An ALM VaR is the NPV loss percentile at the preset confidence level. In the case of interest rate risk, large deviations of interest rates trigger optional risk, from the implicit options (prepayment options) embedded in the banking products. This makes it more relevant to extend simulations to a wide array of possible interest rate scenarios.

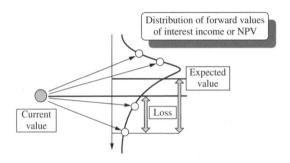

FIGURE 10.2 Forward valuation of target variables (interest income or balance sheet NPV)

To value options for the banking portfolio, the same technique as for single options applies. The NPV is more convenient in order to have a broader view of both loans and options values as of today. Visualizing the portfolio risk–return profile is easy because there is a one-to-one correspondence between interest rate scenarios and the interest income or the NPV, if we ignore business risk (Figure 10.2).

Moreover, assigning probabilities to interest rate scenarios allows us to define the Earnings at Risk (EaR) for interest income, as the lower bound of interest income at a preset confidence level, or the NPV VaR as the lower bound of the NPV at the same preset confidence level.

11

Liquidity Gaps

Liquidity risk results from size and maturity mismatches of assets and liabilities. Liquidity deficits make banks vulnerable to market liquidity risk. Liquid assets protect banks from market tensions because they are an alternative source of funds for facing the near-term obligations.

Whenever assets are greater than resources, deficits appear, necessitating funding in the market. When the opposite occurs, the bank has available excess resources for lending or investing. Both deficits and excesses are liquidity gaps. A time profile of gaps results from projected assets and liabilities at different future time points.

A bank with long-term commitments and short-term resources generates immediate and future deficits. The liquidity risk results from insufficient resources, or outside funds, to fund the loans. It is the risk of additional funding costs because of unexpected funding needs. The standard technique for characterizing liquidity exposure relies on gap time profiles, excesses or deficits of funds, starting from the maturity schedules of existing assets and liabilities.

This time profile results from operating assets and liabilities, which are loans and deposits. Asset–Liability Management (ALM) structures the time schedule of debt issues or investments in order to close the deficits or excess liquidity gaps. Cash matching designates the reference situation such that the time profile of liabilities mirrors that of assets. It is a key benchmark because it implies, if there are no new loans and deposits, a balance sheet without any deficit or excess of funds.

Future deficits require raising funds at rates unknown as of today. Future excesses of funds require investing in the future. Hence, liquidity risk triggers interest rate risk because future funding and investment contracts have unknown rates, unless ALM sets up hedges.

The next chapters discuss the interest rate risk. This chapter focuses on the liquidity position of the banking portfolio. The first section introduces the time profile of liquidity gaps, which are the projected differences between asset and liability time profiles. The second section discusses 'cash matching' between assets and liabilities. The third section discusses the limitations of liquidity gaps, which result mainly from lines without contractual time profiles.

THE LIQUIDITY GAP

Liquidity gaps are the differences, at all future dates, between assets and liabilities of the banking portfolio. Gaps generate liquidity risk, the risk of not being able to raise funds without excess costs. Controlling liquidity risk implies spreading over time amounts of funding, avoiding unexpected important market funding and maintaining a 'cushion' of liquid short-term assets, so that selling them provides liquidity without incurring capital gains and losses. Liquidity risk exists when there are deficits of funds, since excess of funds results in interest rate risk, the risk of not knowing in advance the rate of lending or investing these funds. There are two types of liquidity gaps. Static liquidity gaps result from existing assets and liabilities only. Dynamic liquidity gaps add the projected new credits and new deposits to the amortization profiles of existing assets.

The Definition of Liquidity Gaps

Liquidity gaps are differences between the outstanding balances of assets and liabilities, or between their changes over time. The convention used below is to calculate gaps as algebraic differences between assets and liabilities. Therefore, at any date, a positive gap between assets and liabilities is equivalent to a deficit, and vice versa.

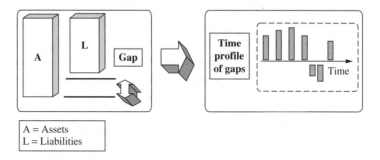

FIGURE 11.1   Liquidity gaps and time profile of gaps

Marginal, or incremental, gaps are the differences between the changes in assets and liabilities during a given period (Figure 11.1). A positive marginal gap means that the algebraic variation of assets exceeds the algebraic variation of liabilities. When assets and liabilities amortize over time, such variations are negative, and a positive gap is equivalent to an outflow[1].

The fixed assets and the equity also affect liquidity gaps. Considering equity and fixed assets given at any date, the gap breaks down as in Figure 11.2, isolating the gap between

---

[1] For instance, if the amortization of assets is 3, and that of liabilities is 5, the algebraic marginal gap, as defined above, is $-3 - (-5) = +2$, and it is an outflow. Sometimes the gaps are calculated as the opposite difference. It is important to keep a clear convention, so that the figures can easily be interpreted.

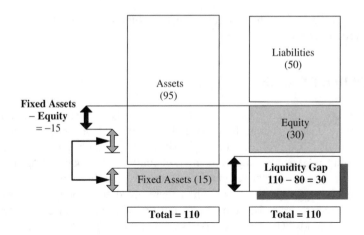

FIGURE 11.2   The structure of the balance sheet and liquidity gap

fixed assets and equity and the liquidity gap generated by commercial transactions. In what follows, we ignore the bottom section of the balance sheet, but liquidity gaps should include the fixed assets equity gap.

Static and Dynamic Gaps

Liquidity gaps exist for all future dates. The gaps based on existing assets and liabilities are 'static gaps'. They provide the image of the liquidity posture of the bank. 'Static gaps' are time profiles of future gaps under cessation of all new business, implying a progressive melt-down of the balance sheet.

When new assets and liabilities, derived from commercial projections, cumulate with existing assets and liabilities, the gap profile changes completely. Both assets and liabilities, existing plus new ones, tend to increase, rather than amortize. This new gap is the 'dynamic gap'. Gaps for both existing and new assets and liabilities are required to project the total excesses or deficits of funds. However, it is a common practice to focus first on the existing assets and liabilities to calculate the gap profile. One reason is that there is no need to obtain funds in advance for new transactions, or to invest resources that are not yet collected. Instead, funding the deficits or investing excesses from new business occurs when they appear in the balance sheet. Another reason is that the dynamic gaps depend on commercial uncertainties.

Example

As mentioned before, both simple and marginal gaps are calculated. The marginal gaps result from variations of outstanding balances. Therefore, the cumulated value over time of the marginal gaps is equal to the gap based on the outstanding balances of assets and liabilities. Table 11.1 is an example of a gap time profile.

TABLE 11.1 Time profiles of outstanding assets and liabilities and of liquidity gaps

Dates	1	2	3	4	5	6
Assets	100	900	700	650	500	300
Liabilities	100	800	500	400	350	100
Gap[a]	0	100	200	250	150	200
Asset amortization		−10	−20	−50	−15	−20
Liability amortization		−20	−30	−10	−50	−25
Marginal gap[b]		100	100	50	−10	50
Cumulated marginal gap[c]		100	200	250	150	200

[a]Calculated as the difference between assets and liabilities. A positive gap is a deficit that requires funding. A negative gap is an excess of resources to be invested.
[b]Calculated as the algebraic variation of assets minus the algebraic variation of liabilities between t and $t − 1$. With this convention, a positive gap is an outflow and a negative gap is an inflow.
[c]The cumulated marginal gaps are identical to the gaps calculated with the outstanding balances of assets and liabilities.

In this example, assets amortize quicker than liabilities. Therefore, the inflows from repayments of assets are less than the outflows used to repay the debts calculated with the outstanding balances of assets and liabilities. Hence, a deficit cumulates from one period to the next, except in period 5. Figures 11.3 and 11.4 show the gaps time profile.

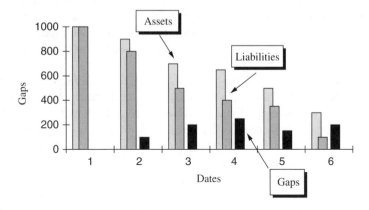

FIGURE 11.3   Time profile of liquidity gaps

Liquidity Gaps and Liquidity Risk

When liabilities exceed assets, there is an excess of funds. Such excesses generate interest rate risk since the revenues from the investments of these excess assets are uncertain. When assets exceed liabilities, there is a deficit. This means that the bank has long-run commitments, which existing resources do not fund entirely. There is a liquidity risk generated by raising funds in the future to match the size of assets. The bank faces the

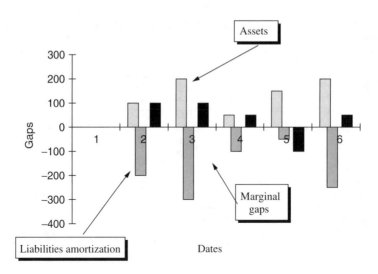

FIGURE 11.4   Time profile of marginal liquidity gaps

risk of not being able to obtain the liquidity on the markets, and the risk of paying higher than normal costs to meet this requirement.

In addition, it has exposure to interest rate risk. Liquidity gaps generate funding requirements, or investments of excess funds, in the future. Such financial transactions occur in the future, at interest rates not yet known, unless hedging them today. Liquidity gaps generate interest rate risk because of the uncertainty in interest revenues or costs generated by these transactions.

In a universe of fixed rates, any liquidity gap generates an interest rate risk. A projected deficit necessitates raising funds at rates unknown as of today. A projected excess of resources will result in investments at unknown rates as well. With deficits, the margin decreases if interest rates increase. With excess resources, the margin decreases when interest rates decrease. Hence, the liquidity exposure and the interest rate exposure are interdependent in a fixed rate universe.

In a floating rate universe, there is no need to match liquidity to cancel out any interest rate risk. First, if a short debt funds a long asset, the margin is not subject to interest rate risk since the rollover of debt continues at the prevailing interest rates. If the rate of assets increases, the new debt will also cost more. This is true only if the same reference rates apply on both sides of the balance sheet. However, any mismatch between reset dates and/or a mismatch of interest references, puts the interest margin at risk. For instance, if the asset return indexed is the 3-month LIBOR, and the debt rate refers to 1-month LIBOR, the margin is sensitive to changes in interest rate.

It is possible to match liquidity without matching interest rates. For instance, a long fixed rate loan funded through a series of 3-month loans carrying the 3-month LIBOR. In this case, there is no liquidity risk but there is an interest rate risk.

Sometimes, future excesses or deficits of liquidity motivate early decisions, before they actually appear. It might be advisable to lock in an interest rate for these excesses and deficits without waiting. Such decisions depend on interest rate expectations, plus the bank policy with respect to interest rate risk.

Gap Profiles and Funding

In the example of deficits, gaps represent the cumulated needs for funds required at all dates. Cumulated funding is not identical to the new funding required at each period because the debt funding gaps of previous periods do not necessarily amortize over subsequent periods. For instance, a new funding of 100, say between the dates 2 and 3, is not the cumulated deficit between dates 1 and 3, for example 200, because the debt contracted at date 2, 100, does not necessarily amortize at date 3. If the debt is still outstanding at date 3, the deficit at date 3 is only 100. Conversely, if the previous debt amortizes after one period, the total amount to fund would be 200, that is the new funding required during the last period, plus any repayment of the previous debt.

The marginal gaps represent the new funds required, or the new excess funds available for investing. A positive cumulated gap is the cumulated deficit from the starting date, without taking into consideration the debt contracted between this date and today. This is the rationale for using marginal gaps. These are the amounts to raise or invest during the period, and for which new decisions are necessary. The cumulated gaps are easier to interpret, however.

Liquidity Gaps and Maturity Mismatch

An alternative view of the liquidity gap is the gap between the average maturity dates of assets and liabilities. If all assets and liabilities have matching maturities, the difference in average maturity dates would be zero. If there is a time mismatch, the average maturity dates differ. For instance, if assets amortize slower than liabilities, their average maturity is higher than that of liabilities, and vice versa. The average maturity date calculation weights maturity with the book value of outstanding balances of assets and liabilities (Figure 11.5).

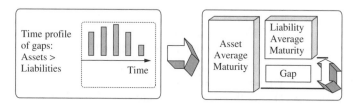

FIGURE 11.5 Liquidity gaps and gaps between average maturity dates of assets and liabilities

In a universe of fixed rates, the gap between average maturities provides information on the average location of assets and liabilities along the yield curve, which provides the market rates for all maturities. Note that averages can be arithmetic or, better, weighted by the outstanding volumes of assets and liabilities.

CASH MATCHING

Cash matching is a basic concept for the management of liquidity and interest rate risks. It implies that the time profiles of amortization of assets and liabilities are identical. The nature of interest applicable to assets and maturities might also match: fixed rates with fixed rates, floating rates revised periodically with floating rates revised at the same dates using the same reference rate. In such a case, the replication of assets' maturities extends to interest characteristics. We focus below on cash matching only, when the repayment schedule of debt replicates the repayment schedule of assets. Any deviation from the cash matching benchmark generates interest rate risk, unless setting up hedges.

The Benefits of Cash Matching

With cash matching, liquidity gaps are equal to zero. When the balance sheet amortizes over time, it does not generate any deficit or excess of funds. If, in addition, the interest rate resets are similar (both dates and nature of interest rate match), or if they are fixed interest rates, on both sides, the interest margin cannot change over time. Full matching of both cash and interest rates locks in the interest income.

Cash matching is only a reference. In general, deposits do not match loans. Both result from the customers' behaviour. However, it is feasible to structure the financial debt in order to replicate the assets' time profile, given the amortization schedule of the portfolio of commercial assets and liabilities.

Cash matching also applies to individual transactions. For instance, a bullet loan funded by a bullet debt having the same amount and maturity results in cash matching between the loan and the debt. However, there is no need to match cash flows of individual transactions. A new deposit with the same amount and maturity can match a new loan. Implementing cash matching makes sense after netting assets and liabilities. Otherwise, any new loan will necessitate a new debt, which is neither economical nor necessary.

The Global Liquidity Posture of the Balance Sheet

The entire gap profile characterizes the liquidity posture of a bank. The zero liquidity gaps are the benchmark. In a fixed rate universe, there would not be any interest rate risk. In a floating rate universe, there is no interest risk either if reset dates and the interest index are identical for assets and liabilities.

Figures 11.6 to 11.8 summarize various typical situations. The assumption is that any excess funds, or any deficits, at the starting date are fully funded or invested. Therefore,

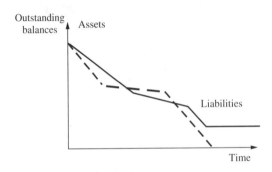

FIGURE 11.6   Gaps profile close to zero

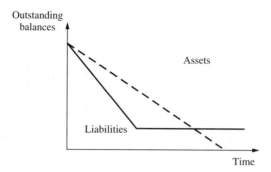

FIGURE 11.7   Deficits

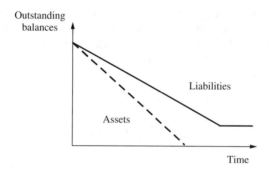

FIGURE 11.8   Excess funds

the current gap is zero, and non-zero gaps appear only in the future. In the figures, the liability time profile hits the level of capital once all debts amortize completely. The figures ignore the gap between fixed assets and equity, which varies across time because both change.

New Business Flows

With new business transactions, the shapes of the time profiles of total assets and liabilities change. The new gap profile is dynamic! Total assets can increase over time, as well as depositors' balances. Figure 11.9 shows the new transactions plus the existing assets and liabilities. The amortization schedules of existing assets and liabilities are close to each other. Therefore, the static gaps, between existing assets and liabilities, are small. The funding requirements are equal to netted total assets and liabilities. Since total assets increase more than total resources from customers, the overall liquidity gap increases with the horizon. The difference between total assets and existing assets, at any date, represents the new business. To be accurate, when projecting new business, volumes should be net from the amortization of the new loans and the new deposits, since the amortization starts from the origination date of these transactions.

When time passes, the gap profile changes: existing assets and liabilities amortize and new business comes in. The gap, which starts from 0 at t, widens up to some positive

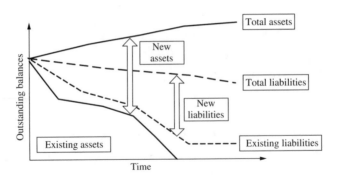

FIGURE 11.9   Gap profile with existing and new business

value at $t + 1$. The positive gap at $t + 1$ is a pre-funding gap, or ex ante. In reality, the funding closes the gap at the same time that new business and amortization open it. The gap at $t + 1$ is positive before funding, and it is identical to the former gap projected, at this date, in the prior periods (Figure 11.10).

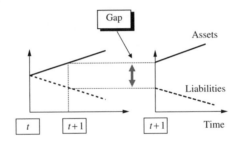

FIGURE 11.10   The gap profile when time passes

LIQUIDITY MANAGEMENT

Liquidity management is the continuous process of raising new funds, in case of a deficit, or investing excess resources when there are excesses of funds. The end of this section briefly discusses the case of investments. The benchmark remains the cash matching case, where both assets and liabilities amortize in parallel.

Funding a Deficit

In the case of a deficit, global liquidity management aims at a target time profile of gaps after raising new resources. In Figure 11.10, the gap at date t is funded so that, at the current date, assets and liabilities are equal. However, at date $t + 1$, a new deficit appears, which requires new funding. The liquidity decision covers both the total amount required to bridge the gap at $t + 1$ and its structuring across maturities. The funding decision reshapes the entire amortization profile of liabilities. The total amount of the new debt is the periodic gap. Nevertheless, this overall amount piles up 'layers' of bullet debts with varying maturities. Whenever a layer amortizes, there is a downside step in the amortization profile of the debt.

The amount of funds that the bank can raise during a given period is limited. There is some upper bound, depending on the bank's size, credit standing and market liquidity. In addition, the cost of liquidity is important, so that the bank does not want to raise big amounts abruptly for fear of paying the additional costs if market liquidity is tight. If 1000 is a reasonable monthly amount, the maximum one-period liquidity gap is 1000. When extending the horizon, sticking to this upper bound implies that the cumulated amount raised is proportional to the monthly amount. This maximum cumulated amount is 2000 for 2 months, 3000 for 3 months, and so on. The broken line shows what happens when we cumulate a constant periodical amount, such as 1000, to the existing resources profile. The length of vertical arrows increases over time. Starting from existing resources, if we always use the 'maximum' amount, we obtain an upper bound for the resources profiles. This is the upper broken line. The upper bound of the resources time profile should always be above the assets time profile, otherwise we hit the upper bound and raising more funds might imply a higher cost. In Figure 11.11, the upper bound for resources exceeds the assets profile. Hence there is no need to raise the full amount authorized.

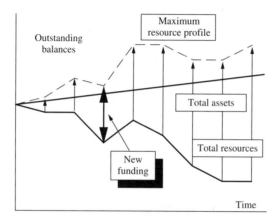

FIGURE 11.11   The gap and resources time profiles

Cash Matching in a Fixed Rate Universe

This subsection refers to a situation where resources collected from customers are lower than loans, generating a liquidity deficit. The target funding profile depends on whether ALM wishes to close all liquidity gaps, or maintain a mismatch. Any mismatch implies consistency with expectations on interest rates. For instance, keeping a balance sheet underfunded makes sense only when betting on declining interest rates, so that deferring funding costs less than now. Making the balance sheet overfunded implies expectations of raising interest rates, because the investment will occur in the future. Sometimes the balance sheet remains overfunded because there is an excess of deposits over loans. In such a case, the investment policy should follow guidelines with respect to target interest revenue and interest rate risk on future investments.

Structuring the Funding

Below we give two examples of profiles of existing assets and liabilities. In both cases, the resources amortize quicker than assets. The amortization of the balance sheet generates new deficits at each period. In a universe of fixed rates, such a situation could make sense if the ALM unit decided to try to bet on decreasing interest rates.

We assume that ALM wishes to raise the resources profile up to that of assets because expectations have changed, and because the new goal is to fully hedge the interest margin. The issue is to define the structuring of the new debts consistent with such a new goal. The target resources profile becomes that of assets. The process needs to define a horizon. Then, the treasurer piles up 'layers' of debts, starting from the longest horizon.

Figure 11.12 illustrates two different cases. On the left-hand side, the gap decreases continuously until the horizon. Then, layers of debts, raised today, pile up, moving backwards from the horizon, so that the resources' amortization profile replicates the asset profile. Of course, there are small steps, so this hedge is not perfect. In the second case (right-hand side), it is not feasible to hit the target assets' profile with debt contracted as of today (spot debt). This is because the gap increases with time, peaks and then narrows up to the management horizon. Starting from the end works only partially, since filling completely the gap at the horizon would imply raising excess funds today. This would be inconsistent with cash matching. On the other hand, limiting funds to what is necessary today does not fill the gap in intermediate periods between now and the horizon.

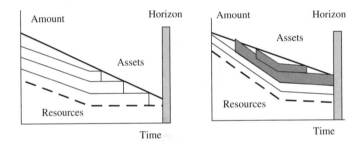

FIGURE 11.12   Neutralizing the liquidity gap (deficit)

In a fixed rate universe, this intermediate mismatch generates interest rate risk. Hence, 'immunization' of the interest margin requires locking in as of today the rates on the future resources required. This is feasible with forward hedges (see Chapter 14). The hedge has to start at different dates and correspond to the amounts of debts represented in grey.

Numerical Example

Table 11.2 shows a numerical example of the first case above with three periods. The existing gap is 200, and the cash matching funding necessitates debts of various maturities. The 'layer 1' is a bullet debt extending from now to the end of period 3. Its amount is equal to the gap at period 3, or 50. A second bullet debt from now to period 2, of amount 50, bridges the gap at period 2. Once these debts are in place, there is still a 100 gap left for period 1. In the end, the treasurer contracts three bullet debts: 50 for three periods, 50 for two periods, and 100 for one period. Once this is done, the time profile of resources becomes identical to that of assets over the total horizon.

In the second case of the preceding subsection, the same process does not apply because the gap increases and, after a while, decreases until the horizon. It is not possible to reach

TABLE 11.2   Bridging the liquidity gap: example

Period	1	2	3
Assets	1000	750	500
Resources	800	650	450
Gap	200	100	50
New funding:			
Debt 1	50	50	50
Debt 2	50	50	
Debt 3	100		
Total funding	200	100	50
Gap after funding	0	0	0

cash matching with resources raised today. One bullet debt, of 100, bridges partially the gaps from now up to the final horizon. A second 100 bullet debt starts today until the end of period 2. Then, the treasurer needs a third forward starting debt of 150. In a fixed rate universe, a forward contract should lock in its rate as of today. However, effective raising of liquidity occurs only at the beginning of period date 2 up to the end of period 2 (Table 11.3).

TABLE 11.3   Bridging the liquidity gap: example

Period	1	2	3
Assets	1000	750	500
Resources	800	400	400
Gap	200	350	100
New funding:			
Debt 1	100	100	100
Debt 2	100	100	
Debt 3	0	150	
Total funding	200	350	100
Gap after funding	0	0	0

Structural Excesses of Liquidity

Similar problems arise when there are excesses of funds. Either some funds are re-routed to investments in the market, or there are simply more resources than uses of funds. ALM should structure the timing of investments and their maturities according to guidelines. This problem also arises for equity funds because banks do not want to expose capital to credit risk by lending these funds. It becomes necessary to structure a dedicated portfolio of investments matching equity.

The expectations about interest rates are important since the interest rates vary across maturities. Some common practices are to spread securing investments over successive periods. A fraction of the available funds is invested up to 1 year, another fraction for 2 years, and so on until a management horizon. Spreading each periodical investment over all maturities avoids locking in the rate of a single maturity and the potential drawback of renewing entirely the investment at the selected maturity at uncertain rates. Doing so for periodical investments avoids crystallizing the current yield curve in the investment portfolio. This policy smooths the changes of the yield curve shape over time up to the selected longest maturity. There are variations around this policy, such as concentrating the investments at both short and long ends of the maturity structure of interest rates. Policies that are more speculative imply views on interest rates and betting on expectations. We address the issue again when dealing with interest rate risk.

THE COST OF THE LIQUIDITY RATIO

The cost of liquidity for banks often refers to another concept: the cost of maintaining the liquidity ratio at a minimum level. The liquidity ratio is the ratio of short-term assets to short-term liabilities, and it should be above one. When a bank initiates a combination of transactions such as borrowing short and lending long, the liquidity ratio deteriorates because the short liabilities increase without a matching increase in short-term assets. This is a typical transaction in commercial banking since the average maturity of loans is often longer than the average maturity of resources.

In order to maintain the level of the liquidity ratio, it is necessary to have additional short-term assets, for instance 1000 if the loan is 1000, without changing the short-term debt, in order to restore the ratio to the value before lending (1000). Borrowing long and investing short is one way to improve the liquidity ratio. The consequence is a mismatch between the long rate, of the borrowing side, and the short rate, of the lending side. The cost of restoring the liquidity ratio to its previous level is the cost of neutralizing the mismatch. Bid–ask spreads might increase that cost, since the bank borrows and lends at the same time. Finally, borrowing implies paying a credit spread, which might not be present in the interest of short-term assets, such as Treasury bills. Therefore, the cost of borrowing includes the bank's credit spread.

The first cost component is the spread between long-term rates and short-term rates. In addition, borrowing long at a fixed rate to invest short also generates interest rate risk since assets roll over faster than debt. Neutralizing interest rate risk implies receiving a fixed rate from assets rather that a rate reset periodically. A swap receiving the fixed rate and paying the variable rate makes this feasible (see Chapter 14). The swap eliminates the interest rate risk and exchanges the short-term rate received by assets for a long-term rate, thereby eliminating also any spread between long-term rates and short-term rates. The cost of the swap is the margin over market rates charged by the issuer of the swap.

Finally, the cost of the liquidity ratio is the cost of the swap plus the credit spread of borrowing (if there is none on investments) plus the bid–ask spread. The cost of maintaining the liquidity ratio is a component of the 'all-in' cost of funds, that serves for pricing loans. Any long-term loan implies swapping short-term assets for a loan, thereby deteriorating the liquidity ratio.

ISSUES FOR DETERMINING THE LIQUIDITY GAP TIME PROFILE

The outstanding balances of all existing assets and liabilities and their maturity schedules are the basic inputs to build the gap profile. Existing balances are known, but not necessarily their maturity. Many assets and liabilities have a contractual repayments schedule.

However, many others have no explicit maturity. Such assets without maturity are over-drafts, credit card consumer loans, renewed lines of credit, committed lines of credit or other loans without specific dates. Demand deposits are liabilities without maturity. Deriving liquidity gaps necessitates assumptions, conventions or projections for the items with no explicit maturity. These are:

- Demand deposits. These have no contractual maturity and can be withdrawn instantly from the bank. They can also increase immediately. However, a large fraction of current deposits is stable over time, and represents the 'core deposit base'.
- Contingencies such as committed lines of credit. The usage of these lines depends on customer initiative, subject to the limit set by the lender.
- Prepayment options embedded in loans. Even when the maturity schedule is contractual, it is subject to uncertainty due to prepayment options. The effective maturity is uncertain.

Demand Deposits

There are several solutions to deal with deposits without maturity. The simplest technique is to group all outstanding balances into one maturity bucket at a future date, which can be the horizon of the bank or beyond. This excludes the influence of demand deposit fluctuations from the gap profile, which is neither realistic nor acceptable. Another solution is to make conventions with respect to their amortization, for example, using a yearly amortization rate of 5% or 10%. This convention generates an additional liquidity gap equal to this amortization forfeit every year which, in general, is not in line with reality.

A better approach is to divide deposits into stable and unstable balances. The core deposits represent the stable balance that remains constantly as a permanent resource. The volatile fraction is treated as short-term debt. Separating core deposits from others is closer to reality than the above assumptions, even though the rule for splitting deposits into core deposits and the remaining balance might be crude.

The last approach is to make projections modelled with some observable variables correlated with the outstanding balances of deposits. Such variables include the trend of economic conditions and some proxy for their short-term variations. Such analyses use multiple regression techniques, or time series analyses. There are some obvious limitations to this approach. All parameters that have an impact on the market share deposits are not explicitly considered. New fiscal regulations on specific tax-free interest earnings of deposits, alter the allocation of customers' resources between types of deposits. However, this approach is closer to reality than any other.

Contingencies Given (Off-balance Sheet)

Contingencies generate outflows of funds that are uncertain by definition, since they are contingent upon some event, such as the willingness of the borrower to use committed lines of credit. There are many such lines of credit, including rollover short-term debts, or any undrawn fraction of a committed credit line. Only the authorization and its expiry date are fixed. Statistics, experience, knowledge of customers' accounts (individuals or corporate borrowers) and of their needs help to make projections on the usage of such lines. Otherwise, assumptions are required. However, most of these facilities are variable rate, and drawings are necessarily funded at unknown rates. Matching both variable rates on uncertain drawings of lines eliminates interest rate risk.

Amortizing Loans

When maturities are contractual, they can vary considerably from one loan to another. There are bullet loans, and others that amortize progressively. Prepayment risk results in an effective maturity different from the contractual maturity at origination. The effective maturity schedule is more realistic. Historical data help to define such effective maturities. Prepayment models also help. Some are simple, such as the usage of a constant prepayment ratio applicable to the overall outstanding balances. Others are more sophisticated because they make prepayments dependent on several variables, such as the interest rate differential between the loan and the market, or the time elapsed since origination, and so on. The interest income of the bank is at risk whenever a fixed rate loan is renegotiated at a lower rate than the original fixed rate. Section 7 of this book discusses the pricing of this risk.

Multiple Scenarios

Whenever the future outstanding balances are uncertain, it is tempting to use conventions and make assumptions. The problem with such conventions and assumptions is that they hide the risks. Making these risks explicit with several scenarios is a better solution. For instance, if the deposit balances are quite uncertain, the uncertainty can be captured by a set of scenarios, such as a base case plus other cases where the deposit balances are higher or lower. If prepayments are uncertain, multiple scenarios could cover high, average and low prepayment rate assumptions.

The use of multiple scenarios makes more explicit the risk with respect to the future volumes of assets and liabilities. The price to pay is an additional complexity. The scenarios are judgmental, making the approach less objective. The choices should combine multiple sources of uncertainty, such as volume uncertainty, prepayment uncertainty, plus the uncertainty of all commercial projections for new business. In addition, it is not easy to deal with interest rate uncertainty with more than one scenario. There are relatively simple techniques for dealing with multiple scenarios, embedded in ALM models detailed in Chapter 17.

12

The Term Structure of Interest Rates

The yield curve is the entire range of market interest rates across all maturities. Understanding the term structure of interest rates, or yield curve, is essential for appraising the interest rate risk of banks because:

- Banks' interest income is at risk essentially because of the continuous movements of interest rates.
- Future interest rates of borrowing or lending–investing are unknown, if no hedge is contracted before.
- Commercial banks tend to lend long and borrow short. When long-term interest rates are above short-term interest rates, this 'natural exposure' of commercial banks looks beneficial. Often, banks effectively lend at higher rates than the cost of their debts because of a positive spread between long-term rates and short-term rates. Unfortunately, the bank's interest income is at risk with the changes of shape and slope of the yield curve.
- All funding or investing decisions resulting from liquidity gaps have an impact on interest rate risk.

Banks are net lenders, when they have excess funds, or net borrowers, when they have future deficits. As any lender or borrower, they cannot eliminate interest rate risk. A variable rate borrower faces the risk of interest rate rises. A fixed rate borrower faces the risk of paying a fixed rate above declining rates. The exposure of the lender is symmetrical. The consequence is that there is no way to neutralize interest rate risk. The only available options are to choose the best exposure according to management criteria.

The purpose of controlling interest rate risk is to adopt this 'best' exposure. The prerequisite is measuring the interest rate exposure. Defining this 'best' exposure requires understanding the mechanisms driving the yield curve and making choices on views of what future rates could be. This chapter addresses both issues. Subsequent chapters describe the management implications and the techniques for controlling interest rate risk.

The expectation theory of interest rates states that there are no risk-free arbitrage opportunities for investors and lenders 'riding' the spot yield curve, which is the term structure of interest rates. The theory has four main applications:

- Making lending–borrowing decisions based on 'views' of interest rates compared to 'forward rates' defined from the yield curve.
- Locking in a rate at a future date, as of the current date.
- Extending lending–borrowing opportunities to the forward transactions, future transactions of which terms are defined today, based on these forward rates.

The first section discusses the nature of interest rate references, such as variable rates, fixed rates, market rates and customer rates. The second section discusses interest rate risk and shows that any lender–borrower has exposure to this risk. The third section discusses the term structure of market interest rates, or the 'spot' yield curve. It focuses on the implications of the spreads between short-term rates and long-term rates for lenders and borrowers. The fourth section defines forward rates, rates set as of today for future transactions, and how these rates derive from the spot yield curve. The fifth section presents the main applications for taking interest rate exposures. The last section summarizes some practical observations on economic drivers of interest rates, providing a minimum background underlying 'view' on future interest rates, which guide interest rate policies.

INTEREST RATES

To define which assets and liabilities are interest-sensitive, interest rates qualify as 'variable' or 'fixed'. This basic distinction needs some refining.

Variable rates change periodically, for instance every month if they are indexed to a 1-month market rate. They remain fixed between any two reset dates. The distinction, 'fixed' or 'variable', is therefore meaningless unless a horizon is specified. Any variable rate is fixed between now and the next reset date. A variable rate usually refers to a periodically reset market rate, such as the 1-month LIBOR, 1-year LIBOR or, for the long-term, bond yields. The frequency of resets can be as small as 1 day. The longer the period between two reset dates, the longer the period within which the value of the 'variable' rate remains 'fixed'.

In some cases, the period between resets varies. The prime rate, the rate charged to the best borrowers, or the rates of regulated saving accounts (usually with tax-free interest earnings) can change at any time. The changes depend on the decision of banks or regulating bodies. Such rates are not really fixed. In some cases, they change rather frequently, such as the prime rate of banks. In others, the changes are much less frequent and do not happen on a regular basis. In the recent period, it has become permitted to make regulated rates variable according to market benchmarks. The motivation is that rates in Euroland have decreased to unprecedented levels, comparable to regulated rates. This phenomenon impairs the profitability of banks collecting this kind of resource.

Finally, among rates periodically reset to market, some are determined at the beginning of the period and others at the end. Most rates are set at the beginning of the period. However, in some countries, some market indexes are an average of the rates observed during the elapsed period. For instance, a 1-month rate can be the average of the last month's daily rates. In such cases, the uncertainty is resolved only at the end of the current period, and these rates remain uncertain until the end of the period. On the other hand, predetermined rates are set at the beginning of the current period and until the next reset date.

From an interest rate risk perspective, the relevant distinction is between certain and uncertain rates over a given horizon. A predetermined variable rate turns fixed after the reset date and until the next reset date. The 'fixed rate' of a future fixed rate loan is actually interest rate-sensitive since the rate is not set as of today, but some time in the future. All rates of new assets and liabilities originated in the future are uncertain as of today, even though some will be those of fixed rate transactions. The only way to fix the rates of future transactions as of today is through hedging. The nature of rates, fixed or variable, is therefore not always relevant from an interest risk standpoint. The important distinction is between unknown rates and interest rates whose value is certain over a given horizon.

As shown in Figure 12.1, there are a limited number of cases where future rates are certain and a large number of other rates indexed to markets, or subject to uncertain changes. In the following, both distinctions 'fixed versus variable' and 'certain versus uncertain' are used. Without specifying, we use the convention that fixed rates are certain and variable rates are uncertain as of today.

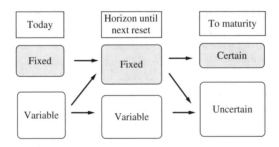

FIGURE 12.1   Interest rates, revision periods and maturity

INTEREST RATE RISK

Intuition suggests that fixed rate borrowers and lenders have no risk exposure because they have certain contractual rates. In fact, fixed rate lenders could benefit from higher rates. If rates rise, lenders suffer from the 'opportunity cost' of not lending at these higher rates. Fixed rate borrowers have certain interest costs. If rates decline, they suffer from not taking advantage of lower rates. They also face the 'opportunity cost' because they do not take advantage of this opportunity. Variable rate borrowers and lenders have interest costs or revenues indexed to market rates. Borrowers suffer from rising rates and lenders from declining rates. Future (forward) borrowers benefit from declining rates, just as variable rate borrowers do. Future (forward) lenders suffer from declining rates, just as variable rate lenders do. The matrix in Table 12.1 summarizes these exposures, with '+'

TABLE 12.1   Exposure to Interest Rate Risk (IRR)

Rate	Change of rates	Lender	Borrower
		Existing exposure	
Floating rate	Rate ↑	+	−
	Rate ↓	−	+
Fixed rate[a]	Rate ↑	−	+
	Rate ↓	+	−
		Projected exposure (same as current + floating)	
—	Rate ↑	+	−
—	Rate ↓	−	+

[a]Uncertainty with respect to opportunity cost of debt only.
+ gain, − loss.

representing gains and '−' losses, both gains and losses being direct or opportunity gains and costs.

A striking feature of this matrix is that there is no 'zero' gain or loss. The implication is that there is no way to escape interest rate risk. The only options for lenders and borrowers are to choose their exposure. The next issue is to make a decision with respect to their exposures.

THE TERM STRUCTURE OF INTEREST RATES

Liquidity management decisions raise fundamental issues with respect to interest rates. First, funding or investing decisions require a choice of maturity plus the choice of locking in a rate, or of using floating rates. The choice of a fixed or a floating rate requires a comparison between current and expected future rates.

The interest rate structure is the basic input to make such decisions. It provides the set of rates available across the maturities range. In addition, it embeds information on expected future rates that is necessary to make a decision on interest rate exposure. After discussing the term structure of interest rates, we move on to the arbitrage issue between fixed and variable rates.

The Spot Yield Curve

There are several types of rates, or yields. The yield to maturity of a bond is the discount rate that makes the present value of future cash flows identical to its price. The zero-coupon rates are those discount rates that apply to a unique future flow to derive its present value. The yield to maturity embeds assumptions with respect to reinvestment revenues of all intermediate flows up to maturity[1]. The yield to maturity also changes

---

[1] The yield to maturity is the value of y that makes the present value of future flows equal to the price of a bond: price $= \sum_{t=1}^{n} CF_t/(1 + y)^t$ where CF_t are the cash flows of date t and y is the yield to maturity. This equation can also be written as: price $= \sum_{t=1}^{n} CF_t(1 + y)^{n-t}/(1 + y)^n$. The equation shows that the price is also the present value of all flows reinvested until maturity at the yield y. Since the future reinvestment of

with the credit standing of the issue. The spread between riskless yields, such as those applicable to government bonds, and the yields of private issues is the credit spread. Yields typically derive from bond prices, given their future cash flows. The zero-coupon yields can be derived from yields to maturity observed for a given risk class using an iterative process[2]. The set of yields from now to any future maturity is the yield curve. The yield curve can have various shapes, as shown in Figure 12.2.

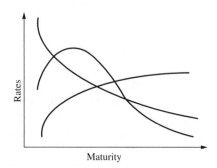

FIGURE 12.2   The term structure of interest rates

Interest Rate Arbitrage for Lenders and Borrowers

The difference in rates of different maturities raises the issue of the best choice of maturity for lending or borrowing over a given horizon. An upward sloping yield curve means that long rates are above short rates. In such a situation, the long-term lender could think that the best solution is to lend immediately over the long-term. The alternative choice would be to lend short-term and renew the lending up to the horizon of the lender. The loan is rolled over at unknown rates, making the end result unknown. This basic problem requires more attention than the simple comparison between short-term rates and long-term rates.

We make the issue more explicit with the basic example of a lender whose horizon is 2 years. Either he lends straight over 2 years, or he lends for 1 year and rolls the loan over after 1 year. The lender for 2 years has a fixed interest rate over the horizon, which is above the current 1-year rate. If he lends for 1 year, the first year's revenue will be lower since the current spot rate for 1 year is lower than the 2-year rate. At the beginning of the second year, he reinvests at the prevailing rate. If the 1-year rate, 1 year from now, increases sufficiently, it is conceivable that the second choice beats the first. There is a minimum value of the yearly rate, 1 year from now, that will provide more revenue at the end of the 2-year horizon than the straight 2-year loan.

---

intermediate flows will not occur at this yield y, but at the prevailing rates at the date when reinvestments occur, this assumption is unrealistic.

[2] Zero-coupon rates apply to a single flow. Such rates derive from the observed bond yields. The one-period yield to maturity is a zero-coupon rate since the first flows occur at the end of the first period. In the following, this period is 1 year. Starting with this first zero-coupon rate, we can derive the others. A 2-year instrument generates two flows, one at date 1, CF_1, and one at date 2, CF_2. The present value of the flow CF_1 uses the 1-year rate z_1. This value is $CF_1/(1 + z_1)$. By borrowing this amount at date 0, we cancel the flow CF_1 of the bond. Then, the present value of CF_2 discounts this flow at the unknown zero-coupon rate for date 2. This present value should be equal to the price (for example 1) minus the present value of the flow CF_1. Using the equality: $1 - CF_1/(1 + z_1) = CF_2/(1 + z_2)^2$, we obtain the value of the zero-coupon rate for date 2, z_2.

The same reasoning applies to a borrower. A borrower can borrow short-term, even though he has a long-term liquidity deficit because the short-term rates are below the long-term rates. Again, he will have to roll over the debt for another year after 1 year. The outcome depends on what happens to interest rates at the end of the first year. If the rates increase significantly, the short-term borrower who rolls over the debt can have borrowing costs above those of a straight 2-year debt.

In the above example, we compare a long transaction with a series of short-term transactions. The two options differ with respect to interest rate risk and liquidity risk. Liquidity risk should be zero to have a pure interest rate risk. If the borrower needs the funds for 2 years, he should borrow for 2 years. There is still a choice to make since he can borrow with a floating or a fixed rate. The floating rate choice generates interest rate risk, but no liquidity risk. From a liquidity standpoint, short-term transactions rolled over and long-term floating rate transactions are equivalent (with the same frequency of rollover and interest rate reset). The subsequent examples compare long to short-term transactions.

The issue is to determine whether taking interest risk leads to an expected gain over the alternative solution of a straight 2-year transaction. The choice depends first on expectations. The short-term lender hopes that interest rates will increase. The short-term borrower hopes that they will decrease. Nevertheless, it is not sufficient that interest rates change in the expected direction to obtain a gain. It is also necessary that the rate variation be large enough, either upward or downward. There exists a break-even value of the future rate such that the succession of short-term transactions, or a floating rate transaction—with the same frequency of resets as the rollover transaction—is equivalent to a long fixed rate transaction. The choice depends on whether the expected rates are above or below such break-even rates. The break-even rate is the 'forward rate'. It derives from the term structure of interest rates.

INTEREST RATE EXPECTATIONS AND FORWARD RATES

The term structure of interest rates used hereafter is the set of zero-coupon rates derived from government, or risk-free, assets. The zero-coupon rates apply to single future flows and are pure fixed rate transactions. The expectation theory considers that rates of various maturities are such that there is no possible risk-free arbitrage across rates. Forward rates result directly from such an absence of risk-free arbitrage opportunities. A risk-free arbitrage generates a profit without risk, based upon the gap between observed rates and their equilibrium value. Today, we observe only current spot rates and future spot rates are uncertain. Even though they are uncertain, they have some expected value, resulting from the expectations of all market players. This principle allows us to derive the relation between today's spot rates and future expected rates. The latter are the implicit, or forward, rates.

The standard example of a simple transaction covering two periods, such as investing for 2 years, illustrates the principle. For simplicity, we assume this is a risk-neutral world.

Risk-neutrality

Risk-neutrality is a critical concept for arbitrage issues. When playing heads and tails, we toss a coin. Let's say we gain if we have heads and lose in the case of tails. There is a 50% chance of winning or losing. The gain is 100 if we win and -50 if we lose. The expected gain is $0.5 \times 100 + 0.5 \times (-50) = 25$. A risk-neutral player is, by definition, indifferent, between a certain outcome of 25 and this uncertain outcome. A risk-adverse investor is not. He might prefer to hold 20 for sure rather than betting. The difference between 25 and 20 is the value of risk aversion. Since investors are risk averse, we need to adjust expectations for risk aversion. For the sake of simplicity, we explain arbitrage in a risk-neutral world.

Arbitrage across Maturities

Two alternative choices are investigated: investing straight for 2 years or twice for 1 year. These two choices should provide the same future value to eliminate arbitrage opportunities. The mechanism extends over any succession of periods for any horizon. Forward rates depend on the starting date and the horizon after the starting date, and require two indexes to define them. We use the following notations:

- The future uncertain *spot* rate from date t up to date $t + n$ is $_t\mathbf{i}_{t+n}$[3]. The current spot rates for 1 and 2 years are known and designated by $_0i_1$ and $_0i_2$ respectively. Future spot rates are evidently random.
- The *forward* rate from date t up to date $t + n$ is $_t F_{t+n}$[4]. This rate results from current spot rates, as shown below, and has a certain value as of today. The forward rate for 1 year and starting 1 year from now is $_1 F_2$, and so on.

For instance, the spot rates for 1 and 2 years could be 10% and 11%. The future value, 2 years from now, should be the same using the two paths, straight investment over 2 years or a 1-year investment rolled over an additional year. The condition is: $(1 + 11\%)^2 = (1 + 10\%)[1 + E(_1\mathbf{i}_2)]$. Since $_1\mathbf{i}_2$ remains uncertain as of today, we need the expectation of this random variable. The rate 1 year from now for 1 year $_1\mathbf{i}_2$ is uncertain, and its expected value is $E(_1\mathbf{i}_2)$. According to this equation, this expected value is around 12% (the accurate value is 12.009%). If not, there is an arbitrage opportunity. The reasoning would be the same for borrowing. If the 1-year spot rate is 10% and the future rate is 12% (approximately), it is equivalent to borrow for 2 years directly or to borrow for 1 year and roll over the debt for another year. This applies under risk-neutrality, since we use expectations as if they were certain values, which they are not.

The expected value that makes the arbitrage unprofitable is the expected rate by the market, or by all market players. Some expect that the future rate $_1\mathbf{i}_2$ will be higher, others that it will be lower, but the net effect of expectations is the 12% value. It is also the value of $_1\mathbf{i}_2$ making arbitrage unprofitable between a 1-year transaction and a 2-year transaction in a risk-neutral world.

The determination of forward rates extends to any maturity through an iterative process. For instance, if the spot rate $_0i_1$ is 10% and the spot rate $_0i_2$ is 11%, we can derive the forward rate $_2 F_3$ from the spot rate for date 3, or $_0i_3$. The return over the last year would be the forward rate $_2 F_3 = E(_2\mathbf{i}_3)$. Therefore, the condition of non-profitable arbitrage becomes:

$$(1 + _0i_3)^3 = (1 + _0i_2)^2[1 + E(_2\mathbf{i}_3)] = (1 + _0i_2)^2(1 + _2 F_3)$$

It gives $_2 F_3$ from the two spot rates.

---

[3] Bold letter $\mathbf{i}$ indicates a random variable, italic letter i indicates any particular value it might have.

[4] An alternative notation would be $_n\mathbf{i}_t$, n being the period and t the starting date. We prefer to use date notations, t and $t + n$, to avoid any ambiguity between dates and periods.

Expected Rates

The implications of the expectation theory of the term structure are important to choose the maturity of transactions and/or the nature, fixed or variable, of interest rates. The long-run rates are geometric averages of short-run rates[5] following the rule of no risk-free arbitrage across spot rates. If the yield curve is upward sloping, the forward rates are above the spot rates and expectations are that interest rates will rise. If the yield curve is downward sloping, forward rates are below the spot rates and expectations are that interest rates will fall (Figure 12.3).

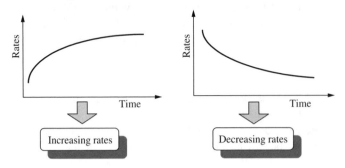

FIGURE 12.3   Term structure of interest rates and future expected rates

If the market expectations are true, the outcome is identical for long transactions and a rollover of short transactions. This results from the rule of no profitable risk-free arbitrage. The future rates consistent with this situation are the forward rates, which are also the expected values of uncertain future rates. The limit of the expectation theory is that forward rates are not necessarily identical to future spot rates, which creates the possibility of profitable opportunities.

The expectation theory does not work too well when expectations are heterogeneous. The European yield curve was upward sloping in recent years, and the level of rates declined for all maturities over several years, until 1999. This demonstrates the limitations of the predictive power of the expectation theory. It works necessarily if expectations are homogeneous. If everyone believes that rates will increase, they will, because everyone tries to borrow before the increase. This is the rationale of the 'self-fulfilling prophecy'. On the other hand, if some believe that rates might increase because they seem to have reached a bottom line and others predict further declines, the picture becomes fuzzy. In the late nineties, while Europe converged towards the euro, expectations were unclear.

FORWARD RATES APPLICATIONS

The forward rates, embedded in the spot yield curves, serve a number of purposes:

- They are the break-even rates for comparing expectations with market rates and arbitraging the market rates.
- It is possible to effectively lock in forward rates for a future period as of today.

---

[5] This is because the reasoning can extend from two periods to any number of periods. The average is a geometric average.

- They provide lending–borrowing opportunities rather than simply lending–borrowing cash at the current spot rates.

Forward Rates as Break-even Rates for Interest Rate Arbitrage

The rule is to compare, under risk-neutrality, the investor's expectation of the future spot rate with the forward rate, which serves as a break-even rate. In the example of two periods:

- If investor's expectation is above the forward rate $_1F_1$, lending short and rolling over the loan beats the straight 2-year investment.
- If investor's expectation is below the forward rate $_1F_1$, lending long for 2 years beats the short-term loan renewed for 1 year.
- If investor's expectation matches the break-even rate, investors are indifferent between going short and going long.

If a lender believes that, 1 year from now, the rate will be above the forward rate for the same future period, he expects to gain by rolling over short transactions. If the borrower expects that, 1 year from now, the rate will be below the forward rate, he expects to gain by rolling over short-term transactions. Whether the borrower or the lender will actually gain or not depends on the spot rates that actually prevail in the future. The price to pay for expected gains is uncertainty.

For those willing to take interest rate risk, the benchmarks for their decisions are the forward rates. The lender makes short transactions if expected future rates are above forward rates. The lender prefers a long transaction at the spot rate if expected future rates are below the forward rates. Similar rules apply to borrowers.

Hence, expectations of interest rises or declines are not sufficient for making a decision. Expectations should state whether the future rates would be above or below the forward rates. Otherwise, the decision to take interest rate risk or not remains not fully documented (Figure 12.4). These are simplified examples, with two periods only. Real decisions cover multiple periods of varying lengths[6].

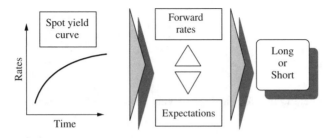

FIGURE 12.4 Expectations and decisions

---

[6] For instance, over a horizon of 10 years, the choice could be to use a 1-year floating rate, currently at 4%, or to borrow at a fixed rate for 10 years at 6%. Again, the choice depends on expectations with respect to the 9-year rate 1 year from now. The break-even rate, or forward rate, for 9 years 1 year from now is such that: $(1 + 4\%)(1 + _1F_9\%)^9 = (1 + 6\%)^{10}$. The yearly forward rate $_1F_9$ is 6.225%. If the borrower believes

Locking in a Forward Rate as of Today

It is possible to lock in a rate for a future date. This rate is the forward rate derived from the spot yield curve. We assume that an investor has 1000 to invest 1 year from now and for 1 year. He will receive this flow in 1 year. The investor fears that interest rates will decline. Therefore, he prefers to lock in a rate as of today. The trick is to make two transactions that cancel out as of today and result, by netting, in a forward investment 1 year from now and for 1 year. The spot rates are 4% for 1 year and 6% for 2 years. In addition, borrowing and lending are at the same rate. Since the investor wants to lend, he lends today for 2 years. In order to do so, he needs to borrow the money invested for 1 year, since he gets an inflow 1 year from now. The amount borrowed today against the future inflow of 1000 is $1000/(1+4\%) = 961.54$. This results in a repayment of 1000 in 1 year. Simultaneously, he lends for 2 years resulting in an inflow of $961.54(1+6\%)^2 = 1080.385$ 2 years from now. The result is lending up to date 2 a flow of 1000 at date 1 to get 1080.385. This is a yearly rate of 8.0385%. This rate is also the forward rate resulting from the equation:

$$(1 + 4\%)(1 + {}_1F_2) = (1 + 6\%)^2$$

Since $(1 + {}_1F_2) = (1 + 6\%)^2/(1 + 4\%) = 1.1236/1.04 = 1.80385$.

Therefore forward rates 'exist' and are more than the result of a calculation (Figure 12.5).

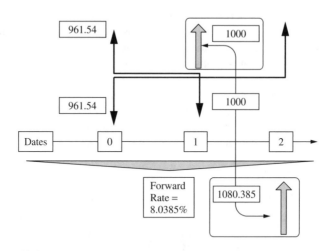

FIGURE 12.5   Locking in a forward rate 1 year from now for 1 year

that 1 year from now the yearly rate for a maturity of 9 years will be above 6.225%, he or she should borrow fixed. Otherwise, he or she should use a floating rate debt. With a spread of 2% between short-run and long-run rates, intuition suggests that borrowing fixed today is probably very costly. A fixed debt has a yearly additional cost over short-run debt, which is $6\% - 4\% = 2\%$. However, the difference in yearly rate does not provide a true picture because we are comparing periods of very different lengths. The 2% additional cost is a yearly cost. If the long rate (9 years) actually increases to 6.225%, the additional cost of borrowing fixed 1 year later will be 0.225% per year. This additional cost cumulates over the 9 years. In other words, the loss of 2% over 1 year should be compared to a potential loss of 0.225% over 9 years.

The Spot and Forward Yield Curves

There is a mechanical relationship between spot rates and forward rates of future dates.

The Relative Positions of the Spot and Forward Yield Curves

When spot yield curves are upward sloping, the forward rates are above the spot yield curve. Conversely, with an inverted spot yield curve, the forward rates are below the spot yield curve. When the spot yield curve is flat, both spot and forward yields become identical (Figure 12.6).

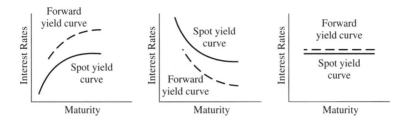

FIGURE 12.6 The relative positions of the spot and forward yield curves

When investing and borrowing, it is important to consider whether it is more beneficial to ride the spot or the forward yield curves, depending on expectations about future spot rates. Since banks often have non-zero liquidity gaps, they are net forward borrowers when they have positive liquidity gaps (assets higher than liabilities) and net forward lenders when they have negative liquidity gaps (assets lower than liabilities). The spot yield curve plus the forward yield curves starting at various future dates chart all funding–investment opportunities.

Example of Calculating the Forward Yield Curves

The spot yield curve provides all yields by maturity. Forward yield curves derive from the set of spot yields for various combinations of dates. The calculations in Table 12.2 provide an example of a forward yield curve 1 year from now and all subsequent maturities, as well as 2 years from now and all subsequent maturities. In the first case, we plot the forward rates starting 1 year from now and for 1 year (date 2), 2 years (date 3), 3 years (date 4), and so on. In the second case, the forward rates are 2 years from now and for maturities of 1 year (date 3), 2 years (date 4), and so on. The general formulas use the

TABLE 12.2 The spot and forward yield curves

Date t	0	1	2	3	4	5
Spot yield	3.50%	4.35%	5.25%	6.15%	6.80%	7.30%
Forward $_tF_1$		5.21%	6.14%	7.05%	7.64%	8.08%
Forward $_{t+2}F_1$			7.98%	8.28%	8.57%	8.82%

term structure relationships. For instance, the forward rates between dates 1 and 3 (1 year from now for 2 years) and between dates 1 and 4 (1 year from now for 3 years) are such that:

$$(1 + {}_1F_3)^2 = (1 + {}_0i_3)^3/(1 + {}_0i_1)$$

$$(1 + {}_1F_4)^3 = (1 + {}_0i_4)^4/(1 + {}_0i_1)$$

If we deal with yields 2 years from now, we divide all terms such as $(1 + {}_0i_1)$ by $(1 + {}_0i_t)^2$ to obtain $1 + {}_2F_t$, when $t \geq 2$.

All forward rates are above the spot rates since the spot yield curve is upward sloping (Figure 12.7). In addition, the further we look forward, the lower is the slope of the forward curve.

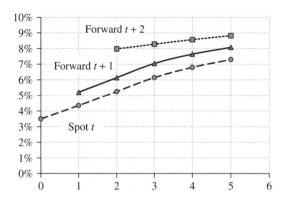

FIGURE 12.7   Spot and forward yield curves

Forward yield curves start later than the spot yield curves because they show forward investment opportunities. The graph provides a broad picture of spot and forward investment opportunities.

VIEWS ON INTEREST RATES

A major Asset–Liability Management (ALM) choice is in forming views about future rates. Interest rate models do not predict what future rates will be. However, most ALM managers will face the issue of taking views of future rates. Not having views on future rates implies a 'neutral' ALM policy considering all outcomes equally likely and smoothing variations in the long-term. Any deviations from that policy imply an opinion on future interest rates. Various theories on interest rates might help. However, forming 'views' on future rates is more a common sense exercise.

The old segmentation theory of interest rates is a good introduction. The segmentation approach considers that rates of different maturities vary independently of each other because there are market compartments, and because the drivers of rates in each different compartment are different. For instance, short-term rates depend on the current economic conditions and monetary policy, while long-term rates are representative of the fundamentals of the economy and/or depend on budget deficits. This view conflicts with the arbitrage theory and with practice, which makes it obvious that rates of different maturities are interdependent.

Drifts of interest rates follow the law of supply and demand. Large borrowings shift yields upwards, and conversely. Hence, large budget deficits tend to increase rates. Still, arbitraging long and short interest rates happens continuously, interlinking all yields across maturities. The shape of the yield curve changes. Monetary policy mechanisms tend to make short interest rates more volatile. They work through the 'open market' policy. When the central bank wants to raise interest rates, it simply increases its borrowing, drying up the market. This explains the high levels of interest rates in some special situations. Traditional policies fight inflation through higher interest rates in the United States. In Europe, some countries used short-term interest rates to manage exchange rates before 'Euroland' formed as a monetary entity. If a local currency depreciates against the USD, for example, a rise in interest rates makes it more attractive to investors to buy the local currency for investing. This increases the demand for the local currency, facilitating its appreciation, or reducing its depreciation. The capability of the central banks to influence strongly interest rates results from their very large borrowing capacity. Long-term interest rates are more stable in general. They might relate more to the fundamentals of the economy than short-term rates.

Such observations help us to understand why the yield curve is upward sloping or downward sloping. Whenever short rates jump to high levels because of monetary policy, the yield curve tends to be 'inverted', with a downward slope. Otherwise, it has a flat shape or a positive slope. However, there is no mechanism making it always upward sloping. Unfortunately, this is not enough to predict what is going to happen to the yield curve. The driving forces might be identifiable, but not their magnitude, or the timing of central interventions.

All the above observations are consistent with arbitraging rates of different maturities. They also help in deciding whether there is potential for future spot rates to be above or below forward rates. Expectations and comparisons with objective benchmarks remain critical for making sound decisions.

13

Interest Rate Gaps

The interest 'variable rate gap' of a period is the difference between all assets and liabilities whose interest rate reset dates are within the period. There are as many interest rate gaps as there are interest rate references. The 'fixed rate gap' is the difference between all assets and liabilities whose interest rates remain fixed within a period. There is only one fixed rate gap, which is the mirror image of all variable rate gaps.

Gaps provide a global view of the balance sheet exposure to interest rates. The underlying rationale of interest rate gaps is to measure the difference between the balances of assets and liabilities that are either 'interest rate-sensitive' or 'insensitive'. If assets and liabilities have interest revenues and costs indexed to the same rate, this interest rate drives the interest income mechanically. If the balances of these assets and liabilities match, the interest income is insensitive to rates because interest revenues and costs vary in line. If there is a mismatch, the interest income sensitivity is the gap. The rationale for interest rate gaps is that they link the variations of the interest margin to the variations of interest rates. This single property makes interest rate gaps very attractive.

The 'gap' concept has a central place in Asset–Liability Management (ALM) for two main reasons:

- It is the simplest measure of exposure to interest rate risk.
- It is the simplest model relating interest rate changes to interest income.

Interest rate derivatives directly alter the interest rate gaps, providing easy and straightforward techniques for altering the interest rate exposure of the banking portfolio.

However, gaps have several drawbacks due to:

- Volume and maturity uncertainties as for liquidity gaps: the solution is multiple scenarios, as suggested for liquidity gaps.

- The existence of options: implicit options on-balance sheet and optional derivatives off-balance sheet. A fixed rate loan is subject to potential renegotiation of rates, it remains a fixed rate asset whether or not the likelihood of renegotiation is high or low. Obviously, when current rates are well below the fixed rate of the loan, the asset is closer to a variable rate asset than a fixed rate one. Such options create 'convexity risk', developed later.
- Mapping assets and liabilities to selected interest rates rather than using the actual rates of individual assets and liabilities.
- Intermediate flows within time bands selected for determining gaps.

The first section introduces the gap model. The second section explains how gaps link interest income to the level of interest rates. The third section explains the relationship between liquidity and interest rate gaps. The fourth section details the direct calculation of interest income and of their variations with interest rates. The fifth section discusses hedging. The last section discusses the drawbacks and limitations of interest rate gaps.

THE DEFINITION OF INTEREST RATE GAPS

The interest rate gap is a standard measure of the exposure to interest rate risk. There are two types of gaps:

- The fixed interest rate gap for a given period: the difference between fixed rate assets and fixed rate liabilities.
- The variable interest rate gap: the difference between interest-sensitive assets and interest-sensitive liabilities. There are as many variable interest rate gaps as there are variable rates (1-month LIBOR, 1-year LIBOR, etc.).

Both differences are identical in absolute value when total assets are equal to total liabilities. However, they differ when there is a liquidity gap, and the difference is the amount of the liquidity gap. The convention in this text is to calculate interest rate gaps as a difference between assets and liabilities. Therefore, when there is no liquidity gap, the variable rate gap is the opposite of the fixed rate gap because they sum up to zero.

Specifying horizons is necessary for calculating the interest rate gaps. Otherwise, it is not possible to determine which rate is variable and which rate remains fixed between today and the horizon. The longer the horizon, the larger the volumes of interest-sensitive assets and liabilities, because longer periods allow more interest rate resets than shorter periods (Figure 13.1).

An alternative view of the interest rate gap is the gap between the average reset dates of assets and liabilities. With fixed rate assets and liabilities, the difference between the reset dates is the difference between the average maturity dates of assets and liabilities. If the variable fraction of assets grows to some positive value, whether all liabilities remain fixed rate or not, the average reset maturity of assets shortens because rate resets occur before asset maturity. With variable rate assets and liabilities, the variable interest rate gap, for a given variable rate reference, roughly increases with the gap between reset dates of assets and liabilities, if average reset dates are weighted by sizes of assets and

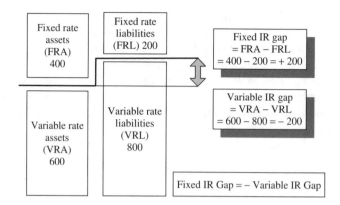

FIGURE 13.1   Interest rate gap with total assets equal to total liabilities

liabilities. The gap between average reset dates of assets and maturities is a crude measure of interest rate risk. Should they coincide, there would be no interest rate risk on average since rate resets would occur approximately simultaneously. In Figure 13.2 the positive variable rate gaps imply that variable rate assets are larger than variable rate liabilities. This is equivalent to a faster reset frequency of assets. The average reset dates show approximately where asset and liability rates are positioned along the yield curve.

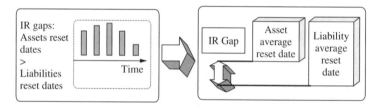

FIGURE 13.2   Interest rate gaps and gaps between average reset dates
***Note:* For a single variable rate reference for assets and liabilities.**

INTEREST RATE GAP AND VARIATIONS OF THE INTEREST MARGIN

The interest rate gap is the sensitivity of the interest income when interest rates change. When the variable rate gap (interest rate-sensitive assets minus interest rate-sensitive liabilities) is positive, the base of assets that are rate-sensitive is larger than the base of liabilities that are rate-sensitive. If the index is common to both assets and liabilities, the interest income increases mechanically with interest rates. The opposite happens when the variable rate gap is negative. When the interest rate gap is zero, the interest income is insensitive to changes in interest rates. In this specific case, the interest margin is 'immune' to variations of rates.

In the above example, the gap between interest-sensitive assets and liabilities is +200. The interest income is the difference between interest revenues and charges over the period. The calculation of the variation of the margin is simple under the set of assumptions below:

- The gap is constant over the period. This implies that the reset dates are identical for assets and liabilities.
- The rates of interest-sensitive assets and liabilities are sensitive to a common rate, i.

We use the notation: IM, Interest Margin; VRA, Variable Rate Assets; VRL, Variable Rate Liabilities; i, interest rate. The change in IM due to the change in interest rate, Δi, is:

$$\Delta IM = (VRA - VRL)\Delta i = +200\Delta i$$

VRA and VRL are the outstanding balances of variable rate assets and liabilities. The variation of the margin in the above example is 2 when the rate changes by 1%. The basic formula relating the variable rate gap to interest margin is:

$$\Delta IM = (VRA - VRL)\Delta i = (\text{interest rate gap})\Delta i$$

The above formula is only an approximation because there is no such thing as a single interest rate. It applies however when there is a parallel shift of all rates. The formula applies whenever the variable interest rate gap relates to a specific market rate. A major implication for hedging interest rate risk is that making the interest margin 'immune' to interest rate changes simply implies neutralizing the gap. This makes the sensitivity of the margin to interest rate variations equal to zero.

INTEREST GAP CALCULATIONS

Interest rate and liquidity gaps are interrelated since any future debt or investment will carry an unknown rate as of today. The calculation of gaps requires assumptions and conventions for implementation purposes. Some items of the balance sheet require a treatment consistent with the calculation rules. Interest rate gaps, like liquidity gaps, are differences between outstanding balances of assets and liabilities, incremental or marginal gaps derived from variations of volumes between two dates, or gaps calculated from flows.

Fixed versus Variable Interest Rate Gaps

The 'fixed rate' gap is the opposite of the 'variable rate' gap when assets and liabilities are equal. A future deficit implies funding the deficit with liabilities whose rate is still unknown. This funding is a variable rate liability, unless locking in the rate before funding. Accordingly, the variable rate gap decreases post-funding while the fixed rate gap does not change. The gap implications are symmetrical when there is an excess of liquidity: the interest rate of the future investment is unknown. The variable rate gap increases while the fixed rate gap remains unchanged. The fixed rate gap is consistent with an ex ante view, when no hedge is yet in place. Hedging modifies the interest rate structure of the balance sheet ex post.

In addition, the fixed rate calculation is convenient because there is no need to deal with the variety of interest rates that are 'variable'. It excludes all interest rate-sensitive assets and liabilities within the period whatever the underlying variable rates. However, this is a drawback of the fixed rate calculation since interest rate-sensitive assets and liabilities are sensitive to different indexes. Therefore, deriving the interest margin sensitivity from the fixed rate gap is only a crude proxy because it synthesizes the variations of all variable rates into a single index. In reality, accuracy would require calculating all variable interest rate gaps corresponding to each one of these market rates.

The interest rate gap is similar to the liquidity gap, except that it isolates fixed rate from variable rate assets and liabilities. Conversely, the liquidity gap combines all of them, whatever the nature of rates. Another difference is that any interest rate gap requires us to define a period because of the fixed rate–variable rate distinction. Liquidity gaps consider amortization dates only. Interest rate gaps require all amortization dates and all reset dates. Both gap calculations require the prior definition of time bands.

Time Bands for Gap Calculation

Liquidity gaps consider that all amortization dates occur at some conventional dates within time bands. Interest rate gaps assume that resets also occur somewhere within a time band. In fact, there are reset dates in between the start and end dates. The calculation requires the prior definition of time bands plus mapping reset and amortization dates to such time bands. Operational models calculate gaps at all dates and aggregate them over narrow time bands for improving accuracy. In addition, calculations of interest revenues and interest costs require exact dates, which is feasible with the detailed data on individual transactions independent of the necessity of providing usable reports grouping dates in time bands.

Interdependency between Liquidity Gaps and Interest Rate Gaps

For future dates, any liquidity gap generates an interest rate gap. A projected deficit of funds is equivalent to an interest-sensitive liability. An excess of funds is equivalent to an interest-sensitive asset. However, in both cases, the fixed rate interest gap is the same. This is not the case with variable rate gaps if they isolate various interest rates. Liquidity gaps have no specific variable rate ex ante, since the funding or the investment is still undefined. In the example below, there is a projected deficit. Variable interest rate gaps pre-funding differ from post-funding gaps. The interest rate gap derived from interest-sensitive assets and liabilities is the gap before funding minus the liquidity gap, as Figure 13.3 shows.

Specific items deserve some attention, the main ones being equity and fixed assets. These are not interest-earning assets or liabilities and should be included from interest rate gaps, but not from liquidity gaps. They influence the interest rate gaps through the liquidity gaps. Some consider equity as a fixed rate liability, perhaps because equity requires a fixed target return. In fact, this compensation does not have much to do with a fixed rate. Since it depends on the interest margin, the effective return is not the target return and it is interest rate-sensitive. We stick to the simple rule that interest rate gaps use only interest rate assets and liabilities and exclude non-interest-bearing items. We illustrate below the detailed calculations of both liquidity and interest rate gaps:

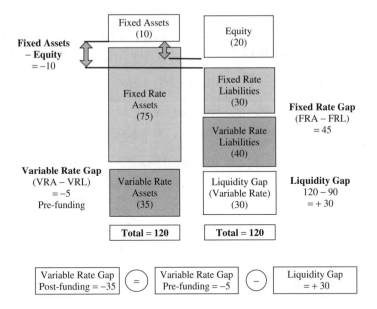

FIGURE 13.3   The balance sheet structure and gaps

Liquidity gaps $=$ total assets $-$ total liabilities

$$= 10 + 75 + 35 - (20 + 30 + 40) = 120 - 90$$

$$= +30 \text{ (a deficit of liquidity)}$$

$a = $ (interest rate assets $-$ interest rate liabilities) $+$ (fixed assets $-$ equity)

$$= (75 + 35 - 30 - 40) + (10 - 20) = +30$$

Fixed interest rate gap $=$ fixed rate assets $-$ fixed rate liabilities

(excluding non-interest-bearing items)

$$= 75 - 30 = 45$$

Variable interest rate gap $=$ variable rate assets $-$ variable rate liabilities

$$= 35 - 40 = -5 \text{ without the liquidity gap}$$

$$= -5 - 30 = -35 \text{ with the liquidity gap}$$

Therefore, the general formula applies:

Variable interest rate gap post-funding $=$ fixed interest rate gap $-$ liquidity gap

In the example, $-35 = -5 - 30$.

Cumulative and Marginal Gaps

Gaps are differences between outstanding balances at one given date, or differences of variations of those balances over a period. Gaps calculated from variations between two dates are 'marginal gaps', or differences of flows rather than volumes. For a unique given period, the variation of the interest margin is equal to the gap times the interest rate variation. For a succession of periods, it becomes necessary to break down the same types of calculations by period.

The gaps change with time. When the gap is assumed constant over one period, it means that the volume of interest-sensitive assets and liabilities does not change. If not, splitting the period into smaller subperiods makes the constant gap assumption realistic. The example below demonstrates the impact of varying gaps over time (Table 13.1). There are three balance sheets available at three dates. The variations of assets and liabilities are differences between two consecutive dates. The data are as follows:

TABLE 13.1   Interest rate gaps, cumulative and marginal

End of period	Month 1	Month 2	Month 3
Variable rate assets	0	250	300
Variable rate liabilities	200	200	200
Cumulative gaps	−200	+50	+100
Marginal gaps	−200	+250	+50

- The total period is 3 months long.
- The total assets and liabilities are 1000 and do not change. All items mature beyond the 3-month horizon and there is no new business. The liquidity gap is zero for all 3 months.
- The interest rate increases during the first day of the first month and remains stable after.
- The interest-sensitive liabilities are constant and equal to 200.
- The interest-sensitive assets change over time. The fluctuation of interest-sensitive assets is the only source of variation of the gap.

MARGIN VALUES AND GAPS

All the above calculations aim to determine variations of margins generated by a variation of interest rates. They do not give the values of the margins. The example below shows the calculation of the margins and reconciles the gap analysis with the direct calculations of margins. The margins, expressed in percentages of volumes of assets and liabilities, are the starting point. They are the differences between the customer rates and the market rates. The market rate is equal to 10% and changes by 1%. If the commercial margins are 2% for loans and −4% for deposits, the customer rates are, on average, $10 + 2 = 12\%$ for loans and $10 - 4 = 6\%$ for liabilities. The negative commercial margins for liabilities mean that rates paid to customers are below market rates. The values of margins are given in Table 13.2.

The initial margin in value is $1000(10\% + 2\%) - 1000(10\% - 4\%) = 60$. If the interest rate changes by 1%, only the rates of interest rate-sensitive assets and liabilities change, while others keep their original rates. New customer rates result from the variation of the reference rate plus constant percentage margins. The change in interest margin is $+1$. This is consistent with an interest rate gap of 100, combined with a 1% variation of interest rate since $100 \times 1\% = 1$ (Table 13.3).

TABLE 13.2 Balance sheets and margins: example

Assets	Outstanding balances	Margins
Fixed rate	700	+2%
Variable rate	300	+2%
Total assets	1000	
Liabilities	Outstanding balances	Margins
Fixed rate	800	−4%
Variable rate	200	−4%
Total liabilities	1000	
Variable rate gap	+100	

TABLE 13.3 Calculation of interest margin before and after an interest rate rise

Rate		10%		11%		Variation
		Assets:				
Fixed rate	700	700 × 12%	84	700 × 12%	84	0
Variable rate	300	300 × 12%	36	300 × 13%	39	+3
Total assets			120		123	+3
		Liabilities:				
Fixed rate	800	800 × 6%	48	800 × 6%	48	0
Variable rate	200	200 × 6%	12	200 × 7%	14	+2
Total liabilities			60		62	+2
Margin			60		61	+1

The Interest Margin Variations and the Gap Time Profile

Over a given period, with a constant gap and a variation of interest rate Δi, the revenues change by VRA $\times \Delta i$ and the costs by VRL $\times \Delta i$. Hence the variation in IM is the difference:

$$\Delta IM = (VRA - VRL)\Delta i = gap \times \Delta i$$

Over a multi-periodic horizon, subperiod calculations are necessary. When interest rates rise, the cost increase depends on the date of the rate reset. At the beginning of month 1, an amount of liabilities equal to 200 is interest rate-sensitive. It generates an increase in charges equal to 200 × 1%[1] (yearly value) over the first month only. At the beginning of month 2, the gap becomes 50, generating an additional revenue of 50 × 1% = 0.5 for the current month. Finally, the last gap generates a change in margin equal to 100 × 1% for the last month. The variation of the cumulative margin over the 3-month period is the total of all monthly variations of the margin. Monthly variations are 1/12 times the yearly variations. This calculation uses cumulative gaps (Table 13.4). In practice, the gaps should be available on a monthly or a quarterly basis, to capture the exposure time profile with accuracy.

Table 13.4 also shows that the calculation of the cumulative variation of the margin over the total 3-month period can follow either one of two ways. The first calculation is

---

[1] Calculations are in yearly values. The actual revenues and charges are calculated over a quarter only.

TABLE 13.4 Cumulative gaps and monthly changes in interest margins

Month	Cumulative gaps	Monthly variation of the margin	
1	−200	−200 × 1%	−2.0
2	+50	+50 × 1%	+0.5
3	+100	+100 × 1%	+1.0
		Total	−0.5

as above. Using cumulative gaps over time, the total variation is the sum of the monthly variations of the margins. Another equivalent calculation uses marginal gaps to obtain the margin change over the residual period to maturity. It calculates the variation of the margin over the entire 3-month period due to each monthly gap. The original gap of −200 has an impact on the margin over 3 periods. The second marginal gap of +250 alters the margin during 2 periods. The third marginal gap influences only the last period's margin. The cumulative variation of the 3-period margin is the product of the periodical marginal gaps times the change in rate, and times the number of periods until maturity[2]. Monthly calculations derive from the above annual values.

INTEREST RATE GAPS AND HEDGING

One appealing feature of gaps is the simplicity of using them for hedging purposes. Hedging often aims at reducing the interest income volatility. Since the latter depends linearly on the interest rate volatility through gaps, controlling the gaps suffices for hedging or changing the exposure using derivatives. Simple examples and definitions suffice to illustrate the simplicity of gap usage.

Hedging over a Single Period

It is possible to neutralize the interest rate gap through funding, without using any interest rate derivative. We assume that the liquidity gap is +30 and that the variable rate gap is

---

[2] The calculation with marginal gaps would be as follows. The marginal gaps apply to residual maturity:

$$[(-200 \times 3) + (250 \times 2) + (50 \times 1)] \times 1\% = -0.5$$

With cumulated gaps, the calculation is:

$$[(-200) + (+250 - 200) + (+50 + 250 - 200)] \times 1\% = -0.5$$

These are two equivalent calculations, resulting from the equality of the sum of marginal gaps, weighted by residual maturities, with the sum of cumulated gaps of each period. The periodic gaps are g_1, g_2 and g_3. The cumulated gaps are $G_1 = g_1$, $G_2 = g_1 + g_2$, $G_3 = g_1 + g_2 + g_3$. The total of cumulated gaps is:

$$G_1 + G_2 + G_3 = g_1 + (g_1 + g_2) + (g_1 + g_2 + g_3)$$

which is identical to:

$$3 \times g_1 + 2 \times g_2 + 1 \times g_3$$

+20 before funding and −10 after funding with a variable rate debt. The bank wishes to hedge its sensitivity to interest rates. If the bank raises floating rate funds, it has too many floating rate liabilities, exactly 10. If the bank raises floating rate debt for 20 and locks in the rate for the remaining 10, as of today, the interest rate gap post-funding and hedging becomes 0. The interest rate margin is 'immune' to interest rate changes. In order to lock in a fixed rate for 10 at the future date of the gap calculation, it is necessary to use a Forward Rate Agreement (FRA).

If we change the data, this type of hedge does not work any more. We now assume that we still have a funding gap of +30, but that variable interest rate gap is +45 pre-funding and +15 post-funding with floating rate debt. The bank has too many floating rate assets, and even though it does not do anything to lock in a rate for the debt, it is still interest rate-sensitive. The excess of floating rate assets post-funding is +15. The bank receives too much floating rate revenue. To neutralize the gap, it is necessary to convert the 15 variable rate assets into fixed rate assets. Of course, the assets do not change. The only way to do this conversion is through a derivative. The derivative should receive the fixed rate and pay the floating rate. The asset plus the derivative generates a neutralized net floating rate flow and a net fixed rate flow. This derivative is an Interest Rate Swap (IRS) receiving the fixed rate and paying the floating rate (Figure 13.4).

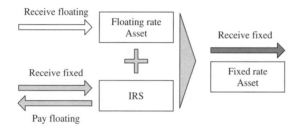

FIGURE 13.4   Hedging interest rate risk with an interest rate swap

Hedging over Multiple Periods

Figure 13.5 shows the time profiles of both marginal and cumulated gaps over multiple periods for the previous example. The cumulated gap is negative at the end of the first month, and becomes positive later.

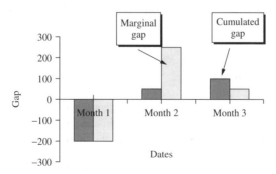

FIGURE 13.5   Interest rate gap profiles

Immunization of the interest margin requires setting the gap to zero at all periods. For instance, at period 1, a swap with a notional of 200, paying the fixed rate and receiving the floating rate, would set the gap to zero at period 1. The next period, a new swap paying the floating rate and receiving the fixed rate, with a notional of 250, neutralizes the interest rate gap. Actually, the second swap should be contracted from date 0 and take effect at the end of month 1. This is a forward swap[3] starting 1 month after date 0. A third swap starting at the end of month 2, and maturing at the end of month 3, neutralizes the gap of month 3. Since the forward swap starting at the beginning of month 2 can extend to hedge the risk of month 3, the third new swap has a notional of only 50.

The marginal gaps represent the notionals of the different swaps required at the beginning of each period, assuming that the previous hedges stay in place. The usage of marginal interest rate gaps is similar to that of marginal liquidity gaps, these representing the new debts or investments assuming that the previous ones do not expire.

The gap model provides the time profile of exposures to interest rate risk. Very simple rules suffice for hedging these exposures. The start dates and the termination dates of such hedges result from the gap profile. The hedge can be total or partial. The residual exposure, after contracting a hedge for a given amount, is readily available from the gap profile combined with the characteristics of the hedge.

LIMITATIONS OF INTEREST RATE GAPS

Gaps are a simple and intuitive tool. Unfortunately, gaps have several limitations. Most of them result from assumptions and conventions required to build the gap profile. The main difficulties are:

- Volume and maturity uncertainties as for liquidity gaps: the solution lies in assumptions and multiple scenarios, as suggested for liquidity gaps.
- Dealing with options: implicit options on-balance sheet and optional derivatives off-balance sheet. These options create 'convexity risk', developed later.
- Mapping assets and liabilities to selected interest rates as opposed to using the actual rates of individual assets and liabilities.
- Dealing with intermediate flows within time bands selected for determining gaps.

We deal with the latter three issues, the first one having been discussed previously with liquidity gaps.

Derivatives and Options

Some derivative instruments do not raise any specific difficulties. A swap substitutes a variable rate for a fixed rate. The impact on the interest rate gap follows immediately.

Other optional instruments raise issues. Caps and floors set maximum and minimum values of interest rates. They change the interest sensitivity depending on whether the level

---

[3] A forward swap is similar to a spot swap, but starts at a forward date.

of the interest rate makes them in-the-money or not. When they are out-of-the-money, options do not change the prevailing rates. When they are in-the-money, caps make assets interest rate-insensitive. In other words, options behave sometimes as variable rate items and sometimes as fixed rate items, when the interest rates hit the guaranteed rates. The interest rate gap changes with the level of interest rates. This is a serious limitation to the 'gap picture', because the gap value varies with interest rates!

There are many of embedded or implicit options in the balance sheet. Prepayments of fixed rate mortgage loans when interest rates decrease are options held by the customers. Some regulated term deposits offer the option of entering into a mortgage with a subsidized rate. Customers can shift funds from non-interest-bearing deposits to interest-earning deposits when rates increase. When sticking to simple gap models, in the presence of options, assumptions with respect to their exercise are necessary. The simplest way to deal with options is to assume that they are exercised whenever they are in-the-money. However, this ignores the value of waiting for the option to get more valuable as time passes. Historical data on the effective behaviour might document these assumptions and bring them close to reality.

The prepayment issue is a well-known one, and there are techniques for pricing implicit options held by customers. Another implication is that options modify the interest rate risk, since they create 'convexity risk'. Measuring, modelling and controlling this optional risk are dealt with in related chapters (see Chapters 20 and 21 for pricing risk, Chapter 24 for measuring optional risk at the balance sheet level).

Mapping Assets and Liabilities to Interest Rates

Interest rate gaps assume that variable rate assets and liabilities carry rates following selected indexes. The process requires mapping the actual rates to selected rates of the yield curve. It creates basis risk if both rates differ. Sensitivities, relating actual rates to selected rates, correct basis risk. The technique serves for calculating 'standardized gaps'[4]. The alternative solution is to use directly the contractual rate references of contracts at the level of individual transactions, raising Information Technology (IT) issues.

Sensitivities

The average rate of return of a subportfolio, for a product family for instance, is the ratio of interest revenues (or costs) to the total outstanding balance. It is feasible to construct time series of such average rates over as many periods as necessary. A statistical fit to observed data provides the relationship between the average rate of the portfolio and the selected market indexes. A linear relation is such that:

$$\text{Rate} = a_0 + a_1 \times \text{index}_1 + \text{'random residual'}$$

The coefficient a_1 is the sensitivity of the loan portfolio rate with respect to index_1. The residual is the random deviation between actual data and the fitted model. A variation of

---

[4] Sensitivities measure correlations between actual and selected rates. A basis risk remains because correlations are never perfect (equal to 1). See Chapter 28.

the market index of 1% generates a variation of the rate of the loan portfolio of a_1%. The same methodology extends notably to transaction rates, which are not market rates, such as the prime rate. The prime rate variations depend on the variations of two market rates. The loan balances indexed with the prime rate behave as a composite portfolio of loans indexed with the market $index_1$ and a portfolio of loans indexed with the market $index_2$. The statistical relationship becomes:

$$\text{Prime rate} = a_0 + a_1 \times index_1 + a_2 \times index_2 + \text{'random residual'}$$

Such statistical relations can vary over time, and need periodical adjustments. The sensitivities are the coefficients of the statistical model.

Standardized Gaps

With sensitivities, the true relationships between the interest margin and the reference interest rates are the standardized gaps, rather than the simple differences between assets and liabilities. Standardized gaps are gaps calculated with assets and liabilities weighted by sensitivities. For instance, if the sensitivity of a loan portfolio is 0.5, and if the outstanding balance is 100, the loan portfolio weighted with its sensitivity becomes 50. With interest rate-sensitive assets of 100 with a sensitivity of 0.5, and interest rate-sensitive liabilities of 80 with a sensitivity of 0.8, the simple gap is $100 - 80 = 20$ and the standardized gap is:
$$0.5 \times 100 - 0.8 \times 80 = 50 - 64 = -14$$

This is because a variation of the interest rate i generates a variation of the interest on assets which is $0.5\Delta i$ and a variation of the rate on liabilities which is $0.8\Delta i$. The resulting variation of the margin is:

$$\Delta IM = 100 \times 0.5 + 80 \times 0.8\Delta i = (0.5 \times 100 - 0.8 \times 80)\Delta i$$

$$\Delta IM = (\text{standardized gap})\Delta i$$

In this example, the simple gap and the standardized gap have opposite signs. This illustrates the importance of sensitivities when dealing with aggregated portfolios of transactions rather than using the actual rate references.

Intermediate Flows and Margin Calculations

The gap model does not date accurately the flows within a period. It does not capture the effect of the reinvestment or the funding of flows across periods. In some cases, both approximations can have a significant impact over margins. This section expands possible refinements.

Intra-periodic Flows

Gaps group flows within time bands as if they were simultaneous. In reality, there are different reset dates for liquidity flows and interest rates. They generate interest revenues

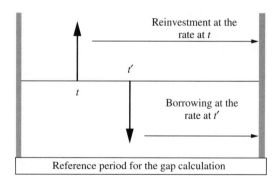

FIGURE 13.6   Interest rate risk depends on the positioning of flows across time

or costs, which are not valued in the gap–margin relationship. Figure 13.6 shows that revenues and costs assigned to intermediate reinvestments or borrowings depend on the length of the period elapsed between the date of a flow and the final horizon.

A flow with reset date at the end of the period has a negligible influence on the current period margin. Conversely, when the reset occurs at the beginning of the period, it has a significant impact on the margin. The simple gap model considers that these flows have the same influence. For instance, a flow of 1000 might appear at the beginning of the period, and another flow of 1000, with an opposite sign, at the end of the period. The periodic gap of the entire period will be zero. Nevertheless, the interest margin of the period will be interest-sensitive since the first flow generates interest revenues over the whole period, and such revenues do not match the negligible interest cost of the second flow (Figure 13.7).

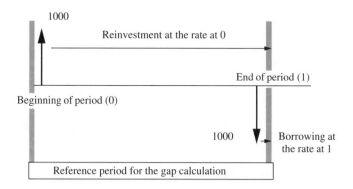

FIGURE 13.7   Zero gap combined with an interest-sensitive margin

The example below illustrates the error when the goal is to immunize the interest margin. In the preceding example, the gap was zero, but the margin was interest-sensitive. In the example below, we have the opposite situation. The gap differs from zero, but the interest margin is immune to interest rate changes. The gap is negative, which suggests that the margin should increase when the interest rate decreases, for example from 10% to 8%. However, this ignores the reinvestment of the positive intermediate flow of date 90 at a lower rate for 270 days. On the other hand, the negative flow generates a debt that costs less over the remaining 180 days. The margin is interest rate-sensitive if we calculate interest revenues and costs using the accurate dates of flows (Figure 13.8).

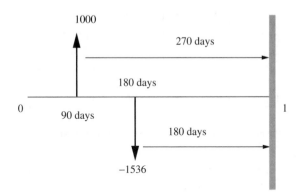

FIGURE 13.8 Negative cumulative gap and rate-insensitive margin

The changes of interest revenues and costs, due to a shift of rates from 8% to 10%, are:

$$\text{Inflow at day } 90: \quad 1000(1.10^{270/360} - 1.08^{270/360}) = -14.70$$

$$\text{Outflow at day } 180: \quad -1536(1.10^{180/360} - 1.08^{180/360}) = +14.70$$

In this example, the decline of funding costs matches the decline of interest revenues. This outcome is intuitive. The interest revenues and costs are proportional to the size of flows and to the residual period over which reinvestment or funding occurs. The first flow is less important than the second flow. However, it generates interest revenues over a longer period. The values are such that the residual maturity differential compensates exactly the size differential. The outflow is 'equivalent' to a smaller outflow occurring before, or the inflow is 'equivalent' to a smaller inflow occurring after.

The example shows how 'gap plugging', or direct gap management, generates errors. In the first example, the margin is interest-sensitive, which is inconsistent with a zero gap. In the second example, the gap model suggests plugging another flow of 536 to hedge the margin. Actually, doing so would put the margin at risk! The exact condition under which the margin is insensitive to interest rates is relatively easy to derive for any set of flows. It differs from the zero gap rule (see appendix to Chapter 23). The condition uses the duration concept, discussed in Chapter 22.

Interest Cash Flows and Interest Rate Gaps

The flows used to calculate interest rate gaps are variations of assets and liabilities only. However, all assets and liabilities generate interest revenues (or costs), received (or paid), at some dates. Only the cash payments of interest count, not the accrued accounting interest flows. Gap profiles based on capital flows only ignore these flows for the sake of simplicity. Gaps should include such interest payments, as the mark-to-market value of the balance sheet does.

Floating rate assets or liabilities generate interest flows as well. A common practice is to project the stream of interest flows using the current value of the floating rate. It 'crystallizes' the current rates up to the horizon. Forward rates would serve the same purpose and are conceptually more appropriate since they are the image of the market expectations. Nevertheless, when the interest rate changes, floating rate flows change as well, and change both the liquidity and interest rate gap profiles.

14

Hedging and Derivatives

Derivatives alter interest rate exposures and allow us to hedge exposures and make interest income independent of rates. This does not eliminate risk, however, since hedges might have opportunity costs because they set the interest income at lower levels than rates could allow.

There are two main types of derivatives: forward instruments are forward rate agreements or swaps; optional instruments allow capping the interest rate (caps) or setting a minimum guaranteed rate (floors). Forward instruments allow us to change and reverse exposures, such as turning a floating rate exposure into a fixed rate one, so that the bank can turn an adverse scenario into a favourable one. However, hedging with forward instruments implies a bet on the future and still leaves the bank unprotected against adverse interest rate movements if the bet goes wrong. Optional instruments allow us to capture the best of both worlds: getting the upside of favourable interest rate movements and having protection against the downside of adverse deviations, with a cost commensurable with such benefits. Derivatives serve to alter the exposure, to resize or reverse it, and to modify the risk–return profile of the balance sheet as a whole. Futures are instruments traded on organized markets. They perform similar functions.

Since there is no way to eliminate interest rate risk, the only option is to modify the exposure according to the management views. To choose an adequate hedging policy, Asset–Liability Management (ALM) needs to investigate the payoff profiles of alternative policies under various interest rate scenarios. Examples demonstrate that each policy implies a bet that rates will not hit some break-even value depending on the particular hedge examined and its cost. This break-even value is such that the payoff for the bank is identical with and without the hedge. Decision-making necessitates comparing the break-even value of rates with the management views on interest rates.

Foreign exchange derivatives perform similar functions, although the mechanisms of forward contracts differ from those of interest rate contracts. There is a mechanical connection between interest rates in two currencies, spot and forward exchange rates. This allows shifting exposures from one currency to the other, and facilitates multi-currency ALM.

This chapter provides the essentials for understanding the implementation of these hedging instruments. The first section discusses alternative 'hedging' policies. The next two sections explain the mechanisms that allow derivatives to alter the exposure profile, starting with forward instruments and moving on to options. Both sections detail the payoffs of hedges depending on interest rate scenarios. The fourth section introduces definitions about future markets, explaining how they serve for hedging. The last section deals with currency risk, using the analogy with interest rate hedging instruments. It details the mechanisms of foreign exchange forward contracts and of options on currency exchange rates.

INTEREST RATE RISK MANAGEMENT

This section discusses interest rate exposure and hedging policies. There are two alternative objectives of hedging policies:

- To take advantage of opportunities and take risks.
- A prudent management aimed at hedging risks, totally or partially (to avoid adverse market movements and benefit others).

In the second case, policies aim to:

- Lock in interest rates over a given horizon using derivatives or forward contracts.
- Hedge adverse movements only, while having the option to benefit from other favourable market movements.

There are two types of derivative instruments:

- Forward hedges lock in future rates, but the drawback lies in giving up the possibility of benefiting from the upside of favourable movements in rates (opportunity cost or risk).
- Optional hedges provide protection against adverse moves and allow us to take advantage of favourable market movements (no opportunity cost), but their cost (the premium to pay when buying an option) is much higher.

In addition, futures also allow us to implement hedging policies. The futures market trades standard contracts, while derivatives might be 'plain vanilla' (standard) or customized[1].

---

[1] See Figlewski (1986) for both theoretical and practical aspects of hedging with futures for financial institutions.

FORWARD INTEREST RATE INSTRUMENTS

Forward instruments aim at locking the rate of exposure. Whether the hedge is profitable or not depends on the subsequent variations of interest rates. Forward hedges lock in rates, but they do not allow borrowers and lenders to benefit from the upside, as options do. Therefore, there are benchmarks to consider when setting up such hedges. The universal principle that applies is to make sure, as far as possible, that expected interest rates would be above, or below, some break-even values. These break-even values are the interest rates making the hedge unfavourable, since contracting a hedge implies contracting an interest rate. We present the basic mechanisms with examples only. The most common instruments are forward rate agreements and swaps[2].

Interest Rate Swaps

The objective is to exchange a floating rate for a fixed rate, and vice versa, or one floating rate for another (a 1-month rate against a 1-year rate). The example is that of a firm that borrows fixed rate and thinks rates will decline. The firm swaps its fixed rate for a floating rate in order to take advantage of the expected decline.

The fixed rate debt pays 11%, originally contracted for 5 years. The firm would prefer to borrow at the 1-year LIBOR. The residual life of the debt is 3 years. The current 3-year spot rate is 10%. The 1-year LIBOR is 9%.

The swap exchanges the current 3-year fixed rate for the 1-year LIBOR. The treasurer still pays the old fixed rate of 11%, but receives from the counterparty (a bank) the current 3-year fixed rate of 10% and pays LIBOR to the bank. Since the original debt is still there, the borrower has to pay the agreed rate. The cost of the 'original debt plus swap' is:

1-year LIBOR (paid to bank) + 11% (original debt) − 10% (received from bank)

The borrower now pays LIBOR (9%) plus the rate differential between the original fixed rate (5 years, 11%) and the current spot rate (3 years, 10%), or 1%. The total current cost is LIBOR + 1% = 10%. The treasurer has an interest rate risk since he pays a rate reset every 3 months. As long as LIBOR is 9%, he now saves 1% over the original cost of the debt. However, if LIBOR increases over 10%, the new variable cost increases beyond the original 11%.

The 10% value is the break-even rate to consider before entering into the swap. The treasurer bets that LIBOR will remain below 10%. If it moves above, the cost of the joint combination 'original debt plus swap' increases above the original cost. If this happens, and lasts for a long period, the only choice left is to enter into a reverse swap. The reverse swap exchanges the floating rate with the current fixed rate. Forward hedges are reversible, but there is a cost in doing so. The cost of the swap is the spread earned by the counterparty, a spread deducted from the rate received by the swap.

The above swap receives the fixed rate and pays the floating rate. Other swaps do the reverse. In addition, swaps might exchange one floating rate for another. There are

---

[2] See Hull (2000) for an overview of derivative definitions and pricing.

also differed swaps, or forward starting swaps. These swaps use the forward market rates, minus any retained spread by the counterparty. Swaptions are options on swaps, or options of entering into a swap contract at a deferred date.

For a bank, the application is straightforward. Banks have both assets and liabilities, which result in interest rate gaps. The interest rate gap is like a debt or an investment. When the variable rate gap is positive, the bank is adversely exposed to interest rate declines and conversely. If the variable rate gap is negative, the bank fears an increase in interest rates. This happens when the variable debt is larger than the variable rate assets. The exposure is similar to that of the above borrower. Therefore, banks can swap fixed rates of assets or liabilities to adjust the gap. They can swap different variable rates and transform a floating rate gap, say on 1-month LIBOR, into a floating rate gap, for instance 3-month LIBOR.

Forward Contracts

Such contracts allow us to lock in a future rate, for example locking in the rate of lending for 6 months in 3 months from now. These contracts are Forward Rate Agreements (FRAs). The technology of such contracts is similar to locking in a forward rate through cash transactions, except that cash transactions are not necessary.

To offer a guaranteed rate, the basic mechanism would be that the bank borrows for 9 months, lends to a third party for 3 months, and lends to the borrower when the third party reimburses after 3 months. The cost of forward contracts is the spread between the 9-month and 3-month interest rates. Since this would imply cash transactions increasing the size of the bank balance sheet, they are lending costs for the bank because of regulations. Hence, the technology for FRAs is to separate liquidity from interest rate exposure, and the bank saves the cost of carrying a loan.

A future borrower might buy an FRA if he fears that rates will increase. A future lender might enter into an FRA if he fears that rates will decline. As usual, the FRA has a direct cost and an opportunity cost. When the guaranteed rate is 9%, the bank pays the difference between the current rate, for instance 9.25%, and 9% to the borrower. Should the rate be 8%, the borrower will have to pay to the counterparty the 1% differential. In such a case, the borrower loses with the FRA. The break-even rate is that of the FRA.

OPTIONAL INTEREST RATE INSTRUMENTS

An option is the right, but not the obligation, to buy (call) or sell (put) at a given price a given asset at (European option), or up to (American option), a given date. Options exist for stocks, bonds, interest rates, exchange rates and futures.

Terminology

The following are the basic definitions for understanding options. A call option is the right, but not the obligation, to buy the underlying at a fixed exercise price. The exercise price is the price to pay the underlying if the holder of the option exercises it.

The payoff, or liquidation value, of the option is the gain between the strike price and the underlying price, netted from the premium paid. The option value is higher by its 'time value', or the value of waiting for better payoffs. A put option is the right, but not the obligation, to sell the underlying. Options are in-the-money when they provide a gain, which is when the liquidation value is higher than the exercise price. Options are out-of-the-money when the underlying value is below the exercise price. Such options have only time value, since their payoff would be negative. Options have various underlyings: stock, interest rate or currency. Hence, optional strategies serve for hedging interest rate risk and foreign exchange risk, market risk and, more recently, credit risk[3].

Figure 14.1 illustrates the case of a call option on stock that is in-the-money.

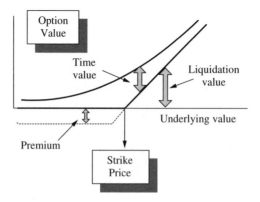

FIGURE 14.1   Option value, liquidation value and payoff

Interest Rate Options

Common interest rate options are caps and floors. A cap sets up a guaranteed maximum rate. It protects the borrower from an increase of rates, while allowing him to take advantage of declines of rates. The borrower benefits from the protection against increasing rates without giving up the upside gain of declining rates. This benefit over forward hedges has a higher cost, which is the premium to pay to buy the cap. A floor sets up a minimum guaranteed rate. It protects the lender from a decline of rates and allows him to take advantage of increasing rates. As for caps, this double benefit has a higher cost than forwards do. Figure 14.2 visualizes the gains and the protection.

Since buying caps and floors is expensive, it is common to minimize the cost of an optional hedge by selling one and buying the other. For instance, a floating rate borrower buys a cap for protection and sells a put to minimize the cost of the hedge. Of course, the rate guaranteed by the cap has to be higher than the rate that the borrower guarantees to the buyer of the floor. Hence, there is no benefit from a decline in rates below the guaranteed rate of the put sold. Figure 14.2 visualizes the collar together with the cap and floor guaranteed rates.

---

[3] See Hull (2000), Cox and Rubinstein (1985) and Chance (1990) for introductions to options.

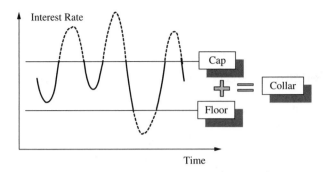

FIGURE 14.2 Cap, floor and collar

Optional Strategies

Optional strategies might be directional, on volatility, or aim to minimize the cost of hedges. Directional policies are adequate when a trend appears likely. Buying a cap is consistent with a bet on interest rate increases. Betting on volatility makes sense when interest rates are unstable and when the current information does not permit identification of a direction. Both an increase and a decrease of rates might occur beyond some upper and lower bounds. For instance, buying a cap at 10% combined with the purchase of a put at 8% provides a gain if volatility drives the interest rate beyond these boundary values. The higher the volatility, the higher are the chances that the underlying moves beyond these upper and lower bounds. Minimizing costs requires collars. The benefit is a cost saving since X buys one option (cap) and sells the other (floor). The net cost is: premium of cap−premium of floor. The drawback is that the interest rate might decline beyond the strike of the floor. Then, the seller of the floor pays the difference between the interest rate and the strike of the floor.

Example: Hedging an Increase of Rates with a Cap

The borrower X has 200 million USD floating rate debt LIBOR 1-month + 1.50% maturing in 1 year. X fears a jump in interest rates. He buys a cap with a guaranteed maximum rate of 8% yearly, costing a premium of 1.54%. After 1 year, the average value of LIBOR becomes 10%. Then X pays 11.50% to the original lender and 1.54% to the seller of the cap. He receives from the seller of the cap: 10% − 8% = 2%, the interest rate differential between the guaranteed rate of 8% and the current rate of 10%. The effective rate averaged is 10% + 1.5% + 1.54% − 2% = 11.04% instead of 11.50% without the cap. This is a winning bet. Payments are the notional 200 million USD times the percentages above.

Now assume that after 1 year the average value of LIBOR becomes 7%. X pays 8.50% to the lender and 1.54% to the seller of the cap. X does not receive anything from the seller of the cap. The effective rate averaged over a year is: 7% + 1.50% + 1.54% = 10.04% instead of 8.50% without the cap! The break-even value of the yearly average of the LIBOR is 9.54% to have a winning optional hedge, or 'guaranteed rate

8% + premium 1.54%'. Before contracting the cap, the borrower should bet that rates would be above 9.54%.

Example: Hedging an Increase of Rates with a Collar

The collar minimizes the direct cost of the optional hedge. The drawback is that the rates should not drop down to the minimum guaranteed rate to the buyer of the put, since the seller has to pay this minimum rate. Hence, there is no gain below that rate.

For example, the debt rate is the LIBOR 1-year, with a residual maturity of 5 years, and an amount of 200 million USD. X buys a 5-year cap, with a strike at 10%, costing 2% and sells a floor with a strike at 7%, receiving the premium of 1%. The net cost is 1%. If the interest rate declines below 7%, the seller of the floor pays the buyer 7%. The maximum (but unlikely) loss is 7% if rates fall close to zero.

Exotic Options

There are plenty of variations around 'plain vanilla' derivatives, called 'exotic' derivatives. There is no point in listing them all. Each one should correspond to a particular view of the derivative user. For instance, 'diff swaps', or 'quanto swaps', swap the interest percentage in one currency for an interest rate percentage in another currency, but all payments are in the local currency. Such options look very exotic at first, but it makes a lot of sense in some cases. Consider the passage to the euro ex ante. Sometimes before, this event was uncertain. We consider the case of a local borrower in France. Possible events were easy to identify. If the euro did not exist, the chances are that the local French interest rate would increase a lot, because the FRF tended to depreciate. In the event of depreciation, the French rate would jump to very high levels to create incentives for not selling FRF. With the euro, on the other hand, the rates would remain stable and perhaps converge to the relatively low German rates, since the DEM was a strong currency. Without the euro, a floating rate borrower faced the risk of paying a very high interest rate. Swapping to a fixed rate did not allow any advantage to be taken of the decline in rates that prevailed during the years preceding the euro. Swapping a French interest rate for a German interest rate did not offer real protection, because, even though the German rate was expected to remain lower than the French rate, the interest payment in depreciated FRF would not protect the borrower against the euro risk.

The 'diff swap' solves this issue. It swaps the French rate into the German rate, but payments are in FRF. In other words, the French borrower pays the German percentage interest rate in FRF, using as notional the FRF debt. The diff swap split the currency risk from the interest rate risk. It allowed to pay in FRF the low German rate without suffering from the potential FRF depreciation. Hence, the view on risks makes the choice of this exotic product perfectly clear. Of course, should the euro come into force, the borrower does not have to use the diff swap.

The general message on derivatives, whether plain vanilla or exotic, is that such hedges require taking 'views' on risks. Plain vanilla derivatives have implied break-even values of rates turning potential gains into losses if expectations do not materialize. This applies also to exotic products.

FUTURES MARKETS

Unlike over-the-counter derivatives, futures are standard contracts sold in organized markets. The major difference between over-the-counter derivatives and futures is the customization of derivatives versus standardized future contracts.

Future Contracts

A future contract is a double transaction consisting of:

- A commitment over a price and a delivery at a given maturity for a given asset.
- Settling the transaction at the committed date and under the agreed terms.

For instance, it is possible to buy today a government debt delivered in 1 year at a price of 90 with a future. If, between now and 1 year, the interest rate declines, the transaction generates a profit by buying at 90 a debt valued higher in the market. The reverse contract is to sell today a government debt at a price of 90 decided today. If, between now and 1 year, the interest rate increases, the transaction generates a profit by selling at 90 a debt valued lower in the market. The main features of futures markets[4] are:

- Standard contracts.
- Supply and demand centralized.
- All counterparties face the same clearinghouse.
- The clearinghouse allocates the gains and losses among counterparties and hedges them with the collaterals (margin calls) provided by counterparties.

A typical contract necessitates the definition of the 'notional' underlying the contract. The notional is a fictitious bond, or Treasury bill, continuously revalued. Maturities extend over variable periods, with intermediate dates (quarterly for instance). Note that forward prices and futures should relate to each other since they provide alternative ways to provide the same outcome, allowing arbitrage to bring them in line for the same reference rate and the same delivery date[5].

Hedging with Futures

The facility to buy or sell futures allows us to make a profit or loss depending on the interest rate movements. Adjusting this profit to compensate exactly for the initial exposure makes the contract a hedge. The adjustment involves a number of technicalities, such as defining the number of contracts that matches as closely as possible the amount to be hedged and limiting basis risk, the risk that the underlying of the contract does not track perfectly the underlying risk of the transactions to be hedged (interest rates are different for example).

---

[4] See Hull (2000) for a review of the futures market.

[5] See, for example, French (1983) for a comparison of forward and futures prices.

Since a contract consists of buying or selling a notional debt at a future date, the value of the debt changes with interest rates. These changes of values should match the changes of the transaction to hedge. For instance, for a borrower fearing interest rate increases, buying a contract at a preset price is a hedge because the value of the notional declines if interest rates increase. For a lender fearing that interest rates will decline, selling a contract is a hedge because the value of the notional increases if they do, providing a gain (Table 14.1).

TABLE 14.1 Hedging interest rate transactions on the futures market

Hedge against[a]:	
Increase of rates	*Decrease of rates*
Lender buys a contract	Borrower sells a contract
• Buy forward at 100 what should be valued more (110) if interest rate decreases	• Sell forward at 100 what should be valued less (90) if interest rate increases
• Hence, there is a gain if interest rate decreases	• Hence, there is a gain if interest rate increases

[a]Lender and borrower have variable rate debts.

CURRENCY RISK

As with interest rates, there are forward and optional hedges. Most of the notions apply, so that we simply highlight the analogies, without getting into any further detail.

The Mechanisms of Forward Exchange Rates

The forward exchange rate is the exchange rate, for a couple of currencies, with market quote today for a given horizon. Forward rates serve to lock in an exchange rate for a future commercial transaction. Forward rates can be above or below spot exchange rates. There is a mechanical relationship between spot and forward exchange rates. The mechanisms of the 'forex' (foreign exchange) and the interest rates markets of two countries create these relationships between the spot and forward exchange rates, according to the interest rate differential between currencies. The only major difference with interest rate contracts is that there is a market of forward exchange rates, resulting from the interaction of interest rate differentials differing from the mechanisms of forward interest rates (Figure 14.3).

Hedging Instruments

Forward rates lock in the exchange rate of a future flow. Swaps exchange one currency for another. This is equivalent to changing the currency of debt or investment into another one. Options allow us to take advantage of the upside together with protection against downside risk.

In the case of currencies, the receiver of a foreign currency flow will buy a put option to sell this foreign currency against the local currency at a given strike price. Being long

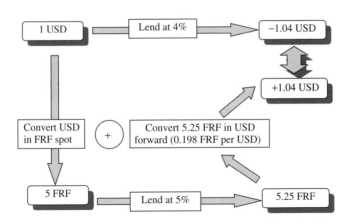

FIGURE 14.3   Spot, forward exchange rates and interest rates

in a currency means receiving the foreign currency, while being short means having to pay in a foreign currency. Hedging with derivatives is straightforward. For instance, X is long 200 million USD. A decline of USD is possible. The spot rate is 0.95 EUR/USD. The forward rate is 0.88 EUR/USD. The alternative choices are:

- Sell forward at 0.88 EUR/USD. This generates an opportunity cost if the USD moves up rather than down because the sale remains at 0.88.
- Buy a put (sale option) with a premium of 2% at strike 6.27 EUR/USD. The put allows the buyer to benefit from favourable upward movements of USD without suffering from adverse downside moves. On the other hand, it costs more than a forward hedge (not considering the opportunity cost of the latter). Embedded in the put are break-even values of the exchange rate. In order to make a gain, the buyer of the put needs to make a gain higher or equal to the premium paid. The premium is 2%, so the USD has to move by 2% or more to compensate the cost. Otherwise, X is better off without the put than with it.

As usual, X needs a view on risk before entering into a hedge. There are plenty of variations around these plain vanilla transactions. We leave it to the reader to examine them.

SECTION 6

Asset–Liability Management Models

15

Overview of ALM Models

Asset–Liability Management (ALM) decisions extend to hedging, or off-balance sheet policies, and to business, or on-balance sheet policies. ALM simulations model the behaviour of the balance sheet under various interest rate scenarios to obtain the risk and the expected values of the target variables, interest income or the mark-to-market value of the balance sheet at market rates. Without simulations, the ALM Committee (ALCO) would not have a full visibility on future profitability and risk, making it difficult to set up guidelines for business policy and hedging programmes.

ALM simulation scope extends to both interest rate risk and business risk. ALM policies are medium-term, which implies considering the banking portfolio changes due to new business over at least 2 to 3 years. Simulations have various outputs:

- They provide projected values of target variables for all scenarios.
- They measure the exposure of the bank to both interest rate and business risk.
- They serve to 'optimize' the risk and return trade-off, measured by the expected values and the distributions of the target variables across scenarios.

Simulation techniques allow us to explore all relevant combinations of interest rate scenarios, business scenarios and alternative hedging policies, to find those which enhance the risk–return profile of the banking portfolio.

Three chapters detail the simulation methodology applied to ALM. The first chapter (Chapter 17) explains the specifics of typical exposures to interest rate risk of commercial banks. The second chapter (Chapter 18) explains how to derive risk and expected profitability profiles from simulations, ignoring business risk. A simplified example illustrates the entire process. The third chapter (Chapter 19) extends the approach to business risk, building on the same example. The examples use the interest income as target variable, but they apply to the balance sheet mark-to-market value ('NPV') as well. These chapters ignore optional risk, dealt with subsequently.

This chapter provides an overview of the process. The first section describes the various steps of simulations. The second section discusses the definition of interest rate scenarios, which are critical inputs to the simulation process. The third section discusses the joint view on interest rate risk and business risk. The fourth section explains how ALM simulations help enhance the risk–return profile of the bank's portfolio, by combining interest rate scenarios, business scenarios and alternative hedging policies. Finally, the last section briefly describes the inputs for conducting ALM simulations.

OVERVIEW OF ALM SIMULATIONS

Simulations serve to construct the risk–return profile of the banking portfolio. Therefore, full-blown ALM simulations proceed through several steps:

- Select the target variables, interest income and the balance sheet NPV.
- Define interest rate scenarios.
- Build business projections of the future balance sheets. The process either uses one single base business scenario, or extends to several business scenarios. For each business scenario, the goal is to project the balance sheet structure at different time points.
- Project margins and net income, or the balance sheet NPV, given interest rates and balance sheet scenarios. The process necessitates calculations of interest revenues and costs, with all detailed information available on transactions.
- When considering optional risk, include valuing options using more comprehensive interest rate scenarios than for 'direct' interest rate risk. Simulations consider optional risks by making interest income, or balance sheet NPV, calculations dependent on the time path of interest rates.
- Combine all steps with hedging scenarios to explore the entire set of feasible risk and return combinations.
- Jointly select the best business and hedging scenarios according to the risk and return goals of the ALCO.

Once the risk–return combinations are generated by multiple simulations, it becomes feasible to examine which are the best hedging policies, according to whether or not they enhance the risk–return profile, and whether they fit the management goals. The last step requires an adequate technique for handling the large number of simulations resulting from this process. A simple and efficient technique consists of building up through simulations the expected profitability and its volatility, for each hedging policy, under business risk, in order to identify the best solutions. The same technique applies to both interest income and NPV as target variables. Figure 15.1 summarizes the process.

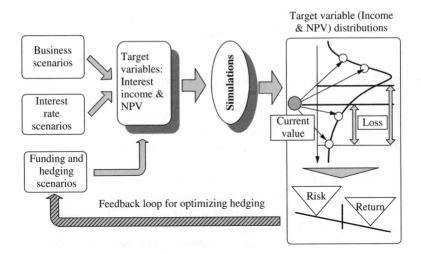

FIGURE 15.1 Overview of the ALM simulation process

Multiple simulations accommodate a large number of scenarios. Manipulating the large number of scenarios requires a methodology. This chapter and the next develop such methodology gradually using examples. The examples are simplified. Nevertheless, they are representative of real world implementations. The latter involve a much larger amount of information, but the methodology is similar.

The technical tools for exploring potential outcomes range from simple gaps to full-blown simulations. Gaps are attractive but have drawbacks depending on uncertainties with respect to the volumes of future assets and liabilities, which relate to business risks. There are as many gaps as there are multiple balance sheet scenarios. Gaps do not capture the risk from options embedded in banking products. Optional risks make asset liabilities sensitive to interest rates in some ranges of values and insensitive in others.

Simulations correct the limitations of the simple gap model in various ways. First, they extend to various business scenarios if needed, allowing gaps to depend on the volume uncertainties of future assets and liabilities. Second, they calculate directly the target variable values, without necessarily relying on gaps only to derive new values of margins when interest rates change. This is feasible by embedding in the calculation any specific condition that influences the interest revenues and costs. Such conditions apply to options, when it is necessary to make rates dependent on the possibility of exercising prepayment options.

ALM simulations focus on selected target variables. They include the interest margins over several periods, the net income, the mark-to-market value of the balance sheet (NPV). For a long-term view, the NPV is the best target variable. Medium to long-term horizons make the numerous periodical interest margins more difficult to handle. Because the NPV summarizes the entire stream of these interest incomes over future years (see Chapter 21), it provides an elegant and simple way to handle all future margins. Since both short and long-term views are valuable, it makes sense to use interest income as a target variable for the near future, and the NPV for the long-term view. Technically, this implies conducting both calculations, which ALM models excel in doing.

INTEREST RATE SCENARIOS AND ALM POLICIES

Interest rate scenarios are a critical input for ALM simulations since they aim to model the interest income or the balance sheet NPV. The discussion on interest rate scenarios is expanded further in subsequent chapters, through examples. The current section is an overview only.

ALM simulations might use only a small number of yield curve scenarios, based on judgmental views of future rates, or consider a large number of values to have a comprehensive view of all possible outcomes. The definitions of interest rate scenarios depend on the purpose. Typical ALM simulations aim to model the values of the target variables and discuss the results, the underlying assumptions and the views behind interest rate scenarios. This does not necessitate full-blown simulation of rates. On the other hand, valuing interest rate options or finding full distributions of target variable values requires generating a large number of scenarios.

Discrete scenarios imply picking various yield curve scenarios that are judgment based. The major benefit of this method is that there are few scenarios to explore, making it easier to understand what happens when one or another materializes. The drawback is that the method does not provide a comprehensive coverage of future outcomes. Increasing the number of scenarios is the natural remedy to this incomplete coverage.

Multiple simulations address valuation of options, which requires modelling the entire time path of interest rates. Options embed a hidden risk that does not materialize until there are large variations of interest rates. Valuing implicit options necessitates exploring a large spectrum of interest rate variations. Models help to generate a comprehensive array of scenarios. Chapter 20 illustrates the valuation process of implicit options using a simple 'binomial' model of interest rates.

Finding an ALM 'Value at Risk' (VaR), defined as a downside variation of the balance sheet NPV at a preset confidence level, also requires a large number of interest rate values for all maturities, in order to define the downside variation percentiles.

When considering changes of interest rates, it is also important to consider shifts over all maturities and changes of slopes. 'Parallel shifts' assume that the yield curve retains the same shape but its level varies. Parallel shifts are a common way to measure sensitivity to interest rate variations. Changing slopes of the yield curve drive the spread between long and short rates, a spread that is critical in commercial banking, since banks borrow short to lend long. During the recent history of rates in Euroland, up to the date when the euro substituted all currencies in the financial industry, the yield curve shifted downwards and its slope flattened. These moves adversely affected the interest income of positive gap banks, because it embeds the spread between the long and short rates.

Interest rate modelling raises a number of issues, ranging from model specifications to practical implementations. First-generation ALM models used a small number of interest rate scenarios to project the ALM target variables. New models integrate interest rate models, allowing us to perform a full valuation of all possible outcomes, while complying with the consistency of rates across the term structure and the observed rate volatilities. Interest rate models serve to provide common interest rate scenarios for ALM simulations, for the valuation of implicit options and consistent with market risk models used for calculating market risk VaR[1].

Models help because they make the entire structure of interest rates a function of one or several factors, plus a random error term measuring the discrepancy between modelled values and actual values. The high sensitivity to both the level and slope of the yield curve of the interest margin rules out some models that tend to model rates based on the current curve[2]. In many instances, as indicated above, the shape of the yield curve changes significantly. Some models help by generating a large number of yield curve scenarios without preserving the current yield curve structure[3]. On the other hand, they do not allow us to use yield curve scenarios that match the management views on interest rate, which is a drawback for ALCO discussions of future outcomes. In addition, business risk makes the volumes of assets and liabilities uncertain, which makes it less important to focus excessively on interest rate uncertainty. For such reasons, traditional ALM models use judgmental yield curve scenarios as inputs rather than full-blown simulations of interest rates.

Models excel for valuing implicit options, and for exploring a wide array of interest outcomes, for instance when calculating an ALM VaR. Historical simulations use interest data from observed time series to draw scenarios from these observations. Models allow the generation of random values of interest rates for all maturities, mimicking the actual behaviour of interest rates. Correlation matrices allow the associations between rates of different maturities to be captured. Principal component analysis allows modelling of the major changes of the yield curves: parallel shifts, slopes and bumps. Chapter 30 provides further details on Monte Carlo simulations of rates. Chapters 20 and 21 show how models help in valuing implicit options. In what follows, we stick to discrete interest rate scenarios, which is a common practice.

JOINT VIEWS ON INTEREST RATES AND BUSINESS UNCERTAINTIES

Restricting the scope to pure 'financial' policies leads to modelling the risk–return profile of the banking portfolio under a given business policy, with one base scenario for the banking portfolio. Simulations allow us to explore the entire set of risk–return combinations under this single business scenario. They show all feasible combinations making up the risk–return profile of the banking portfolio without hedging, or without modifying the existing hedging programme.

Obtaining this risk–return profile is a prerequisite for defining hedging policies. When considering a single business scenario, and a single period, the interest margin is a linear function of the corresponding gap if there are no options. For a single gap value, the interest income varies linearly with the interest rates. The distribution of net income values provides a view on its risk, while its expected value across all interest rate scenarios is the expected profitability. Modifying the gap through derivatives changes the interest

---

[1] Market risk VaR models need to simulate interest rates, but it is not practical to use full-blown models with all interest rates. The principal component technique, using a factor model of the yield curve, is easier to handle (Chapter 30). The same technique would apply to ALM models.

[2] An example is the Ho and Lee (1986) model.

[3] See Hull (2000) for a review of all interest rate models.

income distribution, as well as its expected profitability. Each gap value corresponds to a 'risk plus expected return' combination. It becomes possible to characterize the risk with simple measures, such as the volatility of the target variable, or its downside deviation at a preset confidence level. This converts the distribution of target variable values resulting from interest rate uncertainty into a simple risk–return pair of values. Varying the gap allows us to see how the risk–return combination moves within this familiar space. The last step consists in selecting the subset of 'best' combinations and retaining the corresponding hedging solution (Figure 15.2). A full example of this technique is developed in Chapter 17, dealing with business risk.

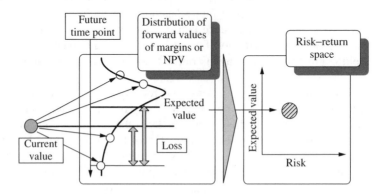

FIGURE 15.2   Forward valuation of ALM target variables

When the gap becomes a poor measure of exposure because there is optional risk, simulations require calculating the interest income for various interest rate scenarios, without using gaps. The calculation requires assumptions with respect to the behaviour of borrowers in exercising their right to reset their borrowing rate.

The ALCO might find none of these risk–return profiles acceptable, because of the risk–return trade-off. Hedging risk might require sacrificing too much expected profitability, or the target profitability might require taking on too much risk, or simply remain beyond reach when looking at a single business scenario and altering risk and return through hedging policies only. The ALCO might wish to revise the business policy in such cases. Extending the simulation process to business scenarios has a twofold motivation:

- Addressing ALCO demand for exploring various business scenarios, and allowing recommendations to be made for on-balance sheet policies as well as for off-balance sheet policies. Under this view, ALCO requires additional 'what if' simulations for making joint on and off-balance sheet decisions.
- Addressing the interaction between business risk and interest rate risk by exploring business uncertainties with several business scenarios. Under this second view, the goal is to find the optimal hedging solutions given two sources of uncertainties, interest rate and business.

ALM simulations address business risk through projections of the banking portfolio. This is a specific feature of ALM, compared to similar techniques applied to market risk and credit risk. When dealing with market or credit risk, simulations apply to a 'crystallized' portfolio, as of current date, ignoring medium-term business scenarios. Because of the ALCO willingness to explore various projections, and because of business risk in the medium and long-term, it is necessary to extend simulations to explicit projections of the banking portfolio over 2 to 3 years. Scenarios differ because they consider various new business assumptions and various product–market mixes. Since there are many business scenarios, there are many distributions of the target variables.

Exposure uncertainty is another motive for multiple balance sheet scenarios. Existing assets and liabilities have no contractual maturities making gaps undefined. New business originates new assets and liabilities, whose volume is uncertain. Dealing with a single projection of the balance sheet for future periods 'hides' such uncertainties. A simple way to make them explicit consists of defining various scenarios. Some of them differ because they make different assumptions, for example to deal with lines without maturity.

ENHANCING AND OPTIMIZING RISK–RETURN PROFILES

When the ALCO considers alternative business policies, ALM simulations address both on and off-balance sheet management. The goal becomes the joint optimization of hedging policies and on-balance sheet actions. This requires combining interest rate scenarios with several balance sheet scenarios and hedging solutions. The methodology for tackling the resulting increase in the number of simulations as illustrated in Chapter 18. For each pair of business and interest rate scenarios, ALM models determine the value of the target profitability variables. When the interest rate only varies, there is one distribution of values, with an expected value and the dispersion around this average. When there are several balance sheet projections, there are several distributions.

This addresses the first goal of conducting 'what if' simulations to see what happens and make sure that the profitability and the risk remain in line with goals. However, it is not sufficient to derive a hedging policy. This issue requires testing various hedging policies, for instance various values of gaps at different time points, to see how they alter the distribution of the target variable. The process generates new distributions of values of the target variable, each one representing the risk–return profile of the balance sheet given the hedging solution. Each hedging solution value corresponds to a 'risk plus expected return' combination. The last step consists in selecting the subset of 'best' combinations and retaining the corresponding hedging solutions.

The technique accommodates various measures of risks. Since we deal with distributions of values of the target variables at various time points, the volatility or the percentiles of downside deviations of target variables quantify the risk. This allows us to determine an ALM VaR as a maximum downside deviation of the target variable at a preset confidence level. Changing the hedging policy allows us to move in the 'risk–return space', risk being volatility or downside deviations and return being the expected value of interest income or the NPV.

SIMULATIONS AND INFORMATION

Actual projections of the balance sheet require a large set of information. In order to project margins, assumptions are also required on the interest rate sensitivity of transactions and the reference rates. The availability of such information is a critical factor to build an ALM information system. Table 15.1 summarizes the main information types, those relating to the volume of transactions and rates, plus the product–market information necessary to move back and forth from the purely financial view to the business view of future outcomes.

TABLE 15.1   Information by transaction

Transaction	Type of transaction and product
Volume	Initial outstanding balance
	Amortization schedule
	Renewal and expected usage
	Options[a]
	Currency
Rates	Reference rate
	Margin, guaranteed historical rate, historical target rate
	Nature of rate (calculation mode)
	Interest rate profile[b]
	Sensitivity to reference rates
	Options characteristics
Customers	Customers, product–market segments

[a] Prepayment, etc.
[b] Frequency and reset dates.

The nature of the transactions is necessary to project exposure and margins. Amortizing loans and bullet loans do not generate the same gap profiles. Projected margins also depend on differentiated spreads across bank facilities. In addition, reporting should be capable of highlighting the contributions of various products or market segments to both gaps and margins. The information on rates is obviously critical for interest rate risk. Margin calculations require using all formulas to calculate effective rates (pre-determined, post-determined, number of days, reset dates, options altering the nature of the rate, complex indexation formulas over several rates, and so on). The rate level is important for margin calculations and to assess the prepayment, or renegotiation, likelihood, since the gap with current rates commands the benefit of renegotiating the loan for mortgages. Sensitivities are required when balance sheet items map to a restricted set of selected reference rates. Options characteristics refer to strike price and the nature of the options for off-balance sheet hedging and embedded options in banking products, such as contractual caps on variable rates paid by borrowers.

16

Hedging Issues

Typically, banks behave as net lenders when they have positive variable rate gaps and as net borrowers when they have negative variable rate gaps. A net lender, like a lender, prefers interest rate increases and needs to hedge against declines. A net borrower, like a borrower, prefers interest rate declines and needs protection against increases. However, the sensitivity to variations of rates is not sufficient to characterize the exposure of a 'typical' commercial bank and to decide which hedging policy is the best.

A 'typical' commercial bank pays short-term rates, or zero rates, on deposits and receive longer-term rates from loans. An upward sloping curve allows these banks to earn more from assets than they pay for liabilities, even if commercial margins are zero. Commercial banks capture a positive maturity spread. Simultaneously, the interest income is sensitive to both shifts and steepness of the yield curve.

This variable gap depends on the nature of the rate paid on the core deposit base. If the rates are zero or fixed (regulated rates), the variable rate gap tends to be positive. If the rate is a short-term rate, the variable rate gap tends to become negative. In both cases, banks still capture the positive maturity spread, but the sensitivity to parallel shifts of the curve changes. The joint view of variable rate gap plus the gap between liability average rates and asset average rates characterizes the sensitivity of interest income of banks to shifts and slope changes of the yield curve.

Deposits blur the image of liquidity and interest rate gaps because they have no maturity. Core deposits remain for a long period, earn either a short-term or a zero rate and tend to narrow the liquidity gap. Zero-rate deposits widen the variable rate gap, and interest-earning deposits narrow it. Such an economic view contrasts with the legal (zero maturity) or conventional (amortizing deposits) views.

Net lender banks, with a large deposit base, are adversely exposed to declining rates, and vice versa. High long-term rates increase income. They are also adversely exposed to a decline in steepness of the yield curve. When rates decline, net lenders face the dilemma of waiting *versus* hedging. Early hedges protect them while late hedges are inefficient because they lock the low rates into interest income. Moreover, banks with excess funds face arbitrage opportunities between riding the spot or the forward yield curves, dependent on both the level and slope of yield curves. For such reasons, hedging policies are highly dependent on interest rate 'views' and goals.

This chapter addresses these common dilemmas of traditional commercial banks. The first section details the joint view on interest rate gaps and yield curve, with a joint sensitivity to shifts of yield curve level and steepness. The second section shows how conventions on deposits alter the economic view of the bank's exposure. The third section details hedging issues.

INTEREST RATE EXPOSURE

The sensitivity to parallel shifts of the yield curve depends on the sign of the variable interest rate gap, or the gap between the average reset period of assets and that of liabilities. With a positive variable rate gap, banks behave as net lenders. With a negative variable rate gap, banks behave as net borrowers.

Variable rate gaps increase with the gap between the asset reset period and the liability reset period. With more variable rate assets than variable rate liabilities, the reset period of assets becomes shorter than the average reset period of liabilities. With more variable rate liabilities than variable rate assets, liability resets are faster than asset resets. The relation between interest rate gaps and average reset dates is not mechanical. We assume, in what follows, that a positive variable rate gap implies a negative gap between the asset average reset date and the liability average reset date, and conversely. The difference between the two views is that the gap between average reset dates positions the average rates of assets and liabilities along the yield curve. The average dates indicate whether the bank captures a positive or negative yield curve spread, depending on the slope of the yield curve and how sensitive it is to this slope.

Hence, the two views of gaps, variable rate gap and average reset dates gap, complement each other. The first refers to parallel shifts of the curve, while the second relates to its steepness. Figure 16.1 shows the two cases of positive and negative variable rate gaps. If variable rate gaps and reset date gaps have the same sign, the posture of the bank is as follows:

- With a positive variable rate gap, the assets average reset period is shorter than the liabilities average reset period. The bank borrows long and lends short. With an upward sloping yield curve, the interest income of the bank suffers from the negative market spread between short and long rates.
- With a negative variable rate gap, the liabilities average reset period is shorter than the assets average reset period. The bank borrows short and lends long. With an upward sloping yield curve, the interest income of the bank benefits from the positive market spread between short and long rates.

The sensitivity to a change in slope of the yield curve depends on the gap between average reset periods of assets and liabilities.

The hedging policy results from such views of the bank's position. Banks with positive variable rate gaps have increasing interest income with increasing rates and behave as net

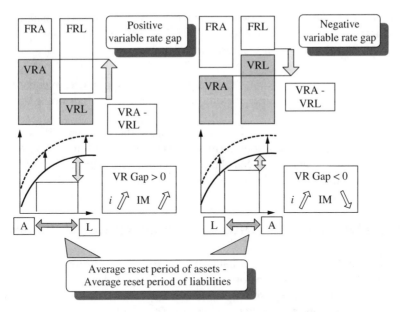

FIGURE 16.1   Interest rate gaps and gaps between average reset periods of assets and liabilities

lenders. If they expect rates to rise, they benefit from maintaining their gaps open. If not, they should close their gaps. Banks with negative variable rates have increasing interest income with decreasing rates and behave as net borrowers. The average reset period of assets is longer than the average reset period of liabilities. If they expect rates to rise, they benefit from closing their gaps. If not, they should open their gaps.

Rules that are more specific follow when considering the forward rates. A bank behaving as a net lender benefits from higher rates. Therefore, if it does not hedge fully its exposures, views on rates drive the hedging policies (Figure 16.2):

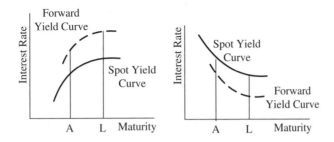

FIGURE 16.2   Bank as net lender: asset reset period is shorter than liability reset period

- With an upward sloping yield curve, forward rates are above spot rates. The bank needs to lock in the current forward rates for future investments if it believes that future spot rates will be below the current forward rates, since these are the break-even rates.

- With an inverted yield curve, forward rates are below spot rates. The bank profits from forward rates for future investments only if it believes that the future spot rates will decrease to a level lower than the current forward rates.

Obviously, if banks expect short rates to be equal to future spot rates are equal to forward rates, they become indifferent since locking in a forward rate or not doing anything are, by definition, equivalent.

When dealing with banks having large deposit bases, the situation differs. Essentially, this is because core deposits are long-term sources of funds earning a short-term rate or a zero rate. The discrepancy between the legal maturity of deposits and their effective maturity blurs the image of the bank's exposure to interest rates.

THE 'NATURAL EXPOSURE' OF A COMMERCIAL BANK

The 'natural liquidity exposure' of a bank results from the maturity gap between assets and liabilities because banks transform maturities. They collect short and lend longer. However, the core demand deposit base is stable. Hence, overfunded banks tend to have a large deposit base. Underfunded banks tend to have a small deposit base. Since deposits have no maturity, conventions alter the liquidity image. Deposits are stable and earn either a small fixed rate or a short-term rate. Therefore, their rate does not match their effective long maturity. This section discusses the 'natural exposure' of commercial banks having a large deposit base and draws implications for their hedging policies.

Liquidity

The views on the liquidity posture depend on the conventions used to determine liquidity gaps. Figure 16.3 shows three different views of the liquidity profile of a bank that has a large deposit base. Core deposits have different economic, conventional and legal maturities. Conventional rules allow for progressive amortization, even though deposits do not amortize. The legal maturity is short-term, as if deposits amortized immediately. This is also unrealistic. The economic maturity of core deposits is long by definition. This is the only valid economic view and we stick to it. Note that this economic view is the

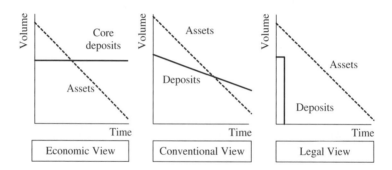

FIGURE 16.3   Liquidity views of a commercial bank

reverse of the view that banks transform maturities by lending long and collecting short resources.

Figure 16.4 shows two possible economic views: an overfunded bank that collects excess deposits and liabilities; an underfunded bank collecting fewer deposits and liabilities than it lends. The situation is either stable through time or reverses after a while. We assume that the total liabilities decrease progressively and slowly because there are some amortizing debts in addition to the large stable deposit base.

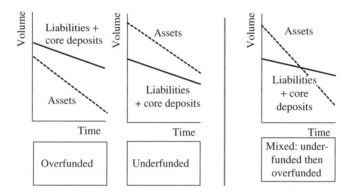

FIGURE 16.4   Underfunded *versus* overfunded commercial bank

Banks with a large core deposit base have excess funds immediately or become progressively overfunded when assets amortize faster than the core deposit base. Banks with a small deposit base are underfunded, at least in the near term, and might become overfunded if assets amortize faster. The interest rate view refers to how the bank captures the maturity spread of interest rates and to its sensitivity to interest rate changes.

Interest Rate Exposure

The exposure to interest rate shifts depends on the variable rate gap or, equivalently, on the gap between the average reset period of assets and the average reset period of liabilities. The larger the variable rate gap, the higher the favourable sensitivity to a parallel upward shift of the yield curve.

Stable deposits do not earn long-term interest rates because their legal maturity is zero, or remains short for term deposits. Many demand deposits have a zero rate. Regulated savings accounts earn a fixed regulated rate in some countries. Demand deposits, subject to certain constraints, earn a short-term rate or a lower rate. In all cases, the stable deposit base has a short-term rate, a fixed rate close to short-term rates or a zero rate. In terms of the yield curve, they behave as if they were on the short end of the curve, rather than on the long end corresponding to their effective maturity. Hence, banks earn the market spread between the zero rate and the average maturity rate of assets, or the spread between the short-term rate of demand deposits and the average maturity rate of assets. For an upward sloping curve, the maturity spread contributes positively to the interest income, and even more so for zero-rate demand deposits.

However, the interest rate gap, or the gap between reset dates of deposits and assets, depends on the rate of deposits. When the rate is a short-term rate, deposits are rate-sensitive liabilities. When the rate is fixed or zero, they are rate-insensitive liabilities. Given their mass in the balance sheet, this changes the interest rate gap of the bank. Banks with zero-rate (or fixed-rate) deposits tend to have a positive variable rate gap, while banks with interest rate-sensitive deposits tend to have a negative variable rate gap. The zero-rate, or fixed-rate, deposits make banks favourably sensitive to a parallel upward shift of the yield curve, while the interest rate-sensitive deposits make banks adversely sensitive to the same parallel upward shift of the yield curve. In both cases, banks benefit from the positive maturity spread of an upward sloping curve (Figure 16.5).

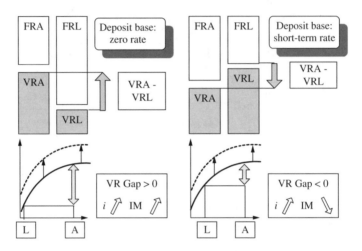

FIGURE 16.5   Interest rate exposure of commercial banks

HEDGING POLICIES

This section makes explicit some general rules driving the hedging policies. Then, we discuss the case of banks behaving as net lenders in continental Europe during the period of declining rates. This is a period of continuous downward shifts of upward sloping yield curves. For several players, it was a period of missed opportunities to take the right exposures and of failures to timely hedge exposures to unfavourable market movements. The context also illustrates why the trade-off between profitability and risks is not the same when rates are low and when rates are high. In times of low rates, hedging locks in a low profitability and increases the opportunity cost of giving up a possible upward move of rates. In times of high rates, the issue might shift more towards reducing the volatility of the margin rather than the level of the profitability.

General Principles

Banks with a large zero-rate deposit base are net lenders, have positive variable rate gaps, and their interest income improves with upward shifts of the yield curve and with an increasing slope of the yield curve. Banks with a large short-term-rate deposit base are also net lenders but have negative variable rate gaps. Their interest income deteriorates with upward shifts of the yield curve and improves with an increasing slope of the yield curve. We now focus only on 'net lender' banks for simplicity.

With the upward sloping yield curves of European countries in the nineties, forward rates were above spot rates. Banks behaving as net lenders faced a progressive decline of the yield curve. They needed to lock in the current forward rates for future investments only if they believed that future spot rates would be below current forward rates. If they expected rates to rise again, the issue would be by how much, since maintaining exposure implies betting on a rise beyond the current forward rates.

Implication for On-balance Sheet Hedging

A net lender bank with a large base of zero-rate deposits tends to have a positive variable rate gap, a negative liquidity gap (excess of funds) and an average reset date of assets shorter than that of liabilities, but they benefit from a positive slope of the yield curve:

- In times of increasing rates, they benefit both from the positive variable rate gap and the asset rate higher than liabilities.
- In times of declining rates, they tend to close the gap, implying looking for fixed rates, lending longer or swapping the received variable rate of assets against the fixed rate.

Note that declining rates right be an opportunity to embed higher margins over market rates in the price of the variable rate loans. In this case, variable rate loans would not reduce the bank's risk but would improve its profitability.

Upward sloping curves theoretically imply that future interest rates will increase to the level of forward rates and that these are the predictors of future rates because of arbitrage. In practice, this is not necessarily true.

The euro term structure remained upward sloping for several years while continuously moving down for years in the late nineties, until short-term rates hit repeatedly historical lows. Rates declined while the yield curve got flatter. Going early towards fixed rates on the asset side was beneficial. After the decline, such hedges became useless because banks could only lock in low rates.

Hedging and the Level of Interest Rates

Hedging policies typically vary when interest rates are low and when they are high. Starting with high interest rates, commercial banks faced a continuous decline of the yield curve, and finally the bottom level, before new hikes in interest levels began to take place in the year 2000.

With high interest rates, interest rate volatility might be higher. This is when hedging policies are most effective. Derivatives reduce the volatility by closing gaps. There are timing issues, since locking fixed rates in revenues is a bet that rates will not keep increasing, otherwise the bank with favourable exposures to interest rate increases would suffer an opportunity cost.

Before reaching low levels, rates decline. Banks acting as net lenders prefer to receive more fixed rates when rates decline and pay variable rates on the liabilities side. Both on-balance sheet and off-balance sheet actions become difficult:

- Banks are reluctant to hedge their current exposures because that would lock in their revenues at the current rates, for instance through swaps, when there is still a chance of hitting a turning point beyond which rates could increase again. This temptation postpones the willingness to set up hedges in time.
- Simultaneously, customers might be reluctant to accept long fixed rates in line with the profitability targets of the bank if they expect rates to keep declining.

Once rates get low, not having set up hedges on time makes them useless later, shifting the pressure from off-balance sheet actions to on-balance sheet actions again. The likelihood of a rise increases, but crystallizing the low rates in the revenues does not make much sense, because the profitability reaches such a low level that it might not suffice any more to absorb the operating costs. There is a break-even value of the interest revenue such that profits net of operating costs hit zero and turn into losses if revenues keep falling. Late forward hedges do not help. Optional hedges are too costly. The European situation illustrates well this dilemma. Many banks waited before setting up hedges because of a fear of missing the opportunity of rates bouncing back up. After a while, they were reluctant to set up forward hedges because low interest revenues from hedges were not economical.

Moreover, institutions collecting regulated deposits pay a regulated rate to customers. This regulated rate remains fixed until regulations change. This makes it uneconomical to collect regulated resources, while depositors find them more attractive because of low short-term rates. The decline in rates puts pressure on deregulating these rates. Because of this pressure, regulated rates become subject to changes, at infrequent intervals, using a formula linking them to market rates.

Riding the Spot and Forward Yield Curves

Riding an upward sloping yield curve offers the benefit of capturing the positive maturity spread, at the cost of interest rate risk. Riding the forward yield curve, with an upward sloping yield curve, offers the benefit of capturing the positive spread between the forward and spot yields. Steeper slopes imply higher spreads between long-term and short-term interest rates. The spot yield curve is not necessarily the best bet for institutions having recurring future excess funds. The difference between forward and spot rates is higher when the slope is steeper. This is an opportunity for forward investments to lock in rates significantly higher than the spot rates. There are 'windows of opportunity' for riding the forward yield curve, rather than the spot yield curve.

A case in point is the transformation of the yield curve in European countries in the late nineties. The slope of the spot yield curve became steep, before decreasing when approaching the euro. When the slope was very steep, there was an opportunity to shift from lending to investing forward.

Banks that faced declining interest rates for lending did not hedge their gaps if they bet that rates were close to the lowest point and would start rising again. An alternative policy to lending was to invest future excess funds at forward rates when the yield curve slope was very steep. These rates ended much higher than the spot rates prevailing later at the forward investment dates, because the yield curves kept shifting downward. Riding

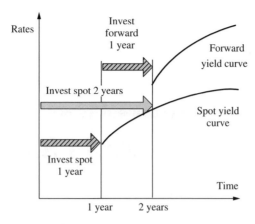

FIGURE 16.6   Comparing spot and forward investments

the forward yield curve was more beneficial than riding the spot yield curve. Figure 16.6 summarizes this policy. Of course, when interest rates reached the bottom line in late 1999 and early 2000, the yield curve had become lower and flatter. The spread between forward and spot rates narrowed. Consequently, the 'window of opportunity' for investing in forward rates higher than subsequent spot rates closed.

17

ALM Simulations

ALM simulations focus on the risk and expected return trade-off under interest rate risk. They also extend to business risk because business uncertainties alter the gap profile of the bank. Return designates the expected value of the target variables, interest income or NPV, and their distribution across scenarios, while volatility of target variables across scenarios characterizes risk. This chapter focuses on interest income.

Simulations project the balance sheet at future horizons and derive the interest income under different interest rate scenarios. When the bank modifies the hedge, it trades off risk and expected profitability, eventually setting the gap to zero and locking in a specific interest income value. For each gap value, the expected interest income and risk result from the set of income values across scenarios. Altering the gap generates various combinations. Not all of them are attractive. Some combinations dominate others because they provide a higher expected income at the same risk or have a lower risk for the same value of expected income. These are the 'efficient' combinations. Choosing one solution within the efficient set, and targeting a particular gap value, becomes a management decision depending on the willingness to take risk.

Simulations with simple examples illustrate these mechanisms. The next chapter extends the scope to business risk. Simple examples involve only one variable rate, as they all vary together. In practice, there are several interest rate scenarios. Multiple variable-rate exposures generate complexity and diversification effects because not all rates vary simultaneously in the same direction.

EaR ('Earnings at Risk'), in this case 'interest income at risk', results from the interest rate distribution given gap and multiple interest rate scenarios. The management can set an upper bound to EaR, for limiting the interest income volatility or imposing a floor to a potential decline. Such gap limits alter the expected interest income.

The first section details balance sheet projections, all necessary inputs, and the projected gaps. The second section details the direct calculations of interest income under different interest rate scenarios. The third section makes explicit the risk–return profile of the balance sheet given interest rate uncertainty and exposure. It also introduces the case of multiple variable-rate gaps. The fourth section shows how controlling the exposure through hedging modifies this profile and implies a trade-off between expected interest income and uncertainty. The last section discusses the hedging policy, from 'immunization' of the interest income to taking exposures depending on the bank's views on interest and setting risk limits.

BALANCE SHEET AND GAP PROJECTIONS

Projections of balance sheets are necessary to project liquidity and interest rate gap profiles and the values of the target variables. Business projections result from the business policy of the bank. Projections include both existing assets and liabilities and new business.

Projections of the Existing Portfolio and of New Transactions

The projection of all existing assets and liabilities determines the liquidity gap time profile. The projection of interest rate gaps requires breaking down assets and liabilities into rate-sensitive items and fixed-rate items, depending on the horizon and starting as of today. The existing portfolio determines the static gaps. The new business increases the volume of the balance sheet while existing assets and liabilities amortize. The new assets and liabilities amortize as soon as they enter the balance sheet. Projections should be net of any amortization of new assets and liabilities. Projecting new business serves to obtain the total volume of funding or excess funds for each future period, as well as the volume of fixed-rate and variable-rate balance sheet items. Projections include both commercial assets and liabilities and financial ones, such as debt and equity. Equity includes retained earnings derived from the projected income statements.

Interest Rate Sensitivity of New and Existing Assets and Liabilities

Interest-sensitive assets and liabilities are those whose rate is reset during each subperiod. Real world projections typically use monthly periods up to 1 or 2 years, and less frequent ones after that. In our example, we consider only a 1-year period. An item is interest rate-sensitive if there is a rate reset before the end of the year.

For new business, all items are interest rate-sensitive, no matter whether the expected rate is fixed or variable. The variable–fixed distinction is not relevant to determine which assets or liabilities are interest-sensitive. A future fixed-rate loan is interest-sensitive, even if its rate remains fixed for its entire life at origination, because origination occurs in the future. The future fixed rate will depend on prevailing market conditions. On the other hand, the fixed–variable distinction, and the breakdown of variable rates for existing assets and liabilities, are necessary to obtain fixed-rate gaps and as many variable-rate gaps as distinct market references. Therefore, interest-sensitive assets and liabilities include variable-rate existing transactions plus all new transactions. Interest-insensitive items include only those existing transactions that have a fixed rate. For simplicity, all sensitivities to the single variable-rate reference are 100% for all balance sheet items in our example.

Table 17.1 provides a sample set of data for a simplified balance sheet, projected at date 1, 1 year from now. There is no need to use the balance sheet at date 0 for gap calculations. All subsequent interest revenue and cost calculations use the end of year balance sheet. We assume there is no hedge contracted for the forthcoming year.

TABLE 17.1   Balance sheet projections for the banking portfolio

Dates	1
Banking portfolio	
Interest rate-insensitive assets (a)	19
Interest rate-sensitive assets (b)	17
Total assets $(c = a + b)$	**36**
Interest rate-insensitive resources (d)	15
Interest rate-sensitive resources (e)	9
Total liabilities $(f = d + e)$	**24**

Projected Gap Profiles

The gaps result from the 1-year balance sheet projections. All gaps are algebraic differences between assets and liabilities. The liquidity gap shows a deficit of 12. The variable-rate gap before funding is +8, but the deficit of 12 counts as a variable-rate liability as long as its rate is not locked in advance, so that the post-funding variable interest rate gap is −4 (Table 17.2).

TABLE 17.2   Gap projections

Dates	1
Banking portfolio	
Interest-insensitive assets (a)	19
Interest-sensitive assets (b)	17
Total assets $(c = a + b)$	**36**
Interest-insensitive resources (d)	15
Interest-sensitive resources (e)	9
Total liabilities $(f = d + e)$	**24**
Liquidity gap $(c - f)$[a]	+12
Variable interest rate gap $(b - e)$	+8
Total balance sheet	
Variable interest rate gap after funding $(b - e) - (c - f)$[b]	−4
Gaps	
Liquidity gap[c]	+12
Interest rate gap[b]	−4

[a]Liquidity gaps are as algebraic differences between assets and liabilities. The +12 value corresponds to a deficit.
[b]Funding is assumed to be variable-rate before any hedging decision is made.
[c]Interest rate gaps are interest-sensitive assets minus interest-sensitive liabilities, or 'variable-rate' interest rate gaps.

INTEREST INCOME PROJECTIONS

The interest margin is the target of financial policy in our example. The margins apply to different levels. The interest margin generated by the banking portfolio (operating assets and liabilities only) is the 'commercial margin'. The interest income is after funding costs, inclusive of all interest revenues or costs from both operating and financial items. In order to calculate margins, we need to relate market rates to customers' rates. The spread between the customers' rates and the market rate is the percentage commercial margin. Such spreads are actually uncertain for the future. Assigning values to future percentage margins requires assumptions, or taking them as equal to the objectives of the commercial policy. Value margins are the product of volume and percentage margins. In this example, we use the market rate as an internal reference rate to calculate the commercial margins. Normally, the Funds Transfer Pricing (FTP) system defines the set of internal transfer prices (see Chapter 26).

Interest Rate Scenarios

In our example, we stick to the simple case of only two yield curve scenarios. The example uses two scenarios for the flat yield curve, at the 8% and 11% levels (Table 17.3).

TABLE 17.3   Interest rate scenarios

Scenarios	Rate (%)
1 (stability)	8
2 (increase)	11

Note: Flat term structure of interest rates.

Commercial and Accounting Margins

The assumptions are simplified. The commercial margins are 3% for assets and −3% for liabilities. This means that the average customer rate for assets is 3% above the market rate, and that the customer rate for demand and term deposits is, on average, 3% less than the market rate. When the market rate is 8%, these rates are 11% and 5%[1]. In practice, percentage margins differ according to the type of asset or liability, but the calculations will be identical. The commercial margin, before the funding cost, results from the customer rates and the outstanding balances of assets and liabilities in the banking portfolio. It is:

$$36 \times 11\% - 24 \times 5\% = 3.96 - 1.20 = 2.76$$

The accounting interest margin is after cost of funding. The cost of funding is the market rate[2]. Since the yield curve is flat, the cost of funds does not depend on maturity in

---

[1] These figures are used to simplify the example. The actual margins obviously differ for various items of assets and liabilities.
[2] Plus any credit spread that applies to the bank, assumed to be included in the rates scenarios.

this example. The interest margin after funding is the commercial margin minus the cost of funding a deficit of 12. This cost is $12 \times 8\% = 0.96$. The net accounting margin is therefore $2.76 - 0.96 = 1.80$.

The Sensitivity of Margins

In this example, we assume that the percentage commercial margins remain constant when the interest rate changes. This is not a very realistic assumption since there are many reasons to relate percentage margins to interest rate levels or competition. For instance, high rates might not be acceptable to customers, and imply percentage margin reductions. For all interest-insensitive items, the customers' rates remain unchanged when market rates move. For interest-sensitive items, the customers' rate variation is identical to the market rate variation because of the assumption of constant commercial margins. The value of the margins after the change in interest rate from 8% to 11% results from the new customers' rates once the market rate rose. It should be consistent with the interest rate gap calculated previously. Detailed calculations are given in Table 17.4.

TABLE 17.4 Margins and rate sensitivity

	Volume	Initial rate	Revenues/ costs	Final rate	Revenues/ costs
Interest-insensitive assets	19	11%	2.09	11%	2.09
Interest-sensitive assets	17	11%	1.87	14%	2.38
Revenues			3.96		4.47
Interest-insensitive resources	15	5%	0.75	5%	0.75
Interest-sensitive resources	9	5%	0.45	8%	0.72
Costs			1.20		1.47
Commercial margin			2.76		3.00
Liquidity gap	12	8%	0.96	11%	1.32
Net interest margin			1.80		1.68

The values of the commercial margins, before and after the interest rate rise, are 2.76 and 3.00. This variation is consistent with the gap model. The change in commercial margin is 0.24 for a rate increase of 3%. According to the gap model, the change is also equal to the interest rate gap times the change in interest rate. The interest rate gap of the commercial portfolio is +8 and the variation of the margin is $8 \times 3\% = 0.24$, in line with the direct calculation.

The net interest margin, after funding costs, decreases by $1.80 - 1.68 = 0.12$. This is because the funding cost of the liquidity gap is indexed to the market rate and increases by $12 \times 3\% = 0.36$. The commercial margin increase of 0.24 minus the cost increase results in the -0.12 change. Alternatively, the interest gap after funding is that of the commercial portfolio alone minus the amount of funding, or $+8 - 12 = -4$. This gap, multiplied by 3%, also results in a -0.12 change in margin. This assumes that the funding cost is fully variable.

THE RISK–RETURN PROFILE

The gaps summarize the balance sheet image and provide a simple technique to derive all possible variations of interest margins. If we know the original interest margin, gaps and interest rate scenarios provide all information necessary to have the risk–return profile of each future time point.

The risk–return profile of the banking portfolio is the image of all attainable combinations of risk and expected return given all possible outcomes. The process requires selecting a target variable, whose set of possible values serves to characterize risk. In the example of this chapter, the interest income is the target variable, but the same approach could use the Net Present Value (NPV) as well. The interest rate changes drive the margin at a given gap. The full distribution of the interest margin values when rates vary characterizes the risk–return profile. Making explicit this trade-off serves to set limits, such as maximum gap values, and assess the consequences on expected net income.

The Risk–Return Profile of the Portfolio given Gaps

Characterizing the risk–return profile is straightforward using the basic relationship:

$$\Delta IM = gap \times \Delta i$$

The margin at date t is random, IM_t, the period is from 0 to t, and the relationship between the variation of the margin and that of interest rates is:

$$\Delta IM = gap \times \Delta i = gap \times (i_t - i_0)$$

To project the interest margin, we need only to combine the original IM_0 at date 0 with the above relations:
$$IM_t = IM_0 + \Delta IM = IM_0 + gap \times \Delta i$$

The expected variation of margin depends on the expected interest rate variation. The final interest rate is a random variable following a probability distribution whose mean and standard deviation are measurable. With a given gap value, the probability distribution of the margin results from that of the interest rate[3]. The change of margin is a linear function of the interest rate change with a preset gap. The expected value of the interest margin at date t, $E(IM_t)$, is the summation of the fixed original margin plus the expected value of its variation between 0 and t. The volatility of the final margin is simply that of the variation. They are:

$$E(\Delta IM) = gap \times E(\Delta i) \quad \text{and} \quad E(IM_t) = IM_0 + gap \times E(\Delta i)$$

$$\sigma(\Delta IM) = |gap| \times \sigma(\Delta i) \quad \text{and} \quad \sigma(IM_t) = |gap| \times \sigma(\Delta i)$$

The vertical bars stand for absolute value, since the volatility is always positive. Consequently, the maximum deviation of the margin at a preset confidence level results directly

---

[3] With the usual notation, the expected rate is $E(i_t)$ and its volatility is $\sigma(i_t)$. When X is a random variable with expectation $E(X)$ and standard deviation $\sigma(X)$, any variable $Y = aX$, a being a constant, follows a distribution with expectation $a \times E(X)$ and volatility $a \times \sigma(X)$. The above formula follows: $E(\Delta IM) = gap \times E(i_t)$ and $\sigma(\Delta IM) = |gap| \times \sigma(i_t)$.

from the maximum deviation of the interest rate at the same confidence level. However, if the gap changes, the interest income distribution also changes. This is the case when the bank modifies the gap through its hedging policy. Figure 17.1 shows the distribution of the interest margin with two different values of the gap. The probabilities of exceeding the upper bound variations are shaded.

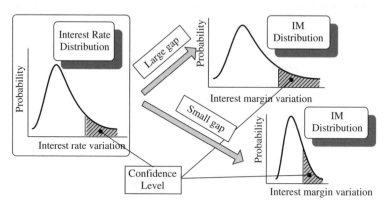

FIGURE 17.1   Distribution of Interest Margin (IM) with random interest rates and a preset gap

Interest Income at Risk and VaR

The usual Value at Risk (VaR), or EaR, framework applies to the interest margin. However, it is possible that no straight loss occurs if we start with a positive interest margin, because the downside deviation might not be large enough to trigger any loss.

The margin volatility results from that of interest rates: $\sigma(\mathbf{IM}) = |\text{gap}| \times \sigma(\mathbf{\Delta i})$. The historical volatility of interest rates is observable from time series. In this example, we assume that the yearly volatility is 1.5%. Using a normal distribution, we can define confidence levels in terms of multiples of the interest rate volatility. The interest rate will be in the range defined by ±2.33 standard deviations from the mean in 1% of all cases. Since the interest margin follows a distribution curve derived from the distribution of interest rates multiplied by the gap, similar intervals apply to the margin distribution of values. With a gap equal to 2000, the margin volatility is: $\sigma(\mathbf{IM}) = 2000 \times 1.5\% = 30$. The upper bound of the one-sided deviation is 2.33 times this amount at the 1% confidence level, or $2.33 \times 30 = 70$ (rounded). The EaR should be the unexpected loss only. This unexpected loss depends on the expected value of the margin at the future time point. Starting from an expected margin at 20, for example, the unexpected loss is only $20 - 70 = -50$.

THE RISK–RETURN TRADE-OFF WHEN HEDGING GAPS

With a given interest rate distribution, the bank alters its risk–return profile by changing its gap with derivatives. Unlike the previous section, the gap becomes variable rather than preset. When altering its exposure, the bank changes both the expected margin and the risk, characterized by margin volatility or a downside deviation at a preset confidence level. In what follows, we ignore the cost of derivatives used to modify the gap and assume that they generate interest payments or revenues with the current flat rate.

The Risk–Return Profile

The basic relationships are $\sigma(\mathbf{IM}) = |\text{gap}| \times \sigma(\mathbf{\Delta i})$ and $E(\mathbf{IM}) = \mathrm{IM}_0 + \text{gap} \times E(\mathbf{\Delta i})$. The gap value, controlled by the bank, appears in both equations and is now variable. Since the volatility is an absolute value, we need to specify the sign of the gap before deriving the relationship between $\sigma(\mathbf{IM})$ and $E(\mathbf{IM})$ because we eliminate the gap between the two equations to find the relationship between expected margin and margin volatility. With a positive gap, the relationship between $E(\mathbf{IM})$ and $\sigma(\mathbf{IM})$ is linear, since gap $= |\text{gap}| = \sigma(\mathbf{IM})/\sigma(\mathbf{\Delta i})$ and:

$$E(\mathbf{IM}) = \mathrm{IM}_0 + [E(\mathbf{\Delta i})/\sigma(\mathbf{\Delta i})] \times \sigma(\mathbf{IM})$$

This relation shows that the expectation of the margin increases linearly with the positive gap. When the gap is negative, $|\text{gap}| = -\text{gap}$ and we have a symmetric straight line with respect to the $\sigma(\mathbf{IM})$ axis. Therefore, with a given gap value, there is a linear relationship between the expected interest margin and its volatility. The risk–return profile in the 'expected margin–volatility of margin' space is a set of two straight lines. If the bank selects a gap value, it also selects an expected interest income. If the bank sets the gap to zero, it fully neutralizes the margin risk. We illustrate such risk–return trade-offs with a simple example when there are only two interest rate scenarios.

Altering the Risk–Return Profile of the Margin through Gaps

In general, there are a large number of interest rate scenarios. In the following example, two possible values of a single rate summarize expectations. The rate increases in the first scenario and remains stable in the second scenario. The probability of each scenario is 0.5. If the upward variation of the interest rate is $+3\%$ in the first scenario, the expected value is 1.5% (Figure 17.2).

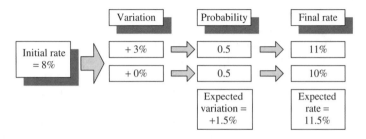

FIGURE 17.2   Interest rate expectations

Swaps serve to adjust the gap to any desired value. For each value of the gap, there are two values of the margin, one for each of the interest rate scenarios, from which the average and the volatility of the margin derive. Gap changes generate combinations of average margin and volatility. The variations of the margins, when the interest rate changes, are equal to the gap times the variation of interest rate: $\Delta IM = \text{gap} \times \Delta i$. If the gap is -4, as in the above example, the variations of the margin are $-4 \times 3\% = -0.12$ and $-4 \times 0\% = 0$, since $+3\%$ and 0% are the only possible deviations of interest rate. Their probabilities are both 0.5. The expected value and the variance are respectively: $0.5 \times (-0.12) + 0.5 \times 0 = -0.06$ and $0.5 \times (-0.12 - 0.06)^2 + 0.5 \times (-0.12 + 0.06)^2 = 0.0036$. The volatility is the square root, or 0.06. With various values of the gap, between $+10$ and -10, the average and the volatility change according to Table 17.5.

TABLE 17.5 Expected margin and margin volatility

Interest rate gap	Volatility of the margin variation	Expected variation of margin
−10	0.15	−0.15
−8	0.12	−0.12
−6	0.09	−0.09
−4	0.06	−0.06
−2	0.03	−0.03
0	0.00	0.00
+2	0.03	+0.03
+4	0.06	+0.06
+6	0.09	+0.09
+8	0.12	+0.12
+10	0.15	+0.15

By plotting the expected margin against volatility, we obtain all combinations in the familiar risk–return space. The combinations fall along two straight lines that intersect at zero volatility when the gap is zero. If the gap differs from zero, there are two attainable values for the expected margin at any given level of volatility. This is because two gaps of opposite sign and the same absolute value, for instance $+6$ and -6, result in the same volatility (0.09) and in symmetrical expected variations of the margin ($+0.09$ and -0.09).

The expected variation of the margin is positive when the gap is positive. This is intuitive since the expectation of interest rate, the average of the two scenarios, is above the current rate. A rise in interest rate results in an increase of the expected margin when the gap is positive. Negative gaps are irrational choices with this view on interest rates. The expected interest rate would make the margin decrease with such gaps.

When, at a given risk, the expected margin is above another combination, the risk–return combination is 'efficient'. In this case, only positive values of the gap generate efficient combinations that dominate others, and negative values of the gap generate inefficient combinations. Therefore, only the upper straight line represents the set of efficient combinations. It corresponds to positive gaps only (Figure 17.3). The optimum depends on the bank's preference. One way to deal with this issue is to set limits on the margin volatility or its maximum downside variation. Such limits set the gap and, therefore, the expected margin.

This result extends over multiple interest rate scenarios since the risk–return profile depends only on the expectation and volatility of interest rate changes. However, the

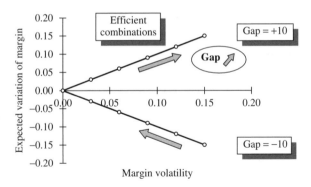

FIGURE 17.3 Risk–return relationships

above calculation applies only with a preset gap controlled by the bank. It does not hold when the gap is random. This is precisely what happens when considering business risk, because it makes future balances of assets and liabilities uncertain. To deal with this double uncertainty, interest rate and business risks, we need a different technique. The multiple interest rate and business scenarios approach addresses this issue (Chapter 18).

Risk–Return Profiles with Multiple Interest Rates

In general, there are multiple gaps for different interest rates. Since all rates vary together, adding up the interest income volatilities due to each exposure, or the worst-case exposures for each gap, would overestimate the risk. This issue is the same for market risk and credit risk when dealing with diversification. The correlation[4] between risk drivers determines the extent of diversification. The two rates might not vary mechanically together, so the chances are that one varies less than the other or in the opposite direction. This reduces the overall exposure of the bank to an exposure lower than the sum of the two gaps. Section 11 of this book provides the extended framework for capturing correlation effects. In the case of interest rates, the analysis relies on gaps.

The following example illustrates these issues. The balance sheet includes two subportfolios that depend on different interest indexes. These indexes are i_1 and i_2. Their yearly volatilities are 3% and 2%. The correlation between these two interest rates can take several values (0, +1, +0.3). The sensitivities of the interest income are the gaps, 100 and 200, relative to those indexes (Table 17.6).

The interest margin variation $\mathbf{\Delta IM}$ becomes a function of both gaps and interest rate changes:

$$\mathbf{\Delta IM} = 100 \times \mathbf{\Delta i_1} + 200 \times \mathbf{\Delta i_2}$$

It is the summation of two random variables, with constant coefficients. The expected variation is simply the weighted summation of the expected variation of both rates, using the gaps as weights. The volatility of the interest margin results from both interest rate volatilities and the correlation. The standalone risk for the first gap is the margin volatility generated by the variation of the first index only, or $100 \times 3\% = 3$. The standalone risk

---

[4] The correlation is a statistical measure of association between two random variables, which is extensively discussed in Chapter 28.

TABLE 17.6 Overall volatility of two interest rate exposures

	Market volatilities	
Rate i_1		$\sigma(\Delta i_1) = 3\%$
Rate i_2		$\sigma(\Delta i_2) = 2\%$
	Exposures	
Exposure 1		$Gap_1 = 100$
Exposure 2		$Gap_2 = 200$
	Portfolio volatility[a]	
Correlation $= 0$		5.00
Correlation $= 1$		7.00
Correlation $= +0.3$		5.67

[a]These values are calculated with the general formula: $\sqrt{[(100 \times 3\%)^2 + (200 \times 2\%)^2 + 2\rho(100 \times 3\%)(200 \times 2\%)]}$ where ρ takes the values 0.1 and 0.3 (see Chapter 28).

for the second exposure is $200 \times 2\% = 4$. The sum of these two volatilities is 7, which overestimates the true risk unless rates are perfectly correlated. The actual volatility is that of a weighted summation of two random variables:

$$\sigma(\mathbf{IM}) = \sqrt{[gap_1 \times \sigma(i_1)]^2 + [gap_2 \times \sigma(i_2)]^2 + 2\rho[gap_1 \times \sigma(i_1)][gap_2 \times \sigma(i_2)]}$$

$$\sigma(\mathbf{IM}) = \sqrt{(100 \times 3\%)^2 + (200 \times 2\%)^2 + 2\rho(100 \times 3\%)(200 \times 2\%)}$$

With a zero correlation the volatility is 5, and with a correlation of 0.3 it becomes 5.67. It reaches the maximum value of 7 when the correlation is 1. The margin volatility is always lower than in the perfect correlation case (7). The difference is the effect of diversification of exposures on less than perfectly correlated rates. The extreme case of a perfect correlation of 1 implies that the two rates are the same. In such a case, the gap collapses to the sum of the two gaps.

When characterizing the risk–return profile of the portfolio of two exposures by the expected margin and its volatility, the latter depends on the correlation between rates. Using a normal distribution as a proxy for rates is acceptable if rates are not too close to zero. In this case, it is a simple matter to generate the distribution of the correlated rates to obtain that of the margin[5].

When considering the hedging issue, one possibility is to neutralize all gaps for full immunization of interest income. Another is to use techniques taking advantage of the correlation between interest rates. In any case, when rates correlation is lower than 1, variable-rate gaps do not add together. Note that using fixed-rate gaps is equivalent to an arithmetic addition of all variable-rate gaps, as if they referred to the same index. This corresponds to a correlation of 1 and overestimates the exposure.

---

[5] Alternatively, interest rates follow a lognormal, more realistic distribution. The changes in interest rates still follow a stochastic process with a random normal factor. It is possible to correlate the rates by correlating their random factor. See Chapter 30 for a description of the main stochastic processes driving rates. Chapter 28 discusses techniques for generating the distribution of a sum of correlated normal variables.

INTEREST RATE POLICY

The ALM unit controls the interest rate exposure by adjusting the gap after funding. This section discusses, through simple examples, various hedging issues: immunization of the interest income; trade-off of the hedging policy when the bank has 'views' on future interest rates; usage of multiple gap exposures; setting limits for interest rate risk.

Hedging

In order to obtain immunization, the post-funding gap should be zero. In other words, the funding and hedging policy should generate a gap offsetting the commercial portfolio positive gap. The funding variable-rate gap is equal to the fraction of debt remaining at variable rate after hedging, with a minus sign since it is a liability. Since the gap is +8 before funding, the variable-rate debt should be set at 8 to fully offset this gap. This means that the remaining fraction of debt, $12 - 8 = 4$, should have an interest rate locked in as of today. An alternative and equivalent approach is to start directly from the post-funding gap. This gap is $+8 - 12 = -4$. Setting this gap to zero requires reducing the amount of floating rate debt from 12 to 8. Therefore, we find again that we need to lock in a rate today for the same fraction of the debt, or 4, leaving the remaining fraction of the debt, 8, with a floating rate.

   In the end, the interest rate gap of the funding solution should be the mirror image of the interest rate gap of the commercial portfolio. Any other solution makes the net margin volatile. The solution 'floating rate for 8 and locked rate for 4' neutralizes both the liquidity gap and the interest rate gap (Table 17.7).

TABLE 17.7 Hedging the liquidity and interest rate gaps

Liquidity gap	+12
Interest rate gap of the banking portfolio	+8
Fixed-rate debt	4
Floating-rate debt	8
Total funding	12
Liquidity gap after funding	0
Interest rate gap after funding and hedging	0

   In order to lock in the rate for an amount of debt of 4, various hedges apply. In this case, we have too many variable-rate liabilities, or not enough variable-rate assets. A forward swap converting 4 of the floating-rate debt into a fixed-rate debt is a solution. The swap would therefore pay the fixed rate and receive the floating rate. Alternatively, we could increase the variable-rate fraction of assets by 4. A swap paying the fixed rate and receiving the variable rate would convert 4 of fixed-rate assets into 4 of variable-rate assets. The same swap applies to both sides.

Hedging Policy

If the amount of floating-rate debt differs from 8, there is an interest rate exposure. The new gap differs from zero. For instance, locking in the rate for an amount of debt of 2 results in a gap which is +2. The margin volatility results directly from the remaining gap after funding. Any increase in rate increases the margin since the variable-rate gap is positive. However, the price to pay is the risk that rates decrease, thereby reducing the margin. Maintaining open a gap makes sense only if it is consistent with an expected gain. In this example, the expectation embedded in the scenarios is a rise of rate, since rates are either stable or increase. A positive variable-rate gap makes sense, but a negative variable-rate gap would be irrational.

The level of interest rates is an important consideration before making a decision to close the gap. A swap would lock in a forward rate. In this case, the locked rate is on the cost side, since the swaps pay the fixed rate. If the forward rate is low, the hedge is acceptable. If the forward rate is high, it will reduce the margin. Using a full hedge for a short horizon only (1 year) provides added flexibility, while later maturities remain open. This allows for the option to hedge at later periods depending on the interest rate moves. Of course, if interest rates keep decreasing, the late hedge would become ineffective.

The exposure to interest rate risks has to be consistent with risk limits. The limits usually imply that adverse deviations of the interest margin remain within given bounds. This sets the volume of the necessary hedge for the corresponding period. Setting the maximum adverse deviation of the target variable, given a confidence level, is equivalent to setting a maximum gap since the margin volatility is proportional to the gap. This maximum gap is the limit.

Setting Limits for Interest Rate Risk

Setting limits involves choosing the maximum volatility, or the maximum downward variation of the margin at a given confidence level. Limits would effectively cap the gap, thereby also influencing the expected income, as demonstrated earlier.

With a given volatility of the margin, the maximum acceptable gap is immediately derived: $\sigma(\mathbf{\Delta IM}) = |gap| \times \sigma(\mathbf{\Delta i})$. If the management caps the volatility of the margin at 20, and the interest rate volatility is 1.5% yearly, the maximum gap is $20/1.5\% = 1333$.

Alternatively, it is common to set a maximum downward variation of the interest margin, say -100. Assuming operating costs independent of interest rates, the percentage variation of pre-tax and post-operating costs income is higher than the percentage change in interest margin at the top of the income statement. For instance, starting with a margin of 200, a maximum downside of 100 represents a 50% decrease. If operating costs are 80, the original pre-tax income is $200 - 80 = 120$. Once the margin declines to 100, the remaining pre-tax income becomes $100 - 80 = 20$. The percentage variation of pre-tax income is $-100/120 = -80\%$, while that of margin is -50%.

If interest rate volatility is 1.5% and confidence level is 2.5%, the upper bound of the interest rate deviation, using the normal distribution proxy for rates, is $1.96 \times 1.5\%$, or approximately 3%. Starting from a maximum decline of the margin set at 100, at the 2.5% confidence level, the maximum sustainable gap is $100/3\% = 3333$. If the interest rate decreases by 3%, the margin declines by $3333 \times 3\% = 100$, which is the maximum.

Hedging Multiple Variable-rate Gaps

For hedging purposes, the simplest way to obtain margin immunization is to neutralize both gaps with respect to the two interest rates. Another option would be to hedge both gaps at the same time using the interest rate correlation. Since rates correlate, a proxy hedge would be to take a mirror exposure to only one of the rates used as a unique driver of the interest rate risk, the size of the hedge being the algebraic summation of all gaps. This is the well-known problem of hedging two correlated exposures, when there is a residual risk (basis risk).

When considering the two variable-rate gaps, respectively 100 and 200 for two different and correlated rates, the basic relationship for the interest margin is:

$$\Delta IM = 100 \times \Delta i_1 + 200 \times \Delta i_2$$

Since the two rates correlate, with ρ_{12} being the correlation coefficient, there is a statistical relationship between the two variations of rates, such that:

$$\Delta i_1 = \beta \Delta i_2 + \varepsilon_{12}$$

$$\Delta IM = 100 \times (\beta \Delta i_2 + \varepsilon_{12}) + 200 \times \Delta i_2$$

The value of the second gap becomes a variable G, since the bank can control it in order to minimize the margin volatility:

$$\Delta IM = 100 \times (\beta \Delta i_2 + \varepsilon_{12}) + G \times \Delta i_2$$

$$\Delta IM = (100 \times \beta + G) \times \Delta i_2 + \varepsilon_{12}$$

The variance of ΔIM is the sum of the variance of the interest rate term and the residual term since they are independent:

$$\sigma^2(\Delta IM) = (100 \times \beta + G)^2 \times \sigma^2(\Delta i_2) + \sigma^2(\varepsilon_{12})$$

There is a value X of the gap G such that this variance is minimum. Using $\beta = 0.5$ and $\sigma^2(\varepsilon_{12}) = 1\%$, we find that $X = -50$ results in a variance of 1. This also has a direct application for setting limits to ALM risk, since the volatility is an important parameter for doing so. Note that hedging two exposures using a single interest rate results in a residual volatility. On the other hand, neutralizing each variable rate gap separately with perfect hedges (same reference rates) neutralizes basis risk. This is a rationale for managing gaps separately.

18

ALM and Business Risk

Since both interest rates and future business volumes and margins are random, banks face the issue of how to jointly optimize, through financial hedges, the resulting uncertainty from these multiple sources of risk. There are practical simulation-based solutions to this joint optimization problem, using financial hedges.

The starting point of the method requires defining a number of interest rate scenarios and business scenarios. The principle consists of simulating all values of the target variable, the interest income or the Net Present Value (NPV) of the balance sheet, across all combinations of interest rate and business scenarios. The resulting set of values is organized in a matrix cross-tabulating business and interest rate scenarios. Such sets of target variable values depend on any hedge that affects interest income or NPV. Since gaps become subject to business risk, it is not feasible any more to fully hedge the interest income.

When hedging solutions change, the entire set of target variable values changes. For turning around the complexity of handling too many combinations of scenarios, it is possible to summarize any set of values of the target of variables within the matrix, by a couple of values. The first is the expected value of the target variable, and the second is its volatility, or any statistics representative of its risk, both calculated across the matrix cells. For each hedging solution, there is such a couple of expected profitability and risk across scenarios. When hedging changes, both expectation and risk change, and move in the 'risk–return' space. The last step consists of selecting the hedging solutions that best suit the goals of the Asset–Liability Management Committee (ALCO), such as minimizing the volatility or targeting a higher expected profitability by increasing the exposure to interest rate risk. Those solutions that maximize expected profitability at constant risk or minimize risk at constant expected profitability make up a set called the 'efficient frontier'. All other hedging solutions are discarded. It is up to the management to decide what level of risk is acceptable. This methodology is flexible and accommodates a large number of simulations.

The technique allows us to investigate the impact on the risk–return profile of the balance sheet under a variety of assumptions, for example: What is the impact on the risk–return profile of assumptions on volumes of demand deposits, loans with prepayment risk or committed lines whose usage depends on customer initiatives? Which funding and hedging solutions minimize the risk when only interest rate risk exists, when there is business risk only and when both interact? How can the hedging solutions help to optimize the risk–return combination?

The Asset–Liability Management (ALM) simulations also extend to optional risks because the direct calculation of interest income or NPV values allows us to consider the effect of caps and floors on interest rates, as explained in Section 7 of this book, which further details these risks. Finally, the ALM simulations provide a unique example of joint control of interest rate and business risks, compared to market risk and credit risk measures, which both rely on a 'crystallized' portfolio as of today.

The first section of this chapter illustrates the methodology in a simple example combining two simple interest rate scenarios with two business scenarios only. It provides the calculation of interest income, and of its summary statistics, expectation and volatility, across the matrix of scenarios. The second section details the calculations when changing the hedging solution, considering only two different hedging solutions for simplicity. The third section summarizes the findings in the risk–return space, demonstrating that extending simulations to a larger number of scenarios does not raise any particular difficulty. It defines the efficient frontier and draws some general conclusions.

MULTIPLE SCENARIOS WITH BUSINESS AND INTEREST RATE RISKS

The previous methodology applies to a unique gap value for a given time point. This is equivalent to considering a unique business scenario as if it were certain, since the unique value of the gap results directly from asset and liability volumes. Ignoring business risk is not realistic, and amounts to hiding risks rather than revealing them when defining an ALM policy. Moreover, the ALM view is medium-term, so that business uncertainty is not negligible. To capture business risk, it is necessary to define multiple business scenarios. Multiple scenarios result in several projections of balance sheets and liquidity and interest rate gap profiles. For hedging purposes, the risk management issue becomes more complex, with interest income volatility resulting from both interest rate risk and business risk. Still, it is possible to characterize the risk–return profile and the hedging policies when both risks influence the interest income and the NPV. Business risk influences the choice of the best hedging policy.

The Risk–Return Profile of the Balance Sheet

When using discrete scenarios for interest rates and for business projections, it is possible to summarize all of them in a matrix cross-tabulating all interest rate scenarios with all business scenarios. For each cell, and for each time point, it is feasible to calculate the margin or the NPV. The process is not fully mechanical, however, because there is a need to make assumptions on funding and interest rate management. Constructing a risk–return profile and hedging are two different steps. For the first step, we consider that there are no new hedges other than the existing ones. Hence, all future liquidity gaps result in funding or investing at prevailing rates. The ultimate goal of the simulations remains to define the 'best' hedge.

If we calculate an interest income value or NPV for each cell of the matrix, we still face the issue of summarizing the findings in a meaningful way in terms of return and risk. A simple way to summarize all values resulting from all combinations of scenarios is to convert the matrix into a couple of parameters: the expected interest income (or NPV) and the interest income (or NPV) volatility across scenarios. This process summarizes the entire matrix, whatever its dimensions, into a single pair of values (Figure 18.1). The volatility measures the risk and the expectation measures the return. This technique accommodates any number of scenarios. It is possible to assign probabilities to each scenario instead of considering that all are equally probable, and both expected margin and margin volatility would depend on such probabilities. If all combinations have the same probability, the arithmetic average and the volatility are sufficient.

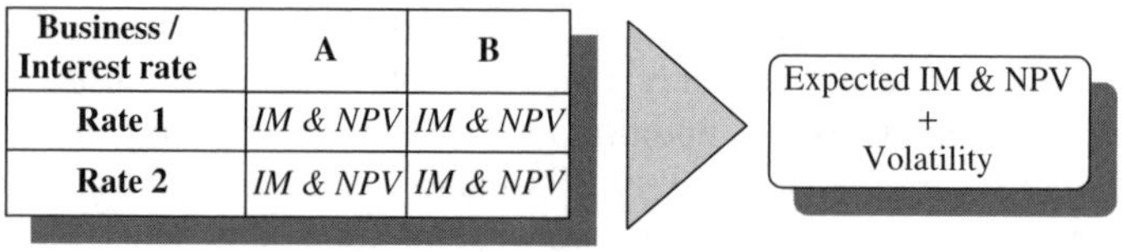

Business / Interest rate	A	B
Rate 1	*IM & NPV*	*IM & NPV*
Rate 2	*IM & NPV*	*IM & NPV*

Expected IM & NPV
+
Volatility

FIGURE 18.1 **Matrix of scenarios: cross-tabulating business scenarios and interest rate scenarios**

However, since the interest income or NPV depends on the funding, investing and hedging choices, there are as many matrices as there are ways of managing the liquidity and the interest rate gaps. We address this issue in a second step, when looking for, and defining, the 'best' policies.

The Matrix Approach

A simple example details the methodology. When using two scenarios, there are only two columns and two rows. It is possible to summarize each business scenario by a gap value. Referring to the example detailed, we use two such gap values: −4 and −8 cross-tabulated with two interest rate scenarios, with +8% and +11% as flat rates. The original value of the margin with rate at 8% is 1.80 with a gap equal to −4. When rates vary, it is easy to derive the new margin value within each column, since the gap is constant along a column. The matrix in this very simple case is as given in Table 18.1, with the corresponding expectation and volatility on the right-hand side, for a single time point 1 year from now.

Using two business scenarios, with net gaps of −4 and −8, and two interest rate scenarios, at +8% and +11%, we find the expectations of the margin change and of the margin volatility in Table 18.1. The variations are respectively −0.12 and −0.24 when the rate moves up from 8% to 11%. Starting from a margin of 1.80, the corresponding final

TABLE 18.1   Matrix of margins: two interest rate scenarios and a single business scenario

Rate	Scenario		Risk–return profile	
	Gap $= -4$	Gap $= -8$		
8%	+1.80	1.80	E(**IM**)	1.7100
11%	+1.68	1.56	σ(**IM**)	0.1149

margins are 1.68 and 1.56. The expected margin and its volatility across the four cells are respectively 1.7100 and 0.1149[1]. In the range of scenarios considered, the worst-case value of the margin is 1.56. By multiplying the number of scenarios, we could get many more margin values, and find a wider distribution than the three values above. In the current simple set of four cases, we have a 2×2 matrix of margins for each financing solution. If we change the financing solution, we obtain a new matrix. There are as many matrices as there are financing solutions.

Handling Multiple Simulations and Business Risk

The matrix approach serves best for handling multiple business scenarios as well as multiple yield curve scenarios. There is no limitation on the number of discrete scenarios. The drawback of the matrix approach is that it summarizes the risk–return profile of the portfolio using two parameters only, which is attractive but incomplete. To characterize the full portfolio risk, we would prefer to have a large distribution of values for each future time point. In addition, probabilities are subjective for business scenarios.

This approach contrasts with the market risk 'Value at Risk' (VaR) and the credit risk VaR techniques, because they use only a 'crystallized' portfolio as of today. With a single business scenario, we could proceed with the same technique to derive an ALM VaR with full probability distributions of all yield curves. This would allow us to generate distributions of margins, or of the NPV, at all forward time points fully complying with observed rates. The adverse deviations at a preset confidence level derive from such simulations. We use this technique when detailing later the specifics of NPV VaR with given asset and liability structures.

However, ignoring business risk is not realistic with ALM. It does not make much sense to generate a very large number of interest rate scenarios if we ignore business risk, since there is no point in being comprehensive with rates if we ignore another significant risk. The next chapter details how the matrix methodology helps in selecting the 'best' hedging solutions.

HEDGING BOTH INTEREST RATE AND BUSINESS RISKS

For any given scenario, there is a unique hedging solution immunizing the margin against changes in interest rates. This hedging solution is the one that offsets the interest rate gap. With several scenarios, it is not possible to lock in the margin for all scenarios by

---

[1] The standard deviation uses the formula for a sample, not over the entire population of outcomes (i.e. it divides the squared deviations from the mean by 3, not 4).

hedges, because gaps differ from one business scenario to another. To determine hedging solutions, we need to simulate how changing the hedge alters the entire risk–return profile corresponding to each business scenario.

The Matrix Technique, Business Risk and Hedging

When ignoring new hedges, we generate a number of values for the target variables identical to the number of combinations of interest rate and business scenarios, conveniently summarized into a couple of statistics, the 'expected value' and 'volatility'. When modifying the hedge, we change the entire matrix of values. There are as many matrices of values of the target variables, interest income or NPV, as there are hedging solutions. Summarizing each set of new values in a risk–return space allows us to determine which hedges result in better risk–return profiles than others. Figure 18.2 illustrates the process.

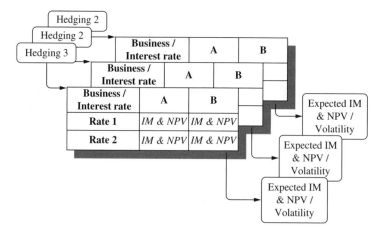

FIGURE 18.2   Matrix of scenarios: cross-tabulating business scenarios and interest rate scenarios

Simulations offer the maximum flexibility for testing all possible combinations of assumptions. Multiplying the number of scenarios leads to a large number of simulations. Two business scenarios and two interest rate scenarios generate four combinations. With two hedging scenarios, there are eight combinations. The number of simulations could increase drastically, making the interpretation of the results too complex. To handle this complexity, summarizing each matrix using a pair of values helps greatly. Only the risk–return combinations generated for each hedging solution serve, independently of the size of the matrix. The approach facilitates the identification of the best solutions within this array of combinations.

In what follows, we ignore probabilities assigned to business scenarios. Using probabilities would require assigning probabilities to each interest rate scenario and to each business scenario. Therefore, each cell of the matrix has a probability of occurrence that becomes the joint probability of the particular pair of business and interest rate scenarios. In the case of uniform probabilities, there is no need to worry about different likelihoods of occurrence when using the matrix technique. Otherwise, we should derive these joint probabilities. Under independence between business scenarios and interest rate scenarios, these would be the product of the probabilities assigned to the particular business scenario and the particular interest rate scenario, as explained in Chapter 28.

Business Scenarios

The interest rate scenarios are those of the first analysis with only one base case for business projections (interest scenarios 1 and 2). One business scenario (A) is identical to that used in the previous chapter. A second business scenario (B) is considered. Each business scenario corresponds to one set of projected balance sheet, liquidity gap and interest rate gap. The scenario B is shown in Table 18.2. The starting points are the liquidity gaps and the interest rate gaps of the banking portfolio for scenarios A and B.

TABLE 18.2   Two business scenarios

Projected balance sheet	Scenario A	Scenario B
Interest-insensitive assets	19	22
Interest-sensitive assets	17	17
Interest-insensitive resources	15	14
Interest-sensitive resources	9	13
Total assets	36	39
Total liabilities	24	27
Gaps		
Liquidity gaps	12	12
Interest rate gap—banking portfolio	8	4
Interest rate gap—total balance sheet	−4	−8

We use the same 3% commercial margins to obtain customer rates and margins in value. For instance, with scenario B, at the 8% rate, the value of the commercial margin is $39 \times 11\% - 27 \times 5\% = 4.29 - 1.35 = 2.94$, and the net margin, after funding costs, is $2.94 - 0.96 = 1.98$. The margins are different between scenarios A and B because the volumes of assets and liabilities generating these margins are different (Table 18.3).

TABLE 18.3   Interest margins: interest rate scenario 1

	A	B
Interest rate gap (banking portfolio)	+8	+4
Initial commercial margin[a]	2.76	2.94
Liquidity gap (a)	+12	+12
Cost of funding (a) × 8%	0.96	0.96
Net interest margin after funding	1.80	1.98

[a]The initial margins correspond to an interest rate of 8%.

When the interest rate changes, the variations of margins result from the interest rate gaps. The cost of funding depends on the hedging solution. The fraction of the total funding whose rate is locked in through swaps defines a hedging solution.

Hedging Scenarios

There are two hedging scenarios. The first solution locks in the interest rate for a debt of 4. The remaining debt, $12 - 4 = 8$, required to bridge the liquidity gap is a floating rate debt. The second solution locks in the interest rate for an amount of 8, the remaining 4 being floating rate debt. These are the H1 and H2 hedging solutions. It is possible to think of the first hedging scenario as the existing hedge in place and of H2 as an alternative solution (Table 18.4).

TABLE 18.4 Funding scenarios

Scenario	A	B
Interest rate gap (banking portfolio)	+8	+8
Liquidity gap	−12	−12
Hedging[a]		
Hedging H1	8vr + 4fr	
Hedging H2	4vr + 8fr	
Interest rate gap after hedging[b]		
Hedging H1	0	+4
Hedging H2	+4	0

[a] The hedging solution is the fraction of total funding whose rate is locked in. 'fr' and 'vr' designate respectively the fractions of debt with fixed rate and variable rate.
[b] The interest rate gap is that of the banking portfolio less the floating rate debt.

The interest rate gap after funding is the difference between the commercial portfolio gap and the gap resulting from the funding solution. This gap is simply the floating rate debt with a minus sign. With the hedging solution H1, the floating rate debt is 8. The interest rate gap post-funding is therefore $+8 - 8 = 0$. In scenario B, the solution H1 results in an interest rate gap post-funding of $+8 - 4 = +4$.

The Matrices of Net Interest Margins

The banking portfolio margins and the net interest margins derive from the initial values of margins using the gaps and the variation of the interest rate. For scenario A, the initial value of the net margin, with interest of 8%, is 1.80. For scenario B, the net margin with initial interest rate of 8% is 1.98. The margin variation with a change in interest rates of $\Delta i = +3\%$ is:

$$\Delta(\text{Net interest margin}) = \text{gap} \times \Delta i$$

It is easier to derive the matrix of net margins from initial margins and gaps than to recalculate all margins directly. A first matrix cross-tabulates the business scenarios A and B with the interest rate values of 8% and 11%, given the hedging solution H1. The second matrix uses the hedging solution H2. For instance, with the business scenario A and the hedging solution H1, both the initial net margin and the final margin, after an interest rate increase of 3%, are equal. With the hedging solution H2 and the scenario B, the initial margin is 1.98. Since the interest rate gap after hedging is −4, the final margin is $1.98 - 4 \times 3\% = 1.86$ when the rate increases by 3% (Table 18.5).

TABLE 18.5 The net margin matrix after hedging

Business scenario	A	B
Fixed rate amount: 4	Hedging H1	Hedging H2
Net margin	$1.80 + 0 \times \Delta i$	$1.80 - 4 \times \Delta i$
Rate 1: 8%	1.80	1.98
Rate 2: 11%	1.80	1.86
Business scenario	A	B
Fixed rate amount: 8	Hedging H1	Hedging H2
Net margin	$1.80 + 4 \times \Delta i$	$1.98 + 0 \times \Delta i$
Rate 1: 8%	1.80	1.98
Rate 2: 11%	1.92	1.98

In order to define the best hedging solutions, we need to compare the risk–return combinations.

RISK–RETURN COMBINATIONS

First, the risk–return profiles generated by the two hedging solutions are calculated. By comparing them, we see how several funding and hedging solutions compare, and how to optimize the solution given a target risk level. For each matrix, the average value of the margins and the volatility[2] across the cells of each matrix are calculated. The Sharpe ratio, the ratio of the expected margin to the margin volatility, is also calculated. This ratio is an example of a risk-adjusted measure of profitability[3]. The results are as given in Table 18.6.

TABLE 18.6 Net margin matrix and risk–return combinations

Hedging H1	A	B	Mean	1.860
Rate 1	1.80	1.98	Volatility	0.085
Rate 2	1.80	1.86	Mean/volatility	21.920
Hedging H2	A	B	Mean	1.920
Rate 1	1.80	1.98	Volatility	0.085
Rate 2	1.92	1.98	Mean/volatility	22.627

The first solution generates a lower average margin with the same risk. The second generates a higher margin, with the same risk. The best solution is therefore H2. The Sharpe ratio is greater with H2.

---

[2] The volatility is the square root of the sum of the squared deviations of the margin from the mean. All values in the matrix have the same probability. The expected value is the arithmetic mean.

[3] The Sharpe ratio is a convenient measure of the risk-adjusted performance of a portfolio. It also serves when modelling the credit risk of the portfolio.

In general, a large number of hedging solutions are considered. When graphed in the risk–return space, they generate a cloud of points[4]. Each dot summarizes a matrix combining several target variable values corresponding to each pair of interest rate scenarios and business scenarios. In spite of the high number of simulations, changing hedging scenarios simply moves the dots in the risk–return space. Some solutions appear inefficient immediately. They are those with an expected return lower than others, at the same risk level or, alternatively, those with the same expected return as others, but with a higher risk. These solutions are inefficient since others dominate them. The only solutions to consider are those that dominate others. The set of these solutions is the 'efficient frontier' (Figure 18.3).

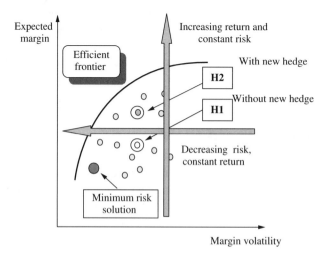

FIGURE 18.3   Risk–return combinations

A risk–return combination is efficient if there is no other better solution at any given level of risk or return. The efficiency criterion leads to several combinations rather than a single one. The optimization problem is as follows:

- Minimize the volatility of the margin subject to the constraint of a constant return.
- Maximize the expected margin subject to the constraint of a constant risk.

For each level of profitability, or of return, there is an optimal solution. When the risk, or the return, varies, the optimum solution moves along the efficient frontier. In order to choose a solution, a risk level has to be set first. For instance, the minimum risk leads to the combination located at the left and on the efficient frontier. When both interest rate and business risks interact, solutions neutralizing the margin risk do not exist. Only a minimum risk solution exists.

---

[4] The graph shows the risk–return profiles in a general case. In the example, the only variable that changes the risk–return combination is the gap after funding. When this gap varies continuously, the risk–return combinations move along a curve. The upper 'leg' of this curve is the efficient frontier of this example.

19

ALM 'Risk and Return' Reporting and Policy

The Asset–Liability Management (ALM) reporting system should provide all elements for decision-making purposes to the ALM Committee (ALCO). The reporting should provide answers to such essential questions as: Why did the interest income vary in the last period? Which interest income drivers caused the variations? Funding, investment and hedging issues necessitate reporting along the two basic financial dimensions, earnings and risks. To move back and forth from a financial perspective, risk and return, to a business policy view, it is also necessary to break down risk and performance measures by transaction, product family, market segment and business line. ALM reporting links gaps, interest incomes and values of transactions to business units, products, markets and business lines. Reports slice gaps, incomes and gaps along these dimensions. To analyse the interest income variations, ALM reports should break down the variations due to the interest income drivers: changes in the structure of the existing by level of interest earned or paid, due to both amortization effects plus new business; changes of the yield curve shape. Moving back and forth from financial to business dimensions, plus the necessity of relating interest margin changes to identified drivers, creates high demands on the ALM information system, which should record all business and financial data.

This chapter provides examples of reporting related to common ALCO issues. The first section lists the typical ALCO agenda for a commercial bank. The second section describes the reporting system specifications. The third and fourth sections illustrate breakdowns of gaps and interest incomes by product family and market segment. The last section focuses on explaining interest income variations.

ALM MISSIONS AND AGENDA

Table 19.1 lists the basic missions and agenda of ALCO. The next subsections discuss them further.

TABLE 19.1   ALM scope and missions

Liquidity management	Funding deficits
	Investing excess funds
	Liquidity ratios
Measuring and controlling interest rate risk	Gaps and NPV reporting
Recommendations off-balance sheet	Hedging policy and instruments
	Hedging programmes
Recommendations on-balance sheet	Flows: new business
	Existing portfolio
Transfer pricing system	Economic prices and benchmarks
	Pricing benchmarks
Preparing the ALCO	Recent history, variance analysis (projections versus realizations)
	GAP and NPV reports
	'What if' analyses and simulations . . .
Risk-adjusted pricing	Mark-up to transfer prices (from credit risk allocation system)
	Mispricing: gaps target prices versus effective prices
Reporting to general management	

The ALCO Typical Agenda and Issues

Without discussing further some obvious items of the list in Table 19.1, we detail some representative issues that need ALCO attention.

Historical Analysis

Typical questions include the following:

- How do volumes, margins and fees behave?
- How do previous projections differ from realizations, in terms of interest margins, fees and volumes?
- What explains the actual–projected volume gaps, based on actual and projected interest rate gaps, and the product mix changes?

A review of commercial actions and their results is necessary to see which corrective actions or new actions are required. These involve promotions and incentives for customers, or all development policies in terms of product mix. Without this historical, or ex post, analysis, it remains difficult to look forward.

On-balance Sheet Actions

There is an important distinction between existing portfolios, which generate the bulk of revenues, and new business for future developments. Actions on the volume–product mix and pricing have an impact on new business. All future actions need analysis both in business terms and in risk–return terms. New development policies require projections of risk exposure and revenue levels. Conversely, interest rate and liquidity projections help define new business policies. This is a two-way interaction. Interest rate risk and liquidity risk are not the only factors influencing these decisions. However, the new transactions typically represent only a small fraction of the total balance sheet. Other actions on the existing portfolio might be more effective. They include commercial actions, such as incentives for customers to convert some products into others, for example fixed to floating rate loans and vice versa, or increasing the service 'intensity', i.e. the number of services, per customer.

Off-balance Sheet Actions

Off-balance sheet actions are, mainly, hedging policies through derivatives and setting up a hedging programme for both the short and long-term. Hedges crystallize in the revenues the current market conditions, so that there are no substitutes to 'on-balance sheet' actions. In low interest rate environments, forward hedges (swaps) embed current low rates in the future revenues. In high interest rate environments, high interest rate volatility becomes the issue, rather than the interest rate level. The hedging policy arbitrages between revenues level, interest rate risk volatility and the costs of hedging (both opportunity costs and direct costs). The financial policy relates to funding, hedging and investing. However, it depends on business policy guidelines. Defining and revising the hedging programme depends on expectations with respect to interest rates, on the trade-off between hedging risk versus level of revenues, and on the 'risk appetite' of the bank, some willing to neutralize risk and others betting on favourable market movements to various degrees.

OVERVIEW OF THE ALM REPORTING SYSTEM

The ALM reporting system moves from the ALM risk data warehouse down to final reports, some of them being purely financial and others cross-tabulating risk and return with business dimensions. The business perspective requires in fact any type of breakdown of the bank aggregates, by product, market segment and business unit. In addition, reporting the sources of gaps, along any of these relevant dimensions, raises the issue of what contributes to risk and return. Therefore, the system should provide functionalities to 'drill down' into aggregates to zoom in on the detailed data. Moreover, front-ends should include 'what if' and simulation capabilities, notably for decision-making purposes (Figure 19.1).

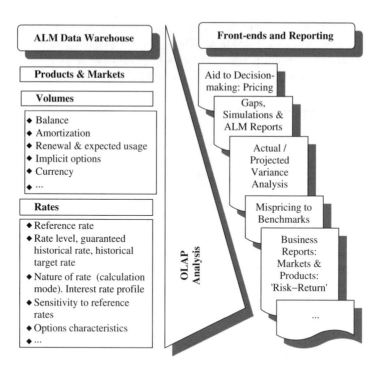

FIGURE 19.1   ALM data warehouse, front-ends and reporting

BREAKING DOWN GAPS BY SEGMENTS

In this section, we illustrate the breakdown of gaps and 'all-in revenues' (interest plus fees) along the product and market dimensions. We show gaps and volumes first, and gaps and volumes in conjunction with 'all-in margins' in a second set of figures. All sample charts focus on risks measured by gaps. Since gaps are differences in volumes of assets and liabilities, there is no difficulty in splitting these aggregates into specific product or market segment contributions measured by their outstanding balances of assets and liabilities.

The time profile of existing assets and liabilities is the static gap profile. Figure 19.2 shows the declining outstanding balances of assets and liabilities. The static gap, measured by assets minus liabilities, tends to be positive in the first periods, which implies a need for new funding. The picture is very different from the dynamic profiles because of the volume of new transactions during each of the first three periods. Figure 19.3 shows total asset and liability values, together with the liquidity gaps and the variable interest rate gaps. Since the total volumes of assets and liabilities are used, these gaps are dynamic. The positive liquidity gaps represent a permanent need for new funds at each period, and the negative variable interest rate gaps show that the bank interest income is adversely influenced by rising interest rates. The dynamic time profile of gaps increases up to period 3 and then declines because we assume that no projections are feasible beyond

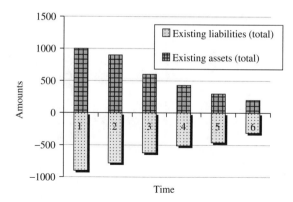

FIGURE 19.2   Static gaps time profile

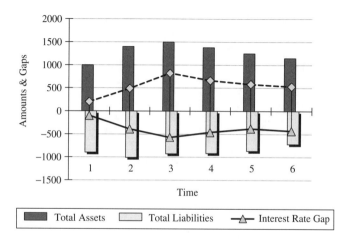

FIGURE 19.3   Assets and liabilities and the liquidity and variable interest rate gaps

period 3. After period 3, the time profile becomes static and total assets and liabilities decline.

Breakdown of Dynamic Gaps by Segments

Figures 19.4 and 19.5 show the dynamic time profiles of assets and liabilities and their breakdown into six hypothetical segments, at each date. Bars represent volumes of assets or liabilities. The differences are the gaps. Each bar is broken down into the six segments of interest. The bar charts show which assets and liabilities contribute more or less to the gap. This type of reporting links the gap and asset and liability time profiles to the commercial policy. For instance, we see that the top segment of each time bar is among the highest volumes of assets contributing to the positive liquidity gap, or the need for

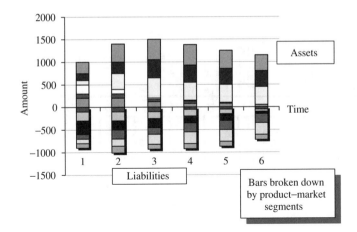

FIGURE 19.4   Breakdown of the liquidity gaps by segments

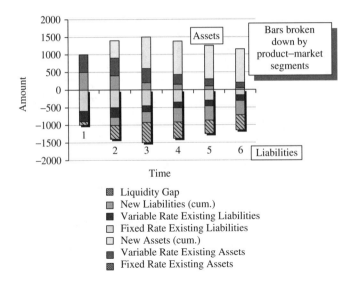

▪ Liquidity Gap
▪ New Liabilities (cum.)
▪ Variable Rate Existing Liabilities
□ Fixed Rate Existing Liabilities
□ New Assets (cum.)
▪ Variable Rate Existing Assets
▪ Fixed Rate Existing Assets

FIGURE 19.5   Breakdown of interest rate gaps and volumes by segments

new funds. Some assets and liabilities are variable rate and others fixed rate. Figure 19.5 shows a similar breakdown using the type of rate, fixed or variable.

These figures are not sufficient, however, since we have only the contributions to gaps without the levels of margins.

BREAKDOWN OF REVENUES AND GAPS, AND THE PRODUCTS–MARKETS MIX

The revenues might be:

- All-in margins, meaning that they combine various sources of revenues.

- Pure interest rate spreads, such as customers' rate minus any internal transfer rate used as the reference for defining commercial margins.
- Pre-operating expenses, and in some cases, post-direct operating expenses.

Breakdown of Interest Income by Segments

Figure 19.6 shows the contributions to the 'all-in margin' (interest margin and fees) of the different types of products or markets across time. The vertical axis shows the all-in revenue divided by the asset volume, and the horizontal axis shows time. The profitability measure is a 'Return On Assets' (ROA). This is not a risk-adjusted measure, since that would require capital allocation. In this case, the total cumulated margin, as a percentage, seems more or less constant at 10%. Hence, the interest incomes in dollars are increasing with volume since the percentage remains constant while volumes grow in the first 3 years.

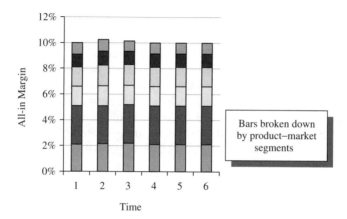

FIGURE 19.6 Breakdown of percentages of 'all-in margins' by segments

This chart shows only interest income contributions, without comparing them with contributions to gaps. Therefore, it is incomplete.

Contributions of Segments to Revenues and Gaps

Figure 19.7 compares both interest income and volumes. The chart brings together contributions to gaps and margins in percentages (of volumes) at a given date. The six segments of the example correspond to the six bars along the horizontal axis. The comparison shows contrasting combinations. Low volume and low margin for the fourth segment make it a loser (relatively), high volume and high margin for the first segment make it a winner (relatively).

'Gap Risk'–Return Profiles

A common financial view plots volumes (gap risk) against incomes (in value) in the same chart. The traditional business view suggests that more volume with high income is

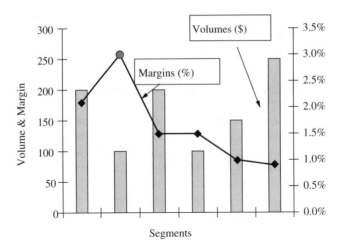

FIGURE 19.7   Comparing margins and volumes by products and market lines

better, and conversely. Under this view, the volume–income space is split into four basic quadrants, and the game is to try to reach the area above the diagonal making volume at least in line with margins: more volume with higher margins and less volume with lower incomes. An alternative view highlights volumes as contributions to gaps. It turns out that this is the same as the risk–income view when volume measures risk, since volume is the contribution to gaps. Hence, the two views are consistent. In Figure 19.8, each dot represents one of the six segments. Some contribute little to gaps and have higher income,

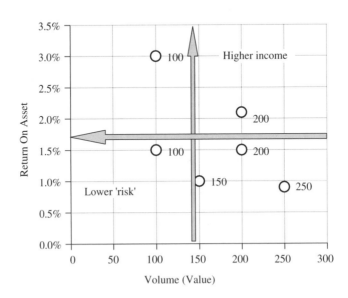

FIGURE 19.8   Margins versus volumes (contribution to liquidity and interest rate risks)

some contribute to both with similar magnitude, and others contribute to gaps and little to income. 'Losers' are the segments combining high volumes with low incomes. The low volume–high income segments are dilemmas, since it might be worth taking on more risk for these. The first diagonal dots are acceptable, with the 'winners' being the high volume–high income combinations.

Another general comment is that the view on risks is truncated. There is not yet any adjustment for credit risk in incomes since gap risk is not credit risk. Hence, credit risk versus income, or the view of Risk-adjusted Return on Capital (RaRoC), provides a global view on the complete risk–return profiles. The conclusion is that the reports of this chapter provide useful views on the sources of gap risk, but they do not serve the purpose of optimizing the portfolio considering all risks. This issue relates more to the credit risk and to the related RaRoC of segments or transactions.

ANALYSIS OF THE VARIATIONS OF INTEREST INCOME

Often, it is necessary to explain the changes in the interest margin between two dates. In addition, with projections and budgets, there are deviations between actual interest income and projected values from the previous projections.

The sources of variations of interest income are: the change in portfolio structure by level of interest rate; the new business of the elapsed period; the changes in the yield curve.

- The amortization of the existing portfolio creates variations of interest income because assets and liabilities earn or pay different interest rates. When they amortize the corresponding revenues or costs disappear. This effect is unrelated to the variations of interest rates. Tracking this variation between any two dates requires having all information on flows resulting from amortization and on the level of rates of each individual asset and liability. To isolate this effect, it is necessary to track the portfolio structure by interest rate level.
- The new business creates variations as well, both because of the pure volume effect on income and costs and because of the new rates of these assets and liabilities. New assets and liabilities substitute progressively for those that amortize, but they earn or pay different rates.
- The changes in the yield curve create variations of the interest income independent of volume variations of assets and liabilities. Note that the gap provides only the change due to a parallel shift of the yield curve, while commercial banks are sensitive to the slope of the yield curve because of the maturity gaps between interest rates of liabilities and assets.

Moreover, the level of interest income depends on the portfolio structure by products and market segments since each of these generates different levels of spread. It becomes necessary to trace back such deviations to the actual versus projected differences between all interest margin drivers, volumes, interest rates and commercial percentage margins. This allows us to allocate the predicted–actual margin variance to errors in past interest expectations and to the actual–predicted variances between volumes and percentage margins. This analysis is required to understand the changes in interest margins between two ALM committees. Corrective actions depend on which drivers explain the variations of the interest margin.

Using gaps to explain the changes in interest income is not sufficient in general. First, gaps show the sensitivity of the interest income due to a parallel shift of the interest rate used as reference. If we use a unique gap, we ignore non-parallel shifts of the yield curve. With as many gaps as there are interest rates, it is feasible to track the change in interest income due to changes of all interest rates used as references. If we assume no portfolio structure change between two dates, implying that the interest margin as a percentage is independent of volume, the change in interest income between any two dates depends on the shifts of interest rates, the change in volumes and the interaction effect of volume–interest rate. This is the usual problem of explaining variances of costs or revenues, resulting from variances of prices, volumes and product mix. In the case of interest income, there is variation due to the pure volume change, the gap effect due to the variations of the interest rates between the two dates, and an interaction effect.

The interaction effect when both price (interest rate) and volume vary results from the simplified equation using a single interest rate:

$$\Delta IM = \Delta[i \times (A - L)] = (A - L) \times \Delta i + i \times \Delta(A - L) + \Delta i \times \Delta(A - L)$$

In the equation, ΔIM is the interest margin, $(A - L)$ is the difference between interest rate-sensitive assets and liabilities, or the variable rate gap, and i is the unique interest rate driver. The interaction term results from the change in product between the gap and the interest rate. Table 19.2 shows how these effects combine when there is no portfolio structure effect.

TABLE 19.2 The analysis of volume and price effects on the variation of interest margin

Actual–predicted variance $\Delta IM = IM_1 - IM_0$	2.80
ΔIM due to interest rate variations at constant margins and volume	−0.90
ΔIM due to volume variations at constant interest rate and margins	3.00
ΔIM due to price variations (interest rate and margins) combined with volume variations (interaction effect)	0.70
ΔIM	2.80

Note that the calculations depend on the numerical values of the start and end values of rates and volumes. In this example, the 2.80 increase of margin is due to:

1. A decrease of −0.90 due to a negative variable rate interest gap at initial date combined with an interest rate increase.
2. An increase of +3.00 due to the expansion of assets and liabilities between initial and final dates.

3. An increase of +0.70 due to the increased customer rates of new assets and liabilities, resulting from the increase in interest rates and from any variation of commercial margins.

In general, there is an additional effect portfolio structure, depending on the amortization of existing assets and liabilities plus the new business. For instance, there are only two assets and a single debt. The two assets earn the rates 10% and 12%, while the debt pays 8%. Total assets are 100, divided into two assets of 50 each, and the debt is 100. At the end of period 1 (between dates 0 and 1), the asset earning 12% amortizes and the bank originates a new loan earning 11%. During period 1, the revenue is $50 \times 10\% + 50 \times 12\% - 100 \times 8\% = 0.050 + 0.060 - 0.080 = 0.030$. Even if there is no change in interest rate and overall volume, the interest income of the next period 2 changes due to the substitution of the old loan by the new loan. The revenue becomes $50 \times 10\% + 50 \times 11\% - 100 \times 8\% = 0.050 + 0.055 - 0.080 = 0.025$. This change is due to the change in portfolio structure by level of interest rates. This change might be independent of interest rate change if, for instance, the new loan earns less than the first one due to increased competition between lenders.

SECTION 7

Options and Convexity Risk in Banking

20

Implicit Options Risk

This chapter explains the nature of embedded, or implicit, options and details their payoff, in the event of exercise for the individual borrower.

Implicit options exist essentially in retail banking and for individuals. A typical example of an implicit option is the facility of prepaying, or renegotiating, a fixed rate loan when rates decline. The borrower's benefit is the interest costs saving, increasing with the gap between current rates and the loan fixed rate, and with the residual maturity of the loan. The cost for the bank is the mirror image of the borrower's benefit. The bank's margin over the fixed rate of debt matching such loans narrows, or eventually turns out negative. Other banking options relate to variable rate loans with caps on interest rates, or to transfers of resources from demand deposits to interest-earning products, when interest rates increase, raising the financial cost to the bank.

Embedded options in banking balance sheets raise a number of issues: What is the cost for the lender and the pricing mark-up that would compensate this cost? What is the risk–return profile of implicit options for the lender? What is the portfolio downside risk for options, or downside 'convexity risk'? How can banks hedge such risks? Because the outstanding balances of loans with embedded options are quite large, several models based on historical data help in assessing the prepayment rates of borrowers. Prepayment models make the option exercise a function of the differential between the rate of loans and the prevailing rates, and of demographic and behavioural factors, which also influence the attitude of individuals. From such prepayments, the payoffs for borrowers and the costs for lenders follow. Payoffs under exercise differ from the value of the option. The value of the option is higher than the payoff as long as there is a chance that future payoffs increase beyond their current value if rates drift further away.

This chapter assesses the benefit to the borrower, calculated as the payoff of the option under various interest rate levels. For a long-term fixed rate loan, the option payoff is the time profile of the differential savings (annuities) after and before exercising the renegotiation option. Alternatively, it is the present value of these cash savings at the date of renegotiation. The payoff increases with the differential between the initial and the new interest rates and the residual maturity of the loan. The next chapter addresses the valuation of options based on the simulation of representative interest rate scenarios.

The first section details the nature of options embedded in various banking and insurance contracts. Subsequent sections illustrate prepayment risk. The second section refers briefly to prepayment models. The last section calculates the payoff of the option under various levels of interest rates, using a simple fixed rate loan as an example.

OPTIONAL RISK: TWO EXAMPLES

The most well known options are the prepayment options embedded in mortgage loans. These represent a large amount of the outstanding balances, and their maturity is usually very long. The prepayment option is quite valuable for fixed rate loans because it usually has a very long horizon and significant chances of being in-the-money during the life of the loan. There are other examples of embedded options. Guaranteed rate insurance contracts are similar for insurance companies, except that they are liabilities instead of assets.

The prepayment option has more value (for a fixed rate loan) when the interest rate decreases. Prepaying the loan and contracting a new loan at a lower rate, eventually with the same bank (renegotiation), might be valuable to the customer. The prepayment usually generates a cost to the borrower, but that cost can be lower than the expected gain from exercise. For instance, a prepayment penalty of 3% of the outstanding balance might be imposed on the borrower. Nevertheless, if the rate declines substantially, this cost does not offset the gain of borrowing at a lower rate.

Prepayments are an issue for the lender if fixed rate borrowings back the existing loans. Initially, there is no interest rate risk and the loan margin remains the original one. However, if the rates decline, customers might substitute a new loan for the old one at a lower price, while the debt stays at the same rate, thereby deteriorating the margin.

For insurance contracts, the issue is symmetrical. The insurance companies provide guaranteed return contracts. In these contracts, the customer benefits from a minimum rate of return over the life of the contract, plus the benefit of a higher return if interest rates increase. In order to have that return, the insurance company invests at a fixed rate to match the interest cost of the contract. If the rate increases, the beneficiary can renew the contract in order to obtain a higher rate. Nevertheless, the insurance company still earns the fixed rate investment in its balance sheet. Hence, the margin declines.

The obvious solution to prepayments of fixed rate loans is to make variable rate loans. However, these do not offer much protection against a rise in interest rates for the borrower, unless covenants are included to cap the rate. Therefore, fixed rate loans or variable rate loans with a cap on the borrower's rate are still common in many countries.

A theoretical way of limiting losses would be to make the customer pay for the option. This implies valuing the option and that competition allows pricing it to customers. Another way would be to hedge the option risk, and pay the cost of hedging. Caps and floors are adapted for such protections. The lender can hedge the risk of a decrease in the rate of the loan by using a floor that guarantees a minimum fixed return, even though the rate of the new loan is lower. An insurance company can use a cap to set a maximum value on the rate guaranteed to customers in the case of a rise in interest rates. However, such hedges have a cost for banks. The underlying issue is to determine the value that customers should pay to compensate the additional cost of options for banks.

MODELLING PREPAYMENTS

The modelling of prepayments is necessary to project the gap profiles. There is a significant difference between contractual flows and effective maturity. The purpose of models is to relate prepayment rates to those factors that influence them[1]. Prepayment models can also help to value the option. If such models capture the relationship between prepayments and interest rate, it becomes easier to value options by simulating a large number of prepayment scenarios.

When prepayments are considered, the expected return of a loan will differ from the original return due to the rollover of the loan at a lower rate at future dates. Models can help to determine the amount subject to renewal, and the actual cost of these loans, as a function of interest scenarios. If multiple scenarios are used, the expected return of the loan is the average over many possible outcomes. The valuation of options follows such lines, except that models are not always available or accurate enough.

Models specify how the prepayment rate, the ratio of prepayment to outstanding balances, changes over time, based on several factors. The simplest model is the Constant Prepayment Rate (CPR) model that simply states that the prepayment at any date is the product of a prepayment rate with the outstanding balances of loans (Figure 20.1). The prepayment rate usually depends on the age of the loans. During the early stages of the loans, the prepayment rate increases. Then, it tends to have a more or less stable value for mature loans. Modifying the model parameters to fit the specifics of a loan portfolio is feasible. The simple prepayment rate model captures the basic features of the renegotiation behaviour: renegotiation does not occur in the early stage of a loan because the rates do not drift suddenly away and because the rate negotiation is still recent. When the loan gets closer to maturity, the renegotiation has fewer benefits for the borrower because savings occur only in the residual time to maturity. Therefore, renegotiation rates increase steadily, reach a level stage and then stay there or eventually level off at periods close to maturity. Hence, the models highlight the role of ageing of loans, as a major input of

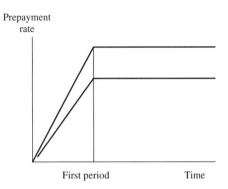

FIGURE 20.1 'Constant Prepayment Rate' models

---

[1] See, for example, Bartlett (1989) for a review of prepayment issues and models serving for securitizations of residential mortgages.

prepayment models, in addition to the rate differentials. This makes it necessary to isolate cohorts of loans, defined by period of origination, to capture the 'seasoning effect', or 'ageing effect', as well as the rate differential, which varies across cohorts.

Other models use such factors as the level of interest rate, the time path of interest rates, the ageing of the loan, the economic conditions and the specifics of customers. These factors serve to fit the modelled prepayment rates to the observed ones. However, such models require a sufficient amount of historical data. An additional complexity is that the time path of interest rates is relevant for options. If the rates decline substantially at the early stage of a loan, they trigger an early prepayment. If the decline occurs later, the prepayment will also occur later. Therefore, the current level of interest rates is not sufficient to capture timing effects. The entire path of interest rates is relevant. This is one reason why the prepayment rate does not relate easily to the current interest level, as intuition might suggest. The valuation of the option uses models of the time path of rates and of the optimum prepayment or renegotiation behaviour (see Chapter 21).

GAINS AND LOSSES FROM THE PREPAYMENT OPTION

In this section, an example serves to make explicit the gains for the borrower and the losses for the lender. The gain is valued under the assumption of immediate exercise once the option is in-the-money. In reality, the option is not exercised as soon as it becomes in-the-money. The exercise behaviour depends on future expected gains, which can be higher or lower than the current gain from immediate exercise. This is the time value of the option. The next chapter captures this feature using a valuation methodology of options.

The example used is that of a fixed rate and amortizing loan, repaid with constant annuities including interest and capital. The customer renews the loan at a new rate if he exercises the prepayment option. The loan might be representative of a generation of loan portfolios. In actual portfolios, the behaviour of different generations of loans (differing by age) will differ. The gain from prepayment results from the characteristics of the new loan. The new loan has a maturity equal to the residual maturity of the original loan at the exercise date. The decision rule is to prepay and renew the debt as soon as the combined operation 'prepayment plus new loan' becomes profitable for the borrower.

If the borrower repays the loan, he might have penalty costs, for instance 3% of the outstanding balance. The gain from prepayment results from the difference between the annuities of the original and the new loan plus the penalty cost. It spreads over the entire time profile of differential annuities between the old and the new loan until maturity. Either we measure these differences or we calculate their present value. The original loan has a 12% fixed rate, with an amount of 1000, and with a maturity of 8 years. Table 20.1 details the repayment schedule of the loan.

The repayment or renegotiation occurs at date 4, when the interest rate decreases to 10%. The new annuities result from the equality between their present value, calculated as of date 4, and the amount borrowed. The amount of the new loan is the outstanding balance at date 4 of the old loan plus the penalty, which is 3% of this principal balance. It is identical to the present value of the new annuities calculated at the date of renewal at the 10% rate until maturity:

Present value of future annuities at $t = 4$, at 10%

$$= \text{outstanding balance at date } 4 \times (1 + 3\%)$$

TABLE 20.1   Repayment schedule of the original loan

Amount 1000		Maturity 8 years			Discount rate 12%				Annuity 201.30	
Date	0	1	2	3	4	5	6	7	8	
PV[a] at 12%	1000									
Annuity (rounded)		201.30	201.30	201.30	201.30	201.30	201.30	201.30	201.30	
Principal repayment		81.30	91.06	101.99	114.22	127.93	143.28	160.48	179.73	
Outstanding balance		918.70	827.64	725.65	611.43	483.50	340.21	179.73	0.00	
Discount rate[b]	12.00%									

[a]PV is the present value of future annuities.
[b]The discount rate is the rate that makes the present value of future annuities equal to the amount borrowed. It is equal in this case to the nominal rate (12%) used to calculate interest payments.

The gain for the borrower is the present value, as of date 4, of the difference between the old and new annuities. The present value of the old annuities at the new rate is the market value of the outstanding debt at date 4. The value of the old debt becomes higher than the outstanding balance if the rate decreases. This change is a gain for the lender and a loss for the borrower. The economic gain from prepayment, for the borrower, as of the rate reset date T, is equal to the difference between the present values of the old and the new debts:

$$PV_{T,\text{new rate}}(\text{old debt}) - PV_{T,\text{new rate}} \text{ (new debt)}$$

$$= PV_{T,\text{new rate}}(\text{old debt}) - \text{outstanding balance} \times (1 + 3\%)$$

$PV_{T,\text{new rate}}$ is the present value at the prepayment date ($T = 4$) and at the new rate (10%).
The calculation of both market values of debt and annuities is shown in Table 20.2. The new annuity is 198.75, lower than the former annuity of 201.30, in spite of the additional

TABLE 20.2   Gains of prepayment for the borrower

Amount			1000		Penalty			3.00%	
Initial rate			12.00%		Date of prepayment			4	
Original maturity in years			8		New rate			10.00%	
Annuity			201						
Schedule									
Date	1	2	3	4	5	6	7	8	
Principal repayment	81.30	91.06	101.99	114.22	127.93	143.28	160.48	179.73	
Outstanding balance	918.70	827.64	725.65	611.43	483.50	340.21	179.73	0.00	
Penalty (3%)	0	0	0	18.34	0	0	0	0	
New debt	0	0	0	629.77	0	0	0	0	
Old annuity	201.30	201.30	201.30	201.30	201.30	201.30	201.30	201.30	
New annuity	0	0	0	0	198.75	198.75	198.75	198.75	
Annuity profile	201.30	201.30	201.30	201.30	198.75	198.75	198.75	198.75	
Differential flows (new−old)	0	0	0	0	2.63	2.63	2.63	2.63	
Gain for the borrower									
Present value at date 4 at the 10% rate									
PV old debt			638.10						
PV new date			629.77						
Present value of gain at 4			8.33						

cost due to the 3% penalty. The annual gain in value is 2.63. The present value of this gain, at date 4, and at the new rate (10%), is 8.33.

The borrower gain increases when the new rate decreases. Above 12%, there is no gain. Below 12%, the gain depends on the difference between the penalty in case of prepayment and the differential gain between the old and the new loans. The gain can be valued at various levels of the new interest rate (Table 20.3).

Table 20.3 gives the value of the old debt at the current new rate. The outstanding balance at date 4 is 611.43. The market value of the debt is equal to 611.43 only when the rate is 12%. The exercise price of the option is equal to the prepayment amount, which is the outstanding balance plus the 3% penalty, or $611.43(1 + 3\%) = 629.77$, rounded to 630. This price is determined by the prepayment date since the amortization schedule is contractual. The present value of gains, at date 4, is the difference between the market value of the old debt and 630, which is the present value of the new debt. The exercise value of the option is the maximum of 0 and the market value of the old debt minus 630. It is given in the last column of Table 20.3.

TABLE 20.3 Borrower gains from prepayment at date 4

New rate	PV(old debt) at 4 12% (a)	PV(new debt) at 4 (b)	PV of gains at 4 (c = b − a)	Exercise value of the option at 4 (d = max[0, c])
6%	698	630	68	68
7%	682	630	52	52
8%	667	630	37	37
9%	652	630	22	22
10%	638	630	8	8
11%	625	630	−5	0
12%	611	630	−18	0
13%	599	630	−31	0
14%	587	630	−43	0

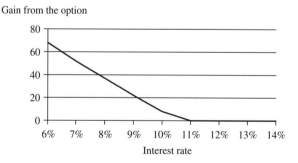

FIGURE 20.2 Payoff profile of the prepayment option

The borrower gains are higher when the interest rate decreases. If the rate increases, the option has a zero exercise value. The profile of payoffs as a function of interest rate has the usual shape of the payoff profile of an option. Positive gains appear when the decline in interest rate below 12% is sufficient to offset the penalty (Figure 20.2).

The same profile is the cost of the exercise of the option for the lender. This cost becomes very important when the decline in rates is significant. If the rate moves down to 8%, the present value of the loss for the bank reaches 37. This is 3.7% of the original capital, or $37/667 = 5.5\%$ of the outstanding capital at date 4. This example is simplified, but it demonstrates the importance of valuing options. The next chapter provides an example of the valuation of a prepayment option.

21

The Value of Implicit Options

The value of an option combines its liquidation value, or the payoff under exercise, plus the value of waiting further for larger payoffs. Valuing an option requires simulating all future outcomes for interest rates, at various periods, to determine when the option is in-the-money and what are the gains under exercise. The option value discounts the expected future gains, using the simulated rates as discount rates. Various interest rate models potentially apply to the valuation of options[1]. The purpose of this chapter is to illustrate how they apply for valuing prepayment options.

The value of options depends on the entire time path of the interest rates from origination to maturity, because interest rate changes can trigger early or late exercise of the option. This is a significant departure from classical balance sheet Asset–Liability Management (ALM) models, which use in general a small number of scenarios. The valuation of options necessitates simulating the future time paths of interest rates and deriving all future corresponding payoffs.

The interest simulation technique applies because it generates the entire spectrum of payoffs of the option up to a certain horizon, including all intermediate values. The valuation is an average of all future payoffs weighted by probabilities of occurrences. In this chapter, we use the simple technique based on 'binomial trees'. Other examples of time path simulations are given in Section 11 of this book.

From a risk perspective, the issue is to find the expected and worst-case values of the option from the distribution of its future values at various time points. From a pricing perspective, the option is an asset for the borrower and it generates an expected cost for the bank, which the bank should charge to borrowers. The worst-case value makes sense in a 'Value at Risk' (VaR) framework, when considering worst-case losses for determining

---

[1] The bibliography is rather exhaustive and technical. A good introduction to the valuation of options is Hull (2000).

economic capital. The sections on Net Present Value (NPV) and optional risk develop this view further.

The expected value of options relates to pricing. Pricing optional risk to borrowers requires converting a single present value as of today into a percentage mark-up. The mark-up reflects the difference in values between a straight fixed rate debt, that the borrower cannot repay[2], and a 'callable debt', which is a straight debt combined with the prepayment option. The callable loan is an asset for the lender that has a lower value than the straight debt for the bank, the difference being the option value. Conversely, the callable loan is a liability for the borrower that has a lower value for him because he can sell it back to the lender (he has a put option).

The percentage mark-up is the 'Option-Adjusted Spread' (OAS). The OAS is the spread added to the loan rate making the value of the 'callable' loan identical to the value of a straight loan. The callable debt, viewed as an asset held by the bank, has a lower value than the straight debt for the lender. To bring the value of the straight debt in line with the value of the debt minus the value of the option, it is necessary to increase the discount rates applied to the future cash flows of the debt. The additional spread is the OAS. For pricing the option, banks add the OAS to the customer rate, if competition allows.

The first section summarizes some basic principles and findings on option valuation. The second section uses the binomial tree technique to simulate the time path of interest rates. The third section derives the value of the prepayment option from the simulated 'tree' of interest rate values. The last section calculates the corresponding OAS.

RISK AND PRICING ISSUES WITH IMPLICIT OPTIONS

The valuation process of implicit options addresses both issues of pricing and of risk simultaneously. From a pricing perspective, the expected value of the option should be a cost transferred to customers. From a risk perspective, the issue is to find the worst-case values of options. In fact, the same technique applies to both issues, since valuation requires simulation of the entire time paths of interest rates to find all possible payoffs.

The valuation issue shows the limitations of the discrete yield curve scenarios used in ALM. The ALCO would like to concentrate on a few major assumptions, while the option risk requires considering a comprehensive set of interest rate time paths. Pricing an option as the expected value of all outcomes requires finding all its potential values under a full range of variations of interest rates. This is why the two blocks of 'ALCO simulations' and 'options valuation' often do not rely on the same technique.

The value of an option is an expected value over all future outcomes. The interest rate risk is that of an increase in that value, since it is a loss for the bank, measured as the loss percentile at a forward horizon. Simulating all interest rate scenarios up to the forward horizon and after provides both.

---

[2] The terminology is confusing. In fact the 'callable loan' is a straight fixed rate loan plus a put option to sell it at a lower than market value when interest rates decline. The value of the loan for the bank (lender) is that of the straight debt minus the put value, which increases when rates decline. It is more like a 'putable loan'.

The value of an interest rate option depends on several parameters. They include the interest rate volatility, the maturity of the option and the exercise price, the risk-free rate. There are many option valuation models. Black's (1976) model allows pricing interest rate options. The model applies to European options, and assumes that the underlying asset has a lognormal distribution at maturity. In the case of loan prepayments, the borrower has the right to sell to the bank the loan for its face value, which is a put option on a bond. Black's model assumes that the bond price is lognormal. This allows us to derive formulas for the option price. In this chapter, we concentrate on numerical techniques, which allow us to show the entire process of simulations, rather than using the closed-form formula. For long-term options, such as mortgage options, the Heath, Jarrow and Morton model (Heath et al., 1992) allows more freedom than previous models in customizing the volatility term structure, and addressing the need to periodically revalue long-term options such as those of mortgage loans. They require using Monte Carlo simulations. However, such advanced models are more difficult to implement. Simple techniques provide reasonable estimates, as shown in the example.

We concentrate on 'American' options allowing exercise at any time between current date and maturity. As soon as the option provides a positive payoff, the option holder faces a dilemma between waiting for a higher payoff and the risk of losing the current option positive liquidation value because of future adverse deviations. The choice of early or late exercise depends on interest rate expectations.

The risk drivers of options are the entire time paths of interest rates up to maturity. The basic valuation process includes several steps, which are identical to those used for measuring market risk VaR, because this implies revaluing a portfolio of market instruments at a forward date. In the current case, we need both the current price for valuing the additional cost charged to borrowers and the distribution of future values for valuing downside risk. The four main steps addressing both valuation as of today and forward downside risk are:

- Simulate the stochastic process of interest rates, through models or Monte Carlo simulations or an intermediate technique, such as 'binomial trees', explained below.
- Revalue the option at each time point between current date and horizon.
- Derive the 'as of date value' from the entire spectrum of future values and their probabilities. The current valuation addresses the pricing issue.
- When the range of values is at a forward date, the process allows us to find potential deviations of values at this horizon. This technique serves for measuring the downside risk rather than the price.

Intermediate techniques, such as binomial trees, are convenient and simple for valuing options[3]. To illustrate the technique, the following section uses the simplest version of the common 'binomial' methodology. The technique of interest rate trees is a discrete time representation of the stochastic process of a short-term rate, such as those mentioned in Chapter 30.

---

[3] There are variations around the basic original binomial model. Hull and White (1994, 1996) provided techniques for building 'general trees' which comply with various modelling constraints on interest rates for incorporating mean-reversion. Mean-reversion designates the fact that interest rates tend to revert to their long-term mean when they drift along time. Some additional details on interest rate models are given in Chapter 31.

A SIMPLE 'BINOMIAL TREE' TECHNIQUE APPLIED TO INTEREST RATES

We use the simplest possible model of interest rates[4] for illustration purposes. We limit the modelling of interest rates to the simple and attractive 'binomial' model. The 'binomial' name of the technique refers to the fact that the interest rate can take only two values at each step, starting from an initial value.

The Binomial Process

Each 'step' is a small interval of time between two consecutive dates t and $t + 1$[5]. Given a current value of the rate at date t, there are only two possible values at $t + 1$. The rate can only move up or down by a fixed amount. After the first step (period), we repeat the process over all periods dividing the horizon of the simulations. The shorter this period, the higher the number of steps[6]. Starting from a given initial value, the interest rate moves up or down at each step. The magnitudes of these movements are u and d. They are percentage coefficients applied to the starting value of the rate to obtain the final values after one step. If i_t is the interest rate at date t:

$$i_{t+1} = u \times i_t \quad \text{or} \quad d \times i_t$$

It is convenient to choose $d = 1/u$. Since $u \times d = 1$, an up step followed by a down step results in a previous value, minimizing the number of nodes. The rate at $t + 1$ is $u \times \text{rate}(t)$ or $d \times \text{rate}(t)$. With several steps, the tree looks like the chart in Figure 21.1. In addition to u and d, we also need to specify what is the probability of an up and of a down move.

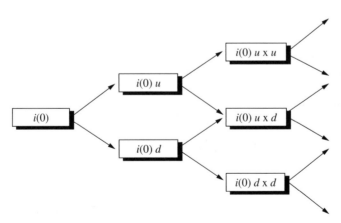

FIGURE 21.1   The binomial tree of rates

[4] See Cornyn and Mays (1997) for a review of interest rate models and their applications to financial institutions.
[5] The literature uses a small interval Δt, which tends towards zero.
[6] The binomial approach to options is expanded in Cox et al. (1979) and Cox and Rubinstein (1985).

Natural and 'Risk-neutral' Probabilities

The 'binomial tree' of rates requires defining the values of the 'up' and 'down' moves, u and d, and of their probabilities consistent with the market. Finding the appropriate values requires referring to risk-neutrality.

This allows us to derive u and d such that the return and volatility are in line with the real world behaviour of interest rates. The financial theory makes a distinction between actual, or 'natural', probabilities and the so-called 'risk-neutral' probabilities.

Risk-neutrality

Risk-neutrality implies indifference between the expected value of an uncertain gain and a certain gain equal to this expected value. Risk aversion implies that the value of the uncertain gain is lower than its expected value. Risk-neutrality implies identity between the expected outcome and the certain outcome (see Chapter 8 for brief definitions). The implication is that, under risk-neutrality, all securities should have the same risk-free return. There exists a set of risk-neutral probabilities such that the expected value equals the value under risk aversion. Intuitively, the risk-neutral probabilities are higher for downside deviations than actual probabilities. For instance, if an investor values a bet providing 150 and 50 with the same probability, his expected gain is 100. Under risk aversion, the value might fall to 90. This value under risk aversion is the expected value under risk-neutral probabilities. This implies that the risk-neutral probability of the down move is higher than the actual natural downside probability, 0.5. The risk-neutral probability of the down move is p^* such that $p^* \times 50 + (1 - p^*) \times 150 = 90$, or $p^* = 0.6$.

The Parameters of the Binomial Model

Risk-neutrality implies that there exists a set of risk-neutral probabilities, p^* and $1 - p^*$, of up and down moves such that:

- The return is the risk-free rate r, or the expectation of the value after one period is $1 + r$.
- The volatility of distribution of the 'up' value and the 'down' value is identical to the market volatility $\sigma \sqrt{\Delta t}$ for a small period t.

The corresponding equations are:

$$p^* u + (1 - p^*)d = 1 + r$$

$$[p^* u^2 + (1 - p^*)d^2] - [p^* u + (1 - p^*)d]^2 = \sigma^2 \Delta t$$

Resulting in:

$$u = \exp[\sigma \sqrt{\Delta t}] \quad \text{and} \quad d = \exp[-\sigma \sqrt{\Delta t}]$$

The derivation of these equations is given in the appendix to this chapter.

Using Numerical Data

In the example used in this section, the yearly volatility is 15% and the steps correspond to a 1-year period. The numerical values selected for u and d are:

$$u = \exp(15\%) = 1.1618 \quad \text{and} \quad d = \exp(15\%) = 0.8607$$

With the above numerical values, the sequence of rates is that of Table 21.1. The risk-neutral probabilities are simply 50% and 50% to make calculations more tractable. This implies that the real world probability of a down jump in interest rate is lower than 50% since the actual risky return should be higher than the risk-free rate in the real market.

TABLE 21.1   The tree of numerical values

Dates	0	1	2
Rates	10.00%	11.62%	13.50%
		8.61%	10.00%
			7.41%

After two up and down steps, the value at date 2 is the initial value, 10%, since $u = 1/d$.

VALUING DEBT AND OPTIONS WITH SIMULATED RATES

In this section, we apply the binomial tree technique to value a risky debt. This implies ensuring that the binomial tree is consistent with market prices. To meet this specification, we need to proceed with various practical steps.

Value of Debt under Uncertainty

Any asset generates future flows and its current value is the discounted value of those flows. The simulated rates serve for discounting. For instance, a zero-coupon bond generates a terminal flow of 100 at date 2. Its current value is equal to the discounted value of this flow of 100 using the rates generated by the simulation. There are as many possible values as there are interest rate paths to arrive at date 2.

In a no-uncertainty world, the time path of rates is unique. When rates are stochastic, the volatility is positive and there are numerous interest rate paths diverging from each other. Each sequence of rates is a realization of uncertain paths of rates over time. For each sequence of rates, there is a discounted value of this stream of flows. With all sequences, there are as many discounted values as there are time paths of rate values. The value of the asset is the average of these values assuming that all time paths of rates are equally probable[7]. The simple zero-coupon bond above illustrates the calculation process. The terminal flow of 100 is certain. Its present value as of date 1 uses the rate at period 2. Its present value as of date 0 uses the rate of period 1, which is the current rate. There are only two possible sequences of rates in this example, and hence two possible values of the same asset:

$$100/[(1 + 10.00\%)(1 + 11.62\%)] = 81.445$$

$$100/[(1 + 10.00\%)(1 + 8.61\%)] = 83.702$$

---

[7] The maximum number of time paths is 2^n where n is the number of periods, since at each date there are twice as many nodes as at the preceding date.

The average value is $(81.445 + 83.702)/2 = 82.574$, which is the expected value given the uncertainty on interest rates (Table 21.2).

TABLE 21.2 Values of the bond at various dates

Dates	0	1	2
Values	82.574	89.590	100
		92.073	100
			100

Another technique for calculating this value serves later. At date 2, the value of the flow is 100 for all time paths of rates. However, this flow has two possible values at date 1 that correspond to the two possible values of the rates: $100/(1 + 11.62\%) = 89.590$ and $100/(1 + 8.61\%) = 92.073$. The current value results from discounting the average value at date 1, using the current rate, which gives $[(89.590 + 92.073)/2]/(1 + 10.00\%) = 82.574$. The result is the same as above, which is obvious in this case. The benefit of this second method lies in calculating a current value using a recursive process starting from the end. From final values, we derive values at preceding dates until the current date. This second technique illustrates the mark-to-future process at date 1. In this case, there are two possible states only at date 1. From this simple distribution, we derive the expected value and the worst-case value. The expected value at date 1 is the average, or $(89.590 + 92.073)/2 = 91.012$. The worst-case value is 89.590.

The binomial model is general. The only difference between a straight debt and an option is that the discounted flows of the option change with rates, instead of being independent of interest rate scenarios. Since it is possible to use flows defined conditionally upon the value of the interest rates, the model applies.

The Global Calibration of the Binomial Tree

The value of listed assets, calculated with all the time paths of interest rates, should replicate those observed on the market. In order to link observed prices and calculated prices, the rates of each node of the tree need an adjustment, which is another piece of the calibration process.

The binomial tree above does not yet include all available information. The rate volatility sets the upward and downward moves at each step. However, this unique adjustment does not capture the trend of rates, any liquidity premium or credit spread observed in markets, and the risk aversion making expected values less than actual values. All factors should show up in simulated rates as they do in the market. Instead of including progressively all factors that influence rates, it is easier to make a global calibration. This captures all missing factors in the model.

In the above example, the zero-coupon value is 82.574. Its actual price might diverge from this. For instance, let us assume that its observed price is 81.5. The simulated rates need adjustment to reconcile the two values. In this example, the simulated rates should be above those used in the example, so that the simulated price decreases until it reaches the observed price. There is no need to change the volatility, since the up and down moves already replicate the market volatility for all rates individually. In the case of zero-coupon maturity at date 2, the initial rate value is 10%, and the rates at period 2 do not count.

Hence, only rates as of date 1 need adjustment. The easiest way to modify them is to add a common constant to both rates at date 1. The constant has an empirical value such that it matches the calculated and observed prices. This constant is the 'drift'. In the example, the drift should be positive to increase the rate and decrease the discounted value. Numerical calculation shows that the required drift is around 1.40% to obtain a value of 81.5. The calibrated rates at 1 become: $i_{1u} = 11.62\% + 1.40\% = 13.02\%$ and $i_{1d} = 8.61\% + 1.40\% = 10.01\%$. Once the rates at date 1 are adjusted, the calibration extends to subsequent periods using the prices of listed assets having longer maturity. It is necessary to repeat this process to extend the adjustment of the whole tree. This technique enforces the 'external' consistency with market data.

The Valuation of Options

In order to obtain an option value, we start from its terminal values given the interest rate values simulated at this date. Once all possible terminal values are determined from the terminal values of rates, the recursive process serves to derive the values at other dates. For American options, whose exercise is feasible at any time between now and maturity, there is a choice at any date when the option is in-the-money. Exercising the option depends on whether the borrower is willing to wait for opportunities that are more profitable or not. An American option has two values at each node (date t) of the tree: a value under no exercise and the exercise value. The value when waiting, rather than exercising immediately, is simply the average of the two possible values at the next date $t + 1$, just as for any other asset. Under immediate exercise, the value is the difference between the strike price and the gain. The optimum rule is to use the maximum of these two values. With this additional rule, the value of the options results from the same backward process along the tree, starting from terminal values.

THE CURRENT VALUATION OF THE PREPAYMENT OPTION

This methodology applies to a loan amortized with constant annuities, whose maturity is 5 years and fixed rate 10%. The current rate is also 10%. The yearly volatility of rates is 15%. The borrower considers a prepayment when the decline in rates generates future savings whose present value exceeds the penalty of 3%. However, being in-the-money does not necessarily trigger exercise, since immediate prepayment may be less profitable than deferred prepayment. The borrower makes the optimal decision by comparing the immediate gain with the expected gains of later periods. The expected gain is the expected value of all discounted gains one period later, while the immediate gain is the exercise value. The process first simulates the rate values at all dates, then revalues the debt accordingly, calculates the strike price as 1.03 times the outstanding principal, and calculates the payoff under immediate exercise. The last step is to calculate the optimum payoff at each node and value the present value of these optimum payoffs to get the option value.

Simulating Rates

Equal yearly periods divide the future. The binomial tree starts at 10%. However, there is a need to adjust the rates with a uniform drift of -0.10% applied to all rates to find the exact value 1000 of the straight debt under interest rate uncertainty. The values of u

TABLE 21.3   The binomial tree of rates (5 years, 1-year rate, initial rate 10%)

Dates (Eoy)	0	1	2	3	4	5
Rates[a]	9.90%	11.52%	13.40%	15.59%	18.12%	21.07%
		8.51%	9.90%	11.52%	13.40%	15.59%
			7.31%	8.51%	9.90%	11.52%
				6.28%	7.31%	8.51%
					5.39%	6.28%
						4.63%

[a] In order to find exactly the value of 1000 when moving along the 'tree' of rates, it is necessary to adjust all rates by deducting a constant drift of −0.10%. Using the original rates starting at 10% results in a value of the debt at date 0 higher than 1000 because we average all debt values which are not a linear function of rates. Instead of starting at 10% we start at 10% − 0.10% = 9.90%. The same drift applies to all rates of the tree. This uniform drift results from a numerical calculation.

and d correspond to a yearly volatility of 15%. The binomial tree is the same as above, and extends over five periods. Dates are at 'end of year' (Eoy), so that date 1 is the end of period 1 (Table 21.3).

The Original Loan

Since dates refer to the end of each year, we also need to specify when exactly the annuity flow occurs. At any date, end of period, the borrower pays immediately the annuity after the date. Hence, the outstanding debt includes this annuity without discounting. The date 0 is the date of origination. The terminal date 5 is the end of the last period, the date of the last annuity, 263.80, completing the amortization. Hence, the last flow, 263.80, occurs at date 5. The value of existing debt is exactly 263.80 before the annuity is paid. Table 21.4 shows the original repayment schedule of the loan. The constant annuity is 263.80 with an original rate of 10%.

TABLE 21.4   Repayment schedule of loan

Dates (Eoy)	0	1	2	3	4	5
Loan	1000					
Annuities		263.80	263.80	263.80	263.80	263.80
Capital reimbursement		163.80	180.18	198.19	218.01	239.82
Outstanding balance		836.20	656.03	457.83	239.82	0.00

The present value of all annuities at a discount rate of 10% is exactly 1000[8].

The Market Value of a Loan, the Exercise Price and the Payoff of the Option

Given the above strike price, the borrower can repurchase the debt and contract a new debt at the new rate. The market value of the old debt varies with interest rates. This market

---

[8] The 1000 values discount all annuities of 263.80, starting at Eoy 1, so that: $1000 = \sum_{t=1}^{5} 263.80/(1+i)^t$.

value is the underlying of the prepayment option. It is the present value of all subsequent annuities, given the market rate. The rate values of each node serve to calculate this time profile of the present value. The gain from prepayment is the difference between the current value of the debt and the current strike price (Table 21.5).

TABLE 21.5 **Market value of loan, exercise price and payoff from immediate exercise**

Dates	0	1	2	3	4	5
			Valuation:			
Value at origination	1000.00	1071.72	881.73	689.25	487.12	263.80
		1126.34	920.29	712.25	496.42	263.80
			951.60	730.78	503.82	263.80
				745.41	509.62	263.80
					514.10	263.80
						263.80
			Exercise price:			
Principal + 3%	1030.00	836.20	656.03	457.83	239.82	0.00
			Payoff from immediate exercise:[a]			
Gains	0.00	0.00	0.00	0.00	0.00	0.00
		26.34	0.47	0.00	0.00	0.00
			31.78	9.15	0.21	0.00
				23.79	6.01	0.00
					10.49	0.00
						0.00

[a]Value = max(market value of debt − strike, 0). The strike is the outstanding balance plus a penalty. The above values are rounded at the second digit: the payoff 26.34 at date 1 is 1126.34 − 263.80 − 836.20 = 26.34.

As an example, the following calculations are detailed at date 1, when the rate is 8.51% (line 2 and column 1 of the binomial tree and of the debt value table): the value of the debt; the exercise price; the payoff from exercise; the value of the option.

Value of Debt

The recursive process starting from the terminal values of the debt applies to the calculation of the debt value along any time path of rates. At date 4, the debt value discounts this 263.80 flow with the interest rates of the binomial tree. The same process applies to all previous dates until date 0. At any intermediate date, the value of the debt includes the annuity of the period, without discounting, plus the average discounted value of the debt at date 2 resulting from previous calculations. This value is:

$$1126.34 = 263.80 + 0.5(920.29 + 951.60)/(1 + 8.51\%)$$

The Payoff from Exercise of the Option

The outstanding balance is the basis for calculating the penalty, set at 3% at any date. The strike price of the option is 1.03 times the outstanding balance at all dates before maturity. The gain, when exercising the prepayment option, is the difference between the market value of existing debt and the exercise price, which is the value of new debt plus penalty. The time profile of the exercise price starts at 1030 and declines until maturity. This difference between market value of debt and strike price is a gain. Otherwise, the exercise value of the option is zero.

A first calculation provides the gain with immediate exercise, without considering further opportunities of exercise. For instance, at date 1 the value of debt, after payment of the annuity, is $1126.34 - 263.80 = 862.54$. The exercise price is 836.20. The liquidation value of the option is $862.54 - 836.20 = 26.34$. In many instances, there is no gain, the option is 'out-of-the-money' and the gain is zero.

Valuation of the Option under Deferred Exercise

The immediate gain is not the optimum gain for the borrower since future rate deviations might generate even bigger gains. The optimum behaviour rule applies. The expected value of deferred gains at the next period is the average of their present values. Finally, the value of the option at t is the maximum between immediate exercise and the present value of expected gains of the next period, or zero. This behavioural rule changes the time profile of gains. The rounded present value of the option as of today is 12.85 (Table 21.6).

TABLE 21.6 The expected gains from the prepayment option[a]

Dates	0	I	2	3	4	5
Value of option	12.85	1.90	0.04	0.00	0.00	0.00
		26.34	4.21	0.09	0.00	0.00
			31.78	9.15	0.21	0.00
				23.79	6.01	0.00
					10.49	0.00
						0.00

[a]Option value = max(exercise value at t, expected exercise values at $t + I$ discounted to t, 0).

The value of the prepayment option is 12.85, for a loan of 1000, or 1.285% of the original value of the loan.

CURRENT VALUE AND RISK-BASED PRICING

Given the value of the option, pricing requires the determination of an additional mark-up corresponding to the expected value to the borrower. This mark-up, equivalent to the current value of the option, is the OAS.

The original loan has a value of 1000 at 10%, equal to its face value when considering a straight debt without the prepayment option. The value of the debt with the prepayment option is equal to the value of the straight debt less the value of the option given away, or $1000 - 12.85 = 987.15$. For the lender, the loan is an asset whose value is less than that of a straight debt of 1000 at 10%, the difference being the value of the prepayment option. For the borrower, the loan is a liability whose value is also lower than the 1000 at 10%. The lender gave away a right whose value is 12.85.

This cost is 1.285% of the current loan principal. With a current rate of 10%, the 'debt plus option' package has a value of 987.15, or only 98.715% of the value of the debt without option. This decline in loan value by the amount of the option value should appear under 'fair value' in the balance sheet. It represents the economic value of the debt, lower than the book value by that of the option given away by the bank. In this case, fair value is a better image than book value, because it makes explicit the losses due to prepayments rather than accruing losses later on when borrowers actually repay or renegotiate their loan rate.

For practical purposes, banks lend 1000 when customer rates are 10%. In fact, the customer rate should be above this value since the 10% does not account for the value of the option. Pricing this prepayment risk necessitates a mark-up over the straight debt price. This periodical mark-up is an additional margin equivalent to the value of the option. The spread required to make the value of the debt alone identical to that of the debt with the option is the OAS. To determine the OAS, we need to find the loan rate making the loan value less the option value equal to 1000. The straight loan value is $1000 + 12.85 = 1012.85$. In order to decrease this value to 1000, we need to increase the yield of the loan. This yield is 10.23%. At this new yield, the annuity is 265.32 instead of 263.80. This is a proxy calculation. The OAS is 23 basis points (Table 21.7).

TABLE 21.7 Summary of characteristics of the loan

A: Loan without prepayment option			
Debt	Maturity	Rate	Annuity
1000	5	10.00%	263.80
B: Loan with prepayment option			
Current rate	Value of option	Value of debt without option	Value of debt with option	OAS
10.00%	12.85	1000	1012.85	0.23%

The methodology used to determine the OAS is similar to that of calibration. However, the goal differs. Calibration serves to link the model to the market. OAS serves to determine the cost of the option embedded in a loan and the required mark-up for pricing it to the borrower.

THE RISK PROFILE OF THE OPTION

To determine the risk profile of the option at a given horizon, we need its distribution. The simulation of interest rate paths provides this distribution. In this simple case, the up and down probabilities are 0.5 each. From these up and down probabilities, we can derive the probabilities of reaching each node of the tree. At any future horizon, the losses are simply the payoffs to the option holder, under exercise.

Using the end of period 3 as a horizon, the probabilities of each payoff depend on how many paths end up with the same value of the debt, remembering that several paths can end up at the same value, because each 'up and down' combination results in the same final value as a 'down and up' combination. At date 3, there are four values of the option payoff. There are more than four time paths leading to these four different values of rates at date 3. The probability of a single time path for three consecutive periods is

$0.5^3 = 12.5\%$ because we use a constant up and down probability of 0.5. When three time paths lead to the same node, the probability is $3 \times 12.5\% = 37.5\%$. At date 3, we have one single path leading to each extreme node and three time paths leading to each of the two intermediate nodes. The probability distribution of reaching each of the four nodes follows. For each node, we have the payoff of the option, which equates the loss for the bank. The distribution of the payoffs, or the bank losses, follows (Table 21.8).

TABLE 21.8   Payoff, or bank's cost, distribution from an option

Date	Probabilities		Bank's cost = option payoff
	0.5^3	12.5%	0.00
	3×0.5^3	37.5%	0.09
	3×0.5^3	37.5%	9.15
	0.5^3	12.5%	23.79
Total		100%	

The lowest value is 23.79 and the worst-case value at the 75% confidence interval is 9.15. Detailed simulations of interest rates would lead to a more continuous distribution. The loss distribution is highly skewed to the left, as for any option, with significant losses for two nodes (9.15 and 23.79) (Figure 21.2).

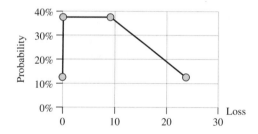

FIGURE 21.2   Standalone risk of the implicit option

Extending the simulation to the entire banking portfolio implicit options would provide the VaR due to option risk. The NPV simulations derive such an ALM VaR for optional risk, as illustrated in Chapter 25.

APPENDIX: THE BINOMIAL MODEL

The natural probability p is that of an up move, while $1 - p$ is the probability of a down move: $p = 1 - p = 50\%$. Similar definitions apply to p^* and $1 - p^*$ in a risk-neutral world. There is a set of risk-neutral probabilities p^* such that the expectation becomes equal to 90:

$$p^* \times 150 + (1 - p^*) \times 50 = 90$$

or:

$$p^* = (90 - 50)/(150 - 50) = 40\%$$

The risk-neutral probability p^* differs from the natural probability $p = 50\%$ of the real world because of risk aversion. Generalizing, the expected value of any security using risk-neutral probabilities is $E^*(V)$, where E is the expectation operator and $*$ stands for the risk-neutral probability in calculating $E^*(V)$. This risk-neutral expected value is such that it provides the risk-free return by definition. Since we know the risk-free return r, we have a first equation specifying that u and d are such that $E^*(V) = 1 + r$ for a unit value. The expectation of the value after one time interval is: $p \times u + (1 - p) \times d = 1 + r$. This is not enough to specify u and d. We need a second equation. A second specification of the problem is that the volatility should mimic the actual volatility of rates.

The volatility in a risk-neutral world is identical to the volatility in the real world. Given natural or risk-neutral probabilities, the variance over a small time interval Δt of the values is[9]:

$$[p^*u^2 + (1 - p^*)d^2] - [p^*u + (1 - p^*)d]^2 = \sigma^2 \Delta t$$

This equality holds with both p and p^*. Under risk-neutrality, the expected return is the risk-free return r. Under risk aversion, it has the higher expected value μ. Therefore, p and p^* are such that:

$$p = (e^{\mu \Delta t} - d)/(u - d)$$
$$p^* = (e^{r \Delta t} - d)/(u - d)$$

Using $p^* \times u + (1 - p^*) \times d = 1 + r$ and $p^* = (e^{r \Delta t} - d)/(u - d)$, we find the values of u and d:

$$u = \exp[\sigma \sqrt{\Delta t}] \quad \text{and} \quad d = \exp[-\sigma \sqrt{\Delta t}]$$

The yearly volatility is σ and Δt is the unit time for one step, say in years. Hence, u and d are such that the volatility is the same in both real and risk-neutral worlds. However, the return has to be the risk-free return in the risk-neutral world and the expected return, above r, in the real world.

---

[9] The variance of a random variable $\mathbf{X}$ is $V(\mathbf{X}) = E(\mathbf{X}^2) - [E(\mathbf{X})]^2$.

SECTION 8

Mark-to-Market Management in Banking

22

Market Value and NPV of the Balance Sheet

The interest income is a popular target of interest rate risk management because it is a simple measure of current profitability that shows up directly in the accounting reports. It has, however, several drawbacks. Interest income characterizes only specific periods, ignoring any income beyond the horizon. Measuring short-term and long-term profitability provides a more comprehensive view of the future.

The present values of assets and liabilities capture all future flows generated by assets and liabilities, from today up to the longest maturity. The mark-to-market value of the balance sheet discounts all future flows using market discount rates. It is the Net Present Value (NPV) of the balance sheet, since it nets liability values from asset values. The calculation of an NPV does not imply any assumption about liquidity of loans. It is a 'fair' or 'economic' value calculation, not the calculation of a price at which assets could trade:

- It differs from the 'fair values' of assets by the value of credit risk of borrowers, because it uses market rates, without differentiating them according to the risk of individual borrowers.
- It also differs from the value of equity because it considers the balance sheet as a portfolio of fixed income assets, long in loans and short in the bank's liabilities, exposed to interest rate risk only, while the stock price depends on equity market parameters and is subject to all bank risks. To put it more simply, NPV can be negative, while stock prices cannot.
- The NPV at market rates represents the summation of all future interest income of assets and liabilities, plus the present value of equity positioned as of the latest date of calculations.

This last property provides a major link between the accounting income measures and the NPV, under some specific assumptions. It makes NPV a relevant long-term target of ALM policy, since controlling the risk of the NPV is equivalent to controlling the risk of the entire stream of interest incomes up to the latest maturity.

The presentation of the NPV comprises two steps. This chapter discusses the interpretation of the NPV and its relationship with net interest margins and accounting profitability.

The first section discusses alternative views of NPV. The second section demonstrates, through examples, the link between NPV at market rates and the discounted value of the future stream of periodical interest incomes up to the longest maturity, plus an adjustment for equity. Chapter 23 deals with the issue of controlling the interest rate risk using the NPV, rather than interest income, as the target variable of ALM. Duration gaps substitute the classical interest rate gaps for this purpose.

VIEWS ON THE NPV

The NPV of the balance sheet is the present value of assets minus the present value of liabilities, excluding equity. This present value can use different discount rates. When using the market rates, we have an 'ALM' NPV that has the properties described below. 'Fair value' calculation would use the yields required by the market dependent on credit spreads of individual assets. This fair value differs from the value of assets under 'ALM' NPV, which is a mark-to-model calculation.

There are various possible views on NPV. We review some of them, focusing on what they imply and eventual inconsistencies. Possible views of NPV are: a mark-to-market value of a portfolio; a measure of performance defined by the gaps between the asset and liability yields and the market rates; a measure of the future stream of interest incomes up to the latest maturity in the banking portfolio.

Definition

The present value of the stream of future flows F_t is:

$$V = \sum_t F_t/(1 + y_t)^t$$

The market rates are the zero-coupon rates y_t derived from yield curves, using the cost of the debts of the bank. The formula provides a value of any asset that generates contractual flows. The NPV of the balance sheet is the value of assets minus that of debts. Both result from the Discounted Cash Flow (DCF) model. The calculation of NPV uses market rates with, eventually, the credit spread of the bank compensating its credit risk. The NPV using market rates, with or without the bank's credit spread, differs from the 'fair value' of the balance sheet. Hence, NPV is more a 'mark-to-model' value whose calculation rules derive from the interpretations of its calculation, as explained below.

NPV as a Portfolio

The NPV is the theoretical value of a portfolio long in assets and short in liabilities. The NPV can be either positive or negative, since the NPV is the net value of assets and liabilities. The change in NPV depends entirely on the sensitivities of these two bonds. A subsequent chapter (Chapter 23) discusses the behaviour of NPV when market rates change.

The NPV 'looks like' a proxy for equity value since it nets the values of assets and debts, so that equity is the initial investment of an investor who buys the assets and borrows the liabilities. However, NPV and market value of equity are not at all identical. First, NPV can be negative whereas equity value is always positive. Second, this interpretation assimilates equity to a bond, which it is not. Using market rates as discount rates is equivalent to considering the investor as a 'net' lender, instead of an equity holder. Since equity investors take on all risks of the bank, the required rate of return should be above the cost of debt. Therefore, it does not make sense to consider the equity investor as a 'pure lender'.

In addition, the NPV at market rates represents the market value of the balance sheet even though assets and liabilities are not actually liquid. If assets and liabilities were marketable, it would be true that an investor could replicate the bank's portfolio with a net bond. In such a case, the market value of equity would be identical to the NPV at market rates because the investor would not be an equity investor. He would actually hold a 'leveraged' portfolio of bonds. The problem is that the market assets do not truly replicate operating assets and liabilities because they are neither liquid nor negotiable.

Hence, the market value of equity is actually different from the theoretical NPV at market rates. The market value of equity is the discounted value of the flows that compensate equity, with a risk-adjusted discount rate. These flows to equity are dividends and capital gains or losses. In addition, the relevant discount rate is not the interest rate, but the required return on equity, given the risk of equity.

NPV and Assets and Liabilities Yields

The NPV at market rates is an economic measure of performance. If the value of assets is above face value, it means that their return is above the market rates, a normal situation if loans generate a margin above market rates. If the bank pays depositors a rate lower than market rates, deposits cost less than market rates and the market value of liabilities is below the face value. This results in a positive NPV, even if there were no equity, because assets are valued above face value and liabilities below face value. Accordingly, when the NPV increases, margins between customer rates and market rates widen, the economic performance improves, and vice versa.

When the bank lends at 10% for 1 year, and borrows in the market at 8%, it gets 1100 as proceeds from the loan in 1 year and repays 1080 for what it borrows. The difference is the margin, 20. In addition, the present value of the asset is $1100/(1 + 8\%) = 1018.52$, above 1000. The gap of 18.52 over face value is the present value of the margin at the prevailing market rate. If asset values at this rate are higher than book values, they provide an excess spread over the bank's cost of debt. If not, they provide a spread that does not compensate the bank's cost of debt. If assets yield exactly the cost of debt for the bank, their value is at par.

The same process applies to bank deposits. When using the market rates for the bank's deposits, their value is under face value. If the bank collects deposits of 1000 for 1 year at 5% when the market rate is 10%, the value of the deposits is $1050/(1 + 8\%) = 972.22$, lower than the face value. The difference is the present value of the margin at the market rate. The interpretation is that lending deposits costing 5% in the market at 10% would provide a margin of $1000 \times 5\% = 50$. This simple reasoning is the foundation of the interpretation of the NPV as the present value of future periodical interest incomes of the bank.

NPV and the Future Stream of Interest Incomes

Since we include all flows in discounting, the NPV should relate to the margins of the various future periods calculated using market rates as references. We show in the next section that the NPV is equal to the discounted value of the future stream of interest incomes, with an adjustment for equity. Since this NPV represents the discounted value of a stream of future interest incomes, all sensitivity measures for the NPV apply to this discounted stream of future margins.

This is an important conclusion since the major shortcoming of the interest margin as a target variable is the limited horizon over which it is calculated. Using NPV instead as a measure of all future margins, the NPV sensitivity applies to the entire stream of margins up to the longest horizon. The next chapter expands the NPV sensitivity as a function of the durations of assets and liabilities.

NPV AND INTEREST INCOME FOR A BANK WITHOUT CAPITAL

The relationship between NPV and interest income provides the link between market and accounting measures. It is easier to discuss this relation in two steps: the case of a bank without equity, which is a pure portfolio of bonds; a bank with equity capital. This section considers only the zero equity case and the next the case where equity differs from zero. The discussion uses an example to make explicit the calculations and assumptions. The discount rate used is a flat market rate of 10% applying to the bank, which can fluctuate.

Sample Bank Balance Sheet

The bank funding is a 1-year debt at the current rate of 9%. This rate is fixed. The asset has a longer maturity than debt. It is a single bullet loan, with 3-year maturity, having a contractual fixed rate of 11%. Hence, the bank charges to customers the current market rate plus a 1% margin. The current market rate is 10%. This margin is immune to interest

**TABLE 22.1   Example of a simpli-
fied balance sheet**

	Assets	Liabilities
Amount	1000	1000
Fixed rate	11%	9%
Maturity	3 years	1 year

rate changes for the first year only, since the debt rate reset occurs only after 1 year. The balance sheet is given in Table 22.1.

The cash flows are not identical to the accounting margins (Table 22.2). The differences are the principal repayments. For instance, at year 1, two cash flows occur: the interest revenue of 110 and the repayment of the bank's debt plus interest cost, or 1110. However, the accounting margin depends only on interest revenues and costs. It is equal to $110 - 90 = 20$. For subsequent years, the projection of margins requires assumptions, since the debt for years 2 and 3 has to be renewed.

**TABLE 22.2   The stream of cash flows gener-
ated by assets and liabilities**

Dates	0	1	2	3
Assets	1000	110	110	1110
Liabilities	1000	1090		

The profile of cash flows remains unchanged even though the interest rate varies. This is not so for margins, after the first period, because they depend on the cost of debt, which can change after the first year. Therefore, projecting margins requires assumptions with respect to the renewal of debt. We assume that the debt rolls over yearly at the market rate prevailing at renewal dates. The horizon is the longest maturity, or 3 years. The cost of debt is 80 if the market rate does not change. If the market rate changes, so does the cost of debt beyond 1 year. The rollover assumption implies that the cash flows change, since there is no repayment at the end of period 1, and until the end of period 3, where the debt ceases to roll over. If the market rate increases by 1%, up to 11%, the cost of debt follows and rises to 10%. The stream of cash flows for the rollover debt becomes (90, 90, 1090) and the margin decreases starting from the second year (Table 22.3).

**TABLE 22.3   The future stream of cash flows and margins generated by
assets and liabilities**

Dates	0	1	2	3
Assets	1000	110	110	1110
Liabilities	1000	90	100	1100
Interest revenues and costs when debt is rolled over at the current rate				
Revenues	—	110	110	110
Costs	—	90	100	100
Margins	—	20	10	10

NPV and Projected Interest Income with Constant Market Rate

The values of assets and liabilities, using the original rate, and the NPV are:

$$PV(\text{asset}) = 110/(1 + 10\%) + 110/(1 + 10\%)^2 + 1110/(1 + 10\%)^3 = 1024.869$$

$$PV(\text{debt}) = 90/(1 + 10\%) + 90/(1 + 10\%)^2 + 1090/(1 + 10\%)^3 = 975.131$$

The NPV is the difference:

$$NPV = PV(\text{asset}) - PV(\text{debt}) = 49.737$$

Next, we calculate the present value of all future interest incomes at the prevailing market rate of 10%:

$$\text{Present value of interest income} = 20/(1 + 10\%) + 20/(1 + 10\%)^2 + 20/(1 + 10\%)^3$$

$$= 49.737$$

These two calculations provide evidence that the NPV from cash flows is exactly equal to the present value of interest incomes at the same rate:

$$NPV = \text{present value of margins} = 49.737$$

NPV and Projected Interest Income with Market Rate Changes

When the market rate changes, the cash flows do not change, but the projected margins change since the costs of debt are subject to resets at the market rates. We assume now parallel shifts of the yield curve. The flat market rate takes the new value of 9% from the end of year 1 and up to maturity. The cost of debt changes accordingly to 8% assuming a constant margin between the cost of debt and the market rate. The flows are as given in Table 22.4.

TABLE 22.4 Flows generated over three years

Periods	0	1	2	3
Assets	1000	110	110	1110
Liabilities	1000	1090		
Rollover of debt at 8%, market rate at 9%				
Revenues	—	110	110	110
Costs	—	90	80	80
Margins	—	20	30	30

The NPV calculation remains based on the same flows, but the discount rate changes. For simplicity, we assume that the rate changes the very first day of the first period. The margins also change with the rate, and the present value discounts them with the new market rate. With a 9% market rate, the margins increase after the first year. The calculations of the NPV and the discounted value of margins are:

$$PV(\text{asset}) = 110/(1 + 9\%) + 110/(1 + 9\%)^2 + 1110/(1 + 9\%)^3 = 1050.626$$

$$PV(\text{debt}) = 90/(1 + 9\%) + 90/(1 + 9\%)^2 + 1090/(1 + 9\%)^3 = 983.861$$

The NPV is the difference:

$$NPV = PV(\text{asset}) - PV(\text{debt}) = 66.765$$

The discounted value of periodical interest incomes is:

$$\text{Discounted margins} = 20/(1 + 9\%) + 30/(1 + 9\%)^2 + 30/(1 + 9\%)^3 = 66.765$$

When the rate changes, the equality still holds. Using the 9% flat rate, or any other rate, shows that this equality holds for any level of market rates.

The Interpretation of the Relationship between Discounted Margins and NPV

For the above equality to hold, we need to reset both the discount rate and the margin values according to rate changes. Taking an extreme example with a sudden large jump of interest rate, we see what a negative NPV means. The negative NPV results from projected margins becoming negative after the first year. Both asset and liability values decline. With a 15% market rate, the projected margins beyond year 1 become $110 - 140 = -30$. The two calculations, discounted flows and discounted margins, provide the same value:

$$NPV = \text{discounted interest incomes}$$
$$= 20/(1 + 15\%) - 30/(1 + 15\%)^2 - 30/(1 + 15\%)^3 = -25.018$$

The change from a positive NPV to a negative NPV is the image of the future negative margins given the rising cost of debt. This results from the discrepancies of the asset and liability maturities and the resulting mismatch between interest rate resets. The short-term debt rolls over sooner than assets, which generate a constant 11% return. The variable interest rate gap is negative, calculated as the difference between interest-sensitive assets and liabilities. This implies that the discounted margins decrease when the rate increases. In the example, discounted margins change from 49.737 to -25.018.

The change in NPV is the difference between variations of the asset and liability values. When rates increase, both decrease. Nevertheless, the asset value decreases more than the debt value. This is why the NPV declines and becomes negative. The sensitivity of the asset value is higher than the sensitivity of the debt value. The following chapter discusses the sensitivity of the mark-to-market value, which is proportional to duration. In the current example, the duration of assets is above that of debt. Accordingly, assets are more sensitive to rate changes than debt.

The above results are obtained for a balance sheet without equity. Similar results are obtained when equity differs from zero, but they require an adjustment for the equity term.

DISCOUNTED MARGINS AND NPV WITH CAPITAL

With capital, the debt is lower than assets and the interest income increases because of the smaller volume of debt. In the example below, equity is 100, debt is 900 and assets are 1000. All other assumptions are unchanged. At the 10% market rate, the first year cost of debt becomes $9\% \times 900 = 81$ instead of 90 because the amount of debt is lower (Table 22.5).

TABLE 22.5 Example of a simplified balance sheet

	Assets	Liabilities
Loans at 11%	1000	
Capital		100
Debt at 9%		900

We can duplicate the same calculations as above with the new set of data. Cash flows and projected margins correspond to the new level of debt:

$$PV(asset) = 110/(1 + 10\%) + 110/(1 + 10\%)^2 + 1110/(1 + 10\%)^3 = 1024.869$$

$$PV(debt) = 81/(1 + 10\%) + 81/(1 + 10\%)^2 + 1081/(1 + 10\%)^3 = 877.618$$

The NPV is the difference:

$$NPV = PV(asset) - PV(debt) = 147.250$$

The stream of future margins becomes 29 for all 3 years. Its discounted value at the market rate of 10% becomes:

$$Discounted\ margins = 29/(1 + 10\%) + 29/(1 + 10\%)^2 + 29/(1 + 10\%)^3 = 72.119$$

The present value of margins becomes lower than the balance sheet NPV. The gap results from equity. The difference between the NPV and the discounted margins is $147.250 - 72.119 = 75.131$. We see that this difference is the present value of the equity, at the market rate, positioned at the latest date of the calculation, at date 3:

$$100/(1 + 10\%)^3 = 75.131$$

Therefore, the NPV is still equivalent to the discounted value of future interest income plus the present value of equity positioned at the latest date of the calculation. Table 22.6 illustrates what happens when the market rate varies, under the same assumptions as above, with a constant margin of −1% for the rollover debt. The discount rate being equal to the market rate, it changes as well.

TABLE 22.6 Discounted values of cash flows and margins at market rates

Market rate	Present value of margins	Present value of 100 at date 3	Present value of margins + capital	NPV
9%	87.932	77.218	165.151	165.151
10%	72.119	75.131	147.250	147.250
11%	56.982	73.119	130.102	130.102

Conclusion

All the above calculations use a very simple balance sheet. However, since all assets and liabilities can be broken down into simple zero-coupon items, the calculations still hold for real balance sheets. In the end, the assumptions required for the equivalence of discounted margins plus capital and NPV are the following:

- Projections of interest income should extend up to the longest maturity of balance sheet items.
- Both the stream of projected margins and the discount rate need adjustment when rates change: future margin resets occur when the current market rate changes until maturity[1].
- The discount rates are the market rates.
- The NPV at market rates, or at the bank's market rates, differs from the 'fair value' which uses rates embedding the credit spreads of the borrower.
- The difference between NPV and discounted margins at market rates is the present value of equity positioned at a date that is the longest maturity of all assets and liabilities.

---

[1] Rate deviations from 8% require adjusting both margins and discount rate.

23

NPV and Interest Rate Risk

The Net Present Value (NPV) is an alternative target variable to interest income. The sensitivity of interest rate assets and liabilities is the 'duration'. Since the NPV is the difference between mark-to-market values of loans and debts, its sensitivity to rate changes depends on their durations.

The duration is the percentage change of a market value for a unit 'parallel' shift of the yield curve (up and down moves of all rates). The duration of assets and liabilities is readily available from their time profile of cash flows and the current rates. Intuitively, the interest rate sensitivity of the NPV depends on mismatches between the duration of assets and the duration of liabilities. Such mismatches are 'duration gaps'.

Controlling duration gaps is similar to controlling interest rate gaps. Derivatives and futures contracts alter the gap. Simple duration formulas allow us to define which gaps are relevant for controlling the sensitivity of several NPV derived target variables. These include the NPV of the balance sheet, the leverage ratio of debt to asset in mark-to-market values, or the duration of 'equity' as the net portfolio of loans minus bank debts. Maintaining adequate duration gaps within bounds through derivatives or futures allows us to control the interest rate sensitivities of mark-to-market target variables.

Duration-based sensitivities do not apply when the yield curve shape changes, or when the interest shock is not small. Durations are, notably, poor proxies of changes with embedded options (for further details see Chapter 24).

This chapter focuses on duration gaps between assets and liabilities, and how to use them. The first section describes duration and its properties. The second section lists NPV derived target variables of the Asset–Liability Management (ALM) policy, and defines the relevant duration gaps to which they are sensitive. Controlling these duration gaps allows us to monitor the risk on such target variables. The last section explains why derivatives and futures modify durations and help to hedge or control the risk of the NPV.

THE SENSITIVITY OF MARKET VALUES AND DURATION

The sensitivity is the change in market value generated by a parallel shift of the yield curve. In technical terms, it is the derivative of the value of the asset with respect to interest rate. The sensitivity is the modified duration of an asset. The duration is the ratio of the present value of future flows, weighted by dates, to the market value of the asset.

The modified duration applies when the yield curve is flat, since it is the ratio of the duration to $(1 + y)$, where y is the flat rate. However, it is always possible to derive a sensitivity formula when the yield curve is not flat, by taking the first derivative with respect to a parallel shift of the entire yield curve. In this case, we consider that a common shock Δy applies to all rates y_t and take the derivative with respect to Δy rather that y. The appendix to this chapter uses this technique to find the condition of immunization of the interest income over a given period when flows do not occur at the same date within the period. The cash flows are F_t for the different dates t, and y_t are the market rates. Then the duration is:

$$\text{Duration} = \sum_{t=1}^{N} \left[t\, F_t / (1 + y_t)^t \right] \bigg/ \left[\sum_{t=1}^{N} F_t / (1 + y_t)^t \right]$$

The duration formula seems complex. In fact, it represents the average maturity of future flows, using the ratio of the present value of each flow to the present value of all flows as weights for the different dates[1]. For a zero-coupon, the duration is identical to maturity. In this case, all intermediate flows are zero. The formula for the duration shows that $D = M$, where M is the zero-coupon maturity.

The duration has several important properties that are explained in specialized texts[2]. Subsequent sections list the properties of duration relevant for ALM. The duration is a 'local' measure. When the rate or the dates change, the duration drifts as well. This makes it less convenient to use with important changes because duration ceases to be constant.

Sensitivity of Market Values to Changes in Interest Rates

The modified duration is the duration multiplied by $1/(1 + y)$. The modified duration is the sensitivity to interest rate changes of the market value and applies when the yield curve is flat. The general formula of sensitivity is:

$$\Delta V / V = -[D / (1 + y)] \times \Delta y$$

The relative change in value, as a percentage, is equal to the modified duration times the absolute percentage interest rate change. This formula results from the differentiation of the value with respect to the interest rate. The sensitivity of the value is the change in value of the asset generated by a unit change in interest rate. This value is equal to the market value of the asset multiplied by the modified duration and by the change in interest rate:

$$\Delta V = -[D / (1 + y)] \times V \times \Delta y$$

---

[1] This is different from the simple time weighted average of flows because of discounting.

[2] Bierwag's (1987) book is entirely dedicated to duration definitions and properties.

The duration of a portfolio is the average of the durations of assets weighted by their market values. This property is convenient to derive the durations of a portfolio as a simple function of the durations of its individual components.

Duration and Return Immunization

The return of an asset calculated over a horizon equal to its duration is immune to any interest rate variation. With fixed rate assets, obtaining the yield to maturity requires holding the asset until maturity. The yield to maturity is the discount rate making the present value of the future cash flow identical to its price. When selling the asset before maturity, the return is uncertain because the price at the date of sale is unknown. This price depends on the prevailing interest rate at this date. The Discounted Cash Flow (DCF) model, using the current market rates as discount rates, provides its value. If the rates increase, the prices decrease, and conversely. The holding period return combines the current yield (the interest paid) and the capital gain or loss at the end of the period.

The total return from holding an asset depends on the usage of intermediate interest flows. Investors might reinvest intermediate interest payments at the prevailing market rate. The return, for a given horizon, results from the capital gain or loss, plus the interest payments, and plus the proceeds of the reinvestments of the intermediate flows up to this horizon. If the interest rate increases during the holding period, there is a capital loss due to the decline in price. Simultaneously, intermediate flows benefit from a higher reinvestment rate up to the horizon at a higher rate. If the interest rate decreases, there is a capital gain at the horizon. At the same time, all intermediate reinvestment rates get lower. These two effects tend to offset each other. There is some horizon such that the net effect on the future value of the proceeds from holding the asset, the reinvestment of the intermediate flows, plus the capital gain or loss cancel out. When this happens, the future value at the horizon is immune to interest rate changes. This horizon is the duration of the asset[3].

Duration and Maturity

The duration increases with maturity, but less than proportionately. It is a 'convex' function of maturity. The change in duration with maturity is the slope of the tangent to the curve that relates the duration to the maturity for a given asset (Figure 23.1).

When time passes, from t to $t + 1$, the residual life of the asset decreases by 1. Nevertheless, the duration decreases by less than 1 because of convexity. If the duration is 2 years in January 1999, it will be more than 1 year after 1 year, because it diminishes less than residual maturity. This phenomenon is the 'duration drift' over time.

Due to duration drift, any constraint on duration that holds at a given date does not after a while. For instance, an investor who wants to lock in a return over a horizon of 5 years will set the duration of the portfolio to 5 at the start date. After 1 year, the residual life decreases by 1 year, but the duration decreases by less than 1 year. The residual time to the horizon is 4 years, but the duration will be somewhere between 5 and 4 years. The portfolio duration needs readjustment to make it equal to the residual time of 4 years. This adjustment is continuous, or frequent, because of duration drift.

---

[3] This is demonstrated in dedicated texts and discussed extensively by Bierwag (1987).

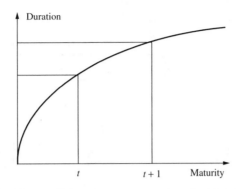

FIGURE 23.1   The relationship between duration and maturity

THE DURATION GAP AND THE TARGETS OF INTEREST RATE POLICY

The target variables of ALM policies include: the interest income over specified periods, the NPV of the balance sheet; the leverage ratio expressed with market values; the market return of the portfolio of assets and liabilities. The immunization conditions for all variables hold under the assumption of parallel shifts in the yield curve.

Immunization of the Interest Margin

With the gap model, all flows within periods are supposed to occur at the same date. This generates errors due to reinvestments or borrowings within the period. The accurate condition of immunization of the interest margin over a given horizon depends on the duration of the flows of assets and liabilities over the period. The condition that makes the margin immune is:

$$VA(1 - D_A) = VL(1 - D_L)$$

where VA and VL are the market values of assets and liabilities, and D_A and D_L are the durations of assets and liabilities. The demonstration of this formula is in the appendix to this chapter. The formula summarizes the streams of flows for both assets and liabilities with two parameters: their market values and their durations. It says that the streams of flows generated by both assets and liabilities match when their durations, weighted by their market values, are equal. Figure 23.2 illustrates the immunization condition that makes market values of assets and liabilities, weighted by duration, equal.

NPV of the Balance Sheet

To neutralize the sensitivity of the market value, the variations in values of assets and liabilities should be identical. This condition implies a relationship between the market values and the duration of assets and liabilities. With a parallel shift of the yield curve equal to Δi, the condition is:

$$\Delta NPV / \Delta i = \Delta (VA - VL) / \Delta i$$

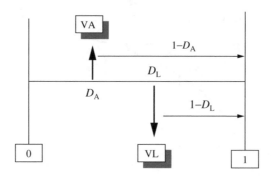

FIGURE 23.2   Summarizing a stream of flows into a single 'equivalent flow'

The changes in values of assets and liabilities result from their durations, D_A and D_L. They are $(-D_A \times VA \times \Delta i)$ and $(-D_L \times VL \times \Delta i)$. If we divide by Δi, we obtain:

$$\Delta NPV/\Delta i = [1/(1+i)][-D_A \times VA + D_L \times VL]$$

The immunization condition is:

$$VA \times D_A = VL \times D_L$$

This condition states that the changes in the market value of assets and liabilities are equal. When considering the net portfolio of assets minus liabilities, the condition stipulates that the change in asset values matches that of liabilities. Note that this duration gap is in value, not in years. When adjusting durations, it is more convenient to manipulate durations in years. The immunization condition is:

$$D_A/D_L = VL/VA$$

The formula stipulates that the ratio of the duration and liabilities should be equal to the ratio of market values of liabilities to assets.

The NPV sensitivity is the sensitivity of the net portfolio of assets minus liabilities. Its duration is a linear function of these, using market value weights:

$$\Delta NPV/NPV = [1/(1+i)]\{[-D_A \times VA + D_L \times VL]/NPV\} \times \Delta i$$

The sensitivity of the NPV has a duration equal to the term in brackets. An alternative designation for the duration of NPV is the 'duration of equity'. It implies dividing the duration gap in value by the NPV. This formula expresses the duration of NPV in years rather than in value. However, it leverages the unweighted duration gap $(D_A - D_L)$ by dividing by the NPV, a lower value than those of assets and liabilities. For instance, using the orders of magnitudes of book values, we can consider approximately that $VL = 96\% \times VA$ since equity is 4% of assets (weighted according to regulatory forfeits). Assuming that the NPV is at par with the book value, it represents around 4% of the balance sheet. If we have a simple duration gap $D_A - D_L = 1$, with $D_A = 2$ while $D_L = 1$, the weighted duration gap is around:

$$-2 \times 100\% + 1 \times 96\% = -1.04$$

The 'equity' or NPV duration is $-1.04/4\% = -26$, which is much higher than the unweighted duration gap because of the leverage effect of equity on debt. On the other hand, the ratio of the durations of assets and liabilities is around $D_A/D_L = 0.96/1$, or 96%.

These conditions are extremely simple. The durations of assets and liabilities are averages of durations of individual lines weighted with their market values. Therefore, the duration of any portfolio is easy to obtain from the durations of the assets. This makes it easy to find out which assets or liabilities create the major imbalances in the portfolio.

Leverage

The leverage is the ratio of debt to equity. With market values, the change of market leverage results from the durations of assets and liabilities. The condition of immunization of the market leverage is very simple, once calculations are done[4]:

$$D_A = D_L$$

This condition says that the durations of assets and liabilities should match, or that the duration gap should be set at zero. By contrast, immunization of the NPV would imply different durations of assets and liabilities, proportional to their relative values, which necessarily differ in general because of equity. The intuition behind this condition is simple. When durations match, any change in rates generates the same percentage change of asset and debt values. Since the change of the debt to asset ratio is the difference between these two percentage changes, it becomes zero. If the debt to asset ratio is constant, the debt to equity ratio is also constant. Hence, leverage is immune to changes in interest rates.

The Market Return on Equity for a Given Horizon

The market return on equity is the return on the net value of assets and liabilities. Its duration is that of the NPV. Setting the duration to the given horizon locks in the return of the portfolio over that horizon:

$$D_E = D_{NPV} = H$$

CONTROLLING DURATION WITH DERIVATIVES

The adjustment of duration necessitates changing the weights of durations of the various items in the balance sheet. Unfortunately, customers determine what they want, which

---

[4] The change in asset to equity ratio is:

$$\Delta[VA/VL]/\Delta i = [-1/E^2]\{E \times \Delta VA/\Delta i - VA \times \Delta E/\Delta i\}$$

$$= -[1/E^2]\{[-E \times VA \times D_A/(1+i)] + [VA \times E \times D_E/(1+i)]\}$$

This can be simplified to:

$$\Delta[VA/E]/\Delta i = [-VA \times E/E^2][1/(1+i)](D_A - D_L)$$

The sensitivity of the ratio is zero when $D_A = D_L$.

sets the duration value. Hence, modifying directly the durations of assets and liabilities is not the easiest way to adjust the portfolio duration.

An alternative method is to use derivatives. Hedges, such as interest rate swaps, modify duration to the extent that they modify the interest flows. When converting a fixed rate asset into a variable rate asset through an interest rate swap, the value becomes insensitive to interest rates, except for the discounted value of the excess margin over the reference rate. In the case where the excess margin is zero, we have a 'floater'. The value of a floater is constant because the discounted value of future cash flows, both variable interest revenues and capital repayments, remains equal to face value. Its duration is zero. When the floater provides an excess margin over the discount rates, the value becomes sensitive to rate because its value is that of a floater plus the discounted value of the constant margin. But its duration becomes much lower than a fixed rate asset with the same face value and the same amortizing profile because the sensitivity relates to the margin amount only, which is much smaller than the face value of the asset.

Future contracts have durations identical to the underlying asset. Any transaction on the futures market is therefore equivalent to lending or borrowing the underlying asset. Hence, futures provide a flexible way to adjust durations through off-balance sheet transactions rather than on-balance sheet adjustments.

APPENDIX: THE IMMUNIZATION OF THE NET MARGIN OVER A PERIOD

The horizon is 1 year. The rate-sensitive assets within this period are A_j for date j and the rate-sensitive liabilities are L_k for date k. Before assets and liabilities mature, it is assumed that the assets generate a fixed return r_j until date j and that the liabilities generate a fixed cost i_j until date j. When they roll over, the rates take the new values prevailing at dates j and k (Figure 23.3).

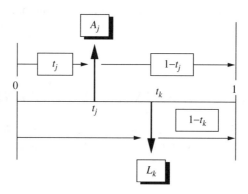

FIGURE 23.3   Time profile of cash flows within a period

The reinvestment of the inflows A_j occurs over the residual period $1 - t_j$. The refunding of the outflows L_k occurs during the residual period $1 - t_k$. Until the revision dates, the return r_j and the costs r_k are fixed. At the time of renewal, rate resets occur according to market conditions. The reinvestment, or the new funding, uses the rates i_j or i_k, assumed constant until the end of the period. The Interest Margin (IM) of the period results from both historical rates and the new rates used for rolling over the flows. The interests and costs accrue from the dates of the flows, j or k, up to 1 year. The residual periods are $1 - t_j$ and $1 - t_k$. The net margin is:

$$\text{IM} = \sum_j \{A_j[(1 + r_j)^{t_j}(1 + i_j)^{1-t_j} - (1 + r_j)^{t_j}]\}$$

$$- \sum_k \{L_k[(1 + r_k)^{t_k}(1 + i_k)^{1-t_k} - (1 + r_k)^{t_k}]\}$$

This expression combines revenues and costs calculated at the historical rates with those calculated after the rollover of transactions at the new rates. For instance, an inflow of 100 occurs at $t_j = 30$, with a historical rate of 10% before renewal. The rate jumps to 12% after reinvestment. The total interest flow up to the end of the period is:

$$100(1 + 10\%)^{30/360}[(1 + 12\%)^{330/360} - 1]$$

The amount $100(1 + 10\%)^{30/360}$ is the future value of the capital at the renewal date. We reinvest this amount up to 1 year at 12%. We deduct the amount of capital from the future value to obtain the interest flows only.

To find out when the net margin is immune to change in interest rates, we calculate the derivative with respect to a change in interest rate and make it equal to zero. The change in rate is a parallel shift λ of the yield curve:

$$i_j \longrightarrow i_j + \lambda$$
$$i_k \longrightarrow i_k + \lambda$$

The derivative of the margin with respect to λ is:

$$\delta\text{IM}/\delta\lambda = \sum_j [A_j(1 + r_j)t_j(1 + i_j) - t_j(1 - t_j)]$$

$$- \sum_k [L_k(1 + r_k)t_k(1 + i_k) - t_k(1 - t_k)]$$

The market values of all assets and liabilities using the historical rates prevailing at the beginning of the period are:

$$\text{VA}_j = A_j(1 + r_j)t_j/(1 + i_j)t_j \quad \text{and} \quad \text{VL}_k = L_k(1 + r_k)t_k/(1 + i_j)t_k$$

Using these market values, the expression of the derivative simplifies and becomes:

$$\delta\text{IM}/\delta\lambda = \sum_j \text{VA}_j(1 - t_j) - \sum_k \text{VL}_k(1 - t_k)$$

This condition becomes, using VA and VL for the market values of all assets and all liabilities:

$$\text{VA} \times \sum_j \left[1 - \sum t_j \text{VA}_j / \text{VA} \right] - \text{VL} \times \sum_k \left[1 - \sum t_k \text{VL}_k / \text{VL} \right] = 0$$

VA and VL are weighted by 1 minus the present values of all assets and liabilities times the reset dates. The weights are equal to 1 minus the duration of assets and liabilities D_A and D_L. This formula is in the text.

24

NPV and Convexity Risks

Using NPV as target variable, its expected value measures profitability, while risk results from the distribution of NPV around its mean resulting from interest rate variations. Market values and interest rates vary inversely because market values discount the future flows with interest rates. The NPV–interest rate profile is an intermediate step visualizing how interest rate deviations alter the NPV. It is convenient for making explicit 'convexity risk'. The NPV risk results from its probability distribution, which can serve for calculating an Asset–Liability Management (ALM) 'Value at Risk' (VaR).

Convexity risk arises from the shape of the relationship between asset and liability values to interest rates. Both values vary inversely with rates, but the slopes as well as the curvatures of the asset–rate curve and the liability–rate curve generally differ. When slopes only differ, the NPV is sensitive to interest rate deviations because there is a mismatch between asset value changes and liability value changes. Controlling the duration gap between assets and liabilities allows us to maintain the overall sensitivities of the NPV within desired bounds. When interest rate drifts get wider, the difference in curvatures, or 'convexities', of the asset–rate and the liability–rate profiles becomes significant, resulting in significant variations of the NPV even when slopes are similar at the current rate. This is 'convexity risk', which becomes relevant in times of high interest rate volatility.

Options magnify convexity risk. 'Gapping' techniques ignore implicit options turning a fixed rate loan into a variable rate one because of renegotiation, or a variable rate loan into a fixed rate one because of a contractual cap on the variable rate. With such options, the NPV variation ceases to be approximately proportional to interest rate deviations, because the NPV durations are not constant when rates vary widely and when options change duration. 'Convexity risk' becomes relevant in the presence of interest rate options even when interest rate volatility remains limited.

Finally, NPV sensitivity results from both duration and convexity mismatches of assets and liabilities. Convexity risk remains hidden unless interest rates vary significantly.

NPV–interest rate profiles visualize this risk. Interest rate volatility and implicit options make a strong case for measuring the downside risk of the balance sheet. NPV is an adequate target variable for revealing such risk because it captures long-term profitability when interest rate shifts become more important. Even though there is no capital requirement for ALM risk, VaR techniques applied to NPV capture this downside risk and value it.

This chapter focuses on the specifics of 'convexity' risk for the banking portfolio starting from the 'market value–interest rate' profiles of assets and liabilities. The first section details the relationship between the market value of the balance sheet and the interest rate. The second section visualizes duration and convexity effects. The third section illustrates how various asset and liability duration and convexity mismatches alter the shape of the NPV–interest rate profile, eventually leading to strong adverse deviations of NPV when interest rates deviate both upwards and downwards. The last section addresses hedging issues in the context of low and high volatility of interest rates. Chapter 25 discusses the valuation of downside NPV risk with VaR techniques.

THE MARKET VALUE OF THE BALANCE SHEET AND THE INTEREST RATE

The sensitivity to interest rate variations of the NPV is interesting because the NPV captures the entire stream of future flows of margins. The easiest way to visualize the interest risk exposure of the NPV is to use the 'market value–interest rate' profile. For any asset, the value varies inversely with interest rates because the value discounts future cash flows with a discount rate that varies. The relationship is not linear (Figure 24.1). The curvature of the shape looks upwards. This profile is a complete representation of the sensitivity of the market value.

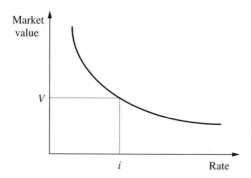

FIGURE 24.1   The market value–interest rate profile

For the NPV, the profile results from the difference of two profiles: the asset profile and the liability profile. If the NPV calculation uses the costs of liabilities (wacc), it is equal to the present value of all streams of margins up to the longest maturity, except for equity. The shape of the NPV profile results from those of the asset and liability profiles, as shown in Figure 24.2.

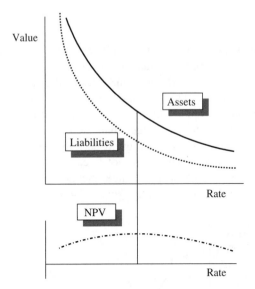

FIGURE 24.2   The NPV–interest rate profile

The two profiles, for assets and liabilities, have the usual shape with an upward looking convexity. However, the difference, the NPV profile, has a shape that depends on the relative curvatures of the profiles of assets and liabilities. Since the market values of assets and liabilities can vary over a large range, and since their curvatures are generally different, the NPV profile can have very different shapes. In Figure 24.2, the NPV is positive, and the curvature of liabilities exceeds that of assets. Nevertheless, this is only an example among many possibilities. In this example, the NPV is almost insensitive to interest rate variations.

The sensitivity analysis of NPV leads to duration gaps and suggests matching the durations of assets and liabilities to make the NPV immune to variations of interest rates. However, this is a 'local' (context-dependent) rule. Sensitivities of both assets and liabilities and, therefore, the sensitivity of the NPV depend on the level of interest rates. When the variation of interest rates becomes important, the overall profile provides a better picture of interest rate risk. Neutralizing the duration gap is acceptable when the variations of interest rates are small. If they get larger, the NPV again becomes sensitive to market movements. The next section discusses duration and convexity.

DURATION AND CONVEXITY

The duration is a good criterion whenever interest rate variations remain small and when the convexity of asset and liability profiles with rates remains small. If one of these two conditions does not hold, matching durations do not make the NPV immune to rate changes and the duration gaps cease to be a good measure of sensitivity. Since the duration is the first derivative of value with respect to interest rate, the second derivative shows how it changes with rates, and there are techniques to overcome the duration limitations and provide a better proxy for the real 'value–rate' profile.

Convexity

The sensitivity of a financial asset is the variation of its value when the market rate moves. Graphically, the slope of the 'market value–interest rate' profile relates to duration. When the interest rate moves, so does the duration. Graphically, the curvature of the profile shows how the slope changes. The curvature means that the sensitivity to downward moves of the interest rate is higher than the sensitivity to upward moves. The effect of a decrease in rates, from 9% to 8%, is bigger than the change generated by a move from 4% to 3%. 'Convexity' measures the change in duration when the rates move. Because of convexity, the market value changes are not linear. For small variations of rates, the duration does capture the change in asset value. Nevertheless, for bigger variations, the convexity alters the sensitivity significantly (Figure 24.3).

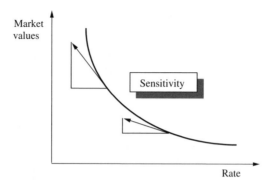

FIGURE 24.3   Sensitivity and the level of interest rates

Visually, convexity is the change in slope that measures duration at various levels of interest rates.

The Sources of Convexity

The first source of convexity is that the relationship between market value and discount rates is not linear. This is obvious since the calculation of a present value uses discount factors, such as $(1 + i)^t$. A fraction of convexity comes from this mathematical formula.

Because of discounting, convexity depends on the dates of flows. The sensitivity is proportional to duration, which represents a market value weighted average maturity of future flows. Convexity, on the other hand, is more a function of the dispersion of flows around that average. Financially speaking, modifying convexity is equivalent to changing the time dispersion of flows.

A third source of convexity is the existence of options. The relationship between the market value of an option and the underlying parameter looks like a broken line. When the option is out-of-the-money, the sensitivity is very low. When the option is in-the-money, the sensitivity is close to 1. Therefore, the 'market value–interest rate' profile is quite different for an option. It shows a very strong curvature when the options are at-the-money. Figure 24.4 shows the profile of a floor that gains value when the interest rate decreases.

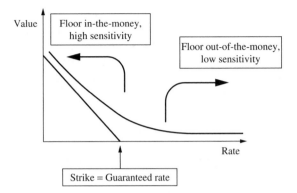

FIGURE 24.4 Market value–interest rate profile: example of a floor

The implication is that, with options embedded in the balance sheet of banks, the convexity effects increase greatly.

The Measure of Convexity

Controlling convexity implies measuring convexity. Mathematically, convexity results, like duration, from the formula that gives the price as the discounted value of future cash flows. The duration is the first-order derivative with respect to the interest rate. The convexity is the second-order derivative. This formula of convexity allows us to calculate it as a function of the cash flows and the interest rate. For options, the convexity results from the equation that relates the price to all parameters that influence its value. Just as for duration, convexity is also a local measure. It depends on the level of interest rate.

Therefore, building the 'market value–interest rate' profile requires changing the yield curve and revaluing the portfolio of assets and liabilities for all values of the interest rates. Simulations allow us to obtain a complete view of the entire profile.

The convexity has value in the market because it provides an additional return when the volatility of interest rates becomes significant. The higher the volatility of interest rates, the higher the value of convexity. The implication is that it is better to have a higher convexity of assets when the interest rate volatility increases, because this would increase the NPV. This intuition results from Figure 24.5. The convexity of assets makes

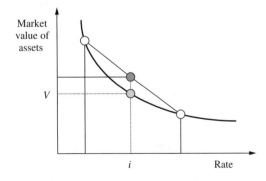

FIGURE 24.5 The value of convexity

the average value of assets between two distant interest rates higher than the current value. Hence, interest rate volatility increases the expected value of assets.

The converse is also true. When convexity is negative, a high volatility of rates results in a lower value of assets, everything else held constant. The value of convexity alters the NPV–rate profile when large deviations of rates occur. The appendix to this chapter expands the visualization with both assets and liabilities having a common duration but different convexities.

THE SENSITIVITY OF NPV

The value–interest profiles of NPV have various shapes depending on the relative durations and relative convexities of the assets and liabilities. Some are desirable profiles and others are unfavourable. What follows describes various situations.

Duration Mismatch

A duration mismatch—weighted by asset and liability values—between assets and liabilities makes the NPV sensitive to rates. The change in NPV is proportional to the change in interest rates since the values of assets and liabilities are approximately linear functions of the rate change. The NPV changes if the durations do not match. Figure 24.6 shows that there is a value of interest rates such that the NPV is zero, reached when rates decrease. When the interest rate increases, the NPV increases.

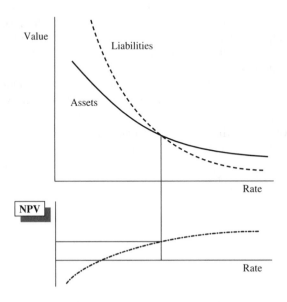

FIGURE 24.6   Value–rate profile and NPV–duration mismatch

By modifying and neutralizing the duration gap, it is possible to have a more favourable case. In Figure 24.7, the convexities are not very important, and the durations of assets

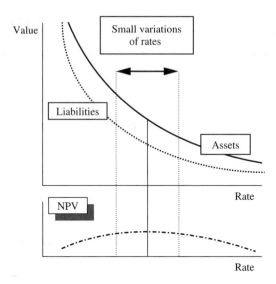

FIGURE 24.7   Variations in NPV with matched durations and different convexities

and liabilities match at the level where the NPV reaches its maximum. With significant changes in interest rates, the NPV remains positive. However, the different convexities weaken the protection of matching durations when interest rates move significantly away from the current value.

With options embedded in the balance sheet, the NPV becomes unstable, because options increase convexity effects. In such cases, the simulation of the entire profile of the NPV becomes important.

The Influence of Implicit Options

Options are the major source of convexity in balance sheets, and the main source of errors when using local measures of sensitivity to determine risk. They cap the values of assets and impose floors on the values of liabilities. For instance, the value of a loan with a prepayment option cannot go above some maximum value since the borrower can repay the loan at a fixed price (outstanding capital plus penalty). Even though the borrower might not react immediately, he will do so beyond some downward variation of the interest rate. In this case, a decline in interest rate generates an increase in the value of the asset, until we reach the cap when renegotiation occurs. The value of a straight debt (without prepayment option) would increase beyond that cap. The difference between the cap and the value of the straight debt is the value of the option.

On the liability side, options generate a floor for the value of some liabilities when the interest rates rise. This can happen with a deposit that earns no return at all, or provides a fixed rate to depositors. Beyond some upper level of market rates, the value of the deposit hits a floor instead of decreasing with the rise in interest rates. This is when depositors shift their funds towards interest-bearing assets. In such a case, even if the resources stay within the bank, they keep from now on a constant value when rates increase since they become variable rate assets.

Everything happens as if fixed rate assets and liabilities behaved as variable rate assets and liabilities beyond some variations of interest rates. The shape of the 'value–interest rate profile' flattens and becomes horizontal when hitting such caps and floors, as shown in Figure 24.8.

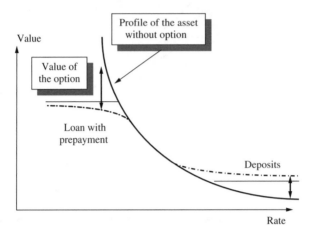

FIGURE 24.8   Values of assets and liabilities under large interest rate shifts

NPV and Optional Risks

The options generate a worst-case situation for banks. The combination of cap values of assets with floor values of liabilities generates a 'scissor effect' on the NPV (Figure 24.9).

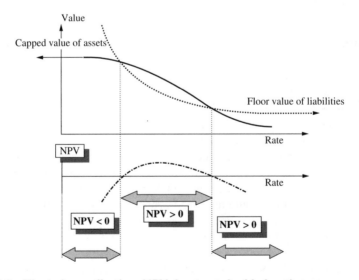

FIGURE 24.9   The 'scissor effect' on NPV due to embedded options

This is because the convexity of the assets is the opposite of the convexity of the liabilities beyond some variations. When the interest rate is in the normal range, the NPV remains positive. However, if it deviates beyond upper and lower bounds, the options gain value. The change in rate generates a negative NPV beyond those values that trigger the caps or floors. This happens for both upward and downward variations of the interest rates. Since there are multiple embedded options with varying exercise prices, the change is progressive.

CONTROLLING AND OPTIMIZING THE NPV RISK–RETURN PROFILE

The goal of interest rate policies is to control the risk of the NPV through both duration and convexity gaps. The common practice is to limit the NPV sensitivity by closing down the duration gap. However, this is not sufficient to narrow the convexity gap. Theoretically, it is, however, possible to eliminate the risk of negative NPV and turn the NPV convexity upside down.

Duration and Convexity Gaps

To immunize the NPV to changes in interest rates, the asset-weighted duration and the liability-weighted duration should match. This policy works for limited variations of rates. In order to keep the NPV immune to interest rates for larger variations, the convexities of assets and liabilities should also match. There is a better solution. When the convexity of assets is higher than the convexity of liabilities, any variation of interest rate increases the NPV as shown in Figure 24.10. The NPV then has a higher expected value when the volatility of rates increases.

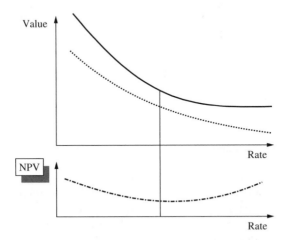

FIGURE 24.10   Convexities and NPV sensitivity to interest rate optimization

Controlling Convexity Risk

The theoretical answer to protect the NPV against duration and convexity risks is to match duration and increase the convexity of assets. Optional hedges allow us to modify the NPV–interest rate profile, to obtain the desired shape. Theoretically, floors protect the lender against a decrease in return from loans. Caps protect the bank against a rise in cost of resources. Floor values will decrease significantly when interest rates decrease significantly. Cap values will increase the NPV when interest rates increase significantly. Both caps and floors correct convexity effects and flatten the asset and liability profiles when rates change.

Since optional hedges are expensive, we face the usual trade-off between the cost of hedging and the gain from hedging. Any technique to reduce the cost of such hedges helps. The simplest is to set up an early hedge out-of-the-money. Doing otherwise might imply a prohibitive decrease in NPV.

APPENDIX: WHERE DOES CONVEXITY VALUE COME FROM?

The value of convexity appears visually when considering the 'market value–interest rate' profile. To make the comparison between two assets of different convexities visible, it is preferable to start with assets of equal value and equal duration, but with different convexities (Figure 24.11).

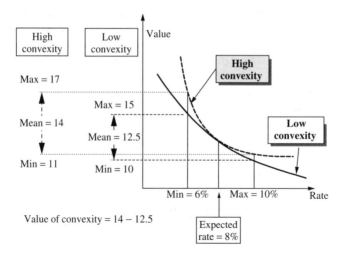

FIGURE 24.11   Expected values of assets of different convexities

It is not obvious how to define assets with the same value and the same duration. One way is to use a zero-coupon and a composite asset called a 'dumbbell'. The zero-coupon duration is equal to its maturity. The dumbbell combines two zero-coupons of different durations. The dumbbell duration is the weighted average of the duration of the two zero-coupons. If the average duration of this portfolio matches that of the zero-coupon, we have portfolios of identical market value and identical duration. A property of zero-coupons is to have the lowest convexity, everything else being equal[1].

The 'market value–interest rate' profiles of these assets, the single zero-coupon and the dumbbell, look like those of Figure 24.11. They intersect at the current price and have

---

[1] What drives convexity is not always intuitive. This property holds only when everything else is equal. Otherwise, it might not be true.

the same tangent at this price, since they have the same sensitivity. However, when the interest rate moves away from its original value, the market values diverge because of the differences in convexity.

Under certainty, the two assets would have the same value. Under uncertainty, they have an expected value. Uncertainty begins with two possible values of interest rate. Two interest rates (6% and 10%) with equal probabilities result in a common expected value of interest rate identical to the current value (8%). Even though the volatility of interest rates increases when the variations from the mean grow bigger, the average value of the interest rate stays the same.

However, the expected value of the asset changes when the rate volatility increases. The reason is that the increase in value when the interest rate declines is higher than the decrease in value when the interest rate moves upwards by the same amount. This asymmetry in the deviation of market values is higher when the convexity (the curvature of the profile) is higher. The expected value of the assets under the two equal probability rate scenarios is the average of the corresponding two values of the assets. The least convex has a value of $(15 + 10)/2 = 12.5$, and the most convex has an expected value of $(17 + 11)/2 = 14$. Therefore, the expected value of the most convex asset (14) is higher than the expected value of the least convex asset (12.5). This difference is the value of convexity (1.5). The value of convexity starts at zero, under certainty, and increases with the volatility of rates.

Convexity explains the behaviour of the NPV when the volatility of rates increases. With the same variations, it depends essentially on the duration gap. With larger deviations of rates, it depends also on the convexity gap.

25

NPV Distribution and VaR

Multiple simulations serve to optimize hedges and determine interest income at risk, or 'Earnings at Risk' (EaR) for interest rate risk as the worst-case deviation with a preset confidence level of interest income. The same technique transposes readily to Net Present Value (NPV) and values downside risk when both duration and convexity mismatches magnify the NPV risk.

The current regulations do not impose capital requirements for Asset–Liability Management (ALM), making the ALM 'Value at Risk' (VaR) of lower priority than market or credit risk VaR. However, the important adverse effects of convexity risk suggest that it is worthwhile, if not necessary, to work out NPV VaR when considering long-term horizons. The construction of a distribution of NPV at future time points follows the same basic steps as other VaR calculations.

The specific of ALM VaR is that interest rate variations beyond some upper and lower bounds trigger adverse effects whatever the direction of interest rate moves, because of convexity risk. Such adverse effects make it necessary both to value this risk and to find these bounds. The same remarks apply for interest income as well, except that NPV crystallizes in a single figure the long-term risk, which short-term simulations of interest income might not reveal or underestimate.

The first section discusses the specifics of NPV downside risk. The second section shows that modelling the NPV VaR uses similar techniques as market risk VaR. The third section illustrates the techniques with a simplified example, in two steps: using the Delta VaR technique designed for market risk (see Section 11 of this book); showing how convexity risk alters the shape of the NPV distribution and the NPV VaR.

OVERVIEW AND SPECIFICS OF NPV RISK AND DOWNSIDE RISK

VaR applies to NPV as it does for other risks, but there are a number of basic differences. They result in an NPV distribution whose profile is highly skewed when the balance sheet embeds a significant convexity risk.

Interest Income and NPV Distributions

The interest income VaR approach looks similar to the EaR approach. In fact, it differs because the interest income results from explicit calculations, whereas EaR concentrates on observed earnings rather than modelling them. In addition, EaR does not use simulations, whereas ALM models do. When transposing the technique to NPV, it is sufficient to identify the main risk drivers and their distributions. These are a small number of correlated interest rates.

Characterizing the NPV risk traditionally uses the NPV sensitivity. The higher the sensitivity, the higher the risk. In addition, setting limits implies bounding this sensitivity. To get downside risk requires going one step further. This is not current practice, but its value is to demonstrate that the same technique applies to various risks and to demonstrate the value of the NPV downside risk. The next step consists of calculating a distribution of NPV values at future time points. The time points need to fit the needs of ALM to have medium-term visibility. A 1 to 2-year horizon is adequate, as for credit risk.

Determining a forward distribution of NPV at the 1-year time point requires considering all cash flows accruing from assets and liabilities up to maturity. ALM models consider business risk over some short to medium-term horizon. Since we need probability distributions, we ignore business risk here, thereby getting closer to the 'crystallized' portfolio approach of market and credit risks. The usual steps are generating correlated distributions of the main interest rate drivers and revaluing the NPV for each scenario. In what follows, we perform the exercise using only a flat yield curve and a single rate. Using correlated interest rates would require the techniques to be expanded for market and credit risks. Because of the relatively high correlations of interest rates for a single currency, parallel shifts of yield curve assuming perfect correlations are acceptable as a first proxy. They do not suffice, however, because a fraction of the interest income results from the maturity gap between assets and liabilities, making both interest income and NPV sensitive to the steepness of the yield curve. Going further would entail using correlations or factor models of the yield curve. For illustration purposes, there is no need to do so here.

Deriving the NPV value from its current sensitivities is not adequate for a medium-term horizon and in the presence of options. Full simulations of the NPV values, requiring revaluations of all assets and liabilities, and of options, are necessary to capture the extreme deviations when discussing VaR. Without option risk, the NPV distribution would be similar to that of interest rates, since interest margin variations remain more or less proportional to interest rate deviations. With options, the NPV distribution drifts away from the interest rate distribution because options break down this simple relationship and introduce abrupt changes in the sensitivity to interest rates. Because of convexity risk, the reason for fat tails in the NPV distributions lies with the adverse effect of large deviations of interest rates on both sides of current interest rates. The fat tails of the NPV distribution result from convexity risk.

Once the NPV distribution is identified, it becomes easy to derive the expected value and the worst-case deviations at preset confidence levels. Since the NPV is usually positive, losses occur once deviations exceed the expected NPV value. The VaR is this adverse deviation minus any positive expected NPV.

Downside Risk and Convexity

Downside risk appears when interest rates deviate both upwards and downwards. From a VaR standpoint, this is a specific situation. It stems from the nature of implicit options, some of them contributing to the decrease in NPV when rates increase, and others when rates decrease. This 'double adverse exposure' results from the implicit options in loans and deposits. As a result, downside risk appears in two worst-case scenarios of rising and decreasing rates. Since it is possible to model interest rate deviations, it is easy to assign probabilities to such deviations and to assign probabilities to the NPV adverse changes.

Note, however, that the 'convexity' risk is not mechanically interest risk-driven. It depends also on behavioural patterns of customers, and demographic or economic factors for prepayments or renegotiations of loans, or on legal and tax factors (for deposits). In addition, we ignore business risk here. We could use business scenarios with assigned probabilities. This would result in several NPV distributions that we should combine into one. For such reasons, the probability distribution of adverse variations of NPV is not purely interest rate-driven.

Figure 25.1 shows the VaR of the NPV at a preset confidence level. Since the NPV is positive, losses occur only when the NPV decreases beyond the positive expected value.

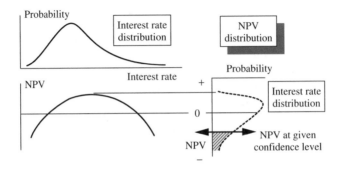

FIGURE 25.1   NPV, implicit options and VaR

NPV VAR

In order to derive the NPV distribution from interest rate distributions, ignoring other risk factors, a first technique mimics the technique for market risk and, notably, Delta VaR as expanded in Section 11 of this book. It relies on the sensitivity, which is the NPV duration. Current durations do not account for changes in sensitivity due to time drift of duration and convexity risk. Forward calculations of duration correct the first drawback. They imply positioning the portfolio at the future time points and recalculating the durations for each value of the future interest rate. We simplify somewhat the technique and assume them given. High interest rate volatility is dealt with through convexity later on. The alternative technique uses multiple simulations of risk drivers plus revaluation of the NPV for each set of trial values of rates, to obtain the NPV distribution, similarly to the simulation technique used for market risk. We summarize here the main steps for both techniques. The process replicates the techniques expanded in Chapter 29 and serves as a transition.

The sensitivity of the NPV is the net duration of assets and liabilities, weighted by the mark-to-market value of assets and liabilities. This allows us to convert any drift of rates into a drift of NPVs. Proceeding along such lines makes the NPV random, as the interest rate is. We use bold characters in what follows for random variables. As usual,

VaR requires looking for the maximum variations of the NPV resulting from the shift of interest rates. Let S_i be the sensitivity of the NPV to interest rate i, this sensitivity resulting from the above duration formula. The volatility of the NPV is:

$$\sigma(\mathbf{NPV}) = S_i \times \sigma(\mathbf{i})$$

With a given interest rate volatility, the maximum change, at a given confidence level, is a multiple of the volatility. The multiple results from the shape of the distribution of interest rates. With a normal curve, as a proxy for simplification, a multiple of 2.33 provides the maximum change at 1% confidence level:

$$\text{VaR} = 2.33 \times S_i \times \sigma(\mathbf{i})$$

When there are several interest rates to consider, and when a common shift is not an acceptable assumption, the proxy for the variation of the NPV is a linear combination of the variations due to a change in each interest rate selected as a risk driver:

$$\mathbf{NPV} = S_1 \times \mathbf{\Delta i_1} + S_2 \times \mathbf{\Delta i_2} + S_3 \times \mathbf{\Delta i_3} + \cdots$$

The indices 1, 2, 3 refer to different interest rates. Since all interest rate changes are uncertain, the volatility of the NPV is the volatility of a sum of random variables. Deriving the volatility of this sum requires assumptions on the correlations between interest rates. The issue is the same for market risk except that interest rates correlate more than other market parameters do. This simple formula is the basic relationship of the simple Delta VaR model for market risk. The distribution of the NPV changes is the sum of the random changes of the mark-to-market values of the individual transactions, which depend on those of underlying rates. Using the normal approximation makes the linear NPV changes normal as well. Figure 25.2 represents the distribution and VaR for NPV at a single time point in the future.

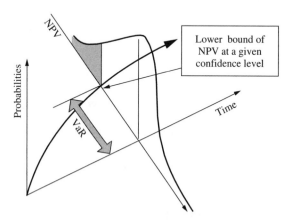

FIGURE 25.2 Projecting NPV at a future horizon (no convexity risk)

In fact, convexity risk plus the long-term horizon makes this technique inappropriate. When time passes, duration drifts. In addition, interest rate volatility grows and activates options. The Delta VaR relationship ceases to apply. Multiple revaluations of NPV for various sets of rates are necessary to capture the changes in durations and NPV. In order to illustrate the effect of convexity risk, we develop in the next section a simplified example.

MULTIPLE SIMULATIONS AND NPV VAR

This section provides simulations of NPV with varying rates and uses Monte Carlo simulation, with a flat yield curve, to calculate the NPV VaR. In order to proceed through the various steps, we need to simulate random values of a single risk driver, which is a flat market rate. The forward revaluation of the NPV is straightforward with only two assets, the loan portfolio and the debt.

Assets and debt are both fixed rate in a first stage. We introduce convexity risk later on in the example using a variable rate loan with a cap on the interest rate of the loan. Using 'with and without' cap simulations illustrates how the cap changes the NPV distribution. Revaluation depends on the interest rates of assets and liabilities. The simulation without cap uses a fixed rate, while the simulation with cap on the variable rate loan necessitates that the loan be variable up to the cap. The first subsection provides a set of simplified data. The next two subsections provide the two simulations.

The Bank's Balance Sheet Data

The bank sample portfolio is as given in Table 25.1.

TABLE 25.1 Sample bank portfolio

	Rate						
Market	8.0%						
	Rate	Amount					
Asset	9.0%	1000.00					
Liability	8.0%	960.00					
Date	0	1	2	3	4	5	
Asset		90.00	90.00	90.00	90.00	1090.00	
Liability		1036.80					

The bank NPV at the flat yield curve, with interest rates at 8%, is the present value at 8% of all asset and liability cash flows, as in Table 25.2.

TABLE 25.2 Sample bank portfolio NPV

	Present value
Asset	1123.12
Liability	1036.80
NPV	86.32

When the interest rate increases, both values of assets and liabilities decrease. There are two cases: without significant convexity risk and with convexity risk for assets due to a prepayment option.

NPV VaR with Fixed Rate Asset and Liability

In the simpler case, without convexity, both asset and debt have fixed rates, the loan yielding a 9% rate and the liability rate being 8%. The NPV calculation is a forward calculation at date 1. Since the liability matures at date 1, its value remains constant whatever the rate value because there is no discounting at this date. Both asset and liability rates are fixed rates. The asset and liability value–rate profiles and the NPV profile when the market rate changes are given in Figure 25.3.

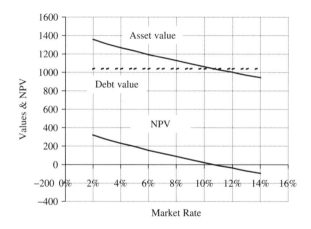

FIGURE 25.3 Asset, debt and NPV values when the market rate changes

The NPV decreases continuously with rates because the asset value decreases, while the debt value remains constant. To calculate the NPV VaR, we vary the interest rate randomly, using a normal curve for the flat rate, with an expected value of 8% and a yearly volatility of 2%[1]. With 1000 simulations, we generate the interest rate values and the corresponding NPV values. With the distribution of NPV values, we derive the NPV at various confidence levels and the VaR at these confidence levels. The break-even rate making the NPV negative is around 11% (Figure 25.4).

The NPV reaches negative values, triggering losses. The VaR requires setting confidence levels. The VaR at various NPV percentiles results from the distribution (Figure 25.5). The graph shows that the NPV VaR at 1% confidence level is close to −60. The NPV expected value is 86.32, and the NPV (1%) shows that the loss from the expected value is close to 146 (86 + 60).

---

[1] We need to ensure that the interest rate does not become negative. We could also use a lognormal curve for the market rate. In this simulation, the rate remains well above 0.

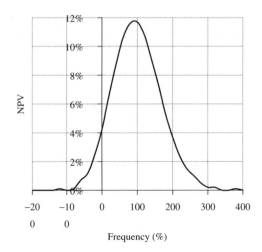

FIGURE 25.4 NPV distribution with market rate changes

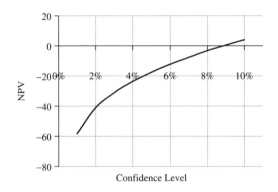

FIGURE 25.5 NPV values and confidence levels

NPV VaR with Convexity Risk in Assets

In the second case, we simulate convexity for the asset by introducing a formula that caps the asset rate: asset rate = max(market rate + 1%, 9%). The asset rate is either the market rate plus a margin of 1% above the market rate, or 9%. It is a floater when the market rate is lower than 8%. When the market rate hits 8%, the loan has a fixed rate equal to 9%. This simulates a prepayment option triggered at 9% by borrowers. The asset value varies when the market rate changes, with a change of slope at 8%. The increase with rate when rate values are lower than 8% results from the discounting flows indexed to rates, and when the asset rate hits the 9% cap the asset value starts decreasing. The liability value remains constant because we have a unique flow at date 1, which is the date for the forward valuation. Consequently, the NPV shows a bump at 8%, and becomes negative when the market rate exceeds some upper bound close to 11% (Figure 25.6). Figure 25.7 shows the NPV bump.

When proceeding with similar simulations of market rate as above, we obtain the NPV distribution and the NPV percentiles for deriving the VaR (Figure 25.8).

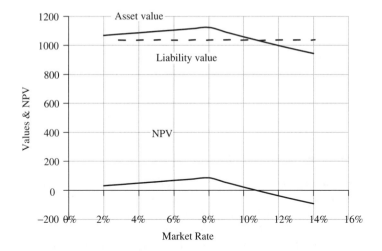

FIGURE 25.6   Asset, debt and NPV values when the market rate changes

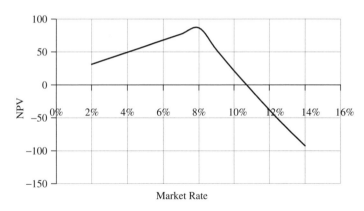

FIGURE 25.7   NPV 'bump' when the market rate changes

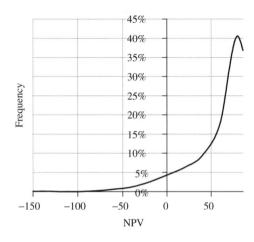

FIGURE 25.8   Distribution of NPV with market rate changes

FIGURE 25.9   NPV values and confidence levels

The NPV distribution becomes highly skewed, illustrating convexity effects. The bump effectively flattens the NPV–rate profile, with a concentration of value around the bump which results in a much higher frequency around the maximum value. On the other hand, both increases and decreases in market rate have an adverse effect due to convexity risk. Hence, there are higher frequencies of adverse deviations and negative values (Figure 25.9).

SECTION 9

Funds Transfer Pricing

26

FTP Systems

The two main tools for integrating global risk management with decision-making are the Funds Transfer Pricing (FTP) system and the capital allocation system. As a reminder, FTP serves to allocate interest income, while the capital allocation system serves to allocate risks.

Transfer prices serve as reference rates for calculating interest income of transactions, product lines, market segments and business units. They also transfer the liquidity and the interest rate risks from the 'business sphere' to Asset–Liability Management (ALM). The capital allocation system is the complement to the FTP system, since it allocates capital, a necessary step for the calculation of risk-based pricing and risk-based performance (ex post). Chapters 51 and 52, discussing 'risk contributions', address the capital allocation issue.

The current chapter addresses three major FTP issues for commercial banking:

- The goals of the transfer pricing system.
- The transfer of funds across business units and with the ALM units.
- The measurement of performance given the transfer price.

It does not address the issue of defining economic transfer prices, deferred to the next chapter, and assumes them given at this first stage. The FTP system specifications are:

- Transferring funds between units.
- Breaking down interest income by transaction or client, or any subportfolio such as business units, product families or market segments.
- Setting target profitability for business units.
- Transferring interest rate risk, which is beyond the control of business units, to ALM. ALM missions are to maintain interest rate risk within limits while minimizing the cost of funding or maximizing the return of investments.

- Pricing funds to business units with economic benchmarks, using economic transfer prices.
- Eventually combining economic prices with commercial incentives.

An internal system exchanges capital between units. Transfers go through ALM. The ALM unit is the central pole buying all resources from business lines, collecting them through deposits and selling funds to the lending business lines. Transfer prices allow the calculation of interest income based on transfer prices, in such a way that the algebraic addition of interest income of all units, including ALM, sums up to the accounting interest income of the overall banking portfolio (because all internal sales and purchases of funds compensate).

The first section introduces the specifications of the transfer pricing system. The second section discusses the netting mechanisms for excesses and deficits of funds within the bank. The third section details the calculation of performance, for business lines as well as for the entire bank, and its breakdown by business units. The fourth section provides simple calculations of interest income, and shows how the interest incomes allocated to business units or individual transactions add up exactly to the bank's overall margin. The fifth section addresses the choice of target profitability and risk limits for ALM and business lines. The last section contrasts the commercial and financial views of transfer prices, and raises the issue of defining 'economic' transfer prices, providing a transition to the next chapter.

THE GOALS OF THE TRANSFER PRICING SYSTEM

The FTP system serves several major purposes, to:

- Allocate funds within the banks.
- Calculate the performance margins of a transaction or any subportfolio of transactions and its contributions to the overall margin of the bank (revenues allocation).
- Define economic benchmarks for pricing and performance measurement purposes. This implies choosing the right reference for economic transfer prices. The 'all-in' cost of funds to the bank provides this reference.
- Define pricing policies: risk-based pricing is the pricing that would compensate the risks of the bank, independent of whether this pricing is effective or not, because of competition, in line with the overall profitability target of the banks.
- Provide incentives or penalties, differentiating the transfer prices to bring them in line with the commercial policy, which may or may not be in line with the target risk-based prices.
- Provide mispricing reports, making explicit the differences between the effective prices and what they should be, that is the target risk-based pricing.
- Transfer liquidity and interest rate risk to the ALM unit, making the performance of business lines independent of market movements that are beyond their control.

The list demonstrates that the FTP system is a strategic tool, and that it is the main interface between the commercial sphere and the financial sphere of the bank. Any malfunctioning or inconsistency in the system interferes with commercial and financial management, and might create a gap between global policies and operations management. Moreover, it is not feasible to implement a risk management system without setting up a consistent and comprehensive FTP system.

All business units of a financial institution share a common resource: liquidity. The first function of FTP is to exchange funds between business units with ALM, since business units do not have balanced uses and resources. The FTP nets the balances of sources and uses of funds within the bank. The exchange of funds between units with ALM requires a pricing system. The FTP system serves the other major purpose of setting up internal transfer prices. Transfer prices serve to calculate revenues as spreads between customers' prices and internal references. Without them, there is no way to calculate internal margins of transactions, product lines, customer or market segments, and business units. Thus, transfer prices provide a major link between the global bank earnings and individual subportfolios or individual transactions. The presentation arranges the above issues in two main groups (Figure 26.1):

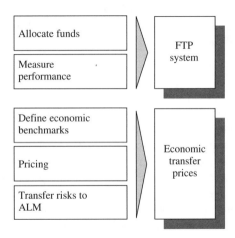

FIGURE 26.1 The 'Funds Transfer Pricing' system and its applications

- The organization of the FTP.
- The definition of economic transfer prices.

THE INTERNAL MANAGEMENT OF FUNDS AND NETTING

Since uses and resources of funds are generally unbalanced for business units, the FTP system allows netting the differences and allocating funds to those having liquidity deficits, or purchasing excesses where they appear. There are several solutions for organizing the system. An important choice is to decide which balances are 'netted' and how.

ALM, Treasury and Management Control

The organization varies across banks although, putting together all interested parties, it should allow us to perform the necessary functions of the FTP. Various entities are potentially interested in an FTP scheme. Since the Treasury is the unit which, in the end, raises debts or invests excesses in the market, it is obviously interested in the netting of cash flows. Since internal prices also serve to monitor commercial margins, management control is also involved. Since ALM is the unit in charge of managing the liquidity and interest rate exposures of the bank, the internal prices should be consistent with the choices of ALM. These various units participate in transfer pricing from various angles. They might have overlapping missions. The organization might change according to specific management choices. The definition of the scope of each unit should avoid any overlapping. In this chapter, we consider that ALM is in charge of the system, and that other management units are end-users of the system.

Internal Pools of Funds

Pools of funds are virtual locations where all funds, excesses and deficits, are centralized. The concept of pools of funds is more analytical than real. It allocates funds and defines the prices of these transfers.

Netting

The FTP nets the excesses of some business units with the deficits of others. This necessitates a central pool of resources to group excesses and deficits and net them. The central pool lends to deficit units and purchases the excesses of others. Starting from scratch, the first thought is to use this simplest system. The simplest solution is to use a unique price for such transfers. The system is 'passive', since it simply records excesses and deficits and nets them. Some systems use several pools of funds, for instance grouping them according to maturity and setting prices by maturity. Moreover, at first sight, it sounds simple to exchange only the net balances of business units (Figure 26.2).

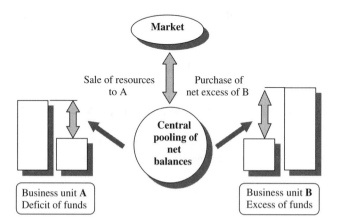

FIGURE 26.2 Transfers of net balances only

Since assets and liabilities are netted before transfer to the central pool, all assets and liabilities, generated by the operations of A and B, do not transit through the system.

Therefore, the transfer prices apply only to net balances. Their impact is limited to netted balances. The system is simple. The flows are consequences of the operations of business units and the fund transfer system does not influence them. A more active management requires a different system.

Pricing all Outstanding Balances

Instead of exchanging only the net excesses or deficits, an alternative is that the ALM purchases all resources and sets a price for all uses of funds of business units, without prior local netting of assets and liabilities. The full amounts of assets and liabilities transit through the central pool. This central pool is the ALM unit. This scheme creates a full internal capital market with internal prices. Post-transfers, the ALM either invests any global excess or funds any global deficit in the capital markets.

This system is an active management tool. It does more than 'record' the balances resulting from the decisions of business units. The major difference with the system exchanging net local balances only is that the internal prices hit all assets and liabilities of each business unit.

By setting transfer prices, the ALM has a powerful leverage on business units. The decision-making process, customer pricing and commercial policy of these units become highly dependent on transfer prices. Transfer prices might also serve as incentives to promote some product lines or market segments through lower prices, or to discourage, through higher prices, the development of others. Such decisions depend on the bank's business policy. Using such a system in a very active manner remains a management decision. In any case, this scheme makes the FTP a very powerful tool to influence the commercial policies of all business units (Figure 26.3).

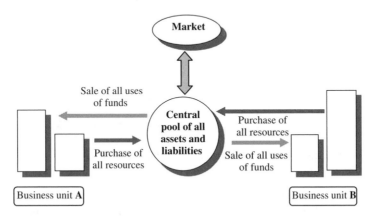

FIGURE 26.3   The central pool of all assets and liabilities

This system serves as a reference in what follows because it 'hits' all assets and liabilities. For instance, it was impossible to calculate a margin of an individual transaction in the previous system, since there was no way to 'hit' that transaction. Now, the FTP system makes it possible, since all transactions transfer through the central pool. This is a critical property to develop the full functions of the FTP system. Given the powerful potential of this solution, the issue of defining relevant economic prices is critical.

MEASURING PERFORMANCE

Any transfer pricing system separates margins into business, or commercial, margins and financial margins. The commercial margin is the spread between customer prices and internal prices. The financial margin is that of ALM, which results from the volumes exchanged plus the spreads between internal prices and the market prices used to borrow or invest. In addition, calculating the spread is feasible for any individual transactions as well as for any subportfolio. This allows the FTP to isolate the contribution to the overall bank margin of all business units and of ALM.

In the FTP, the banking portfolio is the mirror image of the ALM portfolio since ALM buys all liabilities and sells all assets. The sum of the margins generated by the business units and those generated by the ALM balance sheet should be equal to the actual interest margin of the bank (Figure 26.4).

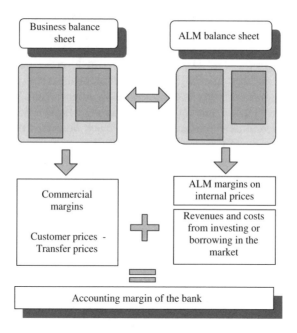

FIGURE 26.4   The bank's balance sheet and the ALM balance sheet

In general, the summation of all business line internal margins calculated over the transfer prices will differ from the accounting margin since it ignores the ALM margin. Without the latter, there is a missing link between the commercial margins and the accounting earnings of the bank. On the other hand, calculating all margins properly, including the ALM margin, makes them sum the accounting margin of the bank because internal transfers neutralize over the entire bank. The FTP implies an internal analytical recording of all revenues to allow reconciliation with the bank's income statement. The next paragraph illustrates this reconciliation process.

The calculations use a simple example. The commercial margin calculation scope is the entire balance sheet of all business units.

- For the bank, we simply sum all revenues and costs from lending and borrowing, including any funding on the market.
- For the business units, revenues result from customer prices minus the cost of any internal purchase of resources by the central unit (ALM). Costs result from the interest paid to customers (depositors) and the revenues of selling these resources to the ALM at transfer prices charged by the ALM.
- For the ALM unit, revenues result from charging the lending units the cost of their funds, and the costs result from purchasing from them their collected resources. In addition, ALM gets a market cost when funding a deficit and a market revenue from investing any global excess of funds.

THE FTP SYSTEM AND MARGIN CALCULATIONS OF BUSINESS UNITS

The margin calculations use a simplified balance sheet. After calculating the bank's accounting margin, we proceed by breaking it down across business units and ALM using the transfer prices. The system accommodates cost allocations for completing the analytical income statements, and any differentiation of multiple transfer prices, down to individual transactions. As long as the ALM records properly internal transactions, the overall accounting profitability reconciles with the interest income breakdown across business lines and transactions.

The Accounting Margin: Example

The business balance sheet generates a deficit funded by ALM. The average customer price for borrowers is 12% and the average customer rate paid to depositors is 6%. The ALM borrows in the market at the 9% current market rate. There is a unique transfer price. It applies to both assets sold by ALM to business units and resources purchased by ALM from business units. This unique value is 9.20%. Note that this value differs from the market rate deliberately. There could be several transfer prices, but the principle would be the same. Table 26.1 shows the balance sheet and the averaged customer rates.

TABLE 26.1   Bank's balance sheet

	Volume	Rate
Assets		
Loans	2000	12.00%
Total	2000	
Resources		
Deposits	1200	6.00%
Funding	800	9.00%
Total	2000	

The full cost of resources is the financial cost plus the operating cost, either direct or indirect. The analytical profitability statements, using both transfer prices and cost allocations, follows. The transfer price mechanism ensures the consistency of all analytical income statements of the business units. If transfer prices change, they simply transfer margins from one unit to another, but they do not change the overall bank margin. Cost allocations add up to the overall costs as well. To illustrate the process, we subdivide the bank into three business units:

- Collecting resources.
- Originating loans.
- ALM, managing financial risks.

Table 26.1 shows the aggregated balance sheet. The volumes of loans, deposits and external funding are under the control of each of the three business units. The direct calculation of the accounting margin is straightforward since it depends only on customer rates and the funding cost by the ALM:

$$2000 \times 12\% - 1200 \times 6\% - 800 \times 9\% = 96$$

Breaking Down the Bank Margin into Contributions of Business Units

From the average customer rates, the transfer price set by the ALM unit and the market rate (assuming a flat yield curve), we calculate the margins for each commercial unit purchasing or selling funds to the ALM. The ALM unit buys and sells funds internally and funds externally the bank's deficit. The corresponding margins are determined using the usual set of calculations detailed in Table 26.2.

TABLE 26.2   The calculation of margins

Market rate	9.00%	
Transfer price	9.20%	
Margin	*Calculation*	*Value*
Direct calculation of margin		
Accounting margin	$2000 \times 12.00\% - 1200 \times 6.00\% - 800 \times 9.00\%$	96.0
Commercial margins		
Loans	$2000 \times (12.00\% - 9.20\%)$	56.0
Deposits	$1200 \times (9.20\% - 6.00\%)$	38.4
Total commercial margin	$2000 \times (12.00\% - 9.20\%) + 1200 \times (9.20\% - 6.00\%)$	94.4
ALM margin	$2000 \times 9.20\% - 1200 \times 9.20\% - 800 \times 9.00\%$	1.6
Bank margin	Commercial margin $+$ ALM margin	96.0

With a unique internal price set at 9.20%, the commercial margin as a percentage is $12\% - 9.20\% = 2.80\%$ for uses of funds and $9.20\% - 6\% = 2.80\%$ for resources. ALM charges the lending activities at the transfer price and purchases the resources collected at this same price. The total commercial margin is 94.4, and is lower than the bank's accounting margin. This total commercial margin adds the contributions of the lending activity and the collection of resources. The lending activity generates a margin of 56.0, while the collection of resources generates 38.4. These two activities could be different business units. The system allocates the business margin to the different business units.

The ALM has symmetrical revenues and costs, plus the cost of funding the deficit of 800 in the market. Its margin is 1.6.

The commercial margin is 94.4, but the accounting margin of the bank is 96.0. This is due to the positive ALM margin, because ALM actually overcharges the market rate to the business units with a transfer price of 9.20%, higher than the market rate (9%). If we add the contributions of business units and the ALM margin, the result is 96.0, the accounting margin. The mechanism reconciles the contribution calculations with the bank's accounting margin.

It is easy to verify that, if the ALM margin is zero, the entire bank's margin becomes equal to the commercial margin. This is a reference case: ALM is neutral and generates neither profit nor loss. Then the entire bank's margin is 'in' the commercial units, as in the calculations below. Note that we keep the customers' rates constant, so that the internal spreads change between customers' rates and transfer prices. They become $9\% - 8\% = 1\%$ for lending and $8\% - 3\% = 5\%$ for collecting deposits. Evidently, since all customers' rates are constant as well as the cost of market funds, the accounting margin remains at 4. Nevertheless, the allocation of this same accounting margin between business units and ALM differs (Table 26.3).

TABLE 26.3   The calculation of margins

Market rate	9.00%	
Transfer price	9.00%	
Margin	*Calculation*	*Value*
Direct calculation of margin		
Accounting margin	$2000 \times 12.00\% - 1200 \times 6.00\% - 800 \times 9.00\%$	96.0
Commercial margins		
Loans	$2000 \times (12.00\% - 9.00\%)$	60.0
Deposits	$1200 \times (9.00\% - 6.00\%)$	36.0
Total commercial margin	$2000 \times (12.00\% - 9.00\%) + 1200 \times (9.00\% - 6.00\%)$	96.0
ALM margin	$2000 \times 9.20\% - 1200 \times 9.20\% - 800 \times 9.00\%$	0.0
Bank margin	Commercial margin + ALM margin	96.0

The above examples show that:

- Transfer prices allocate the bank's margin between the business units and ALM.
- The overall net interest margin is always equal to the sum of the commercial margin and the ALM margin.

Analytical Income Statements

The cost allocation is extremely simplified. We use three different percentages for lending, collecting resources and the ALM units. The percentages apply to volumes (Table 26.4).

Combining the cost allocations with the interest margins, we check that all interest margins add up to the overall bank margin and that the aggregated operating income is the bank operating income (Table 26.5).

TABLE 26.4   Operating costs allocated to business units

Operating cost	Volume		Cost
Loans	2.00%	2000	40.00
Collection of resources	1.80%	1200	21.60
ALM	0.08%	3200	2.56
Total operating cost	3.88%		64.00

TABLE 26.5   Business unit income statements and bank consolidated income statements

Income statement	'Loans'	'Deposits'	'ALM'	'Bank'
Interest margin	56.0	38.4	1.6	96.0
Operating cost (2%)	40.0	26.7	2.6	69.3
Operating income	16.0	11.7	−1.0	26.7

Differentiation of Transfer Prices

The above calculations use a unique transfer price. In practice, it is possible to differentiate the transfer prices by product lines, market segments or individual transactions. If we use a different transfer price for lending and collecting deposits, the customer rates being 12% for lending and 6% for deposits, the margin is:

$$\text{Commercial margin} = \text{assets}(12\% - \text{TP}_{\text{assets}}) + \text{liabilities}(\text{TP}_{\text{liabilities}} - 6\%)$$

$$\text{Commercial margin} = \text{assets} \times \text{assets contribution } (\%)$$

$$+ \text{ resources} \times \text{resources contribution } (\%)$$

The commercial margin depends directly on the transfer prices and it changes if we use different ones. But whatever transfer prices we use, the ALM uses the same. When consolidating business transaction margins and ALM internal transactions, we end up with the accounting margin of the bank. This provides degrees of freedom in setting transfer prices. It is possible to use economic transfer prices differentiated by transaction, as recommended in the next chapter, and still reconcile all transaction margins with the bank's accounting margin through the ALM margin.

The facility of differentiating prices according to activities, product lines or markets, while maintaining reconciliation through the ALM margin, allows us to choose whatever criteria we want for transfer prices. The next chapter shows that economic prices reflecting the 'true' cost of funding are the best ones. However, it might be legitimate to also use transfer prices as commercial signals for developing some markets and products while restricting business on others. As long as we record the transfer prices and their gaps with economic prices, we know the cost of such a commercial policy. Transfer of revenues and costs neutralizes within the bank, whether or not there is a unique transfer price or several. In fact, no matter what the transfer prices are, they allocate the revenues. Setting economic benchmarks for these prices is an issue addressed in the next chapter.

ALM AND BUSINESS UNIT PROFITABILITY GOALS

The overall profitability target should translate into consistent objectives across business units and the ALM unit. We discuss setting objectives for the ALM unit and move on to the definition of business line target profitability levels, from an overall profitability goal. The overall profitability relates to the overall risk of the bank, as target profitability on economic capital. We assume it given, and examine how to break it down.

ALM Profitability and Risks

ALM is a special business unit since it can have various missions. If its target profit is set to zero, it behaves as a cost centre whose responsibility is to minimize the cost of funding and hedge the bank against interest rate risk. If the bank has excess funds, the mission of ALM is still to keep the global interest rate risk within limits, while maximizing the return on excess funds. This is consistent with a strategy that makes commercial banking the core business, and where the ALM policy is to hedge liquidity and interest rate risks with cost-minimizing, or revenue-maximizing, objectives.

However, minimizing the cost of funding could be an incentive for ALM to maintain some exposure to interest rate risk depending on expectations with respect to interest rates. In general, banking portfolios generate either deficits or excesses of funds. Nevertheless, a policy of hedging systematically all exposures, for all future periods, has a cost. This is the opportunity cost of neutralizing any potential gain resulting from market movements. However, without a full hedge, there is an interest rate risk. The ALM unit should be responsible for this risk and benefit from any saving in the cost of funds obtained thanks to maintaining risk exposure. This saving is the difference between the funding cost under full hedging policy and the effective funding cost of the actual policy conducted by ALM. This cost saving is its Profit and Loss (P&L). Since it is not reasonable to speculate on rates, interest rate risk limits should apply to ALM exposures.

Giving such flexibility to ALM turns it into a profit centre, which is in charge of optimizing the funding policy within specified limits on gaps, earnings volatility or 'Value at Risk' (VaR). Making such an organization viable requires several conditions. All liquidity and interest rate risks should actually be under ALM control, and the commercial margins should not have any exposure to interest rate risk. This imposes on the FTP system specifications other than above, developed subsequently. In addition, making the ALM a profit centre subject to limits requires proper monitoring of what the funding costs would be under full hedging over a period. Otherwise, it is not possible to compare the effective funding costs with a benchmark (Figure 26.5).

Setting Target Commercial Margins

Banks have an overall profitability goal. They need to send signals to business units and allocate target contributions to the various business units consistent with this overall goal. These contributions are the spreads over transfer prices times the volume. Assuming transfer prices given, the issue is to define commercial contributions of the various units such that they sum exactly to the target accounting net margin.

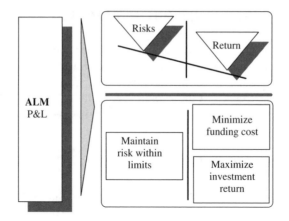

FIGURE 26.5   Policies and profitability of ALM

The accounting net interest margin is the summation of commercial margins, or contributions, and of the ALM margin. If ALM is a pure hedging entity, business units generate the entire margin. In such a case, the sum of commercial margins becomes identical to the target accounting margin. If ALM is a profit centre, any projected profit or loss of ALM plus the commercial margins is necessarily equal to the consolidated margin.

Taking the example of lending only, we have only one business unit. The commercial margin, as a percentage of assets, is the spread between the unknown customer rate and the transfer price, or $X - 8\%$. The value of the margin is the product of this spread with asset volume. The accounting margin is, by definition, the total of the commercial margin of business units and of the ALM margin:

$$M_{\text{bank}} = M_{\text{commercial}} + M_{\text{ALM}}$$

Therefore, the commercial margin is the difference between the accounting margin and the internal ALM margin. The process requires defining what the ALM margin is. The ALM margin might be zero, making the sum of commercial contributions to the margin identical to the accounting margin. This would be the benchmark case, since any P&L of the ALM is a 'speculative' cost saving 'on top' of the net margin of the banking book.

The simple example below shows how to move from a target overall accounting interest margin towards the commercial contributions (margins) of business units. Once these margins are defined, the target customer prices follow, since they are equal to the transfer prices plus the percentage margin on average. We use the following data. The volume of assets is 100, the cost of borrowing in the market is 10% and the internal transfer price is 8%. There is a difference between the market rate and the internal transfer rate to make the argument general. The volume of equity is 4% of assets, or 40. The target net interest margin is 25% of equity, or 10. The outstanding debt is $1000 - 40 = 960$. The cost of debt is $8\% \times 960 = 76.8$. Table 26.6 summarizes the data. The issue is to find the appropriate target commercial margin over transfer price.

The ALM margin is:

$$M_{\text{ALM}} = 8\% \times 1000 - 10\% \times 960 = -16$$

It is negative because the ALM prices internal funds at a rate lower than the market rate and subsidizes the commercial units. The target commercial margin is the difference

TABLE 26.6 Setting a target economic margin

Target accounting margin	10
Cost of debt	10%
Transfer price	8%
Volume of assets	1000
Equity	40
Debt	960
Target commercial margin over transfer price	?

between the targeted accounting margin and that of the ALM:

$$\text{Target IM}_{\text{commercial}} = \text{target IM}_{\text{overall}} - \text{IM}_{\text{ALM}} = 10 - (-16) = 26$$

Given the volume of assets, it is easy to derive the average target customer rate X from this target margin. The margin value 26 represents 2.6% of outstanding assets. The required spread as a percentage of assets is:

$$X - 8\% = 2.6\%$$

The average rate X charged to customers should be 10.6%. It is sufficient to set a target commercial margin at 26, setting some minimum customer rate to avoid selling below cost, so that commercial entities might have flexibility in combining the percentage margin and the volume from one transaction to another as long as they reach the overall 26 goal. We check that the calculation ensures that the net interest margin is 10. It is the total revenue less the cost of debt: $10.6\% \times 1000 - 96 = 10$. This equation allows us to calculate the average customer rate directly since the target accounting margin, the cost of debt and the size of assets are given. It simply says: $(X - 8\%) \times 1000 - 96 = 10$.

The same overall summations hold with multiple transfer prices. Therefore, transfer prices allow us to define the global commercial margin above transfer prices consistent with a given target net accounting margin. Setting the actual business line target contributions to this consolidated margin implies adjusting the profitability to the risk originated by business units. For lending, credit risk is the main one. Within an integrated system, the modulation of target income depends on the risk contributions of business lines to the overall risk of the portfolio (as defined in Chapters 51 and 52).

THE FINANCIAL AND COMMERCIAL RATIONALE OF TRANSFER PRICES

The FTP system is the interface between the commercial universe and the financial universe. In order to serve this purpose, the transfer prices should be in line with both commercial and financial constraints. From a financial standpoint, the intuition is that transfer prices should reflect market conditions. From a commercial standpoint, customer prices should follow business policy guidelines subject to constraints from competition. In other words, transfer prices should be consistent with two different types of benchmarks: those derived from the financial universe and those derived from the commercial policy.

Transfer prices should also be consistent with market rates. The next chapter develops this rationale further. However, the intuition is simple. If transfer prices lead to much higher customer rates than the market offers, it would be impossible to sustain competition and customers would arbitrage them with the market. For buying resources, a similar rationale applies. The alternative uses of resources are lending or investing. If lending provides much less than the market, the bank is better off investing. If the opposite holds, resources priced internally at more than market prices would hurt the lending margin. Hence, the market provides a benchmark.

On the other hand, ignoring competitors' prices does not make much sense. This leads to the usual trade-off between profitability and market share. Banks are reluctant to give up market share, because it would drive them out of business. Since competition and market rates are not easy to reconcile, there has to be some mispricing.

Mispricing is the difference between 'economic prices' and effective pricing. Mispricing is not an error since it is business-driven. Nevertheless, it deserves monitoring for profitability and business management, and preventing mispricing from being too important to be sustainable. Monitoring mispricing implies keeping track of target prices and effective prices, to report any discrepancy between the two. At this stage, the mispricing concept applies to economic transfer prices limited to such benchmarks as the cost of funds for lending and benchmarks of investment return for collecting resources. It extends to risk-based pricing, when target prices charge the credit risk to customers. This has to do with capital allocation.

A logical conclusion is that using two sets of internal prices makes sense. One set of transfer prices should refer to economic benchmarks, such as market rates. The other set of transfer prices serves as commercial signals. Any discrepancy between the two prices is the cost of the commercial policy. These discrepancies are the penalties (mark-up) or subsidies (mark-down) consistent with the commercial policy. This scheme reconciles diverging functions of the transfer prices and makes explicit the cost of enforcing commercial policies that are not in line with market interest rates.

27

Economic Transfer Prices

This chapter focuses on economic benchmarks for transfer prices that comply with all specifications of the transfer pricing scheme. The basic principle for defining such 'economic' transfer prices is to refer to market prices because of arbitrage opportunities between bank rates and market rates whenever discrepancies appear. Economic benchmarks derive from market prices. Mark-ups or mark-downs over the economic benchmarks serve for pricing. There are two types of such add-ons. Some serve for defining risk-based pricing. Others are commercial incentives or penalties resulting from the business policy, driving the product–market segments mix. Note that implementing this second set of commercial mark-ups or mark-downs requires tracking the discrepancies with economic prices which, once aggregated, represent the cost of the commercial policy.

Economic benchmarks for transfer prices are 'all-in' costs of funds. The 'all-in' cost of funds applies to lending activities and represents the cost of obtaining these funds, while complying with all banks' balance sheet constraints, such as liquidity ratio. It is a market-based cost with add-ons for liquidity risk and other constraints. It is the cost of a 'notional' debt mimicking the loans. It is notional because no rule imposes that Asset–Liability Management (ALM) continuously raises such debts. The rationale of this scheme is to make sure that lending provides at least the return the bank could have on the market, making it worthwhile to lend. The target price adds up the cost of funding with mark-ups and mark-downs, plus a target margin in line with the overall profitability goal.

To ensure effective transfer of interest rate risk from business units to ALM, economic prices of individual transactions are historical, calculated from prevailing market rates at origination, and guaranteed over the life of the transaction. The guaranteed prices make the interest incomes of transactions and business lines insensitive to interest rates over subsequent periods until maturity of the transaction.

The cost of funds view applies to lending activities. For excess resources, market rates are the obvious references. The difference is that investments generate interest rate risk and exposure to the credit risk of issuers, while lending generates exposure to the credit risk of borrowers, ALM taking care of interest rate risk. Investments of excess funds raise the issue of defining meaningful risk and return benchmarks. These result, in general, from investment portfolios serving as 'notional' references.

The first section expands the arbitrage argument to define transfer prices referring to market rates. The second section provides an overview of the transfer pricing scheme with all inputs, from the cost of funds to the final customer price, using a sample set of calculations. The third section defines the economic cost of funds, the foundation on which all additional mark-ups and mark-downs pile up. The fourth section makes explicit the conditions for ensuring effective transfer of interest rate risk to the ALM unit.

COMMERCIAL MARGIN AND MATURITY SPREAD

Discrepancies of banks' prices with market prices lead to arbitrage by customers. The drawback of a unique transfer price, equal to the average cost of funds of the bank, is that it would serve as a reference for both long and short loans. If the term structure of market rates is upward sloping, customer prices are below market rates on the long end of the curve and above market rates in the short maturity range (Figure 27.1). The unique transfer subsidizes long-term borrowers and penalizes short-term borrowers. A first conclusion is that transfer prices should differ according to maturities.

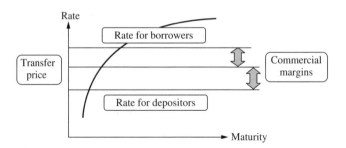

FIGURE 27.1   Drawbacks of a single transfer price

It is sensible to remove the maturity spread from the commercial margins, since this spread is beyond the control of the business lines. The maturity spread depends on market conditions. On the other hand, it is under the control of ALM, which can swap long-term rates against short-term rates, and the spread is in the accounting margin of the bank. Most commercial banks ride the yield curve by lending long and borrowing short, benefiting from this spread. On the other hand, riding the yield curve implies the risk of 'twists' in the curve. The risk of shifts and twists should be under the responsibility of ALM, rather than affecting commercial margins. Otherwise, these would embed interest rate risk. Business lines would appear responsible for financial conditions beyond their control. Making commercial margins subject to shifts and twists of the yield curve would ultimately lead to closing and opening offices according to what happens to the yield curve. The implication is that 'commercial' margins do not include the contribution of the market spread between long and short rates, although it contributes to the accounting margin, and this contribution should be under the control of ALM.

In order to ensure that the bank makes a positive margin whatever the rates, and to isolate the maturity spread from the commercial margin, it is necessary to relate transfer prices to maturity. Bullet loan prices should be above market rates of the same maturity. Term deposit rates should be below the market rate of the same maturity. Demand deposit rates should be below the short-term rate. When lending above the market rate, the bank can borrow the money on the market and have a positive margin whatever the maturity. When collecting resources below market rates, the bank can invest them in the market and make a profit. Figure 27.2 illustrates this pricing scheme.

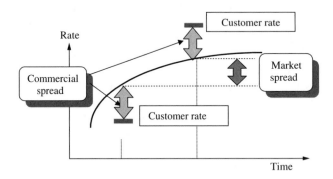

FIGURE 27.2   Commercial and market spreads

This suggests that market rates are the relevant benchmarks. It also illustrates the arbitrage argument making discrepancies irrelevant for both customers and the bank. This basic pricing scheme is the foundation of economic transfer prices, although the relevant benchmarks require further specifications.

PRICING SCHEMES

Transfer prices differ for lending and calculating margins on resources. For assets, transfer prices include all financial costs: they are 'all-in' costs of funds, with all factors influencing this cost. For deposits, the transfer prices should reflect the market rates on investing opportunities concurrent with lending.

Lending Activities

There are several pricing rationales in practice, mixing economic criteria and commercial criteria. It is possible to combine them if we can fully trace the components of pricing and combine them consistently for reporting purposes.

- Risk-based pricing is the benchmark, and should be purely economic. It implies two basic ingredients: the cost of funds plus mark-ups, notably for credit risk in lending. The mark-ups for risk result from the risk allocation system, and derive from capital allocations. We consider them as given here and concentrate on the economic costs of funds.

- Commercial pricing refers to mark-ups and mark-downs over economic benchmarks to drive the business policies through incentives and penalties differentiated by product and market. Such mark-ups and mark-downs are purely business-driven.

A comprehensive pricing scheme might include risk-based references plus such commercial mark-ups and mark-downs. 'Effective pricing' refers to actual prices used by banks. They might differ from the target risk-based prices simply because pricing is subject to competitive pressures. Mispricing is the difference between effective prices and target prices. The 'all-in' cost of funds serves as the foundation for transfer prices. To get the economic transfer price, other economic costs should add up. They include the expected loss on credit risk. Risk-based pricing implies a mark-up related to the credit standing of the borrower. This all-in cost of funding, plus these economic mark-ups, is the foundation of the transfer price.

Note that, at this level, the bank does not earn any profit yet since it simply balances the overall cost of funding and risk. Conventions are necessary at this stage. If the cost of allocated risk includes the target profitability, the bank actually defines a transfer price that provides adequate profitability. An alternative presentation would be to add a margin, which is the target profitability on allocated capital. Such a target margin, or contribution, should be in line with the overall profitability goal of the bank, and absorb the allocated operating costs. We adopt this second presentation below, because it makes a distinction between the economic transfer price and the risk-based price, the difference being precisely the target return on allocated capital. Table 27.1 summarizes the format of the economic income statement.

TABLE 27.1 Risk-based pricing and commercial incentives

Component	%
Cost of funding	
+Cost of liquidity	
='All-in' cost of funding	
−Expected loss from credit risk	
=Economic transfer price	
+Operating allocated costs	
+Risk-based margin for compensating credit risk capital	
=Target risk-based price	
+Business mark-ups or mark-downs	
=Customer price	

Such transfer prices are before any business mark-ups or mark-downs. Additional mark-ups or mark-downs, which result from deliberate commercial policies of providing incentives and penalties, could also affect the prices. Our convention is to consider only the economic transfer price plus a profitability contribution. The rationale is that we need to track these to isolate the cost of the business policy, while other mark-ups or mark-downs are purely business-driven. Moreover, we also need to track mispricing or the gap between effective prices and target risk-based prices for reporting purposes, and take corrective action. Figure 27.3 summarizes all schemes and mispricing.

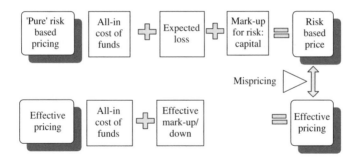

FIGURE 27.3   Pricing schemes and mispricing

At this stage, we have not yet defined the 'all-in' cost of funds. The next section does this.

Transaction versus Client Revenues and Pricing

Risk-based pricing might not be competitive at the individual transaction level simply because market spreads are not high enough to price all costs to a large corporate which has access to markets directly. This is a normal situation, because there is no reason why local markets should price credit risk, as seen in credit spreads, in line with the target of banks based on capital allocation for credit risk. Section 16 of this book addresses again the 'consistency' issue between internal pricing and external pricing of risk.

However, this does not imply that the overall client revenue cannot meet the bank's target profitability. Banks provide products and services and obtain as compensation interest spreads and fees. The overall client revenue is the relevant measure for calculating profitability, because it groups all forms of revenues from all transactions, plus all services resulting from the bank's relationship with its clients. Loans and services are a bundle. Using risk-based pricing at the transaction level might simply drive away business that would be profitable enough at the client level. The client is a better base for assessing profitability than standalone transactions. This is a strong argument for developing economic income statements at the client level.

Target Risk-based Pricing Calculations

Economic pricing for loans includes the cost of funds plus any mark-up for risk plus a target margin in line with the overall profitability goal. The cost of funding depends on rules used to define the funding associated with various loans. The pure economic benchmark is the one notional economic cost of funds, described below, which is the cost of funding that exactly mirrors the loan. We assume here that this cost of funds is 7%. The 'all-in' funding cost of the loan adds up the cost of maintaining the liquidity ratio and the balance sheet structure at their required level. We use here an add-on of 0.2% to obtain an 'all-in' cost of funds of 7.2%. Other relevant items are expected loss and allocated cost. Note that the overall profitability of the bank should also consider an additional contribution for non-allocated operating costs[1].

---

[1] Chapters 53 and 54 provide details on full-blown economic statements pre- or post-operating costs.

The required margin results from the required capital and the target return on that capital. For an outstanding balance of 1000 that requires no capital, the price needs to absorb only the all-in cost of funding.

When there is credit risk, the rationale for defining the target required margin based on allocated capital is as follows. If capital replaces a fraction of debt because the loan is risky, there is an additional cost because capital costs more than debt. The additional cost is the differential cost between equity and debt weighted by the amount of capital required. The same calculations apply to regulatory capital or economic capital. The pre-tax cost of equity is 25% in our example. The additional cost is the amount of equity times the differential between the cost of equity and the cost of debt: (25% − cost of debt) × equity. In order to transform this value into a percentage of the loan outstanding balance, we divide this cost in value by the loan size, assuming that the ratio of equity to assets is 4% for example. This gives the general formula for the risk premium: (25% − cost of debt) × 4%. In this example, the cost of capital is (25% − 7%) × 4% = 0.72%. All components of transfer prices are given in Table 27.2. To obtain a pure economic price, we set commercial incentives to zero.

TABLE 27.2 Components of transfer prices

Component	%
Cost of debt	7.00
+Cost of liquidity	0.20
+Expected losses	0.50
+Operating costs	0.50
=**Transfer price**	**8.20**
+Risk-based margin	0.72
=Target risk-based price	8.92
+Commercial incentives	0
=**Customer rate**	**8.92**

The cost of debt, set to 7%, is the most important item. The next section discusses the all-in cost of funds.

THE COST OF FUNDS FOR LOANS

The transfer price depends on the definition of the funds backing the assets. There are two views on the issue of defining the transaction that best matches the assets or the liabilities. The first is to refer to existing assets and resources. The underlying assumption is that existing resources fund assets. The second view is to define a 'best' funding solution and use the cost of this funding solution as the pure cost of funding.

The Cost of Existing Resources

Using the existing resources sounds intuitively appealing. These resources actually fund assets, so their cost has to be relevant. However, this solution raises conceptual inconsistencies. There are several types of assets and liabilities with different characteristics.

Each type of resource has a different cost. Therefore, we use either the 'weighted average cost of capital' (wacc), the average cost of resources or several costs. We pointed out earlier the shortcomings of a single transfer price. Another solution could be to match assets and resources based on their similar characteristics. For instance, we can try to match long-term resources with long-term assets, and so on for other maturities. This is the rationale for multiple pools of funds based on maturity buckets.

This principle raises several issues:

- Since the volumes of assets and resources of a given category, for instance long-term items, are in general different, the match cannot be exact. If long-term assets have a larger volume than long-term resources, other resources have to fill up the deficit. Rules are required to define which other resources will fund the mismatch, and the resulting cost of funds becomes dependent on such conventions.
- For business units, there is a similar problem. Generally, the balance sheet under the control of a business unit is not balanced. Any deficit needs matching by resources of other business units. However, it does not sound right to assign the cost of funds of another business unit, for instance a unit collecting a lot of 'cheap' deposits, to one that generates a deficit. The collection of cheap resources should rather increase the profitability of the unit getting such resources.
- Any cheap resource, such as deposits, subsidizes the profitability of assets. Matching a long-term loan with the core fraction of demand deposits might be acceptable in terms of maturity. However, this matching actually transfers the low cost of deposits to the margin allocated to loans. Economically, this assumes that new deposits fund each new dollar of loans, which is unrealistic.

This view is inconsistent from both organizational and economic standpoints. It implies a transfer of income from demand deposits to lending. In general, transferring the low cost of some resources to lending does not leave any compensation for collecting such resources. Low cost resources subsidize lending and lose their margin in the process! Given inconsistencies and unrealistic assumptions, the matching of assets with existing resources is not economic. Transfer prices require other benchmarks.

The 'Notional' Funding of Assets

The unique funding solution that neutralizes both liquidity and interest rate risk of a specific asset is the funding that 'mirrors' the time profile of flows and the interest rate nature. For instance, with a fixed rate term loan, the funding should replicate exactly the amortization profile and carry a fixed rate. Such funding is more 'notional' than real. It does not depend on the existing resources. It does not imply either that ALM actually decides to implement full cash flow matching. It serves as a benchmark for determining the cost of funds backing any given asset.

In some cases, the replication is obvious and the cost of funds also. A bullet debt matches a bullet loan. The relevant rate is the market rate corresponding to the maturity of the transaction. In other cases, the notional funding is different. For an amortizing loan, the outstanding balance varies over time until maturity. Therefore, the market rate of this maturity is not adequate. Using it would assume that the loan does not amortize over time. The funding that actually replicates the time profile of the loan is a combination of debts of various maturities. In the example below, a loan of 100 amortizes in 2 years, the repayments of capital being 40 and 60. Figure 27.4 shows the profile of the reference debt. The funding solution combines two spot bullet debts, of 1 and 2-year maturity, contracted at the market rates[2]. This example demonstrates that it is possible to find a unique notional funding for any fixed rate asset whose amortizing schedule is known.

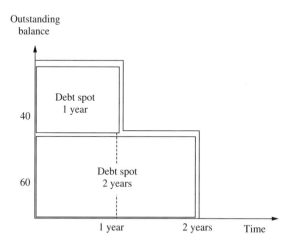

FIGURE 27.4   A 2-year amortizing loan

The solution is even simpler with floating rates than with fixed rates. For floating rate transactions, the replicating funding is a floating rate debt with reset dates matching those of the assets. The amortization profile should mirror that of the floating rate asset. However, for those assets that have no maturity, conventions are necessary.

The Cost of Funds

For a fixed rate loan, the funding solution used as reference has a cost that depends on the combinations of volumes borrowed and maturities. The cost is not a single market rate, but a combination of market rates. In the above example, there are two layers of debt: 60 for 2 years and 40 for 1 year. The relevant rates are the spot rates for these maturities. However, there should be a unique transfer price for a given loan. It is the average cost of funds of the two debts. Its exact definition is that of an actuarial rate. This rate is the discount rate making the present value of the future flows generated by the two debts equal to the amount borrowed.

The future outflows are the capital repayments and interest. The interest flows cumulate those of the 1-year and 2-year market rates. If the debts are zero-coupon, the interest payments are at maturity. The flows are $40(1 + r_1)$ in 1 year and $60(1 + r_2)^2$ in 2 years.

---

[2] There is another solution for backing the loan. For instance, a spot debt for 1 year could be contracted for the full amount of the loan, that is 100 for 1 year at the spot market rate, followed by another 1-year debt, for an amount of 60, starting 1 year from now. Nevertheless, such funding does not replicate the loan, since a fraction of the debt needs renewal for another year at a rate unknown today.

The cost r of this composite funding is a discount rate such that:

$$100 = 40 \times (1 + r_1)/(1 + r) + 60 \times (1 + r_2)^2/(1 + r)^2$$

The discount rate is somewhere between the two market rates. An approximate solution uses a linear approximation of the exact formula:

$$100 = 40(1 + r_1 - r) + 60(1 + 2r_2 - 2r)$$

$$r = (40 \times r_1 + 60 \times 2 \times r_2)/(40 + 2 \times 60)$$

The rate r is the weighted average of the spot rates for 1 and 2 years, using weights combining the size of each debt and its maturity. For instance, r_1 counts roughly twice and r_2 only once. With rates r_1 and r_2 equal to 8% and 9%, $r = 8.75\%$. The rate is closer to 9%, because the 2-year debt is the one whose amount and maturity are the highest. In practice, transfer price tables provide the composite market rates immediately, given the time profile of loans and the current market rates.

The Benefits of Notional Funding

Using the cost of funds of a debt that fully replicates the assets offers numerous economic benefits. Perfect matching implies that:

- The margin of the asset is immune to interest rate movements.
- There is no need for conventions to assign existing resources to usages of funds.
- There is no transfer of income generated by collecting resources to the income of lending activities.
- The calculation of a transfer price is mechanical and easy.

This objective choice avoids possible debates generated by conventions about transfer prices. In addition, this reference actually separates the income of the banking portfolio from those of ALM. It also separates business risk from financial risk and locks in commercial margins at origination of the loan, if we use as transfer price the cost of this notional funding mimicking the loan.

The ALM unit does not have to use a funding policy that actually immunizes the interest margin of the bank. The debt replicating the asset characteristics is a 'notional debt'. The ALM policy generally deviates from perfect matching of the flows of individual assets depending on interest rate views for example. On the other hand, a perfect match is feasible at the consolidated level of the bank for neutralizing both liquidity and interest rate risk. Doing so at the individual transaction level would result in over-hedging because it would ignore the natural offsets between assets and liabilities, resulting in gap profiles.

Comparing the perfect matching cost with the effective cost resulting from the ALM policy determines the performance of the ALM. If ALM policy results in a cost saving compared to the cost of a global perfect match, this saving is the profit of ALM. If the effective policy results in a higher cost, ex post, the cost differential over the benchmark is a loss. This requires keeping track of the cost of funding under perfect matching and the effective cost of funding for the same period. The differential is the ALM contribution.

Transfer Prices for Resources

Assigning transfer prices to resources should follow the same principles, except that some resources have no tangible maturity. The arbitrage rationale suffices to define economic transfer prices to ALM. It is feasible to invest resources with a contractual maturity up to that maturity, so that the corresponding market rate serves as reference.

For resources without maturity, such as the volatile fraction of demand deposits, the maturity is conventional, such as a 1-year maturity, or modelled to some extent according to the effective time profile of resources.

TRANSFERRING LIQUIDITY AND INTEREST RATE RISK TO ALM

Two factors help to fully separate commercial and financial risks. First, the commercial margins become independent of the market maturity spread of interest rates and of the 'twist' of the yield curve. ALM is responsible for managing the spread risk. Second, referring to a debt replicating the asset removes the liquidity and the market risks from the commercial margin. This takes care of the transfer of interest rate risk to ALM. However, guaranteeing this risk transfer requires another piece of the Funds Transfer Pricing (FTP) to actually protect business margins against financial risks.

For instance, if a fixed rate asset generates 11% over a transfer price of 9%, the margin is 2%. Recalculating the margin of the same asset with a new rate at the next period would result in a change, unless the calculation follows a rule consistent with the system. For instance, resetting the transfer price after one period at 10%, because of an upward shift of 1% in the yield curve, results in a decrease of the margin to 1%. This decrease is not acceptable, because it is not under the control of business lines. The philosophy of the system is to draw a clear-cut frontier between commercial and financial risks. An additional component of the FTP scheme allows us to achieve this goal.

The calculation of transfer price as the cost of the mirror debt occurs at the origination date of the asset. This rules out transfer price resets because of market rate changes. The transfer price assigned to a transaction over successive periods is the historical transfer price. Doing otherwise puts the commercial margin at risk, instead of locking it over the life of the transaction. Margins calculated over reset transfer prices are apparent margins. They match current market conditions and change with them.

The FTP system should ensure that transfer prices are assigned to individual transactions for the life of the transactions. These prices are historical prices 'guaranteed' for transactions and business units. Using such historical prices for each transaction puts an additional burden on the information system. Nevertheless, without doing so, the margins lose economic meaning. In addition, the consistency between what business units control by and their performance measures breaks down.

Table 27.3 shows the time profile of both apparent and locked in margins calculated, respectively, over reset prices and guaranteed historical transfer prices. The pricing remains in line with a target margin of 2% over the transfer price. Meeting this goal at origination does not lock in the apparent margin over time. Only the margin over guaranteed prices remains constant.

This last addition makes the transfer pricing system comprehensive and consistent.

TABLE 27.3 Margins on apparent transfer prices and historical transfer prices

Transactions	Period 1	Period 2	Period 3
A	100	100	100
B		100	100
C			100
Current rate	10%	11%	12%
Target % margin	2%	2%	2%
Customer rate	12%	13%	14%
Apparent margin over current rate	$100 \times (12 - 10)$	$100 \times (12 - 11)$ $+100 \times (13 - 11)$	$100 \times (12 - 12) + 100$ $\times(13 - 12) + 100 \times (14 - 12)$
Apparent margin (value)	2	3	3
Apparent margin (%)	$2/100 = 2\%$	$3/200 = 1.5\%$	$3/300 = 1\%$
Margin over guaranteed historical price	$100 \times (12 - 10)$	$100 \times (12 - 10)$ $+100 \times (13 - 11)$	$100 \times (12 - 10) + 100$ $\times(13 - 11) + 100 \times (14 - 12)$
Margin over guaranteed price (value)	2	4	6
Margin over guaranteed price (%)	2%	2%	2%

BENCHMARKS FOR EXCESS RESOURCES

Some banks have structurally excess resources or dedicate deliberately some resources to an investment portfolio, more or less independently of the lending opportunities.

Under a global view, the bank considers global management of both loan and investment portfolios. The management of invested funds integrates with ALM policy. Alternatively, it is common to set up an investment policy independently of the loan portfolio, because there are excess funds structurally, or because the bank wants to have a permanent investment portfolio, independent of lending opportunities. This policy applies for example when investing equity into a segregated risk-free portfolio rather than putting these funds at risk with loans.

The transfer price for the portfolio becomes irrelevant because the issue is to maximize the portfolio return under risk limits, and to evaluate performance in relation to a benchmark return. The benchmark return depends on the risk. The bank needs to define guidelines for investing funds. When minimizing risk is the goal, a common practice consists of smoothing out market rate variations by structuring adequately the investment portfolio. It implies breaking down the investment into several fractions invested over several maturities and rolling them over, like a 'tractor', when each tranche matures. This is the 'ladder' policy. It avoids crystallizing the current yield curve in large blocks of investments. The 'tractor' averages the time series of all yield curves up to the management horizon.

Segregation of assets in different subportfolios creates potential conflicts with the global ALM view of the balance sheet. Any segmentation of the portfolio of assets might result in overall undesired mismatches not in line with global guidelines. For instance requiring a long-term maturity for an investment portfolio, while the loan maturities are business-driven, could increase the gap between the average reset date of assets and that of liabilities. Hedging this gap with derivatives is inconsistent with the long-term goal for the portfolio, because it is equivalent to closing the gap by synthetically creating a short-term rate exposure rather than the long-term one. In general, segmentation of the balance sheet creates mismatch and does not comply with the basic ALM philosophy. If controlling the overall remains the goal, gaps over all compartments should add up. If they do not, the bank maintains an undesired global exposure.

SECTION 10

Portfolio Analysis: Correlations

28

Correlations and Portfolio Effects

Combining risks does not follow the usual arithmetic rules, unlike income. The summation of two risks, each equal to 1, is not 2. It is usually lower because of diversification. Quantification based on correlations shows that the sum is in the range of 0 to 2. This is the essence of diversification and correlations. Diversification reduces the volatility of aggregated portfolio income, or Profit and Loss (P&L) of market values, because these go up for certain transactions and down for others, thereby compensating each other to some extent. Moreover, credit risk losses do not occur simultaneously. In what follows, we simply consider changes of values of transactions, whatever the nature of risk that triggers them.

Portfolio risk results from individual risks. The random future portfolio values, from which potential losses derive, are the algebraic sum of individual random future transaction values or returns. Returns are the relative changes in values between the current date and the horizon selected for measuring risk. The distribution of the portfolio values is the distribution of this sum. The sum of random individual transaction values or returns follows a distribution dependent on the interdependencies, or correlations, between these individual random values. The expected value, or loss, does not depend on correlations. The dispersion around the mean of the portfolio value, or volatility, and the downside risk do.

Individual risks and their correlations drive the portfolio risk and the extent of the diversification effect, which is the difference between the (arithmetic) sum of these individual transaction risks and the risk of the sum. Because portfolio risk depends so much on interdependencies between individual transaction risks, they play a key role in portfolio risk models. Various techniques serve for capturing the correlation, or diversification, effect:

- Correlations quantify interdependencies in statistical terms, and are critical parameters for valuing the random changes in portfolio values. Basic statistical rules allow us to understand how to deal with sums of correlated random individual values of facilities.
- When dealing with discrete default events, the credit standing of individual obligors depend on each other. Conditional probabilities are an alternative view of correlations between individual risks that facilitates the modelling of some random events.
- When looking forward, the 'portfolio risk building block' of models relies on simulations of random future changes of value, or 'returns', of transactions, triggered by risk events. Forward-looking simulations require generating random values of 'risk factors' in order to explore all future scenarios and determine the forward distribution of the portfolio values. Such random scenarios should comply with variance and correlation constraints between risk factors. Special techniques serve to construct such simulations. Several examples use them later on for constructing portfolio loss distributions.

The first section explains why correlations are critical parameters for determining portfolio risk. The second section defines correlations and summarizes the essential formulas applying to sums of correlated random variables. The third section introduces conditional probabilities. The fourth section presents some simple basic techniques, relying on factor models, for generating correlated values of risk drivers.

WHY ARE CORRELATIONS IMPORTANT?

Correlations are measures of the association between changes in any pair of random variables. In the field of risk management, the random variables are individual values of facilities that the random portfolio value aggregates. The subsequent sections expand the essentials for dealing with correlated value changes.

Correlations and Interdependencies between Individual Losses within a Portfolio

For the market portfolio, the P&L is the variation of market values. Market values are market-driven. The issue for measuring downside risk is to quantify the worst-case adverse value deviations of a portfolio of instruments whose individual values are market-driven. It does not make sense to assume that all individual values deviate simultaneously on the 'wrong' side because they depend on market parameter movements, which are interdependent. To measure market risk realistically, we need to assess the magnitudes of the deviations of the market parameters and how they relate to each other. The interdependencies, or correlations, between parameters, plus their volatilities, drive the individual values. This is the major feature of market Value at Risk (VaR) calculations. The modelling relates individual value deviations, or returns, to the market parameter co-movements.

For credit risk, the same phenomenon occurs. It does not make sense to assume that all obligors are going to default at the same time. The principle for modelling simultaneous changes in credit states, including the migrations to the default state, is to relate the credit standing of firms to factors, such as economic–industry conditions, that influence all of them. If these get worse, defaults and credit deteriorations increase, if they improve, the reverse happens. Such dependence creates some association between credit states of all obligors and their possible defaults. This implies that we need to model correlations between credit events, both default and migration events.

In all cases, correlations are key parameters for combining risks within portfolios of transactions, both for market and credit risk. This chapter has the limited goal of summarizing the basics of correlations and the main formulas often used for measuring portfolio statistics, notably volatility of losses. Such definitions are a prerequisite whenever risk aggregation or risk allocation are considered. Throughout the chapter, we use bold characters for random variables and italics or regular characters for their particular values[1].

The Portfolio Values as the Aggregation of Individual Facility Values

In order to proceed, we need the basic definitions, notations and statistical formulas applying to the summation of random variables. As a preliminary step, we show that the portfolio value is the summation of all individual transaction values. The presentation does not depend on whether we deal with market risk or credit risk. In both cases, we have changes of facility values between now (date 0) and a future horizon H. For market risk, the horizon is the liquidation period. For credit risk, it is the horizon necessary to manage the portfolio risk or the capital, typically 1 year in credit portfolio models. For market risk, we link instrument values to the underlying market parameters that drive them. For credit risk, the value changes depend on credit risk migrations, eventually related to factors common to all borrowers such as the economic–industry conditions.

The value change of any transaction i between current date 0 and horizon H is:

$$\Delta \mathbf{V}_i = (\mathbf{V}_{i,H} - V_{i,0}) = V_{i,0} \times \mathbf{y}_i$$

The unit value change $\mathbf{y}_i$ is a random variable independent of the size of exposure i. It is simply the discrete time return of asset i. A loss is a negative variation of value, whether due to default or a downside risk migration.

For market risk, the changes in values of each individual transaction are either gains or losses. The algebraic summation of all gains and losses is the portfolio loss. Since the individual value changes are random, so is the algebraic summation. The distribution of negative changes, or adverse changes, is the loss distribution. The random change portfolio value $\mathbf{V_p}$ is the sum of the random individual losses $\mathbf{V}_i$, and the change in the portfolio value $\Delta \mathbf{V_p}$ is the sum of the changes in all individual transactions $\Delta \mathbf{V}_i$:

$$\mathbf{V_p} = \sum_i \mathbf{V}_i$$

$$\Delta \mathbf{V_p} = \sum_i \Delta \mathbf{V}_i$$

[1] For instance $\mathbf{X}$ is a random variable, and X or X designates a particular numerical value.

The variations of values are $\Delta V_i = (V_{i,H} - V_{i,0}) = V_{i,0} \times y_i$ so that the portfolio return y_p is:

$$y_p = \Delta V_p / V_{p,0} = \sum_i \Delta V_i / V_{p,0} = \sum_i V_{i,0} \times y_i / V_{p,0} = \sum_i w_{i,0} \times y_i$$

In this formula, the portfolio return is the weighted sum of the individual asset returns, the weights $w_{i,0}$ being the ratios of initial exposures to the total portfolio value. By definition, they sum to 1.

The same definitions apply for credit risk, except that credit risk results from credit risk migrations, including the migration to the default state. Whenever there is a risk migration, there is a change in value. Whenever the migration ends in the default state, the value moves down to the loss given default, that is the loss net of recoveries. Models ignoring migrations are default only. In default mode, all changes in values are negative, or losses, and there are only two credit states at the horizon.

PORTFOLIO RISK AS A FUNCTION OF INDIVIDUAL RISKS

This section uses the classical concepts of expectations and variance applied to the portfolio value or loss viewed as the algebraic sum of individual value changes. We provide here only a reminder of basic, but essential, definitions.

Expectation of Portfolio Value or Loss

The expectation of the sum of random variables is the sum of their expectations. This relation holds for any number of random variables. In general, using compact notations for the summation:

$$E\left(\sum_i a_i X_i\right) = \sum_i a_i E(X_i)$$

The immediate application is that the expectation of the change in value of a portfolio is simply the sum of all individual value changes of each individual instrument within the portfolio: $E(\Delta V_p) = \sum_i \Delta V_i$. This result does not depend on any correlation between the individual values or losses.

Correlations

The value or loss volatility of the portfolio measures the dispersion of the distribution of values. The volatility of value is identical to that of value variations because the initial value is certain. The loss volatility, although distinct from loss percentiles, is an intermediate proxy measure to the unexpected loss concept[2]. The portfolio value or loss volatility depends on the correlation between individual values or losses and on their variance–covariance matrix.

The correlation measures the extent to which random variables change together or not, in the same direction or in opposite directions. Two statistics characterize this association: the

---

[2] Loss percentiles are often expressed as a multiple of loss volatility. See Chapters 7 and 50 for specific details.

correlation coefficient and the covariance. A correlation and a covariance characterize pairs of random variables. The covariance is the weighted sum of the products of the deviations from the mean of two variables X and Y, the weights being the joint probabilities of occurrence of each pair of values. The coefficient of correlation is simpler to interpret because it is in the range -1 to $+1$. It is calculated as the ratio of the covariance by the product of the volatilities (which are the square roots of variances) of X and Y. The value $+1$ means that the two variables change together. The correlation -1 means that they always vary in opposite directions. The zero correlation means that they are independent. The formulas are as follows:

$$\sigma_{XY} = \rho_{XY}\sigma_X\sigma_Y$$

where σ_{XY} is the covariance between variables X and Y; ρ_{XY} is the correlation between variables X and Y; σ_X and σ_Y are the standard deviations, or volatilities, of variables X and Y.

Correlation and Volatility of a Sum of Random Variables

The volatility of a sum depends on the correlations between variables. It is the square root of the variance. The variance of a sum is not, in general, the sum of the variances. It is the sum of the variances of each random variable plus all covariance terms for each pair of variables. Therefore, we start with the simple case of a pair of random variables and proceed towards the extension to any number of random variables. The general formula applies for determining the portfolio loss volatility and the risk contributions to the portfolio volatility of each individual exposure. Hence, it is most important.

Two Variables

For two variables, the formulas are as follows:

$$V(X + Y) = \sigma^2(X + Y) = V(X) + V(Y) + 2\,\text{Cov}(X, Y)$$
$$V(X + Y) = \sigma^2(X) + \sigma^2(Y) + 2\rho_{XY}\sigma(X)\sigma(Y)$$

The covariance between X and Y is $\text{Cov}(X, Y)$, $V(X)$ is the variance of X, $\sigma(X)$ is the standard deviation and ρ_{XY} the correlation coefficient. Since the covariance is a function of the correlation coefficient, the two above formulas are identical. If the covariances are not zero, the variance of the sum differs from the sum of variances. The correlation term drops out of the formulas when the two variables are independent:

$$V(X + Y) = \sigma^2(X) + \sigma^2(Y)$$
$$\sigma(X + Y) = \sqrt{\sigma^2(X) + \sigma^2(Y)}$$

The variance of the sum becomes the sum of variances only when all covariances are equal to zero. This result is valid only when all variables move independently of each other. The volatility is the square root of the variance. Since the variance of the sum is the sum of variances and the volatility is less than the sum of volatilities. It is the square root of the sum of the squared values of volatilities.

As an example, the volatilities of two equity returns are 2.601% and 1.826%, and the correlation between returns is 27.901%. The sum of volatilities is $2.601\% + 1.826\% = 4.427\%$. The variance of the sum is:

$$V(\mathbf{X} + \mathbf{Y}) = 2.601\%^2 + 1.826\%^2 + 2 \times 37.901\% \times 1.826\% \times 2.601\% = 0.137\%$$

The volatility is:

$$\sigma(\mathbf{X} + \mathbf{Y}) = \sqrt{0.137\%} = 3.7014\% < 4.427\%$$

This volatility is lower than the sum of volatilities. This is the essence of the diversification effect, since it shows that deviations of $\mathbf{X}$ and $\mathbf{Y}$ compensate to some extent when they vary. Combining risks implies that the risk of the sum, measured by volatility, is less than the sum of risks. Risks do not add arithmetically, except in the extreme case where correlation is perfect (value 1).

Extension to Any Number of Variables

This formula extends the calculation of the variance and of the volatility to any number N of variables $\mathbf{Z}_i$. This is the single most important formula for calculating the portfolio return or value volatility. The portfolio volatility formula also serves for calculating the risk contribution of individual facilities to the total portfolio loss volatility because it adds the contributions of each facility to this volatility. The formula also illustrates why the sum of individual risks is not the risk of the sum, due to the correlation effects embedded in the covariance terms. The general formula is:

$$\sigma^2 \left(\sum_{i=1}^{N} \mathbf{Z}_i \right) = \sum_{i=j=1}^{N} \sigma_i^2 + \sum_{i \neq j} \sigma_{ij} = \sum_{i=j=1}^{N} \sigma_i^2 + \sum_{i \neq j} \rho_{ij} \sigma_i \sigma_i$$

In this formula, σ_i^2 is the variance of parameter i, equal to the square of the standard deviation. σ_i and σ_{ij} are the covariance between variables $\mathbf{Z}_i$ and $\mathbf{Z}_j$. The summation $\sum$ corresponds to a generalized summation over all pairs of random variables $\mathbf{Z}_i$ and $\mathbf{Z}_j$. It collapses to the above simple formulas for two variables. The summation $\sum_{i \neq j}$ is equivalent to the more explicit formula $\sum_{i \neq j}$ with i and $j=1,N$, a summation over all values of i and j, being allowed to vary from 1 to N, but with i not equal to j since, in this case, we have the first variance terms in the above formula. A similar, and more compact, notation writes that the variance of the random variables summing N random variables is the summation of all σ_{ij} using the convention that, whenever $i = j$, we obtain the variance $\sigma_i^2 = \sigma_j^2$:

$$\sigma^2 \left(\sum_{i=1}^{N} \mathbf{Z}_i \right) = \sum_{i,j \text{ with } i \text{ and } j=1,N} \sigma_{ij}$$

Reverting to the portfolio return, we need to include the weights of each individual exposure in the formulas. If we use the portfolio return as the random variable characterizing the relative change in portfolio value, using the simple properties of variances and covariances, we find that:

$$\sigma^2 \left(\sum_{i=1}^{N} \mathbf{Z}_i \right) = \sum_{i=j=1}^{N} w_i^2 \sigma_i^2 + \sum_{i \neq j} w_i w_j \sigma_{ij} = \sum_{i=j=1}^{N} w_i^2 \sigma_i^2 + \sum_{i \neq j} \rho_{ij} w_i w_j \sigma_i \sigma_i$$

The variance σ_i and the covariance σ_{ij} now refer to the individual asset returns. The weights are constant in the formula, which implies a crystallized portfolio, with constant asset structure. This is the basic formula providing the relative portfolio value over a short period. It applies as long as the weights are approximately constant.

Visual Representation of the Diversification Effect

The diversification effect is the gap between the sum of volatilities and the volatility of a sum. In practice, the random variables are the individual values of returns of assets in the portfolio. The diversification effect is the gap between the volatility of the portfolio and the sum of the volatilities of each individual loss.

A simple image visualizes the formula of the standard deviation of a sum of two variables. The visualization shows the impact of correlation on the volatility of a sum. A vector whose length is the volatility represents each variable. The angle between the vectors varies inversely with correlation. The vectors are parallel whenever the correlation is zero and opposed when the correlation is -1. With such conventions, the vector equal to the geometric summation of the two vectors representing each variable represents the overall risk. The length of this vector is identical to the volatility of the sum of the two variables[3]. Visually, its length is less than the sum of the lengths of the two vectors representing volatilities, except when the correlation is equal to $+1$. The geometric visualization shows how the volatility of a sum changes when the correlation changes (Figure 28.1).

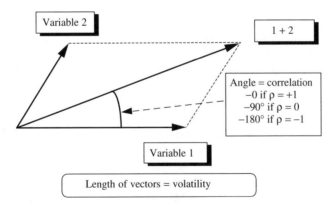

FIGURE 28.1   Geometric representation of the volatility of the sum of two random variables

Figure 28.2 groups different cases. The volatilities of the two variables are set to 1. The only change is that of their correlation changes. The volatility of the sum is the length of the geometric summation of vectors 1 and 2. It varies between 0 when the correlation is -1, up to 2 when the correlation is $+1$. The intermediate case, when correlation is zero, shows that the volatility is $\sqrt{2}$.

---

[3] This result uses the formula for the variance of a sum, expressing the length of the diagonal as a function of the sides of the square of which it is a diagonal.

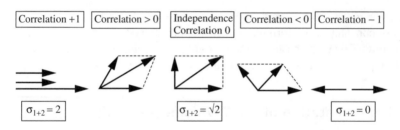

FIGURE 28.2   The change in volatility of a sum when the correlation changes

CONDITIONAL AND UNCONDITIONAL PROBABILITIES

Conditional probabilities provide an alternative view to correlations that serves in several instances. The unconditional probabilities are the 'normal' probabilities, when we have no information on any event that influences the random events, such as defaults. Conditional probabilities, on the other hand, embed the effects of information correlated with the random event.

Conditional Probabilities and Correlations

In the market universe, we have time series of prices and market parameter values, making it easy to see whether they vary together, in the same direction, in opposite directions, or when there is no association at all. The universe of credit risk is less visible. We have information on the assessment of the risk of obligors, but the scarcity of data makes measures of correlations from historical data hazardous. In addition, we cannot observe the correlation between default events of two different firms in general because the joint default of two firms is a very rare event.

Correlation still exists. Typically, the default probabilities vary across economic cycles. Since the credit standing of all firms depends on the state of the economy, the variations of economic conditions create correlations between default events. If economic or industry conditions worsen, all default probabilities tend to increase and vice versa. Therefore, the same default probability should differ when there is no information on future economic conditions and if it is possible to assess how likely the future states of the economy will be, better or worse than average. Probabilities depending on random economic scenarios are conditional probabilities on the state of the economy. In general, when common factors influence various risks, the risks are conditional on the values of these factors. Correlations influence the probability that two obligors default together. Default probabilities depending on the default events of the other firm are conditional probabilities on the status, default or non-default, of the other firm.

The purpose of the next sections is to explain the properties of joint and conditional probabilities, and to illustrate how they relate to correlations. Applications include the definitions of joint default or migration events for a pair of obligors, the derivation of default probabilities conditional on 'scoring models' providing information on the credit standing of borrowers, or making risk events dependent on some common factor, such as the state of the economy, that influences them.

Conditional Probabilities

Conditional probabilities are probabilities conditional on some information that influences this probability. If X is a random event whose probability of occurrence depends on some random scenario S, then the probability of X occurring given S is the conditional probability $P(X|S)$.

We characterize default events by a random variable X taking only two values, default or non-default, or 1 and 0 respectively for these two states. The unconditional default probability of X taking the default value 1 is $P(X)$. This is an unconditional default probability that applies when we have no particular information on whatever influences this probability. The random state of the economy S influences the likelihood of X values. The probability of X defaulting once S is known, or $P(X|S)$, is the conditional default probability of default of X given S.

The conditional probability depends on the correlation between the two events. For example, if economic conditions worsen, the default probability of all firms increases. In such a case, there is a correlation between the default event X and the occurrence of worsening economic conditions, a value of S. If there is no relation, the conditional probability $P(X|S)$ collapses to the unconditional probability $P(X)$. If there is a positive relation, the conditional probability increases above the unconditional probability, and if there is a negative correlation, it decreases. For instance, if the unconditional default probability is 1% for a firm, its conditional probability on S is lower than 1% if the economy improves and higher when it deteriorates.

Joint Probabilities

A joint probability is the probability that two events occur simultaneously. It applies to both continuous and discrete variables. The two random events are X and Y. The relationship between the joint probability that both X and Y occur and the conditional probabilities of X given occurrence of Y, or Y given occurrence of X, is:

$$P(X, Y) = P(X) \times P(Y|X) = P(Y) \times P(X|Y)$$

A first example relates the default probability to the state of the economy. A firm has an 'unconditional' default probability of 1%. The random value F, taking the values 'default' and 'non-default', characterizes the status of the firm. The firm's unconditional default probability $P(F = \text{default}) = 1\%$. The unconditional probability represents the average across all possible states of the economy. Let us now consider three states of the economy: base, optimistic and worst-case. The probability of observing the worst-case state is 20%. Let us assume that the corresponding default probability increases to 2%. This probability is conditional on S. The formula is: $P(F = \text{default}|S = \text{worst-case}) = 2\%$. The joint probability of having simultaneously a default of the firm and a worst-case state of the economy is, by definition:

$$P(F = \text{default}, S = \text{worst-case}) = P(S = \text{worst-case}) \times P(F = \text{default}|S = \text{worst-case})$$

$$= 20\% \times 2\% = 0.4\%$$

As a summary:

$$P(F = \text{default}) = 1\%$$

$$P(\mathbf{F} = \text{default}|\mathbf{S} = \text{worst-case}) = 2\%$$

$$P(\mathbf{F} = \text{default}, \mathbf{S} = \text{worst-case}) = 0.4\%$$

When **X** and **Y** are independent, the joint probability collapses to the product of their standard probabilities, and the conditional probabilities are equal to the standard probabilities:

$$P(\mathbf{X}, \mathbf{Y}) = P(\mathbf{X}) \times P(\mathbf{Y})$$

$$P(\mathbf{X}|\mathbf{Y}) = P(\mathbf{X}) \quad \text{and} \quad P(\mathbf{Y}|\mathbf{X}) = P(\mathbf{Y})$$

If the state of the economy does not influence the credit standing of the firm, the conditional probability of default becomes equal to the unconditional default probability, or 1%. This implies that $P(\mathbf{F} = \text{default}|\mathbf{S} = \text{worst-case}) = P(\mathbf{F} = \text{default}) = 1\%$. As a consequence, the joint probability of having a worst-case situation plus default drops to $P(\mathbf{F} = \text{default}, \mathbf{S} = \text{worst-case}) = 1\% \times 20\% = 0.2\% < 0.4\%$.

The equality of conditional to unconditional probabilities, under independence, is consistent with a joint probability equal to the product of the unconditional probabilities: $P(\mathbf{X}, \mathbf{Y}) = P(\mathbf{X}) \times P(\mathbf{Y})$. With correlated variables **X** and **Y**, the joint probability depends on the correlation. If the correlation is positive, the joint probability increases above the product of the unconditional probabilities. This implies that $P(\mathbf{X}|\mathbf{Y}) > P(\mathbf{X})$ and $P(\mathbf{Y}|\mathbf{X}) > P(\mathbf{Y})$. With positive correlation between **X** and **Y**, conditional probabilities are higher than unconditional probabilities. This is consistent with $P(\mathbf{X}, \mathbf{Y})$ being higher than the product of the unconditional probabilities $P(\mathbf{X})$ and $P(\mathbf{Y})$ since: $P(\mathbf{Y}|\mathbf{X}) = P(\mathbf{X}, \mathbf{Y})/P(\mathbf{X})$ and $P(\mathbf{X}|\mathbf{Y}) = P(\mathbf{X}, \mathbf{Y})/P(\mathbf{Y})$.

In the universe of credit risk, another typical joint probability of interest is the joint default of two obligors **X** and **Y**, or $P(\mathbf{X}, \mathbf{Y})$. If the chance that **X** defaults increases when **Y** does, there is a correlation between the two defaults. This correlation increases the joint probability of default, the conditional probability of **X** defaulting given **Y** defaults, or $P(\mathbf{X}|\mathbf{Y})$, and $P(\mathbf{Y}|\mathbf{X})$ as well. If **X** and **Y** are positively correlated events, the occurrence of **Y** increases the probability of **X** occurring. This is equivalent to increasing the joint default probabilities of **X** and **Y**.

Correlation relates to conditional probabilities. It is equivalent to say that there is a correlation between events **A** and **B**, and to consider that the probability that **B** occurs increases above **B**'s 'unconditional' probability if **A** occurs. For instance, the unconditional probabilities of default of **A** and **B** are 1% and 2% respectively. If the default events **A** and **B** are independent, the Joint Default Probability (JDP) is $2\% \times 1\% = 0.02\%$. However, if the probability that **B** defaults when **A** does becomes 10%, the conditional probability of **B** given **A**'s default $P(\mathbf{B}|\mathbf{A})$ is 10%, much higher than the unconditional probability of **B**'s default, which is $P(\mathbf{B}) = 2\%$. This implies a strong correlation between **A** and **B** default events. Then, the joint default probability becomes:

$$\text{JDP}(\mathbf{A}, \mathbf{B}) = P(\mathbf{A}|\mathbf{B}) \times P(\mathbf{B}) = 10\% \times 1\% = 0.1\%$$

This is much higher than $2\% \times 1\% = 0.02\%$, the joint default probability if the defaults were independent.

Averaging Conditional Probabilities and Bayes' Rule

When inferring probabilities, the rule for averaging conditional probabilities is helpful. Let's assume there are three (or more) possible values for **S**, representing the state of the economy. The default probabilities of firms vary with the state of the economy. If it worsens, the default probabilities increase and vice versa. Let's assume we have only three possible states of the economy, with unconditional probabilities $P(\mathbf{S} = \mathrm{S}1)$, $P(\mathbf{S} = \mathrm{S}2)$ and $P(\mathbf{S} = \mathrm{S}3)$ respectively equal to 50%, 30% and 20%, summing up to 1 since there is no other possible state. The third case is the worst-case scenario of the above. The averaging rule stipulates that the default probability of a firm **F** is such that:

$$P(\mathbf{F}) = P(\mathbf{F}|\mathrm{S}1) \times P(\mathbf{S} = \mathrm{S}1) + P(\mathbf{F}|\mathrm{S}2) \times P(\mathbf{S} = \mathrm{S}2) + P(\mathbf{F}|\mathrm{S}3) \times P(\mathbf{S} = \mathrm{S}3)$$

The probability of **X** defaulting under a particular state of the economy varies with the scenario since we assume a correlation between the two events, default and state of the economy. Taking 0.5%, 1% and 1.5% as conditional default probabilities for the three states respectively, the unconditional default probability has to be:

$$P(\mathbf{F}) = 0.5\% \times 50\% + 1\% \times 30\% + 1.5\% \times 20\% = 0.85\%$$

The unconditional (or standard) default probability is the weighted average of the conditional default probabilities under various states of the economy, the weights being the probabilities of occurrence of each state. Its interpretation is that of an average over several years where all states of the economy occurred. The unconditional probability is the weighted average of all conditional probabilities over all possible states of the economy:

$$P(\mathbf{F}) = \sum_{i=1}^{K} P(\mathbf{F}|Si) \times P(Si)$$

If **S** is a continuous variable, we transform the summation symbol into an integration symbol over all values of **S** using $P(\mathbf{S})$ as the probability of **S** being in the small interval dS:

$$P(\mathbf{X}) = \int P(\mathbf{X}|S) \times P(\mathbf{S})\,\mathrm{d}S$$

Conditioning and Correlation

Correlation implies that conditional probabilities differ from unconditional probabilities, and the converse is true. Correlation and conditional probabilities relate to each other, but they are not identical. Conditional probabilities are within the $(0, 1)$ range, while correlations are within the $(-1, +1)$ range. Therefore, it is not simple to define the exact relationship between conditionality and correlation.

As an illustration of the relation, the joint probability of default of two obligors depends on the correlation and the unconditional default probabilities of the obligors. The relation results from a simple analysis, developed in Chapter 46, explaining the loss distribution for a portfolio of two obligors **X** and **Y**, whose random defaults are variables **X** and **Y** taking the value 1 for default and 0 for non-default. Such 'binary' variables are called Bernoulli variables. For discrete Bernoulli variables, the relationship between the unconditional probabilities and correlation is:

$$P(\mathbf{Y}, \mathbf{Z}) = P(\mathbf{Y}) \times P(\mathbf{Z}) + \rho_{\mathbf{YZ}} \times \sqrt{P(\mathbf{Y})[1 - P(\mathbf{Y})] \times P(\mathbf{Z})[1 - P(\mathbf{Z})]}$$

The joint default probability increases with a positive correlation between default events. However, there are boundary values for correlations and for unconditional default probabilities. Intuitively, a perfect correlation of $+1$ would imply that **X** and **Y** default together. This is possible only to the extent that the default probabilities are identical. Different unconditional probabilities are inconsistent with such perfect correlation.

Conditioning, Expectation and Variance

Some additional formulas serve in applications. The conditional probability distribution of **X** subject to **Y** is the probability distribution of **X** given a value of **Y**. The conditional expectation of **X** results from setting **Y** first, then cumulating ('integrating') over all values of **X**:

$$E(\mathbf{X}) = E[E(\mathbf{X}|\mathbf{Y})]$$

$E(\mathbf{X}|\mathbf{Y}) = E(\mathbf{X})$ implies that **X** does not depend on **Y**. The expectation of a variable can be calculated by taking the expectation of **X** when **Y** is set, then taking the expectation of all expected values of **X** given **Y** when **Y** changes. $E(\mathbf{X}|\mathbf{Y}) = E(\mathbf{X})$ implies that **X** does not depend on **Y**. Conditional expectations are additive, like unconditional expectations. These formulas serve to define the expectation when a loss distribution of a portfolio is conditional on the value of some external factors, such as the state of the economy.

The variance of a random event **X** depending on another event **Y** results from both the variance of **X** given **Y** and the variance of the conditioning factor **Y**:

$$\text{Var}(\mathbf{X}) = \text{Var}[E(\mathbf{X}|\mathbf{Y})] + E[\text{Var}(\mathbf{X}|\mathbf{Y})]$$

It is convenient to use this formula in conjunction with: $\text{Var}(\mathbf{X}) = E(\mathbf{X}^2) - [E(\mathbf{X})]^2$. The variance of **X** is the expectation of the square of **X** minus the square of the expectation. This allows decomposition of the variance into the fraction of variance due to the conditioning factor **Y** and the variance due to the event **X**.

Applications of Joint and Conditional Probabilities for Credit Events

Joint probabilities apply to a wide spectrum of applications. They serve in credit risk analysis when dealing with credit events. Such applications include the following.

The joint default probability of a pair of obligors depends on the correlation between their default events, characterized by probabilities of default conditional on the default or non-default of the second obligor. The two-obligor portfolio is the simplest of all portfolios. Increasing the default probability of an obligor conditional on default of the other increases correlation between defaults. There is a one-to-one correspondence between default correlation and conditional probability, once the unconditional default probabilities are defined.

The same two-obligor portfolio characterizes the borrower–guarantor relation, since default occurs only when both default together. This is the 'double' default event when there are third-party guarantees. The technique allows us to value third-party guarantees in terms of a lower joint default probability.

Modelling default probability from scoring models relies on conditional probabilities given the value of the score, because the score value provides information on the credit standing of a borrower. The score serves for estimating 'posterior' default probabilities, differing from 'prior' probabilities, which are the unconditional probabilities, applying when we do not have the score information.

When defaults are dependent on some common factors, they become conditional on the factor values. This is a simple way to determine the shape of the distribution of correlated portfolio defaults by varying the common factors that influence the credit standing of all obligors within the portfolio.

GENERATING CORRELATED RISK DRIVERS WITH SINGLE FACTOR MODELS

This section shows how to generate, through multiple simulations, two correlated variables, with a given correlation coefficient. The correlation coefficient ρ_{ij} is given. The variables can be credit risk drivers such as asset values of firms or economic factors influencing the default rates of segments.

We first show how to generate two random normal variables having a preset correlation coefficient. Then, we proceed by showing how to generate N random variables having a uniform correlation coefficient. This is a specific extension of the preset pair correlation case. It applies when simulating values of credit risk drivers for a portfolio of obligors with known average correlation. We implement this technique to demonstrate the sensitivity of the loss distribution to the average correlation in Chapters 45–49. Next, we drop the uniform correlation and discuss the case of multiple random variables with different pair correlations. To generate random values complying with a variance–covariance structure, Cholevsky's decomposition is convenient. This technique serves to generate the distribution of correlated variables when conducting Monte Carlo simulations.

Generating Two Correlated Variables

Each random variable $\mathbf{Z}_i$ is a function of a common factor $\mathbf{Z}$ and a specific factor $\boldsymbol{\varepsilon}_i$. The specific factor is independent of the common factor. All cross-correlations between $\mathbf{Z}$ and $\boldsymbol{\varepsilon}_i$ or $\boldsymbol{\varepsilon}_j$ are 0. All random variables are normal standardized, meaning that they have zero mean and variance equal to 1. The correlation is between each $\mathbf{Z}_i$ variable and the common factor is ρ_i, while the correlation between the two random variables $\mathbf{Z}_i$ and $\mathbf{Z}_j \rho_{ij}$.

We use the equations for two different variables $\mathbf{Z}_i$ and $\mathbf{Z}_j$:

$$\mathbf{Z}_i = \rho \times \mathbf{Z} + \sqrt{1 - \rho_{ij}^2} \times \boldsymbol{\varepsilon}_i$$

$$\mathbf{Z}_j = \rho \times \mathbf{Z} + \sqrt{1 - \rho_{ij}^2} \times \boldsymbol{\varepsilon}_j$$

The variance of $\mathbf{Z}_i$ is:

$$\mathrm{Var}(\mathbf{Z}_i) = \rho_i^2 \, \mathrm{Var}(\mathbf{Z}) + (1 - \rho_i^2) \, \mathrm{Var}(\boldsymbol{\varepsilon}_i) + 2\rho_i \sqrt{1 - \rho_i^2} \times \mathrm{Cov}(\mathbf{Z}_i, \boldsymbol{\varepsilon}_i)$$

Given that $\text{Var}(\mathbf{Z}_i) = \text{Var}(\mathbf{Z}) = \text{Var}(\boldsymbol{\varepsilon}_i) = 1$ and $\text{Cov}(\mathbf{Z}_i, \boldsymbol{\varepsilon}_i) = 0$, we have:

$$\text{Var}(\mathbf{Z}_i) = \rho_i^2 + (1 - \rho_i^2) + 0 = 1$$

Risk models make a distinction between the general risk, related to a common factor influencing the values of all transactions, and the specific risk, which depends on the transaction only. If $\mathbf{Z}_i$ represents the transaction 'i' and if $\mathbf{Z}$ represents a factor influencing its risk and that of other transactions, the general risk is the variance of $\mathbf{Z}_i$ due to the factor $\mathbf{Z}$. From above, the general risk is simply equal to the correlation coefficient ρ_i^2 and the specific risk to its complement to 1, or $(1 - \rho_i^2)$. In this very simple case, we have a straightforward decomposition of total risk.

Another correlation of interest is the pair correlations between any pair of variables, $\mathbf{Z}_i$ and $\mathbf{Z}_j$. The covariance and their correlation between these variables derive from their common dependence on the factor $\mathbf{Z}$. All cross-covariances between the factor $\mathbf{Z}$ and the residual terms $\boldsymbol{\varepsilon}_i$ and $\boldsymbol{\varepsilon}_j$ are zero by definition. Therefore:

$$\text{Cov}(\mathbf{Z}_i, \mathbf{Z}_j) = \text{Cov}(\rho_i \times \mathbf{Z} + \sqrt{1 - \rho_{ij}^2} \times \boldsymbol{\varepsilon}_i, \rho_j \times \mathbf{Z} + \sqrt{1 - \rho_{ij}^2} \times \boldsymbol{\varepsilon}_j)$$

$$\text{Cov}(\mathbf{Z}_i, \mathbf{Z}_j) = \text{Cov}(\rho_i \mathbf{Z}, \rho_j \mathbf{Z}) = \rho_i \rho_j \text{Var}(\mathbf{Z}) = \rho_i \rho_j$$

Hence, all pairs such as $\mathbf{Z}_i$ and $\mathbf{Z}_j$ have a predetermined correlation $\rho_{ij} = \rho_i \rho_j \text{Var}(\mathbf{Z})$.

This technique shows how to generate two correlated variables having a predetermined correlation coefficient ρ_{ij} by generating independent normal variables:

- Generate a standardized normal variable $\boldsymbol{\varepsilon}_i$.
- Generate a standardized normal variable $\boldsymbol{\varepsilon}_j$.
- Generate a standardized normal variable $\mathbf{Z}$.

Then $\mathbf{Z}_i$ and $\mathbf{Z}_j$, calculated with the above linear function using ρ_{ij} as the correlation coefficient, have a correlation equal to this ρ_{ij}. The technique applies for generating N correlated variables with various pair correlations.

To use the above technique, we generate independently K random draws of the common factor $\mathbf{Z}$ and K random draws of each of the specific risks $\boldsymbol{\varepsilon}_i$ (N variables) following standardized normal distributions. K is the number of trials or runs. Combining the random values of $\mathbf{Z}$ and $\boldsymbol{\varepsilon}_i$ with the above equation $\mathbf{Z}_i = \rho \times \mathbf{Z} + \sqrt{1 - \rho_i^2} \times \boldsymbol{\varepsilon}_i$, we get K values of the N $\mathbf{Z}_i$. The K values of all $\mathbf{Z}_i$ are such that all cross-correlations are equal to ρ. To generate $K = 1000$ trials for N variables, we need to generate $1000 \times (N + 1)$ values since there are N residuals $\boldsymbol{\varepsilon}_i$ plus the unique common factor.

In the case of a uniform correlation, all pair correlations and covariances of $\mathbf{Z}_i$ and $\mathbf{Z}_j$ are equal to a common ρ. The technique generates random values with standardized normal distributions and all pair correlations equal to a given value ρ. The technique serves for generating samples of N uniformly correlated normal variables. This procedure is implemented in Chapter 48.

Generating Random Values Complying with a Correlation Structure

The correlation structure results from multi-factor modelling of credit drivers and credit events, or any proxy such as the equity return correlations of Credit Metrics. Simulation requires generating risk drivers, such as asset values, complying with this correlation structure. Of course, in such a case, variances and covariances differ across pairs of variables.

Cholevsky's decomposition allows us to impose directly a variance–covariance structure on N random normal variables[4]. It allows us to derive from the generation of N independent variables N other random variables that comply with the given correlation structure, and that are linear functions of the independent variables. The difference with the previous technique is that we start from a full variance–covariance matrix.

First, we generate K independent samples of values of N variables $\mathbf{X}_i$. It is convenient to use normal standardized variables. K is the number of simulation runs. Then, we convert the N $\mathbf{X}_i$ variables into another set of N $\mathbf{Z}_j$ variables. The $\mathbf{Z}_j$ variables are linear combinations of the independent $\mathbf{X}_i$. The Cholevsky decomposition provides the coefficients of these linear combinations. The coefficients are such that the new $\mathbf{Z}_j$ variables comply with the imposed variance–covariance matrix.

The Decomposition Technique

We use the simple case of two random variables. We start from $\mathbf{X}_1$, a normal standardized variable. Once we have $\mathbf{X}_1$, we derive the α_{12} and α_{22} for $\mathbf{X}_2$:

$$\mathbf{Z}_1 = \alpha_{11}\mathbf{X}_1$$

$$\mathbf{Z}_2 = \alpha_{12}\mathbf{X}_1 + \alpha_{22}\mathbf{X}_2$$

These numbers are such that:

$$\mathrm{Var}(\mathbf{Z}_1) = \alpha_{11}^2 = 1$$

This requires $\alpha_{11} = 1$, or $\mathbf{Z}_1 = \mathbf{X}_1$:

$$\mathrm{Var}(\mathbf{Z}_2) = \alpha_{12}^2 + \alpha_{22}^2 = 1$$

$$\mathrm{Cov}(\mathbf{Z}_1, \mathbf{Z}_2) = \mathrm{Cov}(\alpha_{11}\mathbf{X}_1, \alpha_{12}\mathbf{X}_1 + \alpha_{22}\mathbf{X}_2) = \alpha_{11} \times \alpha_{12} = \rho_{12}$$

Since $\alpha_{11} = 1$, we have two equations with two unknown values α_{12} and α_{22}:

$$\alpha_{12}^2 + \alpha_{22}^2 = 1$$

$$\alpha_{12} = \rho_{12}$$

$$\alpha_{22} = \sqrt{1 - \rho_{12}^2}$$

Matrix Format with Two Random Variables

Therefore, the two variables $\mathbf{Z}_1$, $\mathbf{Z}_2$ are linear functions of standardized independent normal variables $\mathbf{X}_1$, $\mathbf{X}_2$ according to:

$$\mathbf{Z}_1 = \mathbf{X}_1$$

$$\mathbf{Z}_2 = \rho\mathbf{X}_2 + \sqrt{1 - \rho^2}\,\mathbf{X}_2$$

---

[4] If all variables are normal standardized, the variance–covariance matrix collapses to the correlation matrix, with correlation coefficients varying for each pair of variables and all diagonal terms equal to 1.

The above equations show that $\mathbf{Z}^T = \mathbf{LX}^T$ using $\mathbf{L}$ as the lower triangular matrix of the α_{ij} coefficients, where $\mathbf{X}^T$ is the column vector of $\mathbf{X}_i$ variables, and $\mathbf{Z}^T$ is also a column vector of $\mathbf{Z}_j$ variables.

Using the matrix format of Cholevsky's decomposition, the process starts from the variance–covariance matrix of two normal standardized variables, which is extremely simple. If $\mathbf{Z}_k$ are standardized normal variables, they have covariance matrix:

$$\Sigma = \begin{pmatrix} 1 & \rho \\ \rho & 1 \end{pmatrix}$$

The Cholevsky decomposition of Σ is:

$$\Sigma = \begin{pmatrix} 1 & \rho \\ \rho & 1 \end{pmatrix} = \begin{pmatrix} 1 & 0 \\ \rho & \sqrt{1-\rho^2} \end{pmatrix} \times \begin{pmatrix} 1 & \rho \\ 0 & \sqrt{1-\rho^2} \end{pmatrix}$$

Therefore, the variables $\mathbf{Z}_1$ and $\mathbf{Z}_2$ having correlation ρ are linear functions of independent standardized normal variables $\mathbf{X}_1$ and $\mathbf{X}_2$ according to the relation:

$$\begin{pmatrix} \mathbf{Z}_1 \\ \mathbf{Z}_2 \end{pmatrix} = \begin{pmatrix} 1 & 0 \\ \rho & \sqrt{1-\rho^2} \end{pmatrix} \times \begin{pmatrix} \mathbf{X}_1 \\ \mathbf{X}_2 \end{pmatrix}$$

Then:

$$\begin{pmatrix} \mathbf{Z}_1 \\ \mathbf{Z}_2 \end{pmatrix} = \begin{pmatrix} \mathbf{X}_1 \\ \rho \mathbf{X}_2 + \sqrt{1-\rho^2}\, \mathbf{X}_2 \end{pmatrix}$$

These are the relations used in preceding sections for generating pairs of correlated variables. The appendix to this chapter provides general formulas with N variables.

APPENDIX: CHOLEVSKY DECOMPOSITION

This appendix shows how to generate any number of correlated normal variables, starting with a set of independent variables and using Cholevsky's distribution to obtain linear combinations of these independent variables complying with a given correlation structure.

The Matrix Format for N Variables

Generalizing to N variables requires an N-dimensional squared variance–covariance matrix Σ. In general, $\mathbf{L}$ and $\mathbf{U}$ stand respectively for 'lower' triangular matrix and 'upper' triangular matrix. The $\mathbf{U}$ matrix is the transpose of the $\mathbf{L}$ matrix: $\mathbf{U} = \mathbf{L}^T$. By construction of $\mathbf{L} = \mathbf{Z}^T(\mathbf{X}^T) - 1$, $\mathbf{LU} = \mathbf{LL}^T$ is the original variance–covariance matrix Σ. The above equations show that $\mathbf{Z}^T = \mathbf{LX}^T$ using $\mathbf{L}$ as the lower triangular matrix of the α_{ij} coefficients, where $\mathbf{X}^T$ is the column vector of $\mathbf{X}_i$ variables, and $\mathbf{Z}^T$ is also a column vector of $\mathbf{Z}_j$ variables. Solving the matrix equation $\mathbf{Z}^T = \mathbf{LX}^T$ determines $\mathbf{L}$:

$$\mathbf{Z}_j = \mathbf{L} \times \mathbf{X}_i$$

$$\begin{pmatrix} \mathbf{Z}_1 \\ \mathbf{Z}_2 \\ \vdots \end{pmatrix} = \begin{pmatrix} \alpha_{11} & 0 & \cdots \\ \alpha_{12} & \alpha_{22} & \cdots \\ \vdots & \vdots & \ddots \end{pmatrix} \times \begin{pmatrix} \mathbf{X}_1 \\ \mathbf{X}_2 \\ \vdots \end{pmatrix}$$

The solution uses an iterative process as indicated below for determining the coefficients, as illustrated with the two-variable case.

Determining the Set of Coefficients of the Cholevsky Decomposition

The Cholevsky decomposition determines the set of coefficients α_{im} of the linear combinations of the X_j such that the Z_j comply with the given variance–covariance structure:

$$Z_j = \sum_{m=1}^{j} \alpha_{im} X_i$$

This set of coefficients transforms the independent variables X_i into correlated variables Z_j. The coefficients result from a set of equations. The variance of Z_j is the sum of the variances of the X_i weighted by the squares of α_{ij}, for i varying from 1 to j. It is equal to 1. This results in a first set of equations, one for each j, with j varying from 1 to N:

$$\text{Var}(Z_j) = \text{Var}\left(\sum_{m=1}^{j} \alpha_{im} X_i\right) = \sum_{m=1}^{j} \alpha_{im}^2 = 1$$

The index m varies from 1 to j, j being the index of Z_j varying from 1 to N because there are as many correlated variables as independent variables X_i. Then, for all i different from j, we impose the correlation structure ρ_{ij}. All variances are 1 and the covariances are equal to the correlation coefficients. The covariance of Z_j and Z_k is:

$$\text{Cov}(Z_j, Z_k) = \text{Cov}\left(\sum_{m=1}^{j} \alpha_{jm} X_i, \sum_{m=1}^{k} \alpha_{jk} X_i\right) = \rho_{ij}$$

This imposes a constraint on the coefficients:

$$\sum_{j \neq m} \alpha_{jm} \alpha_{jk} = \rho_{ij}$$

The problem is to find the set of α_{jm} for each value of j and m, both varying from 1 to N, transforming the independent variables X_i into correlated Z_j that are linear functions of the X_i. These values are the solution of the above set of equations for all α_{im}. Determining these values follows an iterative process.

Example of Cholevsky's Decomposition

The original variance–covariance matrix is Σ. The Cholevsky decomposition of a symmetrical matrix is such that $\Sigma = LU$. The following is an example of such a decomposition using a variance–covariance matrix:

$$\Sigma = L \times U$$

$$\begin{pmatrix} 4 & 2 & 14 \\ 2 & 17 & 5 \\ 14 & 5 & 83 \end{pmatrix} = \begin{pmatrix} 2 & 0 & 0 \\ 1 & 4 & 0 \\ 7 & 3 & 5 \end{pmatrix} \times \begin{pmatrix} 2 & 1 & 7 \\ 0 & 4 & 3 \\ 0 & 0 & 5 \end{pmatrix}$$

If $\mathbf{Z}^{\mathrm{T}}$ is the column vector of the correlated normal $\mathbf{Z}_j$, and $\mathbf{X}^{\mathrm{T}}$ is the column vector of the independent normal $\mathbf{X}_i$ variables, $\mathbf{Z}^{\mathrm{T}}$ derives from the $\mathbf{X}^{\mathrm{T}}$ vector of independent variables through:

$$\mathbf{Z}^{\mathrm{T}} = \mathbf{L}\mathbf{X}^{\mathrm{T}}$$

If we proceed for all $\mathbf{Z}_i$, we find k values for each $\mathbf{Z}_i$, and the values comply with the correlation structure.

Table 28.1 makes two sample calculations of two sets of three values for the three variables $\mathbf{Z}_i$ starting from two sets of three values for each of the three independent variables $\mathbf{X}_m$, of which the $\mathbf{Z}_i$ are linear combinations. The construction of the coefficients of the $\mathbf{L}$ matrix ensures that the values of the $\mathbf{Z}_i$ comply with the original variance–covariance matrix.

TABLE 28.1 The Z values from the values of the independent variable using L

			L		
			2	0	0
			1	4	0
			7	3	5
Column vector **X**:			Column vector **Z = XL**:		
$\mathbf{X}_1$	$\mathbf{X}_2$	$\mathbf{X}_3$	$\mathbf{Z}_1$	$\mathbf{Z}_2$	$\mathbf{Z}_3$
1	3	2	19	18	10
2	1	3	26	13	15
...	...	...	...	...	...
...	...	...	...	...	...

The first row of sample values 19, 18, 10 for $\mathbf{Z}_1, \mathbf{Z}_2, \mathbf{Z}_3$ results from the first row of $\mathbf{X}$ values and the matrix $\mathbf{L}$ coefficients:

$$1 \times 2 + 3 \times 1 + 2 \times 7 = 19$$

$$1 \times 0 + 3 \times 4 + 2 \times 3 = 18$$

$$1 \times 0 + 3 \times 0 + 2 \times 5 = 10$$

We can generate as many values as we need from random trials of normally independent $\mathbf{X}$. The above $\mathbf{Z}$ values comply with the variance–covariance matrix $\Sigma = \mathbf{L}\mathbf{L}^{\mathrm{T}} = \mathbf{L}\mathbf{U}$.

SECTION 11

Market Risk

29

Market Risk Building Blocks

Market risk is the potential downside deviation of the market value of transactions and of the trading portfolio during the liquidation period. Therefore, market risk focuses on market value deviations and market parameters are the main risk drivers.

Figure 29.1 summarizes the specifics of the market risk building blocks using the common structure followed throughout the book for all risks. We focus on the first two main blocks: standalone risk of individual transactions and portfolio risk. The capital allocation and risk–return building blocks are technically identical to that of credit risk.

BLOCK I: STANDALONE RISK

Market risk results from the distribution of the value variations between current date and horizon of individual assets. In percentage terms, these deviations are the random asset returns. Consequently, all we need for measuring risk are the distributions of the returns between now and the future short-term horizon. The risk drivers are all market parameters to which mark-to-market values are sensitive. They include all interest rates by currency, equity indexes and foreign exchange rates.

The exposures are mark-to-market values. Exposure values map to different market parameters, depending on the type of transaction. Simple instruments map to few main parameters, such as equity indexes for stocks. Derivatives are sensitive to several market parameters, such as underlying asset value, underlying asset volatility, interest rate and time to maturity. Mapping exposures to risk drivers is a prerequisite for determining the distribution of random future asset returns.

Valuing risk implies defining the downside deviations between current value and the random market value at the horizon of the liquidation period. These variations of

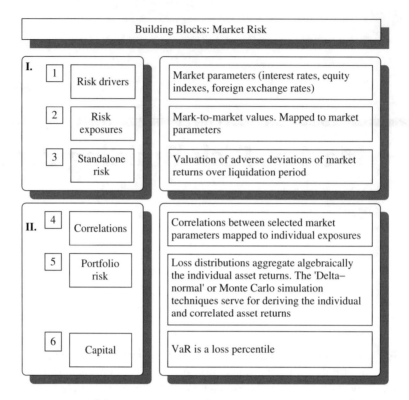

FIGURE 29.1   Major building blocks of market risk

values result directly from the distribution of the future asset returns. Financial models traditionally view small period returns as following specific random processes. Using such processes, it is possible to generate a random set of time paths of market parameter changes or of individual asset returns to obtain their final values at horizon. Then, we can revalue each asset for each final outcome. These are the basics of the full revaluation technique, which is resource intensive.

The Delta 'Value at Risk' (VaR) technique uses several simplifications to bypass full revaluations: mapping individual asset returns to market parameter returns; constant sensitivities of asset returns to underlying value drivers; linear relationship between asset returns and market parameter returns; normal distributions of market parameter returns as a proxy for actual distributions over short horizons. This solution is evidently more economical than full revaluation because there are many fewer market parameters than individual assets. Alternatively, when it is not possible to ignore the changes in sensitivity with market movements, full revaluations at horizon under various scenarios serve for improving the accuracy of the distribution of the simulated values (Figure 29.2).

All loss statistics and loss percentiles derive from the distribution of horizon returns of each individual exposure. The distribution of returns characterizes the standalone risk. When moving on to portfolios, diversification eliminates a large fraction of the sum of individual risks. The portfolio risk building block needs to model correlations and use them to model the distribution of the portfolio return.

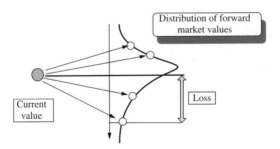

FIGURE 29.2   Forward valuation and loss valuation

BLOCK II: PORTFOLIO RISK

Portfolio risk results from the distributions of all individual and correlated asset returns. In practice, it is more economical to derive asset returns from the common factors that influence them, using sensitivities. These factors, or risk drivers, are the market parameters. Correlations between the returns of individual exposures are derived from those of market parameters.

Sometimes, it is sufficient to observe directly the market parameters for measuring historical correlations. Sometimes, it is necessary to use 'factor models' of market parameters for simulating possible scenarios. Factor models make the market parameters dependent on a common set of factors, thereby correlating them. The most well known single-factor model relates individual equity returns to the single equity index return. Some interest rate models and yield curve models can also serve to capture the distributions of the various rates. Because it is complex to model all rates, other models serve for modelling the random yield curve scenarios from factors that represent the main changes in shape of the yield curve.

This is a two-stage modelling process, from factors to market parameters, and from these risk drivers to individual market values of exposures. Since factors correlate, risk drivers also do, as well as the returns of individual exposures (Figure 29.3).

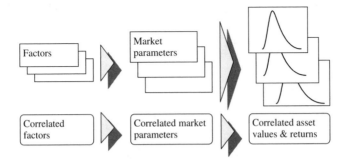

FIGURE 29.3   Modelling risk driver correlations

Portfolio risk results from the forward revaluation of portfolio returns, as the algebraic summation of all individual asset value changes, under various market parameter scenarios. VaR is the loss percentile at the preset confidence level. Generating the various

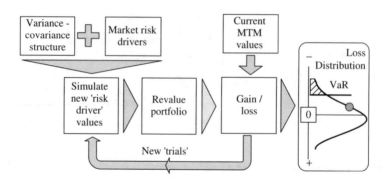

FIGURE 29.4 **The multiple simulation process for generating the market risk value distribution**

scenarios requires techniques for obtaining sets of market parameter values complying with the observed volatilities and correlations.

The Delta VaR methodology, also known as the 'linear–normal model', relates individual transaction returns to market parameter changes through sensitivities. It suffers from limitations due to the assumption of constant sensitivities. Under these simplifying assumptions, the distribution of the portfolio return between current date and horizon is a normal distribution. Loss statistics and loss percentiles, which measure VaR, are obtained from analytical formulas. Nevertheless, the sensitivity-based approach is not appropriate with optional instruments because their sensitivities are not stable.

The multiple simulation methodology (Monte Carlo simulation) remedies the drawback of the attractive, but too simple, linear model. It reverts to the direct modelling of asset values from the underlying random and correlated market parameters. The process implies generating correlated random values of market parameters and deriving, for each set, the values of individual assets. The random risk drivers need to comply with the actual variance–covariance structure observed in the market. Multiplying the number of trials results in a distribution of market parameter values. A distribution of the portfolio returns and value changes is then derived from these runs. This allows us to determine the VaR. The drawback of the Monte Carlo simulation is that it is calculation intensive, so that banks prefer the Delta VaR technique or intermediate techniques whenever possible (Figure 29.4).

30

Standalone Market Risk

This chapter reviews the techniques for measuring the market risk of individual transactions. Market risk results from the distribution of the value variations between current date and horizon of individual assets. In percentage terms, these deviations are the random asset returns. Consequently, all we need for measuring risk are the distributions of the returns of individual assets between the current date and the short-term liquidation horizon. Losses are downside moves from the current value, when ignoring the expected return for the short liquidation period.

The main drivers influencing the returns of market instruments are the market parameters. Individual asset values also serve for options, such as stock options, of which values depend on that of the underlying stock. The literature designates them as 'risk factors': they are 'risk drivers' as well as 'value drivers' because risk materializes as changes of values or of market parameters. The risk measures are loss statistics, such as value volatility and downside variations of values at a preset confidence level. All statistics result from the distribution of the random asset values at the liquidation horizon.

Pricing models in finance consider current prices as the present value of all future outcomes for individual assets. The VaR perspective is the reverse of the pricing perspective. We start from current prices and need to derive all potential adverse deviations of asset values or returns until a future time point. There are two basic techniques for doing so. Full revaluation determines the distribution of all asset values and returns after having modelled the full time path until horizon of those parameters that influence each individual asset price. Partial revaluation relies only on asset returns over the small time period until the liquidation horizon and uses shortcuts to relate these variations directly to market parameter returns over the period through sensitivities.

Full revaluation at a future date for VaR purposes is intensive in terms of resources and often impractical at the full scale of the entire portfolio. Pricing models provide closed-form formulas facilitating revaluation at the horizon once we have the distribution of the parameters that drive values and returns of individual assets. The theoretical process comprises three steps: choosing intermediate time points as 'vertices' for intermediate calculations; generating random time paths of asset and market parameter returns from now to the horizon; revaluing from these time paths the assets at the liquidation horizon.

The Delta VaR technique uses several simplifications for bypassing full revaluations: mapping individual asset returns to market parameter returns; constant sensitivities of asset returns to underlying value drivers; linear relationships between asset returns and market parameter returns; normal distributions of market parameter returns as a proxy for actual distributions over short horizons. This solution is more economical than full revaluation because there are many fewer market parameters than individual assets. The Delta–normal VaR technique that provides an analytically tractable distribution of asset returns and values at the horizon makes it simple to derive value statistics, volatility and value percentiles for a single period. When complex assets, such as exotic options, make this process excessively simplistic, we need to revert to full revaluation.

However, the full power of the Delta–normal technique appears when dealing with portfolios of assets, rather than a single asset, because the portfolio return depends in a linear way on all market parameter returns mapped to the various assets in the portfolio. The values of all instruments depend on a common set of value drivers that comply with the variance–covariance structure. Therefore, we need to mimic this correlation–volatility structure before revaluation. The portfolio return, or final value, sums algebraically all individual asset returns and depends on offsetting effects between positive and negative variations and on correlations between individual asset returns, as subsequent chapters explain. The current chapter shows the process in the case of a single asset, as an intermediate step.

The first section provides an overview of VaR and modelling of returns, and discusses the full valuation technique and the Delta VaR technique. The second section describes well-known stochastic processes for returns, stock prices and interest rates. The third section addresses the volatility measurement issue, which is a major ingredient for modelling variations of returns. The fourth section explains how to derive standalone risk measures from the normal and lognormal distribution of prices. The last section addresses the mapping issues and describes some common sensitivities, which are the foundations of the Delta VaR technique.

VAR AND FUTURE ASSET RETURNS

The market risk loss is the adverse deviation of value due to market movements. This variation is $\Delta V_i = (V_{i,H} - V_{i,0}) = V_{i,0} \times r_i$. It is the deviation from current value or, equivalently, the return times the current value. The return measures the unit deviation of value. Hence, measuring value deviations over short time periods is equivalent to measuring the random returns from the current value in percentage terms. Therefore, to measure market risk VaR, it is sufficient to model random returns between the current date and the horizon. In what follows, we use both value and cumulative returns equivalently since they map on a one-to-one basis at the horizon. The valuation building block of market risk models relies on two basic techniques:

- Full revaluation at a future horizon, set as the liquidation period.
- Partial revaluation of individual asset returns from market movements, also known as the Delta VaR technique, which applies to both single assets and portfolios.

Full Revaluation

The finance literature relies extensively on modelling returns for pricing models. Theoretical finance derives prices from modelled time paths of returns. Returns follow stochastic processes. Stochastic processes specify the distribution of asset returns, or of market parameters, over each time interval, as a function of their expected values and volatilities.

Implementing these stochastic processes allows us to model future outcomes, and to find all future asset payoffs, notably when these payoffs are contingent on outcomes, such as for options. For common assets, including standard options, modelling the stochastic processes of returns results in closed-form pricing formulas. For complex options, the modelling of return processes allows us to conduct simulations of all future outcomes and derive the current price as the expected present value of all option payoffs over this range. Derivative pricing models derive the return of derivatives from the return process of the underlying asset. The most well known example is the pricing of European stock options. The Black–Scholes equation prices a European equity option by modelling the return of the option as a function of the underlying stock return using Itô's lemma. The principle applies to all derivatives[1]. Accordingly, the literature on stochastic processes expanded considerably. Stochastic processes serve for modelling all asset returns and prices. They apply to stock prices, interest rates and derivatives, whose returns depend on the underlying asset return process[2].

The VaR perspective is a sort of 'reverse' pricing perspective. Instead of finding the current price from the present value of all possible future outcomes, we derive all possible asset values for all future outcomes from the current data. There is a duality between cumulative returns and values. The time paths of returns map on a one-to-one basis to future values. This is obvious using the single discrete time formula for the random return $y(0, t) = (V_t - V_0)/V_0$, with V_t and V_0 being random values at date t and the current certain value at date 0. However, discrete time returns have drawbacks, as illustrated in the section on returns below, making it necessary to use small time intervals and construct the time path of returns, over a sequence of small periods. The random cumulative return links final value to initial value. Continuous finance makes extensive use of instantaneous 'logarithmic' returns over small time intervals, rather than arithmetic returns, because they are additive, as demonstrated in the appendix to this chapter.

There are important variations across asset classes for modelling future outcomes. For stocks, we need to model the time path of stock returns and derive the distribution of future prices, given the expected return and its volatility as measured from historical observations. We find, as shown below, that stock prices follow a lognormal distribution whose parameters depend on the expected return and its volatility. For bonds, we need

---

[1] See Hull (2000) and Merton (1990) for comprehensive reviews.
[2] See Neftci (1996) for an introduction to the mathematics of stochastic processes, Smith (1976) and Cox and Ross (1976) for option pricing.

to derive all future interest scenarios at the future date from their stochastic processes to revalue the bond for each of these scenarios by discounting at appropriate market rates the future contractual cash flows. For options, we need to derive all future outcomes for all their value drivers, which include the underlying prices, such as stock prices for equity options, and revalue the options at the future date.

For complex derivatives, the process is the same except that we do not have closed-form pricing formulas. Therefore, we need to revert to simulations of future option payoffs. The difference is that the price as of a given date results from all possible future outcomes. A forward revaluation requires determining all possible outcomes as of this future date. Unfortunately, there are many starting points at future dates, so we need to replicate the process for each of them. This mechanism is a 'simulation within a simulation'. The first simulation provides all outcomes at the horizon. A second set of simulations replicates the process for all dates beyond the horizon starting from each horizon state. Evidently, such a process consumes many resources, making it unpractical. Derivatives looking backward, such as barrier options and 'look back'[3] options, raise different obstacles. The values of these options depend on all intermediate outcomes between the current date and a future date. Revaluation at a future date depends on these intermediate states.

The 'full revaluation' technique requires all outcomes for all ingredients of future prices and recalculates future prices for each scenario. The distribution of future cumulative returns between today and the horizon, provides all that is needed for VaR calculations.

Accordingly, the next section details some basic stochastic processes, those applying to stock prices and those applying to interest rates, to show the implications of using the full revaluation technique. Stochastic processes specify the distribution of asset returns, or of market parameters, over each time interval, as a function of the expected value of the return and its volatility. For stocks, the process allows stock prices to drift away from initial value without imposing any bound on prices. However, the time paths of interest rates follow specific stochastic processes because, unlike stock prices, they tend to revert towards a long-term average value. The next section provides an overview of these basic stochastic processes.

Once stochastic processes of value–risk drivers are specified, the technique implies:

- Choosing intermediate time points as 'vertices' for intermediate calculations.
- Generating random time paths of assets and market parameter returns from now to each time point.
- Revaluing from these time paths the asset at the liquidation horizon.

Partial Revaluation and Delta VaR

It is obvious from the above that the process is resource intensive and impracticable in most cases. Additional shortcuts help resolve such complexities. Partial revaluation uses much simpler techniques. It starts from the observation that all we need for VaR purposes

---

[3] A 'look back' option has a payoff linking to past values of the underlying. For instance, the payoff of a look back equity option could be the maximum of the stock price between inception and the horizon. Barrier options disappear when the underlying hits a barrier, and also depend on the time path of past values.

are variations of values or returns for each individual asset, and that value drivers for assets are market parameters. To be more specific, the drivers of stock returns are the equity indexes. The drivers of interest-bearing assets are the interest rates along the yield curve. The drivers of option values are these market parameters plus the underlying asset prices, for instance an interest rate or a stock price. There are many fewer market parameters than individual assets in a portfolio. Therefore, starting from market parameters to obtain asset returns is evidently more economical than modelling each asset return.

The first prerequisite is to map asset returns to market parameters. Stock returns map to equity indexes, interest-bearing assets map to interest rates, stock options map to the market parameters of interest rates, stock return volatilities and stock prices, and so on for other options. The next step is to relate asset returns to the selected underlying market parameters. Sensitivities provide a simple proxy relationship as long as the variations of market parameters are not too important. This is acceptable in many cases for short-term horizons, except for options when market movements trigger abrupt shifts in sensitivities. Using constant sensitivities makes the relationship between market parameter changes and asset returns linear. This is a major simplification compared to using the pricing formulas of individual assets. The next step is to model the distribution of the market parameter returns.

A normal distribution has very attractive properties: the linear combination of random normal variables is also a normal variable. Combining these shortcuts results in a simple technique. The asset returns follow normal distributions derived from a linear combination of random normal parameter returns. The derivation of all loss statistics and VaR becomes quite easy since we know all percentiles of the normal distribution. For single assets, a single value driver is sufficient. For options, there are several value drivers, but the option returns remain a linear combination of these. For a portfolio, various assets depend on different market parameters, so that we always have a linear function of all of them. These are the foundations of the 'Delta–normal VaR' technique. It provides normal distributions of asset returns from which VaR derives directly.

The Delta VaR technique faces some complexities with interest rates. Modelling future outcomes of the yield curve is not an easy task. Simple interest rate models might suffice, for instance when there are only parallel shifts in the yield curve. In general, however, interest-bearing asset values depend on the entire yield curve. It is not practical to use full-blown yield curve models. One technique consists of selecting only some interest rates along the yield curve for references. An alternative technique consists of using factor models of the yield curve. These make the yield curve a function of a few factors that behave randomly, with specific volatilities, subject to prior fitting to historical data. They allow us to simulate random shocks on the yield curve, including those that alter its shape (level, slope and 'bump'). Converting these factors into yield curves provides the required distribution of selected interest rates.

The partial revaluation process requires the following steps, that substitute for full revaluation:

- Mapping asset returns to value–risk drivers.
- Simple modelling of the market parameter returns.
- Measuring the sensitivities of asset returns to market parameters.
- Deriving the asset return distribution as a linear function of these distributions.

Limitations of the Delta–normal technique are:

- Constant sensitivities.
- Proxy mapping to market parameters, generating basis risk.
- Proxy of actual distributions of value–risk drivers.
- Ignoring 'fat tails' of actual distributions.

Notably, the Delta VaR technique collapses when sensitivities cannot be considered constant, as for options and look back derivatives. Moreover, only on sensitivities for stocks ignores risk unrelated to market parameters, or the specific risk of stocks. The diagonal model of stock returns remedies this drawback, as explained in the next chapter.

Nevertheless, the Delta VaR technique shines for portfolios. Portfolios of assets make the overall return dependent on the entire set of market parameters. Their random movements depend on their correlations. Since the Delta VaR technique makes individual asset returns a linear function of random parameters, it also applies to the portfolio return. The difference when dealing with multiple market parameters resides in correlations affecting their co-movements. Since it is a relatively simple matter to model correlated random variables, using techniques detailed in Chapter 28, the Delta VaR technique allows us to handle correlations without difficulty.

STOCHASTIC PROCESSES OF RETURNS

To fully revaluate asset values at the horizon, the common technique consists of modelling the individual asset returns to derive the value at the horizon by cumulating intermediate returns. This section explains the basic mechanisms of common stochastic processes and how time paths of returns relate to final values. Pricing models view returns as following 'stochastic' processes across successive short time intervals. Measuring risk requires the distribution of cumulative returns to the horizon given the current value. The first subsection illustrates the drawbacks of a single-period discrete return. The next subsections discuss two types of processes serving to model asset returns: the Wiener process for stock prices and processes applicable to interest rates. The last subsection discusses volatility measures, which are critical inputs to risk measures and stochastic models of returns.

Single-period Return

The return over a discrete period is the relative variation of value between two dates. For a short time interval, the single-period return over that period is sufficient to obtain the final value because there is a one-to-one correspondence between the random return value and the final value, according to the above equation. Random returns between dates 0 and H are $\mathbf{y}(0, H)$, values indexed by date are V_0 for the current (certain) value and $\mathbf{V}_H$ for the random value at horizon H. The return $\mathbf{y}$, between any two dates, and the value at the horizon, are:

$$\mathbf{y}(0, H) = (\mathbf{V}_H - V_0)/V_0$$

$$\mathbf{V}_H = V_0(1 + \mathbf{y})$$

With a single-period return, the value distribution at H derives from that of the return because $\mathbf{V}_H = V_0(1 + \mathbf{y})$. The obvious limitation of this technique for modelling returns and final values is that a normal distribution allows the random return to hit values lower than -100%, resulting in non-acceptable negative values of the asset. For a sufficiently short horizon, this formulation is convenient because normal distributions are easier to handle.

When the period gets very small, the return becomes $\mathbf{y} = d\mathbf{V}/V$, where $d\mathbf{V}$ is the small change in value. This makes it more acceptable to use normal distributions. On the other hand, it makes it necessary to use cumulative returns, which are not normally distributed, between discrete dates, current date and horizon.

Stock Return Processes

Under the efficient markets hypothesis, all stock values reflect all past information available. Consequently, variations of values in successive periods are independent from one period to another because the flow of new information, or 'innovations', is random. In addition, small period returns follow approximately normal distributions with a positive mean. This assumption applies notably to stock prices, but it is also a proxy for short-term interest rates. The mean is the expected return, such as the risk-free return for a risk-free asset and the risky expected market yield for risky assets.

Over very small intervals, returns follow stochastic processes. The Wiener process is a common stochastic process, adequate for stock prices:

$$d\mathbf{V}_t = \mu V_t \, dt + \sigma V_t d\mathbf{z}_t$$

This equation stipulates that the small change in value of a stock price V_t is the sum of a term $\mu V_t \, dt$, which reflects the expected return μ per unit time, times the initial stock value, and proportional to the time interval dt, plus a random term. This first term is the expected value of the relative increase $d\mathbf{V}_t/V_t$ of the asset price, because the expected value of the random term $d\mathbf{z}_t$ is zero. The random component of the return is $\sigma V_t d\mathbf{z}_t$, proportional to the return volatility σ, the price $\mathbf{V}_t$ and a random 'noise', $d\mathbf{z}_t$, following a standardized normal variable (mean 0 and volatility 1). This simple process models the behaviour of the price through time. $d\mathbf{V}_t$ follows a 'generalized Wiener process', with drift μ and volatility σ. The process makes the instantaneous return $d\mathbf{V}_t/V_t$ a direct function of its mean and volatility σ:

$$\mathbf{y} = d\mathbf{V}_t/V_t = \mu dt + \sigma d\mathbf{z}_t$$

This equation shows that the return follows a normal distribution around the time drift defined by the expected return $\mu \, dt$. Since dx/x is the derivative of $\ln(x)$, this equation shows that the logarithm of stock price at date t follows a normal distribution[4]. Therefore, the stock price at date t follows a lognormal distribution whose equation is[5]:

$$\mathbf{V}_t = V_0 \exp[(\mu - \tfrac{1}{2}\sigma^2)t + \sigma \mathbf{z}_t]$$

---

[4] This necessitates integration from date 0 to t of the small value increments over each dt.

[5] A lognormal distribution is the distribution of a variable whose logarithm follows a normal distribution. The summation of all $d\mathbf{z}_t$ over time results in a normal variable for $\mathbf{z}_t$. The equation of the final value of the stock results from expressing the logarithm of the stock price as following the process $d[\ln(S)] = [(\mu - \tfrac{1}{2}\sigma^2)dt + \sigma d\mathbf{z}]$.

For stocks, the random process is consistent with the efficient markets hypothesis stating that, if all prices fully reflect the available information, they fluctuate randomly with the flow of new information. Therefore, new prices are dependent only on 'innovations' $\mathbf{dz}_t$, not on past prices. The $\mathbf{dz}_t$ are uncorrelated through time and follow the same distribution at all dates. Under this assumption, the process is 'stationary', meaning that it remains the same through time. Innovations are identically independently distributed (iid). Because the innovations $\mathbf{dz}_t$ are independent variables of variance $(\sigma \, dt)^2$, their sum $\mathbf{z}_t$ has a variance equal to the sum of variances. Using $dt = 1$, and t time intervals, the variance of the cumulated innovations is $t \times \sigma^2$, and the volatility is $\sigma \sqrt{t}$. It increases as the square root of time. This is the 'square root of time' rule for the volatility. It results in an ever-increasing volatility of the random price.

The formula makes it easy to generate time paths of the $\mathbf{S}_t$ by generating normal standardized $\mathbf{dz}_t$ and cumulating them until date t, with preset values of the instantaneous expected return μ and its volatility σ. This simple process is very popular. It applies to asset prices and market parameters whose variance increases over time.

Generating Time Paths of Stock Values: Sample Simulation

The simulation of time paths of value drivers allows us to model the forward values of any asset. We illustrate here the mechanism with the simple Wiener process, which results in a lognormal distribution. The technique comprises three steps:

- Choosing intermediate time points as 'vertices' for intermediate calculations of the returns.
- Generating random time paths of market parameter returns from now to the horizon based on the specific parameters characterizing the asset process.

The final asset value distribution at the horizon results from cumulative returns along each time path. To generate a discrete path, we use a unit value for $\Delta t = t - (t - 1)$ and the standard N(0, 1) normal variable for the innovations $\Delta \mathbf{z}$. With several time intervals, we obtain the intermediate values of the price. The process uses the following inputs:

- Initial price $V_0 = 10$.
- Time interval $\Delta t = 0.1$ year.
- Expected return 10% yearly, or $10\%/10 = 1\%$ per 1/10 of a year.
- Yearly volatility of the random component 20%, or $20\%/10 = 2\%$ per 1/10 of a year.
- The innovation at each time interval $\Delta \mathbf{z}$ as a standardized normal distribution.

The price after one step is:

$$V_t - V_{t-1} = V_{t-1}(\mu + \Delta \mathbf{z} \times \Delta t) = V_{t-1}(1\% \times 0.1 + \Delta \mathbf{z} \times 0.2 \times \sqrt{0.1})$$

Simulating a time path over 1 year consists of generating a time series of 10 random draws of 10 innovation values. Simulating several time paths consists of repeating the process as many times as necessary. This allows us to calculate any final value that depends on past values, such as the value of a look back option on the stock. Figure 30.1 shows various time paths and the final price at date 10.

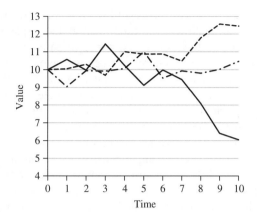

FIGURE 30.1   Time paths of value

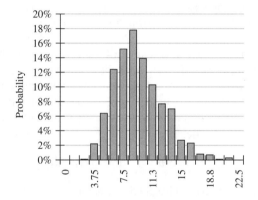

FIGURE 30.2   Distribution of final value

Figure 30.2 shows the simulation of the final prices after 1000 time path simulations, which is a lognormal distribution. The appendix to this chapter shows why logarithmic returns provide good proxies of instantaneous returns and facilitate handling cumulative returns when the number of subperiods makes them small enough. The formulas provide useful shortcuts when modelling cumulative returns.

Interest Rate Processes

Interest rate processes are more complex than the basic stock price processes for two reasons:

- There are several interest rates, so we need to model the behaviour of several parameters rather than only one.
- Interest rates tend to revert to some long-term average over long periods.

To capture the behaviour of interest rates, we need to model the entire time structure of rates, with models using 'mean reverting' stochastic processes. Interest rate models view interest rates as following a stochastic process through time. A stochastic process specifies the change in the rate as a function of the time interval and a random 'noise' mimicking the volatility of rates. Several stochastic processes apply to interest rates. Mean reversion implies that rates revert to some long-term average and avoid extreme variations of the interest rate to mimic the actual behaviour of rates. Mean reverting processes prevent rates from drifting too far away from a central tendency materialized by a long-term rate. This contrasts with stock prices, which can drift away from initial values without bounds.

A 'term structure model' describes the evolution of the yield curve through time. Models generate the entire yield curve using one or two factors. When using models to generate interest rate scenarios, the technique consists of generating random values of the factor(s) driving the rate and the error term. Random interest rate scenarios follow. To find all possible values of a bond at horizon, we need to simulate yield curve scenarios between now and the horizon. For each scenario, there is a unique value of the bond price resulting from its discounting contractual cash flows at maturity with rates of simulated yield curves. Since the same yield curve applies to all interest-driven assets, ignoring the fluctuation of credit spreads, we use the same yield curve scenarios for all bonds. For derivatives, the final values result from the underlying asset values, as for equity derivatives.

One-factor models involve only one source of uncertainty, usually the short-term rate. They assume that all rates move in the same direction. However, the magnitude of the change is not the same for all rates. The following equation represents a one-factor model of short-term rates $\mathbf{r}_t$. Using such a model implies that all rates fully correlate with this short-term rate. The random $\mathbf{dz}_t$ term follows a standardized normal distribution and makes the rate changes stochastic:

$$\mathbf{dr}_t = \kappa(\theta - \mathbf{r}_t)\mathrm{d}t + \sigma(\mathbf{r}_t)^{\gamma}\mathbf{dz}_t$$

The parameter $\kappa < 1$ determines the speed of mean reversion to a long-term mean θ. When the rate is high, the term in parentheses becomes negative, and contributes to a downward move of the rate. When the parameter $\gamma = 0$, the change of rate is normally distributed as the random term. When $\gamma = 1$, the rate $\mathbf{r}_t$ follows a lognormal distribution, as the stock prices do with the standard Wiener process. When $\gamma = 0.5$, the variance of the rate is proportional to its level, implying that low interest rates are less volatile than high interest rates. One-factor models use the following processes:

$$\text{Rendleman and Bartter:} \quad dr = \kappa r \mathrm{d}t + \sigma r \mathbf{dz}$$

$$\text{Vasicek's model:} \quad dr = \kappa(\theta - r)\mathrm{d}t + \sigma \mathbf{dz}$$

$$\text{Cox, Ingersoll and Ross model:} \quad dr = \kappa(\theta - r)\mathrm{d}t + \sigma \sqrt{r}\, \mathbf{dz}$$

Two-factor models assume two sources of uncertainty (Brennan and Schwartz, 1979; Cox et al., 1985; Longstaff and Schwarz, 1992).

The 'no-arbitrage' models start by fitting the current term structure of rates, which provides the benefit of starting from actual rates that can serve for pricing purposes or defining interest rate scenarios from the current state. These models comply with the principle of no risk-free arbitrage across maturities of the spot yield curve. However, this constraint implies that the current shape of the yield curve drives to a certain extent the future short rates. The Ho and Lee (1986) model uses a binomial tree of bond prices. Hull and White extended the original technique[6]. Advanced models allow long-term modelling of the yield curves (Heath et al., 1992).

For VaR purposes, it is not practical to use elaborate interest rate models. Simpler techniques are necessary. Selecting some interest rates as references and allowing them to vary, while complying with given variance–covariance structure, is the simplest technique. Principal component analyses use historical data on market parameters to define components that explain the movements[7]. The application of this technique to term structure modelling shows that the most important factors represent the parallel shifts, twists (slope changes) and curvature of the term structure of yield. Principal component analysis has many attractive properties. The rates of different maturities are a linear function of the factors. The technique provides the sensitivities of rates to each factor and the factor volatilities. Since factors are independent, it is easy to derive the volatility of a rate given sensitivities and factor volatilities. For simulation, allowing factors to vary randomly, as well as the random error, generates a full distribution of yield curves.

MEASURING VOLATILITIES

The volatility is a basic ingredient of all processes leading to the horizon value distribution. There are several techniques to obtain volatilities. The first is to derive them from historical observations of prices and market parameters. More elaborate approaches try to capture the instability of volatility over time. They use moving average, with or without assigning higher weights to the most recent observations, or ARCH–GARCH models of the time behaviour of observed volatilities. A third technique is to use the implicit volatilities embedded in options prices, by reverse engineering pricing models of options to derive from the price the volatility parameter. Implicit volatilities look forward by definition, as market prices do, but they might be very unstable.

Square Root of Time Rule

Historical volatility measures require us to define the horizon of the period of observations and the frequency of observations. The frequency stipulates whether we measure a daily, monthly or yearly volatility. It is easier to use daily measures because there is more information. Then, we move to other periods using the 'square root of time rule' for volatilities. The square root of time rule applies only when there are no bounds to cumulative returns, as mentioned above for stock prices, and if the underlying process is stationary. The rule stems from the independence assumption across time of consecutive value changes. For instance, the change in values between dates 0 and 2, $\Delta V(0, 2)$, is the sum of the change between dates 0 and 1 and between dates 1 and 2 (end of period dates), $\Delta V(0, 1) + \Delta V(1, 2)$. The issue is to find the volatility of the change σ_{02} of $\Delta V(0, 2)$ between 0 and 2 from the volatilities between 0 and 1, σ_{01}, and between 1 and 2, σ_{12}, which are supposed identical, $\sigma_{01} = \sigma_{12} = \sigma_1$, the unit period volatility. A simple rule of summation indicates the volatility of the sum is the square

---

[6] See Hull (2000) for a review of all models and details on the Hull and White extensions.
[7] See Frye (1997) for factor models of interest rates, also Litterman and Scheinkman (1988).

root of the sum of the squared volatilities, or $\sigma_{02} = \sigma_1\sqrt{2}$. The rule extends easily to any number of units of time, if variations across time periods remain independent and have a constant volatility. Using the rule, with a 1% daily volatility, the yearly volatility is $\sigma_{1\text{year}} = \sigma_{1\text{day}}\sqrt{250} = 1\% \times 15.811 = 15.811\%$. This simple rule allows us to convert market volatilities over various lengths of time. The relationship between the volatility σ_t over t periods and the volatility over a unit σ_1 period is $\sigma_t = \sigma_1\sqrt{t}$ (Figure 30.3).

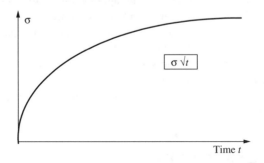

FIGURE 30.3   Volatility time profile of a market parameter over various horizons

Practical rules are helpful, even though reality does not comply with the underlying assumptions. For long-term horizons, the above volatility would become infinite, which is unacceptable. Many phenomena are 'mean reverting', such as interest rates. The above formula provides a practical way to infer short-term volatilities only. In addition, real phenomena are not 'stationary', implying that volatilities are not stable over time, and the assumption does not hold.

Non-stationarity

Various techniques deal with non-stationarity, which designates the fact that the random process from which we sample the volatility observations is not stable over time. Since the VaR is highly sensitive to volatilities of market parameters, it is of major importance to use relevant and conservative values. They extend from simple conservative rules to elaborate models of the time behaviour of volatility, ARCH–GARCH models (Engle, 1993; Nelson, 1990a).

Volatilities are highly unstable. Depending on the period, they can be high or very low. There are a number of techniques for dealing with this issue[8]. Some are very simple, such as taking the highest between a short-term volatility (3 months) and a long-term volatility (say 2 years). If volatility increases, the most recent one serves as a reference. If there are past periods of high volatility, the longer period volatility serves as a reference. Other techniques consist of using moving averages of volatilities. A moving average is the average of a determined number k of successive observations. The average moves with time since the sample of the last k observations moves when time passes. For example, we could have a time series of values such as: 2, 3, 5, 6, 4, 3. A three-period moving average would calculate the average over three consecutive observations. At the third date it is

---

[8] For updating volatilities in simulations, see Hull (2000).

$(2 + 3 + 5)/3$, then it becomes $(3 + 5 + 6)/3$ at the fourth date, $(5 + 6 + 4)/3$ at the fifth date, and finally $(6 + 4 + 3)/3$ at the last date. Moving averages minimize deviations from the long-term mean. Arithmetic moving averages place equal weights on all observations, ignoring the fact that the latest ones convey more information. Exponential smoothing places higher weights on the most recent observations and mimics better the most recent changes. The Exponentially Weighted Moving Average (EWMA) model uses weights decreasing exponentially when moving back in time. Risk Metrics uses a variation of these 'averaging' techniques[9].

The GARCH family of models aims to model the time behaviour of volatility. Volatility seems to follow a mean reverting process, so that high values tend to smooth out after a while. The models attempt to capture these patterns assuming that the variance calculated over a given period as of t depends on the variance as of $t - 1$, over the same horizon, plus the latest available observation. The model equation, using $\mathbf{h}_t$ as the variance and r_t as the return, is:

$$\mathbf{h}_t = \alpha_0 + \alpha_1 r_{t-1}^2 + \alpha_2 \mathbf{h}_{t-1}$$

The variance $\mathbf{h}_t$ is a conditional variance, dependent on past observations. By contrast, the long-term unconditional mean is h, obtained by setting $h = h_t = h_{t-1}$ and observing that $E(r_{t-1}^2) = h : h = \alpha_0 + \alpha_1 h + \alpha_2 h$ implies $h = \alpha_0/(1 - \alpha_1 - \alpha_2)$. The model results in a series of variance shocks followed by smoothed values of variance.

VALUE DISTRIBUTIONS AT THE HORIZON AND STANDALONE MARKET RISK

The measures of standalone market risk of single instruments are loss statistics, loss volatility and loss percentiles, all resulting from the distribution of final values at horizon. Applied to a single asset, we obtain the standalone VaR at a preset confidence level. This section uses the normal and lognormal distributions to derive these measures. The normal distribution has the drawbacks mentioned above, but serves for the Delta–normal technique for a short-term horizon. When reverting to continuous stochastic processes of the time paths of asset returns, we obtain lognormal distributions at the horizon for stock prices. The value percentiles derive from this lognormal distribution.

Normal Values Distribution at Horizon

Return $\mathbf{y}_t$ and value $\mathbf{V}_t$ are such that $\mathbf{V}_t = V_0(1 + \mathbf{y}_t)$ and both follow a normal distribution. The confidence level for the value percentiles is such that:

$$\text{Prob}[\mathbf{V}_t \leq V(\alpha)] = \alpha$$

Converting this equation into a condition on the random return between 0 and t:

$$\text{Prob}[V_0(1 + \mathbf{y}_t) \leq V(\alpha)] = \alpha$$

$$\text{Prob}\{\mathbf{y}_t \leq [V(\alpha) - V_0]/V_0\} = \alpha$$

---

[9] J. P. Morgan, Risk Metrics Monitor, 1995.

y_t follows $N(\mu, \sigma)$ and $z_t = (y_t - \mu)/\sigma$ follows $N(0, 1)$, the normal standardized distribution. Since $y_t = \sigma z_t + \mu$, the preceding inequality becomes:

$$\text{Prob}\{z_t \leq [V(\alpha)/V_0] - (1 + \mu)/\sigma\} = \alpha$$

By definition, $\text{Prob}[z_t \leq z(\alpha)] = \alpha$. The probability of a standardized normal variable being lower than a given threshold $z(\alpha)$ is by definition $\Phi(\alpha)$, where Φ is the cumulative standard distribution. By definition, $z(\alpha) = \Phi^{-1}(\alpha)$, with Φ^{-1} being the standardized normal inverse. This inequality defines $z(\alpha)$ and the value percentile $V(\alpha)$ derives from the linear relationship between $z(\alpha)$ and $V(\alpha)$:

$$z(\alpha) = \Phi^{-1}(\alpha) = [V(\alpha)/V_0 - (1 + \mu)]/\sigma$$

$$V(\alpha)/V_0 = 1 + \mu + \Phi^{-1}(\alpha)\sigma$$

In this formula, $\Phi^{-1}(\alpha)$ is negative, so that the final value can be lower than the initial value as long as the downside deviation exceeds the upside variation due to the asset return.

As an example, let's assume that the expected yearly return μ is 10%, the yearly return volatility σ is 15%, the horizon t is 1 year and the value at date 0, V_0, is 1. This simplifies the formula. If the confidence level is 1%, $\text{Prob}[z_t \leq z(\alpha)] = \alpha$ implies that $z(\alpha) = \Phi^{-1}(\alpha) = -2.3263$. Hence:

$$V(\alpha)/V_0 = 1 + 10\% - 2.3263 \times 15\% = 75.11\%$$

The downside deviation of the value at the preset confidence level of 1% is $1 - 75.11\% = 24.89\%$ in absolute value.

Lognormal Values Distribution at Horizon

When using normal distributions of continuous returns, the distribution at the horizon is a lognormal distribution. The lognormal distribution applies notably to stock prices. Defining the distribution requires the return volatility. Deriving value percentiles from a lognormal distribution is less straightforward than for a normal distribution. If the return follows a Wiener process, the value at date t is:

$$V_t = V_0 \exp[(\mu - \tfrac{1}{2}\sigma^2)t + \sigma\sqrt{t}\, z_t]$$

The random component z_t follows a standardized normal distribution $N(0, 1)$. The parameters μ and σ are the mean and volatility of the instantaneous rate of return of the firm. The value percentile $V(\alpha)$ at the preset confidence level α is such that:

$$\text{Prob}[V_t \leq V(\alpha)] = \alpha$$

From the distribution of the value at t, we derive the value percentile $V(\alpha)$ using the inequality:

$$\text{Prob}\{\exp[(\mu - \tfrac{1}{2}\sigma^2)t + \sigma\sqrt{t}\, z_t] \leq V(\alpha)/V_0\} = \alpha$$

This inequality requires that z_t be such that:

$$\text{Prob}\{(\mu - \tfrac{1}{2}\sigma^2)t + \sigma\sqrt{t}\, z_t \leq \ln[V(\alpha)/V_0]\} = \alpha$$

$$\text{Prob}\{z_t \leq \ln[V(\alpha)/V_0] - (\mu - \tfrac{1}{2}\sigma^2)t/\sigma\sqrt{t}\} = \alpha$$

The probability of a standardized normal variable being lower than a given threshold $z(\alpha)$ is by definition $\Phi(\alpha)$, where Φ is the cumulative standard distribution, and $z(\alpha) = \Phi^{-1}(\alpha)$, with Φ^{-1} being the standardized normal inverse. The equality $\mathrm{Prob}[z_t \leq z(\alpha)] = \alpha$ defines $z(\alpha)$ and, then, the value percentile $V(\alpha)$. This requires determining $z(\alpha)$ first, and moving from there to $V(\alpha)$:

$$z(\alpha) = \Phi^{-1}(\alpha) = \{\ln[V(\alpha)/V_0] - (\mu - \tfrac{1}{2}\sigma^2)t\}/\sigma\sqrt{t}$$

$$\ln[V(\alpha)/V_0] = \Phi^{-1}(\alpha)\sigma\sqrt{t} + (\mu - \tfrac{1}{2}\sigma^2)t$$

$$V(\alpha)/V_0 = \exp[\Phi^{-1}(\alpha)\sigma\sqrt{t} + (\mu - \tfrac{1}{2}\sigma^2)t]$$

In this formula, $\Phi^{-1}(\alpha)$ is negative, so that the final value is lower than the initial value as long as the downside deviation exceeds the upside variation due to the asset return adjusted for the volatility term.

As an example, we assume that the expected yearly return μ is 10%, the yearly return volatility σ is 15%, the horizon t is 1 year and the value at date 0 is 1, so that we have the final value as a percentage of the initial value. This simplifies the formula. If the confidence level is 1%, $z(\alpha) = \Phi^{-1}(\alpha) = -2.3263$. The argument of the exponential above is:

$$\Phi^{-1}(\alpha)\sigma\sqrt{t} + (\mu - \tfrac{1}{2}\sigma^2)t = -2.3263 \times 15\% + (10\% - \tfrac{1}{2} \times 15\%^2) = -0.260195$$

The exponential of this term is 77.09%. The downside deviation of the value at the preset confidence level of 1% is $1 - 77.09\% = 22.91\%$ in absolute value. We observe that this downside deviation is lower than under the normal approximation, because the normal approximation has a 'fatter' downside tail than the lognormal distribution.

MAPPING INSTRUMENTS TO RISK FACTORS

Modelling all individual asset returns within a portfolio is overly complex to handle. Since the number of market indexes is much smaller than that of individual assets, it is more efficient to derive asset returns from the time paths of market parameters that influence their values. On the other hand, it necessitates modelling the relation between asset returns and market parameters. The process requires two steps: identifying those market parameters which influence values, a process called 'mapping'; modelling the sensitivity of individual asset values to market parameters. Mapping and using sensitivities to underlying market parameters is the foundation of the Delta VaR technique. The first subsection describes the mapping process, the second one explains how to derive standalone market risk under the Delta VaR technique with a single asset. The next subsections specify the sensitivities of various types of assets.

The Mapping Process

The mapping process results from pricing models in order to identify the main value drivers of asset values. Mapping individual asset returns to market parameters often uses only a subset of all market parameters for simplification purposes. The subset of interest rates corresponds to selected maturities. For interest rate references that do not correspond to these maturities, it is possible to interpolate a proxy of the corresponding rate using the references. The exclusion of some value drivers results in 'basis risk', since the modelled values do not track exactly the actual asset prices any more.

The variations of value of any market instrument result from its sensitivities to market parameters and the volatility of these parameters. The mapping of individual asset values to market parameters (also designated as risk drivers or risk factors) results from pricing models, showing which parameters influence values. Most relations between asset values and value drivers have a linear approximation. In some cases, the relationship is statistical, and implies always a significant error, such as for stocks. In such cases, it becomes necessary to account for the error in estimating the risk. In other cases, the relation results from a closed-form formula such as for bonds or simple derivatives.

When dealing with derivatives, such as interest rate swaps or foreign exchange swaps, or forward rate agreements, it is necessary to break down the derivative into simpler components to reduce complexity and find direct relations with market parameters driving their values. For example, a forward transaction is a combination of long and short transactions, such as a forward interest rate (lend long until final date and borrow short until start date). An interest rate swap is a combination of fixed and variable flows indexed to the term structure of rates. A forward swap is a combination of a long swap and a short swap.

Sensitivities are unstable because they are local measures. This is a major limitation, notably for options. Their sensitivity with respect to the underlying parameter is the delta of the option. An 'out-of-the-money' option has a relatively stable and low delta. When the option is 'at-the-money', its delta changes significantly with the underlying price. When it is 'in-the-money', the value increases almost proportionally with the market parameter and the delta tends progressively towards 1. With out-of-the-money options, the portfolio behaves as if no options exist. When options are in-the-money, the sensitivity gets close to 1. In other words, the portfolio behaves as if its sensitivity structure changes with variations in the underlying assets. This is the convexity risk, encountered with implicit options in Asset–Liability Management (ALM) models. Whenever convexity is significant within a portfolio, the simple Delta VaR model becomes unreliable[10]. Extensions, as described in the next chapter, partially correct such deficiencies. Sensitivities are 'local' measures that change with the context. Accordingly, calculating the value change of an instrument as a linear function of market parameter changes is only an approximation.

When a model relates the price of an asset to several parameters, the 'Taylor' expansion[11] of the formula is a proxy relationship of the value change resulting from a change in value drivers. It relates the value change to changes in all parameters using all derivatives of the actual function. A Taylor series makes the change of the value of instruments as a function of the first, second, third-order derivatives, and so on. For large changes, it is preferable to consider additional terms of Taylor expansion of the equation beyond

---

[10] Another case in point is the measure of credit risk for options. Since the horizon gets much longer than for market risk, the assumption of constant sensitivities collapses.

[11] See the Taylor expansion formula in Chapter 32.

the first one. Additional terms better proxy the curvature of the relationship between the asset returns and their drivers.

Standalone Risk from Market Returns

The return sensitivity change in asset i is, in general, a function of several market parameters k:

$$\mathbf{y}_i = \Delta \mathbf{V}_i / V_{i0} = \sum_{1}^{K} s_{ik} \times \Delta \mathbf{m}_k / m_{k0}$$

The index k refers to any of the K relevant market parameters, with k varying from 1 to K. The index i refers to any one of N transactions, with i varying from 1 to N. Since one transaction often depends on only one market parameter, and in general on only a small number of them, most of the sensitivities are zero.

The standalone risk of an instrument results directly from the sensitivities and volatilities of market parameters. The equity index return has a volatility of 20%. The volatility of the stock return results from the above relationship:

$$\sigma(\mathbf{y}_i) = \sigma(\Delta \mathbf{V}_i / V_{i0}) = s_{ik} \times \sigma(\Delta \mathbf{m}_k / m_{k0})$$

$$\sigma(\mathbf{V}_i) = \sigma(\mathbf{y}_i) \times V_{i0} = s_{ik} \times \sigma(\Delta \mathbf{m}_k / m_{k0}) \times V_{i0}$$

Let's assume that the stock return has a sensitivity of 2 to the equity index. Then:

$$\sigma(\mathbf{y}_i) = \sigma(\Delta \mathbf{V}_i) / V_{i0} = s_{ik} \times \sigma(\Delta \mathbf{m}_k / m_{k0}) = 2 \times 20\% = 40\%$$

If the initial asset value is 1000, the resulting value volatility is 400. If the value follows approximately a normal distribution, the loss percentile at the 1% confidence level is 2.33×400 in value, or 932. Calculations are very simple because the linear approximation implies that the product of a random normal return by a constant follows also a normal distribution.

Stocks

For stocks, the 'beta' β relates the change in stock price to the change in market index for the same period. It is the sensitivity of the equity return (a percentage change) to the index return (a percentage change). β is the risk measure in the Capital Asset Pricing Model (CAPM), the well-known model[12] that provides the theoretical price of a stock and the required return by the market as a function of risk. It is the coefficient of the regression of the historical equity periodical returns against the similar index return providing β as the coefficient of the regression. The return is the ratio of the variation in stock price, or

---

[12] The original presentation is in Sharpe (1964). See also Sharpe and Alexander (1990) for subsequent developments.

index value, to the original value, for any period. There are as many return observations as periods (daily, weekly, monthly, and so on). β is higher or lower than 1, and it is 1 by definition for the equity index. The return of the stock i and of the index I_m are:

$$\mathbf{r}_i = \Delta \mathbf{P}_i / P_i$$

$$\mathbf{r_m} = \Delta \mathbf{I_m} / I_m$$

β results from a regression on historical returns fitting the equation below to time series of observations:

$$\mathbf{r}_i = \beta_i \mathbf{r_m} + \alpha + \varepsilon_i$$

In the case of stocks, there is no deterministic relationship between the equity index and the stock return. Rather, there is a general risk resulting from general market index changes plus an error term. Ignoring the error term:

$$\Delta \mathbf{r}_i = \beta_i \Delta \mathbf{r_m}$$

β relates the relative price changes of a stock and an equity index, which is the market parameter in this case. If a stock has a β of 1.2, a change in index return Δr_m of 1% results, on average, in a 1.2% increase of the price return r_i. Hence $r_i = \Delta P_i / P_i$ increases by $\Delta r_i = 1.2\%$. Considering the initial stock price as given, the variation ΔP_i is $1.2\% \times P_i$ when the variation of the index ΔI_m is $1\% \times I_m$. Hence, β relates the relative and the absolute changes in stock price and equity index.

Using statistical fits implies an error term. The stock return depends on the equity index return plus a random 'innovation' term, which is independent of the equity index return by definition. The error term is the fraction of return of the stock unexplained by general index variations. This fraction is the specific risk of the stocks, as opposed to the general risk shared by all stocks related to the equity index. The variance of stock return is: $\sigma^2(r_i) = \beta_i \sigma^2(r_m) + \sigma^2(\varepsilon_i)$. It sums the variance due to general risk and specific risk. In practice, since error terms offset to a significant extent, simplified techniques ignore the sum of the specific risks for all stock prices, which is the variance of a sum of independent variables. For portfolio models, the 'diagonal model' of stock returns allows us to consider the specific risk from the innovation term for all stocks.

Bonds and Loans

The sensitivity of bond prices to interest rate shocks, shocks being parallel shifts of the entire spectrum of rates, is the 'duration'. If the duration of a bond is 5, it means the bond value will change by 5% when all rates deviate by 1%. A common measure of sensitivity for bonds is the basis point measure. A basis point (bp) is 1% of 1%, or 0.0001. It is the deviation, expressed in basis points, for a unit basis point change of interest rates. In the previous example, the basis point change of the bond value is 5 bp for a 1 bp change in all interest rates. This is the 'DV01' measure of bond sensitivity.

Sensitivities also apply to credit risk, because bond prices depend on 'credit spreads', the difference between the market rate applying to a risky bond and the risk-free market rate of government bonds. Since bond values are sensitive to credit spread, any widening of spreads reduces the value. The sensitivity of bonds with respect to credit spreads is similar to that of interest rates. For non-tradable assets, such as banking loans, sensitivities to interest rates also apply to their mark-to-market values and are also durations. These sensitivities serve for measuring the risks of the mark-to-market value of the balance sheet, or Net Present Value (NPV).

Durations help when considering only parallel shifts of the yield curves. They do not capture changes in the shape of the curve. Considering all changes in interest rates over all maturities requires the sensitivities to all market rates to obtain proxy asset returns. For the NPV calculations, for ALM, assets and liabilities are fully revalued for each yield curve scenario, without relying on sensitivities. Technically, the change of a single rate along the curve implies a change of the discount factor relative to that rate. For VaR purposes, it is necessary to simulate yield curve changes, either from correlations across rates or from principal components factor models.

Foreign Exchange Exposures

The sensitivity of the dollar value of any exposure labelled in foreign currency to the exchange rate is the variation of this dollar value due to a unit variation of the exchange rate. For instance, the dollar value of 1000 euros, with an exchange rate of 1 EUR/USD, is 1000 USD. If the exchange rate becomes 8 EUR/USD, the dollar value becomes 800 USD. The variation is -20%, which is in value $-1000 \times 20\%$. The relative change in dollar value of exposure and that of the market parameter value are identical to -20%. The value sensitivity of the exposure in USD with respect to the exchange rate is simply 1.

Options

Options are the right, but not the obligation, to buy or sell some underlying parameter. Derivative, and option, sensitivities result from models, or 'pricers', which relate their values to their drivers. The value of options depends on a number of parameters, as shown originally in the Black–Scholes model: the value of the underlying, the horizon to maturity, the volatility of the underlying, the risk-free interest rate. The model is in line with intuition. The option value increases with the underlying asset value, its volatility and maturity, and decreases with interest rate. Option sensitivities are known as the 'Greek letters'.

The sensitivity with respect to the underlying asset is the 'delta' δ. Intuitively, the δ is low if the option is 'out-of-the-money' (asset price below strike) because we do not get any money by exercising unless the asset value changes significantly. However, when exercising provides a positive payoff, the δ gets closer to 1: if strike is 100 and asset price is 120, the payoff is $120 - 100 = 20$; if the asset price increases by 1 to 121, the payoff increases by 1. The sensitivity can be anywhere in the entire range between 0 and 1, when the sensitivity increases from near zero values to values close to one when the option is in-the-money. The variation of δ is the 'convexity' of the option. Gamma (γ) is the change in δ when the underlying changes. It is the change in slope of the curve representing the option value as a function of the underlying. The longer the horizon, the higher the chances that the stock moves above the strike price. Hence, the option is sensitive to the time to maturity, the sensitivity being theta (θ). The shorter the time to maturity, the lower is the value of the option. This value change when time passes is the 'time decay' of the option value. The higher the volatility of the underlying asset, the higher the chances that the value moves above the strike during a given period. Hence, the option has a positive sensitivity to the underlying asset volatility, which is the 'vega' (v). Since any payoff appears only in the future, its value today requires discounting, and so that it varies inversely with the level of interest rates. Rho (ρ) is the change due to a variation of the risk-free rate. The option has several sensitivities, one for each relevant parameter that influences its value.

APPENDIX 1: CUMULATIVE RETURNS OVER TIME PERIODS

When using a single terminal point, we have a straightforward correspondence between the discrete one-period return and the final value. This is not so for cumulative returns over a large number of intervals. Terminal values result from cumulated returns over intermediate periods. In practice, we simulate returns for each set of subperiods, for instance 10 single-period returns, as in the example below, by drawing randomly 10 values from the distribution fitting the stochastic process of returns. Each of the 10 end-of-period values results from the value at the start date times the random percentage return plus 1 ($V_t/V_{t-1} = 1 + y$). Calculating the 10 end-of-period values directly provides the final one at horizon. The example above illustrates the process.

There are shortcuts for obtaining cumulative returns if returns are 'logarithmic' and when using small intervals. The arithmetic return is $y_t = (V_t - V_{t-1})/V_{t-1}$. The logarithm of the price ratio, $\ln(V_t/V_{t-1})$, is identical to $\ln[1 + y(t)]^{13}$. It is approximately equal to the arithmetic return when the return is small because $\ln(1 + y)$ is approximately identical to y. From the logarithmic definition, the value after a time interval Δt is such that: $V_{t+\Delta t} = V_t \exp(y\Delta t)$. With arithmetic return $y_t = (V_t - V_{t-1})/V_{t-1}$, the final value V_t becomes negative for values of y lower than -100%. With logarithmic returns, the final value cannot be negative even with negative returns. This makes the normal distribution for the return $\mathbf{y}$ acceptable. If the logarithm of $\mathbf{V}_t/V_0$ follows a normal distribution of $\mathbf{y}$, $\mathbf{V}_t$ follows a lognormal distribution, by definition.

Finally, logarithmic returns are additive across periods. When combining returns across consecutive periods, the return between dates 0 and t is $\mathbf{y}(0, t) = \ln(\mathbf{V}_t/V_0)$. The logarithmic returns are additive across periods. With two consecutive periods, we have:

$$\mathbf{y}(0, 2) = \ln(\mathbf{V}_2/V_0) = \ln[(\mathbf{V}_2/\mathbf{V}_1) \times (\mathbf{V}_1/V_0)]$$

$$\mathbf{y}(0, 2) = \ln(\mathbf{V}_2/\mathbf{V}_1) + \ln(\mathbf{V}_1/V_0) = \mathbf{y}(0, 1) + \mathbf{y}(1, 2)$$

If, for instance, $V_1/V_0 = 120\%$ and $V_2/V_1 = 90\%$, with $V_0 = 1$, $V_1 = 1.2$ and $V_2 = 90\% \times 1.2 = 1.08$, the overall return is 8%, which differs from the arithmetic summation $20\% - 10\% = 10\%$ because the percentages apply to different initial values. In the

---

[13] The return is $y_t = (V_t - V_{t-1})/V_{t-1}$ and $1 + y_t = 1 + (V_t - V_{t-1})/V_{t-1} = 1 + (V_t/V_{t-1} - 1) = V_t/V_{t-1}$.

example of Table 30.1, the exact cumulative return between initial and final values is 8% from the actual values. This is very close to the logarithm cumulative return of 7.696%, which is the exact summation of single-period logarithmic returns. The arithmetic summation of the single-period arithmetic returns is 10%, significantly above the actual 8%.

TABLE 30.1   Cumulating arithmetic and logarithm returns

	V_t	$V_t/V_{t-1} = 1 + y$	$\ln(V_t/V_{t-1})$	Arithmetic return y_i
V_0	1.00			
V_1	1.20	120.00%	18.232%	20.00%
V_2	1.08	90.00%	−10.536%	−10.00%
		$V_2/V_0 − 1$	$\ln(V_2/V_0)$	$y_1 + y_2$
Cumulative return		8.00%	7.696%	10.00%

Since the sum of random normal variables is also a normal variable, so is $y(0, t)$ for any horizon t. Since $y(0, t) = \ln(V_t/V_0)$ follows a normal distribution, the final value follows a lognormal distribution.

31

Modelling Correlations and Multi-factor Models for Market Risk

To model correlations, the common principle for all portfolio models is to relate the individual risks of each transaction to a set of common factors. For market risk, the market values of individual transactions are sensitive to risk drivers that alter their values. When all risk factors vary, the dependence of the individual asset returns on this set of common factors generates correlations between them. Because common factors influence simultaneously all transaction risks, they create a 'general' risk, defined as the risk common to all assets. The fraction of individual risk unrelated to common factors is 'specific' risk.

Factor models are two-sided, depending on the initial purpose. The first purpose is to model the correlations between risk drivers on which individual risk correlations depend. The second purpose is to construct loss distributions for portfolios. The next chapter explains how to proceed with factor models. We address only the first issue in this chapter.

It is necessary to capture the interdependencies between market parameters to correlate future values of market parameters and assets. Individual asset value variations depend on these correlations, some of them being positive and others negative. They sum algebraically to obtain portfolio values. The diversification effect results from offsetting effects between individual variations.

For market risk, correlations derive directly from observed market prices or market parameters. Pricing models of derivatives or bonds help because they relate in a deterministic way the prices of assets to the market parameters that derive them. In such a case, it is sufficient to correlate the market parameters to obtain correlated individual asset returns (or values) using the pricing models with the correlated market parameter values as inputs. When the relationship to market parameters is stochastic, for example between stock returns and equity indexes, it includes an error term, measuring the random component of individual asset returns unrelated to market parameters.

When using factor models, asset return variations result from the volatility of the factors plus that of the error term, measuring the volatility of the asset return unrelated to factors. The error term contributes to the risk. The volatility of the common factors is the 'general risk', and the volatility of the error term is the 'specific risk'. Specific risk is important for stock returns with general risk driven by equity indexes and specific risk related to each individual stock. These principles underlie the 'diagonal' model for stocks.

Fitting factor models to returns allows us to determine both the return variances plus all their covariance terms from the coefficients of the factor models. In addition, the contribution of common factors to the return volatility is the general risk, while the volatility of the error term is the specific risk. The one-factor model of stocks illustrates these properties. Multi-factor models provide the same information. 'Orthogonal' factor models are the simplest because the factors are independent of each other.

The first section briefly summarizes why correlations between risk drivers are key inputs for capturing diversification effects through variance–covariance matrices. The second section describes the specifics of the 'correlation building block' of market risk. The third section explains how to derive correlations, volatilities and general plus specific risk from factor models of individual asset returns. The appendix describes various types of factor models.

WHY IS THE VARIANCE–COVARIANCE MATRIX NECESSARY FOR MODELLING PORTFOLIO LOSSES?

The risk over a portfolio is the change in all mark-to-market values of individual instruments. The loss of the portfolio is the algebraic sum of all gains and losses for all individual positions. Some exposures gain values, others lose values. These changes are market parameter-driven. Since these correlate, all individual returns correlate as well. When they relate deterministically to risk drivers, the entire value variations result from sensitivities. When there exists only a statistical relationship, the risk drivers generate general risk, to which it is necessary to add specific risk, the fraction of risk not related to the common factors.

A simplistic view would use simultaneous adverse changes, captured as a function of both the risk parameter volatility and the instrument sensitivities. This is a most conservative rule because it is not possible that all market parameters will change simultaneously in such a way that they trigger losses simultaneously for all individual positions. Such arithmetic addition of all risks would greatly over-estimate the portfolio risk. Sensitivities do not add. Adding them is equivalent to assuming that all parameters change simultaneously in adverse directions, which is unrealistic.

The key to measuring portfolio risk lies in capturing the market parameter interdependencies. It is easy to observe that some vary together and others inversely. Sometimes the relationship is strong and sometimes it is loose. The structure of these relationships results in a variance–covariance matrix and a correlation matrix between all market parameters to which the instrument values map. The process for measuring portfolio risk comprises two steps:

- Imposing this variance–covariance structure on market parameter deviations.
- Modelling the portfolio return distribution when all market parameters vary in compliance with such variance–covariance structure.

The correlation methodology aims to replicate realistic simultaneous changes in all market parameters, in line with observed changes. This is a prerequisite for revaluing the portfolio at the horizon. When the correlation structure is available, the correlations between individual asset values result from those of the stochastic processes driving the asset values. Several assets depend on the correlated market parameters, such as equity indexes. It is possible to correlate market parameters and prices, assuming a normal distribution of their values as an approximation.

When implementing full valuation techniques, the issue is to correlate random time paths of returns for different assets. To generate the paths of N correlated assets, indexed i, we use several correlated random processes as follows. The stochastic process driving the market parameter or the individual asset return includes a random term, such as the process applying to stock prices: $\mathbf{y}^i = \mathbf{d}V_t^i / V_t^i = \mu^i \, \mathrm{d}t + \sigma^i \mathbf{dz}_t^i$, where i is the index specific to an individual asset. This process results in the value distribution at a forward date t lognormal distribution of stock prices: $S_{ti} = S_{0i} \exp[(\mu_i - \frac{1}{2}\sigma_i^2)t + \sigma_i \sqrt{t}]$. When considering a pair of stocks, we apply a correlation on the random innovations $\mathbf{dz}_t^i$ of the process. In order to simulate correlated normal innovations, standard procedures apply, such as the Cholevsky decomposition, explained below. The final prices of the pair of stocks correlate even though they follow lognormal distributions.

The techniques for portfolio revaluation at the horizon vary from using sensitivities to value small changes of instrument values to full revaluation of all instruments given multiple correlated scenarios of time paths of the market parameters. The linear relationship between values and underlying market parameters is the foundation of the Delta VaR model. It ends up as an analytical model because the weighted summation of random normal variables is also a normal variable. Hence, only the mean and standard deviation of the portfolio value suffice to define the entire distribution. Monte Carlo simulations allow us to bypass the restrictive assumption that individual returns are linear functions of market parameters. In both cases, the prerequisite is to have the correlations and the variance–covariance matrix of all relevant market parameters.

MODELLING CORRELATIONS BETWEEN INDIVIDUAL ASSET RETURNS AND MARKET PARAMETER RETURNS

Correlations and variances of individual asset returns and market parameters are observable. Therefore, the first technique for obtaining the matrix is to measure it through direct observations, usually on an historical basis. This raises several difficulties. First, the high number of assets makes it unpractical to create a matrix with all pair covariances between individual asset returns. Second, the observed variances and covariances might not comply with the basic property of variance–covariance matrices, that of being semi-definite positive. This happens because some observed parameters correlate strongly[1].

Because of the large number of asset returns, it is more efficient to derive correlations from the correlation of the 'factors' driving these returns. This option requires a prior mapping of asset returns to market parameters. Risk Metrics provides correlations between the main market parameters. Risk drivers are interdependent because they depend on a common set of factors. For instance, all stock returns relate to equity index returns through statistical fitting. The technique extends to multiple factors. One example of a multiple-factor model is the Arbitrage Pricing Theory (APT) model (see Ross, 1976), which considers that more than one factor influences the equity returns. Other factor models model interest rates, making them correlated. Principal Component Analysis (PCA) uses orthogonal factors influencing all rates for generating yield curve changes.

Correlations between instrument returns within each block result from their common dependence on such factors. For market risk, the risk factors are market parameters, or observable parameters that drive the risk. Factors and risk drivers are not necessarily identical however. For example, it is possible to identify a number of factors that influence the equity index returns or the interest rates. Equity indexes and interest rates are the direct drivers of asset returns. On the other hand, factors influence risk drivers without interacting directly with returns as drivers do. They serve to correlate the distributions of risk drivers as an alternative technique to direct measures of correlations. The common dependence of risk drivers, such as interest rates, on a set of factors makes them correlate. Hence, we need to distinguish three levels: factors, risk drivers and market values (Figure 31.1).

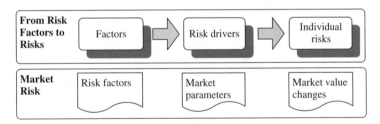

FIGURE 31.1   From risk factors to correlation of individual risks

In many instances, however, risk factors are identical to the risk drivers for market risk. They are the market parameters, under the broad sense of yield curves, foreign exchange rates, equity indexes, plus their volatilities. Since market parameters are directly observable, there is no need to model them. Historical direct observations are feasible. Interest rate models allow us to generate yield curves, such that all interest rates remain consistent with arbitrage relationships.

Factor models offer a convenient alternative technique, notably in two cases:

- For equity returns, the Capital Asset Pricing Model (CAPM) is a single-factor model serving to calculate all variances and covariances of individual stocks, plus the specific

---

[1] When two variables have a correlation of 1, the matrix does not have the desired properties. Measuring errors of highly correlated variables might give a similar result.

risk of each stock. The APT model uses 'orthogonal' factors to achieve the same purpose, using more than one factor to model equity returns.

• For yield curves, multi-factor models help summarize in a convenient way the basic transformation of interest rates, parallel shifts, slope variations and bumps of actual yield curves.

Figure 31.2 provides an overview of the correlation modelling building block of market risk models. The purpose of the 'revaluation' block of models is to link risk drivers to asset returns and values. As such, this revaluation block does not trigger correlations. Correlation between risks results rather from the correlations between the risk drivers. Since returns result from risk drivers through the revaluation process, correlated risk drivers generate return correlations.

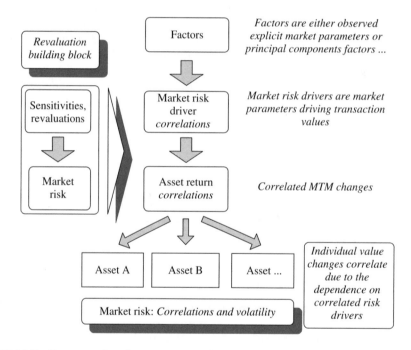

FIGURE 31.2 From market factors to correlated transaction market risk

IMPLEMENTING FACTOR MODELS

Factor models serve, notably, to simplify the modelling of correlations between individual stocks and that of interest rates. In this section we show how to derive correlations from factor models. The main example deals with stock prices. For stocks, it is important both to model correlations and to isolate specific risk, the risk unrelated to common factors. The section addresses the one-factor model of stock returns and multiple-factor models, such as those of PCA.

Deriving the Variance–Covariance for Stocks

The direct measures of the variances–covariances of stock returns would imply measuring N^2 terms, for a portfolio of N stocks. The one-factor model allows us to measure the covariances using a linear relationship between the stock return and the market index return. This is a direct application of a one-factor model, whose formulas are given in the appendix to this chapter. The market model is:

$$\mathbf{r}_i = \alpha_i + \beta_i \mathbf{r_m} + \varepsilon_i$$

The relationships simply indicate that all stock returns co-vary with the index, although their sensitivities β_i vary with each stock[2]. The statistical relationship is a one-factor model, with $\mathbf{r_m}$ being the explicit factor influencing the individual returns. For equity returns, we illustrate first the attractive property of using one factor only and proceed to describe the general 'diagonal' model of stock return correlations.

Pairs of Stocks

By definition of the regression model, the random equity index return is independent of the residual ε_i. As a result, the covariance between any pair of equity returns depends only on the variance of the single factor and the coefficients β_1 and β_2. The covariance and the correlation between any pair of equity returns $\mathbf{r}_1$ and $\mathbf{r}_2$ is simply[3]:

$$\mathrm{Cov}(\mathbf{r}_1, \mathbf{r}_2) = \beta_1 \beta_2 \sigma^2(\mathbf{r_m})$$

$$\rho_{ij} = \mathrm{Cov}(\mathbf{r}_i, \mathbf{r}_j)/\sigma(\mathbf{r}_i)\sigma(\mathbf{r}_j) = \beta_i \beta_j \sigma^2(\mathbf{r_m})/\sigma(\mathbf{r}_i)\sigma(\mathbf{r}_j)$$

Moreover, the volatility of any individual asset return is:

$$[\sigma(\mathbf{r}_i)]^2 = \beta_i^2 [\sigma(\mathbf{r_m})]^2 + [\sigma(\varepsilon_i)]^2$$

The return $\mathbf{r}_i$ volatility is the sum of the systematic variance of the market, the general risk generated by $\mathbf{r_m}$ weighted by the squared sensitivity β_i^2, and of the specific, or idiosyncratic, risk of an individual stock.

Let's assume that all returns are $\mathbf{r}_i$ standardized normal variables, with unit variance, for the index return as well as for the stocks picked. The coefficients are $\beta_i = 1$ and $\beta_j = 1.5$. The $\mathbf{r}_i$ represent the equity returns of two obligors. The model fit sets the volatility of the residual, measuring specific risk:

$$\sigma^2(\mathbf{r}_1) = (1)^2 1 + 1.5 = 2.5 = 1.5812$$

$$\sigma^2(\mathbf{r}_2) = (1.2)^2 1 + 1 = 2.94 = 1.7152$$

$$\mathrm{Cov}(\mathbf{r}_1, \mathbf{r}_2) = 1 \times 1.2 \times 1 = 1.2$$

$$\rho_{12} = 1.2/(1.581 \times 1.715) = 44.25\%$$

---

[2] The CAPM models this empirical finding and shows that the return on any asset i is the risk-free rate $\mathbf{r_f}$ plus a risk premium equal to the differential of the random market return $\mathbf{r_m}$ and the risk-free rate, times the β_i of the asset: $\mathbf{r}_i = \mathbf{r_f} + \beta_i(\mathbf{r_m} - \mathbf{r_f})$.

[3] $\mathrm{Cov}(\mathbf{r}_1, \mathbf{r}_2) = \mathrm{Cov}(\alpha_1 + \beta_1 \mathbf{r_m} + \varepsilon_1, \alpha_2 + \beta_2 \mathbf{r_m} + \varepsilon_2) = \beta_1 \beta_2 \mathrm{Cov}(\mathbf{r_m}, \mathbf{r_m})$ because all cross-covariance terms, $\mathrm{Cov}(\mathbf{r}_1, \varepsilon_1)$, $\mathrm{Cov}(\mathbf{r}_1, \varepsilon_2)$, $\mathrm{Cov}(\varepsilon_1, \varepsilon_2)$, as well as the covariances between $\mathbf{r}_2$ and the residuals, are zero. In addition, $\mathrm{Cov}(\mathbf{r_m}, \mathbf{r_m})$ is the variance of the equity index return.

In the case of the first obligor, the error variance is 1.5 and the variance of the factor is 1. Total variance is 2.5. The R^2 is the ratio of $1/2.5 = 40\%$. In the second case, total variance is 2.94, and the explained variance is 1.44, hence R^2 is $1.44/2.94 = 48.98\%$. The R^2 provides a direct estimate of the general versus specific risk. When no fit is available, for private firms for example, it is necessary to specify the R^2 using for instance the average over all firms, which is in the range of 20% to 30% for listed companies in the main stock exchanges.

Deriving the Variance–Covariance for the Entire Stock Portfolio

The covariance between asset i and asset j returns depends only on β_i and β_j, and on the factor variance. With N assets, there are N variances and $N \times (N - 1)$ covariance terms, a total of N^2 terms in the variance–covariance matrix. Using the one-factor model allows us to calculate the $N \times (N - 1)$ covariance terms from N coefficients β_i plus the factor volatility, or $N + 1$ terms compared to $N \times (N - 1)$. Hence, we summarize N^2 terms of the variance–covariance matrix using only $N + 1$. In matrix format, the variance–covariance matrix becomes:

$$\Sigma = \sigma_m^2 \begin{pmatrix} \beta_1\beta_1 & \beta_1\beta_2 & \beta_1\beta_3 & \cdots \\ \beta_2\beta_1 & \beta_2\beta_2 & \beta_2\beta_3 & \cdots \\ \beta_3\beta_1 & \beta_3\beta_2 & \beta_3\beta_3 & \cdots \\ \vdots & \vdots & \vdots & \ddots \end{pmatrix} + \begin{pmatrix} \sigma(\varepsilon_1)^2 & 0 & 0 & \cdots \\ 0 & \sigma(\varepsilon_2)^2 & 0 & \cdots \\ 0 & 0 & \sigma(\varepsilon_3)^2 & \cdots \\ \vdots & \vdots & \vdots & \ddots \end{pmatrix}$$

All the off-diagonal terms result from the β_i, plus the market index volatility. All the diagonal terms depend on the β_i, plus the market index volatility, plus the specific risk term. This provides the entire matrix. The first term of the matrix is simply $\beta\beta^T \times \sigma_m^2$, where β^T stands for the transpose vector of the sensitivities. This is the 'diagonal' model of stock returns variances and covariances.

The APT Model for Stock Returns

A well-known example of multi-factor modelling is the APT model of equity returns. Contrasting with the CAPM, or the simpler 'market model', the APT model makes the equity returns dependent on several independent factors rather than a single one. Multiple factors generate some additional complexity. Common factors are the source of general credit risk, the risk to which each obligor is subject. The error term is the specific or idiosyncratic risk of asset i. By construction, it is independent of all common factors. The analytical form of risk results from the variance of the Y_i:

$$\sigma^2(Y_1) = (\beta_{i1})^2 \operatorname{Var}(X_1) + (\beta_{i2})^2 \operatorname{Var}(X_2) + (\beta_{i3})^2 \operatorname{Var}(X_3) + \operatorname{Var}(\varepsilon_i)$$

$$\sigma^2(Y_1) = \sum_{i=1}^{K} (\beta_{ik})^2 \operatorname{Var}(X_k) + \operatorname{Var}(\varepsilon_i)$$

The general risk is the sum of the variances of the factors weighted by the model coefficients, and the specific risk is the residual variance. The appendix to this chapter explains how to obtain these formulas.

Orthogonal Multiple-factor Models

A practical model for changing randomly the shape of the yield curve is PCA. In this case, factors are linear functions of observed variables and are independent of each other. In such a case, it is easy to derive the variances and covariances, or correlations, from the factor variances and the model coefficients. We use here a simple example of such calculations, with a two-factor model of two variables. The general formulas are given in the appendix to this chapter. The models for two correlated indexes and two factors are:

$$Y_1 = \beta_{10} + 1 \times X_1 + 1.2 \times X_2 + \varepsilon_1$$

$$Y_2 = \beta_{20} + 0.8 \times X_1 + 0.5 \times X_2 + \varepsilon_2$$

X_1 and X_2 are standardized normal independent factors (zero mean and unit variance). The variances of the residuals $Var(\varepsilon_1)$ and $Var(\varepsilon_2)$ are respectively 1.5 and 1. The cross-covariance between X_1 and X_2 is zero. The volatility of the residuals measures the specific risk and results from the model fit. The variance adds the general factor risk plus the specific risks $Var(\varepsilon_1)$ and $Var(\varepsilon_2)$. The variances of the indexes Y_1 and Y_2 follow:

$$\sigma^2(Y_1) = (1)^2 1 + (1.2)^2 1 + 1.5 = 3.94 \quad \text{and } \sigma(Y_1) = 1.9852$$

$$\sigma^2(Y_2) = (0.8)^2 1 + (0.5)^2 1 + 1 = 0.64 + 0.25 + 1 = 1.89 \quad \text{and } \sigma(Y_2) = 1.3752$$

The R^2 of the regression of Y_1 and Y_2 (Y_i) on X_1 and X_2 (X_k) is the ratio of explained variance by all factors to the error variance or, equivalently, the ratio of general to total risk. In the case of the first asset, the error variance is 1.5 and that of factors X_1 and X_2 is 2.44. Total variance is 3.94. The R^2 is 2.44/3.94 = 61.93%. In the second case, the total variance is 1.89 and the explained variance is 0.89, hence R^2 is 0.89/1.89 = 47.09%. The covariance between Y_1 and Y_2 is:

$$Cov(Y_1, Y_2) = 1 \times 1.2 \times 1 + 0.8 \times 0.5 \times 1 = 1.600$$

The corresponding correlation coefficient is:

$$\rho_{12} = 1.600/(1.985 \times 1.375) = 58.63\%$$

General versus Specific Risk

When relating individual returns to factors, the factors generate general risk, the risk common to all assets, and the residual risk is the specific risk. Specific risk appears only whenever there is no deterministic relationship between the factors and the risk drivers, or between the risk drivers and the returns (such as the closed-form formulas of pricing models). This is the case for stocks, as illustrated above. Specific risk also appears when modelling interest rates from underlying factors. The specific risk is the variance of the error terms in these models. When using the Delta VaR technique, ignoring specific risk underestimates the overall risk. There is always a fraction of the portfolio volatility that does not relate to common factors or risk drivers. The diagonal model described above makes explicit the specific risk component.

APPENDIX: IMPLEMENTING FACTOR MODELS FOR MODELLING CORRELATIONS

Factor models serve to model correlations between risk drivers generating correlated distributions of credit events within a portfolio. To model correlations, we face the issue of constructing a variance–covariance matrix for credit risk drivers, such as asset values or factors that drive the credit standing. From the matrix, we can infer any pair correlation. A distinct, but related, issue is that such a matrix is information intensive for a portfolio. A variance–covariance matrix is squared, and has N^2 terms for a portfolio of N obligors. Therefore, we need to reduce the information to manageable dimensions. Factor models address these issues.

We provide examples of the single-factor model, or orthogonal-factor (independent factors) models obtained with PCA, and of multiple-factor models with correlated factors.

Measuring and Modelling Correlations with Single-factor Models

In the case of a single factor, the decomposition is obvious because the residual term is independent, by definition of the single factor.

The Single-factor Model

We start with this simple case. The one-factor model form is:

$$\mathbf{Y}_i = \beta_{i0} + \beta_i \mathbf{X_1} + \boldsymbol{\varepsilon}_i$$

The variance of $\mathbf{Y}_i$ is simply the sum of the variance due to the single factor and to that of the residual:

$$\sigma^2(\mathbf{Y}_i) = (\beta_i)^2 \, \mathrm{Var}(\mathbf{X_1}) + \mathrm{Var}(\boldsymbol{\varepsilon}_i)$$

The covariance between any two $\mathbf{Y}_i$ and $\mathbf{Y}_j$ is:

$$\mathrm{Cov}(\mathbf{Y}_i, \mathbf{Y}_j) = \mathrm{Cov}(\beta_{i0} + \beta_i \mathbf{X_1} + \boldsymbol{\varepsilon}_i, \beta_{j0} + \beta_j \mathbf{X_1} + \boldsymbol{\varepsilon}_j)$$

$$\mathrm{Cov}(\mathbf{Y}_i, \mathbf{Y}_j) = \beta_i \beta_j \, \mathrm{Var}(\mathbf{X_1})$$

This formula simplifies because all cross-correlations between factors and residuals are zero by construction of the model. All residuals $\boldsymbol{\varepsilon}_i$ are independent of $\mathbf{X_1}$. The correlation between $\mathbf{Y}_i$ and $\mathbf{Y}_j$ is:

$$\rho_{ij} = \mathrm{Cov}(\mathbf{Y}_i, \mathbf{Y}_j)/\sigma(\mathbf{Y}_i)\sigma(\mathbf{Y}_j) = \beta_i \beta_j \, \mathrm{Var}(\mathbf{X_1})/\sigma(\mathbf{Y}_i)\sigma(\mathbf{Y}_j)$$

When the single factor explains a large fraction of the risk driver volatility, the systematic risk is relatively high, and the specific risk is low. The opposite holds when the single factor explains only a small fraction of the volatility. Note that the R^2 of the regression of $\mathbf{Y}_i$ on $\mathbf{X}_i$ is, by definition, the ratio of variance explained by the factor to the total variance or, equivalently, the ratio of general to total risk.

For N assets, there are N variances plus covariances, resulting in N^2 terms. Using the single-factor model, we need only the N β_i, plus the N residual variances, plus the single factor variance, or $2N + 1$ items of information. This is the diagonal model of correlations, as shown when modelling equity risk.

Multi-factor Models for Measuring Correlations

The first subsection extends the definitions to a multi-factor setting. The second subsection shows how to derive variances, covariances and correlations from models using orthogonal factors, and the third subsection is a brief extension to correlated, rather than independent, multiple factors.

General and Specific Risk in Multi-factor Models

In general, a multi-factor model relates some random variable $\mathbf{Y}$ to common factors $\mathbf{X}_k$:

$$\mathbf{Y}_i = \beta_{i0} + \beta_{i1}\mathbf{X_1} + \beta_{i2}\mathbf{X_2} + \beta_{i3}\mathbf{X_3} + \cdots + \varepsilon_i$$

The index i refers to asset returns, while the index k refers to the factor. In the equity universe, the variable explained by factors is the equity return of stocks. They are random just as the factors and the residual are, but they are all sensitive to each of the common factors.

Multiple-factor Models with Orthogonal Factors

To illustrate the general formulas, we use a two-factor model. The two factors are independent, or 'orthogonal'. $\mathbf{Y}_i$ is the random asset return of asset i. The two-factor model is:

$$\mathbf{Y}_i = \beta_{i0} + \beta_{i1}\mathbf{X_1} + \beta_{i2}\mathbf{X_2} + \varepsilon_i$$

The general formula is:

$$\mathbf{Y}_i = \sum_k \beta_{i1}\mathbf{X}_k + \varepsilon_i$$

The index i refers to the assets, while the index k refers to the factor. The R^2 of the regression of $\mathbf{Y}_i$ on $\mathbf{X}_k$ is the ratio of explained variance by all factors to the total variance.

From this general formula, it is easy to derive the variance of $\mathbf{Y}_i$, which simplifies because we have a linear combination of independent variables. For pairs of assets, we derive both covariances and correlations. Again, the formulas simplify because of zero cross-correlations between factors and residuals.

All $\mathbf{X}_k$ are standardized normal orthogonal factors, the variances of the residuals $\sigma^2(\varepsilon_i)$ are respectively 1.5 and 1 for obligors 1 and 2. The cross-covariances between all $\mathbf{X}_k$ are zero. The volatility of the residuals measures the specific risk and results from the model fit. The general formula for the variance of the variable is:

$$\sigma^2(\mathbf{Y_1}) = \text{Cov}(\beta_{11}\mathbf{X_1} + \beta_{12}\mathbf{X_2} + \varepsilon_1, \beta_{11}\mathbf{X_1} + \beta_{12}\mathbf{X_2} + \varepsilon_1)$$

$$\sigma^2(\mathbf{Y_1}) = (\beta_{11})^2 \, \text{Var}(\mathbf{X_1}) + (\beta_{12})^2 \, \text{Var}(\mathbf{X_2}) + \text{Var}(\varepsilon_1)$$

The extension to any number K of factors is straightforward. The variance is the summation of general risk variances plus the specific risk variance of the residual. The variance is:

$$\text{Var}(\mathbf{Y}_i) = \sum_k (\beta_{i1})^2 \ \text{Var}(\mathbf{X}_k) + \text{Var}(\varepsilon_i)$$

With orthogonal factors, all covariances between factors and residuals are zero and the other covariances are:

$$\text{Cov}(\mathbf{Y}_1, \mathbf{Y}_2) = \text{Cov}(\beta_{11}\mathbf{X}_1 + \beta_{12}\mathbf{X}_2 + \varepsilon_1, \beta_{21}\mathbf{X}_1 + \beta_{22}\mathbf{X}_2 + \varepsilon_2)$$

$$= \beta_{11}\beta_{21} \ \text{Var}(\mathbf{X}_1) + \beta_{12}\beta_{22} \ \text{Var}(\mathbf{X}_2)$$

The covariance between $\mathbf{Y}_i$ and $\mathbf{Y}_j$ collapses to:

$$\text{Cov}(\mathbf{Y}_i, \mathbf{Y}_j) = \sum_k \beta_{ik}\beta_{jk} \ \text{Var}(\mathbf{X}_k)$$

The correlation between $\mathbf{Y}_i$ and $\mathbf{Y}_j$ is:

$$\rho_{ij} = \text{Cov}(\mathbf{Y}_i, \mathbf{Y}_j)/\sigma(\mathbf{Y}_i)\sigma(\mathbf{Y}_j)$$

For two assets i and j, the corresponding correlation coefficient is:

$$\rho_{ij} = [\beta_{1i}\beta_{1j} \ \text{Var}(\mathbf{X}_1) + \beta_{2i}\beta_{2j} \ \text{Var}(\mathbf{X}_2)]/\sigma(\mathbf{Y}_i)\sigma(\mathbf{Y}_j)$$

General Multi-factor Models

The models are similar except that there is no simplification due to zero cross-correlations. All formulas for variances, covariances and correlations depend on all cross-correlations, making them more complex. Generally, relating asset returns to market parameters is a multi-factor setting where factors are market parameters. Therefore, we need to account for the observed cross-correlations of market parameters. When factors are not orthogonal, all cross-covariances between factors contribute to both variances and covariances of the $\mathbf{Y}_i$.

Covariances of Risk Drivers

The covariance of two indexes $\mathbf{Y}_1$ and $\mathbf{Y}_2$ is:

$$\text{Cov}(\mathbf{Y}_1, \mathbf{Y}_2) = \text{Cov}(\beta_{10} + \beta_{11}\mathbf{X}_1 + \beta_{12}\mathbf{X}_2 + \varepsilon_1, \beta_{20} + \beta_{21}\mathbf{X}_1 + \beta_{22}\mathbf{X}_2 + \varepsilon_2)$$

All the covariances between constant and any random variables are zero. The covariances between any factor and the residuals are zero because the factors extract the correlations between the random asset values leaving only an uncorrelated residual. We expand all formulas to see the details:

$$\text{Cov}(\mathbf{Y}_1, \mathbf{Y}_2) = \text{Cov}(\beta_{11}\mathbf{X}_1 + \beta_{12}\mathbf{X}_2 + \varepsilon_1, \beta_{21}\mathbf{X}_1 + \beta_{22}\mathbf{X}_2 + \varepsilon_2)$$

Simplifying:

$$\text{Cov}(\mathbf{Y}_1, \mathbf{Y}_2) = \beta_{11}\beta_{21} \ \text{Var}(\mathbf{X}_1) + \beta_{12}\beta_{22} \ \text{Var}(\mathbf{X}_2)$$

$$+ \beta_{11}\beta_{22} \ \text{Cov}(\mathbf{X}_1, \mathbf{X}_2) + \beta_{12}\beta_{21} \ \text{Cov}(\mathbf{X}_2, \mathbf{X}_1) + \beta_{13}\beta_{21} \ \text{Cov}(\mathbf{X}_3, \mathbf{X}_1)$$

All cross-covariances of factors apply for calculating the asset covariance, but all cross-covariances between factors and residuals are zero by construction of the model.

Variances of Risk Drivers

The variance of an asset value results from setting $\mathbf{Y_1} = \mathbf{Y_2}$:

$$\sigma^2(\mathbf{Y_1}) = \text{Cov}(\beta_{11}\mathbf{X_1} + \beta_{12}\mathbf{X_2} + \boldsymbol{\varepsilon_1}, \beta_{11}\mathbf{X_1} + \beta_{12}\mathbf{X_2} + \boldsymbol{\varepsilon_1})$$

Simplifying[4]:

$$\sigma^2(\mathbf{Y_1}) = (\beta_{11})^2 \, \text{Var}(\mathbf{X_1}) + (\beta_{12})^2 \, \text{Var}(\mathbf{X_2}) + 2\beta_{12}\beta_{11} \, \text{Cov}(\mathbf{X_1}, \mathbf{X_2}) + \text{Var}(\boldsymbol{\varepsilon_1})$$

For a single obligor, there are two factor covariance terms, plus two factor variance terms, plus one variance of the error term. The extension to K factors is straightforward. The variance depends on the variances of each factor, plus the covariance terms, plus the variance of the error term representing the specific risk. In general, for each obligor or segment, there are K factor variance terms, plus $K \times (K - 1)$ covariance terms, plus one specific risk term.

Aggregating over the N obligors or segments generates N times these terms. There are $N \times K$ variance terms, plus N specific risk terms, plus $N \times (N - 1) \times K \times (K - 1)$ covariance terms. The $N \times K$ variance terms count less than the covariance terms. This mechanism makes the specific risk much lower than general risk when the number of obligors increases.

---

[4] $\text{Var}(\mathbf{Y_1}) = (\beta_{11})^2 \, \text{Var}(\mathbf{X_1}) + \beta_{11}\beta_{12} \, \text{Cov}(\mathbf{X_1}, \mathbf{X_2}) + \beta_{12}\beta_{11} \, \text{Cov}(\mathbf{X_2}, \mathbf{X_1}) + (\beta_{12})^2 \, \text{Var}(\mathbf{X_2}) + \text{Var}(\boldsymbol{\varepsilon_1})$.

32

Portfolio Market Risk

The goal of modelling portfolio risk is to obtain the distribution of the portfolio returns at the horizon, set at the liquidation period. This implies a forward revaluation at the horizon date of all instruments once market parameters change. Since these are the value drivers of individual assets within the portfolio, the prerequisite is to model the market parameter random deviations complying with their correlation structure. The next step is to derive individual asset return distributions from market parameters to get all possible portfolio returns. Loss statistics and loss percentiles providing the market risk 'Value at Risk' (VaR) derive from the portfolio return distribution. To achieve this ultimate goal, techniques range from the Delta VaR technique to full-blown simulations of market parameters and portfolio values.

Portfolios benefit from diversification. The portfolio return volatility decreases with the number of assets, down to a floor resulting from general risk. However, the value of risk relates to portfolio value rather than return. The portfolio value volatility increases with the number of assets, and the incremental volatility for a new asset increases with the average correlation of the portfolio. When dealing with single assets, there is no need to worry about standalone risk. For portfolios of assets, we need to include the effect of the correlation between individual asset returns and between risk drivers, or market parameters, influencing these individual returns.

The Delta VaR model relates linearly asset returns to market parameter returns using instrument sensitivities. The essentials are that the portfolio return is a linear combination of random normals. Therefore it follows a normal distribution. The volatility of the portfolio return applies to any set of linear combinations of random variables. Since we can calculate the volatility of the portfolio return, and since we know that it is normally distributed, we have all that we need to measure VaR. When the assumptions get unrealistic, we need to extend the simple Delta VaR technique or rely on full revaluation at horizon.

Full-blown simulations consist of generating risk driver returns complying with the variance–covariance structure observed in the markets, and revaluating each individual transaction. Revaluation uses pricing models, or simulation techniques for complex derivatives. The portfolio return distribution results from the full revaluation for all trials. Forward looking simulations generate random market parameter values complying with market volatilities and correlations. Intermediate techniques use sensitivities to save the time intensive calculations. Historical simulations use past values of all risk drivers, which effectively embed existing correlations. Other intermediate techniques include 'Delta–Gamma' techniques, or grid simulations.

Because of model risk, modelled returns deviate from actual returns. This necessitates back testing and stress testing modelled VaR to ensure that tracking errors remain within acceptable bounds.

The first section shows how the portfolio return and the portfolio value volatility vary with the number of assets in a simple portfolio. The second section summarizes the Delta VaR technique. The third section expands fully the calculation of the Delta–normal VaR technique using the simple example of a two-asset portfolio. The fourth section reviews intermediate techniques. The fifth section expands the simulation technique and details some intermediate stages before moving to full-blown Monte Carlo simulations. The last section addresses back and stress testing of market risk VaR.

THE EFFECT OF DIVERSIFICATION AND CORRELATION ON THE PORTFOLIO VOLATILITY

The standard representation of the diversification effect applies to portfolio and asset returns. The principles date from Markowitz principles (see Markowitz, 1952). The portfolio return varies with common factors and because of specific risk, the risk independent of common factors. Extending the number of assets creates diversification because the specific risks of individual asset returns offset each other. The undiversifiable risk is the general risk common to all assets. This well-known result applies notably to stock returns and is the basis for diversification.

When looking at market risk, the focus is more on values than on returns. The diversification reduces the market risk because it reduces the volatility of the market value of the portfolio. When looking at values rather than returns, the same basic mechanisms of diversification apply. Nevertheless, unlike return volatility that declines to a floor corresponding to general risk, the volatility of the value increases with each new asset. The increase in value volatility of the portfolio increases with the portfolio average return correlation. Figures 32.1 and 32.2 show the variation of the portfolio return volatility and of the portfolio value volatility with average correlations of asset returns set to 20% and 0%, respectively. The figures show that the portfolio value volatility varies with the number of assets in both cases of independence and correlated returns (Figure 32.3).

The appendix to this chapter summarizes the calculations of the volatility of the portfolio return and the portfolio value for the simpler case of a portfolio with uniform asset return volatility, asset return correlation and uniform exposure. For a uniform exposure—asset return volatility—asset return correlation, when N gets large, the portfolio value volatility is proportional to the number of assets N. The coefficient is $N \times V_0 \times \sigma \times \sqrt{\rho}$, where V_0, σ and $\sqrt{\rho}$ are the uniform unit asset value, the uniform asset return volatility and the

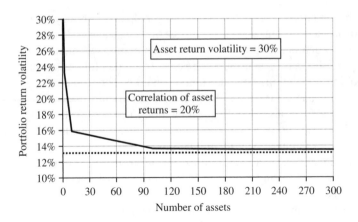

FIGURE 32.1 Portfolio return volatility (asset return volatility 30%, uniform return correlation 20%)

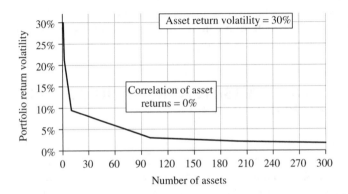

FIGURE 32.2 Portfolio return volatility (asset return volatility 30%, uniform return correlation 0%)

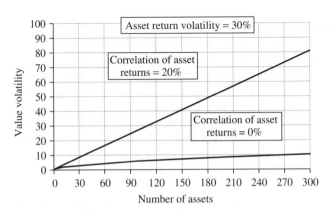

FIGURE 32.3 Portfolio value volatility (asset return volatility 30%, uniform return correlation 20% or 0%)

uniform asset return correlation. When adding one exposure, the additional volatility is simply $V_0 \times \sigma \times \sqrt{\rho}$, and it becomes constant when N is large enough. The volatility is much higher than the volatility under independence, which grows as the square root of N when N becomes large enough.

THE LINEAR MODEL FOR MARKET RISK (DELTA VAR)

Delta VaR makes the individual returns a linear function of market parameter returns. The Delta–normal VaR technique assumes normality of returns distributions, resulting in a normal distribution of the portfolio returns. The volatility of the portfolio return uses the general formula that applies to any set of linear combinations of random variables. Since we can calculate the volatility of the portfolio return and since we know that it is normally distributed, we have all that we need for measuring VaR. The shape of the normal distribution depends on correlations across market parameters. However, the expectation and the volatility suffice to determine the normal distribution of the portfolio return and to derive all loss percentiles and market risk VaR. Since the process does not require any simulation, it is an analytical technique with simple calculations of VaR. The Delta VaR technique contrasts with simulations that generate the portfolio return distribution, and derive empirically from its shape the various loss statistics of interest.

Portfolio Value as a Function of the Set of Market Parameters

The asset returns are a linear function of market parameter changes. Since all assets within the trading portfolio depend on various subsets of the global set of market parameters, its value relates to them through sensitivities as well. The portfolio sensitivities are linear combinations of the various individual transaction sensitivities. When modelling portfolio return, we obtain the $\Delta V_p / V_{p0}$ and derive directly ΔV_p results from the known current value V_{p0}. The formula also includes the specific risk terms when sensitivities capture only a fraction of asset returns (such as for stock return):

$$\Delta V_p / V_{p0} = \sum_{k=1}^{K} \left(\sum_{i=1}^{N} s_{ik} \right) \times \Delta m_k / m_{k0} + \sum_j \varepsilon_j$$

The indices are k (1 to K) for the market parameters and i (1 to N) for the individual transactions. The double summation, first over all transactions, then over all market parameters, results from the fact that any single transaction is a function of a subset of the K market parameters. Since the portfolio includes all transactions, and since all of them depend on various market parameters, the portfolio is sensitive to all market parameter changes. It is convenient to introduce the portfolio sensitivities S_{pk}, which are linear combinations of single transaction sensitivities:

$$\Delta V_p / V_{p0} = \sum_{k=1}^{K} S_{pk} \times \Delta m_k / m_{k0} + \sum_j \varepsilon_j$$

This is a linear relationship between the portfolio value return y_p and the market parameter returns as long as the sensitivities are constant. Since returns are normally distributed, the value changes are $(1 + \mathbf{y_p}) \times V_0$ and are normally distributed as well. However, the volatility of the normal distribution of the portfolio value at the horizon depends on the entire variance–covariance structure of the market parameters.

The Portfolio Value Distribution

The next step is to derive from the linear model the distribution of the portfolio value given the distribution of the individual market parameters. Using normal returns results in a normal distribution. This normal distribution embeds all correlations since the process uses correlated market parameter returns[1]. A linear combination of normally distributed variables also follows a normal distribution, whose expectation and volatility derive from the individual distributions and their variance–covariance matrix. This makes it easy to characterize the portfolio distribution as a function of the market parameters selected for mapping the instrument values and the sensitivities of individual asset returns (Figure 32.4).

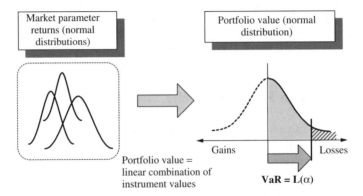

FIGURE 32.4 **From instrument value distributions to portfolio value distribution**

We can use return sensitivities or value sensitivities. The volatility of the variation of the portfolio value is the volatility of a sum of random individual changes weighted by sensitivities:

$$\sigma(\mathbf{V_p}) = \sigma \left(\sum_1^n S_i \times \mathbf{\Delta m_i} \right) = \sum_1^n S_i \times \sigma(\mathbf{\Delta m_i})$$

A similar formula applies to return sensitivities:

$$\sigma(\mathbf{V_p}/V_{p0}) = \sigma \left(\sum_1^n s_i \times \mathbf{\Delta m_i} \right) = \sum_1^n s_i \times \sigma(\mathbf{\Delta m_i}/m_{i0})$$

The derivation of this volatility results from the variance formula for a sum of random variables. The details of this calculation are in the example below. Using the distribution

---

[1] Assuming normal distributions of market parameter returns, combined with constant sensitivities, results in normal distributions of final values of each instrument within the portfolio. However, these distributions correlate. Hence, it is better to start from market parameter correlated distributions to get directly the portfolio value distribution embedding these correlations.

of ΔV_p allows us to define any loss percentiles along the normal distribution. The VaR is a loss percentile $L(\alpha)$ with a given confidence level α. Mapping loss percentiles with multiples of the normal distribution volatility uses the well-known multiples of volatility. Figure 32.4 illustrates the process.

DELTA VAR CALCULATION EXAMPLE

The assumptions of the Delta VaR technique make it 'analytical', using closed-form formulas for determining loss percentiles. Since there are as many covariances and correlations as there are pairs of random variables, it is convenient to group these statistics in matrices. The matrices cross-tabulate the variables in rows and columns. The covariance, or the correlation coefficient, is at the intersection of the row and the column relative to this pair of variables. Since both correlations and covariances do not depend on the sequence of the two variables, the matrix is symmetric around its diagonal. Along the diagonal, the values are the variances of each variable since they are the covariances of each variable with itself. Any variance–covariance matrix needs to comply with such properties[2]. In this example, no specific risk term appears because we use deterministic relationships between two interest rate exposures and the corresponding rates. When there is a specific risk, it is necessary to add to the portfolio volatility all specific risk error volatilities as well as the general risk, since the specific risks are independent of the factors driving general risk.

Example of a Variance–Covariance Matrix

The statistics of the above example correspond to the 2×2 matrices in Table 32.1.

TABLE 32.1 The variance–covariance and correlation matrices: example of interest rates

	Mean	Volatility	Correlation
Rate 1	10.100%	2.601%	37.901%
Rate 2	7.000%	1.826%	

Variance–covariance matrix:			Correlation matrix:		
	Rate 1	Rate 2		Rate 1	Rate 2
Rate 1	0.06767%	0.01800%	Rate 1	100.000%	37.901%
Rate 2	0.01800%	0.03333%	Rate 2	37.901%	100.000%

The variances are along the diagonal. They are $0.06767\% = (2.601\%)^2$ and $0.03333\% = (1.826\%)^2$. The relationship between the correlation coefficient and the covariance is $\sigma_{12} = \rho_{12}\sigma_1\sigma_2$. Hence:

$$0.01800\% = 37.901\% \times 1.826\% \times 2.601\%$$

---

[2] The variance–covariance matrix has to be semi-definite positive, in mathematical terms.

The correlation matrix is easier to interpret since the coefficient has to be compared with the -1, 0 and $+1$ values, but it does not provide variance and covariance terms necessary to value losses. The matrix presentation extends to any set of variables.

Calculation of the Loss Volatility

We calculate the variance and the volatility of a portfolio of two interest rate exposures using a sample set of data. These are market exposures. The same process would apply to mark-to-market values of loans sensitive to interest rate variations. We need to specify the exposures. In order to make explicit calculations, we need to use the property of expectations and volatility when we multiply exposures (certain) with a random variable as in the first section.

Direct Calculation of the Two Exposures Portfolio Volatility

The example is a portfolio of two market exposures to interest rates with zero-coupon bonds of maturities 1 and 5. The sensitivities[3] are 1 and 5. There is a positive correlation between the interest rates for 1 and 5 years. The current market values are 2000 and 1000, with a total portfolio value of 3000. The value sensitivities for a unit change in market rates are 1000 and 5000. It is convenient to define the random value change for a unit size exposure, or return. These unit random losses are the percentage sensitivities, 1 and 5, times the random changes of interest rates, Δi_1 and Δi_2, of the two interest rates.

Unit random returns:

$$\mathbf{u_1} = s_1 \times \Delta i_1 = 1 \times \Delta i_1$$

$$\mathbf{u_2} = s_2 \times \Delta i_2 = 5 \times \Delta i_2$$

The value sensitivities are the value changes for a unit change in interest rates:

$$S_1 = s_1 \times V_1 = 1 \times V_1 = 1 \times 2000 = 2000$$

$$S_2 = s_2 \times V_2 = 5 \times V_2 = 5 \times 1000 = 5000$$

Given these sensitivities, the random variation of the value V of the portfolio is:

$$\mathbf{\Delta V} = V_1 \times \mathbf{u_1} + V_2 \times \mathbf{u_2}$$

Using unit or value sensitivities, this is equal to:

$$\mathbf{\Delta V} = V_1 \times s_1 \times \Delta i_1 + V_2 \times s_2 \times \Delta i_2$$

$$\mathbf{\Delta V} = S_1 \times \Delta i_1 + S_2 \times \Delta i_2$$

$$\mathbf{\Delta V} = 2000 \times \Delta i_1 + 5000 \times \Delta i_2$$

The volatility of the portfolio value is the volatility of this sum of random changes of two interest rates, weighted by sensitivities considered as certain:

$$\mathbf{\Delta V} = 2000 \times \Delta i_1 + 5000 \times \Delta i_2$$

---

[3] We neglect the $(1 + i)$ factor used for modified duration $D/(1 + i)$, which is the actual measure of sensitivity.

Using $\sigma_1 = \sigma(\Delta i_1)$ and $\sigma_2 = \sigma(\Delta i_2)$ as compact notations for volatilities, the portfolio value variance[4] is:

$$\sigma^2(\mathbf{V}) = s_1^2 \times V_1^2 \times \sigma_1^2 + s_2^2 \times V_2^2 \times \sigma_2^2 + 2 \times s_1 \times s_2 \times V_1 \times V_2 \times \sigma_1\sigma_2$$

Or using the value sensitivities of S_1 and S_2:

$$\sigma^2(\mathbf{V}) = S_1^2 \times \sigma_1^2 + S_2^2 \times \sigma_2^2 + 2 \times S_1 \times S_2 \times \sigma_1\sigma_2$$

The numerical calculations are:

$$\sigma^2(\mathbf{V}) = 2000^2 \times 2.601\%^2 + 5000^2 \times 1.826\%^2 + 2 \times 2000 \times 5000 \times 37.901\%$$

$$\times 2.601\% \times 1.826\%$$

$$\sigma^2(\mathbf{V}) = 14\,640$$

$$\sigma(\mathbf{V}) = \sqrt{14\,640} = 120.996$$

This direct calculation extends to any number of exposures and market parameters. The matrix format makes the process simple.

Matrix Format for the Volatility Calculation

The matrix format helps when using a general formula applying to any number of exposures. The starting point is the sensitivity vector of individual exposures. The variance–covariance matrix summarizes the interdependence between the entire set of market parameters. Using the above example, the portfolio volatility is the row vector of sensitivities multiplied by the variance–covariance matrix, times the column vector of sensitivities. The example uses value sensitivities. The intermediate steps of the calculation are identical to the above calculations. The matrix format of Table 32.2 summarizes them.

TABLE 32.2 Determination of the volatility of the portfolio value with the variance–covariance matrix

| | Variance–covariance matrix: | | |
	Rate I	Rate 2	Sensitivities
	0.0677%	0.0180%	2000
	0.0180%	0.0333%	5000
Sensitivities			Variance
2000 5000	2.2533	2.0267	14 640.00
			Volatility
			120.996

---

[4] The portfolio value variance is identical to that of its random variation since the current value is certain, hence $\mathbf{V} = V_0 + \Delta \mathbf{V}$.

The matrix operation is:

$$\text{Variance} = S \times \Sigma \times S^{\mathrm{T}}$$

$$\text{Volatility} = \sqrt{S \times \Sigma \times S^{\mathrm{T}}}$$

where S is the row vector of value sensitivities, S^{T} is the transposed vector and Σ is the variance–covariance matrix of all market parameters.

Note that unit sensitivities necessitate a slightly different format (Table 32.3). The value sensitivity S is the percentage sensitivity times the value. Hence, the vector S is the product of the row vector of unit sensitivities times the row vector of values. The transposed vector S^{T} is the transposed product[5]: $S = sV$ and $S^{\mathrm{T}} = (Vs)^{\mathrm{T}} = V^{\mathrm{T}}s^{\mathrm{T}}$. The variance matrix formula becomes: $\text{Variance} = sV \times \Sigma \times (sV)^{\mathrm{T}}$.

TABLE 32.3 Value sensitivities vector and unit sensitivities and values vectors

	Row vectors: Values V		Column vectors:	
			Unit sensitivities s^{T}	1
	2000	1000		5
Unit sensitivities s	Value sensitivities S		Values V^{T}	Value sensitivities S^{T}
1 5	2000	5000	2000	2000
			1000	5000

The resulting volatility from the example in Table 32.3 is 121 rounded. The same matrix formulas serve for any number of exposures, as long as we stick to the constant sensitivities as a proxy of reality. This concise format serves both for market risk VaR, where volatility is important, and for credit risk VaR, since the portfolio loss volatility is also an important parameter.

For credit risk, the same methodology uses the values of exposures to credit risk to obtain the loss volatility, rather than the value sensitivities as above.

Summary of the Delta–Normal Technique

Figure 32.5 summarizes the methodology. A matrix operation provides the portfolio variance and volatility, using the vector of sensitivities and the variance–covariance matrix:

$$\text{Variance} = S \times \Sigma \times S^{\mathrm{T}}$$

$$\text{Volatility} = \sqrt{S \times \Sigma \times S^{\mathrm{T}}}$$

When there is specific risk, the variance sums the general risk volatility, as derived from sensitivities and the variance–covariance matrix, and the specific risk terms. The variance–covariance matrix embeds these terms in the diagonal, as the diagonal applied to stocks demonstrates. The difference is that the sensitivities do not suffice for capturing total risk, whereas they do in the case of deterministic relationships between individual

---

[5] The transpose of a product is the product of transposed matrices in reverse order: $(Vs)^{\mathrm{T}} = V^{\mathrm{T}}s^{\mathrm{T}}$.

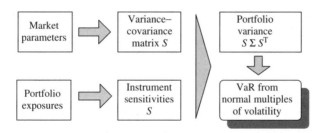

FIGURE 32.5 Delta VaR methodology

risk and market parameters. Since the portfolio value at the horizon is normal, the problem is to find the volatility of the market value of the portfolio in order to derive the VaR. The volatility formula combines the sensitivity vector with a variance–covariance matrix. Then, VaR results from simple multiples of the normal distribution mapped to confidence levels. In the formula, it is easy to use 'value sensitivities', as in the example below. There is no need for simulations, since we use a closed-form expression for portfolio value volatility.

With the above example, the yearly volatility is rounded to 121. The 1% one-tail confidence level is 2.33 for a normal distribution. This would result in a yearly VaR of:

$$\text{VaR}(1\%) = 2.33 \times 121 = 291$$

This yearly volatility has to be converted to fit the shorter period required for market risk VaR, that is 10 days. The simplest conversion rule uses the square root of time coefficient since the period considered for market risk is very short. The 10-day volatility is $\sqrt{10/250} = \sqrt{0.04} = 0.2$ times the yearly volatility 121. Since the VaR is proportional to volatility, the same coefficient applies to obtain the 10-day VaR. With a yearly VaR of 291, we multiply it by 0.2 to get the 10-day VaR, or $0.2 \times 237 = 56.40^6$.

The regulator allows the usage of proprietary models for calculating VaR and economic capital. The quantitative requirements are: a one-tailed confidence level of 99%; a 10-day holding period; observation periods of at least 1 year, with periodical quarterly updates as a minimum; a multiplication factor of 3, possibly adjusted. The multiple covers extreme events, errors, lack of liquidity of markets and of exotic instruments, long periods of adverse market movements. The VaR is the maximum of the last daily VaR and the last 60-day average. The multiple is subject to variations depending on the reliability of the VaR measures, as assessed through back testing. This provides a feedback loop after back testing as well as an incentive to refine the methodology.

EXTENSIONS OF THE DELTA VAR METHODOLOGY

There are several extensions of this basic analytical model. E-VaR is the expectation of VaR conditional on exceeding the threshold at the preset confidence level. It is easy to derive under the normal assumptions. Delta–Gamma VaR relies on shortcuts to capture

---

[6] We could also start from the daily volatilities and multiply by $\sqrt{10} = 3.162$ to get the yearly volatility. Daily volatilities being easier to calculate, this is another common method. Yearly volatilities are $\sqrt{250} = 15.81$ times daily volatilities.

non-linearities. When moving along this path, we soon encounter complexities that lead to the multiple simulation techniques.

E-VaR

E-VaR is the expected value conditional on exceeding a percentile. This is the average size of the loss conditional on exceeding the percentile. With a loss **L** in absolute value:

$$\text{Prob}[\mathbf{L} > L(\alpha)] = \Phi(\alpha)$$

The probability $\text{Prob}(\mathbf{L} = L)$ that the random loss **L** takes the value L conditional on exceeding $L(\alpha)$ is the unconditional probability that the loss has the value L exceeding $L(\alpha)$ divided by the unconditional probability that the loss exceeds $L(\alpha)$, or $\Phi(\alpha)$:

$$\text{Prob}[\mathbf{L} > L | \mathbf{L} > L(\alpha)] = \text{pdf}(\mathbf{L})/\Phi(\alpha)$$

The expectation of the loss given that the loss exceeds the upper bound is the cumulative density function of L, or $\text{Prob}[\mathbf{L} = L | \mathbf{L} > L(\alpha)] = [\int_{L(\alpha)}^{\infty} \mathbf{L} \times \text{pdf}(\mathbf{L})]/\Phi(\alpha)$. This formula requires the calculation of the expectation of a truncated distribution, truncation occurring at $L(\alpha)$. There is a general formula of the expectation for random normal variables. The formula collapses to a simple one when using a normal standardized variable (mean 0 and variance 1) truncated at the lower end by $L(\alpha)$:

$$E[\mathbf{L} | \mathbf{L} > L(\alpha)] = +\text{pdf}(\alpha)/\Phi(\alpha)$$

As an example, the expectation of a random normal standardized loss with a 1% one-tailed confidence level uses $L(\alpha) = 2.33$, the density of the normal distribution at 2.33, which is N(2.33) for the normal standardized:

$$E[\mathbf{L} | \mathbf{L} > L(\alpha)] = 1/\sqrt{2\pi} \times \exp[-1/2 \times 2.33^2]/1\% = 0.026652/0.01 = 2.66652$$

This is a variation of the simple Delta VaR. The E-VaR is above the simple VaR.

Delta–Gamma VaR

A more important variation addresses the 'convexity' issue for options that makes the linear approximation collapse. Because of convexity, sensitivity varies with the underlying parameter. Even with short periods, such variations are not negligible. A proxy of this variation is the Gamma sensitivity. The Gamma is the derivative of Delta with respect to the underlying of an option.

It is therefore possible to extend the Delta VaR to the Delta–Gamma VaR using the Gamma terms. The mathematical formula is the Taylor expansion of the VaR up to the second order[7], while the Delta VaR uses only the first order. The formula is similar

---

[7] Any function $f(x)$ can be expanded around the point x_0 as:

$$f(x) = f(x_0) + 1/1! f'(x_0)(x - x_0) + 1/2! f''(x_0)(x - x_0)^2 + 1/n! f^{(n)}(x_0)(x - x_0)^n + \cdots$$

to the general Delta VaR formula, except that the sensitivity with respect to the underlying of options includes the Delta and the Gamma terms in a linear fashion. Hence, the concept is similar, while using Gamma as a linear proxy for the Delta variation. It is possible to implement a 'semi-full' simulation using the sensitivities to each factor, as linear functions of these factors (delta, gamma, rho, theta) and to recalculate the values. The same technique allows us to decompose the price of derivatives with respect to the 'Greeks'—delta, gamma, nu and rho—as sensitivities of the derivative value with respect to these parameters. These formulas apply to any interest rate security. For an option, we substitute the corresponding 'Greeks' in the coefficients:

$$\mathbf{\Delta V} = \delta \times V_0 \times \mathbf{dm} + 1/2\gamma \times V_0 \times \mathbf{dm}^2 + \cdots$$

For an interest rate asset, the formulas providing the value variation of an option under the Delta and the Delta–Gamma variations are:

$$\mathbf{\Delta V} = -D \times V_0 \times \mathbf{dm} + \cdots$$

$$\mathbf{\Delta V} = -D \times V_0 \times \mathbf{dm} + 1/2C \times V_0 \times \mathbf{dm}^2 + \cdots$$

Unfortunately, the function is not linear any more[8]. The Cornish–Fisher expansion provides a relationship between the moments of a distribution and its percentiles[9].

Moving to Multiple Simulations and Full Revaluations

When the final distribution of the portfolio value is not normal, we cannot rely only on the analytical calculation allowed by normal distributions. The process is similar. Instead of using correlations between market parameter values, we correlate the random terms in the processes mimicking the time paths of market parameters. Asset value changes follow correlated lognormal distributions.

This can be summarized as:

$$f(x) = \sum_{n=0}^{\infty} 1/n! f^{(n)}(x_0)(x - x_0)^n$$

This is simplified for $x_0 = 0$:

$$f(x) = f(0) + 1/1! f'(0)x + 1/2! f''(0)x^2 + 1/n! f^{(n)}(0)x^n + \cdots$$

$$f(x) = \sum_{n=0}^{\infty} 1/n! f^{(n)}(0)x^n$$

[8] Even if $\mathbf{dm}$ is normal, this is not so for $\mathbf{dm}^2$, the square of a normal variable. In addition, the variance of the summation also depends on the covariance term $\text{Cov}(\mathbf{dm}, \mathbf{dm}^2)$. For the variance of the summation, approximations are available. It is also possible to consider $\mathbf{dm}^2$ as approximately normal to revert to the Delta–normal approach.

[9] See Johnson and Kotz (1972). The Cornish–Fisher expansion uses the first three moments of $\mathbf{\Delta V}$. It provides the α percentile distribution of $\mathbf{\Delta V}$ as $\mu_\alpha + w_\alpha \sigma$, with $w_\alpha = z_\alpha + 1/6(z_\alpha^2 - 1)$, z being a function of μ_α and σ_α and $E(\mathbf{\Delta V})$ with z_α being the α percentile of the standard normal distribution $\Phi(0, 1)$.

THE MULTIPLE SIMULATIONS METHODOLOGY

The principle of the simulation method is to test multiple possible outcomes against a portfolio to obtain its risk. A set of future values of market parameters characterizes each scenario. These future values result from time path simulations of their returns if necessary. Each set of parameter values serves for revaluing the portfolio. The revaluation process uses 'pricers', models for valuing instruments and sensitivities for stock prices. By generating a large number of such scenarios, it is possible to generate a large sample of portfolio values. From this distribution of portfolio values, we derive empirically both the volatility of market deviations and the upper bound at a given confidence level.

Principle of Multiple Simulations

The multiple simulation methodology is empirical. There is no need to make assumptions about the shape of portfolio value distributions. This shape results from mechanical revaluations of the portfolio for all runs of market parameters. Then, the determination of the bound for losses is empirical, or 'non-parametric'[10] (Figure 32.6).

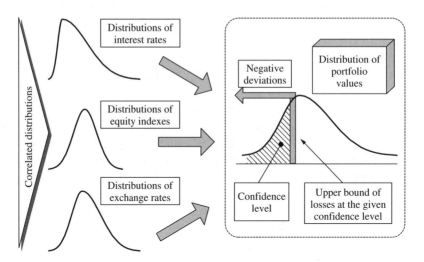

FIGURE 32.6   Multiple simulation methodology

When the linear approximation collapses, as for options, and when we cannot use shortcuts to approximate final values, we need to revert to the full valuation technique. This implies simulating risk drivers, eventually using their entire time path, and obtaining their final values and pricing models for some standard derivatives. The direct revaluation bypasses the proxy formulas using sensitivities, but it makes the process more calculation intensive. Forward revaluation of derivatives might need simulations beyond the horizon, starting from each possible value at the horizon, or 'simulations within simulations', making the process overly complex.

---

[10] This is because it does not depend on the basic parameters, expectation and volatility, of a distribution.

Because of these complexities, several techniques help to simplify the process. One way to address the calculation intensive process is to minimize the number of simulations[11]. There are several variations around these common principles. We review the simplest ones, before addressing the full-blown simulation process. They include:

- Grid simulations.
- Historical simulations.
- Full Monte Carlo simulations.

Grid Simulations

Before generating a very large number of scenarios it is tempting, in order to limit the calculations, to restrict the approach to a small number of scenarios. The grid Monte Carlo approach uses an exact valuation for each grid point and uses a linear interpolation between points.

Grid simulation consists of running a limited number of sets of parameter values. The selected values should cover a maximum range of values of each parameter. Since there is a limited set of values, the process is less calculation intensive than full Monte Carlo simulations that aim for a comprehensive coverage of possible market outcomes. For instance, it is possible to focus on 'shocks' of various parameters to try to capture all main deviations from current value of the portfolio. This is not as powerful as full-blown simulations, because the selection of values might miss some worst-case scenarios.

Some techniques attempt to identify these worst-case situations empirically. As a reminder, it is not feasible to identify worst-case scenarios with a large variety of exposures because of offsetting effects. Stressing one parameter might increase the overall loss. However, for some instruments it generates adverse deviations and for others gains. Therefore, it is possible that a different shock will capture another worst-case situation that is even worse than the previous one. A practical way of identifying such worst-case scenarios is to examine the portfolio structure, to identify its main exposures and their risk drivers, and to try several shocks on various parameters driving the risk of the major exposures. Then, some scenarios will prove worse than others, and selected scenarios for stressing the loss of value of the portfolio could be sampled from this set.

Historical Monte Carlo Simulations

Monte Carlo simulations are more powerful because they explore comprehensively market outcomes. It is common to contrast historical simulations to forward looking Monte Carlo simulations. Historical simulations use actually observed sets of parameter values embedding all volatilities and correlations, over the horizon used for collecting the historical data. The historical simulations use samples from historical data. Future price calculations use historical changes of market parameters applied to the current prices. The last step is to revalue the portfolio using all historically observed sets of values of market parameters over the selected horizon to construct the portfolio value distribution. Using daily observations over 2 years, for example, will provide around 500 sets of values

---

[11] See Jamshidian and Zhu (1997) for techniques limiting the number of simulations. See also Broadie and Glasserman (1998) for simulations and options pricing.

of all market parameters. These observed values embed all correlations observed in the market over the period. They serve for marking-to-market the portfolio 500 times. The risk statistics result from the distribution of these 500 values.

The drawback is that the technique is essentially backward looking. In addition, it averages each observation of market parameters independently of how representative it is of current conditions. The technique is slow in including latest data. In some cases, it is conservative, because historical observations capture market shocks of large magnitude. In others, it averages so much the past values that it misses the current market conditions, which might be an outlier compared to historical scenarios. A large number of observations are necessary to search the 'fat tail' of the VaR measure, and past information over a recent period might not provide enough data. On the other hand, moving too far backwards into the past might capture market behaviour that has become irrelevant. For instance, market liquidity could be poor in the past for new products, and improve when new products disseminate in the market.

Historical simulations provide two benefits:

- They serve for back testing purposes, making sure that the portfolio values include those that would have appeared if the past repeats itself on the current portfolio structure.
- They capture in the simplest possible way all volatilities and correlations linking market parameters to each other.

Full Monte Carlo Simulations

Under full Monte Carlo simulations, the process starts by modelling the stochastic processes of market parameters, doing the best to ensure that they capture recent worst-case situations. It is similar to historical simulations except that we look forward using simulated values rather than historical values. Modelling the inputs is a crucial issue. Inputs include volatilities and correlations whose measures raise issues with respect to their changes over time.

The next stage is the generation of random values of market parameters complying with this input structure. The last stage is the portfolio revaluation for each set of values generated. Since we capture all forward looking information, as well as past information embedded in modelling inputs, we have the best of both worlds. The main drawback of the full-blown simulation is that it is calculation intensive. All instruments should be valued for all sets of market parameter values. The number of runs has to be high enough to provide a sufficient accuracy for the portfolio value distribution. Each set of values implies revaluing each individual instrument within the portfolio.

By contrast, the correlation (Delta VaR) methodology uses a unique variance–covariance matrix for all portfolios and the calculation requires only a product of matrices to obtain the portfolio volatility.

BACK TESTING, EXTREME VAR AND STRESS TESTING

It is important to make a distinction with day-to-day operations VaR and extreme VaR used for capital adequacy purposes. The second form follows the view that VaR is the economic capital that protects the bank from extreme market movements.

VaR and Economic Capital

Day-to-day VaR measures sometimes use low confidence levels, such as the 2.5% level. There are several rationales for adopting low confidence levels. Tight confidence levels result in a higher usage of capital and traders reach their limit VaR quicker than with 'loose' VaR measures, thereby limiting the volume of business. At the extreme, since the VaR is a Profit and Loss (P&L), using a tight VaR implies low P&L, eventually inconsistent with the trading goals. Loose confidence levels make sense if we consider that a single trader might exceed risk limits without deteriorating the credit standing of the bank (although there are examples not supporting this view). However, the entire portfolio VaR cannot rely on a loose confidence level, since it represents the default probability of the trading unit. The regulator recommends the 99% level and makes the measure more conservative by using a multiple to obtain capital. Related issues are the VaR reliability measure, and the extreme VaR or stress testing.

Back Testing

Back testing aims to check that measures are in line with actual portfolio variations of value. Since the portfolio structure changes constantly, the exercise requires using the 'crystallized' structure of the portfolio, looking for what the actual deviations were and comparing them to VaR measures. This allows us to check that the number of outliers is in line with the confidence level. With a 2.5% confidence level, the number of deviations beyond VaR should be less than 2 or 3 out of 100 observations. Running a number of sets of historical parameter values allows us to obtain the distribution of the portfolio values, and check the number of outliers at constant portfolio structure. The test compares the frequency of outliers with the confidence level.

The number of outliers embeds a random error because it results from sampling past values. Therefore, the test is subject to traditional errors of rejecting a good model and accepting a bad one because of the sampling error. This requires using threshold values of the number of outliers, limiting the probability of such errors.

Other techniques compare the actual distribution of portfolio returns, from which the VaR derives the actual distribution, or compare the volatilities of these two distributions.

Extreme VaR and Stress Testing

Stress testing aims to investigate the possibility of exceptional losses by stressing the value of the risk drivers. With a portfolio, it is not simple to identify which deviations of which parameters result in extreme losses because asset value changes are offset within the portfolio.

Extreme VaR measures involve extreme scenarios. Such scenarios might be judgmental and selective. For instance, if the management fears wide variations of selected parameters, these wide variations would serve to revalue the portfolio and see what would be the magnitude of adverse effects. Using the extreme conditions that prevailed historically over a long period is a common way to stress test a portfolio. The idea is to see how it would behave under similar conditions.

There are various practical techniques to explore stressed conditions. A simple one consists of stressing the main risk drivers one at a time. Using a sensitivity analysis allows us to determine which parameters generate the largest changes, and focus on those. Another technique is to select those parameters with the highest values. Cumulating the effects of stressed values of these main parameters might result in worse losses, or losses not depending on the portfolio structure. Losses will increase when all selected parameter deviations alter adversely the values of the assets of the portfolio. Otherwise, they do not.

Extreme VaR techniques differ in that they attempt to model extreme situations, using distributions with fat tails. A common technique uses the Pareto distribution family to fit the fat tail of the distribution. The technique involves 'smoothing the tail' to obtain better estimates of the value percentiles[12]. It allows us to use a known distribution instead of the modelled one, to determine loss percentiles at low confidence levels without requiring calculation intensive simulations. Extreme value theory also provides some techniques for capturing tail effects.

APPENDIX: THE EFFECT OF DIVERSIFICATION ON PORTFOLIO VALUE

This appendix details the usual demonstration of decreasing portfolio return volatility when the number of assets gets large. The portfolio return volatility decreases to a floor set by general risk. When the asset returns are independent, the portfolio return volatility decreases to zero. When there is a common factor affecting all individual returns, the floor is the general risk depending on the correlation level between individual asset returns. By contrast, the portfolio value volatility increases with the number of assets. The sensitivity of the value volatility to the number of assets increases with the average correlation between asset returns.

Asset and Portfolio Returns

The notations are:

$$\text{Asset return} \quad \mathbf{r}_i$$

$$\text{Portfolio return} \quad \mathbf{r_p} = \sum_{i=1}^{n} w_i \mathbf{r}_i$$

The portfolio return is the weighted summation of individual returns, the weights being the ratios of the individual asset values to the initial portfolio value:

$$w_i = V_{i0}/V_{p0}$$

The portfolio value as of current date 0 is the summation of individual values:

$$V_{p0} = \sum_{i=j=1}^{n} V_{i0}$$

---

[12] See Embrechts et al. (1997) for a complete review of extreme value theory.

The first index relates to the individual asset, or to the entire portfolio, and the second index designates the date 0 as the current date. The portfolio value at a future date is random and is the summation of individual values:

$$\mathbf{V_p} = \sum_{i=j=1}^{n} \mathbf{V}_i$$

The relations between values and single period returns of individual assets or of the portfolio are:

$$\mathbf{V}_i = V_{i0}(1 + \mathbf{r}_i)$$

$$\mathbf{V_p} = \sum_{i=1}^{n} V_{i0}(1 + \mathbf{r}_i)$$

The portfolio return and the individual asset returns are such that:

$$\mathbf{r}_i = (\mathbf{V}_i - V_{i0})/V_{i0} = (\mathbf{V}_i / V_{i0}) - 1$$

$$\mathbf{r_p} = (\mathbf{V_p} - V_{p0})/V_{p0} = (\mathbf{V_p}/V_{p0}) - 1$$

Using the standard notations, we can show that the portfolio return variance converges rapidly towards a floor when the number of assets gets large enough. The floor is zero when returns are independent and is proportional to the average portfolio covariance when the correlation is positive.

Portfolio Return Variance

The portfolio return is the weighted average of asset returns:

$$\mathbf{r_p} = \sum_{i=1}^{n} w_i \mathbf{r}_i$$

The weights sum to 1. The portfolio return variance results from the weighted summation of individual asset returns:

$$\sigma^2(\mathbf{r_p}) = \sigma^2 \left(\sum_{i=1}^{n} w_i \mathbf{r}_i \right)$$

$$\sigma^2 \left(\sum_{i=1}^{n} \mathbf{r}_i \right) = \sum_{i=j=1}^{n} w_i^2 \sigma_i^2 + \sum_{i \neq j} w_i w_j \sigma_{ij} = \sum_{i=j=1}^{n} w_i^2 \sigma_i^2 + \sum_{i \neq j} \rho_{ij} w_i w_j \sigma_i \sigma_j$$

In this formula, we use compact notations such that:

$$\sigma^2(\mathbf{r}_i) = \sigma_i$$

The covariance between individual returns of assets i and j is the product of the correlation coefficient ρ_{ij} times the volatilities of returns:

$$\text{Cov}(\mathbf{r}_i, \mathbf{r}_j) = \rho_{ij} w_i w_j \sigma_i \sigma_j$$

All formulas simplify when using a uniform 'exposure–variance–covariance' portfolio. When the variances and the correlations are uniform across the portfolio: $\sigma_i^2 = \sigma^2$ and $\rho_{ij} = \rho$. All weights become equal to $1/N$, so that they still sum to 1: $w_i = 1/N$. All covariance terms are identical to an average uniform covariance term:

$$\text{Cov}(\mathbf{r}_i, \mathbf{r}_j) = \rho_{ij} w_i w_j \sigma_i \sigma_j = \rho \times (1/N)^2 \times \sigma^2$$

The portfolio return variance is:

$$\sigma^2(\mathbf{r_p}) = \sum_{i=j=1}^{n} w_i^2 \sigma^2 + \sum_{i \neq j} \rho w_i w_j \sigma^2$$

There are N variance terms and $N \times (N-1)$ equal covariance terms. The uniform portfolio variance of returns becomes:

$$\sigma^2(\mathbf{r_p}) = N(1/N)^2 \sigma^2 + N(N-1)(1/N)^2 \rho \sigma^2$$

Simplifying:

$$\sigma^2(\mathbf{r_p}) = \{1/N + [1 - (1/N)]\rho\} \times \sigma^2$$

$$\sigma^2(\mathbf{r_p}) = [(1/N)(1 - \rho) + \rho] \times \sigma^2$$

The first term gets close to zero when N grows, while the second term results from the correlation only, and remains constant. Consequently, the portfolio return variance decreases rapidly to this floor when the number of assets grows. The variance of the return collapses: $\sigma^2(\mathbf{r_p}) = \rho \times \sigma^2$ when N becomes large, which is the systematic undiversifiable risk of the portfolio return due to the volatility of the common index driving all individual asset returns. The same property holds when covariances and variances are unequal, but is more difficult to demonstrate.

From Returns to Values

The covariances between individual values derive directly from those of returns between individual assets. The relation results from the linear relation between random returns and random future values:

$$\mathbf{r}_i = (\mathbf{V}_i - V_{i0})/V_{i0} = \mathbf{V}_i/V_{i0} - 1$$

$$\mathbf{r_p} = (\mathbf{V_p} - V_{p0})/V_{p0} = \mathbf{V_p}/V_{p0} - 1$$

The covariances between individual returns and values are such that:

$$\text{Cov}(\mathbf{r}_i, \mathbf{r}_j) = \text{Cov}(\mathbf{V}_i/V_{i0} - 1, \ \mathbf{V}_j/V_{j0} - 1)$$

$$\text{Cov}(\mathbf{r}_i, \mathbf{r}_j) = 1/V_{i0} \times 1/V_{j0} \times \text{Cov}(\mathbf{V}_i, \mathbf{V}_j)$$

The variance of the portfolio value sums the variance of individual values plus the covariances between values:

$$\sigma(\mathbf{V_p})^2 = \sum_{i=j=1}^{n} \sigma(\mathbf{V}_i)^2 + \sum_{i \neq j} \sigma(\mathbf{V}_i, \mathbf{V}_j)$$

The variances and covariances of values and of returns are such that:

$$\text{Cov}(r_i, r_j) = 1/V_{i0} \times 1/V_{j0} \times \text{Cov}(V_i, V_j) \quad \text{or}$$

$$\text{Cov}(V_i, V_j) = V_{i0} \times V_{j0} \times \text{Cov}(r_i, r_j)$$

In general, the portfolio value variance is:

$$\sigma(V_p)^2 = \sum_{i=j=1}^{n} V_{i0}^2 \times \sigma(r_i)^2 + \sum_{i \neq j} V_{i0} \times V_{j0} \times \text{Cov}(r_i, r_j)$$

This formula shows that the variance of the portfolio value derives from the variance–covariance matrix of returns, but the coefficients of these terms are the squared values of assets rather than the squared values of weights. The covariance term is $\text{Cov}(r_i, r_j) = \rho_{ij} w_i w_j \sigma_i \sigma_j$. There are N variance terms and $N(N-1)$ covariance terms.

The Simple Case of a Uniform Exposure, Uniform Volatility and Uniform Correlation Portfolio

All exposures are equal: $V_{i0} = V_{j0} = V_0$ and $V_{p0} = N \times V_0$. All variances and covariances of returns are equal:

$$\sigma(V_i)^2 = V_0^2 \times \sigma^2$$

$$\text{Cov}(r_i, r_j) = \rho_{ij} w_i w_j \sigma_i \sigma_j = \rho \times (1/N)^2 \times \sigma^2$$

$$\sigma(V_i, V_j) = V_0^2 \times \rho \times (1/N)^2 \times \sigma^2$$

When we use the uniform exposure–volatility–correlation portfolio, the portfolio value variance becomes:

$$\sigma(V_p)^2 = \sum_{i=j=1}^{n} V_0^2 \times \sigma^2 + \sum_{i \neq j} V_0^2 \times \rho \times (1/N)^2 \times \sigma^2$$

There are N variance terms and $N(N-1)$ covariance terms, which are identical:

$$\sigma(V_p)^2 = N \times V_0^2 \times \sigma^2 + N(N-1) \times V_0^2 \times \rho \times (1/N)^2 \times \sigma^2$$

$$\sigma(V_p)^2 = N \times V_0^2 \times \sigma^2 \times [(1-\rho) + \rho \times N]$$

With this general formula, we compare the portfolio variance and volatility under independence of returns and when their correlation differs from zero, to show how correlation affects the diversification effect on the portfolio value volatility. When the uniform correlation is zero, the portfolio value variance and the portfolio value volatility become:

$$\sigma(V_p)^2 = N \times V_0^2 \times \sigma^2$$

$$\sigma(V_p) = V_0 \times \sigma \times \sqrt{N}$$

The portfolio value variance increases as the square of the number of assets under independence. The portfolio value volatility increases as the square root of N. When the uniform correlation differs from zero, the portfolio value variance is:

$$\sigma(\mathbf{V_p})^2 = N \times V_0^2 \times \sigma^2 \times [1 + (N - 1) \times \rho]$$

By factoring out N, we find the portfolio value variance and the portfolio value volatility:

$$\sigma(\mathbf{V_p})^2 = N^2 \times V_0^2 \times \sigma^2 \times [(1 - \rho)/N + \rho]$$

$$\sigma(\mathbf{V_p}) = N \times V_0 \times \sigma \times \sqrt{(1 - \rho)/N + \rho}$$

The portfolio value variance increases as the square of the number of assets under independence. The portfolio value volatility increases as the square root of N. This is a growth less than proportional to the number of assets and much lower than the growth of volatility of the portfolio value when the correlation becomes positive, because there is no term proportional to N.

SECTION 12

Credit Risk Models

33

Overview of Credit Risk Models

This chapter provides an overview and a summary of credit risk models, as described in subsequent chapters, and plays a key role in the presentation of credit risk modelling. There is a wide spectrum of credit risk models, addressing different issues with different techniques, making an overview necessary.

Some models serve for defining the credit risk drivers of individual transactions: exposures, recoveries and default plus migration probabilities. Other models use these as inputs for modelling the credit risk of portfolios of loans or bonds. We designate this second category as 'portfolio models'. The chapter describes the major building blocks of credit risk modelling. It details the techniques used for modelling credit risk drivers then the specifics of each of the four major portfolio models (vendors' models). These are Credit Metrics, KMV Portfolio Manager, Credit Portfolio View (CPV) and CreditRisk+.

There are two alternative approaches for presenting portfolio models. The first presents sequentially each of the existing 'vendors' models'. The second details how each existing portfolio model deals with each basic modelling building block, moving from one building block to the next, rather than from one model to the next. This chapter uses the second approach, the 'building block', rather than the more common sequential description of each vendor's model. The rationale for this view by building block, rather than by 'model', is twofold. First, it makes more explicit the alternative methodologies serving similar purposes within each model building block. Second, it facilitates the comparison of techniques across models. The drawback is that this approach is not a substitute for full descriptions of each model. Therefore we provide in this chapter summarized reviews of each of the major models. This allows readers to start with the overview before moving on to details and to easily shift later back and forth from the model view to the building block view.

The first section provides a map of credit risk model building blocks. It is an outline of subsequent chapters. The subsequent sections summarize issues and techniques for each modelling block. Each section is a summary of the subsequent chapters. The last section cross-tabulates vendors' models with the basic techniques that different credit risk models bundle in different ways.

THE BUILDING BLOCKS OF CREDIT RISK MODELS

The general structure by building blocks applies for credit risk as it does for market risk. However, in the case of credit risk there are several vendors' models using different techniques. The first building blocks relate to the inputs to 'portfolio models', such as default probabilities. Credit Monitor from KMV and RiskCalc from Moody's (Moody's Investors Service, 2000b) model default probabilities and there are numerous models using statistical techniques aimed at the same purpose. The second building block deals with portfolio risk. Portfolio models include KMV Portfolio Manager, Credit Metrics (J. P. Morgan, 1997), CPV (Wilson, 1997a, b) and CreditRisk+ (Credit Suisse, 1997).

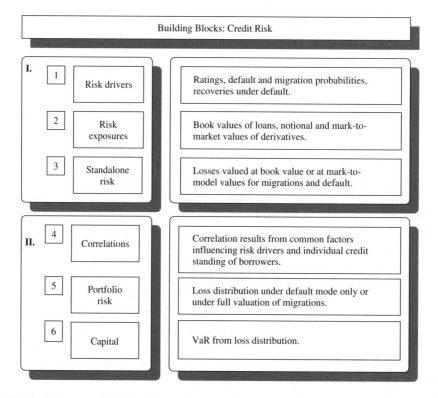

FIGURE 33.1   Major building blocks of credit risk

Portfolio models use exposures, ratings or default probabilities, and recoveries as inputs. Figure 33.1 summarizes the general structure for credit risk, ignoring blocks III (top-down links) and IV (risk–return), which are transversal to all risks. Focusing on the main blocks only, Figure 33.2 shows how the vendors' models map to this general structure.

We focus on the first two main blocks: standalone risk of individual transactions and portfolio risk. Since credit risk portfolio models extend to capital allocation and individual risk-adjusted measures of performance, we add a brief description of building blocks II

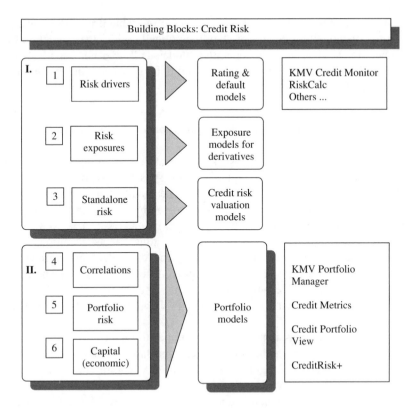

FIGURE 33.2   Major building blocks of credit risk

and IV. The capital allocation and the risk–return building blocks are technically identical for market and credit risk, except that market risk models do not integrate them.

BLOCK I: STANDALONE RISK

This block discusses risk drivers, exposure and credit risk valuation. The credit risk drivers are the factors that trigger credit risk events, default or migrations across risk classes. The exposures to credit risk use either actual or expected exposures, or modelled exposures such as those of over-the-counter derivatives, which are market-driven. Credit valuation implies calculating value changes due to credit events. Under 'default mode', values do not reflect risk migrations. Under full valuation mode, migrations drive value changes.

Modelling Default and Migration Risks

Default and migration probabilities are basic inputs for capturing the risk of a facility as well as the risk of a portfolio. The New Basel Accord considers that assigning default probabilities to borrowers is a requirement for implementing the 'foundation' and 'advanced' approaches, rather than the standardized approach. When implementing portfolio models, it is necessary to specify exposure, recoveries (or loss given default) and the likelihood of default and migrations. This is an area where old scoring and 'rating models', capable of mimicking the ratings assigned by agencies from observable firms' attributes, and new models capable of modelling default probabilities directly with other techniques coexist. Both old generation models and new generation models have expanded at a fast pace since the full recognition of the necessity of ratings and default probabilities by the regulatory authorities in Basel.

Assigning Ratings and Default Probabilities: Judgmental versus Analytical

Ratings rank the credit risk of debt issues. When assigning ratings, there are various dimensions of the risk of a loan to capture. The first is the risk of the borrower. This is a counterparty risk, rather than a facility risk. The facility risk depends on collateral, third-party guarantees and informal support of a holding company. A comprehensive rating scheme should capture the effect of the borrower's risk, a possible supporting entity effect, plus the facility-specific guarantees mitigating effects. Traditionally, external ratings from agencies qualify the risk of issues, the equivalent of facilities within a bank. Several issues from the same borrower have different ratings depending on their seniority level and their secured–unsecured status. The need for issuer, or borrower, ratings became more important because default probabilities are critical inputs, as are recoveries.

The most common way to assign default probabilities to facilities is through the internal rating system of the bank. This is the 'Internal Ratings-Based' (IRB) approach of the New Basel Accord. The forthcoming regulations on credit risk require these internal ratings to better capture risk differentiation than the former Cooke ratio. First from internal ratings to external ratings of rating agencies, and second from these to the historical default frequencies, as recorded historically by agencies for the portfolio of rated entities. Using this 'double' mapping assumes that such portfolios are representative of banks' portfolios, which is not the case in general. For instance, many rated entities are very large companies, while banks' borrowers are not.

The alternative route is to use models to generate internal ratings or default probabilities. When modelling ratings only, the mapping procedure above is again necessary to convert ratings into default probabilities. The difference with a standard internal rating system is the usage of a model to assign the rating, eventually modified by credit officers. The direct modelling of the default probability has existed for a long time. It is currently moving ahead under the incentives of regulators to generalize the usage of default probabilities within banks. There are various ways to reach this stage, with old and new generations of default risk models. Note that KMV is the only firm using a default probability model for listed firms and a portfolio model using the same conceptual framework.

Ratings and Default Models

In general, ratings depend on a number of factors, as explained in Chapter 35. Rating models try to replicate actual ratings using a function of some quantitative financial ratios plus, eventually, other qualitative variables. They use a wide spectrum of techniques, ranging from multivariate statistical analyses, regression analyses, to more elaborate logit–probit techniques, and up to neural network models. Rating models, however, do not suffice for portfolio risk modelling since it remains necessary to transform ratings into default probabilities.

Rather than modelling ratings, default models attempt to predict the default frequency. The main differences are:

- Default events are objective, whereas ratings are somewhat judgmental.
- Modelling directly default events does not require any conventional mapping of ratings to default probabilities.
- Default models provide directly the necessary inputs for portfolio models.
- Nevertheless, a default model requires databases on defaults to fit the models, which is an important difficulty given the relative scarcity of data on defaults and default sources.

Note that default models and rating models use symmetric processes. With rating models, we assign a rating and, through a mapping of ratings with default probabilities, we infer what the default probabilities are. With default models, we model directly the default probability, and then we infer the rating through mapping default probabilities with any rating scale. Default models have extended the range of techniques, using the now famous option model of default, originally presented by Merton (1974), and later made popular by KMV Credit Monitor, as explained below.

Techniques for Modelling Ratings and Default Probabilities

Various techniques apply to the modelling of ratings and of default probabilities, some of them being fairly old and others very recent.

The simple multivariate linear regression provides valuable fits between financial attributes and ratings, and it can extend to qualitative variables as well. This is a good starting point. More elaborated techniques improve the findings or better model default probabilities than ratings.

Scoring applied to firms was developed long ago with the pioneering work of Altman (1968). The technique applies to both default probability and rating modelling. It is still usable and similar techniques apply very well to consumer loans. The score is a function of observable ratios and variables. The rating, or default probability, depends on the score value. The scoring technique uses discriminant analysis to separate defaulting firms from non-defaulting firms. The discriminant function weights a number of observable variables to obtain a score. Depending on the value of the score, the firm is more or less likely to default. Once the score value is known, the default probability, conditional on the score value, differs from one firm to another.

The *logit–probit technique* allows direct modelling of the relationship between the observable variables and the rating class or the default probability. This is the RiskCalc methodology, as implemented by Moody's to measure default probabilities. Logit–probit techniques apply for modelling zero–one variables (default or no default), categories (such as ratings) or numerical values in the zero to one range, such as default probabilities.

The *neural networks approach* offers theoretical benefits over multivariate statistical fits. In general, there are correlations between the firms' attributes influencing statistically the ratings or the default probability. In addition, the relationship between default probabilities and observable attributes of firms is not linear. Neural networks accommodate interdependencies and non-linear relationships. These features might improve accuracy.

The *option theoretic approach to default* considers that equity holders have the option to sell the firm's assets rather than repay the debt if the asset value gets below the debt value. This is the Merton model of default (Merton, 1974). The option theoretic approach sees equity as a put option on the underlying assets of the firm sold to the lender with a strike equal to the debt amount. KMV Credit Monitor made this technique very popular by providing the 'expected default frequency' (Edf ©) using equity prices to derive asset value and compare it to the firm's debt. This is an expected default probability since equity prices look forward, as opposed to historical default statistics. KMV also provides a Private Firm Model that applies to private firms, for which equity values do not exist.

CPV proposes an *econometric modelling of default and transition rates* (Wilson, 1997a, b). The technique links the default rates of portfolio segments to the cyclical dynamics of industries and countries. The model uses two basic blocks. The first block models default rates of segments as a 'logit' function of economic variables (see Chapter 37 for a description of logit functions). The logit function ensures that the default rates are in the range 0 to 1 whatever the economic factor values. The second block uses a time series predictive model of economic factors that are input into the logit function. This allows looking forward and using predicted rather than past values of the economic index used by the logit function. Plugging these predicted values into the logit function results in predicted default rates. The model requires time series of default rates and economic factors that drive the credit standing of all obligors, since they are representative of country–industry conditions. As a prerequisite, it is necessary to measure default rates for portfolios, not individual default events. This makes it necessary to break down the portfolio into subsets by risk class plus any other relevant criteria. Among other contributions, this approach addresses directly the issue of linking default probabilities to the economic cycles, intuitively seen as major determinants of credit risk.

Another modelling technique for default probabilities consists of inferring them from observed market *credit spreads*. Credit spreads are the differences between the risk-free government rates and the yields of risky bonds. Credit spreads value credit risk, both default and migration risk plus recoveries, among other factors such as liquidity and risk aversion. The technique extracts the implied default probabilities from observed spreads. This requires modelling credit spreads as a function of credit risk characteristics. Simple models state that the value of a risky debt is equal to the discounted value of the expected cash flows, given the default probability, at the risk-free rate or, alternatively, to the discounted value at the risky market yield (credit spread included) of the contractual cash flows. From this equality, it is possible to find default probabilities, given a recovery rate, such that this equality holds. Because of market risk aversion, the corresponding default probabilities are 'risk-neutral', meaning that they apply under no risk aversion in the market (see Chapter 42 for details).

Credit Risk Drivers

KMV Portfolio Manager uses the asset value of firms as credit driver. CPV uses country–industry economic variables as risk drivers. Consequently, correlations between the individual credit events result from their dependence on common factors influencing asset values of firms or economic indexes driving the default probabilities. The correlation building of portfolio models uses one of these two approaches. Other models use empirical fits of ratings or defaults to observable attributes, but they do not assume any causal model between these attributes and the modelled ratings or default rates.

Exposure at Default and Recoveries

Most future exposures are uncertain as well as recoveries under default, hence the definitions of the 'Exposure At Default' (EAD) and the loss given default (Lgd) for measuring losses due to credit risk. Exposures at default are future and uncertain, as well as recoveries.

For the banking portfolio, only some contractual exposures are projected. Others require projections, usually based on business rules and assumptions. Exposures at default are time profiles of exposures, either contractual or expected.

For the trading portfolio, the holding period view prevails. Rules stipulate that credit risk is the risk independent of market movements, or specific risk, as defined when discussing market risk. For derivatives, it is not possible to easily trade them, making it necessary to revert to the 'hold to maturity' view of the exposure. Market-driven exposures of derivatives are defined as the time profile of peak positive exposures of instruments during their life, at a given confidence level. It is a common practice to transform uncertain exposures of derivatives into 'loan equivalents' for the horizon considered for credit risk. This bypasses uncertainty, however, because both exposure uncertainty and credit risk interact for determining random losses.

This is a limitation of existing portfolio models. Most models do not really capture exposure uncertainty, except through a judgmental assessment of exposure at default. None of the current versions of portfolio models accommodates derivative exposure risk. All models use the loan equivalent technique to capture derivative exposures, leaving for end-users the definition or the calculation, when adequate tools are available, of this loan equivalent.

Recoveries are a specific issue in credit risk because losses are net of any recovery. Whether or not the borrower defaults, we get back this fraction. The New Basel Accord allows recognition of some reasonably certain recoveries for alleviating capital charge. To some extent, it is possible to model recoveries according to the source of recoveries. In subsequent chapters, we show that some collateral-based transactions have a measurable risk, that the default probability of a primary borrower benefiting from third-party protection derives from the 'double default' rule, or joint default of borrower and guarantor. In other cases, recoveries rely on expert judgment, for assigning a recovery rate. A recovery rate is similar to a facility rating, because it characterizes the facility risk, rather than the obligor's risk, except that it quantifies the risk.

Portfolio models do not get into such details. They use an assigned recovery rate by facility, considered as an input. This is a drawback of models, because recovery is one of the major factors limiting losses, and recognized as such by the regulatory bodies. The only portfolio model that includes recovery uncertainty is KMV Portfolio Manager, which uses a 'beta' distribution for the loss under default, in percentage terms, whose mode is the user-defined expected value.

Credit Risk Valuation

Book value exposures do not change with risk migrations. Models ignoring such value changes are 'default-only' models. CreditRisk+ models defaults only. Marking-to-market values of loans imply that these values change when risk changes. The process uses the basic discounted cash flow model for valuing traded or non-traded facilities, using as discount rates the market risk-free rate plus the credit spread corresponding to the credit risk of the facility. This valuation captures the full effect of risk migrations on value rather than running in default mode only. Techniques for valuing migration range from modelling the distribution of credit risk drivers, such as asset values of firms and economic variables, to the usage of migration matrices, based on historical data, providing the frequencies of migrations for each of the final risk classes. Both expected value and value percentiles characterizing the standalone Value at Risk (VaR) of facilities derive from the distribution of values obtained through any one of these techniques (Figure 33.3).

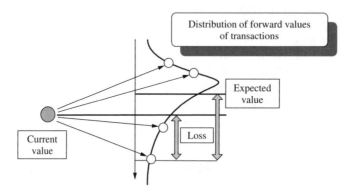

FIGURE 33.3   Forward valuation and loss valuation

Mark-to-market is only an option for modelling migrations of banking exposures. Marking-to-market makes explicit value changes when there are migrations across risk classes. KMV Portfolio Manager, Credit Metrics and CPV are full valuation models. KMV Portfolio Manager models migration by the distribution of the asset values at the horizon. Credit Metrics uses the same technique combined with transition matrices. CPV also uses the transition matrices, linking migration to the economic–industry variables influencing the default rates.

BLOCK II: PORTFOLIO RISK

Portfolio credit risk aggregates individual risks. Unlike market risk, where risk factors are market parameters readily observable, credit risk modelling faces unobservable credit risk drivers, making it necessary to model the underlying factors that drive the credit standing of obligors. Unlike market portfolio losses, which are observable, there is no way to back test credit risk portfolio losses because there is still very little data on such distributions of losses. Although the same basic principles inspire the models, with correlation modelling and generating loss distributions, the techniques differ significantly.

Credit Risk Correlation Modelling

The correlation building block of modelling portfolio credit risk is critical. Casual observation indicates that defaults are more numerous when economic conditions worsen. The observation suggests a positive correlation between default events. Moreover, models show that the loss percentiles measuring the VaR for credit risk are highly sensitive to correlations. Underestimating them would be misleading in terms of capital required to absorb portfolio losses. Note that correlations also apply to migration events in that migrations towards lower ratings are more frequent when economic conditions worsen, just as default rates increase. This is a most challenging conceptual issue, since the observation of joint default events does not happen often. The likelihood of joint default of any two well-established firms is in fact unobservable! The only way to address the correlation issue is therefore to model default events and to infer from the modelled events their joint probability of occurrence.

The correlation building block uses multi-factor models to derive the correlations between the drivers of modelled default events. Such drivers are the asset values of firms under the option theoretic approach and economic factors under the econometric technique. These models make the credit risk drivers dependent on a common set of factors. Since they depend on common factors, they vary in association (Figure 33.4).

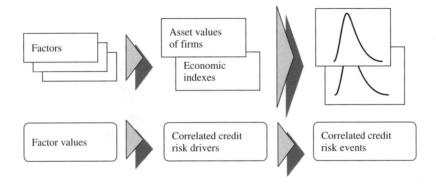

FIGURE 33.4 Modelling risk driver correlations

Modelling Default as an Option

Under the option theoretic approach of default as a put option, the factors driving the defaults are the asset values of firms. Default occurs when asset value falls below debt value. Therefore, correlated asset values trigger correlated default events. This principle applies in KMV Portfolio Manager. Credit Metrics uses the same principle, but uses correlation between equity returns as proxies of correlations of asset returns. In addition, Credit Metrics proposes to use joint migration matrices, providing the joint probabilities that a pair of firms in a given pair of risk classes migrates to any other pair of risk classes. One final class is the default state. Such joint migration probabilities increase with correlations. The dependence of asset returns or equity returns on a common set of factors generates the correlations.

Econometric Approach

The econometric approach of default rates modelling focuses on the relationship between the default rates of portfolio segments and the industry–country conditions. The technique is straightforward. The model uses a first direct logit relation between default rates of portfolio segments and an economic index, which depends on the industry–country economic variables. Since the default rates of different segments depend on a common set of factors, they tend to vary together when these factors change, thereby generating correlations between default rates.

Vendors' Models and Correlations

Other models take correlations as given, without modelling them directly, such as CreditRisk+ (Credit Suisse, 1997). The model applies to portfolio segments, as CPV does. The expanded version uses sensitivities of segment default rates to external factors. The direct connection between default rates and factors generates correlated default rates by segment. However, CreditRisk+ requires end-users to define such a relationship. By contrast, KMV Portfolio Manager and Credit Metrics provide the correlations. CPV provides a framework for modelling both default rates and correlations, but also leaves it to end-users to perform the necessary statistical fits, with end-user-selected variables.

Modelling Loss Distributions

The modelling of loss distributions for portfolios and credit risk is a direct result of correlation modelling in most cases. The VaR methodology necessitates the loss distribution in order to get the loss percentiles measuring capital and VaR. The fat tail of the distribution is critical since this is where large losses appear. Unfortunately, fat tails are difficult to model with accuracy. There are several techniques for modelling loss distributions:

- Using analytical loss distributions, under restrictive assumptions.
- Monte Carlo simulation of credit risk drivers and credit events.
- Modelling all joint transitions of all firms to all states including the default states, using the pair risk correlations.

Analytical Loss Distributions

The analytical approach specifies a parametric loss distribution under a restrictive set of assumptions. CreditRisk+ is the most accomplished example. It is a 'default model' that ignores migrations. It builds on actuarial insurance modelling to specify an analytical loss distribution resulting from the loss distributions of all portfolio segments, plus their eventual dependence on a common set of external factors. The benefit is that the loss distribution is easy and fast to compute. Nevertheless, CreditRisk+ makes simplifying assumptions to obtain an analytically tractable loss distribution and leaves it to the end-user to specify such key inputs as sensitivities of defaults to external factors.

Monte Carlo Simulations

The main technique to obtain correlated loss distributions is to use Monte Carlo simulation. The technique necessitates the correlation structure of the credit risk drivers. When asset values are risk drivers, it becomes a simple matter to generate random asset values such that each firm has a predetermined default probability. For each run, the asset value of each individual firm corresponds to a credit standing of this firm: the risk can improve or deteriorate, or ends up in default state. Implementing this technique requires only the correlation structure of asset values of firms. KMV Portfolio Manager and Credit Metrics (J. P. Morgan, 1997) use this technique.

With CPV, the random values of factors influence the default rates of segments. Under the econometric approach, default rates depend on economic factors that correlate. With the correlation structure, it is feasible to generate random values complying with this structure. With each set of factor values, it is possible to derive the default rates of portfolio segment through the logit function. Therefore loss distributions of portfolio segments correlate.

Modelling Joint Migrations

Another way of generating a loss distribution is the matrix approach proposed by the Credit Metrics technical document. The technique specifies the N possible migrations of each obligor, including to the default state (there are N risk classes). For each obligor, there is a value distribution with N final states, including the default state. For each pair of obligors, there are N^2 risk migrations possible, as many as there are combinations of final credit standing for the pair of obligors.

The transitions to risk classes are sensitive to correlations. If the risks of two firms tend to deteriorate simultaneously, rather than independently, their joint migration towards higher risk will have a probability higher than if their transitions were independent. The technique generates a distribution of values for the portfolio, which includes upward risk migrations (lower risk) resulting in higher mark-to-model values and downward risk migrations (higher risk) resulting in lower mark-to-model values, down to the default states.

Capital and Provisioning

Capital results from the loss distribution. VaR is the loss percentile corresponding to the selected confidence level. It depends on the horizon of the calculation of the loss distribution, on the valuation method of exposures and on the time profile of exposures when mark-to-model applies. Capital measures are: the loss percentile; the loss percentile net of expected loss under economic provisioning; the loss percentile net of expected revenues, minus expected losses, if these can serve for offsetting losses. The final capital measure requires a consistent set of rules.

Most models use a specified horizon, such as 1 year. The loss distribution results from the distribution of asset values at the horizon, using some value as the starting point for counting losses. KMV Portfolio Manager, Credit Metrics and CPV provide a VaR calculation at the horizon, in addition to defaults between the current date and the horizon. CreditRisk+ and CPV theoretically provide loss distributions over various horizons using cumulative default rates.

BLOCK III: CAPITAL ALLOCATION AND RISK CONTRIBUTIONS

The risk contribution of a facility to a reference portfolio is the risk of the facility not diversified away by the portfolio diversification. It is much lower than the standalone risk of the facility. Risk contributions serve several purposes:

- Measuring the risk not diversified away by diversification.
- Allocating capital to existing facilities or segments of the reference portfolio, and defining limits in capital.
- Allocating capital to new facilities or portfolios for decision-making purposes.
- Comparing risk-adjusted performances, for the existing portfolio, or defining risk-based pricing, for new transactions, using Risk-adjusted Return on Capital (RaRoC) measures.

There are different risk contributions:

- Absolute risk contributions sum to the portfolio loss volatility or the portfolio capital.
- Marginal contributions are the incremental risk of a facility or a portfolio segment to the reference portfolio. They are the difference of risks with and without the facility or the subset of facilities selected.

Models derive absolute risk contributions from the formula giving the variance of the portfolio losses as a function of individual facility value variances and covariances. Marginal risk contributions require a 'with and without' calculation of the portfolio risk.

KMV Portfolio Manager calculates the absolute risk contributions, and Credit Metrics provides the marginal risk contributions. Otherwise, end-users can calculate absolute risk contributions to the portfolio loss variance (volatility) using the analytical formula giving the portfolio loss variance (volatility) as a function of pair covariances. Running 'with and without' calculations provides marginal risk contributions.

In Chapters 51 and 52, we show that absolute risk contributions serve for capital allocation within an existing portfolio and that marginal risk contributions serve for risk-based pricing of new facilities.

BLOCK IV: RISK–RETURN VIEW

Once income and risk for a portfolio are available, it becomes possible to alter the risk–return profile of the portfolio by changing the structure of the portfolio. The rationale follows the classical portfolio optimization theory: minimize risk given return or maximize revenues given risk, or maximize the Sharpe ratio (expected return/volatility) of the portfolio.

Within this familiar theoretical framework, it is relatively straightforward to optimize 'mathematically' the portfolio, without integrating any business constraint. Only KMV Portfolio Manager offers a risk–return optimization function, but it ignores such constraints as limits on industries or countries for instance.

In addition, portfolio models serve as 'what if' tools for determining how portfolio management alters the risk–return profile of the portfolio. It becomes possible to find the effect of a securitization or of credit derivatives and insurance on the overall risk–return profile. 'What if' simulations help us to find which portfolio structures are better than others in terms of both risk and return. As such, portfolio models fully address the economics of portfolio management.

OVERVIEW OF TECHNIQUES AND CREDIT RISK MODELS

Table 33.1 maps all techniques subsequently developed in this text to the related specifications of the various vendors' portfolio models. Other commercial models include Credit Monitor from KMV and RiskCalc from Moody's for modelling default probabilities, or several models relating observed ratings to observable characteristics of firms, using various statistical techniques, not included in portfolio models.

TABLE 33.1 Mapping modelling techniques with vendors' models

Techniques	CreditRisk+	KMV Portfolio Manager	Credit Metrics	CPV
Valuation of exposures				
Book value (default model only)	×	×	×	×
Economic valuation (mark-to-model)		×	×	×
Uncertain exposures (derivatives)		Loan equivalents only		
Credit spreads				
Risk-neutral probabilities		×		
As inputs for valuation		×	×	×
Correlation between credit risk events,				
default and risk migrations				
Correlations from firm asset values		×		
Correlations from firm equity values			×	
Correlations from econometric modelling of				×
default rates and transition matrices				
Correlations as inputs only	×			
Recoveries				
Recovery uncertainty				×
Generating loss distribution				
Monte Carlo simulation		×	×	×
Analytical proxy loss distribution		×		
Analytical loss distribution	×			
Capital allocation				
ARC[a]		×		
MRC[a]			×	
Marginal risk contributions: 'with and without'	×	×	×	×
calculations				
RaRoC				
Overall and per facility with ARC		×		
Overall and per facility with MRC	×		×	
Portfolio optimization				
		×		

[a]ARC = Absolute Risk Contribution, MRC = Marginal Risk Contribution.
Notes: CreditRisk+, see Credit Suisse (1997); Credit Metrics, see J. P. Morgan (1997); CPV, see Wilson (1997a, b).

SECTION 13

Credit Risk: 'Standalone Risk'

34

Credit Risk Drivers

This chapter details the various credit risk drivers and discusses measurement issues for standalone risk. It introduces subsequent chapters dealing with the basic credit risk drivers for standalone risk.

Credit risk is the potential loss in the event of default of a borrower, or in the event of a deterioration in credit standing. The discussion extends over four major risk components: 'Exposure At Default' (EAD), default probabilities (DP), loss given default (Lgd) (Figure 34.1).

Exposure characterizes the amount at risk. Default and migration probabilities characterize the chances of defaulting and migrating across risk classes. Recoveries reduce the loss under default. They result from various types of guarantees, from collateral, third-party guarantees or covenants. Subsequent chapters detail each of these in terms of data availability and existing modelling techniques.

The traditional view of credit risk relates to borrowers, individuals, firms or financial institutions. Nevertheless, more and more specialized finance transactions deal with structures whose risk assessment is more challenging. The ultimate issue remains identical: what are the chances of losses and the magnitudes of losses? These depend on bundles of contractual covenants ruling the life of the structure.

The first three sections address the four basic risk drivers. The fourth section describes how standalone risk is measured. The last section addresses the issue of structure 'resiliency'. All sections refer to subsequent chapters, which expand specific issues and models on credit risk drivers.

EXPOSURE RISK

The first ingredient of credit risk is exposure, which is the amount at risk with the counterparty. In practice, exposure is the most common information variable for credit

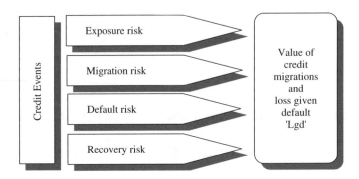

FIGURE 34.1   Credit risk and its underlying risks

risk. Credit risk management imposes limits on exposures by firm, industry or region. Exposure is the 'quantity' of risk. Nevertheless, defining what it is raises issues.

Exposures are either at book value or at mark-to-model values. Valuation of losses under book value ignores migration risk, and results in loss under default only. It is desirable to capture changes in credit standing, which do not materialize in the book value, but alter the default probability of a borrower. Marking-to-model exposures serve for valuing migrations, by discounting future flows from assets at a discount rate, adding the credit risk spread to the risk-free rate. Credit risk models capturing migration are full valuation models. Those using book values are default models. Valuation remains partial only because it usually refers to the credit risk component without considering interest rate movements and their values on the exposures. A full mark-to-market would include interest rates and risk premium changes in valuation, creating value volatility independent of credit risk. This would make it difficult to isolate the credit risk component.

Only future exposures are at risk by definition. This raises the issue of how to deal with uncertain exposures, such as future draws on a credit line for the banking portfolio or derivatives credit risk. Rules serve to characterize the 'Exposure At Default' (EAD).

Exposures for the market portfolio raise other issues because they are market-driven and tradable instruments can be sold at any time. For over-the-counter instruments, any positive liquidation value is the loss in the event of default of the counterparty. These exposures are market-driven, making it necessary to model their time profile under various market conditions. Best practices consider the highest potential values at several time points at a preset confidence level.

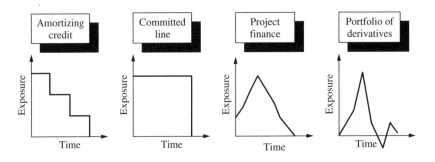

FIGURE 34.2   Time profiles of credit risk exposures: examples

The time profile of exposures varies widely with the type of transactions. Figure 34.2 illustrates some possible shapes based on authorization profiles (not projections), either for amortizing loans or for committed lines whose usage is uncertain.

Chapter 39 develops the modelling of exposures for market instruments.

DEFAULT AND MIGRATION RISKS

Default risk is the probability of the event of default. Several events qualify as 'default', which we review. Migrations are either deteriorations or improvements of the credit standing of obligors, which translate, respectively, into higher or lower default probabilities. For default events, losses are readily observable. For migrations, the valuation of risk necessitates a mark-to-market valuation.

Definitions of Default

There are several possible definitions of 'default': missing a payment obligation for a few days, missing a payment obligation for more than 90 days, filing for bankruptcy, restructuring imposed by lenders, breaking a covenant triggering a cross-default for all lenders to the same entity. It depends on default definition.

A payment delay of a few days for individuals or small businesses is closer to 'delinquency' than default, to the extent that the likelihood of getting the payment remains high. 'Payment default' commonly refers to a minimum period, such as 3 months after due date. Bankruptcy and restructuring are default events, since they follow major failure of payment obligations.

Covenants trigger default events. Nevertheless, there is a wide spectrum of covenants. Many trigger a 'technical' default, requiring a waiver from lenders before continuing operations. Such events usually initiate negotiation, whatever the risk to the borrower's survival. Some covenants trigger cross-default and cross-acceleration. Cross-default implies that a failure of payment with respect to any debt obligation of the lender triggers a default for all lenders. Cross-acceleration specifies that prompt repayments are due immediately, although this might only result in prompt renegotiation with all lenders. Still, without waivers granted by lenders, the borrower becomes bankrupt.

Another view on default is 'economic'. It occurs when the value of the assets of the borrower dips below the value of the debt. This is economic default under the Merton (1974) model, implemented in instrumental default models such as KMV Credit Monitor.

The definition of default is critical for estimating default probabilities and measuring historical default frequencies. Rating agencies usually consider that default occurs when missing a contractual payment. The New Basel Accord includes bankruptcy and restructuring as default events, and makes it necessary to build up histories of such events as well. Economic default differs from legal or conventional default rules, but serves for modelling default.

Finally, securitization structures and funds default when a breach of covenant occurs. The loss under default is more difficult to define than for a loan because default events of structures trigger early amortizations of the notes held by lenders with the amortization of the pool of assets securitized or through liquidation.

Default and Migration Probabilities

The probability that default occurs during a given period characterizes default risk. The probability that a firm migrates from one risk class to any other is a migration. Default is one of these migration states, except that it is an absorbing state.

Under default, the loss materializes and is the amount at risk less recovery. Valuing migrations is different. The migration probabilities result from historical data. Nevertheless, a migration to any state other than the default state does not trigger any loss in book value, although the default probability changes. Marking-to-market transactions value the change in credit quality because it discounts future flows at rates that depend on credit spreads, and credit spreads vary across credit states.

Historical data provide default frequencies according to a specific definition of defaults. Rating agencies provide historical frequencies of defaults of payments exceeding 90 days. Some central banks have default histories of both missed payments and bankruptcies. The drawback of such historical data is that they do not capture expected default rates. The next chapter provides an overview of historical data on defaults and recoveries using rating agencies' data.

A common practice is to map default frequencies with agency ratings. However, a rating is not a direct measure of a default probability of an issuer. Agencies rate the quality of risk of a debt issue, rather than the credit standing of the issuer, defined as the 'severity of losses', which depends on both default probability and recoveries under default. Therefore, ratings of issues in general do not correspond exactly to issuers' ratings and their default probabilities. Nevertheless, they do correlate with historical default frequencies. In practice, banks often assign internal ratings (see Chapter 35) and map them with agency ratings in order to map their own ratings with default frequencies.

This is the route proposed by the 'Internal Ratings-Based' (IRB) approach of the New Basel Accord. The alternative route is to model directly default events, such as KMV Credit Monitor or Moody's RiskCalc.

Several chapters deal with default and migration risk. One provides an overview of the historical data. Another deals with all the techniques for modelling default probabilities or ratings, using statistical techniques, such as RiskCalc and others. A chapter is dedicated to the option view on default used by KMV Credit Monitor.

RECOVERY RISK

The traditional credit culture stipulates that lending is primarily dependent on the credit standing of borrowers, not on covenants or guarantees. The rationale behind this prudent rule is that there is always a residual, small or significant, risk whatever the guarantees. In addition, the credit standing of the borrower ultimately makes the loan perform or not.

However, ignoring the value of guarantees would be misleading given their importance in lending decisions and their mitigating effect on loss under default. The loss in the event of default is the amount at risk at default time less recoveries. The New Basel Accord recognizes that some guarantees deserve recognition in assessing losses.

The main guarantees are:

- Collaterals, which are assets seized by the lender if the borrower defaults.
- Third-party protections. For guarantees, the guarantor fulfils the obligation of the borrower if he defaults. For insurance or credit derivative protections, a third party provides a payment to the lender under default.
- Covenants, which are contractual clauses such as maximum debt cover ratio or a legal obligation not to diversify away from the core business. Breaches of covenants trigger an obligation of prompt repayment, which prevents the borrower from continuing operations unless he gets a waiver. They are strong incentives to renegotiate with lenders in such instances.

Collaterals serve to limit both the lender's loss under default and the borrower's risk-taking propensity. A borrower is reluctant to give up the collateral whenever it has more value than the debt. Whenever the borrower's upside is higher than the value of debt, he has a powerful incentive to comply with the covenants.

On the other hand, a third-party guarantee does not provide any incentive for the lender to limit his risk propensity. However, it does reduce the probability of default, since default occurs only when both the primary borrower and the guarantor default. This is the 'double default' or 'joint default'. It provides a rationale for valuing the third-party guarantee as a reduction of the default probability, moving down from the borrower's default probability to the joint default probability of both obligors. The New Accord simply stipulates that the benefit of the third-party guarantee is a risk transfer to the guarantor. Chapter 40 expands the framework for valuing joint default probabilities in all cases where there is a borrower and a guarantor, which also includes insurance and usage of credit derivatives.

Another credit risk mitigant is the 'support from a third party', often a holding company of a borrower that is a subsidiary. Although support is informal and not contractual, it 'looks like' a third-party guarantee. Its value depends on the supporting entity incentives and willingness to face the obligations of the direct borrower.

The common practical way to value guarantees is to summarize their effects into a recovery rate. The recovery rate is 100% minus the loss given default. The loss in the event of default, or loss under default, is:

$$\text{Loss given default} = \text{exposure} \times (1 - \text{recovery rate } \%) = \text{exposure} \times \text{Lgd } \%$$

Recovery data from historical experience serves for valuing such forfeits. Historical recovery rates are available from rating agencies for bonds. They are the ratio of the post-default price of a bond to its pre-default price. Such rates vary inversely with the level of seniority of debt and are evidently higher for a secured debt than for an unsecured debt. The evidence shows that recovery rates vary widely from one transaction to another, and from one type of guarantee to another. Therefore, there is a need to differentiate the recovery rate by transaction type, seniority level compared to other debts and guarantee type.

Potential recoveries in the event of default are uncertain. Recoveries require legal procedures, expenses and a significant lapse of time. They occur in the future, are context-dependent (the situation of an obligor at the time of default) and depend on the nature of credit risk mitigants. Collateral might not be accessible. Real assets are subject to deterioration simply because there are many incentives to take them away when debtors know that they will loose them. Legal guarantees are subject to enforceability risk, or recourse risk. Covenant values depend on the borrower's ability to recover from credit deterioration at the time of a breach. Related chapters discuss the recovery risks according to the source of recovery (collaterals, guarantees, covenants).

Figure 34.3 summarizes the basic mechanisms of the credit-enhancing effect of guarantees. Collaterals transform credit risk into legal plus asset value risk. Third-party guarantees and support reduce the default probability of the joint entity 'borrower + guarantor'. Covenant values depend on how banks use them to prevent further risk deterioration. Chapters 40 and 41 expand the valuation of guarantees and the modelling recoveries.

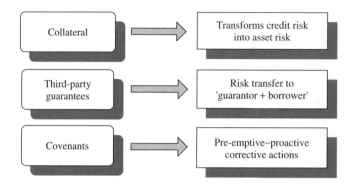

FIGURE 34.3   The risk-enhancing impact of guarantees

STANDALONE RISK

Forward valuation is at the horizon. Under default mode, each transaction has either its book value or its recovery value under default. Under full valuation mode, each transaction has a distribution of values at the horizon resulting from all possible credit risk migrations,

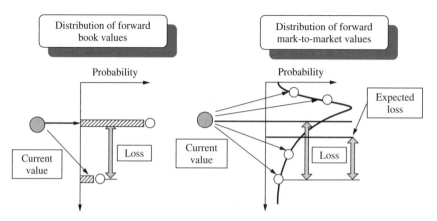

FIGURE 34.4   Forward valuation and loss valuation: with migrations and without migrations

inclusive of the default state. Figure 34.4 shows what happens under default mode only and under full valuation of migration risk. In the first case, value remains at book value and drops to the estimated recovery value under default, while in the second case, value increases occur when there are upward migrations.

The technique of modelling the value distribution at a future time point is implemented in the chapter concluding the review of credit risk drivers by an assessment of standalone credit risk (Chapter 43).

STRUCTURED FINANCE AND SPV

Another situation where credit risk measurement raises technical and specific difficulties is structured finance. Many structured finance transactions use Special Purpose Vehicles (SPVs). As their name indicates, these are dedicated entities to a special operation. SPVs serve in numerous structured transactions:

- Securitizations.
- Project finance.
- Asset financing.
- Leveraged Buy-Out (LBO).

The SPV issues structured notes in the market or gets funding from investors. The purpose of the SPV is to isolate the transaction from its sponsors while, at the same time, providing adequate protection to investors in notes or to lenders. It is bankruptcy remote for the sponsors.

Securitization SPVs differ from other SPVs in that they rely on quantitative models and covenants to define the adequate protection to investors in structured notes. Other SPVs provide protection to lenders and investors based on the insurance mechanisms protecting senior notes by routing first losses to subordinated notes, plus sets of covenants ruling the life of the structure.

Securitizations are non-recourse sales of the assets of a bank to a dedicated vehicle using these assets to provide for the structured note investors an adequate return in line with the risk of each class of note. Rating agencies rate each class of note, except the last one, the most subordinated one. The basic mechanism of structuring is to allocate the first random losses of the portfolio of assets sold to the SPV to the riskiest notes issued to fund the assets according to their seniority level. The first losses hit the subordinated ones first and, if they get bigger, they hit sequentially the notes above. The counterparty of the holders of the notes is the SPV. The SPV has the pool of assets as collateral and covenants rule the functioning of the structure. This is not a classical counterparty, hence the credit risk issue. Quantitative models combined with statistical laws ruling portfolio losses allow us to quantify the credit risk of the various notes. A structure capable of sustaining worst-case assets losses without hitting the notes is 'resilient'. Resiliency is the equivalent of credit risk for securitization SPVs.

In other structures, there is no portfolio of assets as collateral allowing us to use statistical laws to characterize the loss distribution. However, the principle is similar. The SPV might shelter a project in project financing, a fleet of aircraft for asset financing or the shares of a company for LBO. Notes or loans fund the structure.

In project finance, the sponsors put some equity into a project and leverage it with debt. The entire funding is located in the SPV, which is remote from the sponsors. The lenders get repayments from the cash flows of the projects, which are random. Nevertheless, the lenders might force the sponsors to perform some obligations, depending on how the project performs, such as adding more equity. For asset financing, the same basic scheme serves, separating the assets from the sponsors.

In LBO, the purpose is to buy the shares of a target company with the minimum amount of equity. This requires buying, for instance, 50% of the target company with a new holding company dedicated to this transaction (NewCo). The holding company uses a high leverage to minimize the equity required for the purchase of the shares. The profit generated by the target company serves to repay the lenders to the SPV. The LBO is sustainable only if the target company generates enough cash to repay the debt of NewCo, thereby limiting the debt raised by NewCo. Covenants serve to make sure that the actions of the target company do not alter the cash flow and profit of the target company and impair its repayment ability. The SPV is the holding company, whose share values pledged as collateral have no more value than the underlying target company. If the latter fails, the value of shares drops and the standing of the holding company does as well (Figure 34.5).

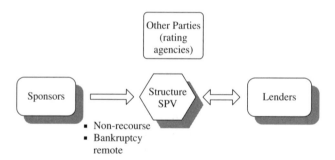

FIGURE 34.5   The common features of SPV structuring

In general, the SPV has no credit standing by itself. Its credit standing derives from the assets held and the various contractual clauses securing the notes issued to investors and rated by agencies when sold in the market.

Securitization SPVs are of interest for credit risk for at least two major reasons:

- They raise the issue of how to assess their credit risk, given that their collateral is a portfolio of assets. This suggests using portfolio models to assess the risk of such structures.
- They serve as vehicles for off-loading credit risk into the market.

For these reasons, we discuss the economics of securitizations in a dedicated chapter, after having reviewed the rationale of portfolio models and economic capital.

35

Rating Systems

Ratings rank the credit standing of debt issues using coded letters for the ratings from agencies. Ranks are 'ordinal numbers', not absolute values of the level of risk, by contrast with default probabilities whose value quantifies the likelihood of default over a given horizon. Internal ratings refer to ratings assigned by banks to their borrowers and their loans. Unlike agency ratings, which use public scales, internal ratings use proprietary scales that vary across banks. Both types of ratings serve as the foundation for the 'Internal Ratings-Based' (IRB) approach of the New Accord and should play an increasing role for differentiating credit risk of loans.

External ratings are those of debt issues, not of issuers. The ratings assigned to senior unsecured debt are close to issuer ratings since the debt defaults only if the issuer does. Subordinated debt might default without a default of senior debt. The secured debts benefit from various guarantees, acting as a 'shield' between the debt's risk and the 'pure' issuer's credit risk. The ratings of issues of facilities capture the 'severity' of losses, which is a combination of default probability and expected recovery.

Rating schemes use various criteria, from qualitative factors, such as strengths or weaknesses of firms, up to financials of corporate borrowers. Internal rating systems should use a rating scheme isolating the various ingredients of credit risk, default probability and recovery rates. This implies distinguishing the intrinsic rating of a borrower, the role of a supporting entity if any and the recoveries resulting from the guarantees attached to each facility. To move back and forth from internal ratings to default probabilities, as the IRB approach of regulators requires, a mapping between external ratings and internal ratings is necessary. It allows us to move from the internal to the external ratings and assign the default frequencies attached, through averages across debt issues, to external ratings. This mapping remains conventional. The alternative route, using directly models of default probabilities, is detailed in Chapter 37.

This chapter provides details about the philosophy underlying ratings and how they help in quantifying risks. The first section details the nature of external ratings. The second section describes the basic scheme underlying internal rating systems. The third section provides an overview of rating criteria. The last section explains how to move from internal ratings to default probabilities, one of the major credit risk drivers in risk models.

EXTERNAL RATINGS

The main, or global, rating agencies are Moody's, Standard & Poor's (S&P) and Fitch. Ratings are assessments of the credit standing of a debt issue, materialized by coded letters (such as Aaa, Aa, etc.) that serve essentially the needs of investors to have a third party view on the credit risk of debt. In addition, ratings rank risk rather than value risk. This is a major distinction between ratings and default probabilities, the latter being a quantification of the default likelihood of a debt issuer.

Rating agencies rate public issues rather than issuers. The same issuer usually has several debt issues, not all of them having the same risk. They all share the risk that the issuer defaults. However, issues differ by seniority levels and guarantees. Senior unsecured ratings are very close to issuer ratings because they benefit from first priority repayments in the event of default. Hence, the likelihood of loss is similar to the default likelihood of the issuer. Secured debts have collateral attached so that, in the event of default of the issuer, they benefit from higher recoveries. Subordinated debts are subject to claims from more senior lenders and have a higher risk. Therefore, the credit risk varies across debt issues of the same issuer, even though they all share the same default risk, which is specific to the issuer. Because senior unsecured debt is first to be repaid and does not benefit from any collateral other than the credit standing of the issuer, it is possible to consider senior unsecured debt ratings as issuers' ratings.

Ratings depend on fundamental analysis under a long-term view. Agencies tend to rate 'through the cycle' based on the long-term view of 'strengths and weaknesses, opportunities and threats' (SWOT) of firms. Hence, ratings do not change frequently under normal conditions because short-term deviations due to current conditions are not relevant as long as they do not alter durably the credit standing of an obligor. However, agencies continuously review their ratings on a periodical basis or under occurrence of contingent events that affect the credit standing of an issuer. An example of such an event is a merger or an acquisition, which changes significantly the risk profile of a corporate borrower. Rating agencies also provide short-term ratings and signal ratings under review to investors.

External ratings apply to various debt issues from: corporate firms; banks and financial institutions; sovereign borrowers (country risk); multilateral development banks. Ratings also apply to currencies, including local currency and foreign currency held locally and subject to transfer risk, the risk of being unable to transfer cash out of the country. By contrast, an issuer's rating characterizes the credit standing of an issuer and should correlate with its default probability.

Ratings from agencies exist only for issues of large listed companies. This creates a bias when assigning default frequencies based on historical default statistics because the sample of counterparties rated by agencies is usually not representative of the banks' portfolios. For bank corporate loans or market counterparties, external agency ratings are usually not available because borrowers are medium or small businesses. Banks need to rely on their own internal rating schemes to differentiate the risk of their exposures to these counterparties.

Internal rating scales differentiate 'investment grade' and 'speculative grade' (riskier) ratings. Moody's simplified rating scale uses three levels for investment grade ratings and the next three levels are 'speculative' grade. Detailed scales include 20 levels, excluding the near default states, for Moody's, S&P and Fitch. The next chapter shows how to map rating scales with historical data on default and migrations. It shows that default frequencies increase drastically when ratings move down along the scale (towards riskier classes).

In general, a typical rating scale uses such general qualifications of credit risk as 'highest', 'high grade', 'some risk' or 'vulnerable', 'highly vulnerable'. The qualifications of various levels do not make fully explicit the criteria used for ratings, although all agencies provide methodology notes. This makes sense given that there is a wide variety of criteria influencing the credit standing of a borrower.

INTERNAL RATING SYSTEMS

Internal rating systems are not public and are customized to each bank's needs. There is a strong tendency towards harmonization due to the new regulations putting the rating system in a central position for evaluating capital requirements. Since capital requirements affect pricing, the banking industry needs common benchmarks. Banks have exposure to all sorts of counterparties and across industries and countries. Therefore, all banks also need ratings for various types of entities: corporate firms; banks; country ratings.

Like external ratings, internal ratings are grades assigned to borrowers or facilities for ranking their risk relative to each other. Unlike external ratings, the counterparties of banks are usually non-rated entities, such as small or medium size businesses. Internal ratings isolate the borrower's risk from the facility risk, which depends on how secured it is. Internal ratings result from a review of both borrowers and facility characteristics.

Typical components of internal rating systems include:

- Borrower's risk.
- Eventual support from a supporting entity, typically a holding company supporting a subsidiary.
- Facility risk (a facility being any transaction), the equivalent to a debt issue for public firms.

The intrinsic borrower's risk is the risk of a corporate as a standalone entity. The support of another entity can strongly affect the risk of the couple 'primary borrower + supporting entity'. Facilities might benefit from a wide spectrum of guarantees, strongly mitigating the credit risk.

Support plays a major role in enhancing intrinsic ratings. The support can be formal, for government owned companies for instance. In general, support designates a less formal relationship linking a holding company to its subsidiary. If the subsidiary is in the core business of the parent company, chances are that the parent company will not let it down. To assess support, it is necessary to assess the credit standing of the direct borrower, that of the supporting entity and the 'strength' of the support. Combining support assessment with intrinsic rating provides the borrower's overall rating.

For facilities, other factors mitigate credit risk, mainly the seniority level and the guarantees attached to single facilities. Hence, a well-collateralized facility might have a good rating even though the borrower has a poor credit standing. Facility ratings are not the rule for banks' internal systems. The risk mitigants of a facility relate directly to recovery in the event of default. Recovery rates based on experience, type of transaction and type of guarantee now serve as a substitute for facility ratings, sometimes used. Chances are that these forfeits will evolve into hard data with historical statistics from default built up under the incentives of the regulators.

Internal ratings of banks should ideally include:

- The intrinsic rating of the borrower.
- In the presence of a supporting entity:
  - The rating of the supporting entity;
  - A rating qualifying the 'intensity' of support of a parent company if any.
- The overall borrower rating, given the intrinsic rating, the supporting entity rating and the assessment of support.
- An assessment of the guarantees, which should be converted into a recovery rate of loss given default rate for capital requirement purposes. It is desirable to differentiate recovery rates according to the nature of guarantees.

Rating systems require business rules for implementation. A common and important example are the rules relating sovereign risk to corporate or banking borrowers. When country risk materializes as transfer risk, it becomes unfeasible to recover cash from a local borrower. This is a rationale for capping intrinsic borrower's ratings by the country rating. If the latter materializes, the lender faces a default due to transfer, even though the borrower's credit standing remains unaffected. There is a strong case, however, for splitting country and borrower risks rather than linking them mechanically, because local borrowers might be in good shape while the country's credit standing has declined. The local borrower's credit standing is probably adversely affected by the country's local situation. Country crises materialize by the deterioration of the credit standing of local private entities. Similar links exist between the quality of banking supervision and banks' ratings. If the supervision process is loose, chances are that the banks' information is less reliable. If it is stringent, using the intrinsic rating of banks and of holding companies based on their financial situation is more reliable. In this case, we split again the rating process into a two-stage process: the assessment of the supervisory process and that of the bank's risk based on the bank's specifics.

Figure 35.1 summarizes a possible structure for a rating system.

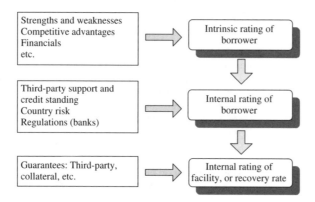

FIGURE 35.1 Internal rating systems

RATING CRITERIA

Rating criteria include both qualitative assessment of the counterparty's credit standing plus quantitative variables, most of them being financial variables. Rating a corporate entity will always involve qualitative and judgmental components, simply because there are too many factors that influence the situation of a corporate and of a financial entity. What follows cannot be comprehensive, but provides an overview of the nature of rating criteria.

The basis for assessing the credit risk of a company does relates to its fundamentals. These include all strengths, weaknesses, opportunities and threats ('SWOT') plus any barriers to entry that provide a shield from competition. Among major factors driving corporate firms' health are: industry, possibly oligopolistic, with few competitors; market share and size; diversification of products and services, and across countries; growth potential; technology; quality of products and services; plus all barriers to entry. Other factors include management quality and record of accomplishment. Some of these factors relate to the firm's future potential as well as to risk. Typical risk factors are business risk, possibly measured with the cyclical dynamics of sales or simply the economics of the industry, some of them being more stable across time than others (capital-intensive industries, consumer durable), or the level of vertical integration which drives the ratio of fixed to variable costs.

Criteria differ depending on the type of counterparty. For financial institutions, some ratios have a specific importance, such as the capital to assets ratio or the ratio of loan loss reserves to total loans. In addition, the relevance of banking information depends on the regulator's requirements. If these impose stringent constraints on local banks, chances are that the bank's information is reliable. If regulation practices are sound, the intrinsic quality of the bank is a major factor. Otherwise, the supervisory system drives the ratings because the information from financial institutions becomes unreliable. It is preferable to look first at the banking industry as a whole and then at country risk.

We provide below a grid of financial criteria applicable to corporate borrowers. This grid ignores such important qualitative variables as management quality or support, because we focus in this sample grid on financial attributes that can serve as inputs in rating models. Evidently, however, such qualitative variables as market outlook, management

TABLE 35.1   Financial attributes affecting the credit standing of corporate firms

Nature of variable	Measures	Comments
Size	In terms of total assets, or sales or profit measures such as Earnings Before Interest, Taxes and Depreciation (EBITDA) or net income	
Operating profitability	Operating return on assets	Operating profitability is before interest, amortization and taxes
	Operating margin or operating profit/sales	
Financial profitability	Return on equity, or net income over equity	Depends on both profitability and leverage or debt to equity ratio
Financial structure	Debt to equity structure, debt/equity	Usually based on financial debt only, ignoring operating debt (payables)
	Debt structure or senior debt to subordinated debt	Seniority structure of debt
	Financial coverage ratio such as EBITDA/interest	Measures the ability to face debt obligations from operating cash flows
Cash flow	Operating cash flow, or free cash flow	'Free cash flow' is the cash flow generated from operations and operations only available to face debt obligations. Operating cash flow is EBITDA minus cash locked into operations (in inventories, receivables minus payables)
Operating efficiency	Inventories turnover	Overall current operations efficiency
	Receivables in days of sales	
	Payables in days of purchases	
	Net cash cycle	
Operating leverage	Ratio of direct and variable cost to fixed costs	Measures flexibility under adverse conditions
Liquidity	Short-term cash and investments over total assets	
	Current ratios and other variations	Ratios of liquid assets over short-term liabilities
Market value	Equity to book value	Measures the market assessment of current and future profitability
	Price to book value	
Volatility of earnings and sales	From time series of sales and profit	Measures the business risk and its effect on profitability

track record, or industry would nicely complement this grid limited to quantitative variables. Note also that all variables refer to corporate borrowers. A different list of financial ratios would be more relevant for banks.

Quantitative variables are mainly financial, although other observable attributes might also convey relevant information. Under a normative view, a grid of financials applying to a corporate borrower could be as in Table 35.1. Note that the models relating observable attributes to ratings do not effectively use all of them. In addition, empirical findings show that some variables discriminate effectively credit standing in some broad classes of firms and not in others. Such broad classes are defined by ratings, i.e. investment grade versus speculative grade, or size bands, i.e. very large firms versus middle sized or small firms. Empirical findings using the techniques of Chapter 37 are that credit standing is sensitive to operating profitability, measured as 'Return On Assets' (ROA), size and financial leverage (debt to equity ratio), and market to book value, when available, which presumably captures the efficiency of capital markets in assessing the strengths and weaknesses of firms. Note also that many of these variables are correlated, i.e. that highly profitable firms have relative leverage and so on.

EXTERNAL RATINGS AND DEFAULT PROBABILITIES

The IRB approach to capital requirements of the New Basel Accord makes the internal ratings a critical building block of the credit risk management within banks. Banks adopting the 'standardized' approach rely only on external ratings, plus the uniform 100% weight for all unrated entities. Since the majority of bank transactions are usually with unrated entities, the standardized approach does not remedy the major drawback of the old system, that of not being risk-sensitive enough. When moving to the foundation and advanced approaches, ratings become the basis for defining default probabilities.

The simplest technique is to map internal ratings to external ratings and use the correspondence between external ratings and default probabilities to obtain the missing link from internal ratings to default probabilities (Figure 35.2). Such techniques assume that the mapping of internal to external ratings is correct and that the mapping of agency ratings to default probabilities is also.

It is easy to challenge both assumptions. Internal rating scales differ from agency rating scales, in terms of what ratings represent, and the correspondence is judgmental. The mapping process necessitates grouping some categories in order to 'match' given external classes. Agency ratings relate to 'severity of losses', a combination of default probability and recovery rate. Unsecured senior ratings should relate better to default frequencies. However, default probability models (Chapter 37) suggest a significant variance of default frequencies of firms within the same rating class.

FIGURE 35.2   From internal ratings to external ratings and default statistics

The expected loss is the product of the default probability and the loss given default:

$$EL = DP \times (1 - Lgd)$$

For instance for the same default probability, say 0.2%, the recovery rate could be 0% or 80% depending on the specifics of a debt issue. The expected losses are respectively $0.2\% \times 100\% = 0.2\%$ and $0.2\% \times 20\% = 0.04\%$. The expected loss quantifies the 'severity of loss', which agencies capture synthetically in their ratings. The merit of the simple expected loss equation is that it illustrates how to separate the issuer's risk from the issue risk. A second application is to assign an equivalent rating from expected loss calculations of debt issues, given their recovery rates. For instance, from Table 36.1, a 0.2% default probability in the simplified rating scale corresponds roughly to a Baa rating and a 0.04% default rate is close to an Aa rating. This allows assigning ratings from expected loss calculations. The 0.2% expected loss percentage maps to a senior unsecured Baa rating. The 0.04% value maps to an equivalent Aa senior unsecured rating. Note that, in this second case, the default probability, 0.2%, remains the same, corresponding to the Baa rating. Because of the higher recovery rate, however, the equivalent rating moves significantly up in the rating scale to a higher grade.

36

Credit Risk: Historical Data

Historical statistics of rating agencies are a first source of data on defaults and migrations based on bond issues. Defaults occur when a borrower fails to comply with a payment obligation. A migration, or a 'transition', is a change of risk class. Historical data for loans also exists in banks. This chapter refers to publicly available data from rating agencies.

Historical data report risk statistics as frequencies (numbers or percentages) of a reference population sample. Percentages are either arithmetic or weighted averages, notably for default rates, using size of defaulting bonds as weights. Agencies group data by risk class, defined by rating, to report default and migration rates over a given period for all ratings. Default and migration 'rates' are historical statistics, as opposed to the predicted 'expected default frequency' (Edf ©) as defined by KMV Corporation. Many applications use such rates as proxies of default and migration probabilities, although historical data are backward looking while probabilities are forward looking.

Rating systems combined with statistics on defaults allow us to relate them to default and migration frequencies. Public historical credit risk statistics include: yearly default rates by rating class; cumulative default rates over time; annualized cumulated default rates; yearly default rate volatilities; transition matrices; averaged recovery rates. Internal bank data warehouses might have detailed credit risk data by borrower and transaction. Banks map their internal ratings to external default frequencies, using an intermediate mapping between their own ratings and those of external agencies.

Some major empirical findings include: default frequencies increase much more than proportionally when moving from good to high risk classes; cumulative default rates increase less than proportionally with horizon for high ratings, and more than proportionally for lower rating classes; default rates relate inversely to the default rate volatility of each risk class.

Transition matrices provide the frequencies of migration between any pair of rating classes, for varying horizons. They serve for valuing migration risk. The value of downside migrations (riskier ratings) results from the wider credit spreads embedded in market rates for discounting future flows when marking to market loans on bonds. The value of the transaction becomes lower than the current value, resulting in a loss. Both cumulative and marginal default rates are useful to characterize default risk through a succession of future periods. Forward default rates are frequencies of default of firms having survived up to a specified date for subsequent periods beyond this starting date.

The first two sections describe the main types of available statistics. The third section addresses migrations across risk classes. The last section addresses the 'term structure of default rates' with cumulative rates over different horizons and marginal default rates, or 'forward default rates', between any two dates in the future.

DEFAULT RISK STATISTICS

The external ratings map to yearly and cumulated default rates, as shown below. Calculations of default rates refer to numbers of firms or are value weighted by size of defaulted issues. When calculating a default rate, it is necessary to refer to a specific number of surviving firms at the beginning of the period. The process implies the following steps:

- Aggregating default data for a given cohort of firms, defined by those firms surviving and rated at the beginning of a given year.
- Breaking down the cohort into subportfolios by rating.
- Calculating the default rate as the ratio of the number of defaults in a given period over the total of surviving firms at the beginning of the period (or a size-weighted ratio).

It is possible to aggregate cohorts across years when using larger populations.

Yearly Default Rates

Yearly default rates are ratios of defaulted firms to surviving firms at the beginning of the year. There are arithmetic default rates and value weighted default rates.

The default rates of a rating class and its volatility over time derive from these statistics. The default rates are close to zero for the best risk qualities. They increase to around 8% a year for the lowest rating class (in the six-class simplified rating scale). Table 36.1 shows the magnitude of yearly default rates for the six rating classes in Moody's simplified rating scale. Actual values vary every year. The top three ratings characterize investment grade borrowers. The other three classes are speculative grade. For investment grade borrowers, the yearly default rate is below 0.1%. For speculative grade borrowers, it ranges from 0.2% to 8% a year.

Figure 36.1 shows the characteristic shape of average default rates by detailed rating class, growing far more than proportionally for the lowest (riskiest) ratings. The increase in default rate when ratings decline has an 'exponential' shape. The increase in default rate from one class to another changes drastically. In order to improve the rating by one grade, the required variation of default rate is around 6% for the last two classes of the

TABLE 36.1   Ratings and default statistics from Moody's

Moody's ratings	Yearly averaged default rates	Yearly volatility of default rates (1970–1997)
Aaa	0.00%	0.00%
Aa	0.05%	0.12%
A	0.08%	0.05%
Baa	0.20%	0.29%
Ba	1.80%	1.40%
B	8.30%	5.03%

Source: Moody's Investors Service, 1997.

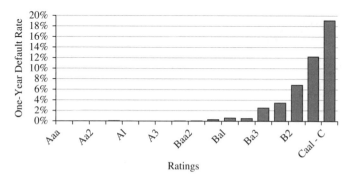

FIGURE 36.1   Yearly default rates and ratings

Source: Adapted from Moody's Investors Service, January 2000.

scale. At the other end of the scale, a small decrease of 0.05% suffices to improve the grade from Aa to Aaa.

Improving the rating of a bank is of major importance. Ratings drive the cost of borrowing for banks and their eligibility to participate in certain activities. Since economic capital calculation uses a confidence level that represents the default risk of the bank, the table shows that targeting investment grade ratings implies very tight confidence levels, way below 0.1%. The required improvement of solvency (default probability) required to gain one rating 'notch' is much higher at the lower (riskier) end of the scale than at the other end. The importance of modelling the fat tail of the loss distribution follows.

Cumulative Default Rates

Default rates cumulate over time. Figure 36.2 shows the characteristic shapes of the default frequency time profiles by rating. The default rates increase with the horizon. The longer the period, the higher the chances of observing a default. The growth of default rates with horizon is not proportional. For high ratings, or low default rates, the increase is more than proportional. For low ratings and high default rates, it is less than proportional. High-risk borrowers improve their risk when they survive for a longer time. Low-risk borrowers face risk deterioration when time passes. All these observable facts are important to differentiate the risks across time and to value both expected and unexpected losses.

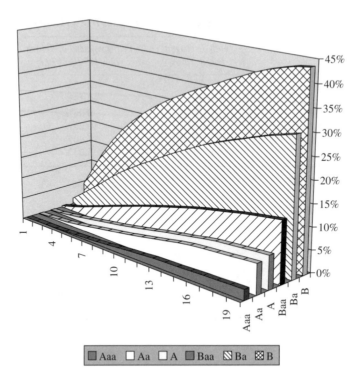

FIGURE 36.2 Average cumulative default rates by letter rating from 1 to 20 years (1920–1999) (%)
Source: Adapted from Moody's Investors Service, January 2000.

Annualized rates serve for constant provisioning across all years and up to maturity. Annualized rates are higher than yearly spot rates when rates increase less than proportionally to the horizon. The opposite holds when rates increase less than proportionally with time. If the cumulated default rate is 3.5% for 2 years, the annualized default rate is 3.5%/2 = 1.75%. It is higher than the spot default rates, for instance 2%. For a 2-year maturity exposure, the annualized default rate will be 1.75%. For a 1-year exposure, it will be higher.

Default Rates Volatility

Default rates are unstable when time passes. The volatility of yearly historical default rates is the standard deviation of observed time series. The volatility increases with the level of default rate, when the rating decreases. Historical volatilities are available from rating agencies for default rates observed across varying horizons. If the volatility is high, the potential deviations of the default rates around the average can be significant. If the volatility is low, deviations are small. The unexpected losses will be higher in the first case (Table 36.2).

Volatility provides a simple way to measure unexpected loss for loan portfolios. The loss volatility is the standard deviation. The expected loss is proportional to the average default rate.

TABLE 36.2 One-year default rate volatility statistics, 1970–1999 (%)

	Aaa	Aa	A	Baa	Ba	B	Caa-C
Median	0.00%	0.00%	0.00%	0.00%	0.84%	5.90%	21.34%
Mean	0.00%	0.03%	0.01%	0.18%	1.34%	6.75%	24.36%
Maximum	0.00%	0.80%	0.35%	1.89%	5.32%	24.00%	67.50%

Source: Moody's Investors Service, January 2000.

The volatility of default rates supports the view of a positive correlation between default events across obligors. The Credit Metrics technical document provides a simple equation to derive the implicit uniform correlation between default probabilities of obligors within the portfolios. The underlying intuition is that the higher the correlation ρ, the higher the volatility of default rates because defaults trigger numerous others if correlation gets higher. The formula below provides the average default correlation ρ for large values of N, the number of names covered by the data, as a function of d, the average default rate over the years, and σ the standard deviation of the default rates observed from year to year[1]:

$$\rho = N\{[\sigma^2/(d - d^2)] - 1\}/(N - 1)$$

RECOVERY STATISTICS

Recovery statistics are based on the prices of defaulted bonds, calculated as the ratio of the defaulted issue to its par value. Recovery rates vary by seniority levels, as shown in Table 36.3. There is a wide variation around the mean, so that the actual ranges across types of debts widely overlap. For instance, 50% of the senior subordinated bonds recovery rates are in the range 20% to 40% (rounded values), while the mean is around 33%. Moreover, recovery rates of senior secured bonds, senior unsecured bonds and senior subordinated bonds. Another empirical fact pointed out by Moody's is that recovery rates seem correlated with economic conditions. Hence, when these worsen, chances are that recoveries also do. Most models using recoveries as an input do not account for such correlations.

TABLE 36.3 Recovery rates by seniority level of debt

	Recovery rates
Senior secured loans	70%
Senior secured bonds	52%
Senior unsecured bonds	49%
Subordinated bonds	33%

Source: Moody's Investors Service, January 2000.

Recoveries are a major determinant of loss under default. Therefore, it is not surprising that the New Accord focuses on building up recovery data. Recovery data by seniority level, types of products and nature of guarantees would help differentiate more significantly average recoveries for these subclasses and cross-sections in the future.

---

[1] From Credit Metrics, Technical Document, April 1997.

TRANSITION MATRICES

When time drifts, the risk either improves or deteriorates. These shifts are captured by the transition frequencies between risk classes. Within a given period, transition rates between classes are transfer frequencies divided by the number of original firms in each risk class. It is possible to map rating classes with observed credit spreads in the market. With such a mapping, we can assign different credit spreads to the final credit state, and value accordingly a loan or a bond. This allows us to generate a distribution of values at a forward horizon for any asset with a given original rating class. This is a common technique for valuing migration risk in credit risk models.

The transition matrices look as in Table 36.4. Since the higher transition frequencies occur mostly in the neighbouring classes of ratings, there is a concentration along the first diagonal of the matrix. Each row and each column is a rating class, the last one of each row being the default state. Each cell, at the crossing of initial rating A and final rating Baa for instance, provides the observed transition rate from the initial rating A to the final rating Baa, or 5.87% (cell with a border). All probabilities sum to 1 across rows because each row lists all possible final states, inclusive of the default state. The default state is an absorbing state. Once in default, there is no way out. Since the default state is an absorbing state, there is a probability of 100% of staying in the default state and zero probability of getting out. The default frequencies for all ratings are in a column at the right-hand side of the table. The last column shows withdrawn ratings. All totals by row are 100%, because the rows show all possible migrations, plus defaults and withdrawals.

TABLE 36.4   All-corporate rating transition matrix, 1999 (%)

Rating from:	Rating to:									
	Aaa	Aa	A	Baa	Ba	B	Caa-C	Default	W[a]	Total
Aaa	95.41%	2.75%	0.00%	0.00%	0.00%	0.00%	0.00%	0.00%	1.83%	100%
Aa	1.99%	88.05%	5.38%	0.00%	0.00%	0.00%	0.00%	0.00%	4.58%	100%
A	0.00%	2.28%	89.02%	5.87%	0.11%	0.33%	0.00%	0.00%	2.39%	100%
Baa	0.12%	0.36%	4.79%	86.11%	5.27%	1.08%	0.00%	0.12%	2.16%	100%
Ba	0.00%	0.14%	0.29%	7.07%	74.46%	9.38%	0.87%	1.01%	6.78%	100%
B	0.00%	0.00%	0.23%	0.35%	3.95%	77.24%	6.50%	5.46%	6.27%	100%
Caa-C	0.00%	0.00%	0.00%	0.00%	0.00%	5.26%	70.33%	18.66%	5.74%	100%
Total	97.52%	93.58%	99.71%	99.40%	83.79%	93.29%	77.70%	25.25%	29.75%	

[a]W=Withdrawn.
Source: Moody's Investors Service, January 2000.

The sum of all migrations to the Aaa class is: $95.41\% + 1.99\% + 0.12\% = 97.52\%$. This is the total of all transition percentages leading to rating class Aaa (total of the first 'Aaa' column). The total percentages ending in each rating class are in the bottom row of the table. Transition matrices are subject to constraints: all rows sum to 1 because they group, together with the default state, all possible migrations; all migration probabilities are positive and lower than 1.

Rating agencies publish several matrices, typically 1 year, 2 years and 5 years. Should the transition probabilities be stationary, we could simply use the same yearly matrix one, two or five times to get a final structure by risk class at the horizon of 5 years. However, the 5-year transition matrix is not a simple (matrix) multiplication of the 1-year transition matrix because transitions and default probabilities are not proportional to time.

THE TERM STRUCTURE OF HISTORICAL DEFAULT RATES

This section shows how to model the term structure of historical default rates from historical raw data. The technique allows us to assign probabilities of default at various forward periods. As mentioned above, there are various default rates, arithmetic or value weighted. The first step is to define the number of firms surviving at the beginning of the period. Statistics follow from this number.

Tables from rating agencies provide cumulative default probabilities from inception of a cohort up to any future date. A cohort groups all rated firms at the beginning of the observation period. We use here only one cohort, created at a past date 0. In fact, there are as many cohorts as there are years of observation.

The following presentation ignores some technicalities, well documented in technical notes of rating agencies. These include rating withdrawals and variations of defaults across cohorts due to changing economic conditions. Rating withdrawals are not defaults and require adjustments to use the actual numbers of rated firms between any two dates. In addition, some cohorts were created at the beginning of an economic cycle, some at a peak cycle and others at the end of a cycle. Figures vary from one cohort to another, reflecting the varying economic conditions across cohorts. We assume that all firms having a rating at date 0 still have one at the current date. We focus only on the calculation of marginal and cumulative default rates over a given population of firms. Finally, we ignore value weighting or issues that defaulted, and limit the presentation to arithmetic calculations.

For the cohort created in 0, counting a number $N(0)$ of firms, we observe defaults every year. The arithmetic default rate at any year t, beginning at date t and ending at date $t + 1$, compares the count of defaults between t and $t + 1$ to the original number of firms within the cohort formed at date 0 and the surviving firms of this cohort at t. We use the following notation: capital letters designate numbers and lowercase letters are rates or percentage ratios. $S(0, t)$ is the number of firms surviving at date t. $S(0, 0) = N(0)$ is the original number of firms of a cohort created at date 0. From these definitions, we derive the cumulative count of defaults from 0 up to t, or $D(0, t)$, and the corresponding default rate $d(0, t)$, as well as the number of surviving firms at t, or $S(0, t)$ and the survival rate $s(0, t)$.

The cumulative number of surviving firms at t is $S(0, t) = N(0) - D(0, t)$. The number of firms $S(0, t)$ surviving at t is lower than the original number of firms $N(0)$. The total number of defaults is the summation of all defaults from 0 to the end of period t, or $D(0, t) = N(0) - S(0, t)$. The ratio of the surviving firms at t, $S(0, t)$, to the original number in the cohort, $N(0)$, is the cumulative survival rate from 0 to t, a percentage: $s(0, t) = S(0, t)/N(0) = [N(0) - D(0, t)]/N(0) = 1 - D(0, t)/N(0)$. Dividing $D(0, t)$ by $N(0)$ provides the cumulative default rate at t: $d(0, t) = [N(0) - S(0, t)]/N(0) = 1 - s(0, t)$.

$D(t, t + k)$ is the number of defaults between dates t and $t + k$. It is a forward count of defaults. For $k = 1$, $D(t, t + 1)$ is the number of defaults within the year starting at date t and ending at $t + 1$, or the marginal rate of default from t to $t + 1$. The marginal default rate between t and $t + 1$, or $d(t, t + 1)$, is the percentage of the number of firms defaulting between t and $t + 1$, or $D(t, t + 1)$, to the number of surviving firms at t, $S(0, t)$. The number of surviving firms at t is $S(0, t) = N(0) - D(0, t)$. The count of defaults between dates t and $t + 1$ is $D(t, t + 1)$ and the forward, or marginal default rate at t up to $t + 1$ is $d(t, t + 1) = D(t, t + 1)/S(0, t) = D(t, t + 1)/[N(0) - D(0, t)]$.

Historical survival rates, marginal or cumulated, or default rates, marginal or cumulated, can serve as survival or default probabilities when looking forward. When looking at historical data, we obtain historical estimates of probabilities. These are estimates of 'natural' or real probabilities.

37

Statistical and Econometric Models of Credit Risk

The usual qualitative assessment of individual risks of borrowers, other than individuals, relies on ratings. However, models of individual risks have existed for a long time. Due to the current emphasis on extensive data on individual borrower's risks, modelling became attractive for assessing risk in a comprehensive and objective manner, and for complying with the New Basel Accord recommendations.

Statistical models link observable attributes of borrowers to actual ratings or to observed default or no default events. The alternative view consists of considering that a drop of the asset value of a firm below the threshold of short-term debt obligations triggers the firm's default. This second approach, based on the Merton (1974) model, relies on values derived from equity prices of publicly listed firms. Statistical techniques do not rely on conceptual models, as the Merton model does, but on statistical fits. This chapter addresses the statistical approaches. There are several generations of models of credit risk and default probabilities, starting from the early statistical models linking ratings to financial characteristics of firms, up to elaborate econometric techniques and neural network models. This chapter focuses on statistical techniques. The next chapter focuses on the option modelling of default probability, its conceptual foundations and implementation techniques.

Rating models make ratings (ordinal numbers) a function of observable attributes of borrowers. Default risk models focus on determining the default probability (cardinal numbers) based on similar attributes. The latter use information on default events rather than ratings, which are more judgmental than factual default events. Banks can map modelled ratings to statistical default rates, although this mapping is not equivalent to modelling directly default probabilities.

Credit scoring uses techniques for discriminating between defaulters and non-defaulters. A 'scoring function' provides a score from observable attributes, which is a number. Score ranges map on a one-to-one basis to ratings or default frequencies. Scores use discriminant analysis to separate defaulters from non-defaulters, as the original Altman's 'zeta score' does. Comparing scores to cut-off values separates firms according to risk. Scoring techniques also provide 'posterior default probabilities', or probabilities of default given the score values. Scoring applies well to individual borrowers in retail banking, because of the large volume of data. It serves when making lending decisions for consumers or mortgage loans to individuals. Scoring also applies to firms, although implementation is more challenging for corporations.

The probit–logit regression models have gained ground for both individual consumers and corporate borrowers. These multivariate techniques use observable attributes and provide similar outputs to those of scoring models, ratings or default probabilities, with a different technique. They apply to default probabilities because defaults are binary events, with probabilities within the 0 to 1 range. The logit–probit technique allows the modelled variable to comply with this specific constraint. This is the methodology of Moody's RiskCalc for modelling default rates.

The econometric techniques allow us to model the default rates of 'portfolio segments', or subpopulations of firms by risk class, from time series of default rates and economic factors. The Credit Portfolio View (CPV) approach illustrates the potential of the intuitive hint that economic cycles relate to default and migration risks. CPV provides a framework for capturing the cyclical dynamics of credit risk. It uses standard time series models combined with a logit model to obtain default rates by portfolio segment. Time series models predict economic variables, industry and economic indexes, later converted into default rates through the logit model. Ultimately, CPV aims at modelling portfolio risk, as detailed in subsequent chapters. Because of its dual contribution in defining inputs for portfolio models and modelling portfolio risk, CPV belongs to both classes of models: default probability and portfolio models.

Neural network techniques are newcomers for modelling ratings and default probabilities. Empirical observations show non-linear relations between financial attributes of firms and their ratings or default frequencies, such as the relationship between size of firms and credit risk. Moreover, financial attributes strongly correlate, which creates weaknesses in statistical models. Such peculiarities do not affect neural networks. The basic tools for measuring accuracy are misclassification matrices and power curves. Misclassification tables simply compare predicted outcomes with actual ones. Power curves characterize the discriminating power of models (between ratings or default–no default states) by a single number. Both techniques apply to all models.

A common feature of all models is that they necessarily make errors in predicting defaults from historical values of attributes of borrowers. However, their added complexity makes it more difficult to interpret why one borrower is more or less risky than another.

The first section explains the basic intuition behind statistical models of ratings or default probability. The second section explains the principle of scoring. The third section discusses the probit–logit techniques and details the basic equations. The fourth section shows how econometric modelling of defaults and migrations by CPV, which captures the cyclical dynamics of credit risk. The fifth section describes the principles of neural networks. Finally, the last section addresses misclassification matrices and 'power curves'. See Caouette et al. (1998) for a comprehensive overview of the statistical techniques.

RISK AND OBSERVABLE ATTRIBUTES

The principle of all statistical models is to fit observable attributes, such as financial variables of firms, to variables to be predicted, such as default or non-default, or the rating of the firm.

The simplest technique for doing so is the simple linear regression, or variations of this technique. This technique provides valuable findings. For instance, it is relatively easy to show that risk decreases when the size of the firm increases, at least over some range of size values, measured by sales or total assets. A common finding of many simple or elaborated models is that the operating profitability, such as operating income or EBITDA to total assets—or Return On Assets (ROA) is a good predictor of risk and of default. Note that such findings are purely empirical, although they comply with intuition. Variables listed in Chapter 35 on rating systems are good candidates for such ingredients of empirical models.

However, simple multivariate analysis (linear regression, because it assumes a linear relation between predicted outputs and inputs) suffers from important limitations. This is why various other techniques were implemented. For instance, the relationship between rating and size, measured by assets or sales of firms, is not linear, but large firms tend to have better ratings. The RiskCalc documentation (Moody's Investors Service, 2000b) visualizes some of them. Size does not discriminate as much against smaller firms, because their credit standing depends on other factors, such as operating profitability and leverage. Note that simple regressions accommodate many non-linear relationships to a certain extent. For example, it is possible to use the logarithm of size, measured by total assets or sales, rather than asset or sale values, to better mimic the actual relations observed.

SCORING AND DISCRIMINANT ANALYSIS

The principle of scoring is to use a metric for dividing 'good' and 'bad' credits into distinct distributions. The statistical technique is the standard discriminant analysis.

Fisher Discriminant Analysis

Discriminant analysis distinguishes statistically between two or more groups of unit observations (firms or individuals). In the case of credit risk, the technique serves to discriminate between firms likely to default and those not likely to default, up to a given horizon, using current and past values of observable attributes such as financial ratios. Discriminant analysis attempts to do this by using characteristics that differ between groups. For credit risk, such variables include profitability, leverage, size and others. For individuals, income, age and professional activities relate to their credit standing.

The technique forms a linear combination of all discriminating variables to obtain a discriminant function. The discriminant function values are the scores. Discriminant analysis works by fitting the function to data, with observations in all classes that we wish to distinguish, such as defaulters versus non-defaulters. Fitting the function to the data also defines cut-off values of the score functions. The model works by calculating the score, comparing its value to cut-off values, and assigning a class based on these cut-off values provided by the model. For instance, firms with high scores could be classified as non-defaulters and conversely. Classification proceeds with functions that generate the probability of being in a given group based on the score value. To illustrate the principle, we limit the presentation to the two-group case, defaulting and non-defaulting firms, and to Fischer's linear discriminant function.

The discriminant function produces a standardized Z score, with mean 0 and standard deviation 1. Averaging each score for one group (such as non-defaulters) provides a mean called the group 'centroid'. The coefficient of the variables of the discriminant function measures the relative contribution of the coefficient to the function. Plotting the number of cases having scores within predefined ranges of values generates the histogram of scores. By plotting scores separately for each group (for instance, defaulters and non-defaulters) we visualize how well the scores differentiate the groups and to what extent they overlap. The wider the gap between the groups' means and the lower the overlap, the better the model performs.

A classification function serves to assign, or classify, a case to a group. A case is predicted to be a member of the group for which the value of its classification function is the highest. For only two groups, the discriminant function is simply the difference between the classification functions for each of the two groups. The score of the Fisher discriminant function relates the score to observable attributes:

$$Z = Z(\text{attributes } X_1, X_2, X_3, \text{ etc.})$$

For every individual, a numerical value of the score results from observed attributes and scores compared to a cut-off value allowing us to assign the firm or individual to one of the two groups. If the value is high, the credit is good, and the higher the score, the higher the quality for the credit. A bad score indicates a lower quality credit.

The outputs of the procedure are the coefficients of the classification function and cut-off values. The coefficients help in interpreting which coefficients best explain the classification, and the posterior probabilities of belonging to a given group. The cut-off values serve to assign a new individual to a group, based on the score value. Posterior probabilities are conditional probabilities of defaulting conditional on the score value. Prior probabilities are default probabilities without any information. For instance, when using a data set of defaulters and non-defaulters, the ratio of defaulters over the total is the prior probability. Since the score value provides information on likelihood of default, the posterior probabilities embed this additional information. Let's assume that high scores relate to bad credit standing. When the company attributes result in a high score value, the posterior probability is higher and vice versa.

Scoring does not use a conceptual framework, such as KMV Credit Monitor, which implements the Merton model. It simply fits a function that best discriminates between high risk and low risk populations. The fit might necessitate repeated calibration to account for changing conditions, although the attributes might also capture the changing conditions.

Therefore, scoring potentially discriminates firms according to their credit standing, and can serve both as a default predictor and as a rating device. For firms, scoring models based on a small number of indicators, such as accounting ratios, have been successful. There are a number of classical studies explaining scoring systems and providing numerical results.

From Scores to Posterior Probabilities

Scoring provides information on the credit standing of a firm. Therefore, the probability of default given the score S differs from the probability of default under no information on S. If we use scoring to discriminate between firms that are likely to default in the future and firms that are not, we can infer from the score the conditional default probabilities given the score value. Without knowledge of the score, we would assign the same default probabilities to all firms. This is the prior probability of default. With scoring, we can differentiate them according to the score values using Bayes' theorem.

Since scores convey information about risk, the probability of default given the score differs from the same probability estimated without having the score value. The posterior probabilities transform the scoring model into a default model. If we pick up a firm, we calculate its score value $Z = z$. The issue is to find the default probability conditional on a score Z greater than the value z obtained for a particular firm. We assume that higher scores correlate with default risk.

Bayes' theorem allows us to move from unconditional, or prior probabilities, to conditional or posterior probabilities, once we add some information relevant to the occurrence of Z. The formula for Bayes' theorem relates unconditional and conditional probabilities of two events, one, D, being a default event, and the other being anything that provides information on the default event, such as a score Z from a scoring model of defaults. Bayes' theorem states that:

$$P(\text{default}|\mathbf{Z} \geq z) = [P(\mathbf{Z} \geq z|\text{default}) \times P(\text{default})]/[P(\mathbf{Z} \geq z|\text{default}) \times P(\text{default})$$

$$+ P(\mathbf{Z} \geq z|\text{no default}) \times P(\text{no default})]$$

In this case, the conditional probabilities serve to convert scores into default probabilities. To do this we need three inputs:

- The probability that a defaulting firm has a score $\mathbf{Z} \geq z$, or $P(\mathbf{Z} \geq z|\text{default})$. This probability comes from the original population serving to fit the scoring model. By cross-tabulating the number of defaulting firms with scores, we find the fraction of defaulting firms having scores above or equal to z, for example 80%.
- The probability that a non-defaulting firm has a score $\mathbf{Z} \geq z$, or $P(\mathbf{Z} \geq z|\text{no default})$. This probability comes from the same cross-tabulation of non-defaulting firms with scores. We derive from this histogram the fraction of non-defaulting firms with a lower score than z, for example 10%.
- The unconditional probability of default that is the average of the entire population, for example 5% or $P(\text{default})$. The unconditional probability of no default is 95%, or $P(\text{no default})$.

Using Bayes' formula:

$$P(\text{default}|\mathbf{Z} \geq z) = [70\% \times 5\%]/[80\% \times 5\% + 10\% \times 95\%] = 4\%/17.5\% = 22.86\%$$

This is a much higher probability than the 5% average. $P(A)$ is an 'unconditional' or 'prior' probability. $P(\text{default}|\mathbf{Z} \geq z)$ is a posterior probability, given the information provided by z, which is also the conditional probability of default given the score value. Discriminating between defaulters and non-defaulters allows us to assign default (posterior) probabilities based on the score value.

The Zeta Score

A famous score is Altman's zeta score (Altman et al., 1977; first contribution 1968). This is a multivariate model built on the values of selected ratios and categorical measures. The Z-score model applies to a large variety of borrowers, from small to medium size firms. The basic Z-score model is public. It uses five variables to discriminate between obligors. These are:

- Working capital/total assets.
- Retained earnings/total assets.
- Earnings Before Interest and Tax (EBIT)/total assets.
- Market value of equity/book value of liabilities.
- Sales/total assets.

The discriminant function is linear. All ratios have a statistical coefficient in the function:

$$Z = F(X_1, X_2, X_3, X_4, X_5)$$

According to the value of Z, the firm is closer or not to the defaulting firm's group characteristics than to the survivor group. The value of Z measures the likelihood of default. High scores indicate low likelihoods of failure, and conversely. The implementation implies that we should define a range of values of Z in order to make a decision. A typical utilization of such a model requires defining boundary values for Z such that:

- Below a lower bound, the firm's likelihood of failure is high.
- Above an upper bound, the firm's likelihood of failure is low.
- Between the upper and lower bounds, we do not know, because the model does not discriminate well the two categories.

These cut-off values of scores serve to classify obligors into good or bad categories, or in between.

Recent versions of the zeta-score model extend the coverage to larger firms than before. Variables are return on assets, stability of earnings, debt coverage ratio, retained earnings, liquidity as measured by the current ratio, capitalization and the logarithm of the size of assets.

The benefit of scoring is to speed up the credit decisions and the rating process. The drawbacks are:

- Some critical characteristics, other than ratios, might be relevant and not included in the discriminant function. For example, management quality for small firms is critical.
- There are no conceptual foundations to scoring, except that the effects of variables are in line with intuition. This is not a drawback as long as the issue is the end result, not the conceptual foundations of the fitting process.

Scoring Consumers

Scoring is widely used for consumer loans. Scoring allows us to automate the credit process because there is no real need to examine in detail the profile of individuals. There are plenty of reliable portfolio loss statistics, given the large number of individuals. The 'intensity' of services provided to customers is a major source of high revenues, both fees and spreads. The relevant criteria combine both the potential revenues, the value added for the bank and the risks. Many fit such conditions. Income per dependent in the family, renting or owning home, marital status, occupation are all criteria for assessing both the credit standing and the potential revenues. Information on other credit cards and loans by other institutions provides information on the exposure to other competitors and the level of debt. Years spent at the same address and years spent in the same job provide information on the mobility to be expected and the length of the financial services to be expected.

The Economics of Scoring Systems

The usage of scoring has economic implications, which are the relative costs of rejecting a good credit and of accepting a bad credit.

Type I and Type II Errors

Scoring is a statistical technique that can fail to make the right predictions, as all do. Beyond some value, the likelihood of failing is negligible, below another lower value, the likelihood is close to 1. In between, we do not know, but we might infer some relationship between default probability and the value of the Z-score. Used in this way, we have both a default predictive tool and a rating device.

Types of errors for cut-off scores are:

- Type I error—accept bad credits.
- Type II error—reject good credits.

Since the costs of the different errors are widely different, the economic side of errors has an influence on the cut-off value of the score.

Scoring Criteria and Revenues

Scoring does not apply only to credit risk measurement. It extends to attributes representative of the potential richness of a customer to the bank. Richness means intensity of services, such as the number of accounts and services with a customer, future transactions expected with the customer, such as new loans and credit card loans. Richness, or service intensity and profitability, are criteria that prove correlated to the personal profile of individuals.

In the end, the modelling provides information on both credit standing and potential richness. An individual can pass the credit standing test and not the richness test. Others might be risky customers, but seem to have plenty of business potential. This extension of the same type of technique can also serve to assess the risk–return profile of individuals. Embedding both revenue and risk criteria in scoring raises the wider issue of the economic implications for individual decisions and for the entire loan portfolio.

For individual decisions, type I errors result in a full loss of principal and interest should risk materialize. Type II error costs are opportunity costs of not lending to a wealthy borrower. The opportunity cost is the lost income. Hence, the cost of a type II error is much lower than that of a type I error. Based on these simple economics, we can tolerate more type II errors than type I errors, because the unit loss is lower. Since the cut-off values of scoring models drive the probabilities of type I and II errors, choosing them depends on both the quality of predictions and the cost of errors.

Rejecting too many good credits results in adverse selection, or taking too many bad credits. Extended at the scale of the portfolio of the banks, this implies that some banks will concentrate on bad credits and others on good credits. If the bank uses risk-based pricing according to credit quality, this is acceptable, since not all banks need to run for the same market segments. Nevertheless, because of competition between banks, pricing might not really differentiate the good and bad accounts. The biased score becomes a problem since pricing does not compensate any more the differential cost of errors. Therefore, the cut-off points should not depend only on the individual loss trade-off between type II errors and type I errors and their frequencies. It should also depend on the portfolio effect once scoring is in force and actually structures the loan portfolio. The portfolio view changes the picture because it relates the implementation of scoring to the portfolio structure and the pricing policy. In addition, it should also extend to any adverse effects of attracting too many bad credits, which influences the bank's reputation.

PROBIT–LOGIT MODELS

There are models dedicated to predicting binary events, such as defaults or non-defaults, or to scaling the probabilities that such events occur. Originally, they were behavioural models, used to predict two or more qualitative choices or behavioural responses, such as voting yes or no, ranking different products by consumer preferences, and so on. These models include the linear probability models and the more adequate logit and probit models. In what follows, 'individual' means individual observation, an observation relating to any type of borrower, consumer or corporate:

- 'Binary models' assume that individuals belong to either one of two categories only, such as defaulting firms and non-defaulting firms, depending on their characteristics.
- 'Multinomial models' accommodate several categories, such as ratings, depending on their characteristics.

In addition, these models apply to:

- Classification in categories: categories (defaulters and non-defaulters) are nominal variables, such as 'yes' and 'no'. The goal is to achieve the highest number of correct classifications.
- Ordinal variables, which measure ranks, such as ratings, or numerical ('cardinal') variables, such as default frequencies. The goal is to minimize the errors between values predicted by the model and actual values.

'Ordered' probit or logit models perform better with ranks (ratings) than other models considering each rating as a separate category, without any rank (ordinal) relation with other ratings. The principle of these models is to determine the probability that an individual with a given set of attributes will make one choice rather than an alternative choice. These models use an adapted multivariate regression technique. The explanatory variables are the attributes X_i.

Use of Logit and Probit Models

In practice, the logit and probit models are adapted for modelling:

- Default frequencies, which have values in the 0 to 1 range.
- Ratings, which are ordinal variables.

Simple regressions have strong limitations when modelling default frequencies, because these are necessarily within the 0 to 1 range. When fitting a linear regression between ratings and financial attributes, size, operating profitability, leverage, and so on, chances are that the model will provide outputs for some combinations of values that lie beyond the 0 and 1 bounds. In such instances, it is necessary to embed the constraints on predicted values from the very beginning. This is where logit and probit, applied to numerical variables, shine. Unlike regression models, which assume that the relation between rating and size, for example, is linear, these models do not suffer from the non-linearities observed between observable attributes.

The 'Basic' Linear Model Drawbacks

The simple linear probability model explains the principles. The linear probability model is the simplest version of models of binary events. It makes the probability P of the event a linear function of one attribute $\mathbf{X}$. In fact, we try to explain a binary variable $\mathbf{Y}$, 0 or 1, with the attribute:

$$\mathbf{Y} = \alpha + \beta \mathbf{X} + \varepsilon$$

Since the expectation of the error term ε_k of the regression is zero:

$$E(\mathbf{Y}) = 1 \times P(\mathbf{Y} = 1) + 0 \times [1 - P(\mathbf{Y} = 0)]$$

$$P(\mathbf{Y} = 1) = \alpha + \beta E(\mathbf{X})$$

The model provides the value of the probability that $\mathbf{Y}$ equals 1. However, it does not comply with the constraint that all values of $\mathbf{Y}$ should be within the 0 to 1 range. This implies truncation to avoid such outliers. The probit–logit models avoid this drawback.

Probit and Logit Models

The probit and logit models address the problem of translating the values of an attribute $\mathbf{X}$, whatever they are, to a probability that ranges between 0 and 1. In addition, an increase of $\mathbf{X}$ should correspond to an increase in probability, which is the dependent variable.

The Linear Model

The categorical variable is **Y**, whose observations are not available directly. Instead, we have data that distinguish only whether individual observations are in one category Y_1 (high values of **Y**) or in a second category Y_2 (low values of **Y**). For credit risk, the categories are default and non-default. The model serves to predict whether one attribute **X** is a good predictor of being a member of a category. The higher the **X**, the higher the probability of being a member of this category. The two basic groups are defaulters and non-defaulters, as in scoring. The first step is to express **Y** as a function of the attribute **X**, just as in the linear model. For simplicity, we write the equation with a single **X**, whereas the general formula would replace $\beta\mathbf{X}$ by $\sum_{i=1}^{n} \mathbf{X}_i$ to model the influence of several **X** characteristics:

$$\mathbf{Y} = \alpha + \beta\mathbf{X} + \varepsilon$$

However, instead of moving directly from **Y** to a probability, we transform the **Y** using a cumulated distribution function, cdf(**Y**). Any cumulated distribution function assigns one value, and only one, between 0 and 1, to any value of the random variable **Y** that it models[1]. Any predicted value of **Y**, without any boundary, corresponds to a probability (within the 0 to 1 range) using a known distribution function. Obviously, the predicted probability depends on the particular distribution used to define the cumulated distribution cdf(**Y**) (Figure 37.1).

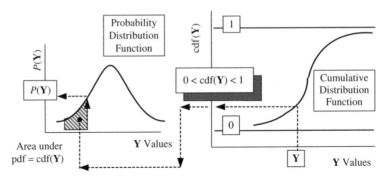

FIGURE 37.1   Converting a modelled variable into a (0, 1) number with a cdf

The Logit Model

The logit model uses the cumulative logistic probability distribution for the cdf. The model fits $\mathbf{Y} = \alpha + \beta\mathbf{X} + \varepsilon$ and calculates the probability of **Y** having a specific categorical value as:

$$P(\mathbf{Y}) = 1/[1 + \exp(-\mathbf{Y})] = 1/\{1 + \exp[-(\alpha + \beta\mathbf{X} + \varepsilon)]\}$$

When **Y** gets very high, the exponential becomes close to 0 and $P(\mathbf{Y})$ tends towards 1. When **Y** gets very negative, the exponential becomes very high and the probability tends

---

[1] Constraining values within a wide range to spread in the 0 to 1 range through a cdf is a technique for generating random values following a specified distribution. The technique generates random uniformly distributed numbers, and converts them into values using the cdf of a specified distribution, such as the normal or the lognormal distribution.

towards 0. Therefore, any value Y of $\mathbf{Y}$ complies with the boundary values of probabilities. $P(\mathbf{Y})$ is the probability of belonging to the particular group having the categorical value Y. Categories can be defaulters or non-defaulters, or various rating classes.

A simple transformation of the logit model shows that:

$$\exp(-\mathbf{Y}) = [1 - P(\mathbf{Y})]/P(\mathbf{Y}) \quad \text{or} \quad \exp(\mathbf{Y}) = P(\mathbf{Y})/[1 - P(\mathbf{Y})]$$

Taking the natural logarithm, we get:

$$\ln\{P(\mathbf{Y})/[1 - P(\mathbf{Y})]\} = \mathbf{Y} = \alpha + \beta\mathbf{X} + \varepsilon$$

This allows an easy interpretation of the model. The argument of the logarithm $P(\mathbf{Y})/[1 - P(\mathbf{Y})]$ is the odds of belonging to one group, or the ratio of the probability of belonging to that group to the probability of not belonging to that group. The logarithm of the odds ratio is the 'logit'. When $\mathbf{Y} = 0$, the logarithm is 1 and the odds ratio is 1, meaning that there are as many chances of belonging to one group as there are of belonging to the other, implying a common value $P(\mathbf{Y} = 0) = 0.5$. One attractive feature of the logit model is that it transforms the issue of predicting probabilities into a linear model predicting the logarithm of the odds of a particular event. Once the model is fitted to data, we have the coefficients. The value $\mathbf{Y} = \alpha + \beta\mathbf{X}$ calculated for particular information is simply the logarithm of the odds ratio, and the exponential is the odds ratio itself.

The logit model has some drawbacks. When $P(\mathbf{Y}) = 0$ or 1, the logarithm is undefined, making the regression inadequate. The remedy is to use grouped observations where we can observe the fraction of observations belonging to one group. This ensures that values will not reach extremes. Note that this applies for credit risk whenever we model the default rate within predefined segments. This applies to CPV. It also applies better to retail banking because segments defined by product type and borrower type are a typical way to model risk. Another drawback is that the variance of the predicted variable varies from one group to the other[2].

The Probit Model

The probit model performs similar functions to the logit model, but uses the normal distribution instead of the logistic distribution. Because the normal distribution is more complex than the logistic distribution, the model looks more complex. However, there are no practical differences with available statistical softwares. The probit model considers $\mathbf{Y}$ as normally distributed and uses the cumulative distribution of the normal distribution. $\mathbf{Y}$ can take any value, negative or positive. Once we have the X value, we have the Y value, and once we have the Y value, we have $P(Y)$ through the equation making Y the normal inverse function of $P(Y)$. There is a one-to-one correspondence between Y, which is unconstrained, and the probability $P(Y)$:

$$P(\mathbf{Y}) = \text{cdf}(\mathbf{Y}) = \text{cdf}(\mathbf{Y} = \alpha + \beta\mathbf{X} + \varepsilon) = (1/\sqrt{2\pi}) \int_{-\infty}^{Y} \exp(-s^2/2)\,ds$$

---

[2] The variance depends on the number of observations within each subset of observations and the fraction in the subset belonging to one group.

The higher $\mathbf{Y}$, the higher the probability that we are in the category corresponding to the upper values of $\mathbf{Y}$:

$$\mathbf{Y} = \mathrm{cdf}^{-1}(\mathbf{P}) = \alpha + \beta \mathbf{X} + \varepsilon$$

For example, if Y is $+2$, the probability of having $\mathrm{cdf}(Y) = +2$ is $P(Y) = 97.7\%$ with the cumulative standardized normal distribution and if Y is 0, $P(0) = \mathrm{cdf}(0) = 0.5$.

In general, $\mathbf{Y}$ is a function of any number of attributes used as predictors of $\mathbf{X}_i$, for instance a linear relationship obtained through a regression analysis to predict $\mathbf{Y}$ from the $\mathbf{X}_i$: $\mathbf{Y} = \beta_0 + \sum_{i=1}^{n} \beta_i \mathbf{X}_i$.

The logit and probit models give very close results. The only difference is that the logit form is easier to manipulate. The logistic function is similar to the normal distribution but has fatter tails. Figure 37.2 illustrates the difference between the shapes of the two cumulative distributions.

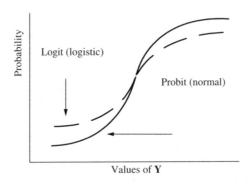

FIGURE 37.2   **Comparison of the cumulated probability distributions: normal and logistic**

ECONOMETRIC MODELLING OF DEFAULT AND MIGRATION RATES OF PORTFOLIO SEGMENTS (CPV)

This section presents the macro-economic modelling of default and migration rates. This is the CPV (Wilson, 1997a, b) framework, which addresses explicitly the cyclical dynamics of these variables. The model focuses on portfolio segments, rather than individual obligors, and default or migration rates rather than probabilities. The underlying assumption is that of the homogeneous behaviour of credit standing of firms within a portfolio segment. This contrasts with the modelling of the credit standing of individual obligors. However, CPV allows us to define segments with more than one criterion, instead of using only risk classes.

The principle underlying CPV is to relate default and migration rates to external factors. Default and migration rates of portfolio segments relate to economic variables through a logit function, to obtain values in the 0 to 1 range. In addition, the model looks forward. Predicted default and migration rates are a function of the predicted values of these factors. Predicting economic variables uses standard time series modelling with Auto Regressive Integrated Moving Average (ARIMA) techniques. We review below the CPV building blocks, related to defaults and migrations, postponing the modelling of correlations to subsequent chapters (44, 45 and 48).

CPV Building Blocks

CPV relies on several modelling options:

- Default events depend on economic conditions materialized by an economic variable Y_i summarizing the influences of country–industry factors X_k, where the index i designates a portfolio segment and k designates each specific factor.
- The default events modelled are default rates, ratios of default frequencies to a subpopulation of firms. Hence, CPV works with grouped data rather than individual data. These subpopulations are banking portfolio segments grouped by risk class for example.
- To look forward, it is necessary to use predicted values of the factors influencing the default rates. For this purpose, CPV needs to model the predicted values of factors using standard time series models.
- To convert the predicted values of factors into default rates, CPV uses the logit form making default rates a logit function of an index summarizing the predicted factors that influence default rates.

The economic factors driving the credit risk of obligors are economic, geographic or industry variables X_k that influence directly or indirectly the credit standing of obligors. This corresponds to the intuition that all firms are sensitive to common external conditions, with a different magnitude, in addition to 'firm-specific' factors. The purpose is to capture the cyclical dynamics of credit risk of firms. The factors X_k represent the 'general' risk of obligors, while the residual of the fit of default rates to Y_i represents the specific risk. The model therefore splits the general and specific components of credit risk explicitly. A major benefit of this modelling technique is to make explicit the cyclical dynamics of credit risk.

CPV uses three main building blocks for modelling default and migration rates of portfolio segments:

- The first block models default rates, at date $t + 1$, $\mathbf{DR}_{i,t+1}$ by portfolio segment i as a function of the economic index $\mathbf{Y}_{i,t+1}$. It uses a logit model to ensure that the default rate remains in the 0 to 1 range of values, no matter what is the predicted $\mathbf{Y}_{i,t+1}$ value. The economic index is a linear combination of several industry–country factors $\mathbf{X}_{k,t+1}$. The index i refers to a portfolio segment and the index k refers to economic factors. The date t is the current date, while $t + 1$ refers to a future date, one period ahead.
- The second block models the future values of the economic–industry factors $\mathbf{X}_{k,t+1}$ as a function of their past values and error terms using an ARIMA time series model. These economic factors are common to all portfolio segments, hence there is no index i. This allows the model to 'look forward' using lagged values of economic factors.
- The third block models the migration probabilities $\mathbf{MR}_{i,t+1}$ of transition matrices consistent with the variations of default rates, allowing the migration probabilities to shift upward or downward according to the values of the default rates.

These three building blocks use three main families of equations: the first family models default rates for each segment as a logit function of $\mathbf{Y}_{i,t+1}$; the second models predicted economic factors $\mathbf{X}_{k,t+1}$ as an ARIMA function of lagged values and errors; the third relates the migration probabilities $\mathbf{MR}_{i,t+1}$ by segment to the modelled default rates. Values of variables are certain as of current date t and random as at future date $t + 1$.

This allows us to extend the model to generate random values at a future horizon, a critical modelling block to obtain a loss distribution and Value at Risk (VaR) for credit risk (see Chapter 48).

The CPV Model

The equations are as follows. The index depends on a set $\mathbf{X}_k$ of common economic factors that influence the credit risk of all portfolio segments:

$$\mathbf{Y}_{i,t+1} = \beta_{i,t} + \beta_{i,1}\mathbf{X}_{1,t+1} + \beta_{i,2}\mathbf{X}_{2,t+1} + \cdots + \beta_{i,k}\mathbf{X}_{k,t+1} + \varepsilon_{i,t+1}$$

Each economic factor predicted value $\mathbf{X}_{j,t+1}$ at date $t+1$ results from an ARIMA time series model, using past observations and past errors as predictors of future values. The general functional form is a linear lagged function of these past observations and errors:

$$\mathbf{X}_{j,t+1} = \alpha_1\mathbf{X}_{j,t} + \alpha_2\mathbf{X}_{j,t-1} + \cdots + \gamma_1\mathbf{e}_{j,t} + \gamma_2\mathbf{e}_{j,t-1} + \mathbf{e}_{j,t+1}$$

The logit model converts predicted values of economic factors into default and migration rates $\mathbf{DR}_i$ for each portfolio segment i:

$$\mathbf{DR}_{i,t+1} = 1/[1 + \exp(-\mathbf{Y}_{i,t+1})]$$

The model differs for investment grade risk classes and speculative grade risk classes. It recognizes that investment grade obligors are less sensitive to economic movements than speculative grade obligors. This is in line with intuition, suggesting that investment grade defaults are more 'unexpected' than speculative grade defaults. The model fit to time series of observations provides the ratios of general to specific risks, since this ratio is that of the variance explained by common factors to the variance of the residual term of the fit.

Econometric Migrations Modelling

Migrations are necessary to find the risk class at the horizon date in order to perform a risk-adjusted valuation of the facilities. The risk status at horizon determines the valuation of the facility using market spreads corresponding to this risk class. In CPV, migration rates are conditional on the state of the economy through the modelled default rates. Credit Portfolio View uses the econometric modelling of default rates to derive what migration rates should be for portfolio segments. Migration rates, just as default rates, depend on country–industry specifics, not risk class only. Details follow on CPV use and integrated econometric modelling of default rates and migration rates.

Existing migration matrices are historical. When using long-term migration statistics, it is possible to consider them as long-term averages, or 'unconditional migration probabilities'. However, migrations are dependent on the state of the economy as much as default rates are. Hence, there is a need to model the migration rates between any pair of risk classes consistently with default rates. Since common factors influence both default and migration rates across risk classes, they correlate them. CPV extends the default rate modelling to migration rates, making them conditional on the state of the economy based on the same factors that influence default probabilities.

Migration rates apply to any pair of classes. The migration rates from segment i to segment j, $\mathbf{MR}_{i,j}$, are random. Consistency with default rates imposes that all migration rates, including the default state, should sum to 1. Therefore, when default rates vary, the sum of all other migration rates across a given risk class should also vary for the sum to remain 1. In order to preserve the consistency of the transition matrix, CPV uses a 'shift' factor that modifies the migration rates in accordance with modelled default rate values.

CPV starts with the long-term average migration matrix, considered as an 'unconditional migration matrix'. The default rates of portfolio segments result from the model. The model shifts the migration rates across risk classes according to their deviation from their long-term values. When the default rates get higher than average, all migration probabilities to non-default states diminish and shift towards lower values. When the default rates get lower than their long-term average, all migration probabilities to the non-default state increase to compensate the default rate decline. The shifts of migration rates are proportional to the deviation of the modelled default rate from its average long-term value.

In addition, CPV considers that investment grade assets are less sensitive to the cyclical dynamics of the economy. This is in line with intuition, suggesting that low risk firms have less predictable defaults than speculative grade firms, who tend to follow more closely the economic cycles. Accordingly, the specific risk, the risk unrelated to external factors, varies across risk classes and increases relative to the upper risk class. CPV provides an adjustment for this higher specific risk of the upper risk class.

Since we use predicted values of factors, the default and migration rates are also predicted variables. They are random as of current date since the factors driving their values are. This allows us to simulate future values complying with the model structure to generate distributions of segment default rates.

THE NEURAL NETWORKS TECHNIQUE

Neural networks (NNs), in their simplest form, are similar to a linear regression (see Principle et al., 2000). The explained variable y is the 'response', while the explaining variables x are the covariates. The linear regression would be:

$$y = w_0 + \sum_{j=1}^{n} w_i x_i$$

The diagram representing this model would be as in Figure 37.3. In the NN literature, this function–diagram is a single unit 'perceptron'. However, an NN is more complex than this plain linear model. Each node processes several inputs that result in several outputs, y, serving as inputs to other nodes of the network, until we reach the final stage where we get the modelled output, as shown in Figure 37.4. When considering a single 'neuron', it receives inputs and transforms them into outputs. We use standard italic letters for inputs to and outputs from a single neuron. The unit receives signals 'x' and transforms them into signals 'y' that serve as inputs to other neurons.

The activation function $f(u)$ takes a specified form, such as the logistic form $f(u) = 1/[1 + \exp(u)]$, which produces a simple output such as 0 or 1. Other functions, with values within the 0 to 1 range, might serve as well. The function $u(x, w)$ might be a linear function of the inputs through the weights (w) plus a constant.

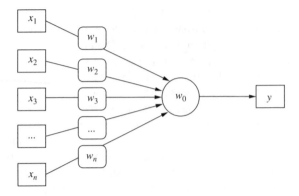

FIGURE 37.3   Simple diagram of a single unit neuronal model

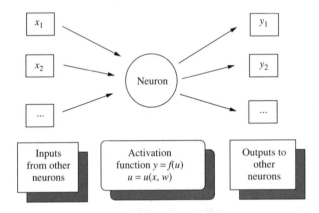

FIGURE 37.4   Inputs and outputs of a single neuron, with an activation function

There are several differences between simple statistical techniques and NNs:

- The relationship between inputs and outputs of each node is not linear, since it combines weights with non-linear functions. Therefore, the final relation between the inputs and the modelled variable is no longer linear.
- The NNs attempt to mimic any function between the original inputs (observable attributes) and the final outputs (modelled variable). To achieve this function approximation, they minimize the error, the gaps between the predicted values and the actual values.

Optimization consists of minimizing this error. To achieve optimization, NNs use a training process, unlike the simple regression method.

The training process uses a feedback loop. For a given set of weights and inputs, the NN produces a set of outputs depending on weights w. Changing the weights changes the outputs. The distance between the actual value and the NN predicted value, at a given stage, triggers or not a change in weights depending on the size of the mismatch. Modifying the weights results in a new set of outputs. If the error produced by the change is high enough, the NN 'learns' by adjusting the weights.

The rule triggering the change in weights is the 'delta rule'. The magnitudes of the weight changes depend on a parameter called the 'learning rate'. The 'delta rule' ensures the fastest convergence towards the best match between modelled and observed outputs. This process is called the steepest 'gradient descent'. The process implies processing each observation in the training set a number of times to reach the highest level of convergence.

Because NNs can replicate closely any function, including complex non-linear functions, it is possible to replicate any kind of output. However, the result would become too dependent on the training sample! The NN could mimic the outputs of the training sample, but it might not do well with new observations. Hence, an NN can 'over-train'. In order to avoid 'over-training', NNs use a cross-validation sample. The cross-validation sample does not serve for training the model. It serves for checking that the error in this second sample does not increase while the NN trains itself through multiple simulations on the training sample. The process prevents the model from 'over-training', since this would result in an increased error in the cross-validation sample.

NN models serve for both classification and function approximation of ordinal or numerical variables. In classification mode, the NN tries to achieve the highest possible level of correct classification. This is attractive for categorical variables, but might result in large errors for incorrect classifications. When running under 'regression' mode, the model recognizes that the size of the error counts. In such a case, an error in predicting a rating of five notches is higher than an error of only two notches. In this mode, the model minimizes the errors over the whole training sample (such as ordered probit–logit models).

This difference is similar to that of using logit and probit models for classification purposes and for modelling ordinal (ranks) or numerical variables (default frequencies). In general, to model ratings or default frequencies out of observable attributes, it makes sense to use ordinal or numerical models.

NNs are appealing because of their capability to tackle very complex issues. In the context of classification, the basic issue for modelling defaults or ratings, NNs have attractive properties with respect to traditional statistics. The observed relationships between the ordinal variables, which characterize credit states, and the observable features are not linear, such as the relation between size and ratings. Moreover, many financial attributes correlate with each other, such as profitability measures, which all depend on some common factors, such as net income of profitability before tax, or Earnings Before Interest, Tax and Depreciation (EBITDA). Multicollinearity is a weakness of linear models as well. NNs take care of non-linear interdependencies, thereby having a higher potential for accuracy. On the other hand, understanding why the modelled risk is high or low, from the input values, gets more complex. This drawback might neutralize the benefits of a higher accuracy. It is still too early to see whether they 'beat' classical statistical models, but their usage extends in the financial universe, notably for standalone credit risk modelling.

MEASURING DEFAULT AND RATING MODELS ACCURACY

The easiest way to visualize accuracy is through a misclassification matrix. The matrix simply cross-tabulates the actual classification versus the predicted classification. The simplest classification uses two categories only, defaulters and non-defaulters. When modelling ratings, there are as many classes as there are different ratings. It is a square matrix. Correct classifications are along the diagonal, since this is where both predicted and actual classes coincide. Errors are above or below the diagonal.

Another standard technique for visualizing and quantifying scoring accuracy is the use of power curves. These apply to any credit risk quality measure, whether from scoring or more involved modelling such as the KMV 'expected default frequency' Edf ©, or agency ratings' predictive ability. The technique measures misclassifications as a single ratio.

Matrices and power curves apply to all types of modelling techniques, multivariate regression, discriminant analyses, multinomial logit or probit, ordered probit and logit, or NN models.

Misclassification Matrices

When modelling ordinal or numerical variables, the further away values are from the diagonal, the larger is the error. Table 37.1 is a simple misclassification matrix for six rating classes. In this case, there are 100 firms, spread over six rating classes. The total of rows shows the total number of firms in each class in this sample. Correct classifications are along the diagonal, and represent 47% of all observations. Since it is interesting to know the number of small errors, say within ± 1 notch, the summary table also provides this total, or 75. Larger errors, within ± 2 notches, are $87 - 75 = 12$. The count of larger errors is 13.

TABLE 37.1 Misclassification matrix for six ratings

Actual	Predicted						Total
	1	2	3	4	5	6	
1	2	2	1				5
2	1	10	5	3	1		20
3		3	11	3	3		20
4		1	2	17	3	2	25
5			2	5	15	3	25
6			1	1	1	2	5
							100

Summary	
Total correct	47
Total within ± 1 notch	75
Total within ± 2 notches	87
Total errors more than ± 2 notches	13

The matrix applies to all models used in classification mode, for classifying in categories, or in ordinal regression mode, for modelling ranks such as ratings. For default models, there are only two cases, default or non-default, and the matrix collapses to 2 rows × 2 columns.

Power Curves

Power curves also visualize errors. Unlike misclassification matrices that provide all details, they summarize the accuracy of a model by a single percentage, which reaches

100% in the extreme case, where the model provides only correct classifications and no errors. These apply to any credit risk quality measure, whether from scoring or more involved modelling such as the KMV Edf, or agency ratings' predictive ability.

Plotting a 'power curve' requires ordering obligors by risk score, from riskiest to safest. For example, the entire population has a small fraction of defaulters, for instance 10%. A model performs well if it classifies all defaulters to the default class. Nevertheless, this default class represents only a small fraction, 10%, of the entire population. Two extreme situations illustrate the shape of the power curve.

Let's assume that we sample 10% of the population among the *riskiest* scores. Since the fraction of defaulters is 10%, a perfect model would find 100% of all defaulters, or 10% of the total population. We plot on the horizontal axis the percentage of sampling from the total population and on the vertical axis the percentage of the total population of defaulters, which is only 10% of the total population. A perfect model would result in a point with 10% of the sample population on the horizontal axis and 100% of defaulters on the vertical axis. This point is at the top of the steepest line starting from the origin and reaching the 10% of population/100% of defaulters population.

No model is perfect. Let's assume that the score does not provide any information on defaulters. We would sample 10% randomly across the population. The average fraction of defaulters would be 10% as well, or $10\% \times 10\% = 1\%$ of the total population. The point with 10% of total population and 10% of total subpopulation of defaulters is on the diagonal of the diagram. Therefore, the worst performing model (without bias) would have all points on the diagonal and not above.

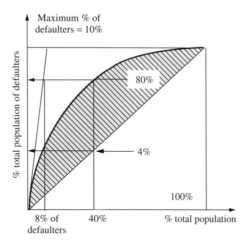

FIGURE 37.5   Predictive power of model and power curve

If the model provides information on who defaults and who does not, we move above the diagonal. In order to understand the shape of the curve when we progressively increase the sampling from the total population, we remark that when we sample the entire population, we necessarily obtain all defaulters, or 100% of them, equivalent to 10% of the total population. Hence, the curve passes through the 100%/100% point. It is between the diagonal and the polygon made of the steep straight line and the horizontal line positioned at 100% of the population. In Figure 37.5, we show a sample of 40% of the population. If the model samples defaulters randomly, we get 40% of them, or 4% of the total population. This point is on the diagonal. If we get all defaulters, we are on the top horizontal line because we have in the sample all defaulters, 100% of them with 10% of the population. If the model discriminates defaulters, we are in between. In this example, we reach around 80% of the defaulters, or $80\% \times 10\% = 8\%$ of the total population.

This rationale underlies using the 'power curve' to measure the accuracy of a model. If the curve is close to the diagonal, the predicting power is close to zero. If it is close to the steepest line, the predicting power is high. Constructing the power curve allows us to see how the model behaves across the entire range of scores. A predictive model has a power curve steeper than the diagonal, but less than the steep straight line. A common way to measure the level of the power curve above the diagonal is the ratio of the area under the power curve and above the diagonal to the area under the steep straight line and above the diagonal. The higher is the ratio, the higher is the accuracy of the model. In the figure, we see that we reach an overall accuracy ratio of around 50% to 60%, using as reference the upper area between the diagonal and the polygon.

38

The Option Approach to Defaults and Migrations

The option theoretic approach to default modelling follows the simple principles set up by R. Merton in his seminal paper of 1974. In short, the option theoretic approach views default as an 'economic' event triggered by a market value of assets lower than the debt value. This approach views a firm's equity as a put option, held by equity holders, to sell assets to lenders with a strike price equal to debt. If equity holders cannot repay the debt, they exercise their option, and the debt holders get the assets. The firm's debt has a value lower than a straight debt by the value of the put option, which increases when the default probability increases. The mirror image of the default option on equity is that the equity holders have a call on the upside of asset value beyond the debt value. The call becomes out-of-the-money when the asset value is lower than the debt, which is when the put payoff becomes positive.

The chances of economic default depend on the asset value, the debt value and the asset volatility. The asset value is that of the future cash flows adjusted for risk.

The option framework values the credit risk as the put option of equity holders on the underlying asset of the firm, making the debt value lower by the value of the put option. The put value is the gap between the values of a risk-free debt and a risky debt. It is equivalent to the credit spread over the risk-free rate, bringing the risky debt value in line with the value of the risk-free debt minus the put value. Any gain of the put value is a loss for the lender. Finally, because there is a link between equity value and asset value, it is conceptually feasible to hedge a borrower's default risk by selling short its equity.

KMV Corporation's Credit Monitor model makes the Merton model instrumental. Credit Monitor uses public equity prices to infer unobservable asset values and their volatility, and traces back the implied default probability embedded in equity prices and debt. The model looks forward because it relies on market data, which embeds market expectation. KMV uses the distance to default as an intermediate step, measured as the gap between the expected asset value and the threshold value of debt triggering default. The distance to default varies inversely with the default probability. The output is the well-known 'expected default frequency' (Edf ©). The Edf is a closed-form expression of the asset value, asset volatility and debt book value. Edfs contrast with historical default rates because they look forward, and with empirical statistical findings because the Edfs rely on conceptual foundations.

Modelling default probabilities also serves to model migrations from the original risk class to any risk class. A migration is simply an upward or a downward move of the asset value relative to debt. The option model applies to migrations because it models default probabilities and because default probabilities map with risk classes.

The first section explains the basic framework of the option theoretic view of risky debt. The second section explains how to infer, unobservable asset values and volatility from equity prices. The third section describes KMV Corporation's Credit Monitor model, which provides the Edf of public companies. The section details: the calculation of 'Edf'; the valuation of the put option value held by equity holders on the assets of the firm; the determination of the equivalent credit spread; the theoretical implications for hedging credit risk by trading stock options. The fourth section summarizes prior and posterior variations of the Merton model. The fifth section introduces a simplified approach for modelling default using a normally distributed asset value plus a predefined default probability. The last section extends the option theoretic framework to migration modelling.

THE OPTION THEORETIC FRAMEWORK FOR VALUATION OF EQUITY AND DEBT

The option theoretic approach to default considers that the equity holders have a put option on the value of the firm's assets, whose strike price is the debt. The rationale is that if the asset value falls below the value of debt, the equity holders are better off by giving the assets to the lenders rather than repaying the debt. The lenders sold the equity holders this option, whose underlying is the firm's asset value. This is an option to default when the asset value gets too low. If the asset value drops below that of debt, the liquidation value of the option is the gap, a value gained by stockholders and lost by lenders. This is the option theoretic framework proposed by Merton (1974) (see the fourth section of this chapter).

Hence, when the firm is close to default, the put gains value and the debt value decreases by the put value increase. The more the asset value moves down, the more the put value increases and the less is the value of debt:

Risky debt = risk-free debt − value of the put option
(selling assets at the value of debt)

An economic default occurs when the economic value of assets drops below the value of outstanding debts. Modelling the behaviour of asset value and debt through time allows us to model default. The original Merton model used a fixed amount of debt. Later extensions extended the framework to random debt values driven by the interest rate. However, the current implementation of the Merton model by KMV assumes debt given and certain. Note that an 'economic' default does not imply any legal action and does not coincide with standard legal definitions of default.

Focusing on asset value implies valuing all future flows of the firm, rather than focusing on a single period. The classical corporate finance approach to default is to project future free cash flows to see whether they allow the timely repayment of debt interest and principal. The relevant cash flows are the future 'free cash flows', or the cash flows from operations left for lenders and equity holders after all economic outflows required to maintain the operating ability of the firm. These future free cash flows should be high enough to face the future debt obligations.

Using the discounted value of free cash flows, which is the firm's asset value, is an elegant way of summarizing the information. A short-term view of cash flows is not a relevant criterion for solvency. A temporary shortage of cash does not trigger default as long as there are chances of improvement in the future. Persistent cash flow deficiencies make default highly likely. Temporary deficiencies do not. The market view synthesizes this information. It is consistent with the view of equity as a call option on asset value. As long as there is an upside potential, the equity has value, even during a transitory shortage of cash. The option view of equity serves for pricing the risky debt (Figure 38.1).

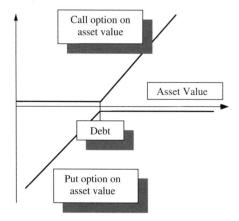

FIGURE 38.1 The call and put options of stockholders and lenders

KMV Corporation made this framework very popular. The basic scheme above serves to extract from equity prices the default probability of the firm. KMV models default as the event that asset values fall below debt value. This is an 'economic default', since it does not coincide with the legal definition of default. KMV calls the 'default point' the value of asset equal to debt. The probability of this event results from the asset value distribution and from the debt value. It is an implied default probability that the KMV Corporation names the Edf. The Credit Monitor model, from KMV Corporation, implements this framework to extract the Edf from observable equity price data. The Edf is forward looking, unlike historical data, because equity prices are forward looking.

Implementing this framework raises difficulties and needs simplification. KMV models default at a given horizon, where the asset value is above or below the debt value. The debt value combines short-term debt plus a fraction of long-term debt. Real situations are more complex. Another technical difficulty is to extract the asset values and distribution characteristics from observable data. The next section addresses this issue.

FROM EQUITY DATA TO ASSET VALUE DATA

It is not possible to observe asset values, since only equity prices are available. It is necessary to extract them from stock values and stock volatilities of publicly listed companies. The structure of equations necessary to extract implied asset values and volatilities from equity values and volatilities is simple in the option theoretic framework. From KMV's public documentation, two equations serve that purpose:

Equity value $= f$(book value of debt, asset value, asset volatility, horizon)

Volatility of equity value $= g$(book value of debt, asset value, asset volatility, horizon t)

In compact notation:
$$\mathbf{E} = f[D_T, \mathbf{A}, \sigma(\mathbf{A}), T]$$

$$\sigma(\mathbf{E}) = g[D_T, \mathbf{A}, \sigma(\mathbf{A}), T]$$

where T is the horizon, D_T is the certain book value of debt, $\mathbf{E}$ is the observed random market value of equity, $\mathbf{A}$ is the unobservable random market value of assets, $\sigma(\mathbf{A})$ is the volatility of the random asset value, $\sigma(\mathbf{E})$ is the volatility of the random equity value.

The underlying asset of the options embedded in equity and debt is the asset value. Equity is a call on asset value, with exercise price equal to book value of debt. The Black–Scholes formula indicates that:

$$E_0 = A_0 N(d_1) - D_T e^{-rT} N(d_2)$$

where D_T is the debt value, or exercise price of the call on the random asset value, and r is the risk-free rate.

The factor e^{-rT} is the discount factor corresponding to the present value of the cost D_T of exercising the option at horizon. $N(d_1)$ and $N(d_2)$ are the Black–Scholes formula coefficients, which depend on asset volatility. The sample calculations below expand the details of the calculation of the call value on asset and of the put value.

We do not know the expected value of $\mathbf{A}$ and $\sigma(\mathbf{A})$. A single equation is not sufficient to find two unknown variables, and we need a second one. Intuition indicates that there is a relation between the volatility of equity $\sigma(\mathbf{E})$ and that of the underlying asset value $\sigma(\mathbf{A})$. This is indeed the case, and the relationship results from the Black–Scholes formula:

$$\sigma(\mathbf{E}) = A_0 \sigma(\mathbf{A}) N(d_1)/E_0$$

From this new equation, we derive the asset volatility:

$$\sigma(\mathbf{A}) = [\sigma(\mathbf{E}) \times E_0]/[A_0 \times N(d_1)]$$

Since we now have two equations, it is possible to obtain the implicit asset value and volatility embedded in the equity price and volatility. The solution can be found easily, using numerical calculations, although these equations are implicit functions A_0 and $\sigma(\mathbf{A})$. However, this simplified model is not sufficient to reconstruct the KMV Edf, since it bypasses the calibration process with actual default data.

THE EDF MODEL

When looking forward at a future date, economic default occurs when the asset value drops below debt. The debt level triggering default is unclear since debt amortizes by fractions according to some schedule. KMV uses a debt value combining short-term debt at horizon plus a fraction of the long-term debt. The issue is to determine the chances that the asset value will fall below that level.

The asset expected value in the future is random. It follows a stochastic process with drift, just as stock prices do. The expected value is normally above the value of debt. The asset value at the horizon follows a lognormal distribution. We need to find the probability that the asset value drops below the debt value at the horizon, which is the theoretical Edf. The asset volatility allows us to use approximations to find this probability. With expected asset value and asset volatility, it is easy to find this probability.

As an example, using the simple normal distribution, instead of the lognormal distribution at horizon[1], it is straightforward to define the intermediate values. Assuming an expected asset value of 100 at the horizon, a debt value at the horizon of 50, and an asset volatility of 21.46[2], the probability of economic default is that the asset value drops by $50/21.46 = 2.33$ standard deviations, or 1% in this case. This is the Edf.

Several adjustments are necessary to mimic the actual default behaviour. The value of debt is the default point. The 'Distance to Default' (DD) is the ratio of the gap between expected asset value and default point to the asset standard deviation. The DD is the downside drop in standard deviation units required for default (2.33 above). This is a theoretical value. In fact, the actual value might differ, so that the calibration of the model requires mapping the distances to default to these actual default observed frequencies. With this mapping, the model replicates the actual default frequencies. The calibration process relies on proprietary default databases. It is necessary to have a sufficient number of defaulted companies to fit the mapping of distances to default to actual default frequencies. Periodical fits are necessary to make sure that the models actually fit the data. Figure 38.2 summarizes the entire process.

The time path of the asset value is stochastic. There are multiple time paths, each one reaching a specific value along the distribution at the horizon. Modelling the time paths as a stochastic process is not necessary as long as we care only about what happens at the horizon. Note that it is possible for the time path of asset value to cross the default point before the horizon. Then, default would occur before the horizon.

The Credit Monitor Edfs do not correspond fairly to default probabilities mapped to the agencies' ratings. The market-based Edf fluctuates continuously, and in spite of recalibration of the KMV proprietary model, there are significant discrepancies with ratings.

---

[1] The subsequent numerical example uses the lognormal distribution.

[2] The numerical value 21.46 makes the multiple of the standard deviation equal to 2.33.

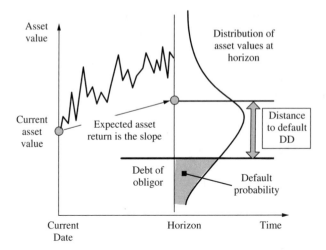

FIGURE 38.2   KMV modelling of Edf

However, this is not an inconsistency. In fact, the market-based Edf should anticipate rating changes, since ratings tend to lag somewhat the changes in credit standing of issues, simply because ratings are supposed to be long-term views of credit risk, not continuously reviewed. Casual observations of Credit Monitor's Edf seem to support this view, that market-based measures lead rating changes to a significant extent. KMV's Credit Monitor provides all the necessary information to make such comparisons: the Edf, the underlying values of the Edf drivers and the rating equivalent. This also allows end-users to better understand the Edf changes.

Of course, there are several studies comparing the KMV Edf with similar results obtained with other techniques, such as scoring. They use, for instance, the 'power curve' to show how well the model discriminates between defaulters and non-defaulters. They suggest that Credit Monitor provides at least a comparable accuracy.

A limitation of Credit Monitor is that it applies to public companies since it uses equity prices. To address the issue of equivalent default risk measures for private companies, KMV Corporation provides another model, the 'Edf Calculator' or 'Private Firm Model', which necessitates minimal information on private companies to model default risk. The basic information is in financial statements. In addition, the usage of the Edf Calculator requires documenting the industry and region of the firm. The principle is to proxy through this information the actual Edf of an 'equivalent' public company.

We calculate below the various variables determining distance to default. Without calibration, the calculation of the theoretical Edf is relatively easy. The process requires the formulas of the put option to default plus the usual assumptions on the asset value stochastic process leading to the lognormal distribution of the asset value at horizon. We summarize below the basic formulas, before making a sample calculation.

The Put and Call Options of Equity Holders

The option framework views the shareholders as having a put option to sell the assets of the firm to the lenders at a strike price equal to the preset book value of debt. The mirror image is that they hold a call option on the asset value, the strike price being the debt. The stockholders benefit from the upside of the asset value, while having a limited liability to lenders. Both options are European: they allow exercise at horizon T only. The lenders hold a debt whose value depends on the default probability. When the default probability gets higher, the put gains value, and the debt value decreases by the gain in the put value. Standard Black–Scholes formulas[3] apply for valuing the call on assets or the put of equity holders. These are:

$$C_0 = A_0 N(d_1) - D_T e^{-rT} N(d_2) = E_0$$

$$P_0 = D_T e^{-rT} N(-d_2) - A_0 N(-d_1)$$

The index stands for the date, 0 for current date and $T = 1$ for horizon. The call represents also the value of equity. The put–call parity is such that:

$$C_0 + D_0 = P_0 + A_0 \quad \text{and} \quad P_0 = C_0 + D_0 - A_0$$

The strike price is the debt at 1, and the value of debt at date 0 is:

$$D_0 = e^{-rT}$$

The values of the options are:

$$C = A_0 N(d_1) - D_1 e^{-rT} N(d_2)$$

$$P = D_1 e^{-rT} N(-d_2) - A_0 N(-d_1)$$

$$d_1 = [\ln(A_0/D_T) + (r + \sigma^2/2)T]/\sigma\sqrt{T}$$

$$d_2 = [\ln(A_0/D_T) + (r - \sigma^2/2)T]/\sigma\sqrt{T} = d_1 - \sigma\sqrt{T}$$

In these formulas, $N(x)$ stands for the standard normal distribution, ln is the Napierian logarithm and r is the risk-free rate. The volatility σ is the volatility of the random asset return. It is useful to note that $N(d_1) = 1 - N(1 - d_1)$ and $N(d_2) = 1 - N(1 - d_2)$. The standard formulas for sensitivities show that the delta of the call is $\Delta \text{call}/\Delta \mathbf{A} = N(d_1)$ and that of the put is $\Delta \text{put}/\Delta \mathbf{A} = N(d_1) - 1 = N(-d_1)$.

In the example below, we choose an expected asset value of 100 and a debt at date 0 of 50, resulting in a leverage ratio of debt to equity of 1 or a ratio of debt to asset of 0.5. The risk-free rate is 10%. There is a continuous rate equivalent to this discrete rate, which is 9.53102%. With this value, we check that the date 1 year from now is:

$$D_T = D_0 e^{-rT} = 50\exp(9.53102\% \times 1) = 55$$

The value of D_1, 55, is the strike price of both options. However, the option formulas require using the current debt value, 50, and the current asset value because they provide the present value of the options.

The firm's asset value follows a standard geometric Brownian motion, starting from the value A_0 at date 0 until date $T = 1$. The firm's asset value is the underlying random asset. What follows uses risk-neutral valuation, so that the asset provides the risk-free return r. The asset value follows a lognormal distribution at the horizon:

$$\mathbf{A} = A_0 \exp[(r - \tfrac{1}{2}\sigma^2)T + \sigma\sqrt{T}\mathbf{z}]$$

---

[3] See Hull (2000) for all basic formulas derived from the Black–Scholes equation.

Since A/A_0 follows a lognormal distribution, the logarithm follows a normal distribution: $\ln(A/A_0) = (r - \frac{1}{2}\sigma^2)T + \sigma\sqrt{t}\,z$. The default point occurs when $A = D_1$, which is when:

$$(r - \tfrac{1}{2}\sigma^2)T + \sigma\sqrt{t}\,z = \ln(D_1/A_0)$$

Or when:

$$z = [\ln(D_1/A_0) - (r - \tfrac{1}{2}\sigma^2)T]/\sigma\sqrt{T}$$

Since z follows N(0, 1), the value of the normalized distance to default is:

$$DD = [\ln(D_1/A_0) - (r - \tfrac{1}{2}\sigma^2)T]/\sigma\sqrt{T} = d_2$$

Hence, the distance to default is simply d_2. The probability of hitting that point is:

$$\text{Prob}\{z \leq -[\ln(A_0/D_1) - (r - \tfrac{1}{2}\sigma^2)T]/\sigma\sqrt{T}\} = \text{Prob}(z \leq DD) = N(-d_2)$$

Therefore, the Edf is $N(-d_2)$, which is the value of the area under the lognormal curve below default point. Because $N(-d_2)$ depends only on leverage, it is insensitive to the scale of asset and debt. This shows that the value of the put is:

$$P_0 = [D_0 - A_0 N(-d_1)/N(-d_2)]N(-d_2)$$

The put is the present value of the cost of default for lenders. It is the product of the default probability times a value of debt lower than the book value at 0. The difference is the expected loss under default, and is equal to the second term of the equation above. The expected loss is lower than the debt because the expected value of debt under default depends on the expected value of asset, conditional on default. Since the asset value triggering default is equal to the debt at date 1, it is still positive, so that lenders recover the expected value of assets conditional on default.

We start from the basic inputs, r, σ, t, A_0 and D_T, and get the Edf as $Edf = N(-d_2)$, which is the value of the area under the lognormal curve below default point. Using a preset value for σ, we derive the values of the call and the put option. Once given these parameters, the volatility of the equity is the volatility of the call option on asset. The relationship between the volatility of the call and that of the asset is:

$$\sigma(E) = A_0\sigma(A)N(d_1)/E_0$$

In the process, we start from the asset value and volatility as inputs. In fact, they derive from the observed equity value and its volatility. When moving from equity data to asset value and volatility, we need to solve the basic equations through an iterative numerical process.

Sample Calculations of the Put and Call Values

The book value of debt is 50 and the value of assets is 100 at date 0. The strike price is 55 at $T = 1$, from the above, if the risk-free rate is 10%. The volatility of equity is 28.099%. This value results in an Edf of 1%, once calculations are done. This is sufficient to derive all the above values (Table 38.1).

The theoretical value E_0 as a call option with the above inputs is 50.043744. It is above the equity value without the put, or $50 = 100 - 50$, because of the upside on asset value.

TABLE 38.1 Equity value as a call option on asset value and default put

$\ln(A_0/D_1)$	0.5978370
$(r + \sigma^2/2) \times T$	0.1347867
$(r - \sigma^2/2) \times T$	0.0558336
$d_1 = [\ln(A_0/D_1) + (r + \sigma^2/2) \times T]/\sigma\sqrt{T}$	2.6073327
$d_2 = [\ln(A_0/D_1) + (r - \sigma^2/2) \times T]/\sigma\sqrt{T}$	2.3263468
$N(d_1)$	0.9954374
$N(d_2)$	0.9900000
Call on asset $= A_0 N(d_1) - D_1 e^{-rT} N(d_2)$	50.0437440
Put $= D_1 e^{-rT} N(-d_2) - A_0 N(-d_1)$	0.0437435

Note: Values rounded to the seventh decimal digit.

The gain from stockholders is the expected loss from debt holders or the value of the put, 0.0437435, due to the put–call parity: $C_0 + D_0 = P_0 + A_0$. The distance to default is $d_2 = 2.3263468$.

Edf and Expected Loss Calculations

Proceeding to the Edf calculations, we find that the Edf is 1% (rounded to the sixth digit) and that the expected loss is the value of the put, resulting from the 1% Edf and the decrease in value of the debt given default. Note that the Edf value is that of a risk-neutral probability (Table 38.2).

TABLE 38.2 Edf and loss on debt

Expected recovery on debt	45.6256510
Loss given default (Lgd $= 50 -$ recovery)	4.3743490
Probability of default Edf $= N(-d_2)$	1.0000006%
Expected loss $N(-d_2) \times 45.62565127$	0.0437435
Distance to default d_2	2.3263468

The expected recovery is the second term of the put value, $A_0 N(-d_1)/N(-d_2)$, calculating $N(-x) = 1 - N(x)$. The loss under default is 4.374349, and the loss given default times the default probability is 1% of that amount.

Debt Economic Value and Implied Equity Volatility

From these values, we derive: the debt economic value as the book value at date 0 minus the put value at date 0; the implied volatility of equity embedded in the asset volatility (Table 38.3).

TABLE 38.3 Implied equity volatility

Implied equity volatility	55.94078%
Debt value $D_0 -$ put$_0$	49.956257

The implied equity value results from the relationship between the equity, as a call option on asset, and the asset volatility from:

$$\sigma(E) = A_0\sigma(A)N(d_1)/E_0 = (100 \times 28.099\% \times 0.9954374)/50 = 55.94078\%$$

We observe that the equity volatility is much higher than the asset volatility. This is due to the leverage effect, since $N(d_1)$ is very close to 1. This is a general result: leveraged firms have asset volatility lower than equity volatility. This calculation also shows how to work backwards from equity value and volatility to asset value and volatility. There is only one pair of values of these parameters that complies with the structure of all equations.

Risky Debt Value and Credit Spread

Since the debt value is lower than 50, there is a discount rate that makes the present value of 55, as of date 1, equal to the lower present value of 49.956257, lower than the initial 50. The gap between the higher discount rate and the original discount rate is the credit spread. The risky yield making the 55 equal to this last value, using continuous rates, is such that:

$$49.956257 = 55e^{-yT}$$

The risky yield is $y = 9.618544\%$. This rate is higher than the risk-free continuous rate, equivalent to the 10% discrete rate 9.53102%. The gap is the credit spread, 0.08753% in continuous compounding or 8.7 basis points.

Hedging Credit Risk with Short Sale of Equity

The equity value and the put depend on the same terms because of the put–call parity. Therefore, it is possible for lenders to hedge the change in the put value by shorting the equity. We know that the sensitivities of the call (or equity) and of the put are respectively:

$$\Delta\text{Call}/\Delta A = N(d_1)$$

$$\Delta\text{Put}/\Delta A = N(d_1) - 1 = N(-d_1)$$

Therefore, we can compensate any increase in put value by shorting the equity, the ratio being that of sensitivities. Rather than using the theoretical formulas, we provide a numerical example below. The asset value decreases by 1, resulting in a higher default probability and put value. Simultaneously, the stock price or the call on asset value decreases (Table 38.4).

TABLE 38.4   Changes of asset value, Edf, put value and stock value

	Initial	Final	Value changes
Asset	100.0	99.0	−1.000000
Edf(%)	1.000001	1.099387	0.099386
Put	0.043744	0.048552	0.004808
Stock = call on equity	50.043744	49.048554	−0.995192

When the asset value decreases by 1 unit, the equity value decreases by 0.995192 units, and the put value increases by 0.004808. The put value increase is a loss for the lender. Therefore, the bank can compensate this loss by selling short the equity for $0.004808/0.995192 = 0.0048315$ units of stock. This ratio is also approximately $N(-d_1)/N(d_1) = (1 - 0.9954374)/0.9954374 = 0.0045835$. It is necessary to adjust the ratio continuously to mimic the relative changes in values of the equity and the put.

VARIATIONS OF MERTON'S MODEL

Some variations of Merton's model existed before 1974, implying default when asset value goes under a preset value of debt, and others are extensions[4], progressively extending the scope of the model to other variables.

The gambler's ruin model considers that a 'gambler' plays with a cash reserve from which he pays negative payoffs and to which positive payoffs are added. Wilcox (1971, 1973) considers the cash flow to have any one of two values at each gamble. The cash reserve is the equity of the firm. Default occurs when the cash drops to zero. Others have extended the model[5]. In this case, the equity has a preset value, which does not recognize the fact that a firm does not fail simply because it runs out of cash. Firms have upside potential from further opportunities that make the equity market value closer to the economic reality than the book value.

The rationale of relating default probability to observable attributes is not far from the equity cash reserve model. For instance, when looking at the ability to face debt obligation through interest coverage ratios, we get close to the view of an exhausting cash reserve with negative cash flows. If interest coverage ratios get below 1, the firm loses cash flows and uses up entirely its cash reserve, once funding through debt and equity becomes limited.

One benefit of the Merton model is that it looks forward. Another is that asset value captures the present value of the entire stream of future free cash flows. Hence, a single cash flow can make the firm fail, and cumulated cash drains cannot as long as the firm has sufficient upside potential. This is exactly what happens when high growth firms keep having negative profit, and remain 'cash-eating' machines for a while until they finally reach the stage where cash flows become positive, if they succeed in their high expansion phase.

The KMV implementation has several limitations due to the necessity of making it instrumental. For example, default occurs at a given horizon, where the asset value is above or below the debt value. Real situations are more complex than considering debt as a bullet bond with exercise at some horizon. There is no such thing as a simple bullet debt amortized only once with a certain value. In fact, both the asset value and the debt value, linked to interest rates and default risk, follow a stochastic process. In addition, the value of debt, in the KMV model, is a combination of short-term debt and a fraction of long-term debt. This is only a proxy of the actual time structure of debt repayments. Therefore, the simple model falls short of the reality, although the concepts are robust. Moreover, the time path of asset value crosses the default point before the

---

[4] We discuss here only some of them. Other related contributions include those of Galai and Masulis (1976), Shimko et al. (1993), Johnson and Stulz (1987), Cooper and Mello (1991).

[5] They include Santomero and Vinso (1977), Vinso (1979), Benishay (1973), Katz et al. (1985).

horizon. Therefore, default could occur before the horizon. Modelling such a probability that the asset value hits the default point at any time between now and the horizon requires simulating all time paths. This would add complexity since the default point (debt) also changes with time. Finally, the KMV model ignores such contractual clauses as cross-default on all debts.

Beyond Merton's model, variations exist trying to extend the original framework to new variables. Black and Cox (1976) model default as the asset value going under a preset boundary value. Longstaff and Schwartz (1995) model default with the same rule, but the risk-free rate is stochastic and follows the one-factor Vasicek model. In addition, they include a correlation between the interest rate and the asset value processes. This allows us to explore what happens to credit spreads when the firm gets closer to default. Other models have introduced various variations. For instance, the boundary value triggering default could relate to the market value of debt. In fact, this would make the valuation of assets comparable to debt, when combined with interest rate volatility. Others consider the influence of the cost of bankruptcy and taxes in the trade-off of borrowers considering exercising their default option.

MAPPING DEFAULT PROBABILITY TO THE STANDARDIZED NORMAL DISTANCE TO DEFAULT

In the KMV universe of listed firms, it is always possible to use the modelled Edf. In the private firm universe, there are no equity prices. Few firms belong to the KMV universe of modelled individual asset returns, among those of banks' portfolios. In addition, credit officers prefer to assign ratings using both quantitative criteria and judgmental information to capture all credit risk dimensions, rather than using mechanical models. In this case, a common practice is to map internal ratings to default probabilities. Outside the KMV universe, it becomes necessary to 'de-link' the model from asset values because they are unobservable, and to 're-link' the option model of default to the preset default probability. The option framework extends, in a simplified version, to the modelling correlations between credit events, migrations and defaults, of different firms when preset default probabilities are assigned rather than modelled.

Chapter 44 explains how to derive correlated default events using the simplified model. The solution is to use a simplified default option framework, given that the 'assigned' default probability embeds all relevant information about the underlying asset value. This simplified model assumes that asset values follow standardized normal distributions (expectation 0 and standard deviation 1). Threshold values corresponding to a given default probability derive from the tables of the standardized normal distribution. If the default probability is 2.5%, the corresponding standardized asset value is -1.96; if the probability of default is 1%, it becomes -2.33. If the asset value falls between two threshold values, we are in the risk class bounded by the upper and lower default probabilities. Considering only one obligor, there is a one-to-one correspondence between the asset value A_X triggering the default of obligor X and the default probability DP_X if we stick to a standardized distribution of asset values (mean 0 and volatility 1) (Figure 38.3).

This correspondence results from: Prob(asset value $\leq A_X$) $= DP_X$. Formally, $\Phi(A_X) = DP_X$ is equivalent to $A_X = \Phi^{-1}(DP_X)$, where $\Phi(A_X)$ is the cumulative function of a

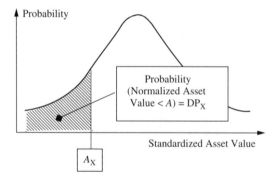

FIGURE 38.3 Asset value and default probability

standard normal distribution, of mean 0 and volatility 1. The absolute values of A_X deviations and the corresponding default probabilities are given in Table 38.5 and Figure 38.4.

TABLE 38.5 Default probability and standardized default point of asset value (normal curve)

Multiple of volatility $A_X = \Phi^{-1}(DP_X)$	$\Phi(A_X) = DP_X(\%)$[a]
1.00	16.00
1.28	10.00
1.65	4.95
1.96	2.50
2.33	1.00
2.57	0.51
2.70	0.35
2.90	0.19
3.00	0.14
3.20	0.07
3.40	0.03
3.60	0.02
3.80	0.01

[a]Probability of asset value being lower than the default point A_i as a multiple of the unit volatility.

As an example, an obligor X has a 1% default probability. Under the simplified standardized distance to default model, the current distance to default is 2.33. The standardized asset value should move down by 2.33 to trigger default or, equivalently, the default threshold for X's asset value is $A_X = -2.33$. The financial interpretation is that the debt value is lower than the asset value by 2.33 units. The initial default probability suffices entirely to define a standardized normal distribution of asset values. The next section uses this model to derive transition probabilities from an initial state defined by a preset default probability.

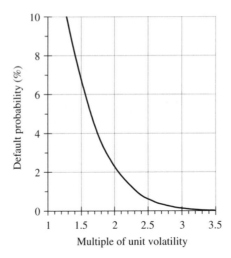

FIGURE 38.4   Relationships between multiples of volatility and default frequency (standardized normal distribution)

MODELLING MIGRATIONS UNDER THE OPTION MODEL OF DEFAULT

Migration matrices group historical frequencies of transitions across risk classes over a specified horizon, for example 1 year. A migration frequency is the count of firms migrating from one risk class to another risk class, or the ratio of these firms to the original firms in the initial risk class. Starting from one risk class, there are as many migrations as there are final states. The final states include all risk classes plus the default state. The default option model applies to migrations since it models the default probabilities that map with risk classes.

The option framework helps to model migrations in two ways. The first application moves from modelled asset values to migration probabilities. The process implies modelling the distribution of asset values at the horizon. This provides three different results: the expected value, from which the expected default probability results; the distribution of probabilities of migrating to any of the values in the spectrum of final asset values, which are the migration probabilities; the corresponding distance to default and the related default probabilities. Since default probabilities map to ratings, it is possible to convert any band of final default probabilities into a final rating.

The second application moves in the opposite direction, from observed default and migration probabilities across ratings classes to the asset value bands and standardized distances to default at the horizon corresponding to final default probabilities. The process is the reverse of the preceding one. It moves from given migration probabilities to probabilities of reaching bands of asset values at the horizon. The purpose is the same as the simplified model of the section above. It allows us to model correlations between migrations of pairs of firms from correlations of their unobservable asset values once we know their initial default probabilities.

From Modelled Asset Values to Migration Probabilities

In the KMV universe of firms, modelled asset returns result in a distribution of final values at the horizon. Each corresponds to a distance to default and a default probability. Hence, the same process that generates the expected value at the horizon to obtain the expected default probability also provides the migration probabilities for all asset levels and the corresponding default probabilities. In Figure 38.5, the distance to default decreases when moving downward from one time path of asset returns to a lower one. Accordingly, the default probability increases. The distribution of asset values at the horizon is identical to the distribution of migrations, and provides the migration probabilities. Notice that the default probability expected at the horizon results from one single asset value, which is the expected asset value. When the time path hits a level other than this expected value, it does not change the default probability between the current date and the horizon, but it does change it from the horizon to the next period. For each new asset value along the unique distribution at the horizon, there is a subsequent distribution which is higher or lower than the one at the horizon, depending on where the asset value ends up at the horizon. Figure 38.5 shows the unique expected default probability at the horizon, not the different future default probabilities corresponding to each final state.

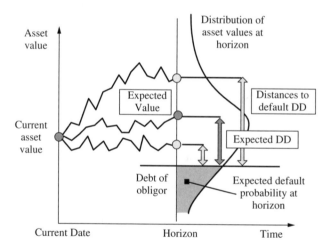

FIGURE 38.5   Modelling horizon asset values and migrations

From Migration Probabilities to Standardized Distances to Default

Transition probabilities map to final asset values, using the standardized distance to default model. Table 38.6 reproduces a transition matrix, with fictitious data. The row 'F' provides all migrations from this credit state to all others, including the default state, the sum of the frequencies as a percentage along the row totalling 100%.

TABLE 38.6 Sample transition matrix

	\multicolumn{8}{c}{Transition matrix}								Sum of probabilities
	A	B	C	D	E	F	G	Default	
A	89.4%	9.8%	0.6%	0.2%	0.0%	0.0%	0.0%	0.0%	100%
B	0.9%	90.9%	7.1%	0.8%	0.1%	0.2%	0.0%	0.0%	100%
C	0.1%	2.6%	90.1%	6.0%	0.8%	0.3%	0.0%	0.1%	100%
D	0.1%	0.3%	6.3%	85.1%	6.3%	1.5%	0.2%	0.2%	100%
E	0.0%	0.2%	0.6%	7.4%	78.9%	10.2%	1.2%	1.5%	100%
F	**0.0%**	**0.1%**	**0.4%**	**0.6%**	**6.1%**	**83.0%**	**3.8%**	**6.0%**	**100%**
G	0.2%	0.0%	0.2%	1.0%	1.5%	12.0%	66.0%	19.1%	100%

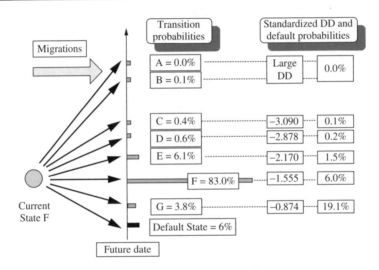

FIGURE 38.6 From migration probabilities to standardized distances to default

The distribution in Figure 38.6 is extracted from the row, in bold characters, of the full transition matrix showing where an 'F' firm migrates, including to the default state. The distribution of migration probabilities is skewed and the mode is in the same risk class as the initial one, meaning that the absence of migration is the most likely event.

Once the distribution of final states is defined, we have the default probabilities of each rating from historical data. These default probabilities map to the threshold of standardized asset values from a normal standardized distribution. Figure 38.6 shows the corresponding values of the implicit asset threshold triggering default for each migration for which the default probabilities differ from zero. The higher the asset value, the lower the risk, and the larger the downside move of the standardized asset value triggering default. The standardized distance to default results directly from the assigned default probabilities for each final state. For example, when the final state, starting from 'F', is C, the default probability is 0.1%, requiring a downward move of the standardized distance to default of -3.09, from the standardized normal inverse distribution. When the final state is E, with a probability of migration to this state of 6.1%, the final default probability is 1.5%, and the standardized distance to default is -2.170.

39

Credit Risk Exposure

Exposures are future amounts at risk. They are valued at book value in the banking portfolio and at market value, or liquidation value, for the trading portfolio. Current exposures are not sufficient to describe exposure risk, since 'Exposure At Default' (EAD) is a future, hence uncertain, exposure. Ideally, the time profile of exposures is the adequate input for measuring risk. This is easy with term loans, with a contractual amortization profile. However, most exposures are uncertain for future dates.

The exposures for the trading portfolio are market-driven and subject to uncertainty as well. For traded instruments, exposure to credit risk remains limited to the holding period. For over-the-counter derivatives, it extends to the entire maturity. Exposure risk relates the uncertainty of future exposures arising from contingent events for the banking portfolio and from market movements for the trading portfolio.

This chapter discusses the exposure measurement for banking products, traded instruments and over-the-counter derivatives.

For the banking portfolio, the on-balance sheet and off-balance sheet exposure uncertainties depend on uncertain events requiring business rules for measurements.

For the market portfolio, exposures are market-driven. For the short holding periods of traded instruments, stocks and bonds, the exposure is the current value, and the credit risk is the fraction of the price variation related to credit risk only. Chapter 43 explains how to isolate these price fluctuations from those related to general market moves.

For over-the-counter derivatives, the exposure is also market-driven, but it extends until maturity. These exposures are 'two-way' exposures. If the liquidation value of the instrument is positive, the bank is at risk, otherwise the counterparty, not the bank, is at risk. Because derivative exposures are market-driven, they vary significantly with time, depending on the volatility of the underlying market parameters. The current risk is the current liquidation value. The potential risk is the time profile is the upper bound of positive exposures, at a given confidence level, as obtained from distributions of values at future time points. These principles follow the guidelines set up by the G30 group.

This chapter comprises three main sections addressing, respectively, exposure uncertainty for banking exposures, tradable instrument exposures and derivative credit exposures. The second section is only an introduction to the detailed discussion of specific risk of tradable instruments in Chapter 43.

BANKING EXPOSURES

There are many contractual exposures since term loans represent a large fraction of outstanding loans. Most other products raise exposure measurement issues because the amount at risk is unknown in advance. For banking credit exposures, relevant distinctions are 'on-balance sheet' versus 'off-balance sheet' transactions. In most cases, there are always hard data that bound exposures in time and amount. In addition, exposures are at book values or mark-to-model.

The 'hard' data for banking exposures are:

- The amount and maturity of committed lines.
- The amortization schedule for term loans.
- The maturity of the authorizations.
- The dates of reviewing the authorizations.
- The current usage of committed lines.

Because of economic measures of exposures, there is a mismatch issue between these and the basis for calculating revenues addressed in the last subsection.

On-balance Sheet

In general, exposure differs from current usage because the amount at risk at future dates is uncertain. Exposure risk appears when we do not know the future usage of a banking line. The notable exception is term loans. Their amortization profile is a good proxy for the future exposures. Still, contractual repayments are subject to prepayments, and the effective maturity is a substitute. Effective maturity results from experience or models for mortgages. For many other credit lines, there is a commitment of the bank to let the borrower increase the usage by drawing on a credit line up to a certain amount left at the initiative of the borrower. Overdrafts, consumer loans and credit card balances are subject to renewal, and borrowers can make new drawings at their initiative. Rollover lines generate a long-term exposure, beyond the rollover dates. Committed lines of credit are on-balance sheet for the used fraction and off-balance sheet for the unused portion of the line. Borrowers draw a committed line whenever they need to, up to the maximum amount authorized. Project financing is subject to exposure uncertainty both for the construction phase and for the subsequent operation phase when the repayments occur. Uncertain exposures are the rule more than the exception.

In all cases, the current usage of the line might differ from the future usage. It is necessary to define what are the expected exposures at future horizons and the exposure under default, which might increase when credit risk deteriorates. The New Basel Accord stipulates that EAD is a key input to the risk assessment process.

A facility has only two characteristics bounding the exposure set from inception: maturity and authorization. For non-committed lines of credit, the current and expected usages are acceptable measures, although choosing which one is relevant is judgmental. The next date for reviewing the authorization is a good candidate for maturity, since the bank does not need to extend credit beyond this. The authorization remains a cap to all measures. The case of committed lines of credit differs from the above, even when the current usage differs from the authorization. The undrawn portion of the line is off-balance sheet, and the subsequent section addresses this special case.

Off-balance Sheet

The basic issue with off-balance sheet exposures is that it is never certain, and sometimes highly unlikely, that such contingencies given will move up to being on-balance sheet. Because of this uncertainty, the common rule is to assign weights lower than 1 to off-balance sheet contingencies to differentiate them from on-balance sheet exposures. This is similar to defining loan equivalents of smaller exposures. This is the regulatory treatment of off-balance sheet exposures, with the 50% factor.

Because of the diversity of off-balance sheet commitments, it makes sense to differentiate their economic treatment. For committed lines of credit, the economic exposure is 100% of the commitment since the bank is contractually at risk for this total amount, even if there is no current usage. Regulations allow us to use a lower percentage because the likelihood of maximum usage remains remote in many cases. However, a borrower getting close to default is likely to fully draw the line.

Third-party guarantees given have only a remote possibility of exercise, since only the default of the borrower triggers exercise. However, they are similar to direct exposures since the borrower's default triggers the guarantee as if there was a direct exposure. The regulatory view on guarantees given to a third party is that the risk is equivalent to a direct exposure. However, there is a wide spectrum of third-party guarantees, ranging from simple letters of comfort to first recourse 'full' guarantees. The former does not carry any real risk because there is no legal commitment. Legal commitments are equivalent to lending directly. Because of these wide variations of the 'legal strength' of bank commitments, there is a case for differentiating the risks.

Other commitments, such as backup lines of liquidity for issuing commercial paper, look more like financial services than 'true' exposures. What triggers drawing is not the default of the client but a need to draw liquidity triggered by unlikely events. Hence, there is a case for differentiating them from other guarantees, but assessing the likelihood of materialization of the risk remains judgmental.

Revenues and Exposure Mismatches in Projections

Since exposure to credit risk is not the usage of lines, there is a mismatch between projected revenues and exposures considered for assessing credit risk. There is a contractual link between the effective exposure and the revenues. In the example of committed lines of credit, the undrawn portion receives a low fee while the drawn fraction receives full interest rate payment. If 100% of the line is at risk, the revenues no longer match the exposure because the calculation uses the effective amount drawn. In general, exposures at default might differ from projected exposures for calculating revenues. The mismatch between projected revenues and exposures alters the risk–return profile of all transactions and of the entire portfolio. However, it is a consequence of the prudent rules applying to risk measures and to revenue measures.

TRADABLE INSTRUMENTS

When dealing with tradable market instruments, the exposure is the price. Exposure uncertainty results from market-driven prices. The major differences with the banking portfolio are:

- For tradable market instruments, the 'hold to maturity' view is irrelevant. Traders make money from taking positions, not holding them. They can sell them at any time, notably when they fear adverse credit conditions. If they do not, the loss from default is the difference between the pre-default price and the post-default price. The loss from an adverse rating migration is also the difference between the pre-migration price and the post-migration price.
- Market risk is not credit risk, even though both result from variations of market values. Market risk is the potential loss resulting from adverse market movements over the liquidation period. Credit risk is the potential loss resulting only from a change in credit standing over the holding period.

The 'hold to maturity' view does not hold because it is possible to get rid of the exposure whenever a warning light turns on. The exposure is the current price.

Note that the credit risk is not the exposure. It is the fluctuation of the price over the holding period relating to credit risk events only. Chapter 43 expands the discussion and the case for measuring credit risk by the 'specific risk' of such instruments, that is the component of price risk unrelated to general market movements.

DERIVATIVE EXPOSURES

Derivatives include currency and interest swaps, options and any combination of these building blocks. Swaps exchange interest flows based on different rates, or flows in different currencies. Options allow us to buy or sell an asset at a stated price. The credit risk of derivatives results from the buy and hold view applicable to over-the-counter instruments since they are not traded in organized markets. For derivatives, the 'originate and hold' policy prevails, and the risk is the potential positive liquidation value of instruments until maturity. Credit risk of derivatives has two salient features:

- It is a two-way credit risk, which shifts from one counterparty to another depending on who owns the positive liquidation value. The liquidation value can be both positive or negative, depending, for example, on the relative values of the paying and the receiving legs of an interest rate swap.

- It is interactive with market risk because liquidation values depend on market parameters.

Current and potential exposures differ. The current risk is the time profile of the liquidation value at the prevailing market conditions. The potential risk is the time profile of the upper bounds of positive exposures, at a given confidence level, obtained by generating distributions of values at future time points. This section deals with the modelling of such time profiles.

The first subsection details the specifics of credit risk for derivatives. The second subsection explains the rationale for the determination of current and potential risk, following the guidelines set by the regulatory or advisory bodies. The third subsection illustrates the implementation of this methodology with simple examples. The last two subsections discuss portfolio effects and the netting of exposures within International Swap Dealers Association (ISDA) contracts, allowing us to reduce the risk by offsetting opposite exposures of different deals within the same ISDA contract.

Credit Risk for Derivatives: Methodology

All derivatives have a liquidation value. The familiar Discounted Cash Flow (DCF) model allows valuation of swaps. The stream of flows includes fixed flows and those indexed on market rates or currency exchange rates. Options have a value which combines the value of the right to exercise plus the payoff under immediate exercise (the difference between the actual value of the underlying parameter and the exercise value).

Credit Risk and Liquidation Values

Derivative exposures are subject to a paradox. They can have both positive and negative values since the liquidation value of a swap is the difference between the values of its two legs. Taking the example of an interest rate swap, we assume that the bank receives the floating rate and pays the fixed rate. Should the floating rate be above the fixed rate, the bank is a net receiver of cash. The liquidation value of its contract is positive. It is an asset. The usual view on credit risk is to value it as the difference between what happens in the case of no default and in the case of default. The bank holds an asset and makes a gain under no default. Under default, it loses this gain.

Since the difference can move from positive to negative, the credit risk is a two-way risk, shifting from one counterparty to the other depending on who owns the positive liquidation value. The bank with the positive liquidation value is the one at risk with the counterparty. If the liquidation value is negative, the counterparty is at risk with the bank. Sometimes, 'counterparty risk' qualifies credit risk for derivatives, suggesting the symmetrical two-way risk exposure.

For options, the risk is different. Options purchased have either zero or positive liquidation values, when they are in-the-money. In this case, the buyer is at risk because the counterparty might default on its obligation to pay if the buyer exercises the option. The seller has no risk since, should the buyer default, since there is nothing to pay to him.

The exposure to credit risk is the positive liquidation value owned by the bank at risk. Hence, credit risk for derivatives is market-driven. This interaction with market movements necessitates modelling of future exposures. Liquidation values fluctuate with markets, being sometimes positive and sometimes negative for swaps.

The Potential Risk and Forward Values

Since the credit risk of derivatives has increased a lot with the development of these instruments, an adequate methodology is required to capture the actual potential risk. Guidelines exist to achieve such objectives[1], as described in subsequent subsections.

The issue is to find the future worst-case exposures—or the maximum positive values—given market parameter behaviour. This methodology requires valuing the forward values of these instruments, at all future dates until maturity. These are 'mark-to-future' values, since the potential values are forward values at all intermediate dates between today and maturity. The future exposures are the upper bounds of positive liquidation values, at each time point until maturity, given a confidence level. The methodology generates time profiles of liquidation values, whose shapes depend on the nature of the instrument. Interest rate swaps have bell-shaped exposures, while currency swaps have an ever-increasing exposure with time, as explained in subsequent subsections.

The risk exists for the whole holding period, over which the liquidation value can change drastically with time. According to standard terminology, the current time profile of the liquidation values is the 'current risk' and the possible upward change in value generates an additional 'potential risk'. The overall risk at any point in time is the sum of the current and the potential risks.

Loan Equivalents: Usage and Issues

For implementation purposes, it is not easy to manipulate entire time profiles, so it is a common practice to derive 'loan equivalents', using the peak or the average exposure over time. Loan equivalents summarize modelled time profiles of exposures. They differ from conventional forfeits, which are crude estimates of future exposures without actually modelling them.

Credit equivalents are in percentage of notional. Conventional forfeits have major draw-backs. They do not capture the real risk of individual transactions, since they rely on conventions. For portfolios of transactions, measuring the risk suggests adding all individual transaction forfeits. This practice ignores offsetting effects. Liquidation values can change in opposite ways within portfolios. Moreover, netting allows us to net positive and negative liquidation values within an ISDA agreement. Without the values and signs of exposures, the individual forfeit system falls short of capturing portfolio effects, netting effects and correlations between the market values of the instruments. Modelling future exposures and how they 'sum up' over a portfolio makes it feasible to use loan equivalents that effectively measure the potential worst-case values and calibrate on the market. For netting agreements, the loan equivalent has to be post-netting.

---

[1] The guidelines were defined by the G30 (Group of Thirty, 1993).

Calculating Credit Risk Exposure of Derivatives

All derivative transactions have a notional amount that measures the size of the transaction. The notional is the base which, combined with market parameters, determines the interest flows or the currency flows of swaps, or the size of an optional transaction in terms of the underlying. Banks hold such instruments until maturity, which ranges from a few months up to 10 or 15 years.

Exposure and Liquidation Value of Derivatives

Over the long run, the liquidation value of derivative instruments can increase considerably. For example, a currency swap exchanges 1 million USD (the notional) against the equivalent in euros. With an exchange rate of 0.9 EUR/USD, a flow would be valued at 0.9 million EUR, if the exchange took place today. However, if the exchange rate fluctuates, the differential flow changes. If the USD reaches 1 EUR, the buyer of EUR is entitled to a gain of $0.1/0.9 = 0.111$ million EUR. This is the amount of the loss if the counterparty defaults. By definition, it is the amount at risk, or exposure. Of course, if the exchange rate varies in the opposite direction, the buyer of EUR has no risk since he owns a 'negative' liquidation value. The credit risk shifts to the counterparty who owns the positive liquidation value.

The same happens with options. The buyer of an option expects that the seller will pay him the difference between the exercise price and the current price of the underlying parameter. The buyer of a cap at 5% with a notional of 1 000 000 USD expects to receive the difference between the current interest rate, 6% for example, times the notional. This is an amount equal to $1\% \times 1\,000\,000$ USD $= 10\,000$ USD for each period. Should the counterparty default, the buyer of the option loses that amount, which is the exposure. The risk exists only when the option is in-the-money. If the option is out-of-the-money, there is no current benefit from exercise. The value drops to the time value of the option. The time value is the discounted value of future possibilities that the option becomes in-the-money between now and maturity. In addition, only the buyer of an option is at risk. He is the one who is entitled to receive some value. The seller's obligation is to pay, which does not generate any credit risk for him.

Credit Risk Management for Derivatives

Financial institutions have to comply with strict rules to limit risk. For their internal management they also need better measures of risk. For instance, the limit system is adequate only if the risk measures are correct. For derivatives, the usage of risk limits is difficult to measure. The notional does not represent the actual exposure. The current exposure is the value. However, the potential exposures arise from future increases in liquidation values. If the measure of potential exposure overestimates the actual risk, the usage of credit lines hits the limit too early, which constrains the volume of business. If the measure understates the actual risk, the limits system becomes inefficient because it does not actually limit the credit risk of transactions.

Current and Potential Risks

The mark-to-market value of a swap is the discounted value of future flows indexed with market parameters. It increases if the present value of future flows increases. At inception, it is zero since the swap exchanges the prevailing market rates. Afterwards, the liquidation value changes. For instance, the value of a swap receiving a floating rate and paying a fixed rate increases when the rate increases. The reverse is true when the swap pays the floating rate and receives the fixed. Swaps have positive or negative values depending on the direction and magnitude of the changes in interest rates. The value also changes with the time to maturity. For interest rate swaps, the number of cash flows decreases when the time to maturity decreases. For currency swaps, the main flow occurs at maturity. Only intermediate interest flows amortize over time. In the end, the risk should be valued at all dates between now and maturity.

The overall risk is the sum of the current and the potential risk. The potential risk is the possible increase in mark-to-market value of the instruments due to market movements. The potential risk of upside deviations of the mark-to-market value is the 'add-on'.

Both the current and the potential risks are time profiles of values. Even if the market parameters do not deviate from their value as of today, the swap value changes with the date due to the amortization effect and the discounting effect of future flows. The current liquidation value of the swap, as of today, does not suffice to fully capture the current risk. At all future dates until maturity, the same swap has different values even though we keep the same values of the market parameters. The swap has a time profile of liquidation values calculated with the current market parameters. The same is true with potential risk. Given a set of values of market parameters, the swap value changes at all future dates. Potential risk is also a time profile of values. In addition, there are many sets of possible market values for each future date, since these parameters are uncertain as of today.

Potential Risk

The potential risk should capture the upward deviations of market values, since only upside moves increase risk. The higher the swap value, the higher the possible amount at risk. However, there are as many future values, at any future date, as there are possible values for market parameters at those dates. As usual, a rule is required to define a 'maximum value'.

The rule is similar to that of the Value at Risk (VaR) methodology. The upper bound for the mark-to-market value of the swap is the upper bound at a given confidence level. For an individual transaction, this upper bound results from the upper or lower bounds of the underlying market parameters, modelled as a confidence interval. The upper and lower of the swap, at the same given confidence level, results from revaluation of the derivatives with these values of market parameters. For future dates, the value is 'mark-to-future' since it requires all flows plus the forward parameters.

An example illustrates the principle. The volatility of the exchange rate of the dollar against the euro is 10%, for instance, with a current exchange rate of 0.9 EUR/USD. The volatility is therefore 0.09 EUR/USD. Under the assumption of a normal distribution of exchange rate, it will not exceed $(0.9 + 0.1764) = 1.0764$ EUR/USD, or the current rate plus two standard deviations, in more than 2.5% of all cases. With this upper bound for the exchange rate, a year from now, the upper bound for the currency swap is $(1.0764 - 0.9)$EUR/USD $\times$ 1 million USD = 0.1764 million EUR. This liquidation value is the upper bound for the mark-to-market value of the swap 1 year from now, at the 2.5% (one-tailed) confidence level.

This upward deviation of the liquidation value is the potential risk. It is also the add-on for the date considered in the calculation (1 year). The add-on is both in dollar value and as a fraction in percentage of the notional. For instance, the 0.1764 million EUR deviation of liquidation value is 20% of the notional value of the swap. It is necessary to calculate the add-ons for all future dates until maturity.

When the horizon extends beyond 1 year, the market volatility increases. It can be derived from the 1-year volatility through the formula: $\sigma_t = \sigma_1 \sqrt{t}$, where t is in years. It is possible to refine all assumptions to accommodate the specifics of the problem. Since the horizon is long-term, pure extrapolation of current values might be inadequate. Mean reverting effects result in lower upper bounds than the above simple extrapolation rule. Nevertheless, the general methodology does not change (Figure 39.1).

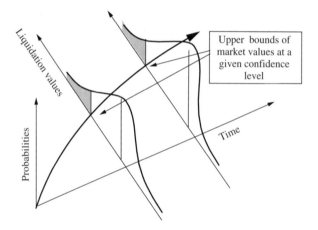

FIGURE 39.1   The upper bounds of mark-to-market values of derivatives

When we look at the time profile generated as above, exposures reach a maximum value at a given confidence level at each time point. In fact, the probability of continuously hitting all maximum exposures at all time points is much lower than the confidence level, so the approach sounds too conservative. On the other hand, if we hit the highest potential exposure at date 1, chances are that we go beyond this exposure later, making the approach appear not conservative enough.

Formally, the probability of hitting the original maximum exposure at date 2, conditional on having hit the maximum exposure at date 1, is much higher than the confidence level corresponding to the upper bound of exposure at date 1. If the process follows a zero drift time path, the probability of exceeding the original date 2 potential exposure if we have done so at date 1 is roughly 50%, because there are roughly as many chances of going above the date 1 liquidation value at date 2 as there are of going below.

In reality, we should simulate time paths of market parameters rather than distributions at several time points. The preset confidence level becomes the fraction of time paths simulated up to date 1, up to date 2, etc. Moreover, certain derivatives look backwards because their value at a future date depends on historical values of the underlying. These require using time path simulations rather than single time point distributions. This would be more calculation intensive. Another simple way to limit the calculation of the time profile is simply to update it when moving forward in time, as illustrated in the next subsection.

Worst-case exposures serve to measure worst-case losses. When looking at expected loss, the expected exposure is a best measure. The expected exposure results from the distribution at any time point, except that positive values only are relevant. Hence, the expected exposure at this time point is the expected value of truncated distribution at the zero value[2].

The Time Profile of Exposure and Time Drift

The time profile of exposure drifts with time, while current value drifts. A continuous, or frequent, update of the time profiles when time passes addresses the issue. Figure 39.2 shows several scenarios depending on whether the liquidation value increases or decreases with time. At each time point, it is necessary to revalue the entire worst-case time profile of exposure, starting from the new value. In the figure, we assume that the original exposure is zero because the derivative is a swap with a zero liquidation value at origination. The derivative is a currency swap, whose value increases until maturity, as shown in the next subsection.

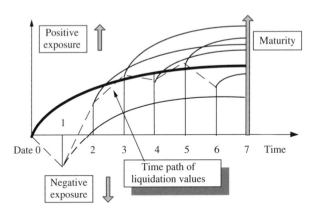

FIGURE 39.2   The time profiles of potential exposures of swaps with drifts of time

The revalued liquidation serves as the basis for the new time profile, which can move downwards or upwards. If the liquidation value increases with time, the time profiles of worst-case exposures increase beyond the original values. On the other hand, negative exposures correspond to a zero risk for the bank, as illustrated by the dashed line, whenever the liquidation value is negative. The dashed straight line shows the liquidation values at revaluation time points. The exposure drops below the line at the first time points

---

[2] The expected value of the exposure normally distributed is $\sigma/\sqrt{2\pi}$. We need to multiply this value by the notional and add any positive current value to get the expected value exposure.

then increases. Accordingly, the maximum exposure reconstructed over a time prior gets shorter when we get closer to maturity.

Implementation

Grids of add-on, expressed in percentages of notional, are 'credit equivalents' or 'loan equivalents'. Such grids result from the nature of the derivative (interest rate or currency swap for instance), the residual time to maturity, the volatility of the market parameters and the various forward sensitivities of the derivatives at all time points. They also depend on the current yield curves (both spot and forward) because the liquidation values are the discounted future flows using the interest rates.

Calculating Credit Risk

The total risk is the sum of the current risk and the potential risk at the date considered. For instance, the current risk at date 2 of the liquidation value, using the current market parameter values, is 10 000. The add-on at the same date is 8%. If the notional is 100 000, for example, the value of the add-on, or potential risk, is $8\% \times 1\,000\,000 = 8000$. The overall, or total, risk at date 2 is:

$$\text{Total risk} = \text{current risk} + \text{potential risk} = 10\,000 + 8000 = 18\,000$$

Since there is a time profile of add-ons, there is a time profile of total risk as well. Sometimes the entire time profile is used, and sometimes only the peak value is considered.

Credit Risk Time Profiles

The time profiles of add-ons for swaps have different shapes. When the last flows are the most important, the risk usually increases with time because of the effect of increased volatility of this last flow. This is the usual profile of currency swaps. When amortizing effects are important, the number of flows decreases with time. Simultaneously, the volatility of market parameters increases with time. These two factors have offsetting effects on the deviations of the liquidation value. When amortization is negligible, the increase in volatility results in increased deviations of liquidation value with time. When the amortization effect dominates, the liquidation values obtained from the bounds of market parameters decline. Hence, there is a maximum for the deviations of the liquidation value of the swap somewhere between now and maturity. Potential risk usually peaks between 1/3 and 1/2 of the residual life (Figure 39.3).

Credit Risk Exposure for Portfolios of Derivatives

With derivative portfolios, the total liquidation value is the sum of individual liquidation values. With 'netting' agreements, positive deviations net against negative deviations. In addition, individual deviations depend on each other, since they are market-driven and market parameter variations comply with a correlation structure.

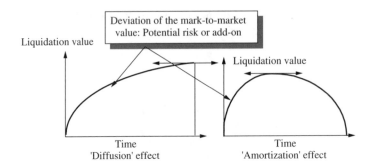

FIGURE 39.3   Time profiles of credit risks of swaps

Netting

With netting agreements, banks exchange only the netted value of instruments. For instance, if A has two transactions with B whose liquidation values are 50 and −20, the risk exposure is the netted value, or +30. This is because only netted flows count. Without netting agreement, only positive liquidation values are at risk. In the above example, the risk will be +50 and 0 for the second transaction. The exposures are added according to the rule of positive liquidation values. Since netting agreements reduce the risk exposure, adding individual forfeit measures of credit risk is not adequate. The liquidation value of the portfolio at any future date should net the liquidation values of individual instruments. This requires direct measures of the current and potential risks for the entire subportfolio subject to netting.

Portfolio Exposure and Correlation between Market Parameters

The evaluation of offsetting effects within portfolios is not simple because the individual instrument deviations do not add. Summing individual risks would mean that all instruments reach their upper bound values at the same time. This is an unrealistic assumption since the different instruments depend on different market parameters that cannot deviate simultaneously in the most adverse direction.

The interdependency between market parameters is a necessary input for defining the upper bound of the portfolio value. Interest rates in one currency correlate, exchange rates correlate with interest rate differentials across currencies, and so on. The issue is to determine the upper bound of the mark-to-market value of the portfolio given such correlations.

The adequate methodology relies on correlations between market parameters or on full simulations. The methodology is the same as that used to value the VaR for market risk for portfolios. The correlation methodology determines the volatility of the mark-to-market value of the portfolio given market parameters, their interdependencies and the sensitivities of the instruments of the portfolio to the different market parameters. Note that sensitivities change at different time points because of the amortization of cash flows. In addition, they change over long periods because they are local measures.

The simulation methodology (Monte Carlo) tests all possible values using sets of market parameter values consistent with their interdependencies. Both the generation of random values constrained by the correlation structure and historical sets of observed values work.

The multiple simulation technique is capable of handling options. The technique generates a distribution of the possible values of the portfolio for each future date. The upper bound at a given confidence level results from this distribution. The composition of the portfolio changes over time. Some derivatives reach maturity and their liquidation value vanishes at that time. Therefore, the time profile of exposures has no typical shape because the portfolio amortization combined with netting effects generates any shape for the time profile (Figure 39.4).

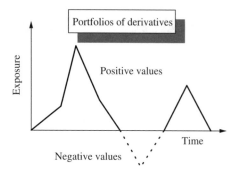

FIGURE 39.4   Time profiles of credit risk exposure: example

A final remark is that credit risk looks for positive variations of market values, whereas market risk cares for negative variations. Hence, there is a case for netting the market risk and the credit risk of derivatives. However, this is both complex and not necessarily relevant. The short-term horizon of market risk does not compare, in terms of deviations of values, with the long-term horizon of derivatives. The small adjustment might not be worth the effort. In addition, it is conservative to add both risks, rather than net them.

40

From Guarantees to Structures

Collaterals, loan contracts and covenants serve to control the borrower's risk-taking propensity and increase recoveries under default. Structures are Special Purpose Vehicles (SPVs) that have no credit standing by themselves: they offer credit risk protection from collateral and from covenants ruling the life of the SPV, which customizes both default probabilities and recoveries according to the seniority level of lenders.

The regulators recognized the risk mitigating effects of various forms of guarantees received in the 'foundation' approach of the New Basel Accord of 2001. Recoveries reduce loss under default and if their value is reasonably certain, they reduce the capital charge. Losses for credit risk depend directly on recovery rates, making these key inputs for measuring credit risk. The New Accord provides strong incentives for building up data on recoveries. Recoveries depend on the nature of protection, making it necessary to differentiate them according to the nature of guarantees.

Collaterals are assets seized by lenders in the event of default.

Third-party guarantees are contractual obligations of a guarantor to act as a substitute for the primary borrower if he defaults on his payment obligations. A third-party guarantee is a legal obligation. Support, from the head of a group to a subsidiary, is informal. It designates the supportive behaviour of holding companies towards subsidiaries whose credit standing deteriorates up to default. Support is like third-party guarantees except that there is no binding legal agreement.

Credit derivatives are similar to guarantees and insurances, but they are distinct contracts from loans and relate to underlying assets that are not necessarily those of lenders. Sellers of credit derivatives are sellers of a protection, or insurers, buyers of credit derivatives are buyers of protection.

Whenever there is an exposure to the risk of a pair of obligors, through guarantees or credit derivatives, default occurs when both obligors default. This is a 'double', or 'joint', default event of the primary borrower and the guarantor. Its probability depends on how interdependent their risks are.

Covenants are contractual clauses, imposed on borrowers, the breach of which triggers a prompt repayment of outstanding debt. Covenant breaches require waivers from lenders, implying renegotiation, to continue operations.

Structures are the ultimate stage of protection shield for lenders. The SPV protects lenders with covenants ruling the structure's behaviour, allowing for early default events before potential losses of lenders get too high and corrective actions triggered by breaches of covenants.

This chapter describes the various credit risk mitigants and serves as an introduction to valuation, when feasible, addressed in the next chapter. The sections address sequentially collateral, third-party guarantees, covenants and structures with SPVs.

COLLATERAL

Collaterals are assets that the lender seizes and sells if the borrower fails to perform his debt obligations. The original credit risk turns into a recovery risk plus an asset value risk. Collateral is also an incentive for the borrower to fulfil debt obligations effectively, mitigating moral hazard in lending. Should he fail in his obligation, the borrower loses if the value of the collateral is higher than debt.

Collateral Risks

The existence of collateral minimizes credit risk if the collateral can easily be taken over and sold at some significant value. Collateralization is a widespread and common way to mitigate credit risk. There are many types of collaterals:

- Real assets, from houses for mortgages to aircraft and commodities in other business lines.
- Securities, mainly for market transactions, the most common example being that of repos.
- Commodities, when a cargo is financed, or in oil and gas financing.
- Receivables from a pool of assets in securitization, when credit card or mortgage receivables are securitized. Pools of assets include bonds and loans as well as structures used to sell these types of assets in the market.
- Margin borrowing.

Specialized finance makes wide usage of collaterals. In some cases, these are tangible assets. Assets financing is collateral-based, whether assets are ships, aircraft or assets of a corporation. In many other cases, there are intangible collaterals. Corporate acquisitions (Leveraged Buy-Outs, LBOs) or project finance pledge the cash flows from assets. Nevertheless, future cash flows are uncertain. Covenants help in structuring the transactions to minimize the risks. The collateralized assets are subject to a number of risks:

- Accessibility risk, since it might be difficult to effectively seize the collateral.
- Integrity risk, the risk of damage to the collateral.

- Legal risk, which is the risk of disputes arising from the various laws at play in international transactions.
- Valuation risk, since the liquidation value of a collateral depends on the existence of a secondary market and the price volatility of such a market.

Legal Risk

Legal risk results from the risk of dispute to access the collateral. In addition, the collateral in international transactions is subject to a number of laws, such as that of the lender, of the borrower, of the place where the collateral is located and the law of the contract.

The Ability to Physically Access the Collateral

Legal access to the collateral is one issue. Physical access might be another, since accessing the collateral might be straightforward or very difficult. With cash collateral or securities, the collateral is posted with a custodian, or the lender, and access is not an issue. When physical collateral is planes or ships, access might be an issue, because these assets can be moved away from their usual location. The case of aircraft is the best illustration. Aircrafts can be seized in airports where legal procedures can be enforced. When planes fly only within a foreign country using local airports, they might be impossible to find and seize. Flying through international airports is an important aspect of risk in such a case. Real estate is the opposite case. By definition, it stays where it is built and there is no physical access issue. Also, it is common to hide away collateralized inventories and equipment in distressed firms since everyone knows that these assets will be taken away. Although this is illegal, the risk always exists.

Integrity Risk

Collateral might be damaged, either through normal deterioration because of a lack of maintenance, or deliberately. Whenever equipment has valuable parts, there is an incentive to move them away once it is known that all equipment will be seized.

Price Risk

The collateral has a liquidation value, which is subject to price risk. Price risk for liquid assets is market-driven, since there are various periods to consider before liquidation can be effective:

- The grace period allowed for lenders before recognizing default of payment.
- The time to work out legal procedures as they are needed. With market transactions, the securities posted as collateral are readily available once a breach in the obligations of the lender has occurred.
- The time to liquidate the collateral depends on market liquidity. It is more difficult to sell large blocks of securities than small quantities. For large blocks, there might be an additional delay because it is worthwhile to sell slowly rather than selling fast and triggering a significant price decline.

The level of posted collateral depends on these factors. Whenever there is a secondary market, the time required to sell allows the price to deviate adversely because of market movements. Even after a worst-case adverse move of liquidation value, the collateral should still absorb the loss under default. Both market liquidity and price volatility are important parameters to define the adequate amount of securities pledged as collateral. Cash liquidation value is risk-free, at least in the local currency. Typical assets subject to measurable price risk include: securities, commodities, oil and gas, aircraft and ships, real estate, standardized equipment.

Market Collateral Transactions

Many transactions use market instruments as collateral, since they are liquid assets easy to sell and since their price is continuously observed. Individuals holding portfolios of securities have margin accounts, which they can use to borrow a fraction of their holdings. Financial institutions or funds can pledge the securities that they hold. Inter-bank transactions require pledging liquid collaterals. Broker financing and margin calls in futures markets are also collateral-based. Brokers pledge their securities. Margin calls in organized futures markets are set to absorb 1-day market volatility, 1 day being the minimum period between two successive adjustments.

The main collateral risk in such cases is price risk, since only liquid assets are generally eligible for collateralization. The principle is to set up a collateral, whose value is higher than the borrower's debt. In the event where the collateral value falls below a preset threshold, the lender can sell the securities to reduce the debt or to get repaid in the event of default.

In order to maintain a 'safety cushion' between collateral and debt value, given that the collateral value moves constantly, there are rules triggering the sale of securities. In some cases, the collateral value is much higher than the debt value at inception. It is typical to borrow no more than 50% of the value of securities held by individuals. In other cases, the collateral value to debt value ratio is smaller. Various rules serve to keep collateral above debt when its value changes. A common rule is to post an additional amount of collateral when the existing security value falls below a threshold level. The excess of collateral value over debt value depends on the delay between the collateral deficiency event and all necessary corrective actions. This delay includes the minimum time required to notify deficiency to the borrower, plus some time to post additional collateral, plus the delay for selling the pledged securities under no corrective action. The difference between collateral and debt value ('haircut' in percentage terms) also depends on the securities' price volatilities. The longer the delay and the larger the volatility, the larger the potential downside move of the collateral value under adverse conditions. Since the final value of the collateral at the time of the sale of securities should be above the debt, the required collateral increases with both delay and securities' volatilities. The next chapter expands this simple model, determining the minimum value of pledged securities given volatilities and total period before sale.

THIRD-PARTY PROTECTIONS

Third-party protections include guarantees, support of a parent company, insurance and protection against credit risk from the seller of credit derivatives. The latter is a much newer concept than the others, and has different characteristics detailed in subsequent chapters (58 and 59).

Third-party guarantees are commitments, ranging from very formal obligations to simple statements, to face the obligations of a primary borrower if he fails to do so. Support is informal. It designates the 'willingness' of a parent company to support a subsidiary unable to face its debt obligations. Legally enforceable guarantees imply a contract, even though the enforcement of this contract is subject to various legal uncertainties. Hence, all formal third-party protections are subject to legal risk.

When effective, third-party protections transform the credit risk on the borrower into a credit risk on both borrower and guarantor. Default occurs only if both borrower and provider of protection default together (double default). The corresponding default probability becomes a joint probability of default of both of them. This joint default risk of the borrower and guarantor is different from a pure transfer of risk to the guarantor, because such a transfer would simply consider that the exposure is on the guarantor rather than on the borrower, which is not the economic reality. However, the New Basel Accord adopts this second view and does not grant 'joint default probability' benefits.

Guarantees

Guarantees allow entering into transactions that would not be feasible without them. A simple guarantee is an obligation of a third party to fulfil the obligation of a borrower if he does not comply with his debt obligation.

Guarantees are widely used in common transactions or in more structured deals such as back-to-back deals. In trade financing, they play a key role since they make trade financing feasible. In back-to-back deals, X does not want to lend directly to Y, but might be willing to lend to a higher credit standing third party. The third party T lends to Y and repays X and, in exchange for this service, gets a spread. Instead of issuing a formal guarantee that Y will repay X, the third party makes the market between counterparties that would not enter into a transaction directly.

Few contractual guarantees can be enforced easily. Some are binding, when the guarantor has to fulfil the obligations of a defaulting borrower. However, the range of guarantees covers a wide spectrum of obligation levels. Letters of intention, as their name implies, are not binding. Some guarantees are dependent on recourses of third parties other than the guarantor. The 'strength' of a guarantee is context-dependent: it depends on its nature, the legal environment(s) that is (are) relevant, current practices and the context when the lender exercises his right.

Support

Support designates an informal relationship. Usually, 'support' applies between a parent company and subsidiaries within a group. A holding company might not let a subsidiary default, although there is no binding rule applied to this. The effectiveness of support depends on intra-group economic links and the behaviour of the supporting entity. In addition, there are various types of support to consider and qualify:

- The support mitigates effectively the borrower risk, and is similar to a guarantee, when the holding company supports the failing subsidiary, whatever the reason (strategy, belonging to a core business of the group).

- Conversely, when the holding company does not support the failing subsidiary at all, for whatever reason (not belonging to core business for instance), without interfering negatively with the borrower, the lender faces the 'standalone' borrower risk only, and the value of support is zero. When the subsidiary default triggers the parent company default, because the subsidiary is so big that the holding company cannot survive if it defaults, the risk remains the standalone credit risk of the direct borrower, and the value of support is zero.
- When the subsidiary credit standing is entirely dependent on the holding company, the holding company default triggers subsidiary default. The lender to the primary borrower, the subsidiary, ends up at risk with both holding company and borrower even though there is no exposure to the holding company!
- The holding company might deteriorate the credit standing of the subsidiary if it decides to dispose of its assets to improve its own standing. Not all legal frameworks allow this. Using other companies' assets is illegal in some countries, if it jeopardizes the future of this entity. If it is feasible, the support becomes 'negative' and increases the risk.

Rating Policy Implications

The implication is that direct exposures are not enough to specify risk. Often, the risk depends on third parties. Sometimes this dependency mitigates the risk with the borrower, sometimes it increases it. The risk assessment process should look at the borrower as a standalone entity and at relationships with third parties that mitigate or aggravate this risk. Table 40.1 summarizes the various cases. The practical implications are that both borrower and guarantor ratings, their intrinsic issuer ratings, are necessary as well as a 'rating' of the value of support, in order to get the overall subsidiary rating.

TABLE 40.1   Third-party guarantee and intra-group support

Influence on borrower's risk		Support		
	Guarantee	Positive	Neutral	Negative
Formal	+			
Behavioural	−	+	0	−

The support concept requires consistency with rating policy. For instance, it may be that a subsidiary has both a poor intrinsic rating and a good rating, thanks to the support of a highly rated parent company. On the other hand, the parent company might be poorly rated, but a subsidiary might have a good credit standing by itself. If support is neutral or positive, the subsidiary deserves a higher rating. If support is negative, this means that the parent company can weaken the subsidiary credit standing if it faces problems. Therefore, the subsidiary ratings cannot be higher than the rating of the parent company. The rule that caps ratings of subsidiaries based on the rating of the parent implies negative support. Nevertheless, this rule does not recognize that the resulting overall rating (or risk) might actually be worse than the parent company rating (or risk).

There are similarities with sovereign risk and corporate ratings. Capping a corporate rating to the sovereign country risk implies a negative support for companies of good credit standing. In this case, negative support might be the rule, since the materialization of transfer risk will result in risk materialization for any lender to any local company.

COVENANTS AND STRUCTURING

Covenants are obligations for borrowers and options for lenders. Covenant breaches trigger prompt repayment of outstanding debt, making it mandatory for the borrower to renegotiate with the lender for continuing operations. The borrower needs a waiver to continue operations. A breach in a covenant is, for instance, a ratio falling below a threshold value, such as a 'Debt–Cover Ratio' (DCR). Covenants are options for lenders since they have the right to grant waivers or to ignore breaches of covenants.

The rationale of covenants is twofold. Covenants help to protect the lender from any significant deterioration in the risk profile of the transaction without prior agreement. They allow lenders to impose a restructuring of the transaction in such instances. Covenants also make it costlier for the borrower to default, because he loses the value of continuing operations even though this value is superior to the debt value. Covenants are incentives against moral hazard, as collaterals are, since they restrict borrowers from taking additional risks or actions that would increase the lenders' risk.

Under 'active' credit risk management, lenders use covenants as a pre-emptive device before losses occur. As such, covenants differ from guarantees and collaterals that are similar to insurance policies. The next section lists and defines some standard covenants. Covenants become essential whenever the credit standing of the borrower and/or the collateral do not provide adequate protection. In such cases, they make deals feasible, even though these would not be by classical standards.

Covenant Types

Covenants are either financial or qualitative. 'Financial' covenants refer to minimum values of ratios or key parameters. For instance, the DCR should not decrease beyond a certain value. Others are qualitative in nature. For instance, the lender might have no right to diversify while a transaction is still alive. If there is a breach, the lender has the right to accelerate repayment of the loan. The borrower needs to interact with the lender and renegotiate some aspects of the transaction in order to get a waiver, allowing continuing operations without loan repayment. The goal of the covenant is not to exercise the loan repayment obligation, but to make the borrower dependent on the lender if his credit standing deteriorates or if the risk profile of the transaction changes.

Covenants effectiveness depends on: how 'tight' or 'loose' they are for the borrower; the bank's attitude towards risk; or its willingness to exercise the right to impose some restructuring (of debt for example) on the borrower. Often, covenants appear less powerful risk mitigants than collaterals or guarantees because they always remain subject to intangible factors. This explains why rating agencies sometimes consider that certain covenants have no credit mitigating value. However, the usage of covenants is widespread.

Covenants usually fall within four categories: affirmative covenants, restrictive clauses, negative covenants and default provisions. All follow simple rationales. Affirmative covenants are obligations imposed on the borrower, such as communicating information to lenders. Quantitative financial clauses, such as a minimum financial ratio, are a special class of affirmative covenants. The restrictive covenants aim to protect the bank by prohibiting the borrower from taking actions that could adversely affect the likelihood of repayment, such as diversifying into areas other than the core business that could alter his risk profile. By agreeing to loan covenants that limit his actions, the borrower commits not to make choices that might reduce the wealth from the lender. The adverse effect of such covenants is that they may deprive the borrower of valuable investment options and strategies. Negative covenants specifically prohibit certain actions, such as not posting the same collateral as a guarantee for multiple lenders. Default or credit event covenants trigger a default dependent on specific clauses. Default event rules stipulate what happens under default.

Affirmative Covenants

These are obligations imposed on the borrower to provide periodical information. A commonly used covenant in this group is the requirement of communicating periodical financial statements. Keeping track of the borrower's financial condition enables preventive timely actions. In project finance, structured finance and other complex transactions, the obligation extends to comprehensive and detailed monitoring of transactions. In securitizations, investors have periodic reports on the portfolio serving as collateral for the structured notes or any other relevant information.

Financial Covenants

Financial covenants are obligations to comply with certain values of financial ratios. Typically, the DCR of a project should be higher than a certain value, such as 1.4. Other ratios extend to debt–equity structure, payout ratios of dividends and similar. The underlying rationale is self-explanatory. The protection potential of such covenants is highly dependent on how 'tight' they are. A DCR of 1.4 provides more protection than a DCR of 1.2.

Restrictive Clauses

Restrictive clauses limit the borrower's actions. Since borrowers tend to divert liquidity and net worth to shareholders rather than keeping it within the firm to protect creditors, a common restrictive clause limits the dividends to shareholders. It is also common for the bank to restrict salaries, bonuses and advances to employees of the firm. Other covenants limit specific types of investments or diversification away from the core business of the borrower because such developments alter the firm's risk profile, possibly to the creditor's detriment.

Negative Covenants

While restrictive covenants limit certain actions, negative covenants prohibit them. A common negative covenant is the negative pledge clause, usually found in unsecured loans. Under the clause, the borrower cannot pledge any of his assets as security to other lenders because the value of the collateral substantially diminishes if it is subject to claims from others. The fewer the assets of the firm pledged for other loans, the greater the share available to the bank in the event of bankruptcy. There may also be prohibitions regarding mergers, consolidations and sales of assets, diversification out of the core business of the borrower. It is also common for the bank to prohibit borrowers from making loans to others or guaranteeing debts to others. Such actions protect the lender's claim.

Default and Credit Event Provisions

These are event-triggered clauses rather than obligations limiting 'ex ante' the risk of such events. Such clauses make the entire debt immediately due and payable under certain conditions. Ordinarily, even though the bank has covenants for governing the borrower's behaviour, violation does not automatically allow the bank to call the loan as long as scheduled payments occur.

The 'pari passu' covenant stipulates that the default on any debt triggers default events on all other debts. Effective violation of such a covenant automatically makes full payment due immediately, or 'accelerates' all loan repayments. This pre-emptive clause allows lenders to take corrective timely actions that would become impossible once the deterioration materializes in missed payments. Because corrective actions take place earlier, they avoid further deteriorations of the borrower, that make recoveries lower. The acceleration clause does not trigger an effective repayment as long as the lenders and borrowers find a common interest in pursuing operations. Rather, it makes it an obligation for the borrower to obtain a waiver, once there is a covenant breach, thereby necessitating renegotiation of the debt terms and restructuring. The lenders look for additional security provisions before allowing the borrower to continue. Typically, this might include raising more equity by the sponsors of a project, getting more information, imposing new restrictions, and so on. Restructuring a loan becomes an obligation under such covenant clauses, if the lenders require it. Restructuring can also take place without any contractual obligations, simply when the lender perceives a deterioration and initiates a negotiation on corrective actions with the borrower.

All credit event provisions apply to events differing from default. Common definitions of default events, that are not very different, include the absence of payment for a minimum period after the date payment is due (for example 3 months) or filing for bankruptcy, which is the ultimate stage of default. Credit events designate a broader range of events, all of them possibly triggering acceleration clauses:

- Failure to make timely payments.
- Inaccuracy in representations and warranties.
- Impairment of collateral, invalidity of a guarantee and/or security agreement.
- Failure to pay other indebtedness when due or to perform under related agreements.
- Change of management or ownership.
- Expropriation of assets.

These credit events become, with acceleration clauses, similar to default events. In some cases, the loan agreement provides the borrower with a grace period to correct his default. If the borrower fails to do so, the bank may terminate the lending relationship. Though banks rarely exercise the right to accelerate loan repayment, having this right substantially strengthens a lender's position. Common related clauses include:

- Cross-default—gives the bank the right to declare an event of default when the borrower defaults with a third party (another lender). It implies that a default with any specific lender is equivalent to a default event for all other lenders. Hence, a default with lender X triggers a default with lender Y as well, even though Y did not suffer from any payment deficiency.
- Cross-acceleration—means that the acceleration of repayments also applies to all lenders equally.

Cross-acceleration and cross-default ensure the equal treatment of all lenders when the borrower defaults on any one of his obligations. It also precludes some lenders from initiating claims earlier than others.

Other Parameters of the Loan Agreement

Loan agreements have many provisions other than amount and price that must be negotiated between the bank and the borrower. Some of the more important parameters of the loan agreement are:

- The time schedule for withdrawing funds from the bank.
- The time schedule for paying back the interest and principal.
- A compensating balance requirement: an obligation by the borrower to maintain deposits at the lending bank.
- A prepayment penalty for repaying a loan before it matures.

Standard covenants are commonly used. The emergence of new structures gave birth to entirely new term sheets making the SPV entirely ruled by covenants. With new vehicles, the role of covenants changes. Instead of being simple enhancements to transactions, they have the role of governance of the structure. In practice, term sheets and public information disclosure fully detail the covenant ruling structures, SPVs, Collateralized Debt Obligation (CDO) structures and liquidity lines.

STRUCTURED TRANSACTIONS AND SECURITIZATIONS

Structured finance designates all specialized finance where credit risk is entirely dependent on a 'structure resiliency', the ability of this dedicated entity to sustain stressed conditions, rather than on the credit standing of a firm. The lender is not at risk with a counterparty that is a firm, as usual, but with an entity that has no credit standing by itself, that is an SPV. In all cases, structures are bundles of covenants and SPVs, which rule the functioning of the structure. Covenants play a key role in structured transactions since, without them, there would be no way to set up the transactions.

SPVs represent the most advanced stage of 'structuring'. Securitizations are special kinds of transactions using SPVs. Securitizations allow banks to sell their assets, or to sell the risks of these assets, to an SPV that issues 'structured' notes in the market bought by investors funding the assets or bearing their risks. They address portfolio management because securitizations are tools that reshape the bank's portfolio risk–return profile.

Other classical structured transactions, such as project finance and LBOs, help in setting up loans that would be too risky without such special features.

The first subsection reviews the nature of structured transactions and the role of the SPV in LBOs and others. The second subsection describes securitizations and their basic mechanisms. The third subsection briefly reviews structure covenants.

Project Finance, LBOs and Others

SPVs serve in a variety of situations: as shields between high-risk projects and lenders. Examples are LBOs and project or asset financing, although they are very different transactions.

In project finance, the risk of the project, its size and characteristics would make standard loans prohibitively risky. The project sponsors create an SPV that acts as a shield, allowing risk reduction and sharing by several participants. The SPV serves to isolate the project free cash flows and allocate them to debt repayments.

For LBOs, the SPV serves for acquiring another company. The SPV is the holding company, NewCo, which gets a majority of voting rights of the target company. NewCo needs to hold at least 50% of equity of the target company. With assets of the target company worth 100, and equity equal to 50, the value of debt is the difference, 50. The investment in the target company shares necessary to control 50% is $50\% \times 50 = 25$ of the equity. With a leverage of 4, we need only 10 to finance the 50 of equity, and the rest is a debt of 40. With 10, we acquire a total value of 100. NewCo's purpose is to buy the shares of the target company using both equity and debt. A highly leveraged LBO uses a lot of debt, thereby minimizing the amount of equity committed for purchasing the target company. Leverage minimizes the amount of cash invested to acquire control. Since NewCo's purpose is this acquisition only, it is possible to structure its debt and covenants in the best way for all lenders, senior ones as well as those willing to take more risk. Pledging NewCo's assets to lenders does not provide much protection since these assets are shares of the target company. Should the target company fail to generate enough cash for NewCo to repay lenders, the shares would have little value.

In both examples of project finance and LBOs, the SPV is a 'bankruptcy remote' structure, such that the failure of the SPV does not imply the failure of the sponsors. In project finance, the sponsors share the risk with lenders and investors. However, the project or the LBO failure would generate significant losses for the sponsors of the project, in addition to lenders, or to the shareholders of NewCo.

Structures and Securitizations

Other types of SPV, or funds, serve as vehicles for securitizations. Securitizations are transactions that transfer the funding and the risk of a pool of assets, originally held by a 'seller', to the market. The assets are consumer loans, mortgages, lease receivables, term loans and bonds, and receivables of a corporate firm (which becomes the seller in this latter case). The first step is a non-recourse sale to an SPV issuing, in the second step, 'structured' notes to finance the sold assets that investors buy in the market. 'Securitization' means turning illiquid assets into securities. The cash flows generated by the pool of assets serve to provide principal and interest payments to the note holders. Notes are 'structured' because they differ in terms of seniority levels with respect to their prioritized access to the cash flows generated by the pool of assets of the SPV. In addition, several covenants rule the functioning of the structure during its life.

By customizing the risk–return profiles of these notes, the structuring of the transactions makes these notes tradable, hence the name securitization. The rationale for selling assets or risks is to arbitrage the cost of funding on-balance sheet and into the market, and/or off-load risks into the market to free up capital.

The structuring of notes issued by the SPV defines the amount, maturity and risk–return profile of each class of structured notes. The structured notes have various seniority levels, the subordinated notes providing a credit enhancement to the upper senior notes. Because subordinated notes have a subordinated claim on cash flows, any cash flow deficiency hits them first. When the deficiency gets larger, it hits sequentially all upper level notes. Senior notes are investment grade, while the last equity tranche concentrates a lot of risk. Return is commensurate with these differentiated risks in line with market risk–return trade-offs. The 'waterfall' of cash flows ensures that the cash from the pool of assets flows first to senior notes and then to subordinated notes.

All securitizations, whether or not they serve for arbitraging the costs of funding, also off-load risk and free up capital. There are several types of securitizations. Securitizations allow funding in the market, through structured notes, of various kinds of assets: residential or commercial mortgages, lease receivables, consumer loans and credit card receivables, account receivables of corporate firms, loans of bonds. For short-term assets, it is necessary to reload periodically the SPV with new assets to prolong its maturity. Such securitizations are 'revolving'. Amortizing transactions securitize long-term assets, and amortize the notes at the pace dictated by the amortization of long-term assets.

CLO (Collateralized Loan Obligation), CDO or CBO (Collateralized Bond Obligation) follow the same principles of a non-recourse sale of assets to a fund, and the financing through structured notes issued in the market. The assets sold, loans, bonds, high yield bonds, might be very risky. Risk depends on the nature of assets, tradable or not (loans) for the same reasons that make market risk differ from credit risk. Cash CDOs imply the actual sale of assets from seller to the fund. Synthetic CDOs transfer the risks only to the SPV, which frees up capital as well as cash securitizations. The mechanism relies on credit derivatives for the risk transfer from seller to the fund[1]. They develop whenever it is difficult to sell assets, for instance if an agreement with the borrower is a prerequisite to a sale. The credit derivatives serve as an insurance mechanism to provide the necessary credit enhancement for the notes issued by the fund.

Structure Covenants

Structure covenants rule the 'governance' of the SPV. They ensure that the structure complies with all constraints that bound its various risks throughout its life. The covenants of structures depend on their types.

For LBOs or project finance, covenants pledge the future cash flows to repayments, and prevent any action that might reduce the lender's wealth, or any action that changes the

---

[1] See the mechanism of credit linked notes, which is similar, in the credit derivative chapter and the analysis of the economics of a securitization in the chapter dedicated to this issue.

risk–return profile of the transaction. They include limitations to cash outflows, diversification, dividends, and so on. A minimum DCR is common in cash flow-based structures. Any drop of this key ratio beyond a preset value would entail the repayment ability. A minimum multiple of Earnings Before Interest, Tax, Depreciation and Amortization (EBITDA) is also a common protecting clause.

For securitizations, covenants specify rules for the ramp-up period, when the portfolio of assets builds up over time at the early stage, whether repayments of all classes of notes occur in parallel, or sequentially (senior notes first and subordinated notes last), and what triggers a 'payout event' during the subsequent life of the structure. A payout event implies early amortization of notes, letting all assets amortize progressively and repaying the principal and interest due on the various classes of notes, following the seniority rules of the term sheet.

This is a difference from loan covenants, where the covenants trigger cross-default and cross-acceleration, but do not necessarily result in a default because the philosophy is more to restructure the loan rather than suffer from an overall immediate loss. In structures, covenants effectively trigger early amortization. Such payout events avoid waiting too long before triggering amortization, which could result in further deterioration of risk and larger losses. For securitizations, many covenants tend to be quantitative.

For CDO-type structures, covenants include: over-collateralization ratios guaranteeing a minimum 'safety cushion'; minimum diversification (quantified by a diversity score, as defined in Chapters 55 and 56) of the portfolio of assets; caps on individual risk concentrations of exposures; liquidation of collateral when its value declines below a certain threshold. For credit card-backed securitizations, target variables trigger the build-up of spread accounts, whose cash amounts serve as a first level of protection for note holders. The trigger variable is the 'excess spread', or the excess of the asset portfolio yield over charge-offs plus the weighted average cost of funding.

41

Modelling Recoveries

This chapter addresses the economic issue of guarantee values. The qualitative assessment of guarantees is the rule in most cases due to multiple intangible factors that affect their values. The quantitative assessment of guarantees is developing the extent feasible, for several reasons:

- A distinctive feature of the foundation approach consists of assigning recovery rates to facilities, and alleviating capital charge accordingly, which provides strong incentives for quantification.
- Certain guarantees are tangible enough to deserve recognition and valuation.
- The loss given default, or exposure minus recoveries, is a critical input for assessing credit risk.
- The expected loss is the product of the loss given default with default probabilities. It is the basis for economic provisioning.
- The expected loss as a percentage is equal to the default probability with zero recovery, and lower if recoveries are positive. Recovery rates allow us to define ratings with both default probability and loss under default, through the expected loss, which combines both. This provides a simple foundation for rating policies in the presence of guarantees.

In several instances, recoveries are reasonably certain, so that netting the exposures with recoveries is acceptable. With tangible securities as collateral, a common practice is to set the excess of collateral value over debt ('haircut') at a level guaranteeing zero loss under default with a given confidence level.

Third-party protections relate to guarantees, support, insurances and credit derivatives. The value of these guarantees results from the gain in default probability that they provide. This gain is the difference between the borrower's default probability and the joint default probability of both borrower and guarantor, if we ignore legal risks. The New Accord does not recognize the full benefit of the 'double default' probability and only allows us to assign the guarantor's risk to the guaranteed facility. However, joint default probabilities are key inputs to evaluate all forms of insurance, making it worthwhile to relate them to their determinants: obligor's default probabilities and correlations between their defaults.

Unlike third-party legal protection support might aggravate the risk while the former cannot. Support is so common that it deserves a separate assessment in the internal rating process qualifying its nature, its 'strength', and the credit standing of the supporting entity.

Covenants are obligations of borrowers and options for lenders contingent on many uncertainties, so that assessing their value remains beyond reach. However, it is relatively easy to specify how binding certain covenants are.

Finally, it is common to model recovery uncertainty by using a loss under default distribution. Recovery uncertainty increases the loss volatility. The beta distribution seems convenient because it fits various types of empirical recovery distributions, even though its usage remains tentative because of scarcity of data.

This chapter comprises six main sections addressing respectively: recoveries and rating policy; liquid collateral; third-party protections; support; recovery risk and its contribution to loss volatility and the beta distributions for modelling recovery risk; covenants.

RECOVERY AND EXPECTED LOSS

In addition to being a major ingredient of loss under default, the recovery rate serves to calculate expected loss, which characterizes the risk of facilities. The expected loss is as the product of a default probability DP and expected recovery rate $1 - \mathrm{Lgd}$[1]. For instance, a 3% default probability combined with an expected recovery rate of 70% results in an expected loss of $30\% \times 3\% = 0.09\%$. This percentage corresponds to the default probability of a rating close to investment grade, whereas the default probability alone would correspond to a speculative grade in the rating scales. Default probabilities better characterize issuer's risk. Expected loss better characterizes facility or issue risk. Both inputs, default probability and recovery rate or loss under default, provide an easy link towards ratings, by mapping expected loss percentages to ratings. The mapping is identical to the mapping between ratings and default probabilities of unsecured loans. When there is no recovery, the expected loss becomes $100\% \times \mathrm{DP}$, or the default probability, which characterizes the issuer.

COLLATERALIZED SECURITIES RISK MODELLING

In collateral agreements, the borrower is committed to post at any time a quantity of securities such that the debt remains below a certain agreed percentage, lower than 100%, of the value of pledged assets or, equivalently, such that the posted collateral remains above 100% of the loan. What follows applies to margin borrowing, lending and borrowing of securities (repos).

---

[1] This is the simplest definition. It applies to individual transactions when there are only two possible outcomes: default or non-default. In other cases, and for portfolios, more elaborated calculations are necessary. See Chapter 46 for examples and Chapter 55 for a portfolio overview of loss statistics.

If the collateral amount is set only once, at origination of the debt, there is a significant chance that the collateral value will fall below the outstanding debt when time passes. In such cases, the safety cushion, defined as the excess collateral (collateral value posted minus debt), should be high enough (200% of the debt, for example) to absorb most long-term fluctuations of the market. To avoid such high over-collateralization, contractual rules impose frequent adjustments of the collateral value, by pledging more, or less, securities. If 100% represents the reference debt amount, the posted collateral has to be above 100%. The excess amount of collateral above debt depends on worst-case calculations of the deviation of its value between consecutive revaluations. For instance, if the debt is 1 million EUR and the collateral is 120%, its value is 1 200 000 EUR. If the collateral value falls below 1 200 000 EUR, the lender should post additional securities or repay a fraction of the debt. It is necessary to consider various parameters to decide what is the adequate level of over-collateralization:

- The notification period, necessary to notify the lender of a collateral deficiency. We consider here that it is zero for simplicity. The notification date is t_0.
- The period T_1 allowed as a grace period for the borrower to respond to a call (a small number of days, such as 2). At the end of period T_1, liquidation of securities begins if the borrower does not respond. This date is $t_1 = t_0 + T_1$.
- The length of time required to liquidate the collateral, constrained by the market liquidity and the volume of securities. For instance, we might consider selling no more than 20% of the daily trading volume to avoid large price declines, and a liquidation period T_2 of 3 days. At date $t_2 = t_0 + T_1 + T_2$, the liquidation is complete.
- The market volatilities and the sensitivity of the pool of securities pledged against the debt.

The total amount of time T that elapses before selling the collateral sums up the grace period T_1 and the liquidation period T_2: $T = T_1 + T_2$.

The collateral value is volatile. Its overall sensitivity to the underlying market parameters as a percentage is s. The daily volatility of the market parameter is σ_m. The daily volatility of the collateral value, for a given time period in days, is $s \times T$. If the collateral value follows a simple normal distribution, the loss percentile at the 1% confidence level is $2.33 \times s \times \sigma_m \sqrt{T}$. The downward deviation of the collateral value at this confidence level is $2.33 \times s \times \sigma_m \sqrt{T}$. From this value, we find the required level of collateral and the trigger threshold for calling additional collateral. The collateral value should be $[(2.33 \times s \times \sigma_m \sqrt{T}) + 1] \times$ debt. If $T = 5$ days, and the daily volatility is 1.58% (or $25\% \times \sqrt{250}$, with a yearly volatility of 25%), the 5-day volatility is 7.91% and the value triggering a call for more collateral is 107.91%. In the above example, the collateral is 120%. The call for additional collateral occurs at 107.91%, to have less than a 1% chance of loss if the borrower fails to adjust the collateral.

This is a simple calculation. Notification occurs at date t_0, liquidation begins at date t_1 and lasts for a period equal to $T_2 - T_1$. During this liquidation period, the securities price keeps falling, but remains above the debt value. At the end of the liquidation period, the average sale price moves somewhere within the price at date T_1 and the price at $T = T_1 + T_2$. Hence, the proceeds from liquidation are above the debt value, so that the above rule is conservative (Figure 41.1).

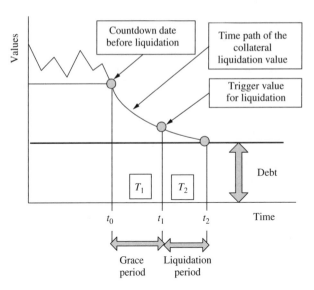

FIGURE 41.1   Determination of the values of collateral triggering call and liquidation (fixed liquidation period)

VALUATION OF CREDIT RISK GUARANTEES, INSURANCE OR CREDIT DERIVATIVES

The valuation of insurance, guarantee or credit derivative depends on the correlation between the credit risk of the two parties, the risk seller/buyer of a protection and the risk buyer/seller of a protection. Whether the protection is a third-party guarantee, an insurance or results from a credit derivative does not matter in terms of valuation. The main issue is what becomes of the joint default probability of the buyer of the protection and the seller of the protection. In general, it decreases far below the default probability of the borrower, which is the key to valuing third-party protection. The regulators do not provide full recognition of this 'double default' effect and consider that the exposure transfers to the guarantor, which is inexact, even though it is more practical than a joint default probability calculation. This section focuses on the technical ways of valuing the joint default probabilities and on correlations that influence this probability. It does not address the legal risk issue, whose assessment is essentially qualitative. The first appendix to this chapter provides details of the calculations of joint default probabilities, and only the essentials are given in the main text.

The Valuation of Joint Defaults

The buyer of a protection, such as an insurance against the default of a direct borrower, hopes that the insurer (the guarantor) will not default if the direct borrower does. If the insurer's probability of default does not depend on the borrower's default, the probability of both defaults is the product of the unconditional default probabilities and is very small. If the default of the borrower and the default of the guarantor correlate, the insurance gets weaker because the likelihood of the insurer's default when the borrower defaults increases. Under positive correlation, the conditional probability of default of the insurer is higher when the borrower defaults than when he does not. A simple way to express default correlation is to assign a value to the conditional probability of default of the insurer given the default probability of the borrower.

To value guarantees, support, insurance and protection through credit derivatives, it is possible to recalculate the joint default probability of the pair of obligors, borrower and provider of protection, given correlation effects. The value of the protection is the difference between the standalone default probability of the borrower and the joint default probability, which is lower (unless support is negative), as shown below. The latter depends on the correlation between the risks of borrower and guarantor. This section uses this principle to value a guarantee. It ignores legal risk and the 'strength' of the support relationship, because their assessment depends on legal issues and judgmental assessment. This allows us to address the valuation issue under a zero enforcement risk, but an assessment of this risk is necessary independently from any valuation of recoveries.

For rating purposes, it is possible to qualify and rate the borrower–third party relationship, based on the joint default probability since the specifics of the relationship are known by credit officers. A comprehensive rating system should include this component since the effects on risk might be very significant in many instances.

Joint Default Probabilities, Conditional Probabilities and Default Correlation

From an economic standpoint, any positive correlation between guarantor and direct borrower weakens the value of the guarantee, as intuition suggests. However, even a low credit standing guarantor can provide an efficient guarantee as long as his chances of defaulting when the borrower does are low. This is because joint default probabilities are, in general, much lower than standalone default probabilities.

The Joint Default Probability (JDP) is:

$$\text{JDP(both default)} = P(\text{borrower defaults } and \text{ guarantor defaults})$$

It depends on the correlation between the default of the primary borrower and that of the guarantor. Usually, the correlation between the default events is positive because of underlying factors influencing credit standing, such as belonging to the same country–industry segment. If default events are independent, the joint default probability is the product of the standalone default probabilities. If there is a positive correlation, the joint default probability is higher than this product. Such principles are not equivalent, in general, to what intuition would qualify as a 'risk transfer'. This intuition suggests that the lender is at risk with the indirect exposure on the insurer rather than on the primary borrower. This is not correct in general, but might be a proxy in some cases.

This section details joint default probabilities and conditional default probabilities. We use the following notation: B is the primary borrower, G is the guarantor or seller of protection (default derivative), $b = P(\text{B defaults})$ and $g = P(\text{G defaults})$ are the two default probabilities of B and G, $P(\text{B, G}) = \text{joint default probability of B and G} = \text{JDP(B, G)}$, $P(\text{G|B}) = \text{conditional probability of default of G if B defaults}$, $\rho = \text{correlation}$ between default events of two entities.

Using our notation rules, bold characters are random variables and italic characters their values. Default events are Bernoulli random variables $\mathbf{d}$, whose values are either 1 for default or 0 for no default. Accordingly, $\mathbf{d_B}$ and $\mathbf{d_G}$ represent the random default events of B and G. There are straightforward relationships between conditional default probabilities and correlations. The second appendix to this chapter shows that joint default probabilities are easy to derive for a pair of obligors. The formula providing the default probability of a primary borrower B benefiting from a fully enforceable guarantee from the guarantor G is:

$$P(\text{B, G}) = b \times g + \rho\sqrt{b(1-b) + g(1-g)}$$

It is not possible to assign default probabilities and correlations independently. There are internal consistency constraints because the correlation coefficient has to be within the $[-1, +1]$ range, while the conditional probabilities have to be within the $[0, 1]$ range. Furthermore, there are relationships between conditional probabilities and correlations between default events:

$$P(\text{G}|\text{B}) = P(\text{B, G})/P(\text{B}) = g + \rho(1/b^2)\sqrt{b(1-b) + g(1-g)}$$

$$P(\text{B}|\text{G}) = P(\text{B, G})/P(\text{G}) = b + \rho(1/g^2)\sqrt{b(1-b) + g(1-g)}$$

These relationships derive from the arithmetic of conditional probabilities.

The Joint Default Probability of the Borrower and the Guarantor

The numerical example below uses the general format for calculating numerically conditional probabilities based on unconditional probabilities and the correlation between credit events. The example starts from unconditional default probabilities. Defining at least one conditional default probability, plus the standalone default probabilities, is sufficient to obtain the full set of conditional probabilities and the joint default probability, as shown in the second appendix. In the example, we start from the conditional probability that G defaults given B defaults, here 20%. The entire set of joint probabilities follows, including the correlation between default events. The example is in Table 41.1.

In the table, the inputs are in bold:

- Standalone default probabilities of B and G, respectively $b = 3\%$ and $g = 2\%$.
- Conditional default probability of G, given B defaults, $P(\text{G}|\text{B}) = 20\%$.

The final result is that the default correlation is 22.61% and the joint default probability of B and G is $P(\text{B, G}) = 0.60\%$, much lower than the higher standalone default probabilities of B and G, respectively 3% and 2%. The 'value' of the guarantee is the gain in default probability of lending to B alone versus lending to B with a guarantee from G. This gain is $3\% - 0.60\% = 2.40\%$. In terms of rating the credit to B, this is a very high increase in rating.

TABLE 41.1 Consistent values of correlation, standalone and conditional probabilities (inputs in bold)

Standalone default probability					Conditional default probability	Joint default probability
Borrower		Guarantor				
N	**3.00%**	D	**2.00%**		**20.00%**	0.60%
		ND	. 98.00%		80.00%	2.40%
				Total		3.00%
ND	97.00%	D	2.00%		1.44%	1.40%
		ND	98.00%		98.56%	95.60%
				Total		97.00%

		Matrix of default probabilities:		Correlation between default events
		Guarantor		
		D	ND	
Borrower	N	0.60%	2.40%	3.00%
	ND	1.40%	95.60%	97.00%
		2.00%	98.00%	100.00%	22.61%

The Value of Third-party Guarantees and Correlations

When the correlation is 0, the default events are independent, the joint probability $P(B, G)$ collapses to $P(B) \times P(G)$ and the conditional default probabilities become identical to the standalone default probabilities. The default of either one obligor has no influence on the default probability of the other. Under independence, the joint default probability is 2% × 3% = 0.06%. The default risk becomes 10 times lower than in the case where $P(G|B) = 20\%$. The gain in default probability of B, compared to the case with no guarantee, is 2% − 0.06% = 1.94%. The guarantee turns a speculative grade rating into an equivalent Aa rating. This result holds even though the guarantor has a 3% default probability, equivalent to a speculative grade rating. An important conclusion is that a poor rating guarantor actually enhances significantly the default probability of the borrower.

When the correlation becomes positive, the joint default probability increases with the correlation. Figure 41.2 shows the relationship between the joint default probability of the primary borrower and the guarantor. The correlation increases the joint default probability, thereby decreasing the value of the guarantee. This relationship is linear, according to the above formulas. The unconditional default probabilities of B and G are respectively 3% and 2%. There are consistency constraints between unconditional probabilities, conditional probabilities and the correlation coefficient values. Therefore, it is not possible to pick these values independently. These constraints are explicit in the second appendix.

Implications

In order to convert the joint default probability into a rating, it is possible to use the rating that corresponds to a default probability equal to this joint default probability.

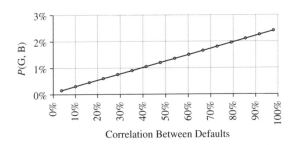

FIGURE 41.2 Joint default probability of borrower and guarantor

This adjusts the default probability of the guaranteed exposure, not its recovery rate. If the exposure guarantee is so strong that the joint probability of default drops to zero, the guaranteed exposure becomes nearly risk-free. It makes sense, in this case, to consider the exposure netted from the guaranteed fraction, which is equivalent to a certain recovery rate equal to this guaranteed exposure. This applies for government guarantees, for instance government owned entities providing guarantees for export–import finance.

A third-party guarantee does not transfer risk to the guarantor to the extent that the joint default probability is much lower than the guarantor's default probability. The intuitive notion of risk transfer towards the guarantor overestimates the true risk of primary borrower exposure[2]. Using the guarantor default probability would imply that the joint default probability is equal to that of the guarantor. This cannot be true unless both borrower and guarantor have the same default probability, in addition to perfect correlation. Therefore, this is not an acceptable solution in general unless the guarantor has a zero risk, implying also a zero risk for the exposure.

SUPPORT

Support is not identical to third-party protection because it can be negative. A positive support is similar to a guarantee. The value of support depends on the joint default probability of the borrower and the supporting entity. The negative support case necessitates a specific analysis:

- Under negative support, the supporting entity's default triggers the default of the borrower.
- Under dependency of the supporting entity on the borrower's default, the borrower's default triggers the supporting entity's default.

These are extreme cases, since such relations are not deterministic. Support changes in the conditional default probability given either the default of the supporting entity or the default of the borrower. For simplification, we consider only the extreme deterministic relationships. With negative support, the risk is more an 'either/or risk': either the borrower's default or the insurer's default triggers a default event for the lender.

---

[2] Using the data of the example, the part of Table 41.1 showing the joint default probability as a function of default correlation indicates that a default correlation of 81% would match the joint default probability of 2%, the guarantor default probability. This is excessively high for a default correlation.

'Either/or' events follow different rules from 'and' rules for combining default probabilities. The probability that either B or G defaults is the sum of their default probabilities minus the probability that both occur. The general corresponding formula is:

$$P(\text{borrower defaults } or \text{ supporting entity defaults}) = P(\text{borrower defaults})$$
$$+ P(\text{supporting entity defaults}) - \text{JDP(both default)}$$

The correlation still influences the risk through the joint default probability. The formula is consistent with the intuition that the lenders face both risks since the joint default probability is generally small, unless correlation is high. Therefore, the default event probability becomes approximately equal to the sum of the standalone probabilities of the borrower and the guarantor. The following calculations consider that the default probabilities are:

$$P(\text{B}) = 3\%$$
$$P(\text{G}) = 2\%$$
$$P(\text{B, G}) = 0.60\%$$
$$P(\text{B } or \text{ G}) = 3\% + 2\% - 0.60\% = 4.40\%$$

The default probability under support is much higher than any one of the standalone default probabilities. The gain is negative, consistent with a negative support.

The usage of the above relationship is subtle. In fact, if we consider that a single default, either that of B or of G, deterministically triggers the default of the other, the correlation is 1. If the correlation is 1, consistency constraints imply that both default probabilities are equal and that their values are equal to the joint default probability. When either B or G triggers the default of the other, it becomes impossible that the standalone probabilities differ from each other. This is a limit case. In practice, the relationship is not necessarily symmetrical. It is possible that the supporting entity default triggers that of the borrower while the reverse is not true. The correlation coefficient does not reflect this asymmetry of causalities.

MODELLING THE EFFECT OF RANDOM RECOVERIES

Since recovery uncertainty results from a number of sources of risk, modelling some of them is not sufficient to capture the overall recovery risk. For instance, we made a number of restrictive assumptions on the valuation of guarantees and support above. In such instances, it is more practical to model the overall recovery risk using expected values plus some distribution around this value. The consequence is that the loss volatility and the loss distribution now depend on the uncertainty of the loss under default. We show how recovery uncertainty influences the loss volatility, before describing the beta distribution, a distribution that seems to fit observed recovery distributions.

Extension of Loss Volatility with Uncertain Lgd

A random loss given default intuitively increases the loss volatility. The value under default is uncertain because of recoveries, and the value under no default is uncertain because of migrations. The loss volatility results from simple calculations under 'default mode'. A simple technique for calculating the increase is to calculate the variance of the random value $\mathbf{V}$ as a conditional variance upon another random variable $\mathbf{D}$ measuring default or no default[3]. The formula is:

$$\text{Var}(\mathbf{V}) = \text{Var}[E(\mathbf{V}|\mathbf{D})] + E[\text{Var}(\mathbf{V}|\mathbf{D})]$$

$$\text{Var}(\mathbf{V}|\mathbf{D}) = E(\mathbf{V}^2|\mathbf{D}) - [E(\mathbf{V}|\mathbf{D})]^2$$

$$\text{Var}(\mathbf{V}) = \text{Var}[E(\mathbf{V}|\mathbf{D})] + E(\mathbf{V}^2|\mathbf{D}) - [E(\mathbf{V}|\mathbf{D})]^2$$

The third appendix to this chapter develops the calculation. The volatility of the value increases to 0.12329 instead of the 0.0872 found directly before. There is an additional term due to the variance of the expected value conditional on default.

The Beta Distribution for Recoveries

Recovery rates might follow some predetermined distributions fitting historical data. The statistics provide both means by debt category and volatility around the mean. It is possible to fit a distribution to both moments, so that the fitted distribution has the same average and volatility as the empirical distributions observed. The beta distribution has the attractive property of being representative of any shape of recovery distributions. These can be U-shaped, representative of the fact that 'either we recover something or not'. They can also be bell-shaped or highly skewed. For example, in some cases, there is no reason why recovery should be significant, like with unsecured transactions. The mode gets close to zero. Nevertheless, due to uncertainties, we still might recover more than that.

The beta distribution depends on two parameters n and r. The formula of the beta density is:

$$\text{pdf}(\mathbf{RR}) = [(n-1)!/(r-1)!(n-r-1)!]\mathbf{RR}^{r-1}(1-\mathbf{RR})^{n-r-1}$$

In this formula, pdf designates the probability density function and $\mathbf{RR}$ is the random recovery rate value, between 0 and 1. The expectation and the variance of the beta distribution are:

$$E(\mathbf{RR}) = r/n$$

$$V(\mathbf{RR}) = r(n-r)/n^2(n+1)$$

The mean and variance formulas depend on two variables, r and n, making it possible to fit a beta distribution using these two values only. The shape depends on the combination of r and n. The expected value of the distribution is $r = k/n$. This ratio is used as a control parameter when we have the average recovery from empirical observations. The variance is a function of k, since $r = nk$:

$$V(\mathbf{RR}) = r(n-r)/n^2(n+1) = nk(n-nk)/n^2(n+1) = k(1-k)/(n+1)$$

---

[3] The variance of $\mathbf{Y}$ conditional on $\mathbf{Z}$ is in general: $\text{Var}(\mathbf{Y}) = \text{Var}[E(\mathbf{Y}|\mathbf{Z})] + E[\text{Var}(\mathbf{Y}|\mathbf{Z})]$. The conditional variance is: $\text{Var}(\mathbf{Y}|\mathbf{Z}) = E\{[\mathbf{Y} - E(\mathbf{Y}|\mathbf{Y})]|\mathbf{Z}\} = E(\mathbf{Y}^2|\mathbf{Z}) - [E(\mathbf{Y}|\mathbf{Z})]^2$. In this case, we have $\mathbf{Z} = \mathbf{D}$ and $\mathbf{Y} = \mathbf{V}$.

For large n, the variance of the recovery rate tends towards 0. Using a high n implies that recoveries are considered as certain. For smaller n, the distribution can have various shapes.

If $r = 1/2$, the distribution is symmetric. If $r/n < 1/2$, the distribution is positively skewed, with a long tail to the right. In this case, the highest probability is that we do not recover much, but we might have a chance of significant recoveries. If $r/n > 1/2$, the long tail is on the left. This is the case where recoveries are expected to be high, because we have guarantees of some collateral, with a possibility of not getting much. As long as $r > 1$ and $n - r > 1$, the distribution has a single mode, equal to $(r - 1)/(n - 2)$. When $r \leq 1$ or $n - r \leq 1$, the distribution is unimodal with mode equal to either 0 or 1, or U-shaped with modes at 0 and 1. When $r = 1$ and $n = 2$, it becomes the uniform distribution. See Figure 41.3 for these various cases.

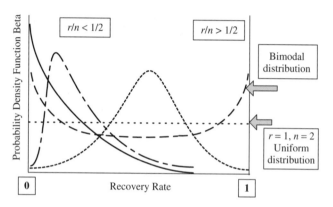

FIGURE 41.3 **The various shapes of the beta distribution**

One simple rule is to use the best guess value of recovery as the mode of the distribution $(r - 1)/(n - 2)$. Then, we can set n so that the recovery volatility is in line with observation. Because of these properties, the beta distribution is widely used in modelling uncertain recoveries.

COVENANTS

Covenants allow for preventive actions. They fit well with active credit management and with a permanent monitoring of risk. The effect is very different from that of collateral and guarantees, because these look more like insurance policies activated only after default occurs. On the other hand, covenants enhance the effect of proactive credit risk management. However, they have no mechanical effects on risk. Their effectiveness depends on many factors such as how constraining they are, the bank's attitude and the context.

Covenants serve for avoiding larger losses due to waiting when credit risk increases. Their value would be the difference between asset values net of recovery costs when a breach occurs, and the value without covenants, when a default event occurs later than a covenant breach. The sooner the breach occurs, the higher should be the recovery of lenders. Moreover, covenants and collateral increase the cost of default of the borrower since they make it an obligation to give up the project or the collateral when these still have a significant value. Hence, one path for valuing covenants would be to increase the recovery rate.

Looking at covenants as tools for restructuring before default occurs, their economic value would be to impose a cap on the default risk of the borrower, equivalent to benefiting from a floor on the default probability. It is difficult to go beyond floors on recovery rates and/or floors on default probabilities. Even such simple rules remain hazardous because of a lack of data.

APPENDIX I: JOINT DEFAULT PROBABILITY

This appendix expands the modelling of the joint default probabilities of two entities, a primary borrower B and a guarantor G. The analysis applies to any pair of entities when considering discrete events, such as defaults or migrations. This important equation is relatively easy to derive.

We consider $P(\mathbf{B})$ and $P(\mathbf{G})$ as the default probabilities of the random events $\mathbf{B}$ and $\mathbf{G}$, where $\mathbf{B}$ and $\mathbf{G}$ are Bernoulli variables taking the values 1 (default, state 'D') or 0 (no default, state 'ND'). We stick to the convention that bold letters are random variables, while italic letters are their values. We simplify the notations using the following rules:

$$P(\mathbf{B} = 1) = P(\mathbf{B}) = b \quad \text{and} \quad P(\mathbf{B} = 0) = 1 - P(\mathbf{B}) = 1 - b$$

$$P(\mathbf{G} = 1) = P(\mathbf{G}) = g \quad \text{and} \quad P(\mathbf{G} = 0) = 1 - P(\mathbf{G}) = 1 - g$$

$P(\mathbf{B})$ is identical to b and $P(\mathbf{G})$ to g, while $\mathbf{B}$ and $\mathbf{G}$ are the random Bernoulli variables, having value 0 (no default) with probability $1 - b$ and 1 (default) with probability $1 - g$. There are four possible situations, as outlined in Table 41.2.

TABLE 41.2 Default events with two entities I

Default events	Probability
B defaults, G does not	b
G defaults, B does not	g
Both B and G default (default event for the lender)	$P(B, G) = JDP(B, G)$
None default	$1 - b - g - P(B, G)$

The correlation ρ is:

$$\rho = \sigma(\mathbf{B}, \mathbf{G})/\sigma(\mathbf{B}) \times \sigma(\mathbf{G})$$

where $\sigma(\mathbf{B}, \mathbf{G})$ is the covariance of the two random variables, or $\sigma_{\mathbf{BG}}$ in compact notation, and where $\sigma(\mathbf{B})$ and $\sigma(\mathbf{G})$ are the standard deviations of $\mathbf{B}$ and $\mathbf{G}$, simplified as $\sigma_{\mathbf{B}}$ and $\sigma_{\mathbf{G}}$. Hence:

$$\rho = \sigma_{\mathbf{BG}}/\sigma_{\mathbf{B}} \times \sigma_{\mathbf{G}}$$

The factors of this equation result from their definitions:

$$\text{Expected value of } \mathbf{B}: \quad E(\mathbf{B}) = 1 \times b + 0 \times (1 - b) = b$$

$$\text{Expected value of } \mathbf{G}: \quad E(\mathbf{G}) = 1 \times g + 0 \times (1 - g) = g$$

The variance is calculated from the formula $V(d) = E(d^2) - [E(d)]^2$:

$$E(\mathbf{B}^2) = 1^2 \times b + 0^2 \times (1-b) = b$$
$$E(\mathbf{G}^2) = 1^2 \times g + 0^2 \times (1-g) = g$$

Note that $E(\mathbf{B}^2) = [E(\mathbf{B})]^2 = b^2$, a convenient intermediate result applying to all Bernoulli variables whose values are 0 and 1.

Variance of $\mathbf{B}$: $V(\mathbf{B}) = E(\mathbf{B}^2) - [E(\mathbf{B})]^2 = b(1-b)$

Variance of $\mathbf{G}$: $V(\mathbf{G}) = E(\mathbf{G}^2) - [E(\mathbf{G})]^2 = g(1-g)$

The covariance relates to ρ using[4]:

$$\sigma_{\mathbf{BG}} = \rho \times \sigma_{\mathbf{B}} \times \sigma_{\mathbf{G}}$$
$$\sigma_{\mathbf{BG}} = \rho \sqrt{b(1-b) \times g(1-g)}$$

Table 41.3 summarizes the various events and their probabilities. All products of the values of the variables are zero, except one whose probability is the joint probability of default:

$$E(\mathbf{B} \times \mathbf{G}) = 1 \times P(\mathbf{B} = 1, \mathbf{G} = 1) = P(\mathbf{B} = 1, \mathbf{G} = 1)$$

TABLE 41.3 Default events with two entities 2

Default events	Values of $\mathbf{B} \times \mathbf{G}$	Probability
B defaults, G does not	$1 \times 0 = 0$	b
G defaults, B does not	$0 \times 1 = 0$	g
Both B and G default	$1 \times 1 = 1$	$P(\text{B, G}) = \text{JDP}(\mathbf{B} = 1, \mathbf{G} = 1)$
None default	$0 \times 0 = 0$	$1 - b - g - P(\text{B, G})$

Since $E(\mathbf{B}) = b$ and $E(\mathbf{G}) = g$, the covariance of default events is:

$$\sigma_{\mathbf{BG}} = P(\text{B, G}) - b \times g$$
$$P(\text{B, G}) = \sigma_{\mathbf{BG}} + b \times g$$

APPENDIX II: CONSISTENCY CONSTRAINTS BETWEEN CORRELATION AND CONDITIONAL DEFAULT PROBABILITIES

From a practical standpoint, it might be easier to define simple values of conditional probabilities than specifying a correlation value between default events. For instance, assigning simple values of conditional probabilities, such as $P(G|B) = 20\%$, is a practical way to rate support. This choice has an intuitive interpretation, since it means that the default probability of the guarantor jumps to 20% if B defaults.

---

[4] The covariance could also be calculated directly using the simplified formula: $\sigma_{\mathbf{XY}} = E(\mathbf{XY}) - E(\mathbf{X})E(\mathbf{Y})$.

The conditional probabilities of default, either $P(G|B)$ or $P(B|G)$, have to be within 0 and 1. Due to these constraints, the correlation ρ and the conditional default probabilities are subject to boundary conditions resulting from the above equations, once the standalone default probabilities of B and G are given. They serve for calculating the boundary values of ρ. An important practical implication is that a correlation coefficient between default events of any pair of obligors, or a conditional probability, cannot be 'picked up' like that. Permissible values depend on the standalone default probabilities of the two obligors[5]. Although this is not so intuitive, it becomes obvious in certain cases. For example, if a counterparty never defaults (zero default probability), such as an Aaa guarantor, there is no correlation at all with any other risky counterparty. This implies that both the correlation and the joint default probability collapse to zero.

The next subsection makes explicit the consistency constraints between probabilities. The second one shows the relationship between the default event correlation and the conditional probabilities.

Unconditional Probabilities, Conditional Probabilities and Correlation

The basic relations are:

$$P(B, G) = P(B) \times P(G|B) = P(G) \times P(B|G)$$

$$P(G|B) = P(B, G)/P(B) = g + \rho(1/b^2)\sqrt{b(1-b) + g(1-g)}$$

$$P(B|G) = P(B, G)/P(G) = b + \rho(1/g^2)\sqrt{b(1-b) + g(1-g)}$$

The example in Table 41.4 further details these interdependencies and constraints, using a consistent set of probabilities. It applies only to the case of discrete events and uses the matrix of four cases, default or no default, for each single firm of a pair.

TABLE 41.4 Default events with two entities B and G

		B		Total
		Default	*No default*	
G	Default	0.9061%	4.0939%	5.0000%
	No default	6.0939%	88.9061%	95.0000%
	Total	7.0000%	93.0000%	

This appears in the matrix constructed from the 'tree' of events used to calculate step-by-step probabilities, as in the main text. The 'tree' shows the sequence of events for the two obligors (default or non-default of B and then of G) resulting in four combinations. The matrix of these four events shows the constraints applying to the assigned probabilities. It applies to any combination of two obligors.

---

[5] It is easier to deal with correlations between continuous variables such as asset values or equity values, because they are observable and because these constraints disappear. Whatever the values are, the correlation coefficient can take any value within the $[-1, +1]$ range. Here, there are permissible ranges $[\rho_{min}(b, g), \rho_{max}(b, g)]$ whose boundary values depend on the unconditional default probabilities of the two obligors (b and g).

Only one conditional probability, in addition to the unconditional default probabilities, is enough to specify all others, given unconditional default probabilities. This is because there is a one-to-one correspondence between the value of the correlation and that of the conditional probabilities once unconditional probabilities are given. All conditional and joint probabilities depend on the unconditional probabilities plus the correlation or, equivalently, one corresponding conditional probability. For instance, the sum of conditional default probabilities of G given B's default (12.944% + 87.056%) has to be equal to 100%. The sum of the joint probabilities that A defaults when B defaults and when B does not is 0.9061% + 6.0939% = 7%, the unconditional default probability of A. The standalone default probability of B is 5%. The same applies to the borrower. These conditions simply state that the sum of the rows and columns of the matrix obtained by cross-tabulating outcomes for B and G are identical to standalone default probabilities and to the standalone non-default probabilities of B and G.

Joint Default Probabilities, Conditional Default Probability and Correlation

Table 41.5 calculates the joint default probabilities when the default correlation and the corresponding conditional default probability of the guarantor given B's default vary. The table also illustrates the existence of boundary values of $P(G|B)$ and $P(G, B)$. These values are such that the conditional probability or the default correlation cannot take unacceptable values outside the allowed ranges, 0 to 1 for conditional probability and -1 to $+1$ for default correlation.

TABLE 41.5 Joint default probabilities, conditional default probability and correlation[a]

ρ	$P(G|B)$	$P(G, B)$
3.768%	5%	0.150%
10.049%	10%	0.300%
16.330%	15%	0.450%
22.611%	20%	0.600%
28.892%	25%	0.750%
35.173%	30%	0.900%
41.453%	35%	1.050%
47.734%	40%	1.200%
54.015%	45%	1.350%
60.296%	50%	1.500%
66.577%	55%	1.650%
72.858%	60%	1.800%
79.138%	65%	1.950%
85.419%	70%	2.100%
91.700%	75%	2.250%
97.981%	80%	2.400%

[a]Standalone default probabilities: 3% for B and 2% for G.

The table shows that the joint default probability is always lower than the 3% standalone probability of B. The guarantee always provides a significant gain, especially when considering that high conditional probabilities or high correlations are unrealistic. As a consequence, the specific case where the conditional probability $P(\mathbf{B} = \mathbf{D}|\mathbf{G} = \mathbf{D})$ is 1, the relationship $P(\mathbf{B} = \mathbf{D}|\mathbf{G} = \mathbf{D}) = P(\mathbf{B} = \mathbf{D}, \mathbf{G} = \mathbf{D})/P(\mathbf{B} = \mathbf{D}) = 1$ implies that the joint default probability and the standalone probabilities become equal. When either B or G triggers the default of the other, it is impossible that the standalone probabilities differ from each other. This is a limit case.

APPENDIX III: COMBINED DEFAULT AND RECOVERY RISKS

Under default mode, there are only two states at the horizon, default and non-default. Under no default, the exposure value is X. Under default, it becomes $X \times \mathbf{Lgd}$, with a random **Lgd**. We assume a given volatility of recoveries $\sigma(\mathbf{Lgd})$ and that the **Lgd** is independent of the default risk. This is a common assumption in several models, although it is unrealistic in all cases where there is a correlation between default and loss under default.

The expected loss value is obtained as above using $E(\mathbf{Lgd})$ instead of the certain Lgd, because the product of expectations is the expectation of the product of independent variables. To calculate the loss volatility, we need to start from the expression of the random value **V**. The value **V** is conditional on default or no default:

$$\mathbf{V} = (\mathbf{V}|\text{default}) \times \mathbf{D} + (\mathbf{V}|\text{no default}) \times (1 - \mathbf{D})$$

The random variable **D** characterizes default, if it equals 0, and non-default, if it equals 1. The probability of default is d. The expectation of **D** equals d, the default probability. When there is no default, the value $\mathbf{V}|\mathbf{D}$ is equal to exposure X. Under default, the value

TABLE 41.6   Calculation of value volatility under loss given default uncertainty

1. Calculation of the expected conditional value						
		D	$E(\mathbf{V}|\mathbf{D}) = \mathbf{V}|\mathbf{D}$	Probability weighted	Random value $(\mathbf{V}^2|\mathbf{D})$	Probability weighted
No default	95%	0	1.00000	0.95000	1.00000	0.95000
Default	5%	1	0.60000	0.03000	0.36000	0.01800
			$E[E(\mathbf{V}|\mathbf{D})]$	0.9800	$E(\mathbf{V}^2|\mathbf{D})$	0.9680
2. Calculation of the conditional variance						
	$E(\mathbf{V}|\mathbf{D}) - E[E(\mathbf{V}|\mathbf{D})]$		$\{E(\mathbf{V}|\mathbf{D}) - E[E(\mathbf{V}|\mathbf{D})]\}^2$		Probability weighted	
No default	0.02000		0.00040		0.00038	
Default	−0.38000		0.14440		0.00722	
			$Var[E(\mathbf{V}|\mathbf{D})]$		0.00760	

3. Calculation of the value variance and volatility
$E(\mathbf{V}^2|\mathbf{D})$ (a)	0.96800
$E(\mathbf{V}|\mathbf{D})^2$ (b)	0.96040
$Var[E(\mathbf{V}|\mathbf{D})]$ (c)	0.00760
$Var(\mathbf{V})$ (a) − (b) + (c)	0.01520
Volatility$(\mathbf{V}) = \sqrt{Var(\mathbf{V})}$	0.12329

$\mathbf{V|D}$ is random because the $\mathbf{Lgd}$ is[6]. Its expectation $E(\mathbf{V|D})$ is, under the independence assumption between default event and loss given default:

$$E(\mathbf{V|D}) = d \times X \times E(\mathbf{V|D} = 0) + (1 - d) \times X \times E(\mathbf{V|D} = 1)$$

Since $E(\mathbf{V|D} = 0) = X$ and $E(\mathbf{V|D} = 1) = E(\mathbf{Lgd})$: $E(\mathbf{V|D}) = X \times [d + (1 - d) \times E(\mathbf{Lgd})]$.

The variance and the volatility result from the formulas giving the conditional variance upon the default event:

$$\mathrm{Var}(\mathbf{V}) = \mathrm{Var}[E(\mathbf{V|D})] + E[\mathrm{Var}(\mathbf{V|D})]$$

$$\mathrm{Var}(\mathbf{V|D}) = E(\mathbf{V}^2|\mathbf{D}) - [E(\mathbf{V|D})]^2$$

$$\mathrm{Var}(\mathbf{V}) = \mathrm{Var}[E(\mathbf{V|D})] + E(\mathbf{V}^2|\mathbf{D}) - [E(\mathbf{V|D})]^2$$

These formulas accommodate any relation between the default event and the random loss under default. The calculations using this formula are given in Table 41.6.

In order to find the loss volatility, when Lgd is certain, the only change is to set the variance of the expected value $\mathbf{V}$ conditional on default to zero. The volatility becomes 0.0872 as found directly before.

---

[6] When $\mathbf{D}$ takes the value 0, the value under migration mode is also random because it is the value at the horizon, which depends on migrations.

42

Credit Risk Valuation and Credit Spreads

Credit risk events, defaults and migrations, result in changes in value of facilities. Between now and the horizon, defaults and migrations are random, so that there is a distribution of the future values at a given horizon over the entire spectrum of risk migrations. This distribution of values at a given horizon serves to determine the potential losses, and the loss statistics and loss percentiles measuring credit risk 'Value at Risk' (VaR). For default-only models, the distribution of values for each facility collapses to two states, default and non-default. For full valuation models, migrations to a different risk class than the original result in changes in values because the risk changes. The most prominent models, KMV Portfolio Manager, Credit Metrics and Credit Portfolio View (CPV) are full economic valuation models. CreditRisk+ is a default model.

Credit risk models value credit risk only, considering that other risks, market risk and interest rate risk, are taken care of by other tools. They use a 'mark-to-model' technique, restricting the mark-to-market of assets to migrations of credit risk only. Valuation at horizon uses the credit spreads of various risk classes for discounting contractual cash flows, or, alternatively, expected cash flows that are lower because of default probabilities. This is a future valuation, or 'mark-to-future', using the entire spectrum of possible credit states at a future time point.

Beyond risk measuring, credit risk valuation serves two other purposes:

- Valuation of traded and non-traded assets in a manner consistent with the market valuation of credit risk.
- Modelling the implied default probabilities in bond prices, as risk-neutral probabilities. The technique makes explicit the relation between spreads, risk-neutral probabilities, rather than natural probabilities, and recovery rates.

The valuation of risky debt uses either one of two equivalent techniques:

- Discounting contractual cash flows using risky yields, risk-free yields plus credit spreads;
- Discounting expected cash flows at the risk-free rates using the 'risk-neutral' probabilities for calculating the expected values of cash flows.

Under risk aversion, the probabilities required to calculate the expected flows are risk-neutral probabilities. Risk-neutral probabilities differ from 'natural' probabilities because they embed the risk aversion of the market. Arbitrage arguments demonstrate that the above two techniques are equivalent. Therefore, credit spreads relate to 'risk-neutral' probabilities and recovery rates.

Valuation is a key building block for determining the value distribution at a forward horizon. In risk models, valuation is forward, at the horizon, for all possible credit risk scenarios, in order to derive a distribution of future values. Matrix valuation refers to the usage of credit spreads for valuing any asset at some horizon, using the array of credit states. The technique combines transition probabilities with the credit spreads corresponding to the final credit states. Most portfolio models use the matrix technique. Implementing the risk-neutral valuation for a future date is more challenging because of the need to have risk-neutral probabilities. Only KMV Portfolio Manager provides risk-neutral valuation as an alternative option to matrix valuation.

The first section defines credit spreads and shows how to derive them from the spot and forward risk-free and risky yield curves. The second section describes the two basic techniques for valuation. The third section discusses the relation between valuation, credit risk and maturity. The last section describes the valuation building blocks of different credit risk models. The appendix to this chapter further details some counterintuitive effects of this mechanism.

CREDIT SPREADS

The market provides yield curves, for the risk-free yields of government debt and for risky debts of all ratings. Standard practices derive risky yields by grouping bonds according to their ratings. Credit spreads are differences between the risky yields and the risk-free yields. This section discusses credit spreads, both spot and forward, from such market yields.

Calculation of Credit Spreads

The calculation of spreads results from spot and forward risky and risk-free yield curves. When using the spot rates, we obtain spot credit spreads. When using the forward yield curves, we obtain forward credit spreads.

Calculation of Spot Spreads

A credit spread is the difference between the yield of a risky debt and the risk-free rate between any two dates. Formally, if y and y_f are the risky yield and the risk-free yield:

$$\text{Credit spread}(t) = y(t) - y_f(t)$$

The calculation is similar for spot credit spreads and forward credit spreads. Using the yields of the risk-free and of the risky debts, spot credit spreads are 0.50% for 1 year, 1% for 2 years and 1.8% for 3 years (Table 42.1).

TABLE 42.1 Term structure of risk-free and risky yields

Periods	1	2	3
Risky yield	5.00%	6.00%	7.00%
Risk-free yield	4.50%	5.00%	6.20%

Calculation of Forward Rates and Spreads

A forward spread is the forward risky debt yield minus the forward risk-free rate. Both risky and risk-free forward rates are derived from the spot yield curves of risky debts and of the risk-free debts. The first step is to calculate forward rates as usual. The forward credit spread is the difference between the risky forward rate and the risk-free forward rates.

Forward rates between any two dates t and $t + n$ derive from spot rates. The forward rate between the future dates t and $t + n$ is $f(t, t + n)$, dates t and $t + n$ being end of period. For instance, $y(1)$ is the yield at date 1, the end of period 1. If the period is 1 year, and we are at date 0 today, $y(1)$ is the spot rate for 1 year, $y(2)$ the spot rate for 2 years, etc. The forward $f(1, 2)$ is the forward 1 year from now and up to the end of year 2, $f(1, 3)$ is the annual forward rate for 2 years $(3 - 1)$, starting 1 year from now. The forward rate $f(1, 3)$ results from the equation $(1 + 5\%)^1[1 + f(1, 3)]^2 = (1 + 7\%)^3$:

$$f(1, 3) = \{[(1 + 7\%)^3/(1 + 5\%)^2]\}^{1/2} - 1$$

We find $f(1, 3) = 8.01\%$. We check that $(1 + 5\%) \times (1 + 8\%)^2 = 1.225043 = (1 + 7\%)^3$. In general, the following formula relates the forward $f(t, t + n)$ to the spot rates $y(t)$ and $y(t + n)$:

$$[1 + y(t)]^t[1 + f(t, n)]^{n-t} = [1 + y(t + n)]^{t+n}$$

So that the forward between t and $t + n$ is:

$$f(t, t + n) = \{[1 + y(t + n)]^{t+n}/[1 + y(t)]^t\}^{1/n} - 1$$

From the yield curves, we derive the forward rates for both the risky and the risk-free debt. The forward $f(1, 3)$ is 8.01%, and substituting the risk-free yield for the risky yield, the forward risk-free yield is 7.06%. Hence, the forward credit spread 1 year from now and for 2 years is 8.00% − 7.06% = 0.95%. Since we can use any two dates in the future to calculate forward yields, both risky and risk-free, we derive credit spreads for any pair of future dates. The shape of the forward and spot yield curves drives the shape of the forward credit spreads term structure. Forward credit spreads result mathematically from the spot yield curves, risky and risk-free. Such mathematical calculations have no reason to be good predictors of the future credit spreads. Therefore, the future credit risk and the forward credit spreads curve are not necessarily in line.

RISK-NEUTRAL VALUATION, SPREADS AND DEFAULT PROBABILITIES

This section addresses the equivalence between credit spreads and default probabilities under risk-neutrality. Risk-neutrality means that investors are indifferent between the expected value of a random flow and the certain flow having a value equal to the expected value of the random one. Since this is unrealistic, 'natural' or 'real' probabilities differ from risk-neutral probabilities. This provides an intermediate step to model credit spreads in relation to the default probabilities and the recovery rate. After introducing notations, we proceed to the calculation of the value of the risky debt.

There are two ways to value risky debt. Either we discount the risk-adjusted flows at the risk-free rate, in practice the expected future flows subject to default risk, or we discount the contractual flows at the risky market rate. Under arbitrage, these two values should be identical. This imposes a condition on the probabilities used to value the expected flows. The corresponding probabilities are 'risk-neutral' probabilities. They differ from 'natural' probabilities because of the market risk aversion. The above equivalence makes it easy to derive 'implied' risk-neutral probabilities from risky debt prices.

The section uses a simple example of a 1-year debt to illustrate the formula. General formulas applying to several periods are given in the last subsection.

Notation

We use the following notation for spot yields and default probabilities.

Notation for spot transactions, the current date being 0:

Risky rate between any two dates: $y(0, t)$
Risk-free rate between any two dates: $y_f(0, t)$
Default probability between any two dates: $d(0, t)$
Recovery rate: $R(\%)$ equal to $1 - \text{Lgd}(\%)$. This parameter is assumed constant over time
Uncertain future flow at date t: $\mathbf{F}_t$

Notation for forward transactions starting at the future date t up to the future date $t + n$:

Risky rate between any two dates: $y(t, t + n)$
Risk-free rate between any two dates: $y_f(t, t + n)$
Default probability between any two dates: $d(t, t + n)$
The other notation is the same as above

Linking market spreads with the underlying credit risk parameters requires making explicit the market valuation as a function of these credit risk parameters. The simplest example would be an investor facing two investment opportunities for 1 year:

- A zero-coupon risky bond, with a 1-year maturity, yielding the risky rate $y = 8\%$.
- A zero-coupon risk-free bond, with a 1-year maturity, yielding the risk-free rate $y_f = 6\%$.

In both cases, the investor invests a value of 1 up to the horizon 1. The investment future value depends on the credit risk of the risky debt, and is the certain value $(1 + y_f)$ with the risk-free debt. The risky debt has a default probability $d(0, 1) = 1.5\%$ between the dates 0 and 1. In the event of default, the recovery rate R is 30%. From the above data, we show that the market requires a credit spread of 2% for the risky debt above the risk-free rate.

The Expected Flow at the Horizon

First, we work out the formula for the expected flow $E(F_t)$ at the end of 1 year. If the risky bond defaults, we get the principal plus interest $(1 + y)$ times the recovery rate, or $(1 + y) \times R$. If the risky bond does not default, we get $1 + y$. If the default probability is $d(0, 1)$, the expected flow at end of year 1 is:

$$E(F_t) = d(0, 1) \times (1 + y) \times R + [1 - d(0, 1)](1 + y)$$

The risk-free debt generates a certain future flow $(1 + y_f)$, equal to $(1 + 6\%) = 1.06$. With $y = 8\%$, $y_f = 6\%$ and $R = 30\%$, the future expected flow with the natural probabilities is:

$$E(F_t) = d(0, 1) \times (1 + 8\%) \times 30\% + [1 - d(0, 1)](1 + 8\%)$$

$$E(F_t) = (1 + 8\%)\{d(0, 1) \times 30\% + [1 - d(0, 1)]\}$$

The Probabilities of Default and Arbitrage

'Natural' default probabilities are the actual ones. If we use the observed historical probability of default of 1.5%, the expected value of the random unit flow of the risky debt is:

$$E(F_t) = 1.5\% \times (1 + 8\%) \times 30\% + 98.5\% \times (1 + 8\%)$$

$$= 1.5\% \times 0.324 + 98.5\% \times 1.08 = 1.06866$$

This future value is above 1.06, that of the risk-free debt. There is no reason to expect that the values will coincide if we use the actual, or 'natural', default probability. Conversely, taking the equality as a constraint, there is a value of the default probability making them equal.

The discrepancy between the two values, 1.06 and 1.06866, cannot hold if it provides investors with a risk-free arbitrage opportunity. They would buy the risk-free asset and short (sell) the risky one to make a mechanical gain. This would increase the price of the risk-free asset and decrease the value of the risky asset. Hence, both values should be equal if there is no risk in the arbitrage. However, there is risk, and this is why the equality does not hold. The expected value of the risky debt, 1.6866, is not certain. The future flow will be either 0.324 or 1.08 with the natural probabilities 8% and 92%. Equality assumes that investors will be happy with 1.06866 in 1 year, even though this value is uncertain.

Risk aversion implies that the certainty equivalent of this flow should be lower. In this case, it has to be 1.06 under risk-neutrality, because investors would not care about risk. Therefore, the market value of the risky flow should be less than its expected value with natural probabilities. This requires changing probabilities, and increasing the down-side probability to bring the expected value in line with 1.06. The risk-neutral default probability is higher than the natural default probability.

Implied or Risk-neutral Probabilities

The risk-neutral default probability is such that the risky debt expected value at the horizon is equal to that of the risk-free debt. The risk-neutral probability from 0 to n is $d^*(0, n)$, instead of $d(0, n)$, the natural default probability. It is such that:

$$d^*(0, 1) \times (1 + 8\%) \times 30\% + [1 - d^*(0, 1)] \times 1.08 = 1.06$$

$$d^*(0, 1) = 2.646\%$$

This risk-neutral default probability is higher than the observed default probability of 1.5%. The risk-neutral probability is the probability that would apply in a risk-neutral universe by definition since it makes equal the expected value with its certainty equivalent.

Natural probabilities are real world probabilities, as opposed to the risk-neutral proba-bilities. Nevertheless, risk-neutral probabilities are also 'real world' probabilities because they are those effectively used by investors to value the risk premium attached to risky flows! Our convention is as follows:

- Risk-neutral default probabilities are the default probabilities adjusted for the risk premium. They serve for valuation using the expected flows and the risk-free rate as discount rate.
- Real world default probabilities, or natural default probabilities, are those effectively observed. These natural probabilities do not serve for valuation. Valuation discounts contractual flows using the risky rate.

Risk aversion implies that investors behave as if they used default probabilities higher than natural default probabilities. In order to find predictors of actual probabilities, we need a correction for risk aversion. The value of risk aversion is the difference between the expected value of the future flow at actual default probabilities and the certain equivalent flow using risk-neutral probabilities. We know the certain equivalent flow, which is 1.06, and the expected flow with actual probabilities, 1.06488. The ratio of the certain equivalent flow to the expected value of the flow is lower than 1. It is:

$$1.06/1.06866 = 0.9895 = 1 - 0.0081$$

The risk premium, as a future value at the horizon, is 0.0081 per unit invested.

Similar calculations could use the credit spreads since they quantify risk aversion. Therefore, in order to derive implied 'natural' default probabilities from the credit spreads, we need to equate the value of the expected flows under risk-neutral probabilities with the value of the contractual flows at the risky yields. However, credit spreads value risk aversion and recovery rate. Unless we know the embedded recovery rate in market spreads, we cannot value risk aversion.

Risk-neutral Probabilities and Recovery Rate

This section uses the general formula, with recovery R, to calculate the risk-neutral default probability of a 1-year zero-coupon bond. The next section uses a formal presentation of such calculations for other maturities. The data is the same as above, with $R = 30\%$. The future flow is equal to the risk-free contractual flow at horizon, $1 + y_f$:

$$\{d^*(0, 1) \times (1 + y) \times 30\% + [1 - d^*(0, 1)] \times (1 + y)\} = (1 + y_f)$$

The difference between y and y_f is the spot credit spread $cs(0, 1)$, so that:

$$cs(0, 1) = y - y_f = 2\%$$

The risk-neutral probability $d^*(0, 1) = d^*$ is:

$$d^*(0, 1) = (y - y_f)/[(1 - R\%) \times (1 + y)]$$

This is 2.646% if $R = 30\%$. Note that:

$$d^*(0, 1) \times (1 - R\%) = (y - y_f)/(1 + y)$$

Since y is small, the product of the default probability times the loss given default (as a percentage, $1 - R\%$) is approximately equal to the credit spread: $d^*(0, 1) \times (1 - R\%) = 2.646\% \times 70\% = 1.852\%$. Hence, credit spreads are close to expected losses. If we set the recovery rate to zero, the implied risk-neutral probability becomes:

$$d^*(0, 1) = (8\% - 6\%)/(1 + 8\%) = 1.852\%$$

The conclusion is that both the risk-neutral probability and the credit spread get closer to 1.5%, the natural default probability when the recovery rate declines. Credit spreads roughly approximate the risk-neutral default probability when the recovery rate is zero. However, they still overstate the natural default probability because of risk aversion.

General Formulas with Multiple Period Horizons

This section makes explicit the relationship between credit spreads and risk-neutral default probabilities, given recovery. It shows the consequences of equating valuation using risky market yields and valuation using risk-neutral probabilities. The example extends to maturities longer than 1 year by splitting them down into zero-coupons of all contractual maturities. Any coupon bond can be stripped into a series of zero-coupons, whose terminal flows are identical to all interest and principal flows, so that the analysis extends to all bonds.

Alternatively, for multiple periods, an equivalent valuation technique uses yields to maturity instead of zero-coupon yields. This formulation extends to multiple periods up to maturity T. The yield to maturity Ytm is such that the present value of a risky debt is equal to its price. This yield to maturity embeds an averaged credit spread. RYV is the value of the risky debt and RFV is the value of the same risk-free debt. In what follows, we use $d^*(0, t) = d_t{}^*$.

Spreads and Risk-neutral Probabilities

The contractual flow at date t is F_t. The actual flow is random, and is $\mathbf{F}_t$, using bold characters. The risk-free value of a risk-free zero-coupon bond is RFV:

$$\text{RFV} = F_t/(1 + y_f)^t$$

The risky value of a risky zero-coupon bond is RYV:

$$\text{RYV} = F_t/(1 + y)^t$$

By definition of credit spread 'cs': $\text{cs} = y - y_f$. The ratio of risk-free debt value to risky debt value is the ratio of the discount factors relative, respectively, to the risky and the risk-free yields.

For the risky bond, the expected flow at maturity is the flow given default times the default probability, plus the flow under no default times the survival probability. The risk-neutral probability $d^*(0, t)$ is adequate for valuation purposes:

$$E^*(\mathbf{F}_t) = [d_t{}^* \times R + (1 - d_t{}^*)] \times F_t$$

$E^*(\mathbf{F}_t)$ represents the expectation with risk-neutral probabilities, lower than the expectation using the natural probabilities. Valuation under no-arbitrage implies that the present value of the expected flow, using risk-neutral probabilities and discounting at the risk-free rate, is equal to the present value of the contractual flow of the risky bond discounted at the risky rate:

$$E^*(\mathbf{F}_t)/(1 + y_f)^t = F_t/(1 + y)^t$$

General Formulas

The general formulas for valuing risky debt follow. We use the yield to maturity as discount rate. The value of the debt is the discounted value of all contractual future flows F_t at the risky yield to maturity:

$$\text{RYV} = \sum_{t=1}^{T} F_t/(1 + y)^t$$

The discount rate y is the risk-free yield y_f plus the credit spread cs: $y = y_f + \text{cs}$. There is a set of risk-neutral default probabilities applicable to each future flow such that the discounted value of the expected flow using these risk-neutral probabilities will be equal to the risky debt value obtained using contractual flows and risky yields:

$$\text{RYV} = \sum_{t=1}^{T} F_t[d_t{}^* \times R + (1 - d_t{}^*)]/(1 + y_f)^t = \sum_{t=1}^{T} F_t/(1 + y)^t$$

The Values of Recoveries and of the Risky Fraction of Debt

What follows shows that these basic formulas are equivalent to the sum of two debts, one risk-free and equal to recoveries, and another risky because it is entirely lost under default. If the debt defaults, we get the recovered flows, and if it does not default, we get them as well. Therefore, the fraction of the flows recovered is not at risk. This recovery is risk-free, whereas the fraction $\text{Lgd} = 1 - R$ of the future flows is actually at risk. The value of the risky debt has two components:

- A fraction R of the debt is risk-free. Its value is the present value of the fraction R of future flows at the risk-free rate.
- Another fraction $\text{Lgd} = 1 - R$ of the debt is risky. Its value is the present value of the fraction $1 - R$ of future flows at the risky rate. Alternatively, it is the present value of the fraction $1 - R$ of the expected future flows, using risk-neutral probabilities, at the risk-free rate.

Using a constant recovery rate applying to interest revenue and principal repayments, the valuation of the risky debt becomes:

$$\text{RYV} = \sum_{t=1}^{T} F_t[R/(1 + y_f)^t + (1 - R)/(1 + y)^t]$$

The first term is the value of the risk-free fraction R of the debt while the second term is the value of the risky fraction $1 - R$ of the debt. The second term is also the risky fraction $1 - R$ of the debt with a recovery rate of zero, since recoveries are already valued. Using the risk-neutral probabilities and the risk-free yield to maturity with a recovery rate of zero:

$$(1 - R) \times F_t/(1 + y)^t = (1 - R)(1 - d_t^*)/(1 + y_f)^t$$

Therefore, we find:

$$\text{RYV} = \sum_{t=1}^{T} F_t \times [R + (1 - R)(1 - d_t^*)]/(1 + y_f)^t$$

The term in brackets is $(1 - d_t^* + Rd_t^*)$. It is exactly the same term as in the general formula of the previous paragraph $[d_t^* \times R + (1 - d_t^*)]$.

The Cumulated Risk-neutral Probabilities and Loss for Default Risk

For any horizon, omitting the time superscript:

$$[d_t^* \times R + (1 - d_t^*) \times 1] \times \text{RFV} = \text{RYV}$$

$$d_t^* = (1 - \text{RYV}/\text{RFV})/(1 - R)$$

The first factor is the loss of value due to default risk expressed as a percentage of the risk-free value. This factor applies to all maturities. The risk-neutral default probability, cumulated from 0 to t, is the loss from default risk divided by the loss given default percentage, since $\text{Lgd} = 1 - R$. This percentage needs to be strictly positive. Should $R = 1$, recoveries would be 100% and the debt would be risk-free. Hence $R < 1$ for a risky debt.

From a pure zero-coupon bond of maturity t:

$$\text{RYV} = F_t[d_t^* \times R + (1 - d_t^*)]/(1 + y_f)^t = F_t/(1 + y)^t$$

$$d_t^* = [1 - (1 + y_f)^t/(1 + y)^t]/(1 - R)$$

When R varies, d_t^* varies, but the ratio RYV / RFV $= (1 + y_f)^t/(1 + y)^t$ does not. Note that the loss from default risk is the same as before. The recovery rate does not change the loss; it changes the implied default probabilities. When R gets close to zero, the formula simplifies. The loss given default becomes 100% and d_t^* is equal to the percentage loss for default risk. In addition, this loss is proportional to:

$$d_t^* = 1 - (1 + y_f)^t/(1 + y)^t = t \times (y - y_f)/(1 + y)^t$$

The risk-neutral probabilities with positive recovery rates are higher than the similar probabilities with a zero recovery rate. The loss is proportional to the cumulated risk-neutral default probability. It is also approximately proportional to the credit spread times the horizon.

Example of Implied Probabilities and Credit Spreads

Table 42.2 calculates the risk-free and the risky value of a risk-free debt and a risky debt having identical contractual cash flows, using different maturities. The loss from default risk is the difference in value of the risky debt and the risk-free debt providing the same flows. It is equal to the risk-neutral default probability if recoveries are zero.

TABLE 42.2 Calculation of implied risk-neutral default probabilities from market spreads–zero recoveries

	1	2	3
Risk-free yield	6.0%	7.0%	8.0%
Risky yield	8.0%	9.5%	10.5%
Recovery rate R	30.0%	30.0%	30.0%
Future value at t	1	1	1
Risk-free debt			
Contractual flows	1	1	1
RFV $= (1 + y_f)^t$	0.94340	0.87344	0.79383
Risky debt			
Contractual flows	1	1	1
RYV $= (1 + y)^t$	0.92593	0.83401	0.74116
Loss from default risk (value)	0.01747	0.03943	0.05267
$d_t^* = [1 - (1 + y_f)^t/(1 + y)^t], R = 0\%$	1.852%	4.514%	6.635%
$d_t^* = [1 - (1 + y_f)^t/(1 + y)^t]/(1 - R), R = 30\%$	2.646%	6.449%	9.478%

FORWARD VALUATION DISTRIBUTIONS AND CREDIT RISK VAR

Full valuation mixes several effects. First, it combines the risk effect with the relative 'richness' or 'poorness' effect, or the influence of the excess spread of an asset over the market required yields. Second, a longer maturity increases the length of exposure to credit risk. Third, the effect of a longer maturity on value depends on excess spread. Finally, migrations alter the risk. The effects of moving forward in time include:

- The drift of time, resulting in a lower number of remaining cash flows and related discount factors. This is the 'roll-down effect', keeping all other parameters constant, or the amortization effect.
- The usage of forward parameters rather than their current values such as the forward yields, both risk-free and risky, and the corresponding credit spreads and risk-neutral probabilities.
- The specifics of the facility, notably its maturity, amortizing schedule and excess spread, or yield minus the market required yield.

The mark-to-model valuation has desirable properties, but also generates interpretation difficulties. Drawbacks in terms of interpretation include deviations from par value resulting from the gap between the facility yield and the risky market yield, the sensitivities of values to maturity, amortization and market spreads combined with the 'roll-down' effect. Some of these are counterintuitive, making it more difficult to understand declines in value.

Two facilities with identical book values and amortization schedules and the same risk can have different economic exposures. This makes sense because a 'rich' facility is more valuable than a 'poor' one. Hence, we lose more if the rich one defaults than if the poor one does. Nevertheless, individual loss values mix the value of richness and the value of risk, possibly resulting in counterintuitive results. The effect of maturity on the loss value is an example.

The difference between rich and poor facilities increases with maturity. The reason is that a rich facility accumulates periodic excess spreads over the entire maturity. Hence, maturity increases any gap between economic value and book value, or between poor and rich facilities. When the excess spread becomes negative, the maturity reduces the value of exposure. Since losses are value-driven, it looks like maturity decreases risk for a poor facility.

The maturity effect looks like a risk effect, but it is not. Rather, it is a pure valuation effect. The value changes even though the risk remains the same (no risk migration). If the excess spread is zero, the facility remains at par whatever the residual maturity. Whenever there is a gap between the facility yield and the market risky yield, the expected forward value becomes sensitive to maturity even though the risk remains the same. Negative excess spreads make the value increase with residual maturity, suggesting less 'losses' with longer maturities. This is exactly the reverse of the expected intuitive effect. In fact, maturity does not decrease the risk as an increase of value would suggest. Rather, it increases the value, which is quite different. In a book value framework, maturity influences credit risk through cumulative default and migration rates only. In an economic value framework, maturity also influences the risk through the value of exposure.

The appendix to this chapter documents further the maturity effect on valuation, using constant market parameters and a time drift. It shows that the pure maturity roll-down effect on value can generate a loss, even though the credit quality remains changed.

IMPLEMENTING THE VALUATION 'BUILDING BLOCK' IN CREDIT RISK MODELS

Valuation is a key building block for determining the value distribution at a forward horizon. In risk models, valuation is forward, at the horizon, for all possible credit risk scenarios, in order to derive a distribution of future values. This section describes how 'matrix valuation', based on transition matrix and credit spreads, and risk-neutral valuation apply to find the distribution of values at a future horizon. It also compares the valuation building block of major models using full valuation of migration risk. The subsections summarize the valuation formulas using contractual flows and market risky yields, to show how matrix valuation operates and indicate which techniques credit risk models use.

Future Valuation

The valuation formulas for a forward date are similar to those providing valuation as of the current date, except that the stream of cash flows rolls down when getting closer to maturity. Formulas use yield to maturity as discount rate. The valuation of the debt as of date 0 is the discounted value of all contractual future flows F_t at the risky yield to maturity. $RYV(t)$ is the value of risky debt at date t. The risk-neutral probability is $d_t^* = d^*(0, t)$ when calculations are as of current date 0, and $d^*(1, t)$ when we are at a forward date 1. Risky yields to maturity y are risk-free yield y_f plus credit spread cs: $y = y_f + cs$, either spot or forward. For a current valuation, we use 0 as the current date. For a mark-to-future valuation at the horizon, we use 1 as the horizon date, and discounting applies to dates 2 and beyond. The formulas for forward valuations are as follows:

$$RYV(1) = \sum_{t=2}^{T} F_t/(1 + y)^t$$

The risk-neutral default probabilities d_t^* are such that the discounted value of the expected flow $E^*(\mathbf{F}_t)$, using these risk-neutral probabilities, is equal to the risky debt value obtained using contractual flows F_t and risky yields:

$$RYV(1) = \sum_{t=2}^{T} F_t[d_t^* \times R + (1 - d_t^*)]/(1 + y_f)^t = \sum_{t=1}^{T} E^*(\mathbf{F}_t)/(1 + y_f)^t$$

$$RYV(1) = \sum_{t=2}^{T} F_t/(1 + y + cs)^t$$

Valuation at a forward date implies using the forward date credit spreads.

Matrix Valuation

When the facility defaults, the loss is net of recoveries, or loss under default. When looking at forward valuation at the horizon, there are as many possible credit states as there are migrations. The distribution of values is the foundation of the credit risk

VaR with full valuation models. There are as many values at the horizon as there are risk classes, including default. Mark-to-future designates the forward valuation for all possible migrations. The principles for valuing a risky debt at the current date and at a forward date are similar, except that the current value is certain while the forward valuation results in an entire distribution of values.

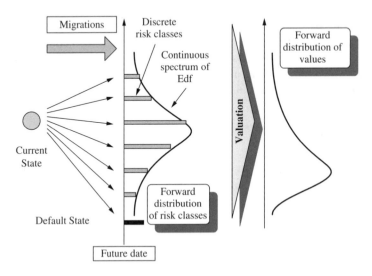

FIGURE 42.1   Migration risk and distribution of future values

Forward valuation applies to debts that do not default between current and forward dates, and to facilities with maturities longer than the horizon. Under the migration matrix technique, there are a finite number of credit states at the horizon. Using the forward credit spreads to discount contractual flows beyond the horizon provides the values at the horizon for all credit states (Figure 42.1).

Risk-neutral Valuation

Under risk-neutral valuation, risk-free rates apply to the expected flows calculated with risk-neutral probabilities. KMV Portfolio Manager provides credit spread valuation and is the only model also providing risk-neutral valuation by modelling risk-neutral probabilities directly.

For each expected default frequency Edf, there is a risk-neutral probability embedding the effect of risk aversion. The risk-neutral probability is such that the asset provides the risk-free yield. It is the probability that the asset falls below the default point when it yields the risk-free rate r_f rather than the expected risky return. We know the default point at the horizon. When the asset provides a risk-free return lower than its actual risky yield, its horizon value is lower than if it provides the risky return. Therefore, the distribution of asset values at the horizon is below the distribution of the risky asset return. With the same default point, this lower distribution results in a higher probability of hitting the default point. This probability, higher than the 'natural' default probability, is the risk-neutral probability. The areas under the two distributions, below the default point 'DP', are the default probabilities, actual or risk-neutral. The risk-neutral probability exceeds the natural probability.

The process needs to price risk aversion. Risk aversion is the difference between the certain equivalent of an uncertain flow and its expected value using natural probabilities. There are several indications of risk aversion. KMV Portfolio Manager uses the risk aversion applicable to equity returns in the Capital Asset Pricing Model (CAPM). In addition, it calibrates this risk aversion on bond data of varying maturities, which is volatile. The risk-neutral probabilities are consistent with this risk aversion. This valuation technique does not require credit spreads (Table 42.3).

TABLE 42.3 Comparisons of valuation techniques across models

Valuation techniques	CreditRisk+	KMV Portfolio Manager	Credit Metrics	CPV
Book value	×	Possible	Possible	Possible
Risk-neutral probabilities	—	×	—	—
Credit spreads	—	×	×	×

APPENDIX: RESIDUAL MATURITY, VALUATION AND RISK MEASURE

In this technical section, we focus on value changes due to a pure maturity roll-down effect. The change in value through time is the basis of loss measures. By controlling all market parameters, we see the pure effect of the difference in valuation dates, as of today and at the horizon, which drives the value-based measure of credit risk loss. It makes it clear that under specific conditions, a loss occurs simply due to time decay.

For this purpose, we use a bullet loan. To isolate the revenue effect, we change some notations. The facility provides a return r. The market risky required yield is y as above, and includes a credit spread. It remains constant through time. The facility yield is a coupon $C = r\% \times K$, where K is the capital repaid once at maturity T. At the end of each period, there is a coupon payment.

The facility value discounts the coupons until maturity, plus the principal at maturity, at the market required rate y. The value discounts the coupons. The capital amortizes once at maturity. The formula for a recurring coupon, plus the terminal discounted term (the capital equal to K) at maturity T is[1]:

---

[1] The discounted summation of all equal coupons is: $1/(1+r) + 1/(1+r)^2 + 1/(1+r)^3 + \cdots + 1/(1+r)^T$. This is a geometrical progression summarized in the simple formula below:

$$S_T = (1/y) \times [1 - 1/(1+y)^T]$$

The general geometric formula is written as follows:

$$S_T = a + aq + aq^2 + aq^3 + \cdots + aq^{T-1}$$

$$S_T = a \times (1 - q^T)/(1 - q)$$

$$V = Y \times \sum_{t=1}^{T} [r \times K/(1+y)^t] + K/(1+y)^t$$

Using the formula in the footnote providing the sum of a geometric progression, we find that:

$$Y \times S_T = (rK/y) \times \{1 - [1/(1+y)^T]\}$$

$$V = Y \times S_T + K/(1+y)^T$$

$$V = K \times \{(1 - r/y) \times [1 - 1/(1+y)^T] + 1/(1+y)^T\}$$

$$V/K = (1 - r/y) \times 1/(1+y)^T + r/y$$

V is sensitive to the facility yield r, the market risky discount rate y and the maturity T. The variation of V with maturity T is straightforward since $1/(1+y)^T$ varies inversely with T:

- The facility yield r is above the market required rate y, $r > y$: V increases with T. This is because $1/(1+y)^T$ decreases with T and this factor times $(1 - r/y)$, a negative factor, increases.
- The facility yield r is below the market required rate y, $r < y$: V decreases with T.
- When the facility yield is equal to the required market yield, valuation is independent of T and remains at par.

The forward valuation depends on the facility return and the market yield. The difference between valuations at 0 and 1 is characterized as a percentage by the ratio $(V_1 - V_0)/V_0$. This is the value change driven only by the drift of time. It is the roll-down effect of moving forward from 0 to 1. It is easy to show that:

$$V_1 - V_0 = (y - r)/(1+y)^T$$

Therefore, the forward change due to drift in time depends again on the sign of the difference between the market required yield and the facility yield. If the facility yields more than the market $(y - r < 0)$, the roll-down effect is negative, and the opposite holds if the facility yields less than the market.

The implications are as follows. A rich facility is such that its revenues will exceed the risky yield, credit spread included. This translates into $r > y$ in the above equation. The value increases with maturity. The longer a rich facility is, the higher its value because we gain more relative to the market when the maturity is longer. The economic amount at risk increases because excess revenues cumulate over longer periods. Conversely, the longer a poor facility is, yielding less than the market for its risk class, the lower is the valuation when maturity increases. This makes sense since we lose less relative to the market if the maturity is shorter. The economic amount at risk decreases because negative excess spreads cumulate over longer periods.

When $a = q = 1/(1+y)$:

$$S_T = 1/(1+y) \times \{[1 - 1/(1+y)^T]/[1 - 1/(1+y)]\}$$

$$S_T = (1/y) \times [1 - 1/(1+y)^T]$$

A reference case is that of a facility remaining at par, when $y = r$. In such a case, the value is constant. When extending the maturity, the risk increases because the cumulated default probability increases, but the debt value remains the same under no migration, implying no loss or gain for a credit risk. However, this remains a theoretical case because a facility at par at origination might not be after migrations, which translate into higher or lower required market yields.

43

Standalone Credit Risk
Distributions

The basic 'economic' measures of risk are the Expected Loss (EL), the standalone Loss Volatility (LV) and the Value at Risk (VaR). The EL serves for economic provisioning, and for statistical loss management, while the LV captures the dispersion of losses around the mean and relates to the unexpected loss concept. VaR measures define capital and are the loss percentile $L(\alpha)$ at various confidence levels α. The determination of the value, or loss, distribution of a transaction at a future horizon is a prerequisite for obtaining such measures. This chapter addresses standalone risk for a single transaction only.

Under default mode only (without valuation of risk migrations), a single banking exposure generates a binary standalone loss distribution with two events: default or no default. When considering the time profile of default risk, the distribution of the future values of a single exposure extends because loss values, as of today, depend on marginal probabilities of default and on discount factors that vary across future dates.

Under full valuation of migrations, there are as many values at the horizon as there are migrations according to the matrix valuation technique. Credit spreads in conjunction with the distribution of final credit states provide the distribution of values at the horizon.

For market exposures, the issue is different because the 'hold to maturity' view collapses for traded instruments. Credit risk is specific risk, or the fraction of the volatility of the value of market instruments unrelated to general market movements. For over-the-counter derivatives, exposures require modelling. Common practices use 'loan equivalents' summarizing the time profiles of derivative exposures and treat them like banking exposures. Loan equivalents should be based on modelled potential exposures (Chapter 39).

The first section discusses loss distributions for a single banking exposure. The second section discusses full migration 'matrix valuation' based on market credit spreads, which assigns values according to the final state post-migration. The third section discusses market instruments and the rationale for using specific risk for traded assets and modelled exposures for over-the-counter derivatives.

STANDALONE BANKING EXPOSURE

This section details the loss distribution relative to a single standalone banking exposure. The subsections address the same issues using a simple portfolio of two exposures only.

Loss Distribution under Default Mode

The standard measure of credit risk is the outstanding balance of cash with the borrower, equal to the book value of exposure. The 'severity of loss' is the ratio of loss to exposure, or 'loss given default' Lgd. With a 100% ratio, the loss under default is the entire exposure and, with a 40% ratio, it is 40% of the exposure. The Lgd as a percentage is equal to $1 - \text{recovery}$ (%). Simple measures of risk combine quantity and quality of risk with various credit data:

Probability of default $= d$
Probability of survival $= 1 - d$
Value of facility (random) $= V$ in value and $V(\%)$ in percentage of exposure
Exposure $= X = 1$
Loss (random) $= L$ in value and $L(\%)$ in percentage of exposure
Loss given default (%) $= \text{Lgd}$ (certain)
Loss given default (value) $= \text{Lgd}(\%) \times X$
Recovery given default (%) $= R = 1 - \text{Lgd}$

The Random Loss

The value V of the facility at the horizon is random because it differs under default and non-default, since it is $\text{Lgd} \times X$ in the first case and X in the second. Using D as a random dummy variable for default ($D = 1$ under default with probability d and 0 otherwise), the value is a random variable:

$$V = X \times \text{Lgd} \times D + X \times (1 - D) \quad \text{and} \quad V(\%) = \text{Lgd} \times D + (1 - D)$$

The expected value of the dummy default variable is d since: $E(D) = d \times 1 + (1 - d) \times 0 = d$. The random value of the facility is the value under no default X multiplied by the dummy variable D plus the value under default $X \times \text{Lgd}$ times d, d being the default probability:

$$V(\%) = (V|\text{default}) \times D + (V|\text{no default}) \times (1 - D)$$

Loss Distribution without Recovery Uncertainty

With a certain Lgd:

$$E(V) = X \times (1 - d) + X \times \text{Lgd} \times d$$

The example uses the values Lgd $= 40\%$ and $1 - \text{Lgd} = 60\%$. X is equal to 1. The loss and the value distributions, as percentages of exposure, follow. The value distribution results from flipping the loss distribution horizontally (Figure 43.1).

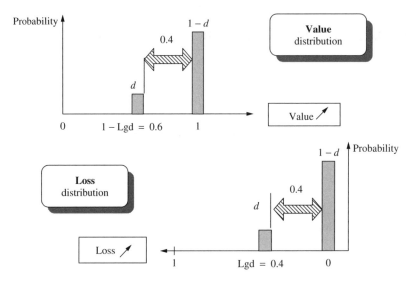

FIGURE 43.1   Probability distribution of loss and value of a standalone facility (default mode)

The value under default is 60% of exposure and the loss under default is 40% of exposure. Under no default, the value is equal to the exposure, and the loss is zero.

Derivation of Expected Value and Loss

The expected value of the exposure is the average of possible values of the facility under default and no default. The expected loss is the averaged values of losses using the default and non-default probabilities. The loss is the exposure times the loss given default percentage. The expected value as a percentage of exposure is:

$$E(\mathbf{V}) = d \times (1 - \text{Lgd}) + (1 - d) \times 1 = 1 - d \times \text{Lgd}$$

The expected value as a percentage of exposure is $(1 - d \times R)$ or $(1 - 5\% \times 40\%) = 98\%$ of X. The expected loss as a percentage of exposure is:

$$\text{EL}(\%) = d \times \text{Lgd} + (1 - d) \times 0 = d \times \text{Lgd} = 40\% \times 5\% = 2\%$$

The loss is $\mathbf{L} = 1 - \mathbf{V}$ and the expected loss is $\text{EL} = 1 - E(\mathbf{V})$. The expected loss is a more comprehensive measure of risk than exposure because it combines quantity and quality of risk.

Derivation of Loss Volatility

Loss volatility captures the potential dispersion of losses around the mean. Since $\mathbf{L} = 1 - \mathbf{V}$, the loss volatility is also equal to the value volatility. For a single facility, without valuing risk migrations, the distribution has only two values corresponding to the default and non-default states. The calculation of the loss volatility with a two-state distribution is straightforward. The loss volatility is the square root of the variance:

$$LV^2 = d \times (\text{Lgd} - d \times \text{Lgd})^2 + (1 - d) \times (0 - d \times \text{Lgd})^2$$

$$LV^2 = d \times (1 - d) \times \text{Lgd}^2$$

$$LV(\%) = \text{Lgd}\sqrt{d \times (1 - d)}$$

The loss volatility in value is $X \times \text{Lgd}\sqrt{d \times (1 - d)}$.
  In the example:

$$LV(\%) = 40\% \times \sqrt{5\% \times (1 - 5\%)} = 8.72\%$$

This calculation assumes certain loss given default. This ignores recovery uncertainty.

Extension to the Time Profile of Exposures

Cumulating risk over several periods changes the binary distribution of a single exposure into a loss distribution with more than two values. Since losses occur at different periods and with different probabilities, they have different present values. This remains true even if exposure is constant, because the discount factors and default probabilities differ from one period to another (Figure 43.2).

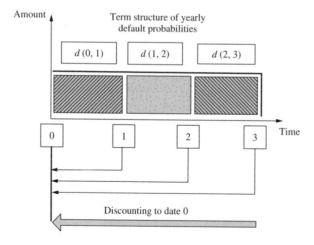

FIGURE 43.2 Stripping default probabilities and discount factors by maturity

  Discounting makes sense if capital should absorb future losses. Since investing capital up to the dates of losses increases its value by the risk-free rate, the future losses are equivalent to present losses calculated at the same risk-free rate. For example, with a risk-free rate of 5%, 100 of current capital becomes 105 1 year from now. Conversely, a current capital of 100 can absorb a 105 loss 1 year from now because it is always possible to invest it risk-free. This is the rationale to discount losses at the risk-free rate[1]. Note that portfolio models designed to estimate economic capital generally calculate losses at a single horizon rather than extending the calculations to maturity, with several subperiods.

FULL VALUATION OF MIGRATION RISK

Under full valuation mode, there are as many values as there are migration states, plus the default state. A single facility has a distribution of values at a preset horizon, one for each migration, including one for the default state. Expected loss, loss volatility and loss percentiles are derived from this loss distribution. Migrations increase the number of values at the horizon. With several period horizons, the number of branches increases as K^N, K being the number of transitions, including the default state, for a single period, and N being the number of periods, since there are K transitions for each period.

The migration risk technique allows us to generate distributions of values at the horizon for single facilities as well as for portfolios of facilities and bonds. Many models use this technique. KMV Portfolio Manager models migrations through asset value changes but allows us to use matrix valuation given the final default probability. All other models value migration risk based on the migration matrix technique.

The following illustrates the mark-to-future process and the VaR for migration risk. The facility is a bullet facility of face value 1000, with maturity 2 years, a coupon of 5.30% corresponding to a rating B. The cash flows generated by the facility are 53 at end of year 1 (Eoy 1) and 1053 at Eoy 2. The risk-free rate is 5%, the credit spread for a B rating is 30 basis points, and the appropriate risky discount rate is 5.30%. The price at date 0 is identical to face value since the facility pays the market yield exactly.

There is a spectrum of values at the end of period 1 since the facility survives up to date 2. Revaluations at the horizon under no default depend on the final risk class and discount the last cash flow of date 2, 1053, at the risky yield corresponding to the risk class at the horizon. For valuation, we do not need the default probabilities at the final horizon. Rather, we need the credit spreads corresponding to each rating[2].

The 1-year transition matrix serves to determine the possible risk classes at the horizon. The credit spreads as end of year 1 correspond to each Eoy 1 credit state. A subset of the transition matrix, starting from rating class B, with final credit classes and corresponding credit spreads is given in Table 43.1. Note that migrations can generate gains as well as losses. The values, after payment of the cash flow of 53 at Eoy 1, discount the last cash flow at Eoy 2 with a discount rate equal to the risk-free rate of 5% plus the credit spread of the final rating at Eoy 1 (Figure 43.3).

In this example of a standalone facility, there are six migrations, with the probabilities from the transition matrix. For each migration, there is a value at date 1. Table 43.1 provides the calculations of all final values. The distribution of the facility values at the horizon, from which all loss statistics derive, follows. As usual for credit risk, the value distribution exhibits skewness and a larger downside tail than upside tail. The losses or gains are the algebraic differences between the final value at Eoy 1 and the current value.

---

[1] The rate has to be risk-free since capital should be invested in risk-free assets. Otherwise, the investments would generate risk and necessitate an additional layer of capital to meet this additional risk.

[2] One of the valuation techniques of the KMV model uses risk-neutral probabilities for valuation at the horizon, as explained in Chapter 8, rather than credit spreads assigned to each rating.

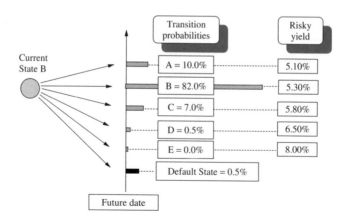

FIGURE 43.3 **Migrations and credit spreads**

TABLE 43.1 **Migrations from rating class B, with transition probabilities and final credit spreads**

Current class	Transition probability	Final rating class at Eoy 1	Yield with credit spread	Values at Eoy 1	Gain (+)/loss (−)
Date 0	10.00%	A	5.10%	1001.903	1.903
B	82.00%	B	5.30%	1000.000	0.000
	7.00%	C	5.80%	995.274	−4.726
	0.50%	D	6.50%	988.732	−11.268
	0.00%	E	8.00%	975.000	−25.000
	0.50%	Default		0.000	−1000.000
Total	100.00%		Mean	994.803	
			Volatility	70.538	

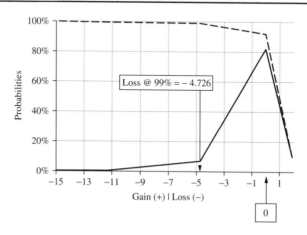

FIGURE 43.4 **Cumulated distribution of values at Eoy 1**

Figure 43.4 provides the probability distribution of gains and losses. The loss percentile at 99% is −4.726, from Table 43.1, using the 1000 value as the origin for counting losses. The loss distribution is highly skewed to the left (losses are on the left-hand side). The various loss statistics deriving from the distribution are: the expected value at Eoy 1, the volatility of the value at Eoy 1 due to migrations plus the loss at a given percentile. Percentile losses are discrete because the number of states at Eoy 1 is small (Table 43.2).

TABLE 43.2 Summary statistics for the value distribution at Eoy 1

Current value	1000.000
Expected loss at Eoy 1	−0.866
Volatility at Eoy 1	70.670
Loss percentiles at 1.0%	−0.866

STANDALONE RISK OF MARKET INSTRUMENTS

The risk of traded instruments exists over the holding period only. The 'hold to maturity' view does not hold because it is possible to get rid of the exposure whenever a warning light turns on. The view on credit risk for such an exposure is that it is the specific risk of value variations unrelated to market movements, as opposed to general risk driven by the market. This section contrasts traded instruments versus banking instruments and specific risk versus general risk. Over-the-counter derivatives do not trade, making it necessary to revert to the 'hold to maturity' view, as explained when modelling their time profile of exposure (see Chapter 39).

Traded Instruments versus Banking Instruments

The loss for credit risk is the adverse change in price of securities due to credit events. It differs from the market risk loss, because the latter results from market movements while the loss from credit risk results only from credit events. Any credit risk event materializes into a price change. The issue is to define which components of price change are due to credit events. This necessitates a distinction between general and specific risk.

Specific and General Risk

In the market universe, risk materializes through adverse price changes. However, price changes result both from market movements and from specific issuer factors. General market movements in interest rate or equity index create general risk. General risk is the fraction of the asset return or of the price volatility related to market movements. By definition, it differs from credit risk, which is issuer-specific. Specific risk is the fraction of the price or return volatility unrelated to the market. It is, by definition, independent of market movements. The prevailing view is that specific risk is the credit risk or, equivalently, issuer risk.

Specific risk materializes differently for bonds or stocks. Holding bonds generates credit risk because the value of the bond changes with risk migrations. Drops in price materialize through a widening of the credit spread, the 'add-on' to the risk-free rate used to get the 'risky discount rates' for pricing the bond. Credit risk models for loans apply to bonds, and model the risk of change in value during a specified horizon due to credit risk migrations.

For stocks, the price embeds credit risk since it reflects any available information on the issuer. Hence, credit risk is the fraction of the price volatility of stocks unexplained by market indexes, or specific risk. Equity prices move down if the credit standing of the issuer deteriorates.

Market risk embeds specific risk since it captures all return variations, whether these are general or specific, over the liquidation period. Under this view, the issuer risk should already be in the market specific risk. However, when considering a holding period longer than the liquidation period, the market specific risk is no longer in line with the actual issuer risk. When dealing with credit risk, we look more at the 'issuer risk' over a holding period than at specific market risk over a liquidation period. Therefore, we prefer to make a distinction between market specific risk and issuer credit risk.

When considering the holding period, specific risk becomes significant for stocks and bonds. The regulatory framework requires a forfeit value for credit risk, but accepts some recognition of the specific risk measures embedded in banks' internal models. The January 1996 Basel Amendment to allow internal models of market risk stipulates the rules as follows:

> '... there needs to be a prudential cushion to address the concern that practice is still developing in this area and that an industry consensus has not yet emerged about how best to model certain elements of specific risk. The Committee has accordingly decided to retain the treatment proposed in the April 1995 consultative document, whereby a modeled treatment of specific risk would be allowed subject to an overall floor on the specific risk charge equal to 50% of the specific risk charge applicable under the standardized approach. Banks whose models take little or no account of specific risk will be subject to the full specific risk charges of the standardized approach. For example, banks with models that are limited to capturing movements in equity indices, or to the spread between the inter-bank or corporate yield curves and that on government securities, should expect to receive the full specific risk charges of the standardized approach.'

Specific Risk for Bonds and Credit Risk VaR

Credit risk models address the issue for bond portfolios as for loans. The horizon is a parameter controlled by the banks. Generally, banks measure credit risk with portfolio models on their loans over a horizon of at least 1 year, because of the 'hold to maturity' philosophy. For bonds, the same models apply. Hence, it is possible to capture credit risk over a portfolio of bonds over any horizon. Most of the section on credit risk deals with measuring credit risk VaR over a specified horizon. It makes a distinction between 'full valuation' models that capture all changes in values due to risk migrations and 'default mode' models that capture loss only in the event of default. Full valuation models include KMV Portfolio Manager or Credit Metrics. They apply to credit risk measurement over a portfolio of bonds for any horizon.

Derivative Credit Risk

For over-the-counter derivatives, the 'hold to maturity' view is relevant and modelling exposures provides the time profile of worst-case exposure at future time points until maturity. A common solution consists of summarizing the time profile of potential exposures at risk into a single value, a loan equivalent, or possibly several for various periods. The process applying to banking exposures applies for loan equivalents of derivatives.

This leaves in the shadow the combination of two risks: the default risk and the exposure risk. If default risk and exposure risk are independent, the problem is similar to the modelling of the volatility of combined default risk and recovery risk.

SECTION 14

Credit Risk: 'Portfolio Risk'

44

Modelling Credit Risk Correlations

The correlation building blocks of models capture the obligors' credit risk correlation across borrowers and/or with external factors. This is a critical modelling block because: the correlations of credit risks are positive, increasing the risk of losses; they drive the shape of loss distributions and generate 'fat tails' highly sensitive to correlations; they relate to external conditions and economic cycles.

The principle for finding unobservable correlations between credit events (default or migrations) or, equivalently, joint default or migration probabilities is to view these credit events as dependent on correlated risk drivers. These are asset values in the option theoretic approach or explicit external economic factors of Credit Portfolio View (CPV). The correlation between credit events derives from the correlations between these common risk drivers.

Credit risk drivers, such as asset values or economic indexes that drive defaults and migrations, are unobservable directly. This contrasts with market parameters, the market risk drivers, whose observations are continuously available. To turn around the difficulty, models measure correlations between the direct drivers of credit risk through their common dependence on observable risk factors.

Correlation modelling for credit risk follows a two-step process: first, from observable risk factors to unobservable 'direct' credit risk drivers and second, from unobservable direct drivers correlations to credit events, defaults and migrations correlations. For this reason, we make a distinction between credit risk 'drivers', intermediate variables influencing 'directly' credit risk events, and observable 'risk factors', or parameters that correlate these risk drivers.

To model correlations, the common principle for all portfolio models is to relate individual risks of each transaction to a set of common factors. The intuition is that such factors as the state of the economy drive the default probabilities. They also affect migration probabilities, since all firms tend to migrate to worse credit states when conditions deteriorate.

KMV uses the option approach to find the joint probability that the correlated values of the assets of two firms hit the threshold value of debts. Credit Metrics uses 'joint migration matrices' providing the 'joint transition probability' of migrating to various credit states for pairs of obligors. The technique models the distribution of pairs of final credit classes for any pair of obligors with given initial credit risk classes. The equity correlations serve as proxies for asset correlations. CPV derives default correlations from their common dependence on economic factors. CreditRisk+ offers the possibility of making default 'intensities' of mixed Poisson distributions of each portfolio segment dependent on common factors. The correlations between risk drivers result from the coefficients of the factor models, and the specific credit risk from the error term that captures the credit risk unrelated to common factors.

The first section details how correlated asset returns drive the correlations between discrete events, such as defaults and migrations. The second section explains how to correlate credit events under the option approach of default. The third section details the Credit Metrics technique, based on joint migration probabilities, for generating correlated migrations for pairs of obligors. The last section addresses multi-factor models of credit risk, with subsections detailing the specifics of credit risk models: KMV Portfolio Manager, Credit Metrics, CPV, CreditRisk+. Chapter 31 summarizes the essentials of multi-factor models.

FACTOR MODELS AND CREDIT RISK CORRELATIONS

Correlating credit risk events, defaults or migrations, necessitates correlating their risk drivers. Unlike market risk drivers, credit risk drivers are unobservable. They are asset values of firms or economic indexes related to country–industry factors (CPV). In addition, the link between credit risk drivers and credit events is not as simple as the variation of value of market instruments sensitive to market parameters. Hence credit risk models face a double difficulty when addressing correlations between credit events: linking risk drivers to credit events; finding correlations between unobservable credit risk drivers.

To address the first difficulty, they use an intermediate 'modelling block' linking the credit risk drivers to credit events. In the option framework, the link with the firm's asset value is the option model of default. In the econometric modelling of CPV, the logit function relates directly an economic index modelled as a function of several economic factors to the default rate of portfolio segments. To address the second difficulty, they model risk drivers as a function of factors which, unlike risk drivers, are observable or derived from observable variables. The intuition is that common factors influence the credit standing of obligors. In some cases, the factors influencing this risk are observable. They are the country or industry indexes that influence the default probability through a logit function. In other cases, factors are derived from observed variables, but are not observable. For instance, KMV Portfolio Manager models asset values as a function of orthogonal factors, composites of observable variables.

The entire process comprises different stages. Credit risk events derive from risk drivers, such as asset values or economic indexes. Correlations between credit events result from correlations between these risk drivers. Correlations between unobservable credit risk drivers result from factor models. For this reason, we refer to risk drivers as variables influencing 'directly' credit risk events, and to the parameters influencing risk drivers as 'risk factors' (Figure 44.1).

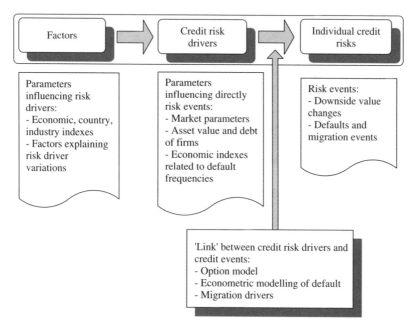

FIGURE 44.1   From factors to credit risk drivers and individual credit risk events

The next sections discuss the module linking credit events to credit risk drivers before moving on to factor models.

MODELLING JOINT MIGRATIONS AND DEFAULTS UNDER THE OPTION THEORETIC FRAMEWORK

This section discusses joint migration probabilities within the option theoretic approach of default and migration. The drivers of credit risk are asset values and the level of debt. Credit risk events include default events and credit migration events. We discuss both sequentially. The principle of the technique is to model the joint probability of the assets of two obligors falling under thresholds triggering either default or migration events.

Correlation and Joint Default Probability

Default events occur whenever the asset value gets lower than the debt. The joint default of a pair of obligors occurs when both of them have asset values under the debt value. This joint probability embeds the correlation of default events. Asset values are uncertain and follow lognormal distributions. The normal distribution is acceptable as a proxy for practical purposes.

The joint probability of default is the area under the left and down rectangle between the origin of the axes and the two lines representing the debt levels of two obligors A and B in Figure 44.2. Both default when the asset value of A falls below its debt and when the same happens simultaneously to B. The area under the distribution curves visualizes these probabilities for A and for B. The figure shows different levels of debt and different values of expected asset values of A and B, as well as different volatilities.

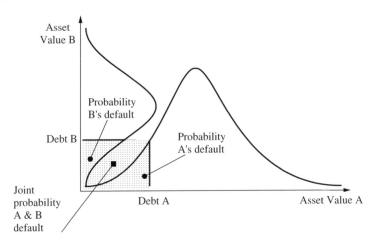

FIGURE 44.2   The joint default probabilities of two obligors and asset correlation

The correlation effect on the joint default probability appears in Figure 44.3. The figure plots the asset values of two obligors on two axes. The 'cloud' of dots is more or less round according to correlation. With a zero correlation, the cloud of dots is a circle. When correlations increase, it tends to spread across the first diagonal. The density of dots in the rectangle represents the joint default probability. The rectangle does not change because it results from fixed values of the debts of A and B. With an elongated cloud of dots, the number of dots inside the rectangle changes, and this number of dots represents the frequency of joint defaults.

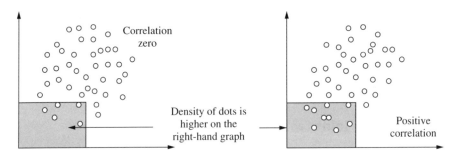

FIGURE 44.3   Visualizing the effect of asset correlation on the joint default probability

Credit Metrics derives the correlations from those of equity returns, using a multi-factor model. By contrast, KMV Portfolio Manager extracts the correlations from the modelled asset returns and uses a multi-factor model with orthogonal (independent) factors.

Correlation and Joint Default and Migration Probabilities

The same model applies to migration correlations derived from asset values. The same model of default correlation extends to correlations between migration events of two obligors. The only difference is that the thresholds driving the final rating differ from that of default. Now the thresholds are such that A gets the expected default frequency Edf_A and B gets Edf_B. Both thresholds are evidently above the default thresholds determined by the debt levels. Correlations determine the density of dots within the new larger rectangle. Asset correlations generate joint migration probabilities as they do for default events. Figure 44.4 uses a presentation similar to that of defaults. Credit Metrics models migrations using various threshold levels to define bands of asset values at the horizon defining the final risk classes.

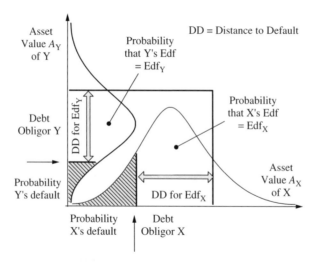

FIGURE 44.4 The joint migration probabilities of two obligors and asset correlation

Calculation of Joint Default Probabilities from the Distributions of Asset Values

In practice, the joint probability of A_X and A_Y being under the default point depends on asset correlations and the distributions of X and Y random asset values, which are A_X and A_Y, respectively. With the normal distribution, the Joint Normal Density (JND) function of the random variables A_X and A_Y has an analytical form:

$$\text{JND}(X, Y) = \left[1/(2\pi\sigma_{AX}\sigma_{AY}\sqrt{1 - \rho^2_{AXAY}})\right] \times \exp[-(1/2)Q(A_X, A_Y)]$$

$$Q(A_X, A_Y) = [1/(1 - \rho^2_{AXAY})]\{[(A_X - E_{AX})/\sigma_{AX}]^2$$
$$- 2\rho_{AXAY}(A_X - E_{AX})(A_Y - E_{AY})/\sigma_{AX}\sigma_{AY} + [(A_Y - E_{AY})/\sigma_{AY}]^2\}$$

In the formula, E_{AX} and σ_{AX} refer to the expectation and standard deviation of **X**, and similar notations apply to **Y**. The correlation coefficient between asset values is ρ_{AXAY}.

The correlation between asset values ρ_{AXAY} differs from the correlation of discrete default or migration events $\rho_{defaultXY}$. If the standalone default probabilities and the default correlation are available, the simple formula for calculating joint default probabilities of discrete events for a borrower B and a guarantor G is, using the compact notation of Chapter 41:

$$P(B, G) = b \times g + \rho\sqrt{b(1 - b) + g(1 - g)}$$

Note the change in notation. The correlation ρ is not the correlation of asset values of **X** and **Y**, but the correlation between their default events. Similarly, b and g are now the default probabilities of obligors B and G. The same formula applies for joint migration probabilities, except that the probabilities $P(X)$ and $P(Y)$ are not the default probabilities of X and Y defaulting, but that of X migrating to a given credit state and Y migrating to another credit state. In this case, since there are many final credit states for each obligor, there are as many joint probabilities as there are pairs of final states. The unconditional migration probabilities $P(X)$ and $P(Y)$ are those of published migration matrices.

The simple standardized distance to default model helps to model migrations with unobservable asset values using:

- The assigned default probabilities, considering that they embed all relevant information.
- A correlation structure between asset values, given from factor models.

Correlations between credit events derive from modelled asset value correlations. Portfolio models simulate correlated asset returns to define the probabilities that two firms migrate jointly to default. For default probabilities equal to 2.5% and 1% respectively, the threshold values are -1.96 and -2.33 respectively with the standardized normal distribution. The process requires simulating standardized asset values and assigning a default value (1 for instance) whenever the simulated asset value falls below the threshold level. This technique serves to model portfolio losses for firms with preset default probabilities. Chapter 46 describes how to generate loss distributions from defaults for a portfolio using this technique for defining default, once the default probability is given. To obtain an analytical derivation of the joint distribution of asset returns, the standardized joint normal distribution applies. The formula above, providing the joint migration probability from the option model of default, simplifies when using standardized normal distributions since their means are 0 and their standard deviations are 1[1]. The formulas require plugging in correlations of asset values as inputs.

---

[1] The formulas are: $Q(A_X, A_Y) = [1/(1 - \rho_{XY}^2)](A_X^2 - 2\rho_{AXAY}A_XA_Y + A_Y^2)$ and $JND(A_X, A_Y) = [1/(2\pi\sqrt{1 - \rho_{AXAY}^2})] \times \exp\{-(1/2)[1/(1 - \rho_{AXAY}^2)](A_X^2 - 2\rho_{AXAY}A_XA_Y + A_Y^2)\}$. In order to find the joint default probability, we need to calculate the cumulative probabilities of A_X and A_Y passing below their threshold values. This requires the numerical integration of the formula to obtain the Joint Cumulative Probability (JCP) that A_X and A_Y fall below the threshold values corresponding to the default probabilities of obligors X and Y. We need to cumulate (integrate) the joint density function within this range to find the joint default probability resulting from asset correlations. The calculation provides the correlation between migration events and their joint probability of occurrence. A similar calculation would provide the correlation between migrations.

CREDIT METRICS CORRELATED JOINT MIGRATION MATRICES

Credit Metrics develops a technique to find the distribution of values of a portfolio at a future time point from transition matrices. The technique requires using correlated transition probabilities for each pair of obligors. Correlated migration probabilities result from the correlations of unobservable asset values. They make it possible to describe all possible credit states for each pair of obligors in a squared matrix called a 'joint migration matrix'. The joint migration matrix shows, for each pair of firms, initially in risk classes i and j, the probabilities of ending in the risk classes k and l, with i, j, k and l being classes of the same rating scale. A transition matrix shows all future states of a single obligor at the horizon. A joint migration matrix shows the joint migration probabilities of any pair of credit states of any pair of obligors. These joint migration probabilities depend on the correlation between the obligors' risks. Details follow with a simplified example.

Credit Metrics Approach

Should the transitions be independent for each obligor, the joint migration probability for any pair of states would be the product of the probabilities of independent migration probabilities. However, the joint migration probabilities differ from this value because of correlations. When economic conditions worsen, chances are that default probabilities increase, and that all downward migrations increase, and they correlate. This is also the principle underlying the CPV view of modelled migrations. This makes it necessary to use correlated joint migration matrices instead of unconditional migrations.

For each initial credit state, we know the unconditional probabilities of moving to other credit states. For instance, the standard transition matrix could tell us that the probability of X moving from A to B is 5% and Y moving from B to C is 4%. If the transitions of firms X and Y are independent, the probability that the pair of obligors moves to the pair of risk classes B and C would be 5% × 4% = 0.2%. From the examples of matrices below, we find that the probability of ending in this state is in fact 0.2%, higher than the product. The reason is that migrations tend to correlate so that the joint migration probability embeds a correlation.

The technique for correlating migrations is to use the correlation between asset values of firms to determine the probability of the pair falling into any combination of two rating classes. To illustrate the process, we use conditional probabilities, which allow us to make explicit all details of the calculations. With zero correlations, the conditional probabilities are equal to the unconditional ones. With positive correlations, they are higher. In the example below, we make explicit the differences between the independent and the correlated case using conditional probabilities to calculate directly the joint probabilities instead of asset value correlations.

Unconditional Migration Matrix

The starting point is the unconditional migration matrix. In this matrix, the default state is C. It is the absorbing state. Once there, there is no way out. All probabilities sum to 100% across rows and across columns (Table 44.1)

TABLE 44.1 Unconditional migration matrix

Risk classes	A	B	C	
A	92%	5%	3%	100%
B	8%	88%	4%	100%
C	0%	0%	100%	100%
	100%	100%	100%	

In order to find the state of a pair of obligors, X and Y, we need to select the initial state of each obligor. We assume that X is in state A and that Y is in state B. The next subsection examines the case of X remaining in state A, while Y migrates upwards from its initial state B to the state A. Due to migrations, the final states follow the migration matrix. We show what happens in the case of independence and of correlated migrations.

Independent Migrations

For example, the first line of Table 44.2 indicates that: the standalone migration probability of X staying in A is 92%; the standalone probability that Y migrates from B to A is 8%; the conditional probability that Y moves from B to A given that X stays in A is 8%. The latter conditional probability, 8%, is equal to the unconditional migration probability that Y migrates from B to A because this migration is assumed, in this table, independent of what happens to X. The general law of conditional probability states that:

$$\text{Prob}(X = A, Y = A) = \text{Prob}(Y = A|X = A) \times \text{Prob}(X = A)$$

The probability of a joint pair of states (A, A) for X and Y is therefore:

$$7.36\% = 8\% \times 8\%$$

TABLE 44.2 Migrations of a pair of obligors: independent case

Initial state: X = **A**, Y = **B**		Standalone migration probabilities		Conditional migration probabilities	Joint migration probabilities
X = **A** to:		Y = **B** to:			
A	92.00%	A	8.00%	8.00%	7.36%
	92.00%	B	88.00%	88.00%	80.96%
	92.00%	C	4.00%	4.00%	3.68%
B	5.00%	A	8.00%	8.00%	0.40%
	5.00%	B	88.00%	88.00%	4.40%
	5.00%	C	4.00%	4.00%	0.20%
C	3.00%	A	8.00%	8.00%	0.24%
	3.00%	B	88.00%	88.00%	2.64%
	3.00%	C	4.00%	4.00%	0.12%
					100.00%

This probability appears in the last column and is the joint migration probability of the pair of states (A, B) to (A, A), where the first state refers to X and the second to Y. As usual with independent events, this is simply the product of the unconditional migration probabilities. It is convenient to group all such joint migration probabilities (JMP) in a matrix, shown in Table 44.3, where each cell provides the joint probability of all nine possible pairs of final states.

The benefit of using the above conditional probability formula becomes clearer when we use conditional migration probabilities that differ from the unconditional ones, in order to capture correlations between migrations. The next subsection shows how figures change in the interdependent case.

TABLE 44.3 Joint migration matrix: independent case

Initial state: X = **A**, Y = **B**		Matrix of JMP independent migrations: Y final state			
		A	B	C	
X final state	A	7.36%	80.96%	3.68%	92.00%
	B	0.40%	4.40%	0.20%	5.00%
	C	0.24%	2.64%	0.12%	3.00%
		8.00%	88.00%	4.00%	100.00%

Correlated Migrations

In order to control the joint migrations, we use conditional probabilities different from the standalone probabilities. In Table 44.4, the columns showing the conditional probabilities and the resulting joint migration probabilities change. The correlation between migration events implied in the joint migration probability results from the formula relating this correlation with unconditional and joint migration probabilities. There is no need to calculate them here, and we focus on the structure of the matrices.

TABLE 44.4 Migrations of a pair of obligors: correlated case

Initial state: X = **A**, Y = **B**		Standalone migration probabilities		Conditional migration probabilities	Joint migration probabilities (correlated)
	X = **A** to:		Y = **B** to:		
1	92.00%	1	8.00%	8.20%	7.54%
	92.00%	2	88.00%	88.30%	81.24%
	92.00%	3	5.00%	3.50%	3.22%
2	5.00%	1	8.00%	9.00%	0.45%
	5.00%	2	88.00%	90.00%	4.50%
	5.00%	3	4.00%	1.00%	0.05%
3	3.00%	1	8.00%	9.00%	0.27%
	3.00%	2	88.00%	90.00%	2.70%
	3.00%	3	4.00%	1.00%	0.03%
					100.00%

The calculations for the first line, X staying in state A and Y upgrading to state A, are:

$$\text{Prob}(X = A, Y = A) = \text{Prob}(Y = A | X = A) \times \text{Prob}(X = A)$$

The values refer to the final state. The calculation is: $\text{Prob}(X = A, Y = A) = 8\% \times$ $8.20\% = 7.54\%$. This joint migration is higher than the previous 7.36% value due to correlations. Note that this is not the case for all joint migration probabilities. When the conditional probabilities are above the standalone probabilities the resulting joint migration probability is above that of the independent case, and conversely. If this were the case for all states, all probabilities would sum to more than 1, which is impossible. Increasing some migration probabilities implies that others decrease. All joint migration probabilities are equal to the product of the unconditional probabilities. Their sum is 100%. This effect appears in Table 44.4 and in the new matrix of pairs of final states (Table 44.5).

TABLE 44.5   Joint migration matrix: correlated case

Initial state: X = **A**, Y = **B**		Matrix of JMP independent migrations: Y final state			
		A	B	C	
X final state	A	7.54%	81.24%	3.22%	92.00%
	B	0.45%	4.50%	0.05%	5.00%
	C	0.27%	2.70%	0.03%	3.00%
		8.26%	88.44%	3.30%	100.00%

The above modelling of defaults serves to generate correlated loss distributions in Chapter 38.

MODELLING CORRELATIONS FROM CREDIT RISK FACTORS

Figure 44.5 provides an overview of the modelling of correlations between individual risks, from common risk drivers and factors. Chapter 31 explains the essentials of factor models. The 'revaluation block' models the relationship between credit risk drivers and credit events, but it does not generate any correlation as such. The purpose of the 'revaluation' building block of models is to link drivers to risks. The revaluation block does not capture correlations. These derive from the correlations of the risk drivers. The next subsections detail the specifics of models related to the correlation building block.

Credit Risk Model Specifics

The different models use different factors to correlate credit drivers and, ultimately, credit events. In the credit risk universe, the random variable Y_i explained by factors is a credit risk driver of obligor i. Credit risk drivers are unobservable asset values in the option theoretic approach, or predicted values of an economic index in the CPV framework.

Multi-factor models relate these credit risk drivers to a number of factors. Some are explicit, such as the observable economic variables of CPV, while asset values are not, but they are all functions of real variables. KMV Portfolio Manager uses orthogonal (independent) factors to model asset returns of obligors. Each factor represents multiple dimensions difficult to disentangle. On the other hand, independent factors make it much easier to model credit risk correlations within a portfolio, as the derivation of correlations

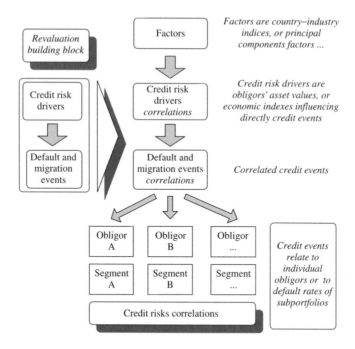

FIGURE 44.5 From factors to obligor's credit events

from the coefficients illustrates in Chapter 31. CPV uses economic indexes to correlate default rates of portfolio segments.

KMV Portfolio Manager

KMV measures correlations between modelled asset values derived from equity and debt values of obligors. The correlations between modelled asset values result from a multi-factor model, using orthogonal factors such as regions, or industry indices, obtained using principal component analysis. Orthogonal factors facilitate the calculation of asset value correlations from the coefficients of the multi-factor model. Asset values are the direct risk drivers, serving to correlate the Edf of different obligors through the option theoretic framework.

Monte Carlo simulation uses random independent asset returns to find, for each run, the risk-adjusted value distribution of a facility. The revaluation block uses either credit spreads and matrix valuation or risk-neutral modelled Edfs. KMV aggregates over the entire portfolio the facility value distributions to obtain that of the portfolio. The R^2 provides a direct estimate of the general versus specific risk. When no fit is available, for private firms for example, it is necessary to specify the R^2, the ratio of general to total risk, using for instance the average over all firms. See Chapter 48 for additional details.

Credit Metrics

Credit Metrics uses observable equity return correlations as proxies of unobservable asset value correlations. To model such correlations, it relies on a multi-factor model. The model derives pair correlations from coefficients of the factor model. The joint migration matrices result from equity return correlations. They serve to simulate the credit standing of pairs of obligors at the horizon, and provide the rating distributions at the horizon for all obligors, from which risk-adjusted facility values derive. Alternatively, Monte Carlo simulations generate correlated asset value returns, using the equity correlation structure.

This procedure does not adjust asset values and correlations for the obligors' leverage that influences both equity values and correlations. By contrast, KMV's usage of asset values and correlations 'undoes' the leverage effect when it relies on unlevered and unobservable asset values.

Credit Portfolio View

CPV models default rates of subportfolios logit functions of an economic index $\mathbf{Y}$. This economic index is a linear function of economic factors, analogous to a multi-factor model. An intermediate building block serves for using predicted values of economic factors, to use predicted values of default rates rather than current ones. The correlations of predicted values result from the multi-factor model. The predicted values of common economic factors derive from Auto Regressive Integrated Moving Average (ARIMA) time series models and depend on their lagged historical values and error terms.

The intermediate risk drivers of the particular portfolio segment i default and migration rates are the future random value of one economic index influencing the credit risk of obligors within this segment, or $\mathbf{CR}_i = \mathbf{Y}_{i,t+1}$. The subscript $t+1$ represents the horizon date and t the current date. This index is a linear function of predicted values of economic factors $\mathbf{X}_{k,t+1}$. Finally, each predicted value of each factor depends on $\mathbf{X}_k$, their lagged values and the residuals. The default rates are a logit function of the predicted index $\mathbf{Y}_{i,t+1}$, which depends on the $\mathbf{X}_{k,t+1}$ through a linear multi-factor model. The economic factors and residuals of the $\mathbf{Y}_{i,t+1}(\mathbf{X}_{1,t+1}, \mathbf{X}_{2,t+1}, \ldots, \mathbf{X}_{k,t+1}, \boldsymbol{\varepsilon}_{i,t+1})$ function are not independent and comply with a variance–covariance structure.

The technique for generating correlations is analogous to those of KMV and Credit Metrics. However, the model differs from these through three major features:

- It measures aggregated default rates, not individual default events. These are observable, unlike individual default events of surviving firms that need modelling.
- It uses economic factors to capture the cyclical dynamics rather than modelling correlated unobservable events. Neither KMV not Credit Metrics link explicitly the credit risk to cyclical dynamics.
- It does not rely on the option framework to derive default rates, but uses a logit function of an economic index linked to economic factors.

CPV provides a framework for model fitting, but leaves it to end-users to choose whatever fit they need depending on available data and portfolio segment definitions. CPV uses Monte Carlo simulations to generate default rate and migration rate distributions for portfolio segments, thereby assigning distributions of correlated final ratings to all facilities. It revalues facilities using the simulated default rates for the entire portfolio to get a portfolio value for each run, and as many as there are runs of simulations. See Chapter 48 for additional details.

CreditRisk+

CreditRisk+ takes another path. Like CPV, it models default rates of subportfolios. Unlike CPV, it requires using size bands as a criterion, in addition to risk class, to create subportfolios. CreditRisk+ models directly loss distributions of subportfolios as mixed Poisson distributions, whose mixed Poisson parameter is $q \times d$, q being the random 'mixing variable' and d being the default intensity analogous to a default probability. The mixing variable allows us to change the default intensity through time for instance.

The 'default intensity' for segment i depends on the 'mixing variable' q_i, which allows the default intensity to vary, where i is the segment index. This distribution has a Poisson parameter, which is the product of the random variable 'q_i', whose expectation is 1, with the usual Poisson parameter. The basic model ignores correlations. The correlation is an add-on to the basic structure.

In order to model correlations, CreditRisk+ makes the mixing variable 'q_i' sensitive to a common set of external factors. The sensitivities to these factors vary across portfolio segments:

$$q_i = \beta_{i1} \times X_1 + \beta_{i2} \times X_2 + \beta_{i3} \times X_3 + \cdots$$

This effectively correlates the mixing variable q_i of segments, resulting in correlated loss distributions per segment. Then, it aggregates the loss distributions of all segments. Since such a linear relationship is deterministic, all credit risk is 'general' and there is no specific risk per segment, which is a risk independent of all factors. CreditRisk+ suggests adding another independent segment for specific risk.

The sensitivities and factors are user-defined, and there is no framework for modelling these factors. CreditRisk+ does provide some guidelines for fitting such factors and default probabilities to observed data. Notably, it suggests linking the random q_i variables to actual observed default volatility as observed from time series. The external parameters as well as the sensitivities to these external factors are end-user-defined. Hence, CreditRisk+ provides a methodology to embed correlations through sensitivities to external factors, but does not specify how to model the sensitivities. The modelled distribution of losses remains entirely analytical (see Chapter 47).

Overview of Portfolio Model Correlation Building Blocks

KMV Portfolio Manager and Credit Metrics are fully self-contained models. CPV provides a modelling framework but lets end-users adjust the fits to selected parameters of their choice. CreditRisk+ remains 'open' for correlation modelling. On the other hand, it provides the easiest calculations, because it uses an analytical loss distribution rather than Monte Carlo simulations. See Table 44.6.

TABLE 44.6   **Credit risk portfolio models and multi-factor models**

	Credit Metrics	KMV Portfolio Manager	CPV	CreditRisk+
In all models, correlations and variances of credit risk are functions of the set of coefficients β_{ik} relating the risk driver $\mathbf{Y}_j$ to the factor $\mathbf{X}_k$				
$\mathbf{X}_k$ = random factors (economic, country– industry specific factors)	Multi-factor model using various industry– country indices	Multi-factor model using various industry– country indices. Factors are orthogonal. Embedded in model	Economic factors of the index driving the default rates. User-defined	User-defined factors
$\mathbf{Y}_j$ = random risk drivers of credit events (asset value or economic index)	Random asset values. Correlations are equity value correlations as proxies for asset value correlations	Random asset values or asset returns. Correlations are modelled asset value correlations	Predicted index value driving the default rates through the logit function	User-defined linear relationship between default 'intensity' of portfolio segments and factors
$\mathbf{Risk}_i$ = random credit events (default or default rate)	Obligor's risk rating or class	Continuous spectrum of obligor's Edf value	Values of segment default and migration rates	Direct analytical modelling of segments and aggregated portfolio loss distribution

Note: The index i refers to obligors or portfolio segments, the index j refers to risk drivers and the index k refers to factors.

General and Specific Risks in Multi-factor Models and Correlation Effects

Normally, the factors influence results from statistical fits. Statistical fits also provide the characteristics of the error terms. This is the case for all firms included in KMV Credit Monitor's universe.

Frequently, the universe of bank portfolios does not include such firms, and there is no modelling available of factor influences. This requires providing an estimate of the fraction of specific variance resulting from the error term (or, alternatively, of the variance from all common factors, which is general risk). In such a case, the specific risk becomes a control parameter of the model. The higher the specific risk, the lower the correlation effect and, conversely, increasing the systematic risk generates a higher correlation. The final loss distribution is very sensitive to the correlation effect, so that the control values used for general risk are important.

Hence, the ratio of specific to total risk becomes an input for private firms whenever there is no model allowing us to capture directly the general risk. KMV Portfolio Manager provides the ratio of general to total risk for end-users and also allows end-users to assign a value to this parameters. The ratio of general risk to total risk is the R^2 of the multi-factor regression model. Stressing this R^2 is equivalent to increasing the general risk and, therefore, the correlations. This increases the portfolio risk. Credit Metrics allows for a similar stress testing of correlations. Similarly, CreditRisk+ does not specify any fit to common factors, making it necessary for the end-user to specify a value for specific risk. The correlations are highly sensitive to this term, and so is the loss distribution of the portfolio.

45

Generating Loss Distributions: Overview

Factor models serve both for modelling correlations between risk drivers and generating correlated credit risk events with simulations to construct the loss distributions of portfolios. This chapter addresses the second issue, assuming that the variance–covariance structure of risk drivers is available from factor models. The generation of correlated loss distributions is critical since all portfolio loss statistics derive from these distributions.

Most vendors' models generate correlated loss distributions with Monte Carlo simulations. The chapter reviews the specifics of different models. KMV Portfolio Manager uses Monte Carlo simulations of modelled asset values of obligors. Credit Metrics uses both Monte Carlo simulations and the joint migration matrix technique. Credit Portfolio View (CPV) uses Monte Carlo simulation of economic factors. CreditRisk+ is a notable exception with its analytical loss distribution. Subsequent chapters further detail the techniques and provide examples of simple implementations. This chapter summarizes all subsequent chapters (46 to 49) detailing the loss distribution modelling techniques.

The principle of simulations is to generate correlated random credit risk drivers complying with a given variance–covariance structure. The risk drivers are asset values for KMV Portfolio Manager and Credit Metrics, although correlations have different bases (asset values versus equity prices). They are the economic variables driving the default rates in CPV.

In many instances, assigned default probabilities summarize all inputs for deriving loss distributions, except correlations between credit risk events. Two techniques serve as a simple correlated default simulator bypassing the unobservable asset values. The simplest solution correlates standardized normal distances to default to obtain correlated defaults. The distance to default measures the risk and varies inversely with default probability. Alternatively, correlating the stochastic processes driving the asset values of each obligor also generates correlated defaults. In this case, asset values follow lognormal distributions. The same general principle applies under the economic framework of CPV. Random values of economic indexes are converted into default rates through the logit function.

Each simulation run comprises four steps:

- Generating a set of correlated values of risk drivers, asset values or economic index values.
- Converting each set of driver values into credit events, default or migration, using the option model (KMV and Credit Metrics) or the logit function (CPV).
- Aggregating the facility values to provide the portfolio value.
- Repeating the process for each new draw of sets of values of credit risk drivers. There are as many portfolio values at the end of the process as there are simulation runs. Together, they make up the portfolio value distribution.

There are analytical proxies of portfolio loss distributions. The most accomplished is that of CreditRisk+. These techniques provide very convenient numerical formulas to determine loss statistics and loss percentiles, bypassing the calculation intensive simulation process. The drawback is that such proxies significantly deviate from simulated distributions, presumed better approximations of unobserved actual distributions.

The first section provides an overview of the loss distribution module. The second section summarizes the specifics of each of the main models.

OVERVIEW

Table 45.1 provides an overview of the model specifics for generating portfolio value distributions at the horizon. The analytical distributions and the joint migration matrices are not as general as the Monte Carlo simulations. For Monte Carlo simulations, multi-factor models serve to generate correlated asset returns of correlated economic indexes, from which defaults and migrations result. The correlations result from the common dependence on several factors of the risk drivers. To generate correlated returns with a preset variance–covariance structure, the Cholevsky decomposition of the variance–covariance matrix is a popular technique. Factor models serve both to measure correlations and to generate correlated factor values by varying the factors on which risk drivers depend. In this case, the Cholevsky decomposition serves to generate correlated factor values converted into risk driver values, and finally into correlated default or migration events.

MODEL SPECIFICS

The following subsections provide a qualitative overview of the various model specifics. Details are given in the corresponding chapters.

KMV Portfolio Manager

KMV Portfolio Manager uses Monte Carlo simulations to generate correlated asset values of each firm. The model operates both within KMV's universe of listed firms and with

TABLE 45.1 Vendors' models: basic techniques for generating loss distributions

	KMV Portfolio Manager	Credit Metrics	CPV	CreditRisk+
Credit events	Default and migration measured as Edf for individual obligors	Default and migration measured as ratings and default probabilities class for individual obligors	Default and migration rates for portfolio segments by country, industry and risk class	Default and migration rates for portfolio segments by country, industry, risk class and band size
Correlation structure	From orthogonal multiple factors model of asset returns	From multiple factors model of equity returns	From economic factors using: • the ARIMA models predicting economic factor values; • the multi-factor model of the index of the logit function	From end-user-defined relations of segment default intensities with external factors
Generation of portfolio value distribution	Monte Carlo simulations of correlated asset values	Simulation of credit states with joint migration matrices. Monte Carlo simulations	Monte Carlo simulation of predicted economic factor values and predicted index values. Segment default and migration rates are a logit function of the predicted index values	Segment-specific defaults follow a mixed Poisson distribution. The mixing variable is a linear function of factors.
Horizon credit state of each facility	Simulated Edf value	Simulated rating class	Simulated default rate of portfolio segments	Default intensity of portfolio segments
Revaluation at the horizon	Using credit spreads or risk-neutral default probabilities according to the horizon Edf	Using credit spreads of the horizon rating class	Using credit spreads of the horizon rating class	No revaluation at the horizon (default mode only)

end-users' preset default probabilities mapped to internal ratings. The end-user can use KMV's modelled 'expected default frequency' (Edf ©) or specify directly the default probabilities through a table mapping internal ratings to Edf. To simulate the asset values at the horizon, KMV uses its multi-factor model of asset values with orthogonal factors. The variances and covariances result from the coefficients of orthogonal factors.

Revaluation at the horizon uses either credit spreads corresponding to the final credit state or the KMV specific 'risk-neutral Edf', allowing risk-neutral revaluation of the bank's transactions at the horizon.

The result is a portfolio value distribution resulting from both migrations altering the value of facilities maturing after the horizon and default events between now and the horizon. The 'value at horizon' statistics, mean, volatility and value percentiles, result from the numerical calculation of the portfolio value distribution. KMV Portfolio Manager also provides an analytical approximation of the loss distribution. Chapter 47 provides an example of such an analytical distribution.

Credit Metrics

Credit Metrics uses both joint migration matrices and Monte Carlo simulations to generate the final credit states of a facility. The joint transition matrix technique serves to determine all possible transitions for any pair of firms, depending on their initial states, between now and the horizon. With a large number of firms, these transitions result in a continuous distribution of the portfolio values. Each final state of an obligor is a rating class. Mapping rating classes with credit spreads allows revaluation according to the horizon credit state. The alternative solution is to use Monte Carlo simulations, as KMV does. The process is similar. The differences are the usage of the equity return correlation structure, and the mapping of final credit states to ratings for a valuation at the horizon based on credit spreads.

Econometric Models

The econometric modelling of the loss distribution (CPV) follows a simple framework. For each portfolio segment, there are default and migration rates. The default rates per segment depend on common economic factors through a logit function. The logit function uses as input an index that is a linear function of economic variables, or factors, and fits the time series of default rates of portfolio segments. By generating random values of economic factors, it becomes possible to generate correlated random values of these default rates. The migration rates change accordingly, so that the sum of all migration rates within a risk class, inclusive of the migration to the default state (with a frequency equal to the modelled default rate), is 1.

The technicalities of the econometric approach result from the multiple models involved in the process. The default rates of portfolio segments are a logit function of an economic index, which is a linear combination of economic factors plus an error term. Looking forward, all economic factors have uncertain values. Therefore, it is necessary to generate the distributions of each of the predicted values of these factors. CPV uses the Auto Regressive Integrated Moving Average (ARIMA) time series model to obtain future predicted values of factors. Future values become conditional on known past values of factors and of error terms of the ARIMA fit. The distribution of the future values of a single economic factor around its predicted value is that of the error term. With only one factor, it is easy to generate such a distribution since we know the standard error of the residual from the fit. With several factors, the problem gets more complex because all factors correlate as well as the error term of each ARIMA model fitting the predicted value of each factor to its past values and errors. Therefore, it becomes necessary to impose the correlation structure on all factors and all ARIMA residuals. CPV uses the Cholevsky decomposition to perform this task. In the end, we obtain correlated values of the indexes that drive the default rates of segments, and correlated values of these default rates through the logit function relating them to the common factors.

The model captures economic trends and cyclical movements, and uses relations between observable variables, making interpretation easy. This feature is an important strength of CPV, since the simulations embed the effects of the economic cycles over future horizons. The model allows us to test explicitly a discrete number of economic scenarios, instead of using the full simulation model, to see how they influence the portfolio. In such a case, instead of drawing a large number of random values of indexes driving default rates, we simply select a discrete scenario made of selected values of economic variables. The process provides a final rating class for each scenario and for each portfolio segment. Revaluation of facilities within the portfolio segments uses the credit spreads corresponding to the simulated values of the default rate. The ultimate result is a portfolio value distribution at the horizon.

The drawback of the technique is that it is data intensive. Also, CPV is an open framework, which is a desirable property since it allows flexibility in model design and variable selection. On the other hand, it is not a self-contained model such as KMV Portfolio Manager, which provides the outputs using its own proprietary model rather than requiring modelling by end-users.

Analytical Distributions and CreditRisk+

The CreditRisk+ approach is an elegant methodology because it is entirely analytical. It relies on the mixed Poisson distribution, whose parameter is the density of defaults per unit of time, a parameter similar to a yearly default probability. This distribution models an independent number of defaults only. This does not capture size discrepancies between exposures, or correlations. To remedy the first limitation, CreditRisk+ requires using portfolio segments by exposure size (in practice, exposure is within predefined bands), risk class and recovery class. This is necessary to convert the number of defaults into losses under defaults given discrepancies in both exposures and loss under default sizes.

Within each segment, the mixed Poisson distribution applies if defaults are independent. Without correlation, it is a simple task to combine the Poisson distributions of the different segments. The sum of Poisson variables is also a Poisson variable whose Poisson default density sums up all Poisson parameters.

The time intensity parameter makes defaults dependent on time, which is a useful feature for modelling the time to default. When aggregating distributions over all segments, we obtain the distribution of the portfolio loss time profile. This can help to schedule provisions or identify worst-case time profiles of losses.

In order to capture correlations, CreditRisk+ uses a property of mixed Poisson distributions. The principle is as follows. A mixed Poisson distribution depends on a default intensity that is the product of a mixing variable and an 'average' default intensity. The mixing variable allows the default intensity to vary depending on whatever factors influence it. A property of mixed Poisson distributions is that a sum of such distributions is also a mixed Poisson distribution, even when the mixed variable depends linearly on external factors. This allows CreditRisk+ to make the mixing variable dependent on user-defined factors. The dependence on a common set of factors makes the mixing variables of all segments correlated. At this stage, it is possible to numerically calculate the loss distribution using the long-term average default intensity per segment plus the user-defined dependency on common factors. To obtain an analytical loss distribution, CreditRisk+ uses another property. When the mixing variable follows a gamma distribution, the resulting loss distribution is a negative binomial distribution.

CreditRisk+ has many appealing properties. Since the loss distribution is analytical, it is simple and fast to calculate. The time intensity parameter makes defaults dependent on time, which is a useful feature for modelling the timing of losses. It is also a simple task to consider various scenarios by changing the values of the mixing variables. On the other hand, CreditRisk+ does not model the relative magnitude of general and specific risk, which is user-defined, and is a default model only. It also imposes restrictions with respect to the definition of portfolio segments and relies on several attractive properties of mixed Poisson distributions, but necessitates restrictive assumptions to implement them.

46

Portfolio Loss Distributions: Example

This chapter details simple examples of loss distributions. Its purpose is twofold:

- To show how correlations alter the loss distribution of portfolios using a very simple portfolio made of two obligors. The credit standings of obligors correlate, which influences the loss distribution. The measures of risk are the Expected Loss (EL), the Loss Volatility (LV) and the Value at Risk (VaR), which results from the loss percentile values $L(\alpha)$ at various preset confidence levels α.
- To provide the full calculation of joint default probabilities and the relations between the default correlation, unconditional and conditional default probabilities of each obligor.

To detail fully the effect of correlations, starting from independent defaults helps. In this case, under default mode only, there are four cases: no default, a single default of the first obligor, a single default of the second obligor, or joint default. This makes it very easy to track any change in loss distribution resulting from correlation. Moreover, the detailed calculation of conditional and unconditional probabilities shows how the probabilities of single or joint defaults within a portfolio relate to the standard (unconditional) default probabilities of obligors and to correlation.

The first section details the loss distribution with a two-obligor portfolio having independent individual risks. The second section constructs a two-obligor loss distribution given default correlation. The next chapters (47 and 49) detail further the correlation effect using the techniques of the main portfolio models.

PORTFOLIO OF TWO OBLIGORS

This section develops the case of a simple portfolio with two obligors A and B subject to correlated default risks. Table 46.1 describes the portfolio, with the unconditional (or standalone) default probabilities and the exposures of each. The loss given default is 100% of exposure.

TABLE 46.1 The portfolio of two obligors

	Default probability	Exposure
A	7.00%	100
B	5.00%	50
ρ_{AB}	0% or 10.00%	

The loss distribution includes four points (values). The table provides the intermediate calculations of the corresponding probabilities. Correlation implies that conditional default probabilities now differ from unconditional default probabilities. In order to calculate the probabilities of the four possible loss values, we use the structure of conditional loss probabilities.

PORTFOLIO OF TWO INDEPENDENT OBLIGORS

The first case deals with independent defaults. In this simple case, all joint probabilities of any pair of credit states of A and B are simply the products of the unconditional probabilities of A and B having the corresponding credit states. A two-obligor portfolio might be a pair consisting of primary borrower+guarantor, or buyer of protection+seller of protection. The analysis illustrates the joint default probability of both entities (or 'double default probability'), which is the unique default event for the lender. The calculations are similar to those detailed in the third-party guarantee analysis.

The Loss Distribution

The calculation of probabilities in Table 46.2 is straightforward since the joint probabilities of two events are the products of the unconditional probabilities of each. The basic relations serving to construct the table are:

$$P(\mathbf{A}, \mathbf{B}) = P(\mathbf{A}) \times P(\mathbf{B})$$

The formula $P(\mathbf{B}|\mathbf{A}) = P(\mathbf{A}, \mathbf{B})/P(\mathbf{A})$ serves to calculate all other probabilities.

The joint default probability is $7\% \times 5\% = 0.35\%$. The joint probability that A defaults and B does not is, similarly, $7\% \times 95\% = 6.65\%$. In addition, the conditional probability $P(\mathbf{A}|\mathbf{B})$ is identical to the unconditional probability in the independent case because $P(\mathbf{A}, \mathbf{B}) = P(\mathbf{A}) \times P(\mathbf{B})$. The values in the table serve for subsequent comparisons with the positive correlation case.

The example of the loss distribution for two obligors shows that unconditional probabilities of obligor defaults and non-defaults are not identical to the default probabilities of each

**TABLE 46.2   Calculation of joint default probabilities of two indepen-
dent obligors**

Unconditional probabilities				Conditional probability B|A	Joint probabilities
A		**B**			
D	**7.00%**	D	**5.00%**	**5.00%**	0.35%
		ND	95.00%	95.00%	6.65%
				100%	P(A)
					7.00%
ND	93.00%	D	5.00%	5.00%	4.65%
		ND	95.00%	95.00%	88.35%
				100%	P(B)
					93.00%

obligor within a portfolio. This is because, within the portfolio, the probability that only
one obligor defaults is conditional upon non-default of the other, and hence different from
the unconditional default probability. Finally, the example provides a general and simple
framework to move from conditional probabilities, that are fairly intuitive, to correlations
that are subject to less intuitive constraints (Tables 46.3 and 46.4, Figure 46.1).

TABLE 46.3   Joint probability matrix: independent defaults

		A		
		Default	No default	
B	Default	0.35%	6.65%	**7.00%**
	No default	4.65%	88.35%	93.00%
		5.00%	95.00%	100.00%

TABLE 46.4   Joint probability matrix: independent defaults

	Loss	Total probabilities	Cumulated probabilities
A & B default	150	0.350%	100.000%
A defaults	100	6.650%	99.650%
B defaults	50	4.650%	93.000%
Neither defaults	0	88.350%	88.350%

The Loss Statistics

The calculation of the EL and LV follows directly from the probabilities of all joint
events. The EL is the weighted average of losses, using probabilities as weights. The LV
is the square root of the loss variance, which is the weighted average of the squares of
deviation from EL, using joint probabilities as weights. Table 46.5 provides the intermediate calculations.

Finally, the loss percentiles derive from the cumulated probabilities. For instance, the
loss percentile $L(99.65\%) = 100$. The next lowest loss percentile is $L(93\%) = 50$. There

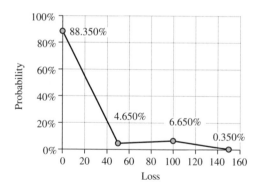

FIGURE 46.1   Loss distribution: independence case

TABLE 46.5   Loss statistics: independence case

	Loss	Joint probabilities	Cumulated probabilities	Prob × loss	Prob × (loss − EL)²
A & B default	150	0.350%	100.000%	0.53	69.09
A defaults	100	6.650%	99.650%	6.65	544.65
B defaults	50	4.650%	93.000%	2.33	76.27
Neither defaults	0	88.350%	88.350%	0.00	79.74
EL		9.50			
LV		27.74			
Loss Var.		769.75			

is a 7% chance that losses exceed 50 and only a 0.35% chance that they exceed 100 (this is the joint default probability). When the confidence level is lower than or equal to 0.35%, the loss percentile is 150, for the double default of A and B.

CORRELATED DEFAULT EVENTS

We proceed with the same portfolio as for the independence case, except that the correlation between default events is now 10%. It is possible to derive all joint event probabilities from the joint default probability as a starting point. The conditional probabilities now differ from the unconditional default probabilities. Correlation increases the joint default probability and the loss volatility and makes the 'fat tail' of the distribution thicker. The framework of calculations is the same as above. In addition, we extend them to show the relationships between the standalone risks of individual obligors measured by expected loss and loss volatility, and the portfolio risk.

Calculation of Joint Default and Conditional Probabilities

The process for calculating all the joint probabilities uses the conditional probabilities of B's credit state given A's credit state. In compact notation, $P(A = D) = a$ designates the unconditional probability that A defaults and $P(A = ND) = 1 - a$ the unconditional probability that A does not default, with similar notation for B [$P(\mathbf{B} = D) = b$ and $P(\mathbf{B} = ND) = 1 - b$].

Three inputs determine all others: the unconditional default probabilities of A and B plus either the conditional probability that B defaults given A defaults, or alternatively the joint probability of default of A and B (using the simple formula applicable to two obligors as in Chapter 41). Table 46.6 shows the detailed calculations. The joint default probability $P(\mathbf{A}, \mathbf{B})$ results from the general formula:

$$P(\mathbf{A}, \mathbf{B}) = a \times b + \rho_{AB}\sqrt{a(1 - a) + b(1 - b)}$$

$$P(\mathbf{A}, \mathbf{B}) = 7\% \times 5\% + 10\%\sqrt{5\%(1 - 5\%) + 7\%(1 - 7\%)}$$

$$= 0.9061\%$$

TABLE 46.6 Unconditional default probabilities, conditional probabilities and default correlation[a]

Unconditional probabilities				Conditional probability B|A	Joint probabilities
A		**B**			
D	7.00%	D	5.00%	12.9440%	0.9061%
		ND	95.00%	87.0560%	6.0939%
				100%	P(A)
					7.0000%
ND	93.00%	D	5.00%	4.4021%	4.0939%
		ND	95.00%	95.5979%	88.9061%
				100%	P(B)
					93.0000%
P(A, B) correlated			0.9061%		
P(A, B) independent			0.3500%		

[a]D = default, ND = no default.

Alternatively, the formula $P(\mathbf{B}|\mathbf{A}) = P(\mathbf{A}, \mathbf{B})/P(\mathbf{A})$ serves for calculating all other probabilities. The conditional probability column provides probabilities conditional on what happens to A. For example, the JDP $(\mathbf{A}, \mathbf{B})$ is equal to $P(\mathbf{A}) \times P(\mathbf{B}|\mathbf{A}) = 7\% \times 12.9440\% = 0.9061\%$. The same joint probability of default results from the correlation formula. Once obtained, the conditional probability that B defaults under A's default derives from the general formula $P(\mathbf{B}|\mathbf{A}) = P(\mathbf{A}, \mathbf{B})/P(\mathbf{A})$:

$$P(\mathbf{B} = D|\mathbf{A} = D) = P(\mathbf{A} = D, \mathbf{B} = D)/P(\mathbf{A} = D) = 0.9061\%/7\% = 12.9440\%$$

The conditional probability that B does not default if A does is simply 1 minus the previous probability, or $P(\mathbf{B} = ND|\mathbf{A} = D) = 1 - P(\mathbf{B} = D|\mathbf{A} = D)$, because default and non-default of B are two exclusive events:

$$P(\mathbf{B} = ND|\mathbf{A} = D) = 1 - 12.9440\% = 87.0560\%$$

Similar calculations apply to B's probabilities conditional on A not defaulting[1]:

$$P(\mathbf{B} = D|\mathbf{A} = ND) = (5\% - 0.9061\%)/93\% = 4.4021\%$$

$$P(\mathbf{B} = ND|\mathbf{A} = ND) = 1 - 4.4021\% = 95.5979\%$$

The sum of conditional probabilities of B defaulting weighted by the probabilities of the conditioning event, A defaulting or not defaulting, is the unconditional default probability of B. The formula below makes this dependence explicit:

$$P(\mathbf{B} = D) = P(\mathbf{B} = D|\mathbf{A} = D) \times P(\mathbf{A} = D) + P(\mathbf{B} = D|\mathbf{A} = ND) \times P(\mathbf{A} = ND)$$

$$P(\mathbf{B} = D) = 0.9061\% + 4.4021\% \times 93\% = 5\%$$

Finally, we check that the unconditional probability of default of A is 7%, identical to the sum of the total probabilities 0.9061% and 6.0900% when B defaults and when B does not default.

Loss Distribution

The process above results in the matrix of Table 46.7 cross-tabulating both entities' credit states showing the joint probabilities, with the margins summarizing the column probabilities and the row probabilities, which equal the unconditional probabilities. This provides the loss distribution.

TABLE 46.7 Joint probability matrix: default correlation 10%

		A		*Total*
		Default	*No default*	
B	Default	0.9061%	4.0939%	5.0000%
	No default	6.0939%	88.9061%	95.0000%
	Total	7.0000%	93.0000%	100.00%

The same observation on single defaults applies to the independent and correlation cases. The single probabilities of default in a portfolio context differ from the unconditional probabilities of default. For instance, the default of A alone has a probability of

---

[1] The conditional probabilities of B are such that:

$$P(\mathbf{B} = D) = P(\mathbf{B} = D|\mathbf{A} = D) \times P(\mathbf{A} = D) + P(\mathbf{B} = D|\mathbf{A} = ND) \times P(\mathbf{A} = ND)$$

The first term is the joint probability of default, so that $P(\mathbf{B} = D|\mathbf{A} = ND)$ is such that:

$$P(\mathbf{B} = D|\mathbf{A} = ND) = [P(\mathbf{B} = D) - P(\mathbf{B} = D, \mathbf{A} = D)]/P(\mathbf{A} = ND)$$

$$P(\mathbf{B} = D|\mathbf{A} = ND) = (5\% - 0.9061\%)/93\% = 4.4021\%$$

Since B either defaults or does not:

$$P(\mathbf{B} = ND|\mathbf{A} = ND) = 1 - 4.4021\% = 95.5979\%$$

6.094%, whereas its unconditional default probability is 7%. How can we explain the paradox of differing single default probabilities of A out of a portfolio and within a portfolio? The explanation is that A defaulting alone, in a portfolio context, is conditional on others not defaulting and is no longer an unconditional probability of default. It is the joint probability of default of A and of others not defaulting.

The standard presentations of the loss distribution, with cumulated probabilities, and the related graph are shown in Table 46.8 and Figure 46.2, respectively.

TABLE 46.8   Loss distribution: default correlation 10%

	Probabilities	Cumulated probabilities
A & B default	0.906%	100.000%
A defaults	6.094%	99.094%
B defaults	4.094%	93.000%
Neither defaults	88.906%	88.906%

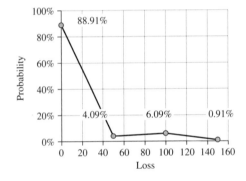

FIGURE 46.2   Loss distribution: default correlation 10%

The Loss Statistics

The calculations show that the EL remains the same as with the independent case, as expected since expectation is not dependent on correlation. The LV and loss percentiles increase with the correlation (Table 46.9). These calculations allow us to relate the portfolio loss statistics to standalone risk measures, such as expected loss and loss volatility, and measure the effect of diversification.

Expected Portfolio Loss and Standalone Expected Loss

The EL of the portfolio results directly from the distribution of losses for the entire portfolio made up of two facilities:

$$EL = 150 \times 0.35\% + 100 \times 6.65\% + 50 \times 93\% + 0 \times 88.35\% = 9.50$$

TABLE 46.9 Loss statistics: default correlation 10%

	Loss	Joint probabilities	Cumulated probabilities	Prob × loss	Prob × (loss − EL)²
A & B default	150	0.906%	100.000%	1.36	178.86
A defaults	100	6.094%	99.094%	6.09	499.11
B defaults	50	4.094%	93.000%	2.05	67.15
Neither defaults	0	88.906%	88.906%	0.00	80.24
EL		9.50			
LV		28.73			
Loss Var.		825.36			

It is easy to check that this is the sum of the standalone expected losses of each facility, or:

$$EL(A) = 0\% \times 100 + 7\% \times 100 = 7.00$$

$$EL(B) = 0\% \times 50 + 5\% \times 50 = 2.50$$

$$EL(A + B) = 7.00 + 2.50 = 9.50$$

This is identical to the result of the direct calculation based on the loss distribution. This value does not depend on the correlation.

Portfolio Loss Volatility and Standalone Loss Volatility

The portfolio loss volatility LV_p is:

$$LV_p^2 = (150 - 9.50)^2 \times 0.906\% + (100 - 9.50)^2 \times 6.094\% + (50 - 9.50)^2 \times 4.094\%$$

$$+ (0 - 9.50)^2 \times 88.906\% = 825.36$$

$$LV_p = 28.729$$

This value depends on loss correlation. If losses were independent, the portfolio loss variance would be the sum of individual facilities' variances. The individual loss variance is $LV = X \times \sqrt{d(1 - d)}$, where X is the exposure and d is the default probability. Hence:

$$LV(A) = 100 \times \sqrt{7\%(1 - 7\%)} = 100 \times \sqrt{0.0651} = 25.515$$

$$LV(A) = 50 \times \sqrt{5\%(1 - 5\%)} = 50 \times \sqrt{0.0475} = 10.897$$

Under independence, the square root of the sum is $LV_p(A + B) = \sqrt{25.515 + 10.897} = \sqrt{36.412} = 27.74$, which is smaller than 28.729.

Portfolio Diversification

The EL is not sensitive to the diversification effect, but the risk reduction effect appears in LV_p since, using the numerical values of the positive correlation case:

$$LV_p(A + B) = 28.729 < LV(A) + LV(B) = 25.515 + 10.897 = 36.412$$

The gain in LV quantifies the diversification effect: $36.412 - 27.744 = 8.668$. Since risks do not add arithmetically, allocating the overall portfolio risk to each obligor is an issue. The risk contributions are risk allocations, dealt with in Chapters 51 and 52.

Comparisons of the Correlation and the Independent Cases

Correlation implies the following changes:

- The joint default probability is now higher than the product of the unconditional (standalone) default probabilities of A and B.
- The conditional default probabilities now differ from the unconditional (standalone) default probabilities.

As a result, the distribution's fat tails gets thicker and the distribution mode shifts to the left-hand side. This results from the higher probability of big losses (150). Table 46.10 shows that the portfolio EL remains the same while the LV increases with correlation. In addition, the probabilities of larger losses are larger, as expected, than in the independent case.

TABLE 46.10 Comparison of loss statistics: independence versus 10% correlation

	Independence	Default correlation 10%
EL	9.50	9.50
Portfolio LV	27.74	28.73

47

Analytical Loss Distributions

This chapter describes some analytical loss distributions when single defaults correlate with each other. The most developed model of analytical distributions is CreditRisk+. Other simple techniques allow us to simulate and visualize the effect of correlation on portfolio risk, measured by loss volatility and loss percentiles, under restrictive assumptions.

The starting point is the simple case of independent losses. The portfolio distribution of the number of defaults is the well-known binomial distribution. This is also a loss distribution applying to uniform (equal) exposures only, since the binomial distribution does not accommodate size discrepancies. The binomial distribution over a uniform portfolio serves as a benchmark for measuring the effect of correlations on the portfolio risk. It also illustrates how the increase in loss volatility, as a percentage of the total portfolio exposure, tends rapidly towards zero when increasing the number of obligors.

The 'limit distribution' corresponds to another simple case with a uniform correlation between uniform exposures, building on a simplified version of the Merton model. To obtain closed-form formulas, we assume that the standardized asset values of firms follow normal distributions with a uniform correlation across firms. The uniform correlation results from the common dependence of all individual asset values on a single factor, representing the state of the economy. This single factor conditions the normal distributions of asset values. When conditions improve, all asset distributions shift upwards, resulting in a lower portfolio default probability than its 'unconditional' long-term value. Conversely, when conditions worsen, the default probability of the portfolio becomes higher than its long-term value. In essence, the technique relies on conditioning the asset value distributions on a single factor. Additional simplifying assumptions allow us to obtain an analytical form of the portfolio value distribution, called the 'limit distribution'. The limit distribution ignores specific risk. An important finding of such distributions, confirmed empirically by full-blown models, is that the 'fat tail' of the loss distribution is highly sensitive to the correlation between defaults.

The next chapters (48 and 49) illustrating Monte Carlo simulations use a similar one-factor model to generate correlated defaults, accommodating unequal exposures and unequal default probabilities of individual obligors.

CreditRisk+ uses actuarial techniques to find the shape of the loss distribution in a more accomplished manner, using the Poisson distribution to model the number of defaults. Starting from independent defaults, CreditRisk+ models defaults using a mixed Poisson distribution. The critical parameter of this distribution is the default intensity per unit of time, analogous to a default probability. It applies only to independent defaults. The mixed Poisson distribution uses as default intensity the product of the long-term (unconditional) default intensity with a multiple called the 'mixing' parameter. The technique accommodates mixing parameters dependent on common factors, resulting in correlated default intensities of the various banks' portfolio segments.

The three sections of this chapter detail respectively: the binomial distribution; the limit distribution; the CreditRisk+ analytical framework.

SIMPLIFIED EXTENSION WITH INDEPENDENT DEFAULT EVENTS

When default events are independent, and have the same probability, the distribution of the number of defaults in a portfolio is the binomial distribution. Unfortunately, the binomial distribution cannot capture the effect of size discrepancies and correlations. We use it here to see what happens when the number of obligors increases.

The Binomial Distribution

Using a simple default probability of 10%, and 100 obligors, Figure 47.1 shows the distribution of the number of defaults. Although the distribution has the fat tail characterizing credit risk loss distributions, this distribution falls short of a realistic correlated loss distribution. Nevertheless, the binomial distribution provides a good introduction to credit risk loss distributions (Table 47.1).

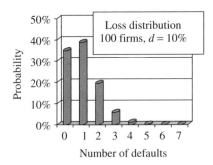

FIGURE 47.1 **The binomial distribution of the number of defaults**

**TABLE 47.1 The binomial distri-
bution of the number of defaults**[a]

Number of defaults	Probability
0	0.3487
1	0.3874
2	0.1937
3	0.0574
4	0.0112
5	0.0015
6	0.0001
7	0.0000
>7	0.0000

[a]Default probability 10%, 100 borrowers.

Simulating Increased Diversification with Loss Independence

Increasing the number of obligors reduces the loss volatility without affecting the mean loss. It is surprising how quickly the loss volatility converges towards zero.

Loss Volatility with a Binomial Distribution

There are two views of the loss distribution of a portfolio when losses are independent. Either we see the total loss as following a binomial distribution, or we consider the same loss as the sum of individual random unit losses. The two approaches are identical.

Looking at the portfolio loss distribution as a binomial distribution, the variance of the distribution is $N \times X^2 \times d \times (1 - d)$, where N is the number of exposures, d is the default probability, $1 - d$ is the non-default probability and X is the uniform exposure on each borrower. Alternatively, the same portfolio loss is the sum of all random individual losses. Each random loss is the exposure X times a Bernoulli variable with value 1 in the event of default (with probability d) and value 0 in the event of no default (with probability $1 - d$). The summation has a variance that is the sum of all individual loss variances, since losses are independent, which is N times the individual identical loss variances. The individual borrower variance is $X^2 \times d \times (1 - d)$ and the portfolio variance is $N \times X^2 \times d \times (1 - d)$, as above. The volatility is the square root of this sum.

With N exposures, of unit value size $X = 2$, the unit variance in value is $10\% \times (1 - 10\%) \times 2^2 = 0.36$ and the total variance is $N \times 0.36$. The loss distribution volatility in value is the square root of this.

The Effect of Diversification

It follows that each additional exposure adds the same constant amount to the portfolio loss variance $X^2 \times d \times (1 - d) = 0.36$. The loss volatility increases as the square root of N, less than the loss variance that is proportional to N. The additional volatility is the difference between the loss volatility with $N + 1$ exposures and the loss volatility with N exposures.

The behaviour of the same statistics as a percentage of the total exposure, or $N \times X$, differs. The portfolio loss variance as a percentage of total exposure is: $[N \times X^2 \times d \times (1 - d)]/[N \times X] = X \times d \times (1 - d)$. This is a constant value since the unit exposure X and d are both constant. This value is $2 \times 10\% \times (1 - 10\%) = 18\%$. The ratio of the portfolio loss variance to the total exposure is proportional to the uniform exposure X.

The ratio of the portfolio loss volatility to the total exposure is:

$$\text{Portfolio loss volatility}/N \times X = \sqrt{N \times X^2 \times p \times (1 - p)}/N \times X = \sqrt{p(1 - p)/N}$$

The portfolio loss volatility, as a percentage of total exposure, decreases with $\sqrt{N}$ and converges to zero when N increases.

In the sample calculation below, N increases from 1 to 10 000, with the same other parameters as above. Table 47.2 shows the variance and the volatility, in value and as a percentage of total exposure, when increasing the number of obligors N from 1 up to 10 000. The ratio of variance to exposure remains constant at 18%. The additional volatility in value is also a constant, and decreases as a percentage (Figures 47.2 and 47.3).

TABLE 47.2 Variation of portfolio loss variance and volatility with diversification and size in dollar value and percentage of portfolio size

N	Variance (value)	Volatility (value)	Variance/ exposure	Volatility/ exposure
1	0.36	0.60	18%	30.00%
2	0.72	0.85	18%	21.21%
10	3.60	1.90	18%	9.49%
100	36.00	6.00	18%	3.00%
200	72.00	8.49	18%	2.12%
1000	360.00	18.97	18%	0.95%
5000	1800.00	42.43	18%	0.42%
10 000	3600.00	60.00	18%	0.30%

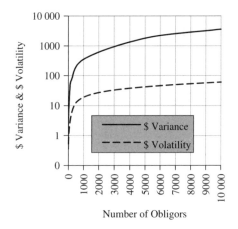

FIGURE 47.2 Variation of portfolio loss variance and volatility in value with diversification

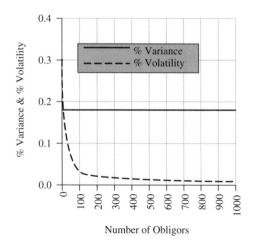

FIGURE 47.3 Variations of portfolio loss variance and volatility as a percentage of portfolio size with diversification

This confirms the well-known result that the loss volatility as a percentage of portfolio size tends towards zero.

THE LIMIT DISTRIBUTION

The limit distribution results from conditioning by one random factor the distribution of asset values within a portfolio. With full Monte Carlo simulations, we need to draw a large number of asset values for each firm consistent with the correlation structure of asset values. Chapter 48 illustrates the technique. We use here the same framework, but constrain the problem to a uniform correlation between all asset values.

The Distribution of Asset Values

The assumptions and notations are the same as for the Monte Carlo simulation, with a uniform default probability. The generation of random correlated values uses the one-factor equation. The one-factor methodology uses the one-factor model. The common factor $\mathbf{Z}$ conditions asset values $\mathbf{A}_i$ of each obligor i according to the following equation:

$$\mathbf{A}_i = \rho \times \mathbf{Z} + \sqrt{(1 - \rho^2)} \times \varepsilon_i$$

In this equation, ρ represents the correlation, ρ^2 is the 'R-square', or R^2, equal to the fraction of the variance of the asset value explained by the common factor, and $1 - \rho^2$ is the specific risk, or the variance unexplained by the common factor.

With the default probability d, there is a value A of the random asset value $\mathbf{A}_i$ such that the confidence level α is equal to the cumulated probability d. If Φ is the cumulated standardized normal distribution, then:

$$\Phi(A) = d \quad \text{or} \quad A = \Phi^{-1}(d)$$

This happens when:

$$A_i = \rho \times Z + \sqrt{(1 - \rho^2)} \times \varepsilon_i < A$$

This requires:

$$\varepsilon_i < (A - \rho \times Z)/\sqrt{(1 - \rho^2)}$$

When Z increases, the residual value triggering default decreases because the asset distribution shifts towards the right, thereby decreasing the chances that default occurs, and conversely.

The Default Point Conditional on the Factor Value

Given Z, and since the residual follows a standardized normal distribution, the probability that this inequality holds is:

$$d(Z) = \Phi(A) = \Phi[(A - \rho \times Z)/\sqrt{(1 - \rho^2)}]$$

As an example, let's assume that $d = 1\%$, $\rho = 54.7\%$ and $\rho^2 = 30\%$, so that $\sqrt{(1 - \rho^2)} = 83.67\%$. The value of A triggering default is -2.33. If $Z = 1$, this corresponds to a residual value lower than:

$$\varepsilon_i < (-2.33 - 54.7\%)/83.67\% = -3.142$$

When Z changes, the default point for ε_i changes accordingly, as shown in Table 47.3.

TABLE 47.3 The default point when the factor increases (standardized normal asset value distribution)

Z	-2	-1	0	1	2
Default point for ε_i	-1.346	-1.945	-2.543	-3.142	-3.741

The probability of default is conditional on the value of Z. When Z increases, the probability of default decreases and when Z decreases, it increases. The intuition is that the normal distribution of asset values shifts to the right when Z decreases, thereby decreasing the probability that the asset value hits the default point.

The Limit Distribution

As an example of an analytical distribution, we assume that the default frequency is exactly $d(Z)$, given Z. This assumes a diversification of the portfolio large enough for the frequency to become almost certain. The portfolio loss becomes $d(Z)$. This implies that the portfolio loss volatility is entirely due to its sensitivity to the factor, and that specific risk tends towards zero. In that case, there is a one-to-one correspondence between the portfolio loss and the Z value. Accordingly, the loss percentiles also correspond to the factor percentiles. The factor percentiles are those of a standardized normal variable. Since the 1% percentile of Z is 2.33, the portfolio 1% loss percentile is $d(2.33)$.

This is a simplification because the actual asset value of a portfolio is not a deterministic function of the factor. It remains random even when the single factor takes a given value because of the residual. Subsequent simulation examples do not bypass the residual factor, and generate fully stochastic asset values, even when conditioning relies on a single factor.

In general, the expected portfolio loss conditional on Z is $d(Z) = \Phi[(A - \rho \times \mathbf{Z})/\sqrt{(1 - \rho^2)}]$. A portfolio loss percentile is an upper bound of loss $L(\alpha)$ such that the probability that the loss exceeds $L(\alpha)$ is equal to or less than the confidence level α. The probability that the loss $d(Z)$ is lower than α is:

$$\text{Prob}[d(Z) < L(\alpha)] \leq \alpha$$

We now use the more compact notation $L(\alpha) = L_\alpha$. The probability that the loss $d(Z)$ will not exceed L_α is:

$$\text{Prob}\{\Phi[(A - \rho \times \mathbf{Z})/\sqrt{(1 - \rho^2)}] < L_\alpha\} \leq \alpha$$

This condition is equivalent to:

$$\text{Prob}[(A - \rho \times \mathbf{Z})/\sqrt{(1 - \rho^2)} < \Phi^{-1}(L_\alpha)] = \text{Prob}\{\mathbf{Z} > [A - \sqrt{(1 - \rho^2)}$$
$$\times \Phi^{-1}(L_\alpha)]/\rho\} \leq \alpha$$

Since:

$$\text{Prob}\{\mathbf{Z} > [A - \sqrt{(1 - \rho^2)} \times \Phi^{-1}(L_\alpha)]/\rho\} = \Phi\{[A - \sqrt{(1 - \rho^2)} \times \Phi^{-1}(L_\alpha)]\} \leq \alpha$$

This equation shows that the loss $d(Z)$ has an upper bound L_α, not exceeded in more than a fraction α of all possibilities, identical to the probability that Z remains above a threshold value depending on the default point A, correlation and L_α. The equation sets the value of L_α once α is set.

Example

As an example, we use a constant loss percentile $L_\alpha = 5\%$, $A = 2.33$, so that the default probability is 1%, and a uniform correlation of 54.7%. The limit distribution provides the probability that the loss remains under the upper bound of 5% of the portfolio exposure when the correlation varies. The sequence of calculations is as follows:

$$\Phi^{-1}(5\%) = -1.6449$$
$$[A - \sqrt{(1 - \rho^2)} \times \Phi^{-1}(L_\alpha)]/\rho = -1.73475$$

The upper bound of loss is 5% of the portfolio exposure and the probability of exceeding this 5% loss is:

$$\Phi\{[A - \sqrt{(1 - \rho^2)} \times \Phi^{-1}(L_\alpha)]/\rho\} = \Phi\{[2.33 - \sqrt{(1 - 54.7\%^2)} \times \Phi^{-1}(5\%)]/54.7\%\}$$
$$= \Phi(-1.73475) = 4.139\%$$

The limit distribution allows us to explore the effect of varying correlations and default probabilities on the probability of exceeding any upper bound. When the correlation increases, the probability that the loss remains under 5% of the portfolio decreases sharply (Table 47.4).

TABLE 47.4 Probability that the loss exceeds 5% of the portfolio when the uniform correlation changes

| Default probability | 1% |
| Upper bound of loss | 5% of portfolio exposure |
Correlation	Prob(loss≤5%)
10%	35.290%
20%	29.144%
30%	24.392%
40%	20.353%
50%	16.762%
60%	13.483%

In this example, we do not exceed a loss of 5% of total exposure with a probability of 35.29% when the asset correlation is 10%. This implies that the loss percentile $L(35.29\%) = 5\%$. When the correlation increases to a more realistic value (for corporate obligors) of 30%, the probability of exceeding the 5% loss drops to 24.392%. Alternatively, the loss percentile $L(24.392\%)$ is equal to 5% of exposure.

CREDITRISK+

CreditRisk+ is a default model that generates loss distributions based on default events, recovery rates and exposure at book value. It is not a full valuation model, since exposure value does not change according to risk.

Major Features

CreditRisk+ utilizes an analytical framework, which makes it easy to manipulate and use numerical calculation algorithms to avoid full-blown Monte Carlo simulations. The next paragraphs summarize the major features of the model.

The mixed Poisson distribution plays a pivotal role in generating independent default events. The Poisson distribution tabulates the frequency of observing k defaults when the default intensity, or the number of defaults per unit time, has a fixed value n. This default intensity is the Poisson parameter. It is analogous to the default probability, except that it is a number of defaults.

The model necessitates dividing the portfolio into segments by risk class and exposure net of recoveries. This allows us to bypass the limitations of the Poisson distribution that generates the distribution of the number of defaults, without considering size discrepancies. This makes it necessary to control both size of exposure, net of recoveries, and default risk before, and model loss within, each band size. In practice, CreditRisk+ requires dividing the portfolio into segments by risk class and loss under default bands.

The mixed Poisson distribution uses a 'mixing variable' **q** that allows the default intensity to vary according to whatever factors are relevant, or to run scenarios of default intensity. This provides the facility to model the default intensity as a function of economic factors.

In the special case where the mixing variable follows a gamma distribution, the resulting mixed Poisson is the negative binomial distribution. Under independence, this completes the analytical modelling of the loss distribution. The purpose of this extension is to allow default rates to vary and to fit the variation to the actual default rate volatility by adjusting accordingly the parameters of the gamma distribution.

The time intensity parameter makes defaults dependent on time, which is a useful feature for modelling the time to default. When aggregating distributions over all segments, it is possible to identify the time profile of default losses. Hence, the same framework provides a loss distribution at a preset horizon and also provides insights into 'time to default' by segment.

Finally, the extended version of the model makes the mixing variable 'q' dependent on a common set of factors to mimic correlations across portfolio segment distributions. To extend the model to correlation, CreditRisk+ makes the mixing variable a linear combination of external 'factors', such as economic conditions, with specific sensitivities. In order to proceed with this extension, CreditRisk+ uses specific properties of the mixed Poisson distribution. One property is that, when individual mixed Poisson distributions are independent, or if they depend on each other through the mixing variables only, the sum of the mixed Poisson distributions remains a mixed Poisson distribution. In addition, the mixing variable is a simple linear function of individual Poisson parameters and mixing variables (Chapter 47 further details these properties). Since CreditRisk+ makes only the mixing variable dependent on external factors, it complies with this condition. This common dependence across segments of the mixing variable on the same factors correlates the default rates. In addition, CreditRisk+ includes specific risk as an uncertainty generated by a factor independent of others. Since interdependency is user-defined, the model does not provide ways to define factors, sensitivities and the magnitude of specific risk. It simply provides an open framework to include these. By contrast, KMV Portfolio Manager is self-contained.

An attractive property is that loss distributions are entirely analytically tractable with adequate assumptions. CreditRisk+ also uses classical numerical algorithms applying to such actuarial distributions to speed up the calculation process.

The subsequent sections discuss these topics further: details of the Poisson distribution, properties of the mixed Poisson distribution, the correlation issue.

The Poisson Distribution

The Poisson distribution is widely used in insurance modelling. It provides the distribution of the number of defaults when defaults are independent. It models a number of defaults, ignoring size discrepancies of losses under default. Hence, it applies to segments, each of them being of uniform size and uniform default probability. CreditRisk+, like Credit Portfolio View (CPV), models default rates, not individual default probabilities.

The density function of the Poisson distribution is:

$$\text{Prob}(\mathbf{k} = k) = e^{-n} n^k / k!$$

where:

- n is the default intensity per unit time, for instance 1 year, or the average number of defaults in a 1-year period. It is also the Poisson parameter.

- **k** is the random number of defaults, from 0 to the maximum number of exposures in a portfolio segment.
- $k!$ is the factorial of k.

If the number of yearly defaults is 3 out of 100 exposures, this corresponds to a yearly default intensity of 3% and a Poisson parameter equal to 3 per year. The probability of observing 8 defaults is:

$$\text{Prob}(\mathbf{k} = 8) = e^{-3}3^8/8! = 0.8\%$$

TABLE 47.5 The Poisson probability function. Poisson parameter 3

Number of defaults k	pdf	cdf
0	4.979%	4.979%
1	14.936%	19.915%
2	22.404%	42.319%
3	22.404%	64.723%
4	16.803%	81.526%
5	10.082%	91.608%
6	5.041%	96.649%
7	2.160%	98.810%
8	0.810%	99.620%
9	0.270%	99.890%
10	0.081%	99.971%
11	0.022%	99.993%
12	0.006%	99.998%
13	0.001%	100.000%

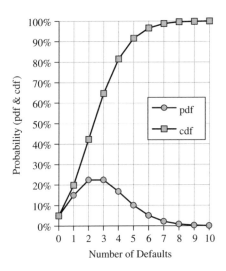

FIGURE 47.4 The Poisson probability function. Poisson parameter 3

The mean of a Poisson distribution is the Poisson parameter, 3 in this case, and its volatility is its square root, or $\sqrt{3} = 1.732$. Table 47.5 shows the probabilities of the various numbers of defaults with a mean of 3 defaults per year, and Figure 47.4 charts the probability density and the cumulative density functions.

The loss percentile corresponding to 99% is around 7 defaults. Converting the loss percentile into loss is straightforward with equal unit sizes. For instance, a $1000 unit loss would result in a $7000 loss percentile at the 1% confidence level.

To develop its analytical framework, CreditRisk+ uses probability generating functions[1] applying to independent events:

$$G(z) = \sum_{n=0}^{\infty} P(\text{loss} = n)z^n$$

To combine all subportfolios, CreditRisk+ uses the fact that the sum of Poisson distributions is also Poisson distributed, with a Poisson parameter equal to the summation of all individual Poisson parameters[2].

The Mixed Poisson Distribution

The mixed Poisson distribution conditions the Poisson parameter with a random mixing variable 'q'. The Poisson parameter becomes $n\mathbf{q}$, instead of the original n. The mixing variable $\mathbf{q}$ can be a simple scaling factor, but it is in general random. This allows the default intensity to fluctuate randomly. To make the analytics simple, it is necessary that $E(\mathbf{q}) = 1$. When $q > 1$, the default intensity increases above the average, and conversely when $q < 1$.

The mixed Poisson has a number of desirable characteristics. The mean of the new distribution becomes $E(\mathbf{q}) \times E(\mathbf{k}) = n$, where $\mathbf{k}$ is the random number of defaults, identical to that of the underlying Poisson distribution. In other words, average default intensity over all $\mathbf{q}$ values remains equal to the long-term average n. The scaling convention implies that $E(\mathbf{qk}) = n$, as with the unconditional distribution. The variance of the number of defaults $\mathbf{k}$ becomes $\sigma(\mathbf{k})^2 = n + n^2\sigma(\mathbf{q})^2$. It is larger than the Poisson variance n due to conditioning by a random variable. The conditioning makes the volatility larger, and the 'fat tail' of the distribution longer than in the simple Poisson distribution.

The mixed Poisson distribution accommodates economic cycle effects, or using a discrete number of scenarios with subjective probabilities assigned to each of them. When allowing the intensity of default to be random, it is necessary to fit the mixing variable to the actual fluctuations observed. This is feasible directly when historical observations

---

[1] The probability generating function of a random discrete variable $\mathbf{X}$ taking values $x = 1, 2, \ldots$ is pgf(z):

$$\text{pgf}(z) = \sum_{x=0}^{\cdots} P(x \text{ defaults})z^x = p_0 x_0 + p_1 x_1 + \cdots$$

pgf(z) = $E[z^x]$. The derivatives of the probability generating functions are the probabilities that $\mathbf{X} = k$: Prob($\mathbf{X} = k$) = $d^{(k)}[\text{pgf}_\mathbf{X}(0)]/dz^k/k!$. A second property of the pgf is to find the moments from the derivatives of the pgf at $z = 0$.

[2] The probability generating function is simply the product of all probability generating functions of individual subportfolios.

are available. However, this is more the case with insurance claims, for which there is plenty of data, than with credit data.

CreditRisk+ uses the attractive properties of the summation of mixed Poisson distributions to obtain the entire portfolio loss distribution. The sum is also a mixed Poisson, if the individual mixed Poisson distributions are independent, or if they depend on each other through the mixing variables only. The sum of the two distributions follows a mixed Poisson with a mixing variable q equal to the weighted average of the individual mixed Poisson variables q_1 and q_2, the weights being the ratios of Poisson parameters n_1 and n_2 of the individual distributions to their sum:

$$q = (n_1 \times q_1 + n_2 \times q_2)/(n_1 + n_2)$$

This allows modelling of the entire aggregated loss distribution over the entire portfolio and opens the door to interdependencies between individual distributions as long as only the mixing variables embed them.

The Analytical Loss Distribution

When using a mixed Poisson, it is not possible in general to stick to analytical loss distributions. Therefore, CreditRisk+ proposes to use a special case that allows a full analytical formulation of the distribution. When the mixing variable follows a standardized gamma distribution, the resulting mixed distribution follows the negative binomial distribution. The gamma distribution is such that:

$$\text{pdf}(\mathbf{X}) = [a^r / \Gamma(r)] \exp(-a\mathbf{X})\mathbf{X}^{r-1} \quad \text{with} \quad \Gamma(r) = \int_0^\infty e^{-u} u^{r-1} du$$

Since the mean value of the gamma distribution is r/a, we should set $r = a$ to adopt the scaling convention of the mixing variable q, so that $E(q) = 1$. Using the common value h for both r and a, the mixing variable function follows Gamma(h, h), and its analytical density function is:

$$H(q) = [1/\Gamma(h)] \int_0^{hq} e^{-z} z^{h-1} dh$$

With these rules, the expectation and the volatility of the mixing variable are:

$$E(q) = 1$$

$$\sigma(q) = 1/\sqrt{h}$$

The expectation and the volatility of the number of defaults following the mixed Poisson, with q following the standardized gamma, are:

$$E(\mathbf{k}) = n \quad \text{and} \quad \sigma^2(\mathbf{k}) = n + n^2/h$$

The smaller h, the larger the standard deviation of $\mathbf{k}$, which corresponds to a larger volatility of Gamma(h, h), the distribution of q. In addition, simple algorithms allow us to calculate the distribution.

The final result is that the mixed Poisson models the default distribution of each portfolio segment, including fluctuations of the default intensity. The distribution has an analytical form as long as we stick to the negative binomial case, implying the usage of a standardized gamma distribution for the conditioning variable **q**. The standardized gamma distributions per segment serve for modelling cyclical fluctuations of **q**.

Aggregating the distributions across portfolio segments requires 'convolution' of the distributions, which is a simple technique applying to independent distributions. Convolution simply says that the joint probability of any number of defaults in one segment and another number in a second segment is the product of the probabilities of having these numbers of defaults.

Correlating Segment Loss Distributions

The CreditRisk+ technique for correlating losses across segments consists of making the mixing variable of individual distributions dependent on a set of common factors. The resulting mixed Poisson has a mixing variable that is a simple linear function of segment-specific mixing variables. Since the conditioning on factors is deterministic, there is no specific risk independent of factors. To correct this, CreditRisk+ adds one sector, which generates a specific random noise. Portfolio segments are not sensitive to this particular factor, so it does add specific risk as an additional segment whose risk is unrelated to others.

48

Loss Distributions: Monte Carlo Simulations

This chapter explains and illustrates the Monte Carlo simulation methodology with two approaches: the option theoretic approach using Monte Carlo simulations of asset values and the econometric modelling of Credit Portfolio View (CPV). In both cases, generating portfolio value distributions requires generating risk drivers complying with a given correlation structure. Both sample simulations use a single-factor model to generate a uniform correlation between the firms of the portfolio.

Asset value simulations use a single-factor model of asset values, with a random specific error term, uniform correlation between assets, uniform sizes of exposures, under default mode only. The asset values are a linear function of a common factor, representing the state of the economy, and of an error term, independent of the state of the economy, representing specific risk. Monte Carlo simulations generate random sets of future values of the economic factor and of the specific risk, from which the asset values derive directly. This is a much more restrictive framework than actual portfolio models. However, it illustrates the essential mechanisms of the process. Moreover, the same technique allows us to vary the default probabilities and the sizes of exposures across exposures, and to use any variance–covariance structure. The examples in Chapters 55 and 56 use the same single-factor model of asset values with differentiated exposures and default probabilities. At this stage, the purpose is only to illustrate the essentials of the technique and the sensitivity of portfolio value distributions to the uniform correlation.

The example shows that the multiple of the loss volatility when moving from independent default to a 30% asset correlation is above 2.5, with a portfolio of uniform default probability equal to 1%. The loss percentile at the 99% confidence level, when moving from independent default to a 30% asset correlation, increases by a scale factor of around 2.5. This illustrates the importance of correlation when looking at extreme losses of portfolios.

For a simplified implementation of simulation under the econometric framework of CPV, the same basic principles apply. A single-factor model drives an economic index directly related to the default rates of two portfolio segments through logit functions. The economic index is a linear function of an economic factor, representing the state of the economy and of an error term, representing specific risk. Monte Carlo simulations generate random sets of future values of the economic factor and of the specific risk, from which the economic index derives. Once the economic index is converted into default rates through logit functions, we obtain correlated distributions of the default rates of two portfolio segments. A large number of trials provides the full distributions of the default rate values of the portfolio segments and of their sum over the entire portfolio. The example does not intend to replicate the CPV framework, but provides a simple illustration.

The first section summarizes the main features of KMV Portfolio Manager and specifies the simplified framework used here to conduct the sample simulations based on random asset values of obligors. The second section provides simple simulations inspired by the CPV approach. The first subsection details the structure of CPV. The second subsection specifies the simplified assumptions used to generate the distributions of segment default rates and of the overall portfolio.

SIMULATION OF ASSET VALUES TO GENERATE LOSS DISTRIBUTIONS

This section provides sample simulations illustrating the generation of value distributions using the option framework of default. The simulations require three steps: summarizing the general framework, defining our set of simplifying assumptions and providing sample simulations.

Simulation of Correlated Losses from the Simulation of Asset Values

In order to obtain the portfolio loss distribution, KMV generates a large number of random standardized asset values of individual obligors from which risk migrations to the horizon derive. The risk migration varies continuously with the generated asset values. The portfolio value V_p is the summation of individual facility values V_i. The individual values V_i result from revaluation at the horizon after risk migrations corresponding to the credit state characterized by the final asset value. The model revalues the facilities according to the final distance to default of each obligor, which corresponds to a credit state characterized by a default probability specific to each obligor. The value under the default state is the exposure X_i times the loss given default percentage Lgd_i: $V_i(\text{default}) = X_i \times \mathrm{Lgd}_i$. In KMV Portfolio Manager, the loss given default is a random variable, following a beta distribution, whose mode is the end-user input. This results in an additional component of the loss volatility, one resulting from the value volatility due to migrations, and another resulting from the independent random Lgd volatility. The portfolio value sums all facility values for each draw of a set of correlated asset values for all facilities $V_p = \sum_{i=1}^{N} V_i$. Generating random standardized asset values complying with the correlation structure of obligors' assets results in the distribution of the portfolio values at the horizon.

The KMV model operates in full valuation mode, using either credit spreads or risk-neutral valuation to revalue any facility at the horizon. Valuation depends on modelled asset values. The modelled asset values are those of the KMV universe, if the user chooses so. If the end-users map default probabilities to internal ratings, the asset values follow standardized normal distributions with a threshold default value corresponding to the preset default probability. Cholevsky's decomposition allows us to generate random correlated asset values at the horizon for each obligor. For each draw of an asset value for a particular obligor, the model revalues the facility according to its risk. The random asset value at the horizon depends on common factors and specific risk. The latter is the volatility due to the error term of the model fitting asset returns to the common orthogonal factors in the KMV universe.

With preset default probabilities, rather than the KMV modelled expected default frequency Edf, the model uses the reduced form of the full model of asset values, considering that all relevant information on asset values is in the assigned default probability. We use this standardized normal distance to default model below.

KMV Portfolio Manager requires specifying the general risk for each facility in the portfolio. The 'R-square' of the regression—measuring general risk—is the output of the multi-factor model linking asset returns to factors. When inputting directly the default probability, general risk becomes an input rather than an output of the multi-factor model in the KMV universe. Increasing the general risk is equivalent to increasing correlation and the dependence on external factors. If this dependence were mechanical, firms' credit standing would be perfectly correlated. For example, country risk creates a 'contagion' effect on firms, increasing the correlation between defaults. A contagion scenario within a country would be reflected in a higher than usual value of the general risk of obligors.

Figure 48.1 summarizes the simulation process. What follows illustrates the process using a much simplified model, but following the rationale of the option theoretic framework.

Simplified Model (Default Mode)

The simplified example differs from the full model:

- The example uses the standardized normal distribution of the 'distance to default' model, given the default probability of obligors.
- The model operates in default mode only, and exposures are at book value.
- There is a uniform preset asset correlation.
- There is a uniform preset default probability.

Asset Distribution and Default Probability

We use the standardized normal 'distance to default' model, considering that the default probability embeds all information relevant to default and on unobservable asset values. With the default probability DP_X, there is a value A_X of the random asset value $\mathbf{A_X}$

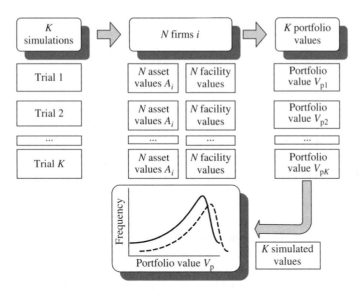

FIGURE 48.1 **Monte Carlo simulation of asset values to generate correlated loss distribution**

such that the default probability is DP_X. If Φ is the cumulated standardized normal distribution, then:

$$\Phi(A_X) = DP_X \quad \text{or} \quad A_X = \Phi^{-1}(DP_X)$$

where Φ^{-1} is the normal inverse distribution. The normal inverse distribution provides the threshold A_X given the default probability DP_X. For instance, with $DP_X = 1\%$, the default point is $A_X = \Phi^{-1}(1\%) = -2.33$, and so on. Generating a default event requires that the asset value A_X be lower than $A_X = \Phi^{-1}(DP_X)$. In practice, a dummy variable represents the default event. It has a value of 1 if the asset value is below the threshold (default) and 0 otherwise (non-default):

$$\mathbf{d_X} = \begin{cases} 1 & \text{if } \mathbf{A_X} \leq A_X = \Phi^{-1}(DP_X) \\ 0 & \text{if } \mathbf{A_X} > A_X = \Phi^{-1}(DP_X) \end{cases}$$

The dummy default event variables are intermediate variables serving to determine the portfolio loss.

Multiple Simulations

A large number of trials generate a portfolio value distribution, later converted into a portfolio distribution. Note that the same procedure allows differentiated default probabilities and different losses under default for the different firms. Such discrepancies exist in the sample portfolio used to illustrate portfolio reporting in the corresponding chapters (Chapters 55 and 56). Here, we ignore such differentiation in order to focus on the correlation effect.

Since asset values trigger default, all we need is to generate correlated asset values for all obligors. When running a default model, the target portfolio variable modelled is the portfolio loss. A random default Bernoulli variable characterizes the default event:

$$\mathbf{d}_i = \begin{cases} 1 & \text{when } \mathbf{Z}_i < A_i \\ 0 & \text{when } \mathbf{Z}_i > A_i \end{cases}$$

A_i is the threshold value triggering default, such that $\text{Prob}(\mathbf{Z}_i < A_i)$ is the preset default probability DP_i of firm i. Each simulated Z_i value determines a 1 or 0 value for $\mathbf{d}_i$. K draws of all $\mathbf{Z}_i$ generate $K \times N$ values of the $\mathbf{d}_i$, one for each of the N obligors, and an aggregated portfolio loss L_p summing up the individual losses for defaulting firms. Each draw of the set of correlated $\mathbf{Z}_i$ provides a simulated portfolio loss value. K draws provide K points representing the simulated portfolio loss distribution. For each one of the K draws, we have N asset values, one for each obligor, as many as there are facilities in the portfolio, plus one portfolio value. Running 10 000 simulations results in $10\,000 \times N$ values of assets, facility migrations, plus 1000 values of $\mathbf{V_p}$, from which we derive the portfolio value distribution, and finally the portfolio loss distribution.

To illustrate the process, we use the one-factor methodology, with a uniform correlation between all pairs of assets and a uniform exposure size in this example, although the technique also accommodates inequality of sizes and of default probabilities. The common factor $\mathbf{Z}$ conditions asset values $\mathbf{A}_i$ of each obligor i according to the following equation:

$$\mathbf{A}_i = \rho \times \mathbf{Z} + \sqrt{(1 - \rho^2)} \times \boldsymbol{\varepsilon}_i$$

The residuals $\boldsymbol{\varepsilon}_i$ follow a standardized normal distribution. The variance of the residual is the specific risk, which depends in a one-factor model on the correlation value. The 'R-square' is the complement to 1. The correlation between any pair of asset values is ρ. To proceed, the sequential steps are:

- Generate a standardized random normal distribution of the common factor $\mathbf{Z}$.
- Generate as many standardized random distributions of the specific residuals $\boldsymbol{\varepsilon}_i$ as there are obligors.
- Calculate the resulting standardized random variable $\mathbf{Z}_i$, which is the asset value of each obligor.
- Transform this asset value, for each obligor, into a default 0–1 variable.
- Calculate the loss for each obligor, given the value of the default variable and the exposure.
- Sum all losses to get one value for portfolio loss for each simulation.
- Repeat the simulation as many times as desired.

In the simulation:

- The correlation coefficient ρ varies between 0% and 50%.
- The number of obligors N is 100.
- The default probability DP_i is uniform across obligors, at 1%, or a threshold value triggering default of assets equal to -2.33 for all obligors.
- The exposures X_i are identical across obligors and equal to 1.
- The number of simulations is 1000, so that we obtain 1000 values of the portfolio loss forming the loss distribution. This is a relatively low value, but it suffices for this example.

This is a simple but powerful way to investigate the correlated loss distributions, since both the average correlation and the average default probability are parameters.

Sample Correlated Loss Distributions

The simulations serve to visualize the distributions with increasing correlation. Generating a range of portfolio loss distributions corresponding to various uniform asset correlations makes it possible to see how loss statistics vary with correlation. Asset correlation varies from 0% to 50% in steps of 10%, generating five loss distributions.

Loss Distributions

When the average uniform correlation of assets increases, the mode of the distribution moves to the left. Simultaneously, the 'fat tail', grouping high losses of low frequencies, extends to the right. To highlight the differences between loss distributions, the X-axis shows only the most frequent losses, losses lower than 10, although the fat tails will extend further to the right (Figure 48.2). In fact, default losses having values higher than 10 occur in the simulation: for a 50% correlation, some simulations generate 40 to 50 defaults, close or equal to half of the total exposure.

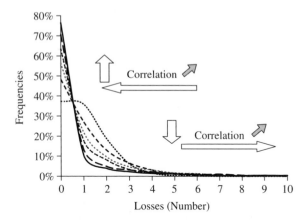

FIGURE 48.2 Loss distribution and loss correlation: uniform portfolio, uniform default probability and uniform asset correlation

Getting to the far end of the right-hand tail implies a much greater number of simulations to stabilize the tail and reduce simulation noise. Simulation noise is the variation of the loss values between different runs of simulations. It decreases proportionally to the square root of the number of simulations.

The lowest mode corresponds to a zero correlation and is very close to the binomial distribution since we use uniform exposure and uniform default probability. From these simulations, we derive sensitivity analyses with respect to the correlation. When correlation increases, the probability of the mode of the loss distribution increases and the tail extends to the right while getting 'thicker'.

Sensitivity of Potential Loss Measures to Correlation

Figures 48.3 and 48.4 show how the portfolio loss volatility and the 99% loss percentile behave when asset correlation increases from 0% to 50%. Common magnitudes for asset correlation are within the range 20% to 40%. The simulation illustrates the sensitivity of loss statistics to asset correlation.

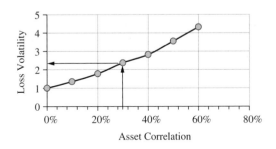

FIGURE 48.3   Sensitivity of loss volatility to asset correlation (default probability 1%)

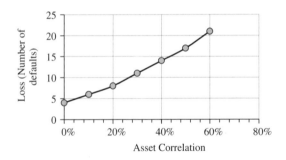

FIGURE 48.4   Sensitivity of the 99% loss percentile to asset correlation (default probability 1%)

With 0% average asset correlation, uniform exposures and an average default rate of 1%, the loss volatility is 1 and the 99% loss percentile is 4, or $4/1 = 4$ times the loss volatility. With 30% average asset correlation, uniform exposures and an average default rate of 1%, the loss volatility is around 2.4 and the 99% loss percentile is 11, or $11/2.4 = 4.6$ times the loss volatility. Both loss volatility and 99% loss percentile increase significantly with correlation. The loss volatility at 30% asset correlation (equal to 2.4) is around 2.4 times the loss volatility under independency (1). The 99% loss percentile increases from 4 to 11, or 2.75 times the initial value. The ratio of 99% loss percentile to loss volatility is rather stable, around 4, because both loss volatility and loss percentile increase with correlation. In any case, it is much higher than the 2.33 ratio applying to the normal distribution. In summary, the loss volatility and the loss percentiles at 1% are roughly 2.5 times the values under independency. This demonstrates that it is critical to model correlations to obtain realistic orders of magnitude, and that ignoring correlations underestimates the loss statistics very strongly.

It is also possible to graph the relationship between loss percentiles and asset correlation. For example, if the 99% loss percentile is around 15% of the portfolio value (15 defaults in Figure 48.4), it is equivalent to an implied 45% asset correlation, and an 8% loss percentile (8 defaults) is equivalent to a 20% asset correlation.

As a reminder, the Chebyshev inequality [$\text{Prob}(|X - \mu| > k\sigma) \leq 1/k^2$] provides an upper bound for a loss percentile. Using only one-sided deviations, the probability of exceeding a deviation of $k \times \sigma$ is:

$$\text{Prob}(X - \mu > k\sigma) \leq \tfrac{1}{2} \times 1/k^2$$

With a confidence level $\alpha = 1\%$, $\tfrac{1}{2} \times 1/k^2 = 1\%$ and we find $k = 7.071$. This value compares with the above multiple of loss volatility equal to 4.6 for an asset value correlation of 30%. The difference is substantial and shows a substantial gain through modelling the loss distribution.

SIMULATIONS BASED ON ECONOMETRIC MODELS

A summarized description of a simplified econometric structure serves to define the simulation framework. After making explicit the set of simplifying assumptions, we present simulations for a two-segment portfolio.

Econometric Modelling Structure

CPV models the default and migration rates of portfolio segments as a function of explicit economic indexes, and allows us to capture the cyclical dynamics of industry–country factors. As a reminder, the CPV structure uses two basic blocks:

- Type '1' models provide the default rates of each segment $\mathbf{DR}_i$ (N segments) as a logit function of an economic index $\mathbf{Y}_i$. There are as many indexes $\mathbf{Y}_i$ as there are segments, or N. Each index $\mathbf{Y}_i$ depends on multiple economic factors $\mathbf{X}_j$ (K factors). There are N models for the N segments. Hence, there are N residuals.
- Type '2' models provide the predicted values of the K economic factors $\mathbf{X}_j$ using an Auto Regressive Integrated Moving Average (ARIMA) fit. There are K economic factors. Hence, there are K models and K new residuals.

To generate a distribution of portfolio values, CPV uses Monte Carlo simulations of the factors influencing the default and migration rates of segments. Due to the dependence on common factors, these simulated rates correlate. The process requires:

- Simulating the predicted values of each factor influencing the index, on which default rates depend, from past values and error terms using time series modelling.
- Simulating the predicted values of segment default rates from the simulated values of the indexes influencing them, the simulated values being generated in the first step above from simulation of future values of country–industry factors.

We use t as the current date and $t + 1$ as the horizon value, by definition a future date when all factors and default rates become random as of today. The three types of equations in CPV are:

$$\mathbf{DR}_{i,t+1} = 1/[1 + \exp(-\mathbf{Y}_{i,t+1})]$$

$$\mathbf{Y}_{i,t+1} = \beta_{i,t} + \beta_{i,1}\mathbf{X}_{1,t+1} + \beta_{i,2}\mathbf{X}_{2,t+1} + \cdots + \beta_{i,k}\mathbf{X}_{k,t+1} + \varepsilon_{i,t+1}$$

$$\mathbf{X}_{k,t+1} = \alpha_1\mathbf{X}_{k,t} + \alpha_2\mathbf{X}_{k,t-1} + \cdots + \gamma_1\mathbf{e}_{k,t} + \gamma_2\mathbf{e}_{k,t-1} + \mathbf{e}_{k,t+1}$$

All $\mathbf{Y}_{i,t+1}$ depend on the same set of factors $\mathbf{X}_{k,t+1}$, which depend on their past values and an error term. To generate a random distribution of the segment default rates, it is necessary to generate random values of the country–industry factors $\mathbf{X}_{k,t+1}$, given their past values up to t, plus the corresponding random values of the indexes $\mathbf{Y}_{i,t+1}$, and finally to derive the random $\mathbf{DR}_{i,t+1}$ from the logit function.

Given the modelling structure, the simulation technique is complex.

We know that within each model, whether logit or ARIMA, the error terms are independent of the explanatory variables. When looking forward (date $t + 1$), taking as given the values as of date t, we generate random values as of date $t + 1$ using the residuals of each model. Each residual has a zero mean and a standard deviation resulting from fitting the model. But the residuals of the different models have no reason to be independent. In general, they correlate. Therefore, we need to generate random values of residuals, of all equations, that comply with their correlation structure. Random values of country–industry indexes conditional on past values of factors and errors result from simulating correlated values of the error term $\mathbf{e}_{k,t+1}$. There are K factors and K residuals $\mathbf{e}_{k,t+1}$. Once this set of correlated predicted values of country–industry factors $\mathbf{X}_{k,t+1}$ is generated, we need to infer the values of the indexes $\mathbf{Y}_{i,t+1}$ by generating random values of the error terms of the fits of indexes to factors, $\varepsilon_{i,t+1}$. There are N segments and N residuals $\varepsilon_{i,t+1}$. Since there are also cross-correlations between the residuals $\mathbf{e}_{k,t+1}$ and $\varepsilon_{i,t+1}$, we need to perform this step in conjunction with the generation of predicted values of factors, in order to preserve both correlations between factor error terms and cross-correlations with index error terms. Finally, the default rate simulated values result from the logit function for all segments. They correlate because they depend on common factors and because of the correlation of the cross-correlation of residuals (Figure 48.5).

The long-term transition matrix serves as the unconditional migration matrix. Short-run migration matrices are conditional on the state of the economy, or default rates. They need to comply with internal consistency constraints since all migration rates have to sum to 1 after adding the default rate for each risk class. They also need to comply with external consistency constraints such as the lower volatility of default rates for investment grade ratings.

The CPV open framework allows customization to any observable data set, but requires modelling as a prerequisite. In addition, it provides an explicit link with the economic cycle dynamics, using observable factors. By contrast, KMV provides the proprietary model bundled in the package, but the interpretation of the 'axes' driving the risk concentrations of the portfolio is not straightforward.

The Simplified Model

We proceed by conducting a sample simulation using, as usual, a much simpler framework. There are two portfolio segments and only one factor driving the index, converted into

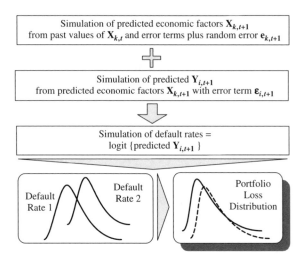

FIGURE 48.5   Simulation of predicted economic factors and default rates

segment default rates through the logit function. We detail the simplified structure of modelling before providing sample simulations.

The Structure

We use a one-factor model for the index $Y_{i,t+1}$, serving as an argument in the logit function to calculate the default rate. There are two portfolio segments '1' and '2', and $i = 1$ or 2. The single common factor X_{t+1} influencing all segment indexes follows a standardized normal distribution. This allows us to omit the k of $X_{k,t+1}$. Using one factor directly driving the default rates through $Y_{i,t+1}$ bypasses the time series model of CPV, which makes this index dependent on past values of other factors and error terms from ARIMA fits. There is no need either to worry about the correlation structure of the multiple error terms of ARIMA models. The index $Y_{i,t+1}$ is a linear function of the X_{t+1} and includes an error term $\varepsilon_{i,t+1}$ as well, independent of the X_{t+1} factor. Generating random values of this error term is equivalent to generating correlated random values of the $Y_{i,t+1}$ converted into correlated default rates of segments. In addition, we assume that the correlation ρ between the index $Y_{i,t+1}$ and the unique factor X_{t+1} is common to the two segments. This is only a convenient simplification. Finally, the model operates in default mode only, without revaluation according to the final credit state. This bypasses the transition matrix modelling and the revaluation block.

The Model

There is a single X_{t+1} factor for the two segments 1 and 2 for default rates indexed DR_i, with i being 1 or 2. The two portfolio segments 1 and 2 have different mean default rates. They represent, for example, two industries whose risk classes differ on average. The default rate DR_i of each segment depends on two economic indexes $Y_{i,t+1}$. Both indexes $Y_{1,t+1}$ and $Y_{2,t+1}$ depend on one common factor X_{t+1} that correlates them. Each industry index is random and drives the corresponding segment default rate through the logit formula. We assume that all inputs to the logit functions $\mathbf{Y}_{1,t+1}$, $\mathbf{Y}_{2,t+1}$ and $\mathbf{X}_{t+1}$ follow normal distributions. However, $\mathbf{Y}_{1,t+1}$ and $\mathbf{Y}_{2,t+1}$ do not follow standardized distributions because we have to adjust their parameters so that the expected segment default rates have realistic values. Finally, we use the simple one-factor model to correlate $\mathbf{Y}_{1,t+1}$ and $\mathbf{Y}_{2,t+1}$. These two dependent variables are a linear function of two independent normal variables, $\mathbf{X}_{t+1}$ and an error term, the coefficients being a function of the correlation coefficient ρ. We end up with two models for each of the two segments:

$$\mathbf{Y}_{1,t+1} = \rho \times \mathbf{X}_{t+1} + \sqrt{(1 - \rho^2)} \times \boldsymbol{\varepsilon}_{1,t+1}$$

$$\mathbf{DR}_1 = 1/[1 + \exp(-\mathbf{Y}_{1,t+1})]$$

$$\mathbf{Y}_{2,t+1} = \rho \times \mathbf{X}_{t+1} + \sqrt{(1 - \rho^2)} \times \boldsymbol{\varepsilon}_{2,t+1}$$

$$\mathbf{DR}_2 = 1/[1 + \exp(-\mathbf{Y}_{2,t+1})]$$

The default rates $\mathbf{DR}_1$ and $\mathbf{DR}_2$ of both segments are logit functions of the random indices $\mathbf{Y}_{1,t+1}$ and $\mathbf{Y}_{2,t+1}$ correlated through the common influence of $\mathbf{X}_{t+1}$. The correlation ρ is an input of this simplified model, rather than resulting from econometric fits. The common correlation between $\mathbf{Y}_{i,t+1}$ and $\mathbf{X}_{t+1}$, ρ, is 40% in this example. In order for the two 'segments' to have different mean default rates, we adjust accordingly the coefficients of the two logit formulas. Segment 1 has a relatively low expected default rate and segment 2 a higher one. The weights of the two portfolio segments in terms of exposure, at book value, are 50% each. The recovery rates are zero.

Converting Index Values into Default Rates

For each set of values of $\mathbf{Y}_{1,t+1}$ and $\mathbf{Y}_{2,t+1}$, we calculate the values of the default rates $\mathbf{DR}_1$ and $\mathbf{DR}_2$ using the logit functions. Due to the transformation by the logit function, the correlation between $\mathbf{DR}_1$ and $\mathbf{DR}_2$ differs from that of $\mathbf{Y}_{1,t+1}$ and $\mathbf{Y}_{2,t+1}$ with $\mathbf{X}_{t+1}$. To obtain realistic values for the expected default rates, we adjust the means of the $\mathbf{Y}_{i,t+1}$. For the purposes of this illustration, $E(\mathbf{Y}_{1,t+1}) = 4.35$ and $E(\mathbf{Y}_{2,t+1}) = 3.615$. This corresponds to expected values of the default rates $E(\mathbf{DR}_1) = 1.274\%$ and $E(\mathbf{DR}_2) = 2.621\%$ using the logit equations for $\mathbf{DR}_i$. Finally, the random loss rate $\mathbf{LR}_{1+2}$ value applicable to the portfolio is the weighted average of $\mathbf{DR}_1$ and $\mathbf{DR}_2$ using the 50% exposure weights, or $\mathbf{LR}_{1+2} = 50\% \times \mathbf{DR}_1 + 50\% \times \mathbf{DR}_2$.

Table 48.1 summarizes the sequential steps of the procedure used to illustrate the methodology. For each segment 1 or 2, we generate random independent values of $\mathbf{X}_{t+1}$ and of the two residuals $\boldsymbol{\varepsilon}_{i,t+1}$ in order to get values of $\mathbf{Y}_{i,t+1}$ correlated with $\mathbf{X}_{t+1}$.

TABLE 48.1   Sample calculation of the portfolio loss rate for each pair of default rate values randomly generated

Simulation number	Default rate 1	Default rate 2	Weighted average $LR_{1+2}(50\%/50\%)$
1	7.090%	17.343%	12.216%
2	1.876%	11.276%	6.576%
. . .	. . .	. . .	. . .

Since both $Y_{1,t+1}$ and $Y_{2,t+1}$ correlate with X_{t+1}, they also correlate with each other. Each value of the pair $Y_{1,t+1}$ and $Y_{2,t+1}$ generates a pair of values of the default rates DR_1 and DR_2 through the specified logit functions. These values also correlate because they both depend on correlated $Y_{i,t+1}$. The weighted average default rate of the portfolio, using exposures as weights, derives from these correlated segment default rate values.

Sample Simulations with Correlated Default Rates

Figures 48.6 and 48.7 show the frequency distributions of the default rates of segments 1 and 2. The distributions of the default rates are highly skewed to the right. It is visible from the frequency distributions that the average value of the default rate of segment 1 is lower than that of segment 2. The scatter plot of one default rate against the other shows how correlated their values are (Figure 48.8). Finally, the loss distribution of the portfolio aggregates the correlated distribution of default rates of the two segments.

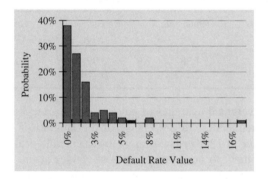

FIGURE 48.6   Frequency distribution of default rate 1

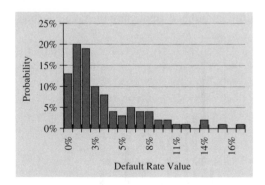

FIGURE 48.7   Frequency distribution of default rate 2

The default rates, with a 40% correlation of factor values, have a correlation of 44%. This is visible in the scatter plot of the two sets of values.

Table 48.2 summarizes the statistics of the simulated default rates and those of the loss rate for the portfolio. The loss distribution presents the characteristic skew to the

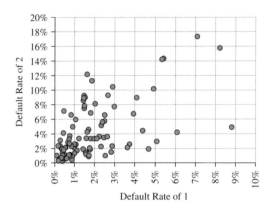

FIGURE 48.8   Scatter plots of default rates 1 and 2

TABLE 48.2   Statistics of the default rates 1 and 2

	Default rate 1	Default rate 2	Loss rate of portfolio
Mean	1.987%	3.991%	2.989%
Volatility	2.342%	3.716%	2.599%

right. The values are weighted averages of pairs of default rate values generated by each simulation run. The frequency is a percentage of the number of obligors. The loss rate peaks, in this simulation, at 12.5%. The peak is lower than the peak values of the segment default rates, because they do not reach their peak values at the same time, so that the overall loss rate average value is lower than the average of the peak values of 1 and 2 default rates. Using a lower correlation between factors driving the default rates would result in a shorter fat tail.

From this loss distribution (Figure 48.9), we derive the cumulated loss distribution (Figure 48.10). This is the cumulated frequency of having values lower than the X-axis

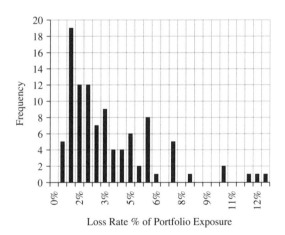

FIGURE 48.9   Loss distribution of the portfolio

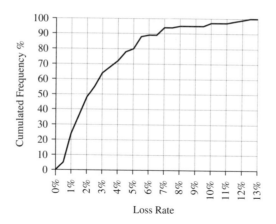

FIGURE 48.10   Cumulative distribution of the portfolio loss rate

percentage. The cumulative distribution visualizes the loss percentiles. For instance, the peak loss in the simulation is 12.5%. The 97.5% loss percentile is 11% and the 95% loss percentile is 10% of the overall loss rate.

Although this is not a comprehensive description of CPV, it illustrates the CPV modelling philosophy. With a simple framework, the technique appears straightforward. In practice, there are difficulties due to the scarcity of data on default rates. If observations are yearly, it is difficult to imagine more than 30 observations. In addition, a long period might make it less relevant for today's measures. Finally, even though CPV provides a comprehensive framework, it lets end-users make the final choices. In spite of these constraints, CPV is the sole model capturing explicitly the cyclical dynamics of default rates.

49

Loss Distribution and Transition Matrices

This chapter explains how to derive distributions of the portfolio values using joint migration matrices. The principle is to find all final risk classes of each firm within the portfolio. The revaluation of assets at the horizon uses the final credit spread that applies to each final risk class. The distribution of portfolio values results from the individual distribution of all states for each facility.

The joint migration matrices determine all possible combinations of migrations of two obligors and assign joint probabilities to each of them. Now, we move one step further, combining joint migration probabilities with revaluation to obtain the loss distribution.

This chapter uses the simple matrix calculated in Chapter 28 to show how to obtain the portfolio value distribution. The first section discusses the joint migration matrix example and the second derives a value distribution for a simple portfolio of two obligors.

JOINT MIGRATION MATRIX VERSUS ASSET CORRELATION

The transition matrices of rating agency data are unconditional on the state of the economy and reflect historical data. They provide the probabilities that an obligor in risk class k moves to risk class l during a certain period. Joint transition matrices provide the probability that a pair of obligors moves from one pair of credit states to another pair of credit states. Credit Metrics derives the probability of joint migrations from the correlated equity returns of firms. Joint migration matrices tabulate the final states of two obligors and assign probabilities to them. The matrix in Table 49.1 is the same one that served as an example when describing the modelling of correlations. We use this matrix to generate a loss distribution.

TABLE 49.1   Joint migration matrix: correlated case

Initial state: X = **A**, Y = **B**		Matrix of JMP correlated migrations: Y final state			
		A	B	C	
X final state	A	7.54%	81.24%	3.22%	92.00%
	B	0.45%	4.50%	0.05%	5.00%
	C	0.27%	2.70%	0.03%	3.00%
		8.26%	88.44%	3.30%	100.00%

This is a simplified matrix. In general, there are more classes. For instance, with six risk classes plus the default state, there are seven transitions. The number of transitions for a two-loan portfolio is $7^2 = 49$. When expanding the portfolio, the number of pairs of firms increases. It is equal to the number of combinations of two facilities among the N facilities in the portfolio, or $N!/[2! \times (N - 2)!]$, where the symbol '!' represents the 'factorial' operator. For $N = 2$, the number of pairs is one, for $N = 3$, it is three, for $N = 4$, it is six and for $N = 5$, it is 10. For large numbers, the number of pairs increases very quickly[1]. Each pair corresponds to 49 transitions, or 490 for five obligors, and so on. This raises the issue of the number of calculations. That is why it might be simpler to use asset correlation to derive the structure of the portfolio by risk class at a given horizon.

SAMPLE TWO-OBLIGOR PORTFOLIO

The example is a portfolio of two obligors X and Y, with a small number of credit states to make the calculations tractable. Using the joint migration matrix above, we have a probability for each cell, and all sum to 1. Mapping credit spreads with ratings serves to value exposures. The spreads by risk class are given in Table 49.2, using only three states, inclusive of the default state (risk class 3).

TABLE 49.2   Transition probabilities and market spreads from current state

Rating	Credit spread over risk-free rate 6.00%
A	1.279%
B	1.379%
C = default	—

The assumptions for the calculations of the value distribution of the portfolio as of end of year 1 (Eoy 1) are:

- All facilities are zero-coupons with 2-year maturity and an identical terminal final flow of 100. The 2-year maturity allows us to conduct value calculations at both the current date and the horizon date, 1 year in the future.

---

[1] The Stirling formula is $n! = \sqrt{2\pi n} \times (n/e)^n$.

- The loss under default is 100% of exposure.
- The risk-free rate is 6% and the yield curve is flat.
- Credit spreads represent the difference between the flat risk-free curve and the risky yield to maturity.
- Credit spreads are also identical for the first year and for the second year.

For the two zero-coupons, the current values discount a final flow of 100 at the risky yield to maturity YTM, including the credit spread. The corresponding values are given in Table 49.3, with a total portfolio value of X + Y of 173.619.

TABLE 49.3   Calculation of current values of X + Y (date 0)

Rating	Credit spread	Risk-free rate	YTM	Value at date 0
A	1.279%	6.000%	7.279%	86.890
B	1.379%	6.000%	7.379%	86.728
C = default	—			0
		Total value		173.619

VALUE DISTRIBUTION AT THE HORIZON

In order to get a value distribution for the portfolio, using the joint migration probability matrix, we consider all combinations of risk classes of X and Y, including default. When a facility defaults, its value drops to zero. When it migrates to the risk class 1 or 2, its value discounts the final 100 flow at the corresponding risky yield to maturity. We assume that credit spreads at Eoy 1 are identical to those of current date. For each combination of final state, we calculate the values as of Eoy 1, of X and Y, and of the portfolio. The probabilities are the joint migration probabilities of the above correlated matrix, arranged in column format (Table 49.4).

TABLE 49.4   Calculation of values of X and Y at Eoy 1

Probability	Risk class X	YTM of X	Risk class Y	YTM of Y	Value X	Value Y	Value X + Y
7.54%	A	7.279%	A	7.279%	93.215	93.215	186.430
0.45%	B	7.379%	A	7.279%	93.128	93.215	186.343
0.27%	C	—	A	7.279%	0.000	93.215	93.215
81.24%	A	7.279%	B	7.379%	93.215	93.128	186.343
4.50%	B	7.379%	B	7.379%	93.128	93.128	186.256
2.70%	C	—	B	7.379%	0.000	93.128	93.128
3.22%	A	7.279%	C	—	93.215	0.000	93.215
0.05%	B	7.379%	C	—	93.128	0.000	93.128
0.03%	C	—	C	—	0.000	0.000	0.000

The table provides the value distribution of the portfolio in the last column. The expected value at Eoy 1 is 180.476. It is above the current value of 173.619 because the final flows gets closer (they are 1 year away from the horizon date) and because of

TABLE 49.5 Probability distribution of the portfolio value

Value X + Y	Probability	Cumulated probability
0	0.030%	100.000%
93.128	2.750%	99.970%
93.215	3.490%	97.220%
186.256	4.500%	93.730%
186.343	81.690%	89.230%
186.430	7.540%	7.540%

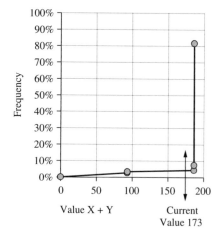

FIGURE 49.1 Portfolio of two obligors' value distribution

migrations and the corresponding discounted values. Note that the loss compared to the current value is negative, since the expected value is higher. Higher default probabilities would make it lower. The probability distribution of the portfolio values is given in Table 49.5. Figure 49.1 shows the usual 'fat tail' to the left of the current value.

Value and Loss Percentiles

The portfolio value volatility is 22.750. The value at 0.03% confidence level value is 93.128, and the 2.78% value percentile is 93.215. These represent losses of around 80.5 from the current value, or 46% of this current value. These values are important because we have a two-obligor portfolio. The loss distribution would be more continuous and loss percentiles would increase more progressively with a diversified portfolio.

Loss Volatility

When the number of obligors increases, the number of horizon values gets very large. Instead of proceeding from the loss distribution to get the loss volatility, Credit Metrics calculates the resulting variance of the distribution from a formula making the variance of a portfolio a function of the variances of all single firms and pairs of firms. For example, with three assets:

$$\sigma(P)^2 = \sigma(V_1)^2 + \sigma(V_2)^2 + \sigma(V_3)^2 + 2\text{Cov}(V_1, V_2) + 2\text{Cov}(V_1, V_3) + 2\text{Cov}(V_2, V_3)$$

Since $\sigma^2(V_1 + V_2) = \sigma^2(V_1) + \sigma^2(V_2) + 2\text{Cov}(V_1, V_2)$:

$$\sigma(P)^2 = \sigma^2(V_1 + V_2) + \sigma^2(V_1 + V_3) + \sigma^2(V_2 + V_3) - \sigma^2(V_1) - \sigma^2(V_2) - \sigma^2(V_3)$$

The formula expresses the portfolio variance in terms of the variances of each facility value and the variances of all two-obligor subportfolios. Using the variances of pairs of obligors allows us to use the same set of data of joint migrations for two-obligor portfolios as above. It facilitates the calculations over a large number of obligors.

Credit Metrics also uses the Monte Carlo simulation technique rather than the joint migration matrices, as KMV does. Joint migration matrices are useful to better understand the migration framework. However, the simulations allow us to achieve the same goal.

50

Capital and Credit Risk VaR

The measures of portfolio risk are statistics, expectation, volatility and percentiles, derived from the portfolio value distributions. Losses derive from setting a value, such as current value, as the zero point for losses. Most portfolio models use a single future horizon to construct the value and the loss distributions and calculate the credit risk 'Value at Risk' (VaR). The loss percentile is $L(\alpha)$, at confidence level α, and the economic capital at the same confidence level is $K(\alpha)$.

Once the value distribution is available, there are still some issues pending to complete the process, including: What is the horizon of the calculations? What are the alternative measures of capital, given economic provisioning policy and portfolio revenues? What are the alternative options for calculating the Risk-adjusted Return on Capital (RaRoC) ratios?

The horizon depends on the portfolio management philosophy. Models capture risk up to a preset horizon that should allow sufficient time to either alter the risk of the portfolio or adjust the capital. The simplest compromise is to use a horizon of 1 to 2 years, together with simple rules for dating default and losses within and beyond this horizon. Note that setting up a horizon shorter than facility maturities does not ignore maturity or actual cash flow dates, because the revaluation at the horizon includes all flows up to maturity. In addition, early losses have more value than late losses, due to discounting.

Once the horizon is set, there are alternative options to determine expected loss and capital, whose choice is a management decision. When looking forward, the portfolio earns income and loses the expected loss. Therefore, capital should be the loss in excess of revenues net of expected loss. Netting expected losses makes sense if economic provisioning is in force. Considering accrued income as a shield against losses assumes that it remains effectively available at the horizon. Modifying the assumptions would require calculating the capital differently.

Under default models, the calculations are straightforward because the loss is the decrease below the current book value due to default. Under full valuation models, the solution is less simple. Using current value for the zero loss point ignores all income from the portfolio. Considering the expected value at the horizon corrects this deficiency, but this value is net of expected loss, which is inconsistent with the need to refer to a zero-loss point. The expected value under no default at the horizon is a better choice. Capital is the excess of loss percentiles of the zero-loss point. The rules directly influence the RaRoC calculations, which depend on all these inputs. Finally, discounting losses to present is necessary to make them comparable with current capital. The calculation should follow a sound rationale for the discount rate consistent with the usage of capital available as of today.

The first section discusses the choice of horizon and details issues related to credit events occurring at intermediate dates for assigning exposures, default probabilities and default dates at intermediate subperiods. The second section reviews the alternative choices for calculating expected loss and capital. The last section discusses the implications for RaRoC calculations of such options.

HORIZON AND TIME PERIODS

Portfolio models generate a loss distribution at a future horizon selected by the end-user. This horizon applies to all facilities regardless of their maturity. Maturities of facilities serve to assign default probabilities as a function of time and to date the exposures.

Horizon

Portfolio management implies continuous restructuring of the risk–return profile of the portfolio through limits, syndications, securitizations, loan trading and usage of credit derivatives. These actions bring the banking portfolio closer to trading. The trend towards more active portfolio management makes the 'buy and hold' philosophy less necessary and less relevant. Sticking to the 'hold to maturity' philosophy creates a bias towards a higher capital charge and is not in line with the facility of restructuring the portfolio risk within a shorter period than maturity.

From a portfolio management perspective, the relevant horizon is a period that allows:

- Restructuring the portfolio to bring its risk in line with bank goals.
- Raising capital, if the existing capital is less than required to ensure adequacy with the portfolio risk.

Both actions take time. Hence, an intermediate period between long maturities and the minimum time to adjust portfolio risk and/or capital seems adequate. Such a horizon might perhaps extend to 1, 2 or 3 years. From a practical standpoint, the 1-year horizon offers many benefits. It is in line with the budget process. It corresponds to the disclosure period of official financial statements. It offers a visibility making assumptions reliable, while longer horizons make them more questionable. Using 1-year or 2-year horizons makes sense, but dealing with amortization over several subperiods is also a desirable specification of portfolio models, even when deviating from the 'buy and hold' principle.

All models require setting a fixed horizon, typically 1 year, and some offer the possibility of making calculations for long periods [CreditRisk+ and Credit Portfolio View (CPV)]. With a fixed horizon, calculations depend on facility maturity:

- If the facility matures before the horizon, the risk exposure goes up to the maturity but the value of the facility at the horizon is zero. In addition, the loss calculation should adjust the default probability to the actual maturity.
- If the facility matures after the horizon, its value at the horizon is random, in full valuation models, due to migration risk. The valuation at the horizon embeds any migration between current dates and the horizon. However, the maturity influences the risk measures and the credit risk VaR through the valuation of the facility at the horizon, which includes the value of all future cash flows up to the final maturity, revalued at the forward time point.

Measuring economic risk suggests differentiating the period of exposure to risk. The longer the exposure, the higher the risk because the default probability increases with the length of exposure. There is a case for capturing risk until the final maturity of all facilities. This is not what most models do when they measure a credit risk VaR. Note that, even with a short 1-year horizon, there is an effect of maturity since the forward valuation at the future date discounts all future cash flows to maturity. Short horizons ignore the migrations and default beyond the horizon, not the maturity. Hence, there is a case for extending the horizon. One reason for sticking to relatively short horizons is the portfolio management philosophy, which deviates from the 'buy and hold' philosophy. Other drawbacks are technical. The drawback of extending the horizon over which we capture migrations and defaults is that calculations get more complex and less intuitive. The excess spread of facilities over market yields creates valuation effects interacting with maturity effects. Long horizons also require longer projections of exposures, whose relevance is questionable. The portfolio amortizes gradually. At the last date of the longer-life facility maturity, the loss distribution narrows down to zero. Hence, we end up with several distributions at various intermediate time points, with data for estimating such distributions less reliable as time passes. Moreover, extending the horizon to long periods would require us to deal with new business. Frequently updated views on the portfolio structure might be more useful than capturing the entire time profile of the portfolio up to the longest maturity. Finally, the longer-life facilities would increase the capital charge, thereby making long maturity deals less attractive. This makes sense, but there is a balance to strike between mechanical penalties assigned to long maturity and business policy.

The regulatory view on maturity is that the capital weights should increase with the maturity of exposures, subject to a cap. This captures the increased period of exposure to credit risk. Ignoring valuation effects, such an increase with maturity is less than proportional for high-risk facilities, and more than proportional for low-risk facilities.

Intermediate Periods before Horizon

When considering long periods, it is necessary to assign default probabilities varying for different periods of exposure and to match them with the time profile of exposures. Amortizing exposures are packages of bullet facilities, so that addressing the issue for bullet facilities is sufficient. In general, the default probabilities broken down by subperiod are the marginal default probabilities applying to each successive period for a given rating class. The first step is to define time points for breaking down the overall maturity into subperiods (Figure 50.1).

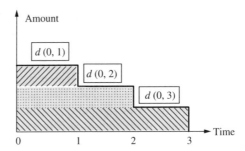

FIGURE 50.1   Stripping amortizing facilities into bullet facilities

In practice, there are two cases to consider depending on whether a bullet facility matures before the horizon or not. If it does mature before the horizon, the default probability should be time-adjusted because it does not make sense to assign a full year default probability to a 3-month exposure. A proportional time adjustment is sufficient for short periods. For instance, with a horizon of $H = 1$ year and a maturity $T < H$, the time-adjusted default probability $d(0, 1) \times T$ suffices. After the horizon, the default probabilities should differ according to subperiods and apply to amortizing balances. In practice, it is easier to assign a single forward default probability $d(1, T)$ from the horizon to maturity.

Assigning default probabilities is not sufficient to date default. Default dates can be at any time between current date and any horizon. They serve for discounting to present future losses. Distinguishing between defaults occurring before and after the horizon, and selecting time points, are necessary. For short maturity facilities, dating default at maturity makes more sense than waiting until the horizon date 1 year ahead. For longer maturities, and a single horizon, the valuation occurs at the horizon. Therefore, both migrations and default are at the horizon. This is consistent with default as a European option exercised at maturity only.

PORTFOLIO VALUE DISTRIBUTIONS, LOSS STATISTICS AND CREDIT RISK VAR

The loss distribution results from the portfolio value distribution. The loss distribution is the mirror image of the portfolio value distribution. From the loss distribution, all loss statistics, including credit risk VaR and economic capital, derive. However, there are several alternative options for calculating them.

Portfolio Value and Loss Distribution

The loss calculations from the value distribution require a starting point to determine the downside variation that counts as a loss. All loss statistics result from the loss distribution and the starting point for calculating losses at the horizon. We discuss alternative choices in the next subsection. The notations used are:

Current date $= 0$
Horizon date $= H$
Portfolio loss percentile at the α confidence level $= L_p(\alpha)$
Portfolio capital at the α confidence level $= K_p(\alpha)$
Portfolio expected loss $= EL_p$
Portfolio contractual revenue $= R_p$
Revenues net of $EL_p =$ expected spread (ES) $= R_p - EL_p$

The capital K_p depends on $L_p(\alpha)$, and on various options for dealing with EL_p and revenues R_p. Figure 50.2 visualizes the various calculations, once the horizon H is specified, for calculating the loss distribution.

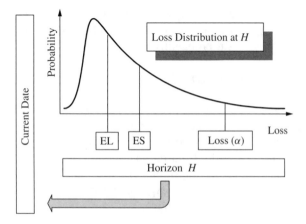

FIGURE 50.2   Future loss distribution and statistics, and the current capital

Calculation of Losses

There is no obvious starting point for the calculation of losses. The loss is a difference between a reference portfolio value, used as origin, and other lower future values. The issue is to choose the reference value from which deviations are losses. The various starting points for calculating losses and capital are:

- The current value of the portfolio.
- The expected value at the horizon date.
- The expected value at the horizon conditional on no prior default.

For a default model and using book values only, the issue is much simpler to solve. The value under no default is the book value. Hence, losses start at aggregated book value as of current date. The accrual revenues serve for absorbing losses, as capital does. However, only excess revenues over expected loss are available for such purposes. Therefore, capital should be net of the excess revenues over expected loss:

$$K_p(\alpha) = L_p(\alpha) + R_p - \mathrm{EL}_p$$

The loss percentile uses the current value V_0 as a zero point for losses.

For a full valuation model, the issue is more complex. The current value of the portfolio appears as a natural reference. However, it differs from the expected value at the horizon due to several factors: revenues between the current date and the horizon that increase the portfolio value at the horizon; migrations; 'roll-down' effect. The expected value at the horizon embeds revenues, is directly comparable to horizon losses because of the time value of money, and appears as a better choice for counting losses. Unfortunately, it also embeds the expected loss instead of providing a clear-cut separation between expected loss and value.

For any facility, the expected value is the expected value under no prior default times the survival probability, plus the value given default, which is recovery, times the default probability (1 minus the survival probability). The equation is:

$$E(\mathbf{V}_H) = E(\mathbf{V}_{H \,|\, \text{no default}}) \times [1 - d(0, H)] + V_{H \,|\, \text{default}} \times d(0, H)$$

Since $\mathbf{V}_{H \,|\, \text{no default}}$ is random, it is necessary to use its expected value. The equation above assumes that $V_{H \,|\, \text{default}}$ is certain, which is only a simplification. The equation shows that the expected value embeds the expected loss. The expected value of the portfolio under no prior default does not. It results from the distribution of values at the horizon under matrix valuation, when eliminating transitions to the default state. It provides a solution for separating the expected loss from the expected value at the horizon.

Capital follows the same equation as above:

$$K_p(\alpha) = L_p(\alpha) + R_p - \mathrm{EL}_p$$

The difference is that the loss percentile results from full valuation at the horizon rather than the initial book value and the expected value under no default is the starting point for counting losses from the value distributions.

KMV Portfolio Manager uses the expected value under no default for counting losses. Credit Metrics shows the current value, and does not calculate the expected value under no prior default. Both current value and expected value conditional on no prior default are feasible choices for calculating the loss distribution.

Expected Loss

For a default model, the expected loss is the expectation of all book value losses at the horizon. Under full valuation, the expected loss depends on the starting point, the current value or the expected value under no prior default. Using the current value as the zero loss point, the expected loss is:

$$\mathrm{EL}_p = \text{expected value of portfolio} - \text{current value}$$

Using the expected value of the portfolio at H under no default as the zero loss point, the expected loss is:

$$\mathrm{EL_p} = E(\mathbf{V}_{H\,|\,\text{no default}}) - V_{H\,|\,\text{default}}$$

KMV Portfolio Manager provides the calculations of both terms to get the expected loss.

Defining Capital

Once the loss distribution and the expected loss are determined, it remains to define the capital. Capital is the gap between a loss percentile $L_p(\alpha)$, if α is the level of confidence, and one of three possible starting points. These are the zero loss point, the expected loss, or the expected revenue. Since revenues might serve to offset some losses, there is a case for calculating capital in excess of expected revenue minus expected loss, which is the definition of the expected excess spread. Adding surviving facility revenues to the value at the horizon would reduce all loss values and shift to the right the loss distribution and its mean. The options are:

- Use capital in excess of the zero loss, when there is no provisioning of expected loss, so that capital absorbs both expected and unexpected losses.
- Use capital in excess of expected loss, if there is economic provisioning.
- Use capital in excess of expected revenue minus expected loss between now and the horizon, considering that revenues serve as a cushion contributing to absorb a fraction of the unexpected losses and that economic provisioning of losses is effective.

These three calculations of capital $K_p(\alpha)$ are:

- Capital including $\mathrm{EL_p}$: $K_p(\alpha) = L_p(\alpha)$.
- Capital in excess of $\mathrm{EL_p}$: $K_p(\alpha) = L_p(\alpha) - \mathrm{EL_p}$.
- Capital in excess of expected revenues: $K_p(\alpha) = L_p(\alpha) - (\text{expected revenues} - \mathrm{EL_p}) = L_p(\alpha) - \mathrm{ES}$.

A common practice is to express capital as a multiple of loss volatility $\mathrm{LV_p}$ of the portfolio. This multiple derives from the prior determination of the loss distribution and the loss statistics serving as the zero point for capital. It is empirical rather than an 'ex ante' multiple such as those of the normal distribution. Once all statistics are calculated, it becomes possible to write capital as a scaled factor of loss volatility:

$$K_p(\alpha) = m(\alpha) \times \mathrm{LV_p}$$

This is a convenient formulation. The most important application of this formulation is capital allocation based on the risk contributions to the portfolio loss volatility. Such risk contributions, properly defined, sum exactly to the portfolio loss volatility (see Chapters 51 and 52). With the multiple $m(\alpha)$, it is easy to convert these 'risk contributions' to the portfolio loss volatility into capital allocations. The loss percentiles result from the simulated distribution of portfolio values.

Discounting Future Losses to Present

Since loss values are at the horizon, they should be brought back to the current date to determine capital properly. A rationale for the choice of discount rate is as follows. Since capital is available today to meet future losses, we can invest it risk-free and get $(1 + y_f)$ times the current capital at the horizon of 1 year. If the risk-free rate is 5% and we have 100 today as capital, we will have 105 in 1 year. Therefore, we need to match the proceeds from investment of capital with horizon losses. This is equivalent to matching the current capital with future losses discounted at the risk-free rate. Therefore, this discount rate is not the cost of capital of the bank, but the risk-free rate. This rule implies that capital should actually be invested in risk-free assets. If not, capital would generate higher revenues than the risk-free revenues, but it would also trigger additional risk, requiring additional capital, etc. The rule has a feedback effect on RaRoC calculations, because it requires adding to the revenues of any facility the revenues from the capital invested in the risk-free asset.

Figure 50.3 shows loss statistics and economic capital.

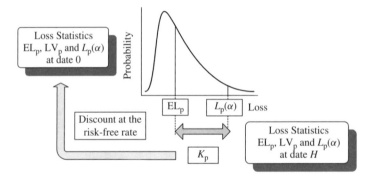

FIGURE 50.3 **From future loss distribution to current loss statistics**

RAROC CALCULATIONS

The RaRoC[1] ratio depends on consistent definitions of the numerator and the denominator.

If the revenues are net of expected loss, the capital should also be, otherwise the expected loss would count twice. If the revenues are the contractual revenues, not netting the expected loss, capital should include both expected and unexpected losses. If the revenues net from expected loss serve to absorb losses, capital should be net of expected revenues. Table 50.1 shows examples of alternative calculations of RaRoC. We assume here that the revenues from capital at the risk-free rate, or $y_f \times K_p(\alpha)$ are included in the total revenue figures.

With revenues netted from capital, the RaRoC ratio is no longer proportional to revenues because revenues are both on the numerator and the denominator. It is easy to increase revenues and observe that all RaRoC ratios still increase with contractual revenues. The RaRoCs based on capital in excess of expected revenues or in excess of EL_p are both lower than the RaRoC based on total expected and unexpected loss because the reduction in numerator has more effect than the reduction in denominator. When netting expected

---

[1] The RaRoC ratio and the SVA are discussed in Chapters 53 and 54.

TABLE 50.1   RaRoC values under various definitions of capital

Revenues (no default)			
R_p	80	80	80
EL_p	50	50	50
$L_p(\alpha)$	400	400	400
Capital	$L_p(\alpha)$	$L_p(\alpha) - EL_p$	$L_p(\alpha) - (R_p - EL_p)$
	400	350	370
RaRoC	Revenues	Revenues $-$ EL	Revenues $-$ EL_p
Numerator	80	30	30
RaRoC formula	$R_p/[L_p(\alpha)]$	$(R_p - EL_p)/[L_p(\alpha) - EL_p]$	$(R_p - EL_p)/[L_p(\alpha) - (R_p - EL_p)]$
RaRoC	20.00%	8.57%	8.11%

loss from revenues, negative values are possible because the expected loss might be bigger than revenues. In addition, risk-free exposures generate a zero capital, or a negative one when considering revenues! RaRoC is irrelevant in such cases, but it is still possible to determine target revenues in line with profitability goals (see Chapters 53 and 54).

The actual RaRoC values within a mark-to-model framework are more complex than they look. Under full economic valuation, the loss percentile and the EL_p both depend on contractual revenues because of the mark-to-model calculation discounting the revenues. Such discounted revenues appear only implicitly in the above ratios because $L_p(\alpha)$ and EL_p derive from mark-to-market values that embed revenues. The above equations look oversimplified given that they do not make explicit these underlying interdependencies.

SECTION 15

Capital Allocation

51

Capital Allocation and Risk Contributions

The standalone risk of a transaction portfolio is intrinsic to a facility and pre-diversification effects within a portfolio. The risk contribution is the risk retained by a facility, or a subportfolio, post-diversification. Risk contributions are the foundation of the capital allocation system and of the risk-adjusted performance measurement system.

Risk contributions are either 'absolute' risk contributions or 'marginal' risk contributions. Marginal risk contributions are the changes in risk 'with and without' an additional unit of exposure, a facility or a subportfolio of facilities. Absolute risk contributions are allocations of the portfolio risk to the existing individual facilities or subportfolios, embedding the correlation structure of the portfolio. Risk contributions are based on such measures as the loss volatility or the portfolio credit risk capital. The loss distribution is a prerequisite for determining risk contributions, since all loss statistics, expected loss, portfolio loss volatility and portfolio capital, derive from the loss distribution.

The mechanisms for calculating risk contributions are similar for market risk and credit risk. They require the loss distributions but do not depend on the actual source of risk. Because of this property, we make no distinction with respect to the nature of risk, market or credit, in this chapter.

Capital allocations are the absolute risk contributions. Only absolute risk contributions add up arithmetically to obtain the overall portfolio risk, while marginal risk contributions do not. Thanks to this attractive property, the risk allocation issue collapses to simple arithmetic operations. Capital allocations are an input to risk-adjusted performance. When considering the existing portfolio only, these measures are 'ex post', once facilities are within the portfolio. By contrast, marginal risk contributions are relevant for pricing purposes, because they apply well to new transactions. Hence, absolute and marginal risk contributions serve different purposes.

The purpose of this chapter is to define risk contributions, both 'absolute' and 'marginal' risk contributions, and to demonstrate their basic properties. The first section discusses briefly the goals and contributions of the capital allocation system. The second section provides specific definitions of risk contributions. The third section focuses on the key properties of absolute versus marginal risk contributions. Subsequent sections focus on absolute risk contributions and capital allocation only. The fifth section expands a full example of capital allocation, starting from constructing the loss distribution of a simple two-obligor portfolio and ending with the detailed calculations of risk contributions to both loss volatility and risk capital. The next chapter details further marginal risk contributions.

CAPITAL ALLOCATION GOALS

Capital allocation aims at allocating both credit and market risk to the business units and the transactions that originate them. They provide the top-down and bottom-up links between the post-diversification risk of the bank and individual transactions. The relationship is far from obvious because the risks do not add up arithmetically, so that the total risk is less than the sum of individual risks. Capital allocation defines meaningful keys for tracing back the overall risk to its sources.

Capital allocations are risk contributions of facilities to the overall portfolio risk. They apply to both credit risk and market risk using the same techniques. The risk contributions should comply with simple constraints to be usable. They should add up arithmetically to obtain the total risk, in order to reconcile allocated risks with overall risk. For pricing purposes, they should also be such that pricing based on risk contributions keeps the portfolio return in line with the overall target. The analytics show that the risk contributions complying with these two objectives differ. To allocate existing risks, absolute risk contributions apply. For pricing purposes, marginal risk contributions apply. This chapter highlights these differences and explains their sources.

The capital allocation system allows us to break down and aggregate risk contributions according to any criteria as long as individual transaction risk contributions are available. These properties allow us to deal with most issues related to allocating risks. For example, portfolios by business unit and portfolios by counterparty do not coincide. They might overlap or not. The implication is that the measures of credit risk and of business unit risk do not refer to the same portfolios in general. The capital allocation system solves the issue. It provides the risk contributions for individual facilities for both market risk and credit risk. If several business units deal with the same customer, it is possible to aggregate the risk contributions of all facilities with this customer into subsets relative to each business unit. When the same customer generates both credit risk and market risk with market transactions, it is possible to allocate both credit and market risk to the corresponding business units.

DEFINITIONS AND NOTATION

In this section, we define the standalone risk of a facility, the risk contribution of an existing facility i within a portfolio P, or RC_i^P, also named 'Absolute Risk Contributions' (ARC), and the marginal risk contribution of the facility f added to a portfolio P, or MRC_f^{P+f}.

Definitions

The main definitions are:

- The standalone risk is the loss volatility of a single facility.
- The marginal risk contribution is the change in portfolio loss volatility when adding a facility f to the portfolio P.
- The absolute risk contribution of an existing facility i to a portfolio P is the covariance of the random loss of this single facility i with the random loss aggregated over the entire portfolio (including i), divided by the loss volatility of this aggregated loss. This risk contribution is also the 'absolute' risk contribution; to avoid confusion it is distinct from the marginal risk contribution.

Among the three definitions above, the two first are intuitive and the third sounds mathematical. The absolute risk contribution captures the risk of a facility given that other facilities diversify away a fraction of its standalone risk.

Risk contributions also depend on the overall measure of portfolio risk to which they contribute. The simplest risk contributions are the contributions to the loss volatility of the portfolio loss. These risk contributions have the attractive property of adding up to the loss volatility of the portfolio. Since it is common to express capital as a multiple of this portfolio loss volatility, risk contributions are converted into capital allocations through the same scaling factor. Since risk contributions sum to the loss volatility, capital allocations also sum to the portfolio capital. Because they add up to the portfolio risk measure post-diversification effects, the absolute risk contributions are a convenient basis for the overall portfolio capital allocation to individual facilities. The concept of risk contribution is intuitive, but calculations use technical formulas requiring us to specify the notation.

Notation

Risk contributions always refer to a facility of obligor i and a reference portfolio P. There are several risk contributions defined below. The portfolio P is made up of N facilities. Each facility i relates to a single obligor. The notation applies to both default models and full valuation mode models. However, all examples use calculations in default mode only for simplicity.

- The losses are random variables. For the single facility i, the loss is $\mathbf{L}_i$. The portfolio loss is the summation of individual obligor losses. The aggregated portfolio loss is $\mathbf{L_p} = \sum_{i=1}^{N} \mathbf{L}_i$ for these i obligors. In default mode, the loss results from default only. In full valuation mode, the loss for one facility follows a distribution.
- The exposures are X_i, $i = 1$ to N. $\mathbf{L}_i$, $i = 1$ to N. Exposures are certain and identical to losses given default, Lgd_i.
- To make random losses distinct from certain exposures, we use $\mathbf{L}_i$ for losses and X_i for exposures. Exposures, equal to Lgd_i, are the actual values potentially lost. Loss is equal the certain exposure X_i times a random variable describing the credit state of the facility. In default models, this variable is a Bernoulli variable, $\mathbf{d}_i$, taking the value

1 in case of default and 0 otherwise, and $\mathbf{L}_i = X_i \mathbf{d}_i$. By convention, d_i designates the value of the random variable. The default probabilities are $E(\mathbf{d}_i) = d_i$ in default mode.

- The loss volatility is the standard deviation of a loss. It is LV_i for a single facility i and LV_P for an entire portfolio P. These notations are equivalent to the more compact notations σ_i and σ_P. LV_i and σ_i, LV_P and σ_P are two different notations for the same volatilities.

- The 'unit exposure' loss volatility of a single facility is the loss volatility for an exposure equal to one unit. In default mode, the unit exposure loss volatility is the usual $\sigma_i^1 = \sqrt{d_i \times (1 - d_i)}$. The superscript 1 differentiates unit exposure volatility from exposure weighted loss volatility, or $LV_i = \sigma_i = X_i \times \sigma_i^1 = X_i \times \sqrt{d_i \times (1 - d_i)}$. This distinction serves for setting a structured and general presentation of all calculations leading to the risk contributions and the portfolio loss volatility.

- The correlation coefficients between individual losses $\mathbf{L}_i$ are $\rho_{ij} = \rho_{ji}$. The standalone loss volatilities are $LV_i = \sigma_i$ calculated with the above standard formulas.

- Since all risk contributions refer to a common portfolio P, it is convenient to use the superscript P to designate the reference portfolio in subsequent notations.

ABSOLUTE AND MARGINAL RISK CONTRIBUTIONS TO PORTFOLIO LOSS VOLATILITY AND CAPITAL

This section summarizes the key definitions of absolute and marginal risk contributions in the first subsection and the key properties of absolute risk contributions to portfolio loss volatility and capital, making them pivotal in the capital allocation system. The demonstration of properties follows.

Risk Contribution Definitions

The standalone risk is the loss volatility of a single facility. The *absolute risk contribution* to the loss volatility of the portfolio is the contribution of an obligor i to the overall loss volatility LV^P. Since it depends on both the portfolio and the obligor, it is useful to use RC_i^P instead of RC_i to make explicit the reference to portfolio P. Absolute risk contributions to the portfolio loss volatility differ from the risk contributions to the portfolio capital, which are the capital allocations. The capital allocations relate to the risk contributions through the portfolio loss volatility. To convert absolute risk contributions to portfolio loss volatility into absolute risk contributions to capital, we multiply them by the ratio $m(\alpha)$ of capital to portfolio loss volatility.

The *marginal risk contribution* to loss volatility is the change in portfolio loss volatility when adding an additional unit of exposure, a new facility, a new obligor, or a new portfolio. For instance, the marginal risk contribution of an obligor f is the variation of the loss volatility with and without the obligor f (or a subset a of obligors). Marginal risk contributions are MRC_f^P below. The marginal risk contribution of obligor f in a portfolio of N obligors without f, and $N + 1$ with f, is:

$$MRC_f^P + f = LV^{P+f} - LV^P$$

The marginal risk contribution to the portfolio loss volatility and the marginal contribution to capital differ. The first is the variation of the portfolio LV^P when adding a facility or obligor, or any subset of facilities. The marginal contribution to capital is the corresponding variation of capital. These distinct marginal contributions do not relate in a simple way. The capital is $K(\alpha)$, with confidence level α. The two marginal risk contributions are:

$$\text{MRC}_f^{P+f}(\text{LV}^P) = \text{LV}^{P+f} - \text{LV}^P$$

$$\text{MRC}_f^{P+f}[K(\alpha)] = K(\alpha)^{P+f} - K(\alpha)^P$$

Unless otherwise specified, we use marginal risk contribution as the marginal change in loss volatility of the portfolio. If the multiple $m(\alpha)$ does not change significantly when the portfolio changes, the marginal contribution to loss volatility times the overall ratio of capital to portfolio loss volatility is a proxy of marginal risk contribution to capital. This approximation is not valid whenever the portfolio changes significantly.

Basic Properties of Risk Contributions

The absolute risk contributions serve to allocate capital. The absolute risk contribution to the portfolio loss volatility of a facility i to a portfolio P is the covariance of the random loss of this single facility i with the aggregated random portfolio loss over the entire portfolio (including i), divided by the loss volatility of this aggregated random loss. The formula for calculating absolute risk contributions results from that of the variance of the portfolio, as explained in subsequent sections: $\text{Var}(L_P) = \sum_{i,j} \sigma_{ij} = \sum_{i,j} \rho_{ij}\sigma_i\sigma_j$. Absolute risk contributions to loss volatility, times the multiple of overall capital to overall portfolio loss volatility, sum exactly to the portfolio capital. This is the key property making them the foundation for the capital allocation system solving the non-intuitive issue of allocating risks.

Marginal risk contributions serve to make incremental decisions and for risk-based pricing. They provide a direct answer to questions such as: What is the additional capital consumed by an additional facility? What is the capital saved by withdrawing a facility or a subportfolio from the current portfolio? Marginal contributions serve for pricing purposes. We show later that:

- Pricing in such a way that the revenues of an additional facility equal the target hurdle rate of return times the marginal risk contribution of the new facility ensures that the target return of the portfolio on capital remains equal to or above the minimum hurdle rate.
- Marginal risk contributions to the portfolio loss volatility are lower than absolute risk contributions to the portfolio loss volatility. However, marginal risk contributions to the portfolio capital can be higher or lower than absolute contributions to the portfolio capital.

The properties of absolute and marginal risk contributions serve to address different issues. The key distinction is 'ex post' versus 'ex ante' applications. Absolute risk contributions serve for ex post allocations of capital based on effective usage of line, while marginal risk contributions serve to make ex ante risk-based pricing decisions (Table 51.1).

A simple example illustrates these properties before deriving general formulas demonstrating the above properties. Using the same example of a very simple portfolio throughout

TABLE 51.1 Absolute and marginal risk contributions and their key properties

	To portfolio loss volatility LV^P or capital K^P
Absolute risk contribution ARC (ex post view)	• Sum up to LV^P • Capital allocation (ex post) • Risk-based performance (ex post)
Marginal risk contribution MRC (ex ante view)	• Do not sum up to LV^P or K^P • Risk-based pricing (ex ante)

the chapter facilitates our understanding of the formulas and shows the calculation details. The reader can skip the formal demonstrations of the above properties, once having reviewed the example. However, demonstrations are given in the main text. We detail more absolute risk contributions in what follows.

Undiversifiable Risk

With an existing facility, the absolute risk contribution is proportional to the standalone risk. The ratio of the risk contribution of a given facility to the facility loss volatility is lower than 1. It measures the diversification effect at the level of a facility. The ratio represents the 'retained risk', or the risk retained within the portfolio as a percentage of the standalone risk of a facility. This ratio, RR_i, measures the undiversifiable risk of the facility by the portfolio:

$$RR_i = \text{undiversifiable risk/standalone risk} = ACR_i / \sigma_i$$

Risk contributions and retained risk have several attractive properties that we demonstrate below. We show that $ARC_i^P = \rho_{iP} \times \sigma_i$. Therefore, RR_i of an individual facility i is simply identical to its correlation coefficient with the entire portfolio P: $RR_i = \rho_{iP}$. Since all correlation coefficients are lower than or equal to 1, this demonstrates the general result that $RC_i^P \leq \sigma_i$. The risk contribution is always lower than, or equal to, the standalone risk. This is intuitively obvious since risk contributions are post-diversification measures of risk.

The facility RR_i depends on the entire correlation structure with the portfolio. The higher the RR_i ratio, the higher the undiversifiable risk of the facility. It is important to track the retained risks to identify facilities contributing more to correlation risk. Conversely, for diversification purposes, using low RR_i guides the choice towards transactions that increase the diversification of the existing portfolio.

As shown below, the summation of all absolute risk contributions is the aggregated loss volatility of the portfolio. Using the retained risk, this loss volatility is:

$$\sigma_P = \sum_i RR_i \times \sigma_i$$

If all cross-correlations are zero, $\rho_{ij} = 0$, the absolute risk contribution becomes $ARC_i^P = \sigma_i^2 / \sigma_P$ and the undiversifiable risk ratio becomes $RR_i = \sigma_i / \sigma_P$, the ratio of the standalone risk of the facility to the portfolio loss volatility. Finally, note that retained risk measures apply only to subportfolios or facilities. For the entire portfolio, the diversification effect is not the total risk contribution to the aggregated loss volatility of the portfolio since this ratio equals 1. For a portfolio, the diversification measure is simply the ratio of the aggregated loss volatility of the portfolio to the summation of all individual facility loss volatilities or standalone risks.

SAMPLE CALCULATIONS OF ABSOLUTE RISK CONTRIBUTIONS

This section uses a simple example to calculate various loss statistics including risk contributions. The example uses a pure default model, building up on the example of the two-obligor portfolio with 10% default correlation identical to that of Chapter 46. We do not replicate all detailed calculations. Rather, we detail the comparison of standalone and portfolio risk measures.

The Portfolio Used as Example

To illustrate the above risk measures, we use the example of a portfolio of two obligors with correlated defaults. Tables 51.2 and 51.3 provide the details of exposures and the loss distribution.

TABLE 51.2 Standalone default probabilities and default correlations

	Default probability	Exposures X_A and X_B
A	7.00%	100
B	5.00%	50
ρ_{AB}	10.00%	

TABLE 51.3 Loss distribution (default correlation 10%)

	Loss	Probabilities	Cumulated probabilities	Confidence level
A & B default	150	0.906%	100.000%	$\leq 0.906\%$
A defaults	100	6.094%	99.094%	$\leq 7.000\%$
B defaults	50	4.094%	93.000%	$\leq 11.094\%$
Neither defaults	0	88.906%	88.906%	Not significant

The cumulated loss probabilities provide the loss percentiles. For instance, the loss at the 7% confidence level is 50, and the loss at the 0.906% confidence level is 100. When we use the second percentile, we consider as a rough proxy of the loss at the 1% confidence level. For confidence levels lower than or equal to 0.906%, the loss is maximum, or 150. Between 7% and less than 0.906%, the loss is 100. Between 11.094% and less than 7.00%, the loss is 50.

Standalone Expected Losses and Portfolio Expected Losses

The expected loss of obligor i is $EL_i = d_i \times Lgd_i$ in value. The expected loss for the portfolio of obligors is the sum of individual obligor expected losses: $EL_P = \sum_i d_i \times Lgd_i$. The expected losses of A and B are the default probabilities times the exposure, or $100 \times 7\% = 7$ and $50 \times 5\% = 2.5$ respectively for A and B. The portfolio expected loss also results directly from the portfolio loss distribution considering all four possible events, with single default probabilities lower than standalone default probabilities. The probability weighted average of the four loss values is also 9.5.

Standalone Loss Volatility and Portfolio Loss Volatility

The standalone loss volatility of obligor i in value is:

$$LV_i = \sigma_i = X_i \times \sqrt{d_i \times (1 - d_i)}$$

The loss volatility of obligor i per unit value is $\sigma_i^1 = \sqrt{d_i \times (1 - d_i)}$, which is a percentage of exposure, and the above is equal to $LV_i = \sigma_i^1 \times X_i$. The convention is that the exposure X_i is identical to Lgd_i, or an exposure with a zero recovery rate. The loss volatilities of A and B are $LV_A = 100 \times \sqrt{7\% \times (1 - 7\%)} = 25.515$ and $LV_B = 50 \times \sqrt{5\% \times (1 - 5\%)} = 10.897$. The unit exposure volatilities are $\sigma_A^1 = \sqrt{P(A)[1 - P(A)]} = 25.515\%$ for A and $\sigma_B^1 = \sqrt{P(B)[1 - P(B)]} = 21.794\%$ for B (Table 51.4).

TABLE 51.4   Unit exposure volatilities and loss volatilities

Facility	Exposure	Default probability	Unit exposure volatility	Exposure weighted loss volatility
A	100	7%	25.515%	25.515
B	50	5%	21.794%	10.897

The direct calculation of loss statistics is replicated in Table 51.5. The loss volatility is the square root of the portfolio loss variance, or 28.73.

TABLE 51.5   Loss distribution statistics

EL	9.50
Loss volatility	28.73
Loss variance	825.36

Portfolio Capital

Capital derives from the loss distributions and the loss percentiles at various confidence levels. The portfolio loss percentile at 1% is approximately $L(1\%) = 100$. The expected losses of A and B are respectively 7.0 and 2.5, totalling 9.5 for the portfolio. Capital is the loss percentile in excess of expected loss, or $100 - 9.5 = 90.5$. If the confidence level changes, the loss percentiles do as well.

THE CAPITAL ALLOCATION MODEL AND ABSOLUTE RISK CONTRIBUTIONS

This section provides the theoretical formulas of portfolio loss variance and volatility and their decomposition in absolute risk contributions, and shows how to derive the capital allocation. This is the basic capital allocation model. The next section illustrates these theoretical formulas and provides a fully detailed numerical example using the above two-obligor portfolio example. Readers can move directly to the numerical examples, but the theoretical properties are relatively easy to demonstrate.

Portfolio Loss Volatility

The loss volatility is a common measure of the risk of the portfolio. All loss volatilities in this section are exposure weighted. The portfolio loss volatility depends on the correlation between obligor losses. It is the square root of the portfolio loss variance σ_{Lp}^2. In what follows, we use σ_P^2 for σ_{Lp}^2. The classical formula for the loss variance of a portfolio P results from its definition:

$$\sigma_P^2 = \mathrm{Cov}(\mathbf{L}_P, \mathbf{L}_P)$$

$$\sigma_P^2 = \mathrm{Cov}\left(\sum_i \mathbf{L}_i, \sum_i \mathbf{L}_j\right) = \sum_i \mathrm{Cov}(\mathbf{L}_i, \mathbf{L}_P)$$

This is the well-known equation of the variance of a portfolio loss as the summation, for all combinations of i and j, of the $\rho_{ij}\sigma_i\sigma_j$ terms:

$$\sigma_P^2 = \sum_i \sum_j \rho_{ij}\sigma_i\sigma_j$$

The correlation coefficient between the losses of i and j is:

$$\rho_{ij} = \mathrm{Cov}(\mathbf{L}_i, \mathbf{L}_j)/\sigma_i\sigma_j$$

The variance of the portfolio loss is the summation of all covariances across the entire set of pairs of facilities. In order to check this formula, it is useful to decompose it into its risk contribution components.

The Absolute Risk Contributions to Portfolio Loss Volatility

The starting point is the standard formula of the portfolio loss volatility in value. All variances and covariances are in value and include the size effect of exposures in this section. The portfolio loss variance is:

$$\sigma_P^2 = \sum_{i=1}^{n} \mathrm{Cov}(\mathbf{L}_i, \mathbf{L}_P)$$

Definition of Absolute Risk Contributions to Volatility

The portfolio loss variance is the sum of all covariances of individual obligor losses with the portfolio. This allows us to utilize a shortcut to demonstrate directly that the absolute risk contributions to loss volatility are additive:

$$\sigma_P^2 = \text{Cov}(\mathbf{L}_P, \mathbf{L}_P) = \text{Cov}\left(\sum_i \mathbf{L}_i, \mathbf{L}_P\right) = \sum_i \text{Cov}(\mathbf{L}_i, \mathbf{L}_P)$$

The loss volatility is, by definition, identical to the loss variance divided by the loss volatility:

$$\sigma_P = \sum_i \text{Cov}(\mathbf{L}_i, \mathbf{L}_P)/\sigma_P$$

Each term of the summation is the covariance of each single obligor and the entire portfolio divided by the portfolio loss volatility. This formula defines the absolute risk contribution to portfolio volatility, ARC_i^P, as above:

$$\text{ARC}_i^P = \text{Cov}(\mathbf{L}_i, \mathbf{L}_P)/\sigma_P$$

Simplified Formulas for Risk Contributions

From this basic formula, we derive practical simplified versions and demonstrate the main properties of the absolute risk contributions. The two main formulas of absolute risk contributions to portfolio volatility are either in terms of the correlation of individual losses with aggregated losses or in terms of the β_i coefficient, which is the coefficient of the relation between individual losses and the portfolio loss.

The analogy with the Capital Asset Pricing Model (CAPM) serves: in this model, the correlation is that of the asset return with the entire market return and the β_i is the coefficient of the regression of the asset return on the market portfolio return, and the measure of systematic risk[1]. In our context, our reference portfolio P is that of the bank instead of the market portfolio.

To find a simple formula, we first write $\text{Cov}(\mathbf{L}_i, \mathbf{L}_P) = \rho_{iP} \times \sigma_i \times \sigma_P$. Dividing both terms by σ_P, we find the first simple relation:

$$\text{ARC}_i^P = \rho_{iP} \times \sigma_i$$

The absolute risk contribution is proportional to the correlation with the rest of the portfolio and with its standalone risk. This is a very simple rule for relating risk contribution to volatility. To find an alternative simple relation, we use the definition of the coefficient β_i:

$$\beta_i = \rho_{im} \times \sigma_i/\sigma_m \quad \text{and} \quad \beta_i \times \sigma_m = \rho_{im} \times \sigma_i$$

Therefore, using P as the reference portfolio instead of the market portfolio:

$$\text{ARC}_i^P = \rho_{iP} \times \sigma_i = \beta_i \times \sigma_P$$

---

[1] See Hull (2000) for these basic properties of the CAPM.

These are very simple and compact relationships. They apply to any variable of interest in terms of risk.

For instance, we can use individual losses, or individual asset returns or 'Earnings at Risk' (EaR) of a subportfolio, such as that of a business line. It is easy to find the 'diversified' contributions of individual losses, individual asset values or business line EaR to the volatility of the aggregated loss, value or EaR of the entire portfolio. We simply measure the correlation ρ_{iP} or the coefficient β_i, and multiply them, respectively, by the standalone volatility or the portfolio volatility. For instance, if we need to find a risk contribution based on EaR volatility, we calculate the volatility of earnings for the entire portfolio, then for a single business line, and then calculate the correlation between EaR$_i$ and EaR$_P$. The standalone EaR$_i$ is undiversified. The diversified value in this case is simply $\rho_{iP} \times$ EaR$_i$.

Risk Contributions Capture Correlation Effects

Risk contributions combine the correlation effect with the portfolio and the magnitude of the standalone risk. The absolute risk contributions sum to the loss volatility of the portfolio, a key property that becomes obvious given the definition of ARC$_i^P$:

$$\sum_i \text{ARC}_i^P = \sum_i \text{Cov}(\mathbf{L}_i, \mathbf{L}_P)/\sigma_P = \sigma_P^2/\sigma_P = \sigma_P$$

$$\sum_i \text{ARC}_i^P = \sigma_P$$

These risk contributions sum to the loss volatility, not the capital. In order to proceed to capital allocation, we need the multiple of loss volatility providing the capital at a given confidence level. The loss distribution provides both loss volatility and capital at a given confidence level, from which the multiple derives.

A specific case is that of independence, where all cross-covariance terms are zero. Then, $\sigma_P^2 = \text{Cov}(\mathbf{L}_P, \mathbf{L}_P) = \text{Cov}\left(\sum_i \mathbf{L}_i, \mathbf{L}_P\right) = \sum_i \text{Var}(\mathbf{L}_i)$. The total portfolio variance is the sum of all individual variances and the portfolio loss volatility becomes the square root of this summation. The absolute risk contribution is $\text{ARC}_i^P = \text{Var}(\mathbf{L}_i)/\sigma_P = \sigma_i^2/\sigma_P$, or the ratio of the standalone variance of the facility to the loss volatility of the portfolio.

From Absolute Risk Contributions to Capital Allocation

If $K(\alpha)$ is the capital at the confidence level α, there is always a multiple $m(\alpha)$ such that $K(\alpha) = m(\alpha) \times \text{LV}_P$. We also know that $\text{LV}_P = \sum_i \text{ARC}_i$. To obtain the capital allocations, we need to multiply the risk contributions by a multiple $m(\alpha)$, the ratio of portfolio capital to loss volatility, both resulting from the loss distribution:

$$K(\alpha) = m(\alpha) \times \text{LV}_P = \sum_i m(\alpha)\text{ARC}_i$$

The capital allocation system simply allocates the fraction $m(\alpha) \times \text{ARC}_i$ as capital to the facility or the subportfolio i. For a subportfolio, such as those of business units, the capital allocation simply sums all $m(\alpha) \times \text{ARC}_i$ over all facilities of the subportfolio, using the additive property of absolute risk contributions (Figure 51.1).

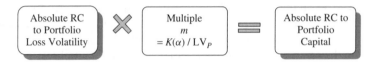

FIGURE 51.1   Absolute risk contributions to portfolio loss volatility and capital allocation

EXAMPLE OF THE CALCULATION OF ABSOLUTE RISK CONTRIBUTIONS

Table 51.6 provides the standalone loss volatilities, the portfolio loss volatility and the absolute risk contributions to loss volatility and capital (the latter being the capital allocations). The example is the same as above.

TABLE 51.6   Absolute risk contributions to the portfolio loss volatility

	A	B	Portfolio
Loss volatility (weighted by exposure)[a]	25.515	10.897	36.412
ARC to loss volatility	23.628	5.101	28.729

[a]The sum of standalone loss volatilities is 36.412, higher than the portfolio loss volatility of 28.729 derived from the loss distribution.

Calculating the Absolute Risk Contributions to Volatility

The important point is how to derive the calculation of the risk contributions. The absolute risk contributions of A and B result from the decomposition of the portfolio loss variance into its different covariance terms, making an adjustment for the loss volatility. They are:

$$\text{ARC}_i^P = \text{Cov}(\mathbf{L}_i, \mathbf{L}_P)/\sigma_P$$
$$= \text{Cov}(\mathbf{L}_i, \mathbf{L_A} + \mathbf{L_B})/\sigma_P$$
$$= [\text{Cov}(\mathbf{L}_i, \mathbf{L_A}) + \text{Cov}(\mathbf{L}_i, \mathbf{L_B})]/\sigma_P$$

The covariances are functions of standalone volatilities and correlation coefficients using:

$$\text{Cov}(\mathbf{L_X}, \mathbf{L_Y}) = \rho_{XY}\sigma_X\sigma_Y$$

The two risk contributions become:

$$\text{ARC}_A^P = [\rho_{AA}\sigma_A\sigma_A + \rho_{AB}\sigma_A\sigma_B]/\sigma_P$$
$$\text{ARC}_B^P = [\rho_{BA}\sigma_B\sigma_A + \rho_{BB}\sigma_B\sigma_B]/\sigma_P$$

Since we know all terms of this equation, we use $\rho_{AA} = \rho_{BB} = 1$ and $\rho_{BA} = \rho_{AB} = 10\%$, plus $\sigma_A = 25.51$ and $\sigma_B = 10.90$. In this case, ARC_A^P and ARC_B^P are[2]:

$$ARC_A^P = (25.51^2 + 10\% \times 25.51 \times 10.90)/28.73 = 23.628$$

$$ARC_B^P = (10\% \times 10.90 \times 25.51 + 10.90^2)/28.73 = 5.101$$

It is easy to verify that the risk contributions sum to the loss volatility:

$$ARC_A^P + ARC_B^P = 28.729$$

Capital Allocation

The ratio of capital to loss volatility depends on the confidence level. With a confidence level of 1%, the loss percentile is 100 and the capital is the loss percentile in excess of the expected loss or, using a rounded value $K(1\%) = 100 - 9.5 = 90.5$. Since the portfolio loss volatility is 28.729, the ratio $m(1\%)$ of capital to loss volatility is $m(1\%) = 90.5/28.73 = 3.150$. Hence, the absolute risk contributions to the portfolio capital are $23.628 \times 3.150 = 74.430$ and $5.101 \times 3.150 = 16.070$, summing to the capital 90.500. These are the capital allocations. We can now complete the previous Table 51.6 with capital allocations (Table 51.7).

TABLE 51.7 Absolute risk contributions to the portfolio loss volatility

	A	B	Portfolio
Loss volatility (weighted by exposure)[a]	25.515	10.897	36.412
ARC to loss volatility	23.628	5.101	28.729
$m(1\%) = 90.5/28.729 = 3.150$			
ARC to capital at 1%	74.430	16.070	90.500

[a] The sum of standalone loss volatilities is 36.412, higher than the portfolio loss volatility of 28.729 derived from the loss distribution.

The capital allocation uses the risk contributions. Nevertheless, we could also use any other criteria such as standalone risk to perform the same task. What are the drawbacks and benefits of these two alternative schemes? The capital allocations based on risk contributions to portfolio loss volatility differ from allocations on standalone risks. The risk contributions of A and B are respectively 23.628 and 5.101, summing to 28.729. The percentage allocations are 23.628/28.729 and 5.101/28.729, or respectively 74.43% and 16.07%. Similar percentage allocations derive from the standalone risks. The standalone loss volatilities of A and B are respectively 25.515 and 10.897, also summing to 36.412 > 28.729. The corresponding percentage allocations would be 25.515/36.412 and 10.897/36.422, or 70.07% and 29.93% respectively. The capital allocation to B with risk contributions is heavier than with standalone risks, and the opposite occurs for A. Both choices are practical.

---

[2] All figures in these calculations are rounded to two decimal places. Table 51.6 provides the same values to three decimal places.

The major difference is that the risk contributions embed the correlation structure, whereas standalone risks do not. For example, two facilities might have the same stand-alone risk, with one being highly correlated with the rest of the portfolio and the other having a lower correlation. The former contributes more to the portfolio risk than the latter. Risk contributions differentiate the two facilities accordingly. On the other hand, the drawback of risk contributions is that they are more difficult to interpret than stand-alone risks. Using standalone risks is simpler, but this reference ignores the differences between two facilities having different correlations with the rest of the portfolio and identical standalone risks.

Calculation of Absolute Risk Contributions from the Variance–Covariance Matrix

The absolute risk contributions derive from the simple matrix formula of the variance of the portfolio loss. This matrix extends to any number of obligors. To proceed, we stick to the default model with two obligors, but the formulas are general and apply to full valuation models as well. The variance of the portfolio loss distribution is:

$$\text{Portfolio loss variance } \sigma_P^2 = X \Sigma X^{\mathrm{T}}$$

where X is the row vector of exposures, or 100 and 50, X^{T} is the column vector of exposures, the transpose of the above, Σ is the unit variance–covariance of the portfolio of exposures, with each term equal to $\rho_{AB}\sigma_A\sigma_B$. ρ_{AB} is the default correlation between A and B (Table 51.8).

TABLE 51.8   Exposures, default probabilities, loss volatilities and default correlation

Exposure	Weight	Default probability	Unit standalone volatility
100	66.67%	7%	25.515%
50	33.33%	5%	21.794%
150	100.00%		
Default correlation ρ_{AB}	10%		

The 'unit exposure' variance–covariance matrix, or Σ, combines the correlation matrix and the unit exposure volatilities. The unit exposure loss volatility of X is $\sqrt{P(X)[1 - P(X)]}$ for any obligor X. The generic formula of covariance: $\text{Cov}(A, B) = \rho_{AB}\sigma_A^1\sigma_B^1$ provides all terms of the unit exposure variance–covariance matrix (Table 51.9). For example:

$$\rho_{AB}\sigma_A^1\sigma_B^1 = 10\% \times 25.515\% \times 21.794\% = 0.5561\%$$

The matrix format applies to the calculation of any portfolio loss volatility, as illustrated in Chapter 28. Here, we focus on a specific additional step allowing us to obtain the vector of risk contributions. The sequential steps are:

TABLE 51.9 'Unit exposure' variance–covariance matrix

6.5100%	0.5561%
0.5561%	4.7500%

- Multiplying the row vector of exposures X by the 'unit' variance–covariance matrix Σ results in a row vector of the unit covariances of individual obligors A and B with the portfolio loss, or 6.788 and 2.931. A sample calculation is as follows. The covariance of A with portfolio $P = A + B$, $\text{Cov}(A, P)$, depends only on unit covariances and on exposures: $\text{Cov}(A, P) = 100 \times 6.51\% \times 50 \times 0.5561\% = 6.788$. In order to find the risk contributions, we simply need to divide these by the portfolio loss volatility obtained in the next step.
- Multiplying this row vector by the transpose of X, we get the variance of the portfolio loss, 825.358, and the square root is the portfolio loss volatility 28.729.

TABLE 51.10 Calculations of portfolio loss variance and volatility and of absolute risk contributions

		Default correlation matrix		
		I	10.00%	
		10.00%	I	
		Variance–covariance matrix (unit exposure)		Transposed X^T vector
		6.5100%	0.5561%	100
		0.5561%	4.7500%	50
	X vector	σ_{AP}	σ_{BP}	Variance
100	50	6.788	2.931	825.358
		$X_A \times \sigma_{AP}^I$	$X_B \times \sigma_{BP}^I$	Variance
		679	147	825.358
		$X_A(\sigma_{AP}^I/\sigma_P)$	$X_B(\sigma_{BP}^I/\sigma_P)$	Volatility
ARC to LV (value)		23.628	5.101	28.729
(sum to portfolio loss volatility)				
		σ_{AP}/σ_P	σ_{BP}/σ_P	
ARC to LV (%)		82.24%	17.76%	100.00%

TABLE 51.11 The absolute risk contributions to loss volatility and capital

Multiple $m(1\%) = 3.15$	A	B	Portfolio
ARC to LV (value)	23.628	5.101	28.729
ARC to capital (value)	74.430	16.070	90.500

- Equivalently, we can directly calculate the covariance of each exposure with the portfolio by the multiplication of unit covariances by the exposure of the obligor, instead of using the entire vector X^T. For example $X_A \times \text{Cov}(A, P) = 100 \times 6.788 = 679$ is the covariance of obligor A with portfolio P. Similarly, $X_B \times \text{Cov}(B, P) = 50 \times 2.931 = 147$. Obviously, these two covariances add up to the same portfolio variance as before, 825.358.

- Dividing these covariances, 679 and 147, by the portfolio loss volatility, we obtain the absolute risk contributions of A and B in value, as a row vector, 23.628 and 5.101. They are $\text{ARC}_A^P = 679/28.729 = 23.628$ and $\text{ARC}_B^P = 147/28.729 = 5.101$.
- Summing these two absolute risk contributions in value, or $23.628 + 5.101$, gives the portfolio loss volatility 28.729.
- Using the absolute risk contributions as a percentage of the portfolio loss volatility, we obtain the capital allocation coefficients based on absolute risk contributions, or 82.24% and 17.76%.
- Finally, the absolute risk contributions to capital are directly derived from the absolute risk contributions to loss volatility using the multiple $m(1\%) = 3.15$, this multiple necessitates a knowledge of the entire loss distribution.

All risk calculations in matrix format are given in Table 51.10. Table 51.11 summarizes the capital allocation process.

52

Marginal Risk Contributions

This chapter focuses on marginal risk contributions, to portfolio loss volatility or to portfolio capital, and compares them with absolute risk contributions. Marginal risk contributions serve essentially for risk-based pricing with an 'ex ante' view of risk decisions, while absolute risk contributions are the basis for the capital allocation system.

They have a number of specific properties, some of them counterintuitive, which make them somewhat difficult to handle at first sight. The marginal risk contributions to the portfolio loss volatilities are lower than the absolute risk contributions and lower than the standalone loss volatilities. They also depend on the order of entrance of facilities or obligors in the portfolio. They sum to less than the capital, or to the portfolio loss volatility, since the absolute contributions, which are larger, do. Nevertheless, marginal risk contributions to capital are the correct references for risk-based pricing.

Pricing based on marginal risk contributions charges to customers a mark-up equal to the risk contribution times the target return on capital. The mark-up guarantees that the return on capital for the entire portfolio will remain in line with the target return when adding new facilities. However, prices based on marginal risk contributions are lower than prices based on absolute risk contributions. This is a paradox, since the absolute risk contributions are the ones that sum to capital! In fact, the new facility diversifies the risk of those facilities existing prior to entrance of the new one. Therefore, adding a new facility results in a decline in all absolute risk contributions of existing facilities. Because of this decline, the overall return of the portfolio remains on target. However, the ex ante measure of risk-based performance, on the marginal contribution, and the ex post measure, on the absolute contribution, differ for the same facility!

The first section defines marginal and absolute risk contributions, illustrates their calculation using sample calculations based on the simple two-obligor portfolio, and summarizes the properties of risk contributions. The second section demonstrates the relationship, and the ranking, between marginal and absolute risk contributions. The third section deals with marginal risk contributions and risk-based pricing, and addresses the 'pricing paradox'. The last section contrasts the implicit underlying philosophies of absolute versus marginal risk contributions, or the 'ex post' view versus the 'ex ante' view.

THE MARGINAL RISK CONTRIBUTIONS

The marginal contributions of a facility, or a subportfolio, to the portfolio loss volatility or to capital are the differences of the portfolio loss volatility, or the portfolio capital, with and without the facility or subportfolio. We calculate below both marginal risk contributions (MRC) to loss volatility and to capital. All calculations use the example of a two-obligor (A and B) portfolio is in the previous chapter (and Chapter 46). They assume that B is the last transaction entered in the portfolio. Its marginal risk contribution is the difference between the loss volatility, and the capital, of the portfolio $A + B$ and the similar values for A only.

Marginal Contributions to Loss Volatility

The marginal contribution of B to the portfolio loss volatility is the latter minus the loss volatility of A, or $28.73 - 25.51 = 3.21$. The marginal risk contribution of A is determined in the same way, $28.73 - 10.90 = 17.83$. The sum of these marginal risk contributions is 21.05, significantly less than the portfolio loss volatility. Table 52.1 compares standalone risk, absolute risk contributions and marginal contributions.

TABLE 52.1   Risk measures for individual obligors and for the portfolio

	A	B	Portfolio	Sum
Loss volatility LV_i	25.515	10.897	28.729	36.412
ARC to loss volatility	23.628	5.101	28.729	28.729
MRC (to loss volatility LV^P)	17.832	3.214	—	21.046

We observe that:

$$\text{MRC}(LV^P) < \text{ARC}(LV^P) < \text{standalone risk}$$

Using A's data for example:

$$17.83 < 23.63 < 25.51$$

The Marginal Risk Contributions to Capital

The portfolio distribution is a prerequisite for defining capital and its relation to loss volatility. Capital derives from the loss distributions and the loss percentiles at various confidence levels. In the preceding chapter, we used the portfolio loss percentile $L(1\%) = 100$. Capital is the loss percentile in excess of expected loss totalling 9.5, or $100 - 9.5 = 90.5$. A second calculation at the 0.5% confidence level results in a maximum portfolio loss of 150 and a capital of $150 - 9.5 = 140.5$.

Marginal contributions to capital require a two-step procedure, since we need to define the 'first-in' obligor. The first-in obligor in the two-obligor portfolio has a capital identical to his marginal risk contribution to capital by definition, following the 'with versus without' principle. When the second-in obligor comes in, his marginal capital contribution follows the 'with and without the second-in' rule. It is the portfolio capital minus the initial capital used up by the first-in obligor. Therefore, marginal risk contributions to capital depend on the order of entrance of a particular obligor into the portfolio, since each obligor has a different 'first-in' marginal risk contribution to capital.

The first calculation uses a 1% confidence level, leading to a loss percentile of 100 for the portfolio A + B and a capital of $100 - 9.5 = 90.5$. A second calculation at a 0.5% confidence level would result in a maximum portfolio loss of 150 and a capital of $150 - 9.5 = 140.5$.

Marginal Risk Contributions to Capital at 1% of A and B

When A only is in the portfolio, the confidence level of 1% is lower than the standalone default probability of A, which is 7%. Therefore, the loss percentile at 1% is 100 and the expected loss is 7, so that capital at 2% is $100.0 - 7.0 = 93.0$. Adding B raises the portfolio capital to 90.5. Hence the marginal contribution to capital of B is $90.5 - 93.0 = -2.5$. The diversification effect makes the incremental contribution of B negative. This non-intuitive result depends on the magnitudes of exposures and expected losses.

Economically, negative marginal risk contributions to capital do make sense. This does not happen with contributions to the loss volatility. First, absolute risk contributions to loss volatility and capital are never negative. Second, marginal contributions to loss volatility are always positive because any new incremental exposure increases the loss volatility unless the correlations with the portfolio are negative. This case applies to insurances or credit derivatives.

If we start with B as the 'first-in' exposure, the capital at the 1% confidence level is the entire exposure of B, whose default probability 5% is higher, minus its expected loss, or $50 - 2.5 = 47.5$. When adding A to B, we reach the capital level of 90.5, resulting in an incremental risk contribution of A of 43.0. This sequential process implies that marginal risk contributions to capital always sum to the capital of the portfolio grouping all exposures, by definition. Table 52.2 summarizes the calculations.

Marginal Risk Contributions to Capital at 0.5% of A and B

For comparison purposes, we conduct similar calculations following exactly the same two-step procedure, with a tighter confidence level of 0.5% and a capital in excess of expected loss 9.5 equal to $150 - 9.5 = 140.5$. Accordingly, all marginal risk contributions to capital increase, and they sum to the capital. However, in this second example, none is negative, whatever the first-in (Table 52.3).

With a very tight confidence level, A and B have positive marginal risk contribution to capital no matter which enters first in the portfolio. The first-in marginal risk contributions of A and B are 93 and 47.5 respectively. In addition, in this case, the marginal capital contributions are identical for a first entrant or a second entrant. For instance, A has 93 when first-in and 93 when second-in as well. The same happens to B. This illustrates

TABLE 52.2 Marginal risk contributions to loss percentiles (confidence level 2%)

	A	B	Portfolio
EL_i and EL_P	7	2.5	9.5
Loss volatility LV_i and LV_P	25.515	10.897	28.729
Confidence level α	1%		
Capital	90.50		
Multiple of loss volatility	3.150		
ARC (to LV^P)	23.628	5.101	28.729
ARC (to LV^P) (%)	82.24%	17.76%	
ARC (to K)	74.431	16.069	90.500
MRC	MRC (first-in)	MRC (second-in)	Total
A then B	93.0	−2.5	90.5
B then A	47.5	43.0	90.5

TABLE 52.3 Marginal risk contributions to loss percentiles (confidence level 0.5%)

	A	B	Portfolio
EL_i and EL_P	7	2.5	9.5
Loss volatility LV_i and LV_P	25.515	10.897	28.729
α	0.50%		
Capital	140.50		
Multiple of loss volatility	4.891		
ARC (to LV^P)	23.628	5.101	28.729
ARC (to LV^P) (%)	82.24%	17.76%	
ARC (to K)	115.553	24.947	140.500
MRC	MRC (first-in)	MRC (second-in)	Total
A then B	93.0	47.5	140.5
B then A	47.5	93.0	140.5

why marginal risk contributions to capital are difficult to tackle, because of unexpected or non-intuitive effects.

General Properties of Marginal Risk Contributions

General properties of marginal risk contributions include:

- The marginal risk contributions to the portfolio loss volatility are lower than the absolute risk contributions and lower than the standalone loss volatilities. Accordingly, marginal risk contributions to portfolio loss volatility add up to a value lower than the portfolio loss volatility. The subsequent sections demonstrate that these properties are general.

- On the other hand, marginal risk contributions to portfolio capital can be higher or lower than absolute risk contributions to capital (derived from absolute risk contributions to volatility). In addition, they add up to portfolio capital if we calculate sequentially the marginal risk contributions of each obligor when he enters the portfolio.

The calculation of marginal contributions to capital in excess of expected loss suggests several observations:

- The marginal risk contributions to capital calculated following the two-step procedure are additive. They sum up by construction to the portfolio capital, and this sum is algebraic (negative incremental risk contributions are possible). This contrasts with the finding that the sum of marginal contributions to the portfolio loss volatility is always lower than, or at most equal to, the portfolio loss volatility.
- The marginal contributions to the portfolio capital can be positive or negative. This depends on the shape of the distribution and on the confidence level selected.
- The marginal contributions to the portfolio capital can be bigger or smaller than the absolute risk contributions to capital. This depends also on the shape of the distribution and the confidence level. This finding contrasts with the property that marginal contributions to loss volatility are always lower than the absolute risk contributions.
- The marginal risk contributions of the first entrant and of the second entrant depend on who is first and who is second, and on the confidence level.

Such properties are non-intuitive. They become apparent here because we use a two-obligor portfolio, and because individual exposures are large compared to total exposure. In real cases, the exposures are very small fractions of the portfolio exposure, and we do not have such drastic concentration effects. Considering these observations, the most representative case is the second one, with a tight confidence level of 0.5% making both A's and B's incremental risk contributions positive.

Implications

The discrepancies between absolute and marginal risk contributions and between contributions to loss volatility and capital raise important issues. These include: risk-based pricing (ex ante decision); risk-based performance, once facilities are in the portfolio (ex post measure); consistency of capital allocation rules with pricing rules. The question is which risk contributions should we use and for what purposes?

For example, when considering risk-based pricing, choosing the right measure of risk contribution is critical. Risk-based pricing means that revenues net of expected loss are at least a minimum percentage of capital. This constraint sometimes has unexpected implications. The negative incremental risk contribution of B in the first case above (capital at 1% confidence level) implies that we can afford negative revenues since we save capital thanks to B. All risk-based performance measures and risk-based pricing implications use the same example as above.

In the next sections, *we refer only to marginal risk contributions to loss volatility.* The discussion of risk contributions to loss volatilities stems from the fact that many transactions are small compared to the reference portfolio and that it is acceptable to use a constant ratio of capital to portfolio loss volatility. Therefore, the marginal risk contributions to capital are always positive, unless we use credit derivatives, which are like negative exposures.

MARGINAL RISK CONTRIBUTIONS TO VOLATILITY VERSUS ABSOLUTE RISK CONTRIBUTIONS TO VOLATILITY

Marginal risk contributions are relevant for such decisions as adding or removing a subportfolio, or pricing a new transaction according to its incremental risk. As with absolute risk contributions, marginal risk contributions refer either to capital or to loss volatility.

With small portfolios, as above, there is no mechanical link between absolute and marginal risk contributions. On the other hand, with large portfolios, the absolute risk contributions to volatility and to capital might proxy marginal risk contributions. The distinction deserves attention because vendors' models provide different outputs in terms of risk contributions. KMV Portfolio Manager calculates absolute risk contributions, while Credit Metrics calculates marginal risk contributions. Since the diversification of banks' portfolios is important, chances are that these measures get close. It is helpful to identify these cases since the calculation of absolute risk contributions, to loss volatility and to capital, is immediate when the loss distribution is available. On the other hand, recalculating the marginal contributions to capital requires repeated and tedious 'with and without' simulations.

Relation between the Marginal and Absolute Risk Contributions

Marginal risk contribution to volatility MRC_a is the difference in loss volatility of the portfolio with and without the facility f. We need a superscript, P or $P + f$, to specify risk contributions because the portfolio changes from P to $P + f$. Nevertheless, the starting point is the existing portfolio P. By definition of MRC_f:

$$MRC_f = \sigma_{P+f} - \sigma_P$$

Also, since all risk contributions within portfolio $P + f$ are additive and sum to the loss volatility of $P + f$:

$$\sigma_{P+f} = ARC_P^{P+f} + ARC_f^{P+f}$$

An important issue is to compare MRC_f to ARC_f^{P+f} since both might serve, a priori, either for capital allocation purposes or for risk-adjusting performance, or both. Combining the above formulas, we see that:

$$MRC_f = ARC_f^{P+f} + [ARC_P^{P+f} - \sigma_P]$$

By definition, ARC_P^{P+f} is lower than σ_P since P is diversified within a portfolio $P + f$ bigger than P alone:

$$ARC_P^{P+f} \leq \sigma_P$$

Marginal versus Absolute Risk Contribution for a New Facility

In the expression of MRC_f, the term in brackets is negative, or exceptionally zero. In general, this implies that the marginal risk contribution MRC_f of facility f is lower than the absolute risk contribution of the facility f, ARC_f^{P+f}, within $P + f$. Another inequality, $\mathrm{ARC}_f^{P+f} \leq \sigma_f$, is obvious given the definition of ARC_f^{P+f}: the standalone loss volatility of facility f is always larger than its risk contribution because the latter is post-diversification effects[1].

Combining both results, we find the general conclusion that the marginal risk contribution to loss volatility is lower than the absolute risk contribution, which is also lower than the standalone loss volatility:

$$\mathrm{MRC}_f < \mathrm{ARC}_f^{P+f} < \sigma_f$$

From the above calculation of MRC_f, the difference between MRC_f and ARC_f^{P+f} is $(\mathrm{ARC}_P^{P+f} - \sigma_P)$, which is negative, so that the gap between absolute and marginal risk contribution is positive and equal to:

$$\mathrm{ARC}_f^{P+f} - \mathrm{MRC}_f = \sigma_P - \mathrm{ARC}_P^{P+f}$$

This difference is the gap between the portfolio loss volatility *before* the addition of facility f and the risk contribution of facility f once it is included in P to make up $P + f$.

Implications

The implications of the above formulations are:

- When the additional facility is small compared to the portfolio, chances are that the gap between the marginal and the absolute risk contribution to loss volatility gets small. This would happen whenever we can consider that $[\mathrm{ARC}_P^{P+f} - \sigma_P]$ is small. This is the case when P and $P + f$ are similar.
- Capital allocation and risk-based performance using absolute risk contributions cannot be equivalent to using marginal risk contributions. Both are useful, and we need to further specify the usage of each of these measures.
- When we add a facility to an existing portfolio, we have two effects. The absolute risk contribution of the new facility, or ARC_f^{P+f}, is positive, which increases the portfolio loss volatility. Simultaneously, the second term, or $[\mathrm{ARC}_P^{P+f} - \sigma_P]$, is negative, which contributes to decrease the portfolio loss volatility.

The interpretation of the last observation is that all existing facilities, before the introduction of the new one, have lower absolute risk contributions because of diversification within a larger portfolio than before the introduction.

---

[1] This is intuitive. We skip a formal demonstration of this inequality resulting from the calculations of covariances and comparisons with variances.

KMV Portfolio Manager provides covariance-based absolute risk contributions to loss volatilities and to capital within a given portfolio. Calculating a marginal risk contribution implies conducting 'with and without' calculations to see the impact on portfolio loss volatility and capital if these differ significantly (the new subportfolio is not a small fraction of the existing portfolio). Credit Metrics provides directly the marginal risk contributions, considering that we can add or remove any facility from the portfolio.

MARGINAL RISK CONTRIBUTIONS AND PRICING

The goal of risk-based pricing is to ensure a minimum target return on capital, in line with shareholders' requirements. A hurdle rate serves as a benchmark for risk-based pricing and for calculating creation or destruction of value with 'Shareholders Value Added' (SVA). It is the target rate of return on existing equity, or the target return on economic capital. Moreover, if the average risk-adjusted return of the portfolio is higher than the minimum, it makes sense to set the hurdle rate at this level.

Risk-based Pricing Requires Marginal Risk Contribution

The existing portfolio is P. Economic capital is a multiple of σ_P, or $m \times \sigma_P$, and m is supposed to be constant. The required pre-tax pre-operating expense return is $r\%$. The target revenue is $r\% \times m \times \sigma_P$. A portfolio has a loss volatility of 100. The multiple capital/loss volatility is 2. The hurdle rate is 25% pre-tax and pre-operating expense. The target net revenue is $25\% \times 2 \times 100 = 50$. A new transaction increases the portfolio loss volatility to 110. The marginal risk contribution to loss volatility of this additional new transaction is 10, and the approximate new capital of this transaction is $2 \times 10 = 20$. The target pre-tax net income on the new portfolio becomes $25\% \times 220 = 55$. This is an increase of $55 - 50 = 5$. This increase is exactly $25\% \times (220 - 200) = 5$. Pricing on a different basis than marginal risk contribution will not maintain the portfolio return.

General Formulation

We use the previous notation. The initial portfolio is P and it becomes $P + f$, f being the new transaction. By definition, $\mathrm{MRC}_f = \sigma_{P+f} - \sigma_P$. What should be the return required for the additional facility f? The hurdle rate is $k\%$ on the capital of the existing portfolio. We assume that capital K is a constant multiple m of the loss volatility with $K = m \times \sigma_P$.

We assume that the existing portfolio provides exactly r, and we look for the minimum return r_f on the new facility f guaranteeing that the return of the portfolio $P + f$ will remain at (at least) $k\%$. The required income in value is $k\% \times m \times \sigma_{P+f}$. The return without the new facility is $k\% \times m \times \sigma_P$. The required return on the new facility $r_f\%$ is such that the return on the portfolio $P + f$, summing the income on the existing portfolio plus the income on the new facility, is $k\% \times m \times \sigma_{P+f}$:

$$k\% \times m \times \sigma_P + r_f\% \times m \times (\sigma_{P+f} - \sigma_P) \geq k\% \times m \times \sigma_{P+f}$$

Dropping the multiple m implies that $r_f\% \geq k\%$. Consequently, the rule is that the risk-adjusted return on marginal risk contribution to volatility, with a constant multiple m, should be at least $k\%$. The implications are:

- The relevant basis for risk-based pricing is the marginal risk contribution to loss volatility.
- Since the absolute risk contribution ARC to the loss volatility is higher, pricing on ARC would overestimate the required revenue. ARC is not the right risk measure for pricing purposes.

The assumption of a constant multiple m is acceptable subject to the size of the facility and its correlation with the rest of the portfolio. New facilities are generally small compared to the size of the portfolio. However, the assumption collapses when considering adding or removing risk concentrations, such as subportfolios, business lines or even single large concentrations of risk. Then, we need to revert to a direct 'with and without' calculation of the marginal risk contribution to capital.

The Pricing Paradox with Risk Contributions

The usage of MRC lower than ARC for pricing purposes sounds puzzling at first. It means that MRC-based pricing is lower than ARC-based pricing. This does not sound consistent with an overall target return on capital, because capital sums up all ARC and not all MRC! This is the pricing paradox of using marginal, rather than absolute, risk contributions.

An example will help us to understand the paradox. Suppose the marginal risk contribution to capital is 15 and the required rate is 20%, resulting in a target income of $20\% \times 15 = 3$. When the facility enters into the portfolio, it has a new absolute risk contribution, for instance 17, higher than its marginal risk contribution of 15. The revenue of 3 does not provide any more than 20% on 17. How could the revenue of 3 maintain the overall portfolio return?

In fact, 3 is the additional revenue required to compensate the overall portfolio capital after inclusion of the new facility. Using fictitious numbers, suppose that all absolute risk contributions *before* including the new facility sum to 100. After inclusion of the new facility, all absolute risk contributions sum to 115, since the MRC, 15, is the incremental overall capital. If the new facility now has an ARC of 17, this implies that the sum of all absolute risk contributions over all facilities existing *before* the inclusion of the new one drops from 100 to 98. This is the only way for the new capital to be 115, given that the incremental capital is 17, since $98 + 17 = 115$. The new facility increases the overall risk incrementally, but simultaneously diversifies the existing risks. This solves the pricing puzzle. Pricing according to the absolute risk contribution of the new facility ignores the fact that all other absolute risk contributions of existing facilities decrease. On the other hand, pricing on marginal risk contribution captures both the incremental risk and the increased diversification or, equivalently, the decrease in all existing facility absolute risk contributions.

CAPITAL ALLOCATION VIEW VERSUS PRICING VIEW

The implication of what precedes is that we need both risk contributions, but for different purposes. Absolute risk contributions are ex post measures. They measure risk contributions for a given set of facilities. Therefore, absolute risk contributions serve to allocate capital for an existing portfolio. Marginal risk contributions are ex ante measures and serve for risk-based pricing.

Ex Ante versus Ex Post Views of Risk and Return

Ex ante marginal risk contributions are adequate for risk-based pricing of new facilities. However, once included in a portfolio, the return of new facilities on their allocated capital becomes lower than the target return obtained on the marginal risk contribution at the pricing time. This is not relevant since all other facility returns over their absolute risk contributions improve because of the dilution of these existing absolute risk contributions within an increasingly diversified portfolio. Therefore:

- Absolute risk contributions serve to allocate capital to existing facilities and to set up limits. This allows us to allocate capital in such a way that all capital allocations sum to the portfolio capital. In addition, limits for an existing portfolio can be set in terms of capital, and compared to the capital usage of each subportfolio.
- Marginal contributions serve for pricing. Marginal risk contributions ensure that the portfolio return remains at least at the target level.

See Figure 52.1.

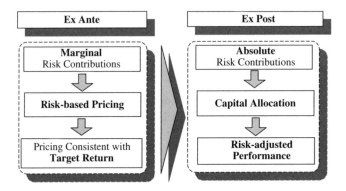

FIGURE 52.1   Ex ante and ex post views on risk contributions and revenues

Capital Allocation

As long as the capital is a multiple of the portfolio loss volatility, allocating the loss volatility provides an allocation proportional to capital. Let capital be $m \times \sigma_P$. Then, if the ARC_i^P are the basis for capital allocation, the sum of all ARC_i^P will be the aggregated loss volatility, and $m \times \mathrm{ARC}_i^P$ will be the capital allocation to facility i. Since all ARC_i^P are additive, they aggregate for any subgroup of facilities, by customer, business units or any other criteria. Since all ARC_i^P are post-diversification effects, they embed more information than the allocation according to the facility standalone risks, which do not include the correlation structure of facilities.

However, it is always possible to allocate capital at the pro rata of exposures, or of standalone risks measured by the standalone loss volatilities. This is a management choice of an appropriate allocation key depending on the trade-off between ease of interpretation and the need to capture differentiated correlation effects.

Risk-adjusted Performance versus Risk-based Pricing

This discussion of risk contributions relates to the distinction between the ex ante measure of risk required to meet a target return on capital, and the ex post risk-based performance using given revenues. Once a facility enters the portfolio, its ex post return, on its allocated capital, drops, compared to the ex ante pricing based on marginal contributions. This phenomenon results from an absolute risk contribution of the new facility higher than the ex ante marginal risk contribution. Nevertheless, the ex post risk-based performances using absolute risk contributions remain necessary for comparing ex post the risk–return profiles of facilities, clients, products and business units.

Without risk-based pricing, we do not know the required revenues. Without ex post risk-adjusted performances based on absolute risk contributions, we cannot compare the risk–return profiles of facilities or subportfolios. Hence, both are necessary because they serve different purposes.

These issues require further developments regarding: the target rate of return on capital for ex ante pricing; the ex post monitoring of risk-adjusted performance; mispricing, defined as the discrepancy between the theoretical target price and the effective price given competition. Chapters 53 and 54 discuss further the ex ante view of the determination of target revenues with risk-based pricing using marginal risk contributions to capital and the ex post view of risk-adjusted performances once revenues are given.

SECTION 16

Risk-adjusted Performance

53

Risk-adjusted Performance

In the financial universe, there is no expected performance without a price to pay in terms of risk. Since only risk–return combinations are meaningful, comparing performances across transactions or business units is inconsistent, and pricing risk to customers without risk adjustment is not feasible. The entire risk–return monitoring and pricing systems depend on such risk adjustments.

Ex post, Risk-Adjusted Performance Measurement (RAPM) serves for comparisons. Ex ante, Risk-Based Pricing (RBP) serves for determining a pricing in line with risk and with the overall profitability goal of the bank. In the first case, income is given, whereas the purpose of RBP is to define what is its minimum level. The risk adjustments are the risk contributions.

Because risk contributions do not depend on the source of risk, market or credit risk, risk-adjusted performance calculations do not either. The same calculations apply to both market and credit risk contributions and performances.

The standard measures of risk-adjusted performance are the 'Risk-adjusted Return on Capital' (RaRoC) and 'Shareholders Value Added' (SVA) (see Bennett, 1991). The first RaRoC ratio is a profitability percentage comparable to minimum risk-adjusted benchmarks, or hurdle rates. The SVA is a value, which combines both percentage profitability and size of transactions, to find whether a transaction or a subportfolio creates or destroys value for shareholders. Both serve in conjunction. The ratio ignores the size effect, so that we do not know whether a transaction with a RaRoC close to the hurdle rate generates much income or not without looking at its size. A high SVA figure does not indicate whether it results from a low percentage RaRoC combined with a large size and vice versa.

Risk adjustments use both expected loss and economic capital allocation. A RaRoC measure nets the expected loss from income and divides the netted income by economic capital. SVA measures net the expected loss plus the cost of economic capital, valued as a hurdle rate times the amount of capital, from income. The reference for the hurdle rate is the cost of capital of the bank.

The hurdle rate, or cost of equity for the bank, is the unit price of risk of each specific bank. This 'price of risk' raises practical and conceptual issues. Market spreads for banks and loans are not in line with the capital charge allocated by banks to transactions and their required return, except by chance. Market spreads are a common reference for all players, while the risk contributions and the cost of equity vary across banks. The risk contributions change because the portfolio structures of banks differ. The cost of equity also changes because the market compensates equity based on the 'general' risk of the banks' equity stocks, the β, as the well-known Capital Asset Pricing Model (CAPM) demonstrates.

This chapter defines the risk-based performance measures and discusses their required inputs. The next chapter provides numerical examples illustrating these definitions. The first section discusses the two basic risk-adjusted performance measures, RaRoC and SVA, their inputs and relative merits. The second section discusses the revenue and cost inputs for determining income. The third section addresses the definition of the hurdle rate, or the 'price of risk', referring to the market cost of equity. The last section discusses the consistency issue between the bank's price of risk versus the market's price of risk, as observed in credit spreads, and its implications.

PROFITABILITY MEASURES

Classical profitability measures include the Return On Equity (ROE) and the Return On Assets (ROA). Risk-based profitability measures embed risk adjustment combining expected loss and economic capital.

Economic Capital

Risk-based measures require quantified risk measures. For credit risk, the risk measures are economic capital and expected loss. Both serve for the banking transactions, at the portfolio level, for any subportfolio, using the risk contribution as the capital base, and for any facility, using also the risk contribution as the capital base. For market risk, capital only is relevant, globally, or allocated to subportfolios or facilities through risk contributions. Both market risk capital and credit risk capital for market transactions serve to adjust Profit and Loss (P&L) for risk.

Using regulatory capital for risk-adjusting measures also makes sense. However, as long as regulatory forfeits do not sufficiently differentiate the risk and are not in line with economic capital, using the regulatory capital results in mispricing risks, which is a competitive 'disadvantage'. Regulatory forfeits are progressively enriched, step-by-step, by regulators. The old forfeits (before the January 2001 guidelines) consider private small business risk as equivalent to the risk of AAA large corporations, which falls short of the essential requirements of RAPM and RBP. However, whatever the regulatory scheme, banks have to meet regulatory capital definitions. Therefore, they still have to obtain a sufficient return on this capital and keep monitoring its cost for transactions and portfolios.

We focus on economic capital as a prerequisite for risk-adjusted measures. Technically, however, the regulatory capital-adjusted measures RaRoC and SVA are easy to obtain by simply substituting regulatory capital for economic capital in the same formulas, so that there is no difficulty in calculating both.

RaRoC Measures

The two basic variants for risk-adjusted ratios are the 'Return on Risk-adjusted Capital' (RoRaC) or RaRoC. The RoRaC is a profitability calculated on risk-based capital. RaRoC adjusts first the return for risk by netting expected loss from income for banking transactions. Both adjustments are necessary for banking transactions, and adjustment for capital only suffices for market transactions. In the following, RaRoC is the generic name for the return on risk-based capital.

We discuss the credit risk case, given that only capital without Expected Loss (EL) adjustment suffices for market risk. The RaRoC ratio adjusts the earnings with EL and uses risk contributions as economic capital. The revenues are the All-In Spread (AIS), which averages all interest revenues and fees into an annualized average. The formula applies both pre-operating costs and post-operating costs:

$$RaRoC = [AIS - EL]/economic\ capital$$

Economic capital is the portfolio capital for the entire portfolio and is the capital allocation, or risk contribution, for subportfolios or facilities. There are two risk contributions, absolute and marginal, each corresponding respectively to ex post measures and ex ante measures. At this stage, we simply use risk contributions, given that we have to use the right one depending on the purpose of the measure:

$$RaRoC = [AIS - EL]/RC(K)$$

where $RC(K)$ is the risk contribution of a facility or subportfolio to the capital K. When considering that the capital allocation $RC(K)$ provides a risk-free return $y_f \times RC(K)$, it should be included in the revenues.

The usage of RaRoC implies the definition of a hurdle rate, $k\%$, which is the minimum risk-adjusted return on a transaction. The EL netted from revenues has different interpretations depending on whether it applies to individual transactions or to portfolios of transactions. For an individual transaction, the EL concept looks theoretical since the loss will either occur or not. In any case, the loss is never equal to the EL, since the actual loss is either zero or the loss given default. For portfolios, EL has a statistical meaning because setting aside a fraction of revenues of all transactions will, after consolidation, result in a sufficient provision for meeting the overall EL requirement (estimated on an ex ante basis).

The fully developed analytical formulas use the following notation:

- Exposure A.
- Asset all-in return r (%).
- Cost of debt i. This cost includes any credit spread applicable to the bank.
- Allocated debt D.
- Operating costs oc (%).
- Expected loss el (%).
- Allocated capital $RC(K) = K$.

- Hurdle rate $k\%$.
- Required rate on capital 20%.

$$\mathrm{RaRoC} = [r \times A - i \times D - \mathrm{el} \times A - \mathrm{oc} \times A]/K$$

Since $A = D + K$, the formula simplifies when dividing by the asset value:

$$\mathrm{RaRoC} = (A/K) \times (r - \mathrm{el} - \mathrm{oc}) - i \times (D/K)$$

$$\mathrm{RaRoC} = i + (A/K) \times (r - i - \mathrm{el} - \mathrm{oc})$$

This shows that the RaRoC is the excess over the cost of debt of the AIS minus the cost of expected loss and operating costs and multiplied by the ratio of assets to capital. This equation serves notably for determining the target customer rate, or spread above the all-in cost of funds, making the RaRoC of the new transaction at least equal to the target return on capital $k\%$.

SVA Measures

The SVA is a value measure. SVA adjusts the revenues with expected loss, then with operating costs, and finally with the cost of unexpected loss, which is the cost of the required risk-based capital, equal to the above hurdle rate:

$$\mathrm{SVA} = \mathrm{earnings} - \mathrm{EL} - k\% \times \mathrm{capital}$$

By definition, when the RaRoC is above the hurdle rate, the SVA is positive, and conversely. However, using both of them improves the reporting by providing both percentage profitability and volume. The SVA is equal to:

$$r \times A - i \times D \geq \mathrm{el} \times A + \mathrm{oc} \times A + k\% \times K$$

The Hurdle Rate

The hurdle rate $k\%$ is the minimum required return as a percentage. There are two important benchmarks for setting this hurdle rate:

- The required return on capital, since this is a shareholder target that indicates whether a particular transaction creates or destroys value.
- The mean return of the bank portfolio, because it is important to know whether a transaction of a subportfolio improves or deteriorates this average.

The first benchmark derives from the price of risk in the capital market from well-known equity return models. It is the return $k\%$ required by shareholders given the risk of the stock as measured by the beta of the bank's stocks, following the CAPM framework or the Arbitrage Pricing Theory (APT) framework. An order of magnitude of such a return is 20–25% before tax. This benchmark applies to revenues net of all operating costs. If revenues are pre-operating costs, the benchmark is higher since it should provide the revenues required to absorb all unallocated costs in addition to providing the required pre-tax income to shareholders. The next section illustrates the simple adjustment required to determine revenues, given the post-operating cost hurdle rate and the non-allocated costs.

RaRoC and SVA

For decision-making purposes and to compare performance to a hurdle rate, RaRoC and SVA are equivalent. By definition, RaRoC $\geq k\%$ is equivalent to SVA at $k\% > 0$. However, they provide different pictures of business volume, risk-free and low-profitability transactions.

Business Volume

A drawback of ratios is that they do not account for size. It is nice to have a RaRoC of 50% with a transaction of 1 million euros. However, it is even nicer if the transaction size is 10 million euros. In order to improve an overall profitability rate, it is always possible to eliminate those transactions that are less profitable and to keep only the rest. In such cases, the portfolio profitability increases at the expense of the volume of business. Since both business volume and profitability are desirable, SVA measures might look appropriate, but they do not provide the percentage profitability, so we cannot tell whether a high SVA results from a large size or from a large percentage profitability.

This is a business issue. If there is a permissible trade-off between percentage profitability and volume, it makes sense to aggregate transactions. For instance, we can have a low RaRoC loan to a customer because it attracts new business later on. Each individual transaction with a customer might not be profitable, once it is risk-adjusted. But all of them might. Client-driven revenues are more relevant than transaction-driven revenues. Therefore client-based profitability is as necessary as transaction-based profitability. This applies also for any business policy aimed at gaining market share. However, this shows that improper usage of risk-adjusted measures could lead to rejecting profitable transactions because of a pure transaction-based reporting.

Risk-free Transactions

A well-known drawback of RaRoC is that the ratio can take very high values for close to zero risk, such as with Aaa counterparties. In addition, it increases to infinity with risk-free transactions. This is more a reporting drawback than a conceptual flaw. It is normal for non-risky borrowers not to consume any capital. RaRoC has no value added in this case. This does not mean that a relevant target pricing is undefined. When capital drops to zero, the risk premium is zero, and the target revenues should still absorb the operating costs, plus the cost of debt, plus any mark-up. Nevertheless, very high RaRoC, infinite ratios or negative ratios appearing in reports create confusion. SVA does not have this flaw. If risk is zero, the SVA equals revenues, pre- or post-operating costs, without deduction of any cost of risk, and remains meaningful. In addition, a negative SVA is also meaningful, while a negative RaRoC is not. The negative SVA means that the business destroys value for shareholders and tells us how much.

Netting EL from Revenues and RaRoC

RaRoC ratios can be negative when revenues do not absorb costs plus expected loss EL. A partial remedy would be to include EL in capital, instead of using capital in excess of EL. This means that capital should absorb both expected and unexpected losses. SVA does not have these drawbacks and is always meaningful. If capital drops to zero because the transaction is risk-free, both EL and cost of capital in the SVA calculations drop to zero, but the other terms remain relevant.

REVENUES AND COSTS

The revenues include the interest margin plus fees. The operating costs allocated to a transaction or portfolios include direct costs and overheads. In addition revenues, costs and risk should relate to the same perimeter. If risk is client-based, there is a case for consolidating all revenues and costs over the client portfolios.

Revenues and Operating Costs

For credit risk, revenues include the interest margin, plus any upfront and recurring fees. The total is the overall revenue generated by a transaction. It is an AIS because it includes all revenues. The upfront fee increases the margin during the early life of the transaction. This makes the AIS higher in the early stages and lower in the later stages. To avoid such distortion, a simple solution is to calculate the average AIS over the life of the transaction to obtain an annualized AIS in value or as a percentage of exposure. For market risk, revenues are the P&L of the period.

To analyse the profitability of a given transaction, or of a product line, it is necessary to allocate costs. The minimum required return depends on which cost allocations are feasible. Revenues should contribute to absorbing direct and fixed operating costs, before obtaining the net required return on capital.

Allocating Costs and Hurdle Rate

If the hurdle rate after operating cost allocation is $k\% = 20\%$, and if the cost allocation to a transaction is 100:

$$\text{Revenues} \geq \text{cost allocation} + k\% \times \text{capital} = 100 + 20\% \times \text{capital}$$

The minimum return based on interest revenues and costs plus fees is higher than 25% in order to absorb the 100 operating cost. If allocating direct costs only is feasible, the minimum required rate remains above 20%, but by a lower amount. For instance, if 50, out of the 100, are direct costs, the minimum profitability should be such that:

$$\text{Revenues} - \text{direct costs} - \text{fixed costs allocation} \geq 20\% \times \text{capital}$$

$$\text{Revenues} - \text{direct costs} \geq 50 + 20\% \times \text{capital}$$

Revenues can be pre- or post-operating costs, depending on whether costs can be allocated without too much distortion because of indirect costs. The minimum benchmark of the ratio differs, to make it consistent with a post-operating cost income target. Finding this benchmark is easy since the capital base is defined. Let's assume that the capital base is

40, so that the pre-tax income is $20\% \times 40 = 8$. Under no allocation of operating costs, it does not make sense to set the target revenues at 8 because there is still a 100 operating cost to absorb. The target revenue should be $100 + 8 = 108$. If this revenue results from a 1000 loan, the required yield, or ROA%, is $108/1000 = 10.8\%$. Therefore, it is easy to adjust the benchmark rate as long as we know the capital base and the unallocated costs.

Client versus Transaction Revenues

Some revenues are independent of exposure or usage of individual credit lines by borrowers. They include the revenues from services and money transfers, which relate to the number of transactions for instance. This is an important consideration for risk-adjusting profitability. Relevant perimeters for calculating the risk adjustment are the client portfolio or other aggregates such as the business unit portfolios. For consistency, the same perimeter should apply to revenues.

The reason for using clients as a reference for consolidating revenues is that individual facility spreads often do not generate a RaRoC in line with target bank risk-adjusted profitability. Market spreads of large corporates do not compensate the bank's risk, although that depends on country and geographic areas. In Europe, typical spreads to large and low risk corporates in the bond market are in the 10 to 20 basis point range, and substantially higher for small businesses. With such values, it is impossible to get a significant RaRoC.

For example, the market spread on a 1000 loan is 0.2%, while the required capital is $4\% \times 1000 = 40$. The capital-based income should be $20\% \times 40 = 8$, or 0.8% of the book value. It is much higher than the market spread over the risk-free rate, that is 0.2%. There is an implied capital in the market spread that would earn the target return. It is equal to the ratio of the given spread, $0.2\% \times 1000 = 2$, to 20%, or $2/20\% = 10$. This technique allows us to tabulate, by spread level and risk class, the implied capital in market spreads and to measure the gap between the implied and the economic capital.

The example illustrates the discrepancy between market price of risk and internal price of risk. It also suggests having client-based revenues as well as transaction-based revenues for reporting purposes to make the risk-adjusted measures meaningful. The picture changes drastically when aggregating all revenues, fees and spreads, over all facilities and services to single customers. Fees increase substantially the profitability and represent an increasing fraction of revenues. Client RaRoC or client SVA probably provide a more relevant image than single facility spreads, RaRoC or SVA.

THE PRICE OF RISK AND THE HURDLE RATE

The definition of a minimum required return for shareholders is a well-known topic with well-known solutions, as mentioned above when referring to the CAPM and APT models of required returns on equity given risk. We focus more here on its implications, first with respect to terms of pricing and second with respect to the capital base. There is a third issue, related to any gaps between the price of risk within the bank and the market, that we tackle in the next section.

Target Profit on Economic Capital

The required profit, after expected losses, cost of debt and operating costs, is 20% of capital. With regulatory capital, the required profit does not change with the risk of those counterparties that share the same weight for calculating the regulatory capital. In Figure 53.1, the target profit is 20% times capital. However, the regulatory capital remains a forfeit while economic capital increases with risk. This is the old Cooke ratio framework. Using regulatory capital as a base for pricing results in systematic mispricing, sometimes underpricing risky borrowers and overpricing the lower-risk borrowers. This is equivalent to attracting risky borrowers and rejecting good borrowers. This demonstrates why an adequate risk-based pricing, and an adequate base for measuring risk, is a true competitive advantage.

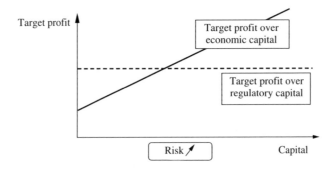

FIGURE 53.1   Target profit, capital and mispricing

The Capital Base

Since the capital base differs when considering regulatory capital, available capital and economic capital, the target profit changes, depending on which one we use as a reference, even though the required percentage return is the same. Hence, it is necessary to choose which capital base serves for defining the target pre-tax profit. Presumably, the goals relate to regulatory or available capital because they are already there. However, risk-based target profitability should refer to economic capital, while being consistent with these other amounts of capital.

If regulatory capital is lower than economic capital, and if the required return over capital is 20%, the return on regulatory capital is higher than 20%, and vice versa. For instance, with a regulatory capital of 120, the target profit is $20\% \times 120 = 24$. If economic capital is lower, for example 100, using the regulatory capital as a reference results in an effective return on economic capital that is higher and equal to $24/100 = 24\%$. If economic capital is 140, the resulting return on economic capital is lower than 20% and equal to $24/140 = 17.14\%$. The return on economic capital results from the return on regulatory capital through the relationship:

$$\text{Return of economic capital} = 20\% \times (\text{regulatory capital/economic capital})$$

If the reference capital base is different from regulatory capital, for instance the available capital, because it is higher, a similar relationship applies. If the reference capital is the economic capital, we use this reference to determine the target profit. The resulting return on regulatory or available capital follows as above. For example, requiring 20% on an economic capital of 140 implies a target profit of $20\% \times 140 = 28$ and a 23.3% return on economic capital of 120.

A side issue is whether such discrepancies make sense economically. For instance, is it normal to require 20% on economic capital because it is greater than regulatory capital? This makes sense only if economic capital decreases down to regulatory capital. The discrepancy is an incentive to take fewer risks because regulatory capital understates the true risk of the portfolio. This is what is going to happen if the available capital is 120 only. In the end, economic capital should tend towards regulatory/available capital. Once they converge, there is a common base. Otherwise, there is room for arbitraging economic and regulatory capital, resulting in mispricing with respect to economic targets.

THE INTERNAL PRICE OF RISK AND THE PRICE OF RISK IN THE CAPITAL MARKETS

According to the CAPM, the required return on capital results from the market price of systematic risk of the stock. The APT model would provide similar benchmarks. Hence, it is possible to define a cost of equity depending on the risk of the bank's stock required return in the equity market. This is the theoretical hurdle rate for RaRoC and SVA. Once this rate is set, for instance at 20%, the internal price of risk follows. It is the required profit by unit of capital, or 20% of capital. This relationship is summarized in Figure 53.2.

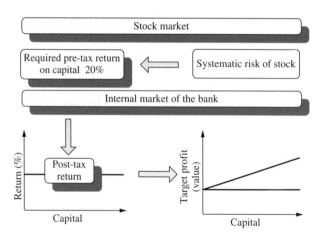

FIGURE 53.2 The market price and the internal price of risk

Different businesses within the same bank require different returns if they have different systematic risks. Making such a differentiation explicit is feasible, legitimate and relevant for those institutions involved in very different businesses. Another issue is subtler. It relates to the potential gap between the internal price of risk derived from economic capital and the market price of credit or market risk.

The internal price of risk is the additional profit per unit of capital, or the additional profit per unit of loss volatility. This is not the market price of equity risk measured by the CAPM or the APT models. These two prices are different. The two notions are distinct. Such discrepancies can lead to conflicting signals for those who make market transactions.

The above example of narrow spreads due to competition illustrates the issue. The issue extends to all market-priced risks. There is no reason why the credit spreads of bonds should match the internally defined credit risk-based price, other than by coincidence. A risky bond has a value of 1000 and the credit spread that prevails in the market for its risk class is 0.5%, or 5. The required capital, economic or regulatory, is $4\% \times 1000 = 40$. The capital-based return should be $20\% \times 40 = 8$, or 0.8% of the bond value. It is different from the 0.5% market spread. Discrepancies can appear with both economic capital and regulatory capital. A portfolio manager trying to meet the internally required return would not do so given the external market conditions.

Discrepancies are not surprising. Economic capital measures the overall volatility of losses post-diversification, whereas bond credit spreads relate to default probabilities, recovery rates and risk aversion. Similarly, the required return on equity of a bank results from the systematic risk of its stock. The economic capital depends on the portfolio risk, and includes both specific and general risk. Nothing ensures a parity between the risk premia required by the bank's shareholders and by the investors in bonds of issuers to whom the bank lends.

It is possible to reconcile the two approaches by adjusting the economic capital to the value that makes 5 equal to the required profit on internal risk. This would be achieved with an economic capital such that $5 = 20\% \times$ capital, or a capital of 25. This is the implied capital in market rates. A 'mathematical' solution for reconciling internal and external prices would be to adjust the confidence level so that the economic capital matches the implied capital in market spreads. This is more a theoretical consideration than a helpful business conclusion.

Making a clear distinction between the two prices of risk helps. If not, the management could assign unrealistic target profitability to those who operate in the market. In addition, it is important to consider other revenue sources than pure spreads. Finally, it makes sense to arbitrage the market valuation of credit risk when the discrepancy is favourable to the bank.

54

Risk-adjusted Performance Implementation

The purpose of this chapter is to present practical calculations when implementing risk contributions and risk-adjusted profitability measures. It details calculations of absolute versus marginal risk contributions, and of risk-based profitability, with ex post performances (Risk-Adjusted Performance Measurement, RAPM) versus ex ante Risk-Based Pricing (RBP). The calculations illustrate the general properties of the risk contributions and of risk-adjusted profitability, as introduced previously.

Economic income statements serve for reporting risk-adjusted measures of performance. Risk-based pricing piles up all costs, including the necessary mark-ups for absorbing risk (EL and capital compensation). Assuming that prices are in line with both risk and the target compensation of risks, ex post Risk-adjusted Return on Capital (RaRoC) and Shareholders Value Added (SVA) measures differ from the ex ante measures because the absolute risk contribution replaces the marginal risk contribution once a facility is in the portfolio. Moreover, these measures drift with time, as risk does spontaneously, when time passes.

The examples demonstrate that RBP using marginal contributions does ensure that the 'ex post' RAPM of the portfolio using absolute contributions is effectively in line with the target return.

The first section details the calculations of RaRoC and SVA and presents economic income statements, or risk-adjusted performance reporting on an ex post basis. The second section shows how to derive the target price from target return and risk, and contrasts ex ante versus ex post views of risk-adjusted measures. The third section compares RaRoC and SVA based on absolute and marginal risk contributions. It also shows through examples that RBP on marginal contributions guarantees the RAPM target under portfolio expansion.

THE CALCULATION OF RAROC AND SVA FOR CREDIT RISK

This section provides sample calculations of RaRoC and SVA using as inputs: interest income and fees measured as an All-In Spread (AIS); expected loss; capital, either regulatory or economic, obtained as a risk contribution from the capital allocation system; operating costs. The calculations apply to a single period. The presentation organizes the calculations into 'economic income statements'. Both RaRoC and SVA formulas are those discussed previously. There is a hurdle rate, set at 20% before tax, to calculate the charge for capital in SVA calculations and compare RaRoC to this minimum threshold target return.

Calculation of RaRoC and SVA

Table 54.1 details a sample calculation. Simplifying assumptions are used. The horizon is 1 year. The loss is identical to exposure (zero recoveries), the AIS is 2% of exposure, the expected loss is 1%, and the economic capital is 3%. The economic capital represents a risk contribution. The cost of capital is the required return on equity, or 25% pre-tax. Finally, this is a pre-operating cost calculation.

TABLE 54.1   RaRoC and SVA calculations over 1 year before operating costs

Year	1
Exposure	1000
Parameters (% of outstanding balances)	
Expected loss	1.0%
Economic capital	3.0%
AIS	3.0%
Cost of capital (before taxes)	20.0%
Yearly RaRoC and SVA	
Expected loss	10
Capital	30
AIS	30
−Expected loss	−10
=Net AIS	20
Cost of capital (20% × 20)	4.0
RaRoC	66.7%
SVA	16

Since RaRoC is above 20%, the SVA is positive. However, the RaRoC is pre-operating costs. However, the hurdle rate is post-operating costs and pre-tax. With pre-operating costs earnings, it should be higher than 20%. Such earnings are contributions margins.

The Economic Income Statement

The economic income statement, based on the economic measures of expected and unexpected losses, summarizes the above calculations. There are two income statements, one truncated as above before cost allocation and another post-operating costs (Table 54.2).

TABLE 54.2 Economic income statement pre-operating costs and pre-tax (risk-adjusted contributions)

+Revenues (margins and fees)	30
−Expected loss	−10
=Contribution before operating costs[a]	20
Capital	30
Cost of capital	6.0
RaRoC pre-operating costs[b]	66.7%
SVA pre-operating costs	14.0

[a]Operating costs not allocated to transactions.
[b]The hurdle is 20% pre-tax and post-operating expenses. It is higher with pre-operating costs, so that the minimum revenues absorb these.

In Table 54.3, operating costs are 5. They include direct costs and overheads. The operating income nets them from revenues before calculating RaRoC and SVA.

TABLE 54.3 Economic income statement post-operating costs

+ Revenues (margins and fees)	30
− Expected loss	10
= Revenues net of expected loss	20
− Direct costs[a]	3
− Overhead allocation	2
= Operating income	15
Capital	30
− Cost of capital[b]	6.0
RaRoC	50%
SVA	9.0

[a]Allocated by product line.
[b]Hurdle rate 20% pre-tax.

RISK-BASED PRICING

A direct application of RaRoC and SVA is to determine the appropriate customer price given risk. The approach is identical to the one used to derive price from a target Return On Equity (ROE) applied to the regulatory capital. The only difference is that economic capital replaces regulatory capital. Instead of moving down from revenues to RaRoC and SVA, we move bottom-up, from target return to target pricing.

The Target Revenues

The target revenues correspond to a RaRoC of 20%, over either regulatory or economic capital. The revenues are net of operating costs:

$$\text{RaRoC} = (\text{revenues} - \text{EL})/\text{capital} \geq 20\%$$

$$\text{SVA} = \text{revenues} - \text{EL} - 20\% \times \text{capital} \geq 0$$

The analytical formulas use the same notation as the previous chapter:

- Exposure A.
- Asset all-in return r (%).
- Cost of debt i. This cost includes any credit spread applicable to the bank.
- Allocated debt D.
- Operating costs oc (%).
- Expected loss el (%).
- Allocated capital $RC(K) = K$.
- Hurdle rate on capital $k\%$.
- Required rate on capital 20%.

We found that the RaRoC and the SVA formulas are:

$$\text{RaRoC} = i + (A/K) \times (r - i - \text{el} - \text{oc})$$

$$\text{SVA} = r \times A - i \times D - \text{el} - \text{oc} \times A - k\% \times K$$

The condition that the RaRoC is higher than $k\%$ becomes:

$$\text{RaRoC} = i + (A/K) \times (r - i - \text{el} - \text{oc}) \geq k\%$$

This relation implies a minimum value of $r\%$ such that:

$$i + (A/K) \times (r - i - \text{el} - \text{oc}) \geq k\%$$

or

$$r \geq i + \text{oc} + \text{el} + K/A \times (k - i)$$

The minimum required return should be the overall cost plus $K/A \times (k - i)$. The last term is the additional cost of risk since it is proportional to the capital charge K. It is called the risk premium, and collapses to zero for a risk-free transaction.

The formula also has a simple financial rationale. When substituting a fraction of debt by capital, rather than using a 100% debt funding, there is an additional cost which is the differential cost of capital over debt, proportional to the ratio of capital to debt. This is the formula for the risk premium.

The Customer Rate

The example in Table 54.4 shows the difference in target prices obtained with regulatory capital and economic capital. Regulatory capital does not differentiate price with risks when two private counterparties belong to different risk classes. Economic capital does.

The example uses an exposure net of recoveries of 100, with a 100% weight for the Cooke ratio, a cost of debt of 10%, and operating costs equal to 2% of exposure. The target customer rate covers the cost of debt and operating expenses, and provides a return on capital of 20% before tax (hurdle rate).

TABLE 54.4   Risk-based pricing (RaRoC $\geq$ 20%)[a]

	Low risk	High risk
Exposure (X)	1000	1000
Regulatory capital	80	80
Economic capital (capital)	40	120
Expected loss (a)	1%	1%
Regulatory capital/X	8%	8%
Capital/X	4%	12%
Minimum RaRoC	20%	20%
Operating costs (oc%) (b)	2%	2%
Cost of debt (10%) (c)	10%	10%
Differential cost of capital (20% − i)	15%	15%
Calculation based on regulatory capital:		
Risk premium regulatory capital × (20% − i)/X (d)	1.2%	1.2%
Price (e = a + b + c + d)	14.2%	14.2%
Margin (e − c)	4.2%	4.2%
Calculation based on economic capital:		
Risk premium capital × (20% − i)/X (f)	0.6%	1.8%
Target price (g = a + b + c + f)	13.6%	14.8%
Target margin (g − c)	3.6%	4.8%

[a]Percentages calculated over exposure 1000.

The calculation of the target customer rate consists of adding the risk premium, as detailed above, to the cost items. The premium collapses to zero when there is no risk, and increases proportionally with capital.

The price is the same for both transactions with regulatory capital. When using economic capital, it increases with risk, due to the risk premium included in the cost of capital. The relationship between risk and price is straightforward. Whenever there is credit risk, the price increases proportionally with the risk premium. In the absence of risk, the (risk-free) price should only cover the cost of debt plus operating costs.

Origination and Post-origination Follow-up

For reporting purposes, the profitability ratios are historical, with values at origination. Moreover, RaRoC and SVA differ at origination and after, because both risks and valuation change when time drifts. Recalculating the RaRoC and SVA of a given facility post-origination would therefore result in values differing from the historical values at the origination date. In other words, RaRoC and SVA measures differ at origination and post-origination and drift with time. The variation results from the normal drift of risk through

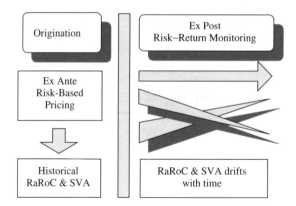

FIGURE 54.1   Ex ante versus ex post risk–reward profiles

time, since risk decreases when residual maturity declines, even if periodical revenues are constant (under constant valuation of exposure[1]) (Figure 54.1).

Post-origination, we know the actual revenues and risk migrations. Hence, periodical recalculations of RaRoC and SVA would result in different values, so that the risk-adjusted performance of the same transaction will drift with time. Ex post risk–return monitoring implies updates as time passes to get the risk–return profile of the portfolio, take corrective action or enter into more active portfolio management. RaRoC and SVA ex post measures allow us to decide whether there is an economic rationale to keep a transaction in the portfolio. If the RaRoC deteriorates because of credit events, there is an incentive to off-load the risk before it decreases further and ultimately defaults. Therefore, there is a rationale for using RaRoC and SVA in ex post reports, to periodically recalculate their values and keep a track record of these values. There is also a case for keeping track of RaRoC and SVA values at origination, and for controlling ex post drifts.

RISK-BASED PERFORMANCE, PRICING AND CAPITAL ALLOCATION

Ex post measures use absolute risk contributions and serve for risk–return monitoring of the existing portfolio (ex post view). Ex ante measures use marginal risk contributions and serve for risk-based pricing (ex ante view).

Using marginal risk contributions makes pricing sensitive to the entrance order in the portfolio. The same facility entering first and second requires a different pricing to obtain a given target overall portfolio return, as explained when discussing risk contributions. However, whatever the entrance rank, risk-based pricing achieves the target overall rate of return over the entire portfolio. The same simple example of a two-obligor portfolio used for illustrating risk contribution properties now illustrates RaRoC calculations, with and without a new facility. After a reminder of the example data, we proceed with the calculations of the ex post risk-based performance and the ex ante risk-based pricing using a target required return on capital.

---

[1] Under full valuation, the drift of time causes the valuation to migrate upwards or downwards, while getting simultaneously closer to maturity. The net effect of valuation and risk drift might be positive or negative.

The Sample Portfolio

The portfolio of two obligors of Chapter 46 (with 10% correlation) is as shown in Table 54.5. We now add revenues as annualized AISs, or interest margins plus any fee averaged over the life of the transaction in Table 54.6.

TABLE 54.5   Portfolio of two obligors

	Default probability	Exposure
A	7.00%	100
B	5.00%	50
ρ_{AB}	10.00%	—

TABLE 54.6   AIS for A and B, ex post

	A	B	Portfolio
AIS	20	9	29

We conducted all detailed calculations to obtain the loss statistics of the portfolio and allocate the capital and loss volatility to each of the two obligors. A summary is given in Table 54.7. There are two cases for economic capital, using the confidence levels 2% and 0.5%.

TABLE 54.7   Loss distribution statistics for the two-obligor portfolio

	A	B	Portfolio
EL_i and EL_p	7.000	2.500	9.500
Loss volatility LV_i and LV_p	25.515	10.897	28.729
ARC (to LV_p)	23.628	5.101	28.729
Capital at 2.00%	—	—	90.5
Multiple $m(2\%) = K(2\%)/LV_p$	—	—	3.150
ARC to K	74.430	16.070	90.500
Capital at 0.50%	—	—	140.5
Multiple $m(0.50\%) = K(0.50\%)/LV_p$	—	—	4.891
ARC to K	115.553	24.947	140.50

To conduct risk-adjusted performance analysis, we need existing revenues. To conduct a risk-based pricing calculation, we need to calculate the required revenues. The first case considers revenues as given ('ex post' view), while the second case determines the required revenues in line with target profitability ('ex ante' view).

Risk-based Performance

Risk-based performance is an ex post measure showing, given past pricing decisions, what are the relative performances of business lines, facilities and so on. All that remains to do is to define the risk measure to compare the performances achieved. The calculation of risk-based performance is straightforward using RaRoC or SVA. We use a target pre-operating expense and pre-tax hurdle rate of 20%. The formulas are:

$$RaRoC(RAPM \text{ ex post view}) = (AIS - EL)/ARC(K)$$

$$SVA(\text{ex post view}) = AIS - EL - 20\% \times ARC(K)$$

where $ARC(K)$ is the absolute risk contribution to capital. All $ARC(K)$ sum to capital (Table 54.8). The two values of economic capital are 90.5 and 140.5.

TABLE 54.8   Ex post RAPM

	A	B	Portfolio
Capital	90.5	—	—
RaRoC on ARC(K)	17.47%	40.45%	21.55%
SVA	−1.886	3.286	1.400
Capital	140.5	—	—
RaRoC on ARC(K)	11.25%	26.06%	13.88%
SVA	−10.111	1.511	−8.600

The overall portfolio performance is 21.55% if capital is 90.5 and 13.88% if it is 140.5. The overall RaRoC of the portfolio is identical to the portfolio Sharpe ratio, which is the ratio of the spread over the risk-free rate to the loss volatility, or the capital. Whenever the RaRoC is below 20%, the transaction destroys value and vice versa. Only B creates values, and less so when capital increases, an obvious effect.

Risk-based Pricing

Risk-based pricing implies pricing according to risk. The starting point becomes the required hurdle rate, set at 20% pre-operating expenses and pre-tax. Then we move to the required revenues that meet this target. The difference with the previous RAPM calculation is that we use the marginal risk contribution to capital, or $MRC(K)$, rather than the absolute risk contribution. We show numerically here several implications: the pricing is not the same, using the unique 20% hurdle rate, when we use absolute or marginal contributions; the pricing depends on the order of entrance into the portfolio; the ex post portfolio RaRoC is in line with the target rate. In order to do so, we need to make a distinction between the events 'A first-in' and 'B first-in'.

The RaRoC formula is:

$$RaRoC = (AIS - EL)/MRC(K)$$

The RaRoC should have the target value of 20%, from which the required unknown AIS derives. It is such that:

$$AIS = EL + k\% \times MRC(K)$$

where $k\%$ is the target return 20%:

$$AIS = EL + 20\% \times MRC(K)$$

TABLE 54.9   Risk-based pricing on ARC and MRC to capital (90.5)

Capital	90.5	—	—
m (2%)	3.150	—	—
	A	B	Portfolio
Target AIS on ARC(K)	21.886	5.714	27.600
RaRoC (on ARC)	20.00%	20.00%	20.00%
Ex ante MRC	MRC(first-in)	MRC(second-in)	Total
A then B	93	−2.5	90.5
Target AIS on MRC(K)	25.60	2.00	27.60
RaRoC (on MRC)	20.00%	20.00%	20.00%
B then A	47.5	43.0	90.5
Target AIS on MRC(K)	16.50	11.10	27.60
RaRoC (on MRC)	20.00%	20.00%	20.00%

TABLE 54.10   Risk-based pricing on ARC and MRC to capital (140.5)

Capital	140.5	—	—
m (0.5%)	4.891	—	—
	A	B	Portfolio
Target AIS on ARC(K)	30.111	7.489	37.600
RaRoC	20.00%	20.00%	20.00%
Ex ante MRC	MRC(A)	MRC(B)	Total
A then B	93	47.5	140.5
Target AIS on MRC(K)	25.60	12.00	37.60
RaRoC	20.00%	20.00%	20.00%
B then A	47.5	93.0	140.5
Target AIS on MRC(K)	16.50	21.10	37.60
RaRoC	20.00%	20.00%	20.00%

Tables 54.9 and 54.10 show two calculations, the first with a capital of 90.5 (2% confidence level) and the second with a capital of 140.5 (0.5% confidence level).

Table 54.9 presents the absolute and the marginal risk contributions of A and B, both when A is first-in and when B is first-in. It shows the values of the required AIS based on both absolute and marginal risk contributions.

The obvious observation are: the target AIS differs when using absolute and marginal risk contributions; the target AIS of A and B also depend, when using marginal risk contributions, on which facility is the first-in the portfolio. Nevertheless, in all cases, the RaRoC is always equal to the target rate 20%, simply because the AIS are derived under this constraint. Calculations differ by their meaning. For risk-based pricing, only marginal risk contributions combined with the hurdle rate count. Note that the absolute risk contributions are unknown before a new transaction is selected, since this new facility changes all of them.

However, it is useful to check that the overall return on capital remains 20%. It is also necessary to see what are the absolute risk contributions after entrance of both exposures into the portfolio. The table summarizes all information.

From an ex ante view, we have to consider a first entrant and then a second one to build up the portfolio. When A enters first and then B, we require a high AIS on A (25.60) and a low AIS on B (2.00) to get the overall 20% return, because of diversification. The example shows that the entrance order changes the marginal contribution of A, or of B, as well as the target AIS. The same transaction, A, requires a different pricing depending on the order of entrance. If transaction A is first-in, it requires a 25.60 AIS and if the same transaction A is second-in requires only 11.10. Still, in both cases we always end up with the overall 20%. All marginal risk contributions to capital sum to the portfolio capital, 90.5, after all transactions are in, by construction. Therefore, necessarily, the sum of the excess spread over expected loss remains 20% of that capital, or $20\% \times 90.5 = 18.10$. The sum of the gross AIS is 27.60. The difference between the sum of the excess spreads and the sum of the AIS is the sum of the EL, or 9.50.

The AIS that would be required using the absolute risk contributions is in the top section. It differs from the AIS required based on marginal risk contributions, because absolute and marginal risk contributions differ radically. However, the AIS values sum to 27.60. This is necessary, since absolute risk contributions sum to capital. Even though they comply with this overall ex post constraint, the required AIS on absolute risk contributions would not guarantee that the portfolio return remains at 20% during its build-up, while the marginal contributions do so.

Note that simple relationships would not hold when using marginal contributions to portfolio loss volatility rather than marginal contributions to portfolio capital. The reason is that the ratio of capital to loss volatility differs substantially when the first-in enters and when the second-in enters.

The second calculation (Table 54.10) uses the 0.5% confidence level, with a capital of 140.5. This calculation illustrates the case where all marginal risk contributions are positive. In this case, the marginal risk contributions to capital are identical for the first-in transaction (93.0), independent of whether it is A or B. Nevertheless, the marginal risk contributions between first-in and second-in always differ. Consequently, the required AIS for A and B changes, depending on which one is first-in. Of course, the overall portfolio RaRoC remains at 20% during the build-up period and after.

SECTION 17

Portfolio and Capital Management (Credit Risk)

55

Portfolio Reporting (1)

Three chapters address portfolio credit risk reporting. This first chapter details the specifics of a sample portfolio and provides an overall reporting on its risk–return profile. This is the top management view of the bank's portfolio. The second chapter 'slices' the portfolio along various risk and business dimensions. The risk dimensions are the various credit risk components, such as exposures, default probabilities and recoveries. The business dimensions refer to the usual product families, market segments and business lines. Reporting requires breaking down the portfolio along these dimensions, to provide the various 'management views' of the portfolio as an aid to business decisions. The third chapter goes beyond these descriptions towards more analytical reports, such as sensitivity and 'what if' analyses.

This chapter provides the portfolio overview using a sample portfolio. The portfolio description is given in the appendices. The major characteristics are: 50 obligors, uniform loss correlation of assets of obligors, two risk classes of default probability, two business units and two industries, unequal exposures and various loss given default percentages. Monte Carlo simulation generates the loss distribution using the simplified asset value model.

The portfolio overview through portfolio models provides a number of portfolio characteristics of interest. They include notably: the expected loss, the portfolio capital, the overall portfolio Risk-adjusted Return on Capital (RaRoC) and Shareholders Value Added (SVA), plus measures of correlation risk and concentration risk. The correlation risk measure is simply the ratio of a measure of overall risk, such as the loss volatility, to the sum of standalone risks of individual transactions, a percentage lower than 1 showing the overall gain from diversification. The size concentration risk addresses pure size discrepancies, summarized in adequate indexes, or with curves showing the percentage of the overall portfolio risk resulting from the largest exposures.

The first section describes the portfolio. The second section summarizes the portfolio overview, with overall statistics such as expected loss, capital and the aggregated portfolio RaRoC. The third section provides additional measures of portfolio concentration risk. The last section is a short transition towards the detailed views of individual facilities of the next chapters.

THE PORTFOLIO

The three chapters use the same sample fictitious portfolio for illustrative purposes. This section briefly summarizes the characteristics of the portfolio.

Portfolio Details

The portfolio used throughout the three chapters, comprising 50 obligors, is detailed in the appendices. There is one facility per obligor, with different exposures, loss given default percentages, default probabilities and All-In Spreads (AISs). The maturity is 1 year for all facilities. Facilities are in two risk classes, whose default probabilities are 1% and 2.5% respectively. There are two business units (V and W) and two industries (A and B). Facilities have unequal exposures, from 50 to 500, and loss given default percentages ranging from 20% to 100%. Exposures are at book value. The portfolio is subject to a uniform correlation of 30% between the obligor's assets. The loss distribution results from a Monte Carlo simulation with 50 000 runs. The methodology for generating the loss distribution uses the simulation of asset values using standardized normal distributions with a uniform correlation of 30% across asset values, and threshold asset values triggering default events adjusted to the 1% and 2.5% default probabilities. The revenues are AISs. The accounting return on asset is the ratio of the AIS over total exposure. The risk-adjusted return is the ratio of AIS minus expected losses to economic capital. The simulation uses the one-factor model, with a common factor for general risk and an independent residual for specific risk.

All portfolio statistics result from the Monte Carlo generated loss distribution. For individual facilities, standalone loss volatility and expected loss result from exposures, loss given default percentages and default probabilities. Economic capital and portfolio loss volatility result from the loss distribution. Capital allocations of overall economic capital are proportional to the standalone loss volatilities of facilities. Such allocations are identical to absolute risk contributions for a uniform correlation portfolio.

Ex post values of RaRoC and SVA for the entire portfolio, and each individual facility from AISs, result from revenues, economic capital and capital allocations. Capital is in excess of expected loss or expected spread. The cost of capital, pre-tax and pre-operating costs, is $k = 25\%$.

Portfolio Loss Distribution

We visualize in Figure 55.1 the entire loss distribution, plus a zoom in on the 'fat tail', for both the probability density distribution and the cumulated distribution. The total

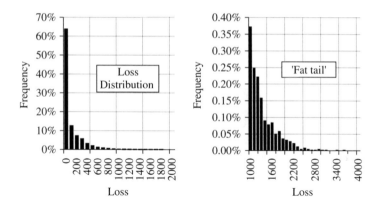

FIGURE 55.1   Portfolio loss distribution: overall distribution 'fat tail'

exposure is 11 000, before recoveries. Figure 55.2 shows the cumulative distribution, from which loss percentiles derive, and the fat tail frequency distribution. The loss at the 99% confidence level is 1055, or 9.59% of the total exposure of 11 000, and 17.58% of the total loss given default of 6000. These are relatively high numbers, resulting from the choice of both a small portfolio and high default probabilities, which are in the speculative grade zone of the rating scale.

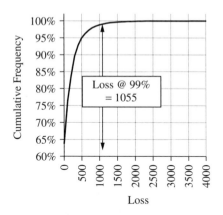

FIGURE 55.2   Loss distribution: cumulative

PORTFOLIO OVERVIEW

The portfolio overview provides some basic aggregated characteristics of the risk–reward profile. Table 55.1 summarizes some of these aggregated characteristics. The loss given default percentages have a direct and very significant effect on losses, but exposures serve to normalize the data since the spreads are exposure-based.

TABLE 55.1   Portfolio overview

Total exposure value X	11 000.00
Total Lgd value	6000.00
Average Lgd%	54.55%
Expected loss value EL	100.58
EL / X	0.91%
Portfolio loss volatility LV_p	221.1
Loss volatility as % of X, LV_p/X	2.01%
Sum of transaction loss volatilities $\sum LV_i$	750.17
Diversification effect, or retained risk $\sum LV_i/LV_p$	29.47%
Loss percentile at 99%, $L(99\%)$	1055.00
$L(99\%)/X$	9.59%
$L(99\%)/LV_p$	1.41
$L(99\%)/\sum LV_i$	4.77
Capital in excess of EL, $K_{EL}(99\%) = L(99\%) - EL$	954.43
$K_{EL}(99\%)/X$	8.674%
$K_{EL}(99\%)/LV_p$	4.32
$K_{EL}(99\%)/\sum LV_i$	1.27
AIS	401.00
Expected spread ES $=$ AIS $-$ EL	300.43
AIS/exposure or ROA	3.65%
ES/X or expected ROA	2.73%
Capital in excess of ES, $K_{ES}(99\%) = L(99\%) - (\text{AIS} - EL)$	654
$K_{ES}(99\%)/X$	5.95%
Cost of capital ρ, pre-tax and pre-operating costs	25%
RaRoC ratio $(\text{AIS} - EL)/[L(99\%) - EL]$	31.48%
SVA $=$ ES $- k \times K_{EL}(99\%)$	61.82

Loss Statistics and Capital

The definitions used in the calculations below are self-explanatory. The expected loss is 101, or 0.91% of exposure. It is lower than the default probabilities, 1% and 2.5%, because of recoveries. The loss percentile $L(99\%)$ is 4.77 times the sum of transaction standalone volatilities, while it is only 1.41 times the portfolio loss volatility LV_p because of the diversification effect. As a reminder, $L(99\%)$ with a normal distribution would be 2.33 times the portfolio loss volatility, in between these two values, the higher multiple 4.77 illustrating the effect of the fat tail and the lower multiple 1.41 measuring the effect of diversification. This shows that normal distribution multiples have finally comparable orders of magnitude to those of the actual correlated loss distribution because the fat tail effect and the diversification effect compensate to some extent.

There are three possible calculations of capital: as a loss percentile at 99%, or $L(99\%)$; as a loss percentile in excess of expected loss, or $K_{EL}(99\%)$; as a loss percentile in excess of expected spread, or $K_{ES}(99\%)$. Their respective values as a percentage of total book value exposure X are 9.59%, 8.67% and 5.95%. The smaller value considers that revenues in excess of expected loss are available to absorb unexpected losses.

Portfolio Risk–Return Profile

The AIS is the annualized revenue from each obligor, including interest margins and fees, both upfront flat fees and recurring fees. The latter should be averages over the maturity of the facility, based on expected values of exposures. The exposures are current or expected. The aggregated contractual spread, or total AIS under no default, is 401, while expected loss is 101. The expected spread is the contractual AIS minus the EL, or $401 - 101 = 300$ (rounded value).

The overall RaRoC over capital in excess of expected loss, or $K_{EL}(99\%)$ is:

$$RaRoC = (AIS - EL)/K_{EL}(99\%) = 31.48\%$$

The SVA is the difference between the AIS and the EL, and the cost of the economic capital of the portfolio, pre-tax and pre-operating costs, set at 25%. Since RaRoC = 31.48% > 25%, the SVA is positive and equal to 62 (rounded). The expected spread ES increases the RaRoC numerator, while decreasing the denominator. The accounting ROA is not risk-adjusted, and is the contractual AIS divided by the total exposure, $401/1055 = 3.65\%$. It is much lower than the Sharpe ratio of 31.48%. The wide gap illustrates the magnitude of differences between economic and accounting measures.

PORTFOLIO CONCENTRATION AND CORRELATION RISK

Both correlation risk and concentration risk are related measures of portfolio risk. Correlation risk relates to the loss association. Concentration risk designates here the effect of size discrepancies. Pure correlation risk is measured by the 30% asset correlation, independent of the sizes of exposures. Pure size concentration is measured by a concentration index, such as the diversity score, or concentration curves.

Diversification and Correlation Effects

In general, when the risks of two obligors correlate, the risk is higher if they have large exposures. There is an interaction between size and correlation. A simple measure combining these effects is the ratio of the portfolio loss volatility, 221.1, to the sum of individual standalone loss volatilities, 750.17 or 29.47% in our example. The portfolio diversifies away close to 70.53% of the standalone loss volatilities.

Concentration Risk: Diversity Score

Concentration characterizes size discrepancies. The individual loss given default weights, ratios of the individual loss given default to the total loss given default of 6000, measure exposure sizes. Synthetic views of portfolio size concentration, other than reporting the largest individual weights, include such measures as the diversity score and concentration curves.

The diversity score is an index synthesizing the discrepancies of exposure of individual facilities. There are as many concentration indices as there are metrics for risk. Alternative metrics include exposure weights, loss given default weights or capital allocation weights, each of them being the ratio of the individual measure to the total portfolio measure. There is a concentration index, or diversity score, for each metric. The diversity score is a number that is always lower than the actual number of facilities, here 50. The lower the ratio, the higher the risk concentration along the selected dimensions. The diversity score is the number of equal size exposures equivalent to the weight profile of individual exposures. The diversity score DS is the following ratio:

$$ DS = 1 \Big/ \sum_{i=1}^{n} w_i^2 $$

The w_i are the weights of facilities, using one risk metric, for instance exposure or loss given default of individual facilities. If all weights were equal to $1/n$, with n the number of obligors, the ratio would be $1/(\sum_{i=1}^{n} 1/n^2)$, or $1/(n/n^2) = n$. The diversity score is commonly interpreted as the number of uniform exposures 'equivalent' to the number of actual unequal exposures. It is a convenient measure to capture pure size concentration effects, as opposed to correlation effects. The ratio of the diversity score to the actual number of exposures is always lower than 1 whenever there are size discrepancies, and the gap measures pure concentration risk[1].

Table 55.2 provides the diversity scores for exposure and capital allocation, respectively equal to 35.02 and 33.22. Both numbers are lower than the actual number of exposures, 50. The ratios of these diversity scores to this actual number of exposures, 50, measure the level of concentration in terms of weight discrepancies. Note that the capital diversity score combines both effects, concentration and diversification, since capital allocations capture the retained risk post-diversification effect.

TABLE 55.2   Concentration risk

Diversity score exposure	35.02
Concentration index exposure	70.04%
Diversity score capital (in excess of EL)	33.22
Concentration index capital	66.45%

Concentration Curves

A second measure of concentration risk is the 'concentration' curve, or 'Gini' curve. The curve shows the cumulated exposure, or any alternative risk metric, such as capital, as

---

[1] As an example, the simple two-obligor portfolio, with exposures of 100 and 50 respectively, used previously as an example, has exposure weights equal to 66.667% (100/50) and 33.333% (50/50). The equivalent number of uniform exposures is the diversity score $DS = \{1/[(1/66.667\%)^2 + (1/33.333\%)^2]\} = 1.80$. The concentration index is the ratio of the diversity score to the actual number of exposures, two in this case. This gives $1.8/2 = 0.9$. The ratio is lower than 1 because the exposures are unequal.

a function of the number of exposures. The curve cumulates the risk metric (exposure) sorted by descending values. A uniform exposure portfolio would have a straight-line concentration curve. The higher the curve above the straight line, the higher the concentration risk.

In the exposure concentration curve of Figure 55.3, the first five biggest obligors represent 21% of the total portfolio exposure, the first 10 biggest obligors represent 40% of the total portfolio exposure, and so on. The curve hits 100% when all 50 exposures cumulate. The slope is steeper at the beginning of the curve because the largest exposures are the first along the X-axis. Steepest slopes also characterize concentration because they imply that a lower number of the largest risks concentrates a larger fraction of the total risk.

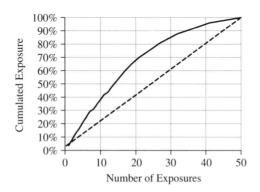

FIGURE 55.3   Gini concentration curves of exposures

FROM PORTFOLIO RISK TO DETAILED FACILITY DATA

Capital allocation figures are ex post absolute risk contributions, or simpler alternative metrics, such as standalone loss volatilities of facilities. In this example, the capital allocation criterion is the standalone loss volatility (equivalent in this case to using risk contributions). The loss volatility of each facility is $Lgd \times \sqrt{Edf(1 - Edf)}$. It is an output of the portfolio report, for each facility. The standalone loss volatility of a facility is intrinsic to that facility and does not depend on any portfolio effect.

Allocating capital to each facility follows the rule of the pro rata of the standalone facilities. For each facility, the ratio of the individual standalone loss volatility to the sum over the entire portfolio serves for allocating the economic capital in excess of expected loss. The capital allocation of each facility is equal to this percentage times the total portfolio capital. Note that, due to uniform correlation, the ratio of capital allocation K_i to portfolio capital K_p, K_i/K_p, is identical to the ratio LV_i/LV_p for all facilities. This ratio appears in the first appendix to this chapter, along with the main inputs.

The facility data, both inputs and outputs, are given in the appendices. Together with the AIS and excess spread, the capital allocation serves to calculate the RaRoC and SVA of each individual facility as well. Once the allocation is available, all facilities have a risk–return profile. Subsequent chapters provide detailed reports on individual facility risk–return profiles.

APPENDIX I: SAMPLE PORTFOLIO INPUTS

Facility	Exposure X	Edf%	Lgd%	X × Lgd	Industry	Spread X%	Business unit	Weight X%
1	400	1.0%	20%	100	A	1.8%	V	3.64%
2	200	1.0%	40%	80	B	1.6%	V	1.82%
3	500	1.0%	80%	400	A	1.5%	W	4.55%
4	100	1.0%	80%	80	A	3.0%	W	0.91%
5	50	1.0%	80%	40	A	3.0%	V	0.45%
6	200	1.0%	80%	160	B	2.2%	W	1.82%
7	50	1.0%	40%	20	A	2.5%	V	0.45%
8	50	1.0%	100%	50	A	4.5%	W	0.45%
9	50	1.0%	100%	50	A	4.0%	W	0.45%
10	100	1.0%	60%	60	B	3.2%	V	0.91%
11	100	1.0%	80%	80	A	2.5%	W	0.91%
12	200	1.0%	20%	80	A	1.8%	V	1.82%
13	350	1.0%	80%	280	B	1.8%	V	3.18%
14	250	1.0%	100%	250	B	1.8%	V	2.27%
15	100	1.0%	100%	100	A	2.2%	W	0.91%
16	100	1.0%	100%	100	A	2.2%	W	0.91%
17	150	1.0%	20%	30	A	2.0%	V	1.36%
18	200	1.0%	60%	120	A	2.0%	V	1.82%
19	200	1.0%	100%	200	A	2.2%	W	1.82%
20	250	1.0%	60%	150	A	2.4%	V	2.27%
21	400	1.0%	60%	240	B	1.2%	W	3.64%
22	400	1.0%	40%	160	A	1.1%	V	3.64%
23	200	1.0%	100%	200	A	1.6%	W	1.82%
24	350	1.0%	50%	175	B	1.2%	V	3.18%
25	450	1.0%	20%	90	A	0.8%	V	4.09%
26	350	2.5%	40%	140	A	2.0%	V	3.18%
27	50	2.5%	100%	50	A	5.0%	W	0.45%
28	50	2.5%	60%	30	B	4.8%	V	0.45%
29	100	2.5%	100%	100	A	5.0%	W	0.91%
30	50	2.5%	80%	40	A	5.0%	W	0.45%
31	400	2.5%	40%	160	A	2.3%	V	3.64%
32	50	2.5%	60%	30	B	2.8%	V	0.45%
33	300	2.5%	50%	150	A	2.0%	W	2.73%
34	50	2.5%	100%	50	B	5.0%	W	0.45%
35	100	2.5%	80%	80	B	3.0%	W	0.91%
36	450	2.5%	50%	225	B	2.2%	W	4.09%
37	100	2.5%	60%	60	B	3.2%	W	0.91%
38	200	2.5%	20%	80	A	2.5%	V	1.82%
39	400	2.5%	80%	300	A	3.0%	W	3.64%
40	100	2.5%	60%	60	B	3.0%	W	0.91%
41	150	2.5%	40%	60	A	3.0%	V	1.36%

(continued)

Facility	Exposure X	Edf%	Lgd%	X × Lgd	Industry	Spread X%	Business unit	Weight X%
42	150	2.5%	40%	60	A	2.0%	V	1.36%
43	150	2.5%	40%	60	A	2.5%	V	1.36%
44	150	2.5%	60%	80	B	3.5%	V	1.36%
45	200	2.5%	80%	160	B	3.3%	W	1.82%
46	350	2.5%	20%	70	B	0.8%	W	3.18%
47	300	2.5%	20%	60	B	0.8%	V	2.73%
48	500	2.5%	20%	100	A	0.7%	V	4.55%
49	400	2.5%	60%	300	B	2.0%	W	3.64%
50	500	2.5%	40%	200	B	1.5%	V	4.55%
	Total			**Total**				**Total**
	11 000			**6000**				**100%**

APPENDIX II: SAMPLE PORTFOLIO OUTPUTS

Facility	Exposure X	Spread X%	$Spread	$EL	$Spread −EL	$UL[a]	$UL × UL% = K%	$K[b]
1	400	3.6%	2.5	1.00	1.50	9.95	1.33%	12.66
2	200	3.4%	6.8	0.80	6.00	7.96	1.06%	10.13
3	500	3.3%	16.5	4.00	12.50	39.80	5.31%	50.64
4	100	4.8%	4.8	0.80	4.00	7.96	1.06%	10.13
5	50	4.8%	2.4	0.40	2.00	3.98	0.53%	5.06
6	200	4.0%	8.0	1.60	6.40	15.92	2.12%	20.25
7	50	4.3%	2.2	0.20	1.95	1.99	0.27%	2.53
8	50	6.3%	3.2	0.50	2.65	4.97	0.66%	6.33
9	50	5.8%	2.9	0.50	2.40	4.97	0.66%	6.33
10	100	5.0%	5.0	0.60	4.40	5.97	0.80%	7.60
11	100	4.3%	4.3	0.80	3.50	7.96	1.0611	10.13
12	200	3.6%	7.2	0.80	6.40	7.96	1.06%	10.13
13	350	3.6%	12.6	2.80	9.80	27.86	3.71%	35.45
14	250	3.6%	9.0	2.50	6.50	24.87	3.32%	31.65
15	100	4.0%	4.0	1.00	3.00	9.95	1.33%	12.66
16	100	4.0%	2.6	1.00	1.60	9.95	1.33%	12.66
17	150	3.8%	5.7	0.30	5.40	2.98	0.40%	3.80
18	200	3.8%	7.6	1.20	6.40	11.94	1.59%	15.19
19	200	4.0%	8.0	2.00	6.00	19.90	2.65%	25.32
20	250	4.2%	10.5	1.50	9.00	14.92	1.99%	18.99
21	400	3.0%	12.0	2.40	9.60	23.88	3.18%	30.38
22	400	2.9%	11.6	1.60	10.00	15.92	2.12%	20.25

(continued overleaf)

(*continued*)

Facility	Exposure X	Spread X%	$Spread	$EL	$Spread −EL	$UL	$UL × UL% = K%	$K
23	200	3.4%	6.8	2.00	4.80	19.90	2.65%	25.32
24	350	3.0%	10.5	1.75	8.75	17.41	2.32%	22.15
25	450	2.6%	11.7	0.90	10.80	8.95	1.19%	11.39
26	350	3.8%	13.3	3.50	9.80	21.86	2.91%	27.81
27	50	6.8%	3.4	1.25	2.15	7.81	1.04%	9.93
28	50	6.6%	3.3	0.75	2.55	4.68	0.62%	5.96
29	100	6.8%	6.8	2.50	4.30	15.61	2.08%	19.86
30	50	6.8%	3.4	1.00	2.40	6.24	0.83%	7.95
31	400	4.1%	16.4	4.00	12.40	24.98	3.33%	31.78
32	50	4.6%	2.3	0.75	1.55	4.68	0.62%	5.96
33	300	3.8%	11.4	3.75	7.65	23.42	3.12%	29.80
34	50	6.8%	3.4	1.25	2.15	7.81	1.04%	9.93
35	100	4.8%	4.8	2.00	2.80	12.49	1.67%	15.89
36	450	4.0%	18.0	5.63	12.38	35.13	4.68%	44.69
37	100	5.0%	5.0	1.50	3.50	9.37	1.25%	11.92
38	200	4.3%	8.6	2.00	6.60	12.49	1.67%	15.89
39	400	4.8%	19.2	7.50	11.70	46.84	6.24%	59.59
40	100	4.8%	4.8	1.50	3.30	9.37	1.25%	11.92
41	150	4.8%	7.2	1.50	5.70	9.37	1.25%	11.92
42	150	3.8%	5.7	1.50	4.20	9.37	1.25%	11.92
43	150	4.3%	6.5	1.50	4.95	9.37	1.25%	11.92
44	150	5.3%	8.0	2.00	5.95	12.49	1.67%	15.89
45	200	5.1%	10.2	4.00	6.20	24.98	3.33%	31.78
46	350	2.6%	9.1	1.75	7.35	10.93	1.46%	13.90
47	300	2.6%	7.8	1.50	6.30	9.37	1.25%	11.92
48	500	2.5%	12.5	2.50	10.00	15.61	2.09%	19.86
49	400	3.8%	15.2	7.50	7.70	46.84	6.25%	59.59
50	500	3.3%	16.5	5.00	11.50	31.22	4.16%	39.73
	Total **11 000**	**Mean A** **4.300%**	**Total** **401.00**	**Total** **100.58**		**Total $UL** **750.17**	**Total%** **100%**	**Total** **954.43**

[a]UL stands for 'Unexpected Loss' measured by loss volatility.
[b]The dollar value of capital, K, is the capital allocation, $K\%$, times total capital 954.43. Figures are rounded.

56

Portfolio Reporting (2)

This chapter provides views on the portfolio structure, slicing the portfolio along various dimensions of interest. These include risk, performance and business dimensions as well. The overall view does not suffice because managers need to 'drill down' in the portfolio to find the sources of excess risks or insufficient returns and decide where they should focus corrective actions.

The Information Technology (IT) architecture needs to accommodate all demands. This necessitates a data warehouse combined with adequate reporting and front-end tools to manipulate simultaneously all risks and business dimensions.

Slicing the portfolio along risk dimensions shows how different risk components, exposure size, default probability or recovery, contribute to risk. Views differ across risk dimensions because each single one does not provide a complete picture. For example, exposure is not risk. It is only a risk component. This raises the issue of how to synthesize risk, paving the way for limits in terms of expected loss or capital, which combine all dimensions.

Performance reports address the mispricing or gaps between target income and actual income or, alternatively, the average portfolio risk-adjusted return. Mispricing reports visualize these gaps and help focus on corrective actions (ex post view) or future decisions (ex ante view). Plain Risk-adjusted Return on Capital (RaRoC) and Shareholders Value Added (SVA) reports show which transactions and subportfolios contribute more or less to the overall portfolio performance.

Finally, reporting risk and return along business dimensions allows managers to move back and forth from financial views to business views.

The first section deals with the information architecture required to monitor risk. The second section provides sample reports on risk and risk-adjusted performance measures.

The last section provides business views of the portfolio segments and sample combinations with risk and return dimensions.

IT ISSUES

Risk information has several characteristics making risk data management a serious challenge: risks are multidimensional, they need interactive investigation by end-users and require moving back and forth from synthetic Value at Risk (VaR) to underlying sources of risk. Identifying the sources of risk conditions the ability to hedge risks, since we cannot hedge directly synthetic metrics combining entangled dimensions. Risk management processes require adequate risk data warehouses, integration of models and interactive front-ends for monitoring risk. IT plays a key role in implementing the entire risk process and provides the necessary interface for data gathering, running models and reporting through interactive front-ends with end-users (Figure 56.1).

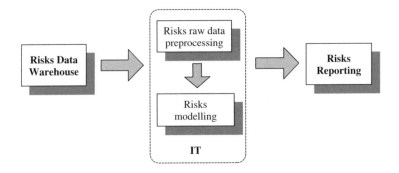

FIGURE 56.1   Risk data, risk modelling, reporting and IT

Credit risk information is a complex set of data. The risk data warehouse is a dedicated database for collecting all risk data in order to analyse it. On-Line Analytical Processing (OLAP) and data mining allow us to perform these analyses along the multiple dimensions relevant for monitoring risk, identifying its sources, detecting patterns across transactions and providing all reports for conducting business.

The criteria for 'slicing' a bank's portfolio are multiple: excess utilization over risk limits, transaction data for risk assessment purposes and preparing credit risk decisions, cross-sectional data by country or rating, or any other relevant dimension, in addition to the usual business views such as customers, products and business units. Moreover, modelling adds new metrics to classical measures, such as economic values of exposures, expected and unexpected losses, capital and so on. This magnifies the number of dimensions of risk to deal with for management purposes. It becomes critical to handle all of them, and to have useful views along all relevant dimensions and risk metrics.

Multiple dimensions magnify the need for filtering the data interactively. Reports provide views on risk and return, and raise issues such as why risks are high or low in portfolio segments, or why mispricing is so important in some business segments. These findings inspire new investigations, making data mining interactive for end-users. Interactivity is necessary whenever the search for new information depends on previous findings suggesting new investigations. Examples abound. Discovering a new excess exposure over limits necessitates understanding why such excesses appear. They might result from new transactions, or simply from the risk drift of existing transactions. Corrective actions depend on the sources of excess risks. Risk management is event-driven.

New measures require two-way processes for implementation. The power of VaR is in combining multiple measures into a single VaR figure. However, this single measure is not a substitute for all others. VaR solves the issue of quantifying the adequate capital. It also provides a single synthesis of multiple measures. The drawback is that it embeds many underlying sources of risk. Synthetic measures are convenient, but not fully explicit. 'Why is risk measured by allocated capital high or low for a particular segment?' is not a simple question any more. How will end-users disentangle the components of risk? Without access to underlying sources of risk, it is not feasible to control VaR. It is not possible to hedge directly VaR. We can only hedge the underlying components. VaR-type measures of risk require a two-way implementation: from underlying parameters to VaR, and from VaR to the different sources of risk that they synthesize (Figure 56.2).

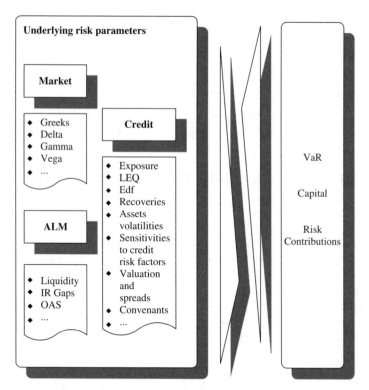

FIGURE 56.2 Two-way view of VaR and underlying risk parameters

OLAP and data mining address these issues efficiently. OLAP allows us to view data along different angles or dimensions. Data mining, drilling-down and slicing risk data help to discern patterns in the data, for example into subsets of risk–return outliers. OLAP can store outputs of scenarios, or even run new scenarios in real time, making powerful 'what if' functions available to end-users in the right reporting format allowing easy interpretation of the outputs. Embedding the risk information in the right architecture, with

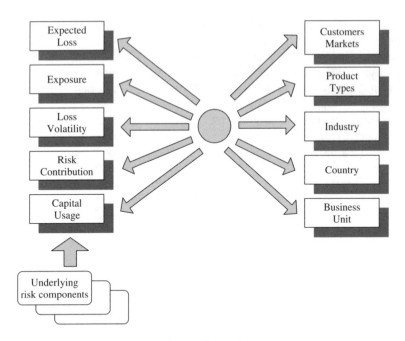

FIGURE 56.3   **Risk–return versus business dimensions**

a number of preset interactive functions, is a prerequisite for making the risk management process a reality through adequate front-ends (Figure 56.3).

REPORTING RISK AND PERFORMANCE MEASURES

The basic risk measures used are:

- Exposure, either in value or as a percentage of total portfolio exposure.
- Capital in excess of expected loss, either in value or as a percentage of total portfolio capital.
- Edf as a percentage.
- Lgd as a percentage of exposure.
- Expected loss and unexpected loss.
- Income measures, either as spreads or risk-adjusted performance measures, namely the RaRoC ratio and SVA.

All dots in the sample charts of this chapter represent individual facilities. Subsequent sections provide sample reporting examples.

Facility Exposures and Risk Components (Edf and Lgd)

Two basic underlying components of credit risk, besides exposure, are the default probability (Edf) and the severity of loss under default, or loss given default (Lgd). They are basic ingredients of the expected loss EL, since Edf $\times$ Lgd measures the loss rate. In this sample portfolio, the default probabilities do not correlate with exposures. However, there are more small exposures in the area of high loss under default (low recovery rate). This is in line with expectations (Figure 56.4).

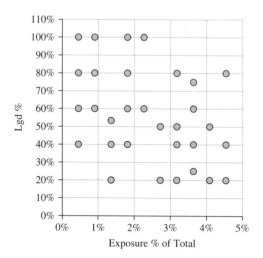

FIGURE 56.4 Facility exposure and loss given default (%) or severity of loss

Setting Up Limits: EL and LV

Expected loss EL as a percentage of exposure is a relevant measure for risk quality, for assigning ratings or setting up limits and delegations. Loss volatility LV, both as a percentage of exposure and in value, synthesizes several risk dimensions, risk quantity, risk quality and capital allocation. Charts visualize the trade-off between risk quality and exposure.

Risk Quality versus Exposure

The EL–exposure graph (Figure 56.5) shows what happens when capping either EL or exposure. There are four quadrants, and points spread over all of them. The best measure of risk quality is EL as a percentage of exposure, while exposure (in value or as a percentage of total) measures the volume of risk. In addition, EL as a percentage is a frequent basis for rating risk because it combines both default probability and severity of loss. The EL in value serves better for economic provisioning. The EL as a percentage possibly serves for setting delegations and limits in terms of risk class. The graph shows EL as a percentage of exposure.

Capping exposure does not eliminate high EL, since there are many high ELs in the small exposure area of the chart. Conversely, capping percentage EL does not eliminate high exposures in general. The graph shows a tendency to take on more exposure for a small EL risk. It also shows that it is not equivalent to set a limit in EL and in exposure. Since 'exposure' is not risk, because it does not embed all relevant risk dimensions, it is worth considering setting limits in EL.

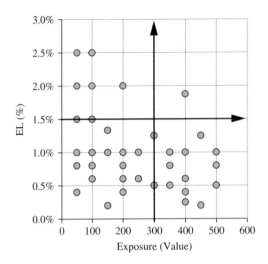

FIGURE 56.5   Expected loss (%) and exposure (value)

The Risk Quality–Exposure Trade-off, LV and Setting Up Limits

The LV(%)–exposure chart shows a similar picture (Figure 56.6). Since LV is the basis of capital allocation, capping LV is another option to up economic risk limits rather than exposure. Note, however, that EL and LV depend on the same risk components—EaD, DP and Lgd—although LV is 'closer' to capital than EL.

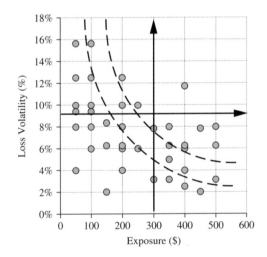

FIGURE 56.6   Setting up limits using LV% and LV value

The graph of LV(%)–exposure value also shows the trade-off between risk quality (EL% or LV%) and risk quantity (exposure). The product LV(%) × exposure is the LV in value. Bounding this product is similar to bounding LV in value. The various levels of LV value in the LV(%)–exposure graphs are hyperboles, each one corresponding to an LV value. Pushing the curve towards the centre limits both quality and quantity of risk. Let's assume that the lower curve shown in the graph is the limit. There are still several points above this curve. The implication is that the subjective trade-off between risk quality and risk quantity does not filter high LV values.

Risk-based limits in LV eliminate some small and large exposures that 'appear' less risky than they are. In order to push the LV value under a preset limit, we have to decrease either the risk quality (EL% or LV%) or the risk quantity (exposure), or both, to move below the risk limit curve. Since LV relates to capital allocation, bounding the LV is a proxy for bounding economic capital allocation.

Risk-adjusted Performance and Mispricing Reports

The performance measures relate revenues to exposure or economic risk measures. Revenues are All-In Spreads (AISs), including interest margins and fees annualized over the life of the facility, either in value or as a percentage of exposure. The percentage measure is the accounting Return On Assets (ROA), which is not risk-adjusted because it relates revenues to the 'volume' on risk only, ignoring risk quality.

The risk-adjusted return is the RaRoC, or Sharpe ratio, of the facility, based on the allocated capital: RaRoC = (AIS − EL)/(allocated capital − EL). The RaRoC should be above the hurdle rate k, representing the target pre-tax and pre-operating expenses return on economic capital. RaRoC can be negative since it is the ratio of a difference in spreads and expected loss to allocated capital. The SVA is AIS − EL − kK. The SVA measure combines both size of transactions and risk-adjusted return. It shows the relative 'richness' of transactions in value: positive SVA indicates creation of value. Unlike negative RaRoC, negative SVA has an interpretation, since it means destruction of value. The SVA minimum line is therefore the zero value horizontal line, a function of the 25% hurdle rate. The average SVA is the ratio of total SVA by the number of exposures, 50, or 1.24.

Risk–return profiles are also mispricing reports since they show gaps between target and effective pricing. Mispricing reports serve to identify which facilities contribute to the 'richness' of the portfolio and which do not. There are two mispricing reports:

- The first mispricing is the gap between the target minimum return and the effective return. For RaRoC, the benchmark is the hurdle rate 25%. For SVA, it is the zero value showing that a facility breaks even on the cost of risk.
- The second mispricing is relative to portfolio average. It shows whether a facility is more or less profitable, after risk adjustment, to the average portfolio risk-adjusted return. For the RaRoC, the reference value is 38%.

For SVA, it is possible to use the average SVA as a benchmark, or 1.24. However, the SVA depends on size, so that the actual reference value for the portfolio should be the SVA per unit of exposure, or 61.82/11 000 = 0.56%. Mispricing would become the gap between the SVA per unit of exposure for each facility and the portfolio average unit exposure SVA.

We provide below representative reports for our sample portfolio (for illustration only).

RaRoC Reports

Figure 56.7 shows that accounting measures of profitability (ROA%) and risk-adjusted measures (RaRoC%) have no relationship. This is the primary reason for risk-adjusting performance measures. Negative RaRoCs appear in real portfolios whenever the spread does not compensate the EL plus allocated costs. When isolating a transaction, the AIS might not exceed EL because market spreads might not compensate risk. The phenomenon often disappears when extending revenues to all transactions and services to a client, because fees and other profitable transactions might more than compensate the lowest profitability transactions originated to build up business volume with a client.

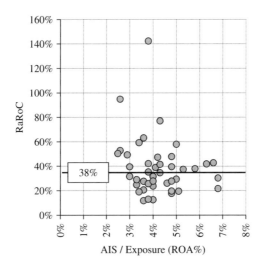

FIGURE 56.7   ROA% or spread% versus RaRoC

AIS − EL in value plotted against capital shows the numerator and the denominator of the RaRoC ratio (Figure 56.8). All points above the 25% line create values and all points below the line destroy values. All points above the 38% line are richer than the portfolio average, and conversely. Mispricings are gaps between the points and the two lines representing 25% × K and 38% × K. The graph shows both what the pricing should be (in terms of risk-adjusted return) and what it is effectively. It also allows us to identify over- and underpriced facilities compared with either the hurdle rate or the average return.

The plot of RaRoC versus exposure provides another view of mispricing (Figure 56.9). It shows which facilities are above the 25% hurdle rate. All points above the horizontal 25% line create values, and all points below destroy values. Similarly, all points above the 38% average contribute to increasing the portfolio RaRoC above the average, and vice versa.

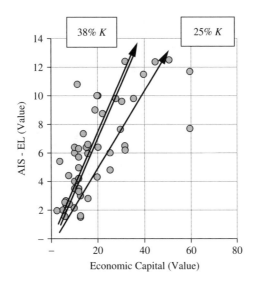

FIGURE 56.8 Expected spread and capital

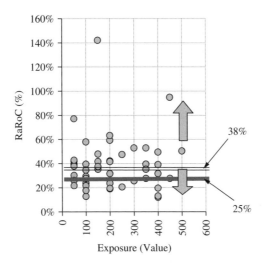

FIGURE 56.9 RaRoC, mispricing and exposure

SVA Reports

The SVA reports are in value (Figure 56.10). The graphs compare each facility SVA
with the arithmetic average of the portfolio. This is convenient, but not accurate, since
the SVA combines both size and profitability. An alternative graph would show the unit
exposure SVA of each facility and compare it with the average unit exposure SVA of
the portfolio. In any case, there are negative SVAs, which correspond to RaRoC points
lower than the 25% hurdle rate. The 25% RaRoC value corresponds here to the zero SVA
value.

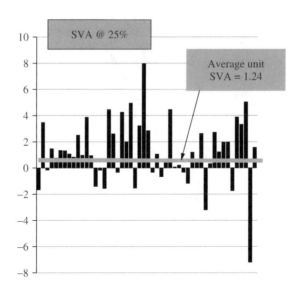

FIGURE 56.10   Facilities SVA at the 25% hurdle rate

REPORTING RISK–RETURN VERSUS BUSINESS DIMENSIONS

Our sample reports use industry and business units as management dimensions and grouping criteria, cross-tabulated with risk and return measures. Using industry and business units we show risks and performance. The risk dimensions include:

- Exposure, using the sum of values for aggregation.
- Capital, using the sum of values for aggregation.
- EL%, using the arithmetic average value in each cell (the exposure weighted average is also suitable).
- Edf%, using the arithmetic average value in each cell (the exposure weighted average is also suitable).
- Lgd%, using the arithmetic average value in each cell (the exposure weighted average is also suitable).

The performance dimensions are risk-adjusted:

- RaRoC%, using the arithmetic average value in each cell (the exposure weighted average is also suitable).
- SVA in value, using the sum of values for aggregation.

Tridimensional representations allow us to show risk or return vertically, aggregated or averaged, for industries A and B versus business units V and W, in the horizontal dimensions. OLAP multidimensional capabilities are valuable from a business standpoint since they allow us to shift from one view to another and drill down in aggregates to understand which are the sources contributing to the risk or performance aggregated measures.

All figures are self-explanatory, mentioning the variables and whether they are aggregates or arithmetic averages. They are illustrations only. Actual reports would be generated with OLAP techniques, using any type of combinations, allowing us to slice the portfolio across any dimension, or drill down in aggregates to find transaction subsets or averages of risk or return, and allowing us to identify dynamically on a front-end which transactions contribute more to risk and return, for example.

Highlighting the risk concentrations and the performances along various management dimensions suggests the path to follow to find the 'whys' of the difference, paving the way directly for management issues and policies. The reports illustrate the multidimensional nature of the portfolio analysis. Segments other than those defined could also be used to deal with such issues as setting limits, setting target revenues, reallocating resources, restructuring the portfolio and so on. Further analysis, such as 'what if' simulations, trading-off exposure from one segment to another to improve the risk–return profile, and 'optimization' would all contribute to the enhancement of the risk–return profile of the portfolio.

Exposures and Capital by Portfolio Segments

The charts show that the ranking across business units and industries differs when using as risk metric exposure weights or capital weights (Figures 56.11 and 56.12).

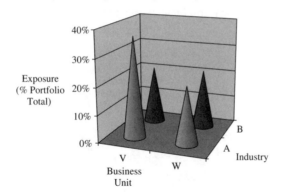

FIGURE 56.11   Exposure by industry and business unit segments

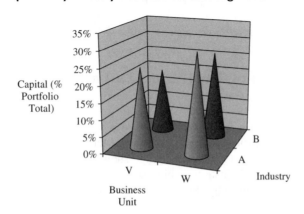

FIGURE 56.12   Capital by industry and business unit segments

Risk Components by Industry–Business Unit Segment

The graphs suggest that higher averaged Edfs correlate with higher averaged Lgds in percentage terms. Checking whether this is an averaging effect or not requires using the scatter plots of Edf versus Lgd in percentage terms (Figures 56.13 and 56.14).

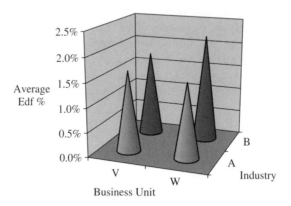

FIGURE 56.13   Edf by industry and business unit segments

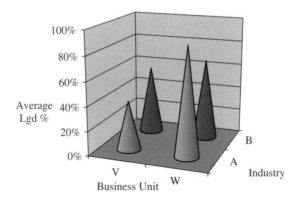

FIGURE 56.14   Lgd by industry and business unit segments

Economic Measures of Risk (EL and UL) by Industry–Business Unit Segments

Figure 56.15 shows how EL as a percentage varies across the portfolio segments. The LV, as a percentage of exposure, has a similar pattern as EL%, because LV and EL depend on the same risk components. The graph shows clearly a higher economic risk in the W business unit across industries, which suggests drilling down to the Edf and Lgd underlying drivers to find out why this pattern appears.

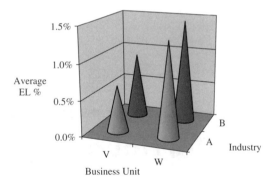

FIGURE 56.15   EL% by industry and business unit segments

Performance Reports

The RaRoC graph shows the W business unit to have a lower risk-adjusted performance across both industries, with a lower than hurdle rate averaged RaRoC, and a slightly negative SVA. For RaRoC, the 25% plane provides the target minimum value, while for SVA it is the zero SVA plane. Most of the created value comes from the 'Industry A–Business Unit V' portfolio segment (Figures 56.16 and 56.17)

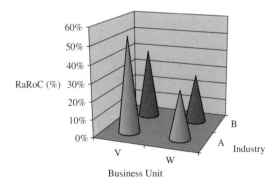

FIGURE 56.16   RaRoC% by industry and business unit segments

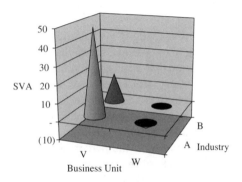

FIGURE 56.17   SVA by industry and business unit segments

57

Portfolio Applications

This chapter details portfolio applications beyond descriptive reports. Its scope extends over three topics:

- Risk-based limits or economic limits of risk resulting from a deterioration of the risk-adjusted performance when the exposure size grows.
- Sensitivity analyses serve to determine to which risk drivers the portfolio risk is most sensitive.
- Risk–return optimization shows how to trade-off risk across exposures to enhance the overall portfolio return. There is potential for enhancement because income is proportional to size while risk is not.

The three sections illustrate these issues.

RISK-BASED LIMITS

We consider a two-segment portfolio, with two exposures: A is an existing exposure, and B is a new exposure of varying size. We examine what happens in terms of return on economic capital when the additional B exposure increases, while its AIS in percentage or, equivalently, its Return on Assets (ROA) remains constant.

A number of simplifying assumptions help without loss of generality. The exposure of A remains constant and equal to 50; the exposure of B is initially 10 and progressively increases; A and B share the same default probability 1% and the same zero recovery rate; the risk of A and B are independent; the percentage AIS or ROA remains constant at 1%; regulatory capital is 4% of exposure; the required return on capital, economic or regulatory, is 25% pre-tax; the loss volatilities, both standalone and marginal, are used as a proxy for economic capital.

We first check that the 1% ROA provides an AIS in line with the target return of A using regulatory capital. For A, the AIS is $1\% \times 50 = 0.5$, the regulatory capital is $4\% \times 50 = 2$, and the ratio AIS/capital is $0.5/2 = 25\%$. The AIS of B is usually proportional to exposure. It would here be $1\% \times$ exposure, resulting in a return to regulatory capital of $1\%/4\% = 25\%$, since regulatory capital is 4% of exposure.

Instead of referring to the contractual AIS, we now look at what it should be when B's exposure increases, using a target return on economic capital of 25%. The required AIS is no longer proportional to exposure because economic capital is not. We simulate the behaviour of the required AIS of B based on a target return on marginal risk contribution to the portfolio loss volatility, when the exposure of B increases.

If the exposure of B is 10, we first derive its marginal contribution to the portfolio volatility. Since the default probabilities are 1%, the standalone unit loss volatilities are $\sqrt{d \times (1-d)} = \sqrt{1\% \times 99\%} = 9.950\%$. Accordingly, the standalone loss volatilities of A and B are respectively $50 \times 9.950\% = 4.975$ and $9.950\% \times 10 = 0.995$. Since risks are independent, the portfolio loss volatility is the square root of the portfolio variance, which sums up the standalone variances. The sum of variances is $24.750 + 0.990 = 25.740$ and the portfolio loss volatility is the square root, or 5.074. The initial portfolio volatility with A only was 4.975. The incremental loss volatility due to B is the difference $5.074 - 4.975 = 0.099$. By contrast, the additional regulatory capital due to B is $10 \times 4\% = 0.04$. It is much lower than its marginal risk contribution.

Now, we increase the size of B's exposure up to 50 and calculate again its marginal risk contribution and its incremental regulatory capital. The new standalone loss volatility of B becomes $50 \times 9.95\% = 4.975$, identical to that of A because exposures share the same characteristics. The portfolio loss variance $24.750 + 24.750 = 49.50$ under independence of risks, and the portfolio loss volatility increases to $\sqrt{49.50} = 7.036$. The marginal risk contribution to volatility is now $7.036 - 4.975 = 2.061$. The marginal regulatory capital is only $4\% \times 50 = 2$. We observe that the marginal risk contribution now gets higher than the marginal capital, whether it was lower when the exposure of B was only 10 or not.

The required AIS on marginal risk contribution is $25\% \times 2.061 = 0.515$, while it is still $25\% \times 2 = 0.5$ for regulatory capital. Conversely, the effective return on marginal risk contribution at the 1% AIS is $1\% \times 50 = 0.5$ and the return on risk contribution is $0.5/2.061 = 24.264\%$, now lower than the current $0.5/2 = 25\%$ on regulatory capital. The size of 50 is very close to the break-even value at which the new exposure fails to meet the target return on economic capital when we stick to a contractual ROA of 1%. Trying a higher size would confirm this finding, the constant 1% ROA providing a decreasing return on economic capital, while maintaining the 25% on regulatory capital. This break-even value is the risk-based limit.

The underlying reason for the existence of this economic limit is that economic capital increases more than proportionally to exposure, while the ROA remains constant. The purpose of this analysis is to demonstrate that setting limits has a purely economic rationale.

In Figure 57.1, the required return as a percentage of exposure based on marginal risk contribution grows with size. The return on exposure (or ROA%) is a constant, implying that revenues grow proportionally with exposure. It is at least above or equal to the minimum return required on capital. There is an optimal size for the transaction since the ROA no longer compensates the additional risk contribution beyond a certain size.

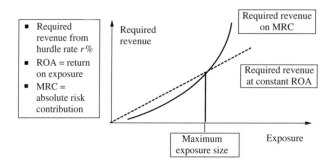

FIGURE 57.1   Risk–return and risk-based limits

Other reasons, such as the size of the exposure relative to the borrowing capacity of the obligor, limit the size per obligor. The economic rationale provides a basis for setting limits, when no other constraint is binding.

For instance, when doubling the exposure, from 50 up to 100, the absolute risk contribution to loss volatility increases from around 5 up to around 15, or three times as much. Hence, the risk–reward profile deteriorates when B's exposure increases.

SENSITIVITY ANALYSIS

Various sensitivity analyses apply to portfolios. To proceed on an orderly basis, we need to refer to a unique base case, and change only one variable at a time. For instance, we can change A's exposure from 100 to 110, then revert to the 100 value for A and change B's exposure from 50 to 55, then revert again to the base case, and change another variable. Several variables are of interest, such as the default probabilities, since they result from judgmental ratings making stress testing useful. In addition, a sensitivity analysis requires us to focus on some relevant variables, such as the portfolio loss volatility, the capital or the RaRoC of the portfolio.

Changing the values of inputs changes the values of the output variables. First, since there are several changes to consider, the number of runs can increase quickly. It is necessary to restrict the number of simulations and 'what if' runs for easy interpretation. Fortunately, there is no need to consider unrealistic values for inputs, and we can restrict them to the range of feasible values. Second, the influence on the target variable can be large or small. Ranking inputs according to the change in target variables is a standard practice for limiting the number of inputs to critical ones that have the most important effect on the target variables.

A convenient representation of this type of analysis is the so-called 'tornado' graph. A 'tornado' graph visualizes, for a given target variable, such as the portfolio loss volatility, the influences of given variations of the inputs. Once a range of variations of an input is given, the variations of the target variable appear ranked from largest to smallest. On top of the 'tornado', large bars represent the largest changes generated by the input variations to which the calculated variable is the most sensitive. Moving down, the sensitivity decreases and the bar gets shorter, providing the 'tornado' image. Critical inputs are on top. In the graph of Figure 57.2, the portfolio loss volatility is sensitive to the exposure of A, to

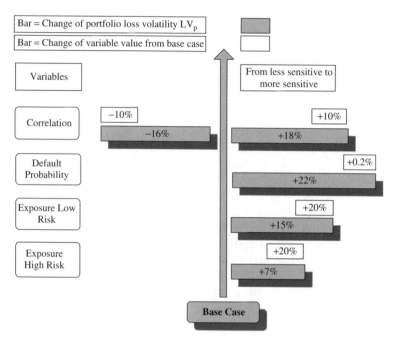

FIGURE 57.2 Tornado graph and sensitivity analysis. Target variable: portfolio loss volatility

the default probability of A and to the default correlation, the other variables being less critical (given the ranges of variations considered).

RISK–RETURN OPTIMIZATION

Enhancing the risk–return profile of the portfolio can minimize risk given return, increase return at constant risk, or improve both if the portfolio structure is inefficient. In addition, when removing funding constraints, it is no longer necessary to trade-off risks and return within the portfolio by changing the exposures. It becomes necessary to decide along which direction portfolio expansion is more efficient. We illustrate through simple examples the trade-off under constraint of risk and return and the case of portfolio expansion.

Trade-off Risks within Limits

We can use the above sensitivity analysis to illustrate what happens when we increase the exposure in different segments. For this purpose, we use a portfolio segmentation into high-risk and low-risk obligors, because it is straightforward.

When we increase exposure on high-risk obligors by 20%, the loss volatility increases by 6.56%. If we increase the exposure by 20% on low-risk obligors, the loss volatility increases by 15.12%. This is more than twice as much. The ratio is $15.12/6.56 = 2.305$. This means that we can trade-off exposures between high-risk and low-risk exposures with a ratio of 2.305 to 1 at constant risk, the risk metric being loss volatility. An additional exposure of 1 on the low-risk obligor is, on average, equivalent to 2.305 of additional exposure on low-risk obligors. This assumes that we hold constant the structure of the exposure and the loss given default. In practice, more accurate calculations are necessary, to revaluate the portfolio loss volatility.

Portfolio Optimization

Portfolio optimization under a global funding constraint means:

- Reducing risk, at a constant return.
- Increasing revenue, at the same risk.

If we assume the spread as a percentage constant, the issue is to define the portfolio weights leading to a more efficient risk–return profile. Formally, this is the well-known problem of maximizing return given risk, or minimizing risk given return, a constrained optimization problem. In practice, enhancing the risk–return profile through trade-off of exposures requires only simple calculations as a first approximation.

From Table 57.1, we see that the capital and Shareholders Value Added (SVA) expand when expanding the exposures. However, expanding the low-risk exposures decreases the RaRoC and the SVA. Therefore, it is better to expand the high-risk exposure, which slightly improves the SVA, even though it deteriorates the overall RaRoC. In this example, the base case is the best of the three cases (Figure 57.3).

TABLE 57.1   Enhancing the risk–return profile of the portfolio

	Base case	High-risk exposure + 20%	Low-risk exposure + 20%
Loss volatility	221	252	244
Portfolio expected loss EL	101	114	107
Loss at 99%	1055	1190	1196
Capital in excess of EL	954	1076	1089
Portfolio All-In Spread (AIS)	401	446	436
Portfolio RaRoC	31.48%	30.81%	30.17%
Portfolio SVA	61.82	62.46	56.27

Portfolio optimization follows these lines. Restructuring exposures generates new risk–return combinations. Some dominate others. These make up the efficient frontier. Then, it becomes technically a simple matter to see how to move to various points on the efficient frontier by changing the portfolio structure. This requires a full optimization module in the portfolio model, because both capital allocation and return are allowed to vary (Figure 57.4).

Optimization under funding constraints differs from optimizing the portfolio expansion. In addition, a full optimization model should recognize the limits imposed on business volume, by risk class, industry and country. Economically, limits are sub-optimal. On the other hand, portfolio expansion remains business-driven, and the 'optimization' should well integrate both the economic efficiency and the business policy. The optimization module helps, but is not a substitute for business policy and limits.

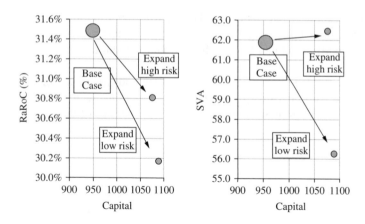

FIGURE 57.3   Efficient portfolio expansions

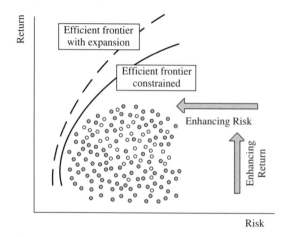

FIGURE 57.4   Optimization functions with portfolio models

KMV Portfolio Manager and Credit Metrics illustrate the two philosophies. The first model embeds a constrained optimization module providing various optimized outputs, such as:

- Optimization at constant risk.
- Optimization at constant return.
- In addition, it visualizes the efficient frontier given the funding constraint.

Modelling the efficient frontier under no expansion guides the rebalancing of the portfolio through exposure sizes. Revising limits, adjusting the 'final take' (the commitment size retained by the leading bank) and securitizations are examples of business transactions that rebalance the portfolio.

Credit Metrics does not offer optimization functions. However, it provides the marginal risk contribution, rather than the absolute risk contribution. This is theoretically more adequate when considering expansion of exposures along various segments or individual obligors.

Both models allow recalculation of the marginal contributions anyway. With small exposures, these do not differ significantly from the absolute risk contributions. With large exposures, the portfolio model has to run with and without new exposures, repeatedly if necessary.

Models provide valuable insights for restructuring and expanding, or contracting, some portfolio segments or individual exposures. In fact, without such models there is no way to compare various 'what if' scenarios and rank them in terms of their risk–return profiles.

58

Credit Derivatives: Definitions

Credit derivatives (CD) are a major innovation in that they offer credit risk protections that were not available until recently. The potential for managing and hedging portfolio credit risk seems considerable. Until the appearance of credit derivatives, and besides insurances, there was no way to hedge credit risk, once originated, other than by restructuring a transaction, which is an uneasy process.

Credit derivatives provide this possibility without altering the actual assets held by a bank. In addition, they benefit from the potential depth of the market, driven by the attractiveness that they provide to sellers, or investors, in these instruments. Because of their innovative characteristics, they offer plenty of new opportunities for major players, such as banks having exposure to credit risk, and for investors willing to sell protection in exchange for a credit exposure and the corresponding return.

Credit derivatives perform classical functions embedded in standard products providing insurance on credit risk. They are like back-to-back deals, where a third party allows its credit standing to be used as a guarantee to make a market between counterparties who, otherwise, would not enter into a transaction directly. Credit derivatives perform similar functions with more flexibility and are not simple substitutes for traditional guarantees. They provide protections for underlying assets that often differ from those effectively held by protection buyers, and they allow both buyers and sellers of protection to customize their credit risk exposures. Credit derivatives are attractive because they provide flexible hedges to the protection seekers and new investment opportunities to the protection sellers. In order to organize and develop the market, the terms of these contracts have evolved sufficiently to make transactions feasible.

There are three basic types of credit derivatives:

- Credit default products providing a specified payment under default events.
- Total return swaps exchanging revenues and capital gains–losses of the underlying assets.
- Credit spread products allowing positions to be taken on future spreads.

The spectrum also extends from credit derivatives to other products providing further flexibility, such as 'basket swaps', credit-linked notes or sovereign risk derivatives.

This chapter is a broad overview of credit derivatives. The first section introduces their specific functions and describes who are the key players. The second section details the main definitions and key terms for understanding the characteristics and mechanisms of these products. Subsequent sections describe the different types of credit derivative products and the rationales of using them as protection buyers or protection sellers.

CREDIT DERIVATIVE FUNCTIONS

This section provides a broad overview of credit derivatives, what functions they fulfil, who has an interest in them and why.

Functions of Credit Derivatives

Credit derivatives are instruments serving to trade credit risk by isolating the credit risk from the underlying transactions. The emergence of credit derivative instruments is a major innovation because, unlike other risks, such as market or interest rate risk, there was no way, until they appeared, to hedge credit risk.

Hence, the first function of credit derivatives for risk takers is hedging. A credit derivative provides protection against other credit events, such as a downgrade or default event. When such an event occurs, the credit derivative provides a payment to the party suffering the loss from the credit event as classical insurances do. But there are many differences. For example, credit derivatives do not necessarily refer to assets held by the bank. Another difference is that credit events need specifications and defining the amount to pay, since it is not straightforward to value a downgrade or a default, because of recovery uncertainty. In addition, there are various ways to define credit events. For example, default can be delays in payment, restructuring or filing for bankruptcy.

Credit derivatives allow us to separate trade in the credit risk of assets from trade in the assets themselves since, like other classical derivatives, it is possible to trade them without trading the reference assets. Another salient feature of credit derivatives is that they are off-balance sheet and do not necessitate entering directly into loan arrangements or purchases of bonds, nor do they necessitate the prior agreement of the issuer of the reference asset. This is why so many synthetic securitizations, structured with credit derivatives, developed in Europe, because such agreements are not yet usual.

The products are generally classified into three broad groups: total return swaps, credit spread products and credit default products. In a total return swap, the protection seeker exchanges the 'total return' of an asset, which combines both current revenues and capital gains or losses, with a fee paid to the protection seller. This provides a protection against a downside move of the value of the reference asset. The investor looks for an enhanced return. Credit spread derivatives exchange a risky spread against the risk-free rate, or a risky spread against another. The protection provider, or investor, looks for enhanced revenue, while the buyer seeks protection against a loss of asset value due to a widening of credit spreads. Credit default products offer payment in the event of default of a reference asset. If the protection provider is rational, he does not believe the event likely enough to absorb the enhanced revenue from the sale of the instrument.

The two parties are:

- The protection seller who sells the credit derivative.
- The protection buyer who pays a premium and/or fees to the protection seller, in exchange for the protection.

The terms of buyer and seller are best thought of as 'buyer of protection' and 'seller of protection'. Alternatively, buying risk means selling protection, and selling risk means buying protection. The terminology is confusing because it often refers to traditional derivatives. For example, premiums paid to get a payment in the event of default suggest more an option than a swap, although the contract is an obligation. In addition, 'premiums' apply for credit swaps, but they are fees and spreads exchanged during the contract life.

Views on Credit Derivatives

Credit derivatives serve for various players, who view them from different angles. Under the insurance view, the credit derivative market is like a market of protections, 'transferring' credit risk between buyers and sellers of credit derivatives. Investors look at these instruments as providing some return enhancements through the revenue attached or as a technique for replicating exposures to which they have no direct access, as well as trading credit exposures.

Insurance View

Credit derivatives look like insurances. They require a regular payment to provide protection against events whose materialization has a perceived low probability. If the event such as a default occurs, the insurer pays the loss given default, net of recoveries. The triangle of insuring credit risk brings together a protection seller, a protection buyer and the underlying reference assets. The intermediate player making the market is the protection seller (Figure 58.1).

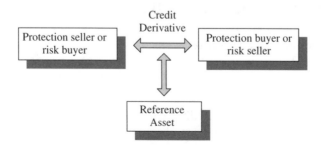

FIGURE 58.1   The triangle: protection seller and buyer, and reference assets

Banks and financial institutions are seekers of protection against credit risk. Corporate entities might use these instruments because they need protection from their customers, especially big customers with whom they have large contracts. Sovereign risk is a case where the size of risk exposure is large enough to warrant a specific protection. All parties are also interested in unbundling the risk components of assets, such as credit and country risks, otherwise tied together in the same loans.

Other Views

Under the investor's view, the market looks at these instruments as promising an attractive and enhanced return when credit events are perceived as having a low probability. The 'search for yield' increases when spreads narrow. If an investor can get a high spread with these instruments, it makes them attractive in spite of default risk. Conversely, when the price of credit risk increases, credit derivatives might be less attractive because they become likely to be 'in-the-money'. Under the risk management view, credit derivatives serve to take or shape credit risk and return, both from a buyer's view and a seller's view of credit derivatives.

The buyer of credit risk actually gains exposure to the risk of the underlying assets. This replicates the risk through an off-balance sheet instrument, so that the exposure is only notional. In addition, buying and selling risk implies the transfer, full or partial, of credit risk. Transferring risk can be of mutual interest. Two banks, one heavily concentrated in industry A and the other in industry B, might be willing to exchange, or transfer, their risks to each other in order to achieve a better balance of their portfolios. In addition, the parties are sensitive to the revenue effect of credit risk derivatives.

In general, through the trading of credit risk, credit derivatives serve for replicating, transferring or hedging credit risks. Simultaneously, trading risks shapes the returns because of the related revenues or costs. The players have other motives than insurance, such as adding value to portfolios by trading credit risk separately, managing credit risk of investments or participating indirectly in the loan market. Credit risk derivatives also facilitate arbitraging the price of credit risk across transactions of market sectors. The market of credit risk is such that expectations about what the credit spreads or the recovery rates should be are heterogeneous. This creates opportunities to arbitrage market spreads against an investor's expectations.

MAIN SPECIFICS AND KEY TERMS

The main specifics of credit derivatives are:

- The underlying assets.
- The payment terms.
- The value of payments under a credit event.
- The conditions defining a credit event.
- The risk materialization.
- Legal issues with respect to risk transfers.

Underlying Assets

The credit derivative contracts exchange payments triggered by a credit event of an underlying asset or a basket of assets. The credit event can be a loss in value, a downgrade or a default. The underlying asset can be a bond, a loan or any credit asset, including baskets of assets. There is no need for the asset to be tradable, although observable prices facilitate the valuation of the asset under no default or under default, as well as the measurement of credit risk loss in the event of migrations. As with other derivatives, there is a notional amount. The notional amount might be identical to the principal of a loan, or it can differ from the value of the underlying asset. This allows leveraging the transaction. For instance, it is possible to insure the spread of a bond for an amount that is a multiple of the face value of the underlying bonds. This allows speculation and return (or loss) enhancement because the ratio notional/face value of the underlying asset is higher than 1.

Credit derivatives include forward instruments, with a forward start. Such contracts start at a future date, instead of the inception date. The term of the contract differs from the maturity of the underlying. It might be shorter and/or start forward, allowing tailored term structures of exposures. However, it cannot exceed the maturity of the underlying, since the reference would disappear if the contract were longer. This does not apply with an underlying made up of pools of assets, since there might be a permanent structure of the pool agreed in advance.

Payment Terms

The investor or, equivalently, the risk buyer, or protection seller, receives fees from the buyer of protection plus the interest payments of the underlying assets. The buyer of protection, or the risk seller, receives from the investor an interest, such as LIBOR plus some margin. Payments are both periodic and at termination. Termination payments are settlement payments if the credit risk of the underlying actually materializes. They require the definition of the post-default value. When assets are tradable with a reasonable liquidity, prices are a sound basis for calculating the payment. This leads to choosing underlying assets complying with such conditions, or agreeing in advance to a payout payment (such as a fixed amount). In addition, the determination of the price based on securities needs to be transparent, necessitating some polling of dealer prices to have an objective reference.

Legal Issues

The legal separation of the derivatives from the underlying loan or bond allows transferring the risks without prior consent of the borrower. This transfer extends to economic rights related to the borrower obligation. Such an extension raises legal issues since the holder of the total return swap might exercise rights that could affect the profile of the obligation (in case of distress restructuring or any dispute). Because of this issue, the investor might not have directly such information and the right of representation.

Credit derivatives allow transferring risk without transferring the cash assets. This offers potential whenever it is more difficult to transfer assets than credit risk through derivatives. The development of synthetic structures in Europe for off-loading credit risk without sales of assets illustrates the benefit of this differential legal treatment.

The Value of Payments under a Credit Event

There is some initial reference price, either a nominal value for a loan or a bond price, reflecting the current credit standing of the issuer as well as the contractual payments of this asset. Since listed assets do not have a single price, several dealers' quotes serve to determine a price. Payments relate to the current value of the asset.

For a credit default option, the buyer and seller agree on the payment value, netted from any recoveries or not. For traded assets, the post-default price defines the loss under default. With total return swaps, payments cumulate the capital appreciation or depreciation with the normal asset return. For credit spread derivatives, the payments are a function of the difference between initial and final credit spreads and need conversion into a value. The value is the difference in spreads times a multiple for converting this change into a price change. The multiplier is the duration since it measures the price sensitivity of a bond to a unit change in discount rate. The determination of the duration requires a rule, because of duration drift across time and because it depends on the interest level.

The relationship to the asset does not imply matching the asset price with the derivative notional. Users can leverage the actual exposure of the underlying by using a notional different from the actual asset value. This allows us to customize the exposure. Lenders can reduce their excess exposures. Investors in credit derivatives can leverage their investment and customize their expected return.

Delivery is in cash, or with securities. The second option raises the usual issue of what to deliver, since the underlying asset might disappear. This requires defining the equivalent assets to deliver in advance.

Credit Events

There are two overlapping categories of credit events: those of the underlying asset credit event and those that trigger a derivative credit event. The second group includes all conditions that trigger exercise of the derivative obligations. The two sets of events normally overlap, but they might differ in practice. The difference might exist because any deterioration of the credit standing of the underlying asset might serve to trigger the derivative obligations. For instance, mergers might weaken the credit standing of firms and be looked at as a potential credit event triggering exercise of a credit derivative, while it is a migration event for credit risk. Furthermore, a merger might not even trigger a migration and still be a credit event for a credit derivative.

For the reference asset, credit events include: payment obligation default; bankruptcy or insolvency event; restructuring or equivalent; rating downgrade beyond a specified threshold; change in credit spread exceeding a specified level; payout event of a struc-ture. Failure to pay is a key credit event. However, a grace period can delay the failure event. Credit events might have a wide scope. Downgrades usually refer to ratings. They differ according to whether they relate to long-term ratings or short-term ratings. Default events are more restrictive than credit events. They relate to any contractual clause that triggers default. The event itself is a payment default obligation or an insolvency event, plus all events that trigger covenants resulting in cross-default and cross-acceleration. Such obligations refer broadly to any borrowings by the reference entity from several lenders. Since they refer to several parties, they are 'cross' obligations.

Materialization

Such events might be difficult to define precisely, because of potential disputes. Materiality clauses help to avoid triggering a 'false' credit event by specifying the observable consequences of a credit event. Common factors are minimum variations of prices or changes in spreads, legal notices and publicly available information. Price materiality refers to a minimum difference between the initial price of the reference asset and the price if the risk materializes. Spread materiality refers to a minimum difference between the spread at inception and the final spread.

However, all are subject to dispute and materialization should be legally acceptable to all parties. This issue is imperfectly solved as of today, although the term sheets of derivative contracts now embed some experience.

CREDIT DEFAULT PRODUCTS

These include credit default swaps, credit default options or indemnity agreements. Conceptually, they are insurance products. The protection buyer looks for insurance in the event of default of the underlying. The seller requires a premium, and/or a periodic fee, for this service.

Although the word 'swap' is used, these products look more like options. The payout of these contracts is a predetermined amount: a percentage of the face value of a loan, or a post-default difference between the pre-default bond price and the post-default bond price. The payment is contingent on the default event of an obligor (Figure 58.2).

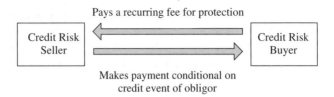

FIGURE 58.2   Credit swap

Default events are specific in that the amount to be paid depends on recovery value post-default. Such a recovery percentage ranges from around 20% for unsecured facilities to 60% and above for secured ones. However, due to recovery risk, this amount is uncertain. Contracts are subject to basis risk since they pay something that might differ from actual recoveries. This is the case for loans, and less so for tradable bonds, since the post-default price exists. Credit events are also specific since they are subject to a variety of covenants that, if breached, trigger a default event.

TOTAL RETURN SWAP

A total return swap exchanges the total return, current yield plus any change in value, whether positive or negative, between two assets. The exchange of cash flows occurs whether or not there is a default event. The swap exchanges flows and capital gains or losses periodically or at some fixed dates. Usually, periodic flows are interest payments and the capital gain or loss exchange occurs at a termination date. The seller of the total return swap is also the seller of the protection and the buyer of risk. The same terminology applies for the buyer of the swap, who is also the buyer of the protection and the seller of risk (Figure 58.3).

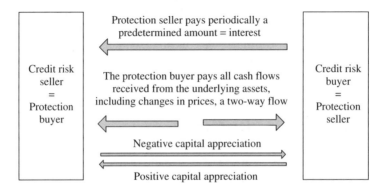

FIGURE 58.3   Two-way flows with a total return swap

Total return swaps exchange returns, including any interest payment and capital appreciation or depreciation. The total return requires payment of a spread over LIBOR. The investor, or credit risk buyer, in the total return swap gains full exposure to the underlying asset. Should the risk materialize through a capital depreciation or a default, the buyer of the protection still receives the interest while the seller suffers a loss. The buyer of a total return swap always pays the seller the interest rate plus the agreed margin. The seller pays a total return to the buyer that can be positive or negative. If there is a capital appreciation, the risk seller pays the buyer. If there is a capital depreciation, the risk buyer pays the depreciation to the risk seller compensating the loss similarly to an insurance contract.

CREDIT SPREAD PRODUCTS

Credit spread derivatives refer to the credit spread relative to the risk-free benchmark or differentials of credit spreads of two risky assets. In addition, there are credit spread forwards and credit spread options. The specifics of credit spread derivatives is that they isolate the effect of spreads as opposed to contracts on prices subject to the entire yield change combining both interest rate variations and spread variations. Spread products are similar to other derivatives. Credit swaps exchange credit spreads, while credit spread options provide the right to buy a future credit spread, as do other forward and option contracts. The difference is that the underlying is a credit spread. The value of a spread variation depends on the duration of the underlying assets.

The seller of a credit spread swap pays the buyer a predetermined fixed spread, while the buyer pays the seller the spread of a risky asset over the risk-free rate, or another security. The buyer is insensitive to spread variations of the reference assets since he gets the fixed spread anyway. The seller gains if the risky spread widens and suffers a loss if the risky spread narrows.

There is a potential for heterogeneous expectations and discrepancies between spreads derived from today's yield curves and tomorrow's credit standing materialized in future spreads. Spread derivatives serve to trade, hedge or arbitrage expectations and market spreads. The buyer of a forward spread bets that credit deterioration or default will occur before the maturity of the contract. The seller of a forward spread hopes the opposite will occur (Figure 58.4).

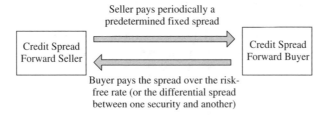

FIGURE 58.4 Credit spread swap

Forward contracts on interest rates are similar, except that such contracts have exposure to interest rate risk, not spread. Locking in a forward rate as of today implies lending long and borrowing short. To isolate the spread effect, it is necessary to sell forward the risky debt and buy forward the risk-free debt. Since the price variations due to yield changes are duration-driven, it is necessary to adjust the amounts to compensate any duration mismatch. The remaining change in price is due to spread variations. Forward contracts on spreads use current spot prices, just as forward rates are implicit in spot rates.

Credit spread options are options whose payoff depends on the spread between a risky bond and a risk-free bond. Cash transactions do not disentangle the price variations due to interest rate variations from spread variations. A put on a risky debt does not sell the spread only because its value depends on both interest rate and spread risk. This is a protection against a fall in the price of the asset without risk if the yield, inclusive of the spread, moves in the opposite direction. Only credit spread options strip the risks and isolate the spread risk. Credit spread options have the usual value drivers: notional, maturity, underlying, strike spread and premium. Duration is important because it measures the sensitivity to a credit spread change.

BASKET SWAPS AND FIRST-TO-DEFAULT

Basket swaps refer to portfolios of asset defaults rather than single asset credit events. The main characteristic of a basket credit derivative relates to the 'first-to-default' concept.

The first-to-default event is the default event of any one asset in the basket, and triggers the derivative as long as it belongs to the basket.

Such characteristics raise the 'correlation paradox' issue. Diversification should intuitively reduce the risk of the basket. In fact, it does so for the basket but not for the derivative. The probability of triggering the derivative is higher than for a single asset. The derivative does not offer protection for a single asset, but for several, by definition, since any default triggers the protection. This suggests that such protection is indeed riskier for the seller than a protection limited to a single reference asset. Second, it is possible to model the phenomenon along the lines applying to the loss distribution of a portfolio.

If we have two independent assets of default probabilities 1% and 2%, their survival probabilities are 1 minus the default probability, or 99% and 98% respectively. The probability that both survive is simply $98\% \times 99\% = 97.02\%$ if the events are independent. The joint default probability is $1\% \times 2\% = 0.02\%$. The probability that any one of the two assets defaults is therefore $1 - 97.02\% = 2.98\%$. This is higher than any one of the two single default probabilities. This demonstrates that the risk of first-to-default baskets is greater than for single assets, and shows that the credit risk of a basket depends on the survival probability of all assets in the basket, with or without correlation.

Correlation effects are counterintuitive in this case. A low correlation helps diversify away some of the portfolio risk, and conversely a high correlation increases the portfolio risk. However, the 'correlation paradox' is that a high correlation increases the risk of the basket but decreases the risk of the basket derivative! Again, simple arithmetic with two assets will make this clear. Let's now assume correlated defaults instead of considering them independent. The joint default probability increases above that of independent default events. Under independence, the joint default risk is $1\% \times 2\% = 0.02\%$. Under correlation, the basket derivative does not default if neither of the two assets defaults. We use the same calculations as for the borrower–guarantor joint default probabilities, to find out the probability that both survive. With a correlation between defaults of 10%, the joint default probability becomes 0.159%, instead of 0.02% under independence. It is consistent with the higher risk of the basket due to correlation. However, the risk of the derivative depends on the survival probability of both. The probability that the riskier asset alone defaults is 1.841% (less than 2% because it is conditional on the survival of the other) and the probability that the other one defaults is 0.841% (again lower than 1%). The survival probability of both is $1 - 0.159\% - 1.841\% - 0.841\% = 97.159\%$. The probability that any one of them defaults is $1 - 97.169\% = 2.841\%$, which is lower than the above 2.98%. Correlation effectively decreases the risk of the basket derivative although it increases that of the basket[1].

This analysis explains the rationale for such derivatives. From the protection buyer's standpoint, there might be very large exposures of high-grade obligors to hedge. Putting them together makes sense. From the protection seller's standpoint, there is some comfort in finding high-grade exposures in the basket. In fact, the portfolio of high-grade exposures has a lower credit quality in terms of first-to-default. Nevertheless, it remains an

---

[1] The probability that either one of two obligors defaults is the sum of the unconditional probabilities that each defaults minus the probability that both default (the joint default probability). This rule provides directly the above result.

eligible investment in low-risk assets with an enhanced return compared to that of individual high-grade assets. However, the return should, in theory, be in line with the true economic risk.

CREDIT-LINKED NOTES

A Credit-Linked Note (CLN) is like a credit derivative. It is a debt with payments linked to the performance of assets. Notes are tradable in the market. Being liquid is a major benefit. Protection buyers dislike looking for investors directly. They prefer to have something traded. CLNs meet this requirement. In order to be tradable, the note needs some special features providing comfort to investors.

The first stage of the structure is a classical default swap, between a highly rated entity providing the insurance and a bank looking for a protection. The protection buyer pays a fee to the entity. The entity selling the protection needs a high rating because it issues the notes to investors, who ultimately bear the credit risk. Alternatively, the issuer of the CLN is a Special Purpose Vehicle (SPV). However, the SPV has no credit standing as such, and it remains necessary to provide investors and the credit risk seller with some payment guarantee.

The SPV issues notes to investors and invests the proceeds from the sale in risk-free assets. These risk-free assets serve both as collateral and to pay the risk-free interest to investors. If investors buy highly rated notes directly, they will not get any excess return. However, since the SPV sold a protection, this enhances the return to investors with the revenues from the sale of the protection. In essence, the process breaks down a risky return into a risk-free interest plus the fees from the protection sale. The investors in the SPV get an enhanced return because of this sale. The credit risk seller pays a spread to the SPV. The excess of the asset spread over the spread paid to the SPV is the excess return to investors (Figure 58.5).

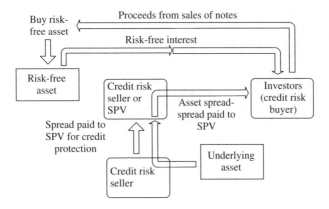

FIGURE 58.5   Credit-linked note

If there is no default event of the reference asset, the structure lives up to maturity, with the third party protected and the return to investors enhanced by the sale of protection by the SPV to the third party. Finally, at maturity, the SPV pays the face value of the asset to investors from the purchased risk-free collateral. If there is a default event, the SPV pays the amount lost, that is the face value of the asset minus recoveries to the buyer of protection and the investors get the recoveries only. The SPV total payment is the same as under no default, since it pays both the recoveries and the loss. Only the recovery fraction goes to investors, because the SPV provides protection to the third party first and because investors agreed to provide the insurance. The buyer of protection does not face the credit risk of investors, and that investors have their principal payments collateralized by risk-free assets, to the extent that there is no default. Investors fund from the very beginning whatever payments are due to both the risk protection buyer and themselves by purchasing the SPV notes. The SPV is capable of facing both obligations. In the end, all parties get some share of the value added of the CLN.

CLN can leverage the return of assets if they have a value lower than the value of assets. If the assets total 100 million USD and the note is 20 million USD, the leverage is 5. If the loss exceeds 20 million, the investors absorb a loss of 20 and the bank absorbs the excess loss beyond 20.

SOVEREIGN RISK CREDIT DERIVATIVES

Sovereign risk has grown with the exposure of emerging markets. Country risk is somehow hybrid in nature. It can be an economic crisis, a currency crisis or a political crisis. Economic crises tend to increase the default rate of all private obligors residing in the country. Another aspect of country risk is inconvertibility risk.

Convertibility products address the ability to make payments in another country. Such events look like political events, but their consequences are equivalent to a credit event. Credit derivatives hedge currency inconvertibility and transfer risks. The agreement provides protection for a determined period. The protection buyer pays a premium. If there is no currency inconvertibility during the agreed period, the contract terminates without benefit to the protection buyer. If there is a currency inconvertibility event, the protection buyer gets the face value of the funds in hard currency. In return, the protection seller gets property to the face value in soft currency. The simplest reference for the exchange rate is the one prevailing at a recent rate. Receiving the strong currency effectively protects the owner of the weak currency from not being able to get the money back. The protection seller should have some local usage of the inconvertible currency to make a deal. Investors in the country might have such a position.

Other derivatives address different dimensions of country risk. Sovereign default has remained scarce, but sovereign crises have happened rather frequently. Derivatives use currency exchange rates as underlying asset.

59

Applications of Credit Derivatives

The applications of credit risk derivatives stem from two main features:

- The capacity to trade credit risk only, in isolation.
- The ability to do so in a liquid fashion, with low transaction costs, since these are off-balance sheet.

Credit derivatives offer innovations beyond hedging credit risk. They allow us to hedge credit risk, trade, customize and create synthetic exposures. The demand for protection is only one side of the coin. Investors have new opportunities to invest, enhance their revenues and arbitrage the credit risk market. They play a double role: selling the protections demanded by others and taking advantage of new investment opportunities. Credit derivatives tailor risk and reshape income, so that the economics of such transactions extend to the whole risk–return profile.

The five main applications are:

- Trading credit risk. The off-balance sheet nature of the transaction allows trading credit risk whenever expectations of future credit risk differ.
- Hedging credit risk. Hedges match the credit risk of actual assets with the mirror credit risk of a credit derivative. There were no hedging instruments before credit derivatives, other than classical insurance contracts (in addition to clauses embedded in loan contracts). Furthermore, credit derivative hedges apply to single assets, baskets of assets or the entire bank's portfolio.
- Active portfolio management. Credit derivatives provide many features necessary to actively reshape the risk–return profile of a portfolio.

- Customizing credit risk. Customization applies to exposure, term structure and credit quality. Customization requires combining actual asset risk profiles with the risk profile of derivatives, resulting in a reshaped combined risk profile. The ability to leverage the exposure by using a notional different from the actual asset value magnifies this capability.
- Creating synthetic exposures and taking credit exposures. The buyer of a credit derivative can take synthetic exposures that would otherwise be out of his direct reach. The seller of a protection gets the exposure to the underlying risk. Instead of buying cash the exposure from a bank, he purchases, for example, a total return swap. On the other side of the deal, the lender hedges his risks.

The sections of this chapter detail the benefits and drawbacks of these five types of applications of credit risk derivatives.

TRADING CREDIT RISK

Credit derivatives allow us to trade credit risk as a commodity, in isolation from the underlying assets, such as interest rate and foreign exchange risks. In addition, there was no way to hedge credit risk until the appearance of credit derivatives. The insurance function of instruments is not the unique key factor. Others are the ability to trade risk off-balance sheet without making cash transactions and the ability to trade different expectations on the same underlying credit risk, making the credit risk market more efficient.

Trading Portfolio Risks

Banks have different costs of funding. Bank A has a relatively low cost of debt, making a loan to customer X profitable enough to compensate the capital charge. Another bank B has a higher cost of funding, making a loan to X not profitable enough to compensate the capital charge, either regulatory or economic. Bank A might lend, keep the loan on its books and sell the credit risk to bank B for a fee. Since bank B is now at risk with bank A, it benefits from a capital saving compared to lending to X as long as the seller bank A has a better rating than the borrower B. In addition, bank B gets the fee. The risk-adjusted return for both banks might increase through such transactions. In addition, bank B now has a way to gain a profitable exposure, which was not possible through X.

We expand the example using regulatory capital. The weight for the private corporation X is 100% and the weight with a banking counterparty drops to 20%. The capital charge with the direct loan is 4% (50% times 8%) and becomes $1/5(4\%) = 0.80\%$ for bank A, the direct lender, when it sells the risk to bank B, the buyer of the risk of A. Bank A's pre-tax revenue decreases by the fee paid for the credit protection by bank B, say 0.80%, while bank B's revenue increases by the same fee. Bank B has no funding cost, has the fee as pre-tax revenue and has a capital charge equal to the full 4%, the same as lending directly to X:

$$\text{ROE(bank A)} = (\text{interest margin} - \text{fee})/\text{capital charge for lending to X}$$

$$\text{ROE(bank B)} = \text{fee}/\text{capital charge for offering protection to A}$$

In the calculations of Table 59.1, we use a client rate of 9.10%, a cost of funding for A of 8% and a cost of funding for B of 8.50%. The capital structure is 96% debt and 4% equity. The cost of debt as a percentage of assets is 96% times the cost of funding, or 96% × 8% = 7.68% for A and 96% × 8.5% = 8.16% for B. The interest margin, the difference between the customer rate and the bank's weighted cost of debt, is 1.42% for A and 0.94% for B. Direct lending to X results in a 30.50% Return On Equity (ROE) for bank A and 16.00% for bank B.

TABLE 59.1 Calculation of the profitability of a direct loan to client X for banks A and B

Direct loan	Bank A			Bank B		
	Weight[a]	Rate	Cost in % of loan	Weight[a]	Rate	Cost in % of loan
Revenue	100%	8.80%	8.80%	100%	8.80%	8.80%
Debt cost	96%	8.00%	7.68%	96%	8.50%	8.16%
Interest margin			1.22%			0.64%
Pre-tax revenue			1.22%			0.64%
Capital			4.00%			4.00%
ROE			30.50%			16.00%

[a]Weights are in percentage of assets.

Post-credit derivative transaction, bank A's revenue diminishes by 0.80% and bank B's revenue becomes 0.80%. Bank A's capital decreases to 1/5(4%) = 0.80% (if the capital charge for bearing the risk of bank B is 1/5 of the capital charge when lending to B) and bank B's is at the full 4%. The resulting ROE becomes 52.5% for bank A and 20% for bank B. The transaction increases the capital profitability of both banks. The same could happen with economic capital, so this capital arbitrage is not only regulatory (Table 59.2).

TABLE 59.2 Economics of the loan plus derivative

Credit derivative	Bank A			Bank B		
	Weight[a]	Rate	Cost in % of loan	Weight[a]	Rate	Cost in % of loan
Revenue	100%	8.80%	8.80%	100%	0.0%	0.00%
Debt cost	96%	8.0%	7.68%	0%	8.6%	0.00%
Interest margin			1.22%			0.00%
Fee paid			0.80%			
Fee received						0.80%
Pre-tax revenue			0.42%			0.80%
Capital			0.80%			4.00%
ROE			52.5%			20.00%

[a]Weights are in percentage of assets.

Trading Expectations on the Same Risks

Default probabilities and recoveries are uncertain parameters. In both cases, statistics remain unreliable and internal ratings or default probability models are not necessarily accurate. Whatever such uncertainties, credit spreads embed expectations of default probabilities and recoveries. If different parties have different views on future recoveries, they can trade these views with default derivatives. Given the individual banks' biases in perceptions of the same risks, there is a market for credit risk expectations.

One way to summarize both uncertainties is to refer to loss rates, or the default rate times the loss given default rate. For instance, a default probability of 1% combined with a recovery rate of 20% results in a loss rate of $(1 - 20\%) \times 1\% = 0.8\%$. Conceptually, the same loss rate should approximately result in the same spread. In practice, this is not so because banks use different combinations of default probability and estimates of recovery rates resulting in different loss rates and pricing. Looking at banks as price makers based on expectations, the differences in loss rates could be arbitraged.

Bank A might estimate a loss rate of 1%, bank B of 0.6%. If this is the case, it is possible to trade the differences in expectations about loss rates. Bank A prices the loan at 1% and bank B at 0.6%. Bank A can sell the deal to bank B at 0.6% or above, as long as it gets a profit of 1%. Since bank B is ready to buy at 0.6%, it can purchase from bank A at higher than 0.6%, as long as it requires less than 1%. This is a direct trading of expectations. Trading can also occur through derivatives. Bank A can enhance its return by selling a protection guaranteeing a net 0.6% to bank B. Bank B will pay the protection. This will enhance bank A's return and decrease bank B's return. If the price of protection is 0.2% for instance, the 0.2% enhances bank A's return up to 1.2% and bank B pays the protection through a lower return $0.8\% - 0.2\% = 0.6\%$.

Note that trading risk expectations is not the same as trading different risk contributions of a given asset to different portfolios. Banks can trade the same asset without any discrepancies in expectations, simply because the same asset has different risk contributions to their specific portfolios.

Trading Credit Spread Expectations

Expectations on future spreads differ from forward spreads. The seller of a forward spread believes that the spread will actually be lower than the buyer does. The buyer fears a spread widening, thereby losing value. The seller bets that future spreads will be lower than the forward.

For instance, a forward spread, 2 years from now, on a longer maturity deal is 40 basis points (bp). The protection buyer fears that the spread will be higher 2 years from now. The seller bets that it will be lower. The seller sells forward this spread. If the future spread happens to be 50 bp, the buyer of protection gets the difference between the 50 bp and 40 bp. The value is the differential times the duration of the reference asset and the notional. If the duration is 3 years, and the notional is 100, the seller pays the buyer $0.1\% \times 3 \times 1000 = 30$. If the future spread is 20 bp, the buyer of protection has to pay the differential with the forward 40 bp to the seller of the forward, or $0.2\% \times 3 \times 1000 = 60$. The seller makes a gain.

With forward spreads, there is a downside for the buyer of protection, making a credit spread put option more attractive for him. Of course, the premiums paid by the buyer of protection will be higher than with a forward contract. The buyer of protection might prefer a collar: he buys a credit spread put option and funds it partially by selling a call option on credit spreads at a different strike value of the spread.

Trading Synthetic Exposures Instead of Illiquid Cash Loans

The 'buy and hold' practice for cash loans does not make it easy to avoid credit risk deterioration. A synthetic exposure does. The renewal of short credit derivative transactions allows us to get revenues as long as the credit standing of the reference assets remains acceptable. If the credit standing deteriorates, there is no renewal. Renewal is an option. This looks like a revolving line, except that it is synthetic and that the reference asset is not in the balance sheet of the bank. Under cash portfolio management, illiquidity might make a cash sale uneconomic.

HEDGING CREDIT RISK

Hedging is the most direct application of credit derivatives for bankers looking to insure against excessive risks or aiming to reshape the risk of their portfolios.

Contributions of Credit Derivatives

Simple transactions cannot disentangle the various risk components embedded in them. We can try to hedge the credit risk of a bond by selling short another similar bond. However, this transaction does not eliminate the specific risk component. If interest rates move, the changes of prices offset if durations match. However, the issue is to neutralize the long credit risk by going short in a similar credit risk for hedging. Using identical rating bonds would not help either, because the credit spreads do not correlate in general. It is possible that both bond spreads will increase by the same magnitude, but there is no mechanism that guarantees this. It would only happen with similar issues from a common issuer. The general credit risk of both assets might offset, but the specific risks will not. All specific risks of all obligors are independent by definition, if measured properly. The implication is that adding an exposure, even if this exposure shorts another exposure in the portfolio, cannot neutralize the risk. There is always an incremental specific risk. If we add many exposures in a largely diversified portfolio, the incremental risk of each additional exposure is always positive. It becomes a smaller fraction of the total risk, but it is never negative. Hence, there is no way to hedge the specific ingredients of credit risk using simple transactions.

Hedging Defaults or Downgrades

Credit default swaps or total return swaps provide hedges against defaults or downgrades. Moreover, credit spread swaps isolate the spread component. This is of direct interest to protection seekers. It also provides additional flexibility to manage portfolios, because transferring the risk helps in developing new transactions. Protections against rating downgrades also provide the possibility to control or get rid of exposures contingent on ratings.

Without such protections, it might be impossible to hold assets subject to a minimum rating constraint. Credit derivatives guarantee that the minimum target rating holds through the horizon of the reference assets. Derivatives formatted as puts to sell the asset at an agreed price terminate the transaction if there is a downgrade. A standard put does not perform the same function since it does not differentiate the effects of credit deterioration and of a change in market rates. These options on spreads work like covenants triggering default if the credit standing deteriorates beyond some threshold. However, covenants necessitate interactions with the lender, with smaller chances of success if the lender cannot do much. Then the loan repayment will simply accelerate and the loss materialize. On the other hand, a spread option will work.

Hedging Sovereign Risk

Exposure to sovereign risk is very common for financial and non-financial organizations. As mentioned previously, country risk is a bundle of political risk, economic risk, default risk related to local economic conditions and convertibility risk. Ignoring the default risk of private obligors, we concentrate on pure sovereign risk. Credit derivatives serve in various ways to provide some, but less than perfect, protections.

A default or downgrade derivative on any sovereign issue provides some protection. However, if the risk materializes without any default or downgrade, the hedge is not effective. Alternative hedges use the prices of the sovereign issues. Risk widens spreads and lowers prices. A spread derivative might be a more attractive protection than a downgrade protection. However, spreads are often related to liquidity, so that a liquidity crunch in an emerging market, unrelated to the credit standing of the sovereign, might not be effective because it will trigger the derivative even if there is real underlying economic risk.

Hedging Syndication Risk

Syndication is the classical process of raising funds with a bank, the underwriter, later sold to other banks for purposes of diversification. The final take is the fraction of the funding retained by the underwriter. Syndication implies several risks: keeping a larger amount of the funds for a longer than expected time; selling a fraction to other banks at a lower than predicted spread, if not agreed in advance. During the process, the bank has a large exposure and is subject to spread risk.

This makes it useful to customize the size of the intermediate exposure, the term of the exposure and the spread. Customization of all three items for the expected horizon of syndication, from inception up to final take, avoids excess exposures. Over-exposure beyond expected volume and horizon freezes other business opportunities because it makes credit lines unavailable. The cost of such excess exposure is both direct, in terms of risk borne by the underwriter, and indirect, in terms of missed opportunities. The economics of the hedging transaction need a careful calculation of all revenues, hedging costs and risks.

Hedging Uncertain Exposures of Derivatives

Credit derivatives can help insure uncertain potential excess exposures arising from the current derivative portfolio. The bank holding these derivatives fears an increase in exposure due to market parameter changes, leading to unacceptable exposures. Instead of insuring the potential excess exposure, the bank enters into a credit default swap on variable exposure. The default payment will be proportional to the variable exposure of the derivatives. The payment can be either the prevailing mark-to-market of the swap, or its excess above a threshold, or the exposure up to a certain amount, minus an agreed recovery rate. Such a credit default swap linked to the swap mark-to-market value differs from a standard swap since exposure is uncertain at inception of the deal.

If there is no excess exposure, there is no payment in the event of the counterparty defaulting on the derivatives held by the first bank. The economics of the transaction depend on the cost versus an insurance against excess exposure, the likelihood of hitting a higher level of exposure. With market-driven exposures, credit risk interacts with market risk so that both expectations on credit risk and market risk play a role in the feasibility of the transaction.

Hedging and Restructuring a Loan

Sometimes loans need restructuring at origination because they do not fit the bank's constraints. Instead of restructuring the transaction with the client, the bank can restructure the transaction with credit derivatives to meet the constraints. Such restructuring means customizing the exposure, the revenues, the spread risk, and the maturity of the commitment with credit derivatives. For instance a forward loan swap, starting 2 years from now, effectively restructures the exposure to this horizon whatever the actual maturity of the loan contracted. Both the total return swap and the credit default derivative serve for such purposes.

Hedging for Corporates

Corporations' usage of credit derivatives is straightforward. Sometimes, firms face country risk to a significant extent. The customers' portfolio of receivables of a corporation has credit risk exposure, making hedging attractive. Dependency on a few major customers, who have significant default risk, is an additional incentive to enter into such transactions. Another important application for corporate entities is protection against the widening of credit spreads, because they influence directly the cost of borrowing, a significant cost item in the income statement of a leveraged company. Just as a forward derivative locks in interest rates for the future, credit spread forwards achieve the same result for this component of the cost of debt.

PORTFOLIO CREDIT RISK MANAGEMENT

Credit derivatives have an obvious potential for portfolio management because they are new tools helping to reshape the risk–return profile of portfolios without cash sales of assets or to extend exposure beyond limits by transferring excess risks to others. They also create an inter-bank market for credit risk, allowing banks to rebalance their specific portfolios by exchanging risk concentrations.

The Rationale for Portfolio Management and Credit Risk Protection

The rationale for portfolio management is to resolve the well-known conflict between relationship banking and diversification. This is the 'credit paradox' of relationship banking versus credit exposure.

Banks rely on lending first and services after. Hence, lending is a prerequisite to further relationship development. The relationship manager wants new deals with big customers, but the credit officer gets worried because a large customer failure gets the bank into serious trouble. Developing business requires diversification, but the credit business creates concentration and specialization instead. The focus on client relationship creates a conflict between origination and diversification requirements. Hence, there is a need to off-load loan concentrations in the market. Trading the credit risk resulting from origination would help the bank to stay within risk limits while maintaining relationship banking.

This is one of the emerging roles of active portfolio management. However, cash portfolio management is not easy, because clients might be reluctant to let banks sell their loans and because loans have a poor liquidity. The usage of credit derivatives eliminates these major obstacles, because they do not require any prior agreement from customers and because the liquidity of the credit derivatives market might be higher than that of loans. Credit derivatives appear as a new way of reconciling these two conflicting sides of relationship banking since they allow the excess exposures to be traded while continuing to develop business with the same customers.

As a result, origination does not imply a 'buy and hold' management philosophy. Portfolio management consists of trading exposures in cash or trading credit risk through credit derivatives. It appears as a natural complement to origination and to the basic lending business. The function helps origination by selling excess exposures and creating diversification through purchases of bonds or loans or using credit derivatives.

Portfolio management gets banks closer to the trading philosophy, since it implies changing the structure of portfolios to optimize the risk–return profile. The portfolio management unit becomes a profit centre and lives with its own goals, tools and techniques to achieve 'optimization'. Credit derivatives facilitate this task and add new degrees of freedom for doing so.

Hedging a Portfolio with a First-to-Default Basket Derivative

If the bank holds a concentration in an industry, it has a number of choices: capping exposures, originating commitments in other industries or hedging the risk of some of the assets held in the industry with credit derivatives.

Credit derivatives offers additional options. Buying direct protection for a number of assets held is a simple but costly solution. Buying protection for a first-to-default basket derivative is more attractive. The contract is simple. The first default is an early warning signal of later defaults. This is a powerful rationale for entering into first-to-default baskets. It allows holders of credit risk to get protection for the first-to-default, thereby neutralizing the risk on subsequent defaults.

When correlation varies, the portfolio risk and the first-to-default basket risk vary inversely. The risk of a basket derivative is higher when correlation decreases, because the joint survival probability decreases, and vice versa. The first-to-default risk behaves as a mirror image of the increasing risk of the portfolio when correlation increases. This makes entering into a credit hedge against correlation attractive to both parties. When correlation increases, the portfolio risk increases, making hedging more necessary. Simultaneously, the first-to-default derivative risk decreases, making it less costly for the seller of protection. Similar hedges can use first-to-downgrade baskets.

CUSTOMIZING CREDIT RISKS

Tailoring and customizing exposures is a major function of credit derivatives. This helps to reshape individual and portfolio credit risk profiles so that they meet eligibility criteria, for both lenders and investors.

Credit Exposures

Credit derivatives serve as insurance for banking loans. A bank entering into a total return swap will pay the total return of the asset to the protection seller, and receive periodic fixed revenues. This shifts the asset exposure to the counterparty. The same occurs if the bank enters into a default option.

This does not eliminate fully the asset credit risk. For credit risk to materialize, there needs to be a joint adverse credit event (downgrade or default) of the original obligor and the seller of protection. The joint risk depends on correlation of credit events of obligor and seller of protection, and is low as long as credit events do not perfectly correlate. Mismatch between asset value and notional of the derivatives allows further customization of exposures.

The economics of such transactions should consider both the risk and the revenue effect of such hedges. Credit derivatives imply measuring the risk contribution saved by shifting the risk from the original obligor to the protection provider. Depending on the cost of the protection and the gain in risk contribution, the transaction might improve or deteriorate the risk–return profile. Revenues are in values. The value of the risk saving is the required rate on capital times the capital saved. If we can consider that the exposure benefiting from a protection has a near zero risk, as long as the obligor and the protection seller are nearly independent, the risk gain amounts to setting the protected exposure to zero. The full economic analysis necessitates measuring the risk contributions with a portfolio model.

Term Structures

Derivatives help to customize the term structure of credit risk, independent of the maturities of the underlying assets, bonds or loans. Credit derivatives allow a better utilization of the current credit capacity, even though there are no cash deals meeting eligibility and maturity criteria.

Let's assume that a bank or an investor has the ability to take forward exposures, while current commitments use up credit lines entirely. A forward start derivative allows a better usage, as of today, of credit lines. As an example, consider the situation where current commitments are for 2 years, credit lines are available for a longer period and there is no usage between the 2-year commitment and the longer maturity of the lines. Instead of waiting for credit lines to be free in 2 years, it is possible to gain exposure as of today 2 years from now, thereby fully utilizing the current credit lines up to their maturity.

When credit lines are relatively short, there might not exist any attractive cash transaction with such short maturity. However, a financial institution could get exposure for 1 year using eligible reference assets, even though they have a longer maturity. This creates in effect a synthetic short exposure through a credit derivative, terminating in 1 year, and meeting any eligibility criteria, even though there is no cash asset meeting both eligibility and maturity constraints.

Customizing Credit Quality

Credit derivatives allow us to engineer the credit risk quality and spreads using baskets. First-to-default baskets have a credit standing lower than any one of the standalone assets in the basket. Therefore, it is possible to engineer any credit standing independent of what exists in the market by customizing the basket so that it has the desired credit standing. This is like creating a portfolio, but with fewer constraints since we build up the rating in constructing the basket.

The reverse holds as well. With assets held in a portfolio, it is feasible to construct a basket meeting investors' requirements exactly. It is easy to proxy the target default probability of a basket as the 'first-to-default' probability. Note that securitizations provide a similar function, since the Special Purpose Vehicle (SPV) issues notes of various levels of seniority, allowing investors to fund the securitized portfolio with tailored default probability.

CREATING SYNTHETIC EXPOSURES

There is no need to stick to cash exposures with credit derivatives. By unbundling the credit risk component from the cash transactions, market players can create synthetic exposures that are not available in the cash market.

Creating a Synthetic Spread

Forward credit spread swaps provide protection against downside moves in credit quality. If a bank fears that the spread on a subset of its loans might widen in the future, it can offset the loss in (mark-to-market) value by entering into a credit spread derivative with a protection seller. This is also feasible for subportfolios, such as loans specific to an industry, using a pool of reference assets as underlying for the derivatives. In such a case, the derivative caps the widening of the credit spreads of the bank's loans, or a credit spread collar keeps them within bounds.

Creating Synthetic Exposures

Without the proper infrastructure, some investors have no access to the loan market. In addition, banks might be willing to create exposures that they do not have. Any investor can create a synthetic exposure by selling credit risk protection without holding the underlying asset. The simplest transaction is to enter into a total return swap that entitles the seller to get the total return, positive or negative, while receiving a preset spread from the buyer of the protection. The seller of the total return swap gains a full synthetic exposure to the underlying asset. However, he has to pay the risk-free rate plus the spread to the protection buyer.

Another way to get a synthetic exposure replicating an existing reference asset is to create a combination of a cash investment and a total return swap or a default option. The investor acquires the total return of the reference asset with a swap and invests simultaneously in risk-free assets. By selling a credit protection, or buying the risk, the investor pays an interest plus some margin to the protection buyer and gets the total return of the reference asset. In order to generate the interest flow due to the credit risk seller (the buyer of protection), the investor enters simultaneously into a cash investment. The interest received serves to fund the interest paid to the buyer of protection. In the end, the investor invests the same amount as in a risky loan, but does so in a risk-free asset.

With a credit default option, the investor insures the risk seller against default, making it necessary to pay the net loss under default if the default occurs. The investor buys an amount of risk-free asset equal to this preset loss under default. He uses the interest proceeds to pay the interest due to the risk seller. In exchange, he receives the fees plus any spread from the credit risk seller. The cash investment by the investor fully funds the acquired exposure to default (Figure 59.1).

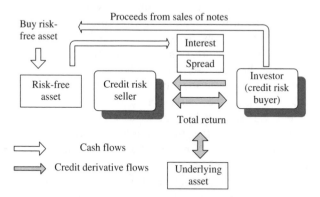

FIGURE 59.1   Creating a funded synthetic exposure

This scheme involves cash transactions on risk-free assets while gaining exposure to credit risk through derivatives. Since the investor is at risk with the credit risk seller, this seller should have a good credit risk standing. This is a generic scheme that also applies to synthetic securitizations (synthetic collateralized loan obligation). Essentially, the cash investment guarantees the cash exposure of investors, using the proceeds from sales of notes to investors, while the credit derivatives reshape the risk–return profile, so that players trade spreads and total returns only.

60

Securitization and Capital Management

Securitization is a technique used to sell balance sheet assets to outside investors. It ensures compensation to investors with cash flows generated by the pool of assets sold. Securitizations issue 'structured notes', funding the securitized assets, over the entire spectrum of credit risks. To differentiate the risk of notes, the structure routes the flows generated by the pool of assets towards notes according to seniority rules. In addition, covenants rule the life of the structure, notably by triggering early amortization whenever the credit risk deteriorates beyond specified thresholds.

The common rationales for securitizations are to arbitrage the cost of funding on-balance sheet with funding in the market or to off-load risks in the market to save capital. Securitizations vary widely by type of assets securitized, from credit cards to loans or leasing receivables, and in the structuring of the notes, by size and seniority level. Structures for off-loading credit risk in the market are Collateralized Debt Obligations (CDOs), Collateralized Bond Obligations (CBOs) and Collateralized Loan Obligations (CLOs). The differences relate to the nature of assets securitized, tradable or not. Cash CDOs rely on the actual sale of assets to the dedicated vehicle issuing structured notes to investors. Synthetic CDOs use credit derivatives to sell only the risk of a pool of assets, or a fraction of their risk, while keeping the assets on-balance sheet, and still saving capital. The economics remain similar however.

The non-recourse sales of assets necessarily save economic capital. Securitizations would be of limited interest unless they improve profitability. This implies looking to the overall economics of the transaction: capital savings; the differential cost of funding on-balance sheet and through the market; the effect on the return on capital; the capital gains or losses from the sale of assets to the SPV; the direct costs of setting up the structure and operating it.

This chapter details the economics of a simple securitization, the nature and the influence of drivers of its profitability.

The first section explains the basic mechanisms of securitization. The second section analyses the economics of the transaction. The third section details, through an example, the cost of the transaction from the asset seller's perspective. The fourth section looks at the risk–return effect on the bank's overall portfolio. The fifth section details the leverage effect of securitization on the return on economic capital of the seller of assets. The last section addresses the issue of structuring the notes, rather than analysing the economics of a transaction given a structure of notes.

SECURITIZATION MECHANISMS

The rationale of securitizations is very simple. The first motivation is arbitraging the cost of funding in the market with funding on-balance sheet, for a bank or a corporate entity. The second motivation is off-loading credit risk to free capital for new operations or to modify the risk–return profile of the loan portfolio of banks.

Figure 60.1 summarizes the basic mechanism of a securitization. The seller of the assets is often a bank, or a corporate firm looking for attractive funding of account receivables. The SPV assets generate cash flows that serve to pay the note holders. The structured notes have different risk–return profiles, and different maturities. Rating agencies provide a rating for each class of structured note, and provide the necessary information to investors to make the notes tradable. The 'arranger' structures the transaction. The 'servicer' takes care of day-to-day operations during the life of the transaction.

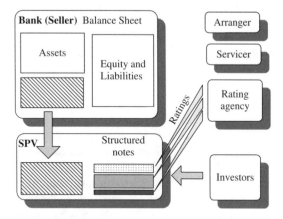

FIGURE 60.1   Structuring a securitization

The SPV isolates the pool of assets from the seller. The non-recourse sale implies that the seller is not responsible for losses by note holders. The SPV, or the fund, is a shield between lenders to the SPV and the seller of assets. The distinction between selling the assets and selling their risk only became practical with the development of synthetic structures in recent years. Sometimes, selling the assets is difficult because the authorization of borrowers is necessary. Selling the risk without selling the assets is feasible with credit derivatives such as credit-linked notes or similar, as detailed in

Chapter 58. The structuring of the transaction relies on covenants that rule the governance of the SPV during its life. It also refers to the structuring of the notes issued to investors: size, seniority level in terms of claims on SPV cash flows, customizing risk–return profiles so they fit the needs of investors. To customize the risk–return profile of the 'structured' notes issued to fund the SPV, it is necessary to set up an 'insurance' mechanism that differentiates their risks, makes them explicit and makes these notes marketable.

The Insurance Mechanism

The basic insurance mechanisms consist of differentiating the seniority levels of notes issued, so that some have a higher priority claim on the cash flows of the SPV, and others a subordinated claim. This differentiates the risks across notes, while simultaneously ensuring a protection for the more senior notes. The protection simply results from the fact that equity and subordinated notes provide 'first loss' protection.

The pool of assets generates future flows of different types: interest, capital repayment and prepayment of existing loans. A fraction of these flows is uncertain since defaults, payment delays and prepayments can happen at any date. However, the grouping of the assets into large pools of transactions makes it feasible to capture such uncertainties through statistics.

The simple way to provide a safety cushion is to use an oversized pool of assets. Since only a fraction of the pool suffices to pay investors, they have a protection against adverse deviations of the flows generated by the pool because of this safety cushion. For instance, a pool of assets can generate 100, and only 90 is necessary to pay off low-risk investors. The risk of loss for these investors materializes when the actual flow goes under 90. The excess of 10 means that the structure pays the flows promised to investors as long as the flows generated by the assets do not decrease by more than 10%. In practice, there are several classes of structured notes ranked by seniority level.

Structured Notes

The structuring of the transaction consists of defining the amounts of the various notes issued and their risk–return profile. The main structuring factors are the seniority levels and the amounts of the notes. All notes subordinated to a given senior note absorb losses first. They act as a safety cushion, protecting the senior note. When cash flows do not suffice to pay all the obligations to all note holders, the deficiencies hit the subordinated notes first. At the lower end of subordination, the risk is maximal, since this range concentrates all the risk of the pool of assets. At the upper range of senior notes, the risk is quasi-zero because it is practically impossible for losses to reach a level such that they would hit this upper class of notes.

The subordination level of a note is the amount (as a percentage of total assets funded) of subordinated notes that protect the senior ones. The higher this 'safety cushion', the lower the risk of the notes protected by the subordinated notes. Agencies rate notes according to risk. The last subordinated note, which is like equity, gets all the first losses and has no rating. Senior notes can be investment grade, because the likelihood that the loss in pool of assets exceeds the safety cushion provided by the subordinated notes is near zero for the highest grades. When moving down the scale of seniority, the loss franchise provided by the subordinated notes shrinks. Either the seller of assets or a third party, acting as a 'credit enhancer' for others, holds the last tranche. Since the equity tranche bears all the risk of the assets, the spread compensating credit enhancers is high.

The Waterfall of Cash Flows and Losses

The structure re-routes the flows generated by the pool of assets to investors using priority rules based on the seniority level of the structured notes, first to senior notes and last to the 'equity' tranche. This is the 'waterfall of cash flows'. The 'waterfall of losses' follows a symmetrical path. First, they hit the credit enhancer, then the subordinated notes and only then the senior notes. The first cash flows go to the senior notes. The first losses go to the subordinated notes (Figure 60.2).

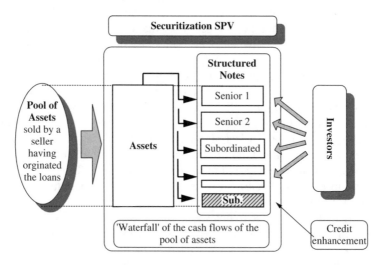

FIGURE 60.2   Securitization and structured notes

Customization of Structured Notes

Structuring through differentiated seniority levels allows the issuance of several types of securities differing in terms of their risk–return profile and maturity. Issuing several classes of structured notes of different seniority levels makes the securities attractive to various populations of investors, over the entire spectrum of risks. High-risk notes are of interest to investors looking for a higher expected spread in compensation for the added risk. Investors in senior notes benefit from a good rating, while having a return higher than with the same rating bonds, perhaps because the market values the risk differently for structured notes and plain bonds. Maturities vary across notes, under the sequential amortization scheme, because the payments flow first to senior notes, thereby amortizing them quicker. The concurrent amortization scheme requires amortizing notes in parallel. The seniority level of a structured note drives the required return, hence its cost.

Resiliency and Stress Testing Securitizations

The resiliency of a structure designates its ability to sustain large variations in risk drivers without generating losses to the various classes of structured notes. Critical parameters that determine the resiliency of structures depend on the type of structure. For consumers or mortgage loans, typical critical parameters include: the delinquency rate (delays in payment), the charge-off rate (losses due to default), the payment rate (both monthly payments of interest and principal), the recovery rate (both percentage amount and timing of recoveries) and the average yield of the portfolio of loans. For other structures such as CDOs, critical parameters include: the degree of over-collateralization, or the excess amount of asset value over note value, the diversification of the portfolio of assets and the interest rate risk.

'Stress' scenarios on critical parameters such as charge-offs and minimum amounts of collateral serve to assess the resiliency of the structure and the risk of the various classes of structured notes issued. A typical way to assess the resiliency of structures by rating agencies consists of stress testing all critical risk drivers, such as the ones above. The same stress tests serve for rating the notes, in addition to measuring the resiliency of the structure.

The first purpose is to check whether each class of structured note suffers from loss when stress testing the values of these risk drivers. A very common way of validating the risk of a structured note is to apply to the portfolio of assets a multiple of the expected charge-off rate and check that notes do not suffer from losses. For a given note, the higher the multiple of charge-offs sustainable by the note without any loss, the higher the rating. For instance, the required multiple for a triple 'AAA scenario' is obviously higher than for a risky subordinated note. The terminology might be confusing. An 'AAA scenario' designates the minimum required multiple to have an AAA rating, and is a highly stressed scenario, because it is the one required to assign the best rating. Typical stress tests apply a high multiple to charge-off rates, for example five or six times the expected average charge-off rate for senior notes.

One easy way to assign ratings to notes is to map these multiples with the note ratings. Evidently, the minimum multiple required to have a given rating also depends on the quality of the assets. Hence, the 'AAA scenario', or the 'AAA multiple' of expected loss, is lower when the average risk of assets is medium or low than when the risk of assets is high (average rating low). This is a practical shortcut to full modelling of the risk of the portfolio of assets in CDOs, as detailed in the following two sections explaining the economics of securitizations for the seller of assets. The full assessment of the structured note ratings requires plugging these scenarios into the 'spreadsheet' model of the waterfall of cash flows and redirecting the loss to the notes, allocating first losses to the lower seniority levels. The simulation tells us whether a loss occurs to notes other than the equity.

THE ECONOMICS OF SECURITIZATION

The issue, when off-loading risks, is whether freeing up capital in this way is economically acceptable. The solution lies in finding out whether this makes the risk–return profile of the banking portfolio more efficient (higher return for the same risk or lower risk for the same return). When using the portfolio Sharpe ratio as the target variable, the issue is to find out whether the securitization improves the bank's portfolio Risk-adjusted Return on Capital (RaRoC) or not.

Through structuring of notes, securitization dissociates the quality of the original flows from the quality of the promise of flows to investors. As a result, funding through securitization has a cost that has no reason to coincide with the cost of funding on-balance sheet for the seller. The cost through securitization combines operating costs plus the cost of funding in the market through the notes. Whether on-balance sheet or in the market, the weighted average cost of funds summarizes the cost of various funding solutions. It is the weighted average of costs of equity and debt in the bank's balance sheet, and the weighted average of the costs of the various notes issued by the securitization. In both cases, we use the familiar 'weighted average cost of capital' (wacc). The next question is to compare the wacc on-balance sheet ($wacc_{on-BS}$) with the wacc of securitization ($wacc_{sec}$), inclusive of operating costs. Intuition suggests that if the $wacc_{sec}$ is below the $wacc_{on-BS}$, the economics of the securitization are favourable, and conversely.

Analysing the economics needs identifies all critical parameters underlying such differences, quantifying the gap between the costs of funding on- or off-balance sheet and the effect on capital and return on capital. Since the securitization triggers savings of capital plus a differential cost of funds, it could well be that capital savings suffice to improve the return on capital (RaRoC or Sharpe ratio of the portfolio remaining with the seller), even though the differential cost of funding is not favourable. This depends on the relative magnitude of the change in net income due to volume and capital gains or losses when selling the assets to the SPV, and on capital savings.

The first securitizations arbitraged the regulatory capital, using the favourable forfeits accepted by regulators for the equity tranche. The capital charge for this tranche was limited, without checking that it could actually cover unexpected losses that might materialize. The regulators increased the capital charges for such credit enhancement tranches, as well as for subordinated notes, by differentiating capital according to ratings. In any case, the true economics of the securitization necessitate developing the analysis on economic capital rather than regulatory capital.

Figure 60.3 summarizes the process of analysing the economics of a securitization for the seller of assets. The figure applies both for classical cash securitization as well as for synthetic securitization aimed at saving capital, because the end result is the same.

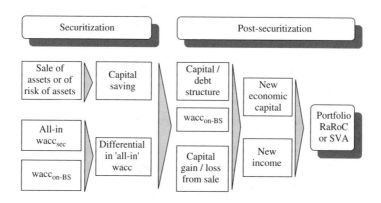

FIGURE 60.3   The economics of a securitization: capital and RaRoC–SVA

Costs and Benefits of Securitization

The potential benefits of securitization are:

- Reducing the cost of funding the assets by going through the market. This is an arbitrage between the cost of funding on and off the seller's balance sheet.
- Saving capital through the non-recourse transfer of credit risk to the SPV, both in classical cash securitizations and synthetic CLOs. These are sometimes called 'balance sheet' securitizations, since they arbitrage the capital load required on and off the balance sheet.
- Optimizing the portfolio risk–return profile, by restructuring the on-balance sheet portfolio and increasing the Sharpe ratio of the portfolio or, in general, moving towards the efficient frontier.

It is not always feasible to meet such goals, because the economics of the transaction have to comply with market conditions. For instance, selling low-yield assets to a fund when high market yields prevail, generating capital losses, so that the yields of notes are in line with the market, thereby destroying value. Still, the securitization would reduce capital, but at an unacceptably high cost. Several parameters influence the economics of the securitization for the seller of assets:

- The risk and return of original assets. They depend on the seller's choice in interaction with the rating agency, which might consider that only some assets are eligible for the project.
- The market credit spreads across rating classes. These are market-driven.
- The potential savings in economic and/or regulatory capital. These depend on the portfolio risk profile of the securitized assets and on their risk contribution to the seller's (bank's) portfolio. Full assessment of the economic capital savings requires running the portfolio model with and without the securitized assets to get their marginal risk contribution to capital. The assessment of the regulatory capital savings is much quicker since it uses forfeits.
- The structuring of the transaction determines the pool composition as well as the profile of the structured notes issued. The first influences capital savings directly. The second influences the cost of funding through securitization directly.
- The costs of creating the structure, of operating the SPV and of servicing the assets. These increase the all-inclusive cost of funding through securitization since they add up to the wacc of issued notes.

Analysing the economics of the transaction requires reviewing all costs and benefits resulting from the specific values of each of these parameters at the time of the transaction.

SECURITIZATION ECONOMICS: THE COST OF FUNDING

The analysis below uses an example. Its purpose is to determine the costs and benefits of the transaction and to assess the impact on return on capital. There are three steps: the description of the original situation before securitization; the calculation of the funding cost for the originating bank; the funding cost through securitization. The impact on the return on capital (Return On Equity, ROE or RaRoC) follows in the next section.

Capital Savings

In this case, we skip the determination of capital saved and simplify it by using a shortcut making capital saved proportional to amount securitized. This is valid for regulatory capital under the old scheme. The new scheme requires assessing the economic capital savings with more risk-sensitive measures. With economic capital, only portfolio models provide capital savings, given correlations and resulting risk contributions. The relationship with size of securitization is no longer proportional, because the risk contribution is not in general. However, once economic capital savings are assessed for different securitization scenarios, the same analysis as below provides the final effect on return on capital. The only change from the analysis below is in substituting the economic capital saved for the value calculated with the above shortcut. The capital saving calculation in the example uses a 4% forfeit applied to the amount sold by the seller to the securitization vehicle, in line with the old regulatory scheme.

The Original Balance Sheet

The bank has a portfolio of mortgaged loans. The regulatory weight for such assets is 50%. The outstanding balance is 10 000. The capital is 400, which is equal to the regulatory capital required, $8\% \times 0.5 \times 10\,000$. The cost of equity is 25% before tax. We assume that this market required yield on stocks is equivalent to minimum accounting ROE of 25%, an assumption valid under specific conditions. The capital includes subordinated debt yielding 10.2%. The other debt cost is 10%. The bank considers a securitization, for an amount of 1000. The portfolio of loans has a theoretical duration of 10 years, but its effective duration is 7 years due to early prepayments. The return net of statistical losses and direct operating costs is 10.20%.

The capital saving with our shortcut is simply $4\% \times 1000 = 40$, 20 of equity and 20 of subordinated debt. The economic capital saving is the marginal risk contribution of the subportfolio of assets sold, as evaluated with a portfolio model. The 4% shortcut is convenient without loss of generality. It should be evaluated as above. The resulting economic capital saving would depend on which assets the sellers select and how they correlate to the existing portfolio.

The Structure

The structure in Table 60.1 is a simple example with only two classes of notes: junior and senior. The junior securities have a BBB rating due to their risk. The senior securities are rated AAA. Given such ratings, the required return for junior securities is 10.61%, and that of senior securities is 9.80%. The latter cost less than the balance sheet debt, that pays 10%. However, to obtain a BBB rating, the rating agency imposes that the junior securities represent at least 10% of the total securitized amount. The direct costs include the initial cost of organizing the structure plus the servicing costs. The yearly servicing cost is 0.20% of the securitized amount.

With an amount of 1000 securitized, the senior securities fund 900 and the junior securities fund 100. The outstanding balance of the loan portfolio of the bank drops from

TABLE 60.1   The original situation

Current funding	
Cost of equity	25%
Cost of subordinated debt	10.20%
Cost of debt	10%
Structure	
Cost of senior securities	9.80%
Weight of seniors	90%
Maturity of seniors	10 years
Cost of junior securities	10.61%
Weight of juniors	10%
Maturity of juniors	10 years
Direct costs of the structure (% of amount)	0.20%
Original assets	
Portfolio yield[a]	10.20%
Portfolio duration	7 years
Outstanding balances	
Outstanding loans	10 000
Securitized amount	1000

[a] Net of average losses and direct operating costs.

TABLE 60.2   Required capital before and after securitization

Outstanding balances	Value		Required capital
Initial portfolio	10 000		400
Securitized amount	1000		40
Senior securities	900	Sold	
Junior securities	100	Sold	
Final portfolio	9000		360
Total assets	9000	—	
Total weighted assets	4500		360

10 000 to 9000. The weighted assets are $0.5 \times 9000 = 4500$. The capital required against this portfolio is $8\% \times 4500 = 360$. With an initial capital of 400, the transaction saves and frees 40 for expansion (Table 60.2).

The Cost of Funds for the Bank (On-balance Sheet)

The cost of funding is the average cost of all funds, or $wacc_{on-BS}$. The funding structure is capital, 4%, divided into 2% equity at 25% and 2% subordinated debt at 10.20%, and 96% debt at 10%. We use book values for weights, which is equivalent to assuming that debt is at par. The weighted cost of funding is:

$$wacc_{on-BS} = 96\% \times 10.00\% + 8\% \times 50\% \times (25\% \times 50\% + 10.20\% \times 50\%) = 10.304\%$$

This average rate is consistent with the 25% before tax ROE. If the assets do not generate this required return, the ROE adjusts. Since the assets generate only 10.20%, lower than the above target of 10.304%, the actual return on equity is lower than 25%. The return actually obtained by shareholders is such that the average cost of funds is identical to the

10.20% return on assets (ROA%). Writing that this effective ROA equates to the average cost of funding on-balance sheet determines the effective ROE%:

$$ROA\% = 96\% \times 10.0\% + 8\% \times 50\% \times (ROE\% \times 50\% + 10.20\% \times 50\%)$$

After calculation, the effective ROE is 19.800% before tax, lower than the 25% required return.

In theory, it would be impossible to raise new capital since the portfolio return does not compensate its risk. Therefore, the bank cannot originate any additional asset without securitization. In addition, the securitization needs to improve the return to shareholders from the remaining portfolio of assets.

The Cost of Funding through Securitization

The potential benefit of securitization is a reduction in the cost of funding. The cost of funding through securitization ($wacc_{sec}$) is the weighted cost of the junior securities and of the senior securities, plus any additional cost of the structure (0.20%). The cost of senior securities is 9.80% and that of junior securities is 10.61% (ignoring differences in duration). The weighted average is the $wacc_{sec}$ before operating costs:

$$90\% \times 9.80\% + 10\% \times 10.61\% = 9.881\%$$

The overall cost of securitization is this weighted average plus the yearly 0.20% of structure costs averaged over the life of the transaction. This overall cost becomes the all-inclusive weighted cost of funds through securitization, or:

$$wacc_{AI-sec} = wacc_{sec} + 0.200\% = 9.881\% + 0.200\% = 10.081\%$$

From this finding, we draw some preliminary conclusions:

- The overall cost is less than the cost of funding on-balance sheet, which is 10.304%. This is sufficient to create a financial benefit for securitization.
- In addition, the cost of funding through securitization is lower than the portfolio yield. Therefore, selling the original loans to the structure that issues the securities generates a capital gain. This gain improves the profitability of the bank.
- However, the change in ROE or RaRoC remains to be quantified.

In general, not all effects will be positive because it could be that the cost of funding through securitization falls below the cost on-balance sheet, but is still higher than the portfolio yield, thereby generating a loss when selling the assets to the SPV. Even if the cost of funding through securitization was higher than on-balance sheet, there would be room to improve the seller's portfolio RaRoC because of capital savings. Hence, this example is not representative of all possible situations.

SECURITIZATION ECONOMICS: THE RETURN ON EQUITY

In our example, the influence on the equity return results from both the lower level of equity and the reduced cost of funding through securitization. The gain value is either a present value or an improvement of yearly margins averaged over the life of the transaction. The capital saving is a preset forfeit percentage, used as an input, in the example. When considering the global economic picture, this same percentage of assets would result from modelling economic capital and would be an output of a portfolio model. In both cases, analysing the economics of the transaction aims at finding whether the securitization improves the risk–return profile of the bank's portfolio. Enhancing the risk–return profile means getting closer to the efficient frontier or increasing the RaRoC or Sharpe ratio of the bank's portfolio. This would imply calculating RaRoCs both pre- and post-diversification and comparing them.

The Gain/Loss of the Sale of Assets for Bank's Shareholders

The value of assets is the discounted value of cash flows calculated at a rate equal to the required return to investors. The average required return by the outside investors, who buy the securities issued from securitization, is 10.081%. For the lenders and shareholders who fund the bank, the average asset return is 10.20%. But the existing shareholders would like to have 25% instead of the 19.80% resulting from the insufficient return on assets of 10.20%. In order to obtain 25%, the return on assets of the bank should be higher and reach 10.304%.

The present value of the securitized assets for outside investors is the discounted value of future flows at 10.08%. The value of the same assets for those who fund the balance sheet results from discounting the same cash flows at 10.20%, either with the current effective ROE of 19.80%, or 10.30% with a required ROE of 25%. In both cases, the average cost of funds for the bank is higher than the cost of funding through securitization. Therefore, the price of existing assets, at the 10.08% discount rate required by outside investors, will be higher that the price calculated with either 10.20% or 10.304%. The difference is a capital gain for the existing shareholders of the bank.

Since the details of projected cash flows generated by assets are unknown, an accurate calculation of their present value is not feasible. In practice, a securitization model generates the entire cash flows, with all interest received from assets, prepayments, defaults and recoveries, and interest from the pool of assets. For this example, we collapse the entire process into a small number of very simple shortcuts, bypassing the technicalities of structure models. The easiest way to get a valuation is through the duration formula. We know that the discounted value of future flows generated by the assets at 10.20% is exactly 1000 because they yield 10.20%. With another discount rate, the present value differs from this face value. An approximation of this new value derives from the duration formula, since:

$$(V - 100)/100 = -\text{duration}/(1 + i)(y - r)$$

The present value of assets is V. The ratio $(V - 100\%)/100\%$ provides this value as a percentage of the face value. The portfolio yield is r and the discount rate is y. The duration formula provides V given all three other parameters:

$$V(\% \text{ of face value}) = 100\% + \text{duration}(r\% - y\%)$$

Since the yield is $r = 10.200\%$, the value of the assets at the discount rate $y = 10.08\%$ is:

$$100\% + 7 \times (10.200\% - 10.081\%) = 100.833\%$$

This means that the sale of the assets to the securitization structure generates a capital gain of 0.833% over an amount of 1000, or 8.33 in value.

The Conditions of a Profitable Securitization

The sale of assets will generate a capital gain for the seller only when the all-in cost of funding with securitization is lower than the asset yield, which is 10.20% in this case:

$$\text{wacc}_{\text{AI-sec}} < \text{wacc}_{\text{on-BS}} = 10.20\%$$

In this case, the capital gain from the sale will effectively increase the revenues, thereby increasing the average return of assets on the balance sheet. This is a sufficient condition to improve the ROE under present assumptions. The reason is that the effective ROE remains a linear function of the effective yield on assets, inclusive of capital gains from sales of assets to the SPV, as long as the weights used to calculate it from the ROA as a percentage of total assets remain approximately constant. This relation remains:

$$\text{Effective ROA}\% = 96\% \times 10.0\% + 8\% \times 50\% \times (\text{effective ROE} \times 50\%$$
$$+ 10.20\% \times 50\%)$$

This is true as long as the equity is proportional to the amount securitized, which is the case in the example. However, in general, economic capital is not proportional to the amount securitized, and the linear relationship collapses. 'What if' scenarios are required to determine the effective yields on equity.

Note that the current average cost of on-balance sheet funding is 10.20%, by definition, since it equates the yield of assets with the balance sheet wacc: effective ROA% = effective $\text{wacc}_{\text{on-BS}}\%$. The implied return to shareholders is 19.80%. Whenever the all-in cost of funding through securitization is lower than the yield of assets, it is by definition also lower than the effective on-balance sheet cost of funds.

If the shareholders obtained their required rate of 25%, instead of the effective 19.80% only, the average cost of funding on-balance sheet would become 10.30%. The securitization would be profitable as long as $\text{wacc}_{\text{AI-sec}} < 10.30\%$. Since, in this case, the all-inclusive $\text{wacc}_{\text{AI-sec}}$ is 10.08%, the transaction meets both conditions. However, the first one only is sufficient to generate a capital gain.

Using the current effective ROE of 19.80%, we find that the one-shot capital gain when selling the assets is 0.84% (Table 60.3) using figures rounded to two digits.

TABLE 60.3   Costs–benefits from securitization

$\text{wacc}_{\text{on-BS}}$	10.20%
Cost of juniors	10.61%
wacc(junior + senior)	9.88%
$\text{wacc}_{\text{AI-sec}}$ (direct costs included)	10.08%
Portfolio value at current $\text{wacc}_{\text{on-BS}}$ (% of nominal)	100.00%
Portfolio value at $\text{wacc}_{\text{AI-sec}}$ (% of nominal)	100.84%
Capital gain from sale	0.84%

The Additional Annualized Return from Securitization

It is possible to convert the gain from securitization into an additional annualized margin obtained over the life of the transaction. A simple proxy for this yearly margin is equal to the instantaneous capital gain averaged over the life of the transactions (ignoring the time value of money). The gain is $0.84\% \times 1000 = 8.4$ in value.

This implies that after securitization, the assets provide the 10.20% plus the yearly return of 0.0833% applicable only to the fraction, 1000, securitized. Once securitization is done, the size of the balance sheet drops to 9000. These 9000 assets still provide 10.20%. There is an additional return due to the capital gain. Since this annualized capital gain is 0.0833% of 1000, it is $(0.0833\%/1000) \times 9000$ in percentage of remaining assets, or 0.00926% applicable to 9000. Accordingly the asset all-in yield increases from 10.200% up to 10.20926% post-securitization. This increased yield also implies a higher return on capital, reviewed next.

ENHANCING RETURN ON CAPITAL THROUGH SECURITIZATION

Under a forfeit valuation of capital as a function of the amount securitized, it is relatively easy to determine whether the securitization enhances the ROE, by how much, and what are the limitations. Under full economic capital analysis, the capital results from a direct calculation with a portfolio model pre- and post-securitization. The enhancement issue consists of finding out whether the securitization enhances the risk–return profile of the bank's portfolio, and more practically, whether the post-securitization RaRoC is higher or lower than the pre-securitization RaRoC. We address both issues sequentially. The next subsection details the effect on the return on capital of the securitization.

The Effect of Securitization on the Return on Capital

Table 60.4 shows the income statement pre- and post-securitization. The debt, the subordinated debt and the equity represent the same percentages of total assets, respectively 96%, 2% and 2%. Their costs are identical to above. Pre-securitization, assets yield 10.200%. Post-securitization, we found above that the assets yield more, or 10.2093%. The gain influences directly the return on capital, which increases from 19.800% to 20.263%.

In general, the effect of an increase of asset yield on capital return is not mechanical because the capital gain is the marginal risk contribution of the subportfolio securitized. Therefore an increase of asset yield due to a capital gain from sale to the SPV might not increase the return on capital if the capital saving is lower. For instance, if the capital decreases only to 190, and subordinated debt does also, the remaining debt being the complement to 9000 or 9620, the same calculations would show that the new return on capital becomes $37.5/190 = 19.712\%$. This is a lower value than the original 19.800%. It is necessary to determine the economic capital pre- and post-securitization, both to determine the magnitude of the capital savings and to perform return calculations on new capital post-securitization. Once economic capital is determined and converted into a percentage of assets, we are back to the same type of formula as above.

TABLE 60.4   Effect of securitization on the return of capital

	Balances	Revenue and costs (%)	Revenue and costs
Pre-securitization of 1000			
Assets	10 000	10.200%	1020.0
Debt	9600	−10.000%	−960.0
Subordinated debt	200	−10.200%	−20.4
Equity	200		39.6
Return on capital			**19.800%**
Assets	9000	10.209%	918.833
Debt	8640	10.000%	−864.000
Subordinated debt	180	10.200%	−18.360
Equity	180		36.5
Return on capital			**20.263%**
Assets	9000	10.209%	918.8
Debt	8620	10.000%	−862.0
Subordinated debt	190	10.200%	−19.4
Equity	190		37.5
Return on capital			**19.712%**

The Leverage Effect on ROE of Securitization

If securitization improves the ROE, it is tempting to increase the amount securitized. The bank would benefit even more from the positive relationship between the amount securitized and the ROE. This is the leverage effect of securitization. Leverage is positive as long as the cost of funding through securitization remains fixed at the 10.08% obtained above. If we consider this figure as given, the higher the amount securitized, the higher the final ROE after securitization.

For instance, using the above example, securitizing 2000 instead of 1000, and keeping the same proportions of assets for debts and capital, would mechanically increase the ROE. This increase does not result from an additional capital gain in percentage of assets securitized, since this gain remains 0.833% of assets (one-shot). Rather it results from the fact that the additional annualized yield is proportional to the ratio of assets pre- and post-securitization. In the example, with 1000 securitized, the additional annualized yield in percentage of assets post-securization is $0.0833\% \times 1000/9000 = 0.00926\%$ of assets. Should we sell 2000, the same percentage of assets post-securitization would increase to $0.0833\% \times 2000/9000 = 0.02082\%$, the EBT would become 33.346 and the return on capital (now 160) would be $33.346/160 = 20.841\%$. Another quick simulation would show that securitizing 5000 out of 10,000 would provide an EBT of 23.965 and a return on capital of 23.965%. In fact securitizing 5553 would allow hitting the 25% target return on remaining assets. This is the leverage effect of securitization, which is more than proportional to the amount securitized.

However, there are limits to the leverage effect. First, a bank securitizing all assets changes its business. It becomes a pure originator reselling new business to outside investors. Origination and lending, collecting deposits and providing financial services to customers, are the core businesses of commercial banking. Keeping loans on-balance sheet is part of the core business. This is a first reason for not going all the way to securitizing the entire balance sheet. Second, the originators need to replenish the pool of securitized receivables. In order to do so, they need to keep assets on-balance sheet. This happens when securitizing credit cards that amortize much quicker than mortgages. In such cases, the pool of credit card receivables rolls over with time and fluctuates depending on the customers' behaviour. The bank needs a pool of credit card receivables to replenish the pool of securitized assets. Third, increasing securitization significantly would result in a significant change in business and might change the investors' perception of the seller, modifying his cost of funds. This is not necessarily true, however, depending on the usage of capital savings.

STRUCTURING CDO NOTES

Structuring notes requires defining the number and size of each note based on the risk characteristics of the portfolio of assets serving as collateral. The common philosophy for structuring and rating notes is to use stressed, unexpected losses to check that each class of note sustains such stresses without loss. The rating depends on the level of stressed losses that triggers the first loss of various seniority level notes. The actual practice uses a more comprehensive testing of all scenarios possible for all relevant variables, including the effects of all covenants, in order to check that the assigned rating corresponds to the resiliency of each note.

Portfolio models because they provide the entire distribution of losses, unexpected losses and their probabilities, rather than single stressed values whose low probability of occurrence is largely judgmental.

This section illustrates the potential contribution of portfolio models for structuring and rating notes of CDOs. Nevertheless, it remains much simplified because it ignores the technicalities and effects of covenants.

The Principle

The principle is to generate a loss distribution and to allocate each random value of the portfolio loss to each one of the structured notes, following the 'waterfall' of losses according to their seniority levels. However, this simple example ignores covenants and simply passes on the portfolio losses to notes.

It is possible to derive the loss distributions of each structured note from the portfolio loss distribution. This makes the calculation of the average loss of each structured note feasible, providing an objective basis for rating them. This avoids the judgmental component of selecting 'ad hoc' stressed values of unexpected losses, based on history or experience. To redesign the structuring of tranches, for example changing their sizes, it is possible to test several size structures and find what minimum sizes guarantee a given rating, depending on the risk characteristics of the portfolio.

The next subsection explains how to derive the loss distribution of each structured note from the portfolio loss distribution. The third subsection shows how to generate a sample loss distribution for a fictitious simple portfolio and how to calculate the expected loss of all five classes of structured notes in the example. The fourth subsection provides an example of the calculation of structured note expected losses using a Monte Carlo simulation to generate the portfolio loss distribution.

The Portfolio Loss Allocation to Structured Notes

The loss of any structured note depends on the aggregated level of losses of a portfolio of loans. Losses flow to structured notes according to their seniority level. Any note benefits from the protection of all subordinated notes, whose total size determines the level of over-collateralization of the structured note, characterizing its the seniority level. The total size of all subordinated notes under a specific note is a loss franchise benefiting the next senior tranche.

The loss allocation is very simple. A portfolio has a size of 100. There are five classes of structured notes, each having an equal size of 20. A tranche gets more senior when moving up. The lowest tranche is 'Sub 1', serving as 'equity' for the others since it gets hit by any first loss of the portfolio. The most senior tranche is 'Senior 3', on top (Table 60.5).

TABLE 60.5   Example of a simple structuring of notes

Structured notes	Size
Senior 3	20
Senior 2	20
Senior 1	20
Sub 2	20
Sub 1, or equity	20
Total	100

The exercise is to allocate loss. The portfolio loss can range from 0 up to 100, although this 100 loss will never happen. If the loss is lower than 20, it hits Sub 1. If it is above 20, the excess over 20 hits the upper tranche. Hence a 25 portfolio loss results in a total loss of 20 for Sub 1 and $25 - 20 = 5$ for Sub 2. Following the same rationale, the allocation of a large portfolio loss of 45 would be 20 for Sub 1, 20 for Sub 2, 5 for Senior 1 and 0 for both Senior 2 and 3. Of course, the likelihood of these losses varies, with high losses exceptional and small losses frequent, as usual.

The Loss Distribution of Structured Notes

Using this mechanism, we can reconstruct the loss distribution for each structured note, and derive from this loss distribution its expected loss.

The loss distribution of each note has a lower bound of zero. This corresponds to a portfolio loss equal to or lower than the seniority level measured by the total size of lower rated notes. For example, the Senior 1 note has a loss of 0 when the portfolio loss is 40 and a loss of 1 when the portfolio loss reaches 41. Simultaneously, each note loss has an upper bound, which is simply its size. In our example, Senior 1 cannot lose more than 20. In order to have this 100% loss level, the portfolio loss should hit the value 60.

The random loss of the portfolio is L_p, the random loss for the note N_{ab} benefiting from the seniority level a and of size $b - a$ is L_{ab}. The size of the note is $N_{ab} = b - a$, and this difference is the maximum loss of the note. For any given portfolio loss L_p, we

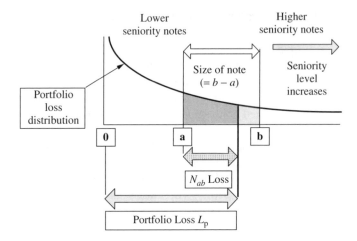

FIGURE 60.4   **Loss distributions of the portfolio and of a structured note**

can calculate the loss for the structured note N_{ab}. Figure 60.4 shows both the portfolio loss and the loss for note N_{ab}.

Analytically, the loss for the note is $L_{ab} = \min[\max(L_p - a, 0), b - a]$. The first loss appears only when L_p passes the lower bound a. If the portfolio loss L_p gets bigger, it remains bounded by $b - a$, the size of the note N_{ab}. Any excess above this cap hits the next structured note. The expected loss results from the portfolio loss distribution truncated at the levels a and b[1].

Example of Structured Note Loss Distributions and Expected Losses

In order to illustrate the above methodology, we use the example of the portfolio funded by five classes of structured notes, inclusive of equity (note 'Sub 1'). The portfolio characteristics are: 100 obligors, uniform unit exposure, uniform default probability of 5%, recoveries of zero and a uniform asset correlation of 30%.

In order to determine expected losses, we generate a loss distribution using the simplified asset model. The number of simulations is 1000. By allocating the portfolio loss to all structured notes at each run, we also generate the loss distributions of the structured notes. The expected loss of each note is simply the arithmetic average of losses hitting each tranche across all 1000 trials. Table 60.6 summarizes the results.

TABLE 60.6   **Simulation of the expected loss of a portfolio and a series of five structured notes issued to fund the portfolio**

	Portfolio loss	Senior 3	Senior 2	Senior 1	Sub 2	Sub 1 (equity)
Maximum	58.00%	0.00%	0.00%	18.00%	17.00%	19.00%
Mean	4.98%	0.00%	0.00%	0.06%	0.21%	3.71%

[1] Formally, if $f(L_p)$ is the pdf of the portfolio loss: $E(L_{ab}) = \int_a^b L_p f(L_p) \, d(L_p)$.

With 30% correlation, there is no loss in the 1000 trials for Senior 1 and Senior 2. The three most senior notes are investment grade, since the expected loss is 0.059% (rounded to 0.06%) for Senior 3. For the subordinated notes, the expected loss is much higher. Surprisingly, it is always lower than the average loss of the portfolio. This average simulated loss is 4.98%, very close to the 5% value. This results from the upper bound of loss that exists for each note. There is no way to lose more than the amount of the note, or 20% of the total portfolio size.

For moving from expected loss of each note to its rating, we can use the equivalence between the default probability of a senior unsecured issue and the default probability. According to the default frequencies from rating agencies of Chapter 36, note Senior 1 has a rating slightly better than a single A in the simplified scale of six rating classes, Sub 2 is a Baa note, and the equity tranche is a single B.

The process models the expected loss and the rating equivalent of all notes issued from the loss distribution of the collateralized portfolio. The mechanisms apply whatever the sizes of structured notes and allow us to test various structures or target the structure of notes according to desired ratings and the targeted clientele of investors. The limitations of this simple model are that it does not embed all covenants that also mitigate the credit losses and trigger early termination. Subject to this limitation, it covers the spectrum of all loss scenarios rather than using discrete stress scenarios selected judgementally among all possible scenarios included in the simulations.

Bibliography

Ahm D., Boudoukh J., Richardson M. and Whitelow R.F. (1997) Optimal risk management using options, NBER Working Paper No. 6158, National Bureau of Economic Research, Cambridge, MA.

Ahn M.J. and Falloon W.D. (1991) Valuing fixed income investments and derivatives, in Allen S.L. and Kleinstein A.D. (eds), *Strategic Risk Management*, Probus, Chicago, IL.

Alexander C. (1998) Volatility and correlation: measurement, models and applications, in Alexander C. (ed.), *Risk Management and Analysis*, Wiley, Chichester.

Alexander C. (ed.) (1998) *Risk Management and Analysis*, Wiley, Chichester.

Alici Y. (1995) Neural networks in corporate failure prediction: the UK experience, Working Paper, University of Exeter.

Allayannis G. and Weston J. (2001) The use of foreign currency derivatives and firm market value, *Review of Financial Studies*, in press.

Allen S.L. and Kleinstein A.D. (1991) *Valuing Fixed Income Investments and Derivative Securities: Cash Flow Analysis and Calculations*, Simon and Schuster, New York.

Altman E.I. (1968) Financial ratios, discriminant analysis and the prediction of corporate bankruptcy, *Journal of Finance*, September, 589–609.

Altman E.I., Haldeman R. and Narayanan P. (1977) ZETA analysis: a new model to identify bankruptcy risk of corporations, *Journal of Banking and Finance*, 29–55.

Altman E.I. and Nammacher S.A. (1985) The default rate experience of high-yield corporate debt, *Financial Analysts Journal*, July/August, 25–41.

Altman E.I. (1987) The anatomy of the high-yield bank market, *Financial Analysts Journal*, July/August, 12–25.

Altman E.I. (1989) Measuring corporate bond mortality and performance, *Journal of Finance*, September, 909–922.

Altman E.I. and Kao D.L. (1992a) The implications of corporate bond ratings drift, *Financial Analysts Journal*, 48, 64–75.

Altman E.I. and Kao D.L. (1992b) Rating drift in high yield bonds, *The Journal of Fixed Income*, March, 15–20.

Altman E.I. (1993a) *Corporate Financial Distress and Bankruptcy: A Complete Guide to Predicting and Avoiding Distress*, Wiley, New York.

Altman E.I. (1993b) Defaulted bonds: demand, supply and performance, 1987–1992, *Financial Analysts Journal*, May/June, 55–60.

Altman E.I. and Eberhart A.C. (1994) Do seniority provisions protect bondholders' investments?, *Journal of Portfolio Management*, Summer, 67–75.

Altman E.I. and Bencivenga J.C. (1995) A yield premium model for the high-yield debt market, *Financial Analysts Journal*, September/October, 49–56.

Altman E.I. and Kishore V. (1996) Almost everything you wanted to know about recoveries on defaulted bonds, *Financial Analysts Journal*, 52(6), November/December, 57–64.

Altman E.I. and Saunders A. (1997) Credit risk measurement: developments over the last 20 years, *Journal of Banking and Finance*, 21, 1721–1742.

Altman E.I. (1998) The importance and subtlety of credit rating migration, *Journal of Banking and Finance*, 22, 1231–1247.

Altman E.I. and Kishore V. (1998) Defaults and returns on high yield bonds: analysis through 1997, Working Paper No. S-98-1, Salomon Center, New York University.

Altman N.S. (1992) An introduction to kernel and nearest-neighbor nonparametric regression, *The American Statistician*, 46, 175–185.

Anderson R.W. and Sundaresan S.M. (1996) Design and valuation of debt contracts, *Review of Financial Studies*, 9(1), 37–68.

Antonov I. (2000) Crafting a market landscape, *The Journal of Lending & Credit Risk Management*, February.

Artzner P., Delbaen F., Eber J.M. and Heath D. (1999) Coherent measures of risk, *Mathematical Finance*, 9, July, 203–228.

Asarnow E. (1994/1995) Measuring the hidden risks in corporate loans, *Commercial Lending Review*, 10(1), Winter, 24–32.

Asarnow E. (1995) Measuring loss on defaulted bank loans: a 24-year study, *The Journal of Commercial Lending*, March.

Asarnow E. and Marker J. (1995) Historical performance of the US corporate loan market: 1988–1993, *The Journal of Commercial Lending*, 10(2), Spring, 13–32.

Asarnow E. (1996) Best practices in loan portfolio management, *Journal of Lending and Credit Risk Management*, March, 14–24.

Asquith P., Mullins D.W. and Wolff E.D. (1989) Original issue high yield bonds: aging analysis of defaults, exchanges, and calls, *The Journal of Finance*, September, 923–952.

Asquith P., Gertner R. and Scharfstein D. (1994) Anatomy of financial distress: an examination of junk-bond issuers, *Quarterly Journal of Economics*, August, 625–657.

Austin D.G. (1992) Use migration analysis to refine estimates of future loan losses, *Commercial Lending Review*, 7(2), Spring, 34–43.

Avery R.B. and Berger A.N. (1991) Loan commitments and bank risk exposure, *Journal of Banking and Finance*, 15, 173–192.

Baestaens D.-E. (1999) Credit risk strategies: the road to serfdom?, *International Journal of Intelligent Systems in Accounting, Finance and Management*, 8, 225–235.

Bahar R. and Gold M. (1995) Structuring derivative product companies: risks and safeguards, in *Derivative Credit Risk: Advances in Measurement and Management*, Risk Books, London.

Bair S. and Milligan S. (1996) Voluntary efforts to provide oversight of OTC derivatives activities, in Klein R. and Lederman J. (eds), *Derivatives Risk and Responsibility*, Irwin, Chicago, IL.

Bangia A., Diebold F., Schuermann T. and Stroughair J. (1999) Liquidity on the outside, *Risk*, 12, June, 68–73.

Bank of England (1995) *Report of the Board of Banking Supervision Inquiry into the Circumstances of the Collapse of Barings*, HMSO Publications, London.

Banks E. (1993) *Volatility and Credit Risk in the Capital Markets*, Probus, Chicago, IL.

Banks E. (1994) *Complex Derivatives*, Probus, Chicago, IL.

Banz R. (1981) The relationship between return and market value of common stocks, *Journal of Financial Economics*, 9, 3–18.

Barclay M.J. and Smith C.W. (1995) The priority structure of corporate liabilities, *Journal of Finance*, L(3), July, 899–917.

Barniv R. (1989) Identifying financial distress: a new nonparametric approach, *Journal of Business Finance and Accounting*, 361–383.

Bartlett W.W. (1989) *Mortgage-Backed Securities*, New York Institute of Finance, New York.

Baruch (1988) Toward a theory of equitable and efficient accounting policy, *Accounting Review*, 63, January, 1–22.

Basel Committee on Banking Supervision (1988) International Convergence of Capital Measurement and Capital Standards, Basel Committee on Banking Supervision, Basel, Switzerland.

Basel Committee on Banking Supervision (1994) Risk Management Guidelines for Derivatives, BIS, Basel, Switzerland.

Basel Committee on Banking Supervision (1995a) Public Disclosure of the Trading and Derivatives Activities of Banks and Securities Firms, BIS, Basel, Switzerland.

Basel Committee on Banking Supervision (1995b) Basel Capital Accord: Treatment of Potential Exposure for Off-Balance-Sheet Items, BIS, Basel, Switzerland.

Basel Committee on Banking Supervision (1995c) An Internal Model-Based Approach to Market Risk Capital Requirements, Basel Committee on Banking Supervision, Basel, Switzerland.

Basel Committee on Banking Supervision (1996a) Supervisory Framework for the Use of 'Back Testing' in Conjunction with the Internal Models Approach to Market Risk Capital Requirements, BIS, Basel, Switzerland.

Basel Committee on Banking Supervision (1996b) Amendment to the Capital Accord to Incorporate Market Risks, Basel Committee on Banking Supervision, Basel, Switzerland.

Basel Committee on Banking Supervision (1998a) Amendment to the Basel Capital Accord of July 1988, BIS, Basel, Switzerland.

Basel Committee on Banking Supervision (1998b) Enhancing Bank Transparency, BIS, Basel, Switzerland.

Basel Committee on Banking Supervision (1998c) Framework for International Control Systems in Banking Organizations, Basel Committee on Banking Supervision, Basel, Switzerland.

Basel Committee on Banking Supervision (1998d) Framework for the Evaluation of Internal Control Systems, BIS, Basel, Switzerland.

Basel Committee on Banking Supervision (1998e) Operational Risk Management, Basel Committee on Banking Supervision, Basel, Switzerland.

Basel Committee on Banking Supervision (1998f) Operational Risk Management, BIS, Basel, Switzerland.

Basel Committee on Banking Supervision (1999a) Performance of Model-Based Capital Charges for Market Risk, 1 July–31 December 1998, BIS, Basel, Switzerland.

Basel Committee on Banking Supervision (1999b) Credit Risk Modeling: Current Practices and Applications, BIS, Basel, Switzerland.

Basel Committee on Banking Supervision (1999c) Recommendations for Public Disclosure of Trading and Derivatives Activities of Banks and Securities Firms, BIS, Basel, Switzerland.

Basel Committee on Banking Supervision (1999d) A New Capital Adequacy Framework, Basel Committee on Banking Supervision, Basel, Switzerland.

Basel Committee on Banking Supervision (1999e) Banks' Interactions with Highly Leveraged Institutions, Basel Committee on Banking Supervision, Basel, Switzerland.

Basel Committee on Banking Supervision (1999f) Capital Requirements and Bank Behavior: The Impact of the Basel Accord, Working Paper, BIS, Basel, Switzerland.

Basel Committee on Banking Supervision (1999g) Credit Risk Modelling: Current Practices and Applications, Basel Committee on Banking Supervision, Basel, Switzerland.

Basel Committee on Banking Supervision (2000a) Best Practices for Credit Risk Disclosure, BIS, Basel, Switzerland, February.

Basel Committee on Banking Supervision (2000b) Overview of the Amendment to the Capital Accord to Incorporate Market Risks, BIS, Basel, Switzerland, February.

Basel Committee on Banking Supervision (2000c) Treatment of Potential Exposure for Off-Balance-Sheet Items, BIS, Basel, Switzerland, February.

Basel Committee on Banking Supervision (2000d) Sound Practices for Managing Liquidity in Banking Organizations, BIS, Basel, Switzerland, February.

Basel Committee on Banking Supervision (2000e) The Relationship Between Banking Supervisors and Banks' External Auditors, BIS, Basel, Switzerland, February.

Basel Committee on Banking Supervision (2000f) Report to G7 Finance Ministers and Central Bank Governors on International Accounting Standards, BIS, Basel, Switzerland, April.

Basel Committee on Banking Supervision (2000g) Operational Risk, BIS, Basel, Switzerland, April.

Basel Committee on Banking Supervision (2000h) Best Practices for Credit Risk Disclosure, BIS, Basel, Switzerland, September.

Basel Committee on Banking Supervision (2000i) Principles for the Management of Credit Risk, BIS, Basel, Switzerland, September.

Basel Committee on Banking Supervision (2001a) The New Basel Accord, BIS, Basel, Switzerland, January.

Basel Committee on Banking Supervision (2001b) Principles for the Management and Supervision of Interest Rate Risk, BIS, Basel, Switzerland, January.

Basel Committee on Banking Supervision (2001c) The Standardized Approach to Credit Risk, BIS, Basel, Switzerland, January.

Basel Committee on Banking Supervision (2001d) The Internal Ratings-Based Approach, BIS, Basel, Switzerland, January.

Basel Committee on Banking Supervision (2001e) Risk Concentration Principles, BIS, Basel, Switzerland, January.

Basel Committee on Banking Supervision (2001f) Industry Views on Credit Risk Mitigation, BIS, Basel, Switzerland, January.

Basel Committee on Banking Supervision (2001g) Pillar 2 (Supervisory Review Process), BIS, Basel, Switzerland, January.

Basel Committee on Banking Supervision (2001h) Pillar 3 (Market Discipline), BIS, Basel, Switzerland, January.

Basel Committee on Banking Supervision (2001i) Overview of the New Basel Capital Accord, BIS, Basel, Switzerland, January.

Basel Committee on Banking Supervision (2001j) The New Basel Capital Accord: An Explanatory Note, BIS, Basel, Switzerland, January.

Basel Committee on Banking Supervision (2001k) Asset Securitisation, BIS, Basel, Switzerland, January.

Bates D. (1995) Testing option pricing models, NBER Working Paper No. 5129, Cambridge, MA.

Baumol W. (1963) An expected gain–confidence limit criterion for portfolio selection, *Management Science*, 11, 174–182.

Beaver W. (1966) Financial ratios as predictors of failure, *Journal of Accounting Research*, Supplement on Empirical Research in Accounting, 71–111.

Beaver W.H. and Parker G. (eds) (1995) *Risk Management: Problems & Solutions*, McGraw-Hill, New York.

Beckstrom R. and Campbell A. (eds) (1995) *An Introduction to VAR*, CATS Software, Palo Alto, CA.

Beder T. (1995) VAR: seductive but dangerous, *Financial Analysts Journal*, 51, 12–24.

Begley J., Ming J. and Watts S. (1996) Bankruptcy classification errors in the 1980s: an empirical analysis of Altman's and Ohlson's models, *Review of Accounting Studies*, 1, 267–284.

Beidleman C.R. (ed.) (1991) *Interest Rate Swaps*, Business One Irwin, Chicago, IL.

Benishay H. (1973) Discussion of a prediction of business failure using accounting data, *Journal of Accounting Research*, Supplement on Empirical Research in Accounting, 180–182.

Bennet P. (1984) Applying portfolio theory to global bank lending, *Journal of Banking and Finance*, 8(2), 153–169.

Bennett B. (1986) Off-balance-sheet risk in banking: the case of standby letters of credit, *Economic Review, Federal Reserve Bank of San Francisco*, Winter, 19–29.

Bennett III S.G. (1991) *The Quest for Value. A Guide for Senior Managers*, Harper Collins, New York.

Bensoussan A., Crouhy M. and Galai D. (1994) Stochastic equity volatility related to the leverage effect, *Applied Mathematical Finance*, 1(1), September, 63–85.

Berger A.N. and Udell G.F. (1990) Collateral, loan quality, and bank risk, *Journal of Monetary Economics*, 25, 21–42.

Berger A.N. and Udell G.F. (1995) Relationship lending and lines of credit in small firm finance, *Journal of Business*, 68, 351–381.

Berger A.N., Herring R.J. and Szego G.P. (1995) The role of capital in financial institutions, *Journal of Banking and Finance*, 19(3/4), June, 393–430.

Berkman H. and Bradbury M. (1996) Empirical evidence on the corporate use of derivatives, *Financial Management*, 25(2), Summer, 5–13.

Berkowitz J. (2000) A coherent framework for stress testing, *Journal of Risk*, 2, Winter, 5–15.

Berlin M. and Mester L. (1992) Debt covenants and renegotiation, *Journal of Financial Intermediation*, 2/3, June, 95–133.

Bernstein P.L. (1996) *Against the Gods: The Remarkable Story of Risk*, Wiley, New York.

Berry M., Burmeister F. and McElroy M. (1988) Sorting our risks using known APT factors, *Financial Analysts Journal*, 44(2), March/April, 29–42.

Bessembinder H. (1991) Forward contracts and firm value: investment incentive and contracting effects, *Journal of Financial and Quantitative Analysis*, 26(4), December, 519–532.

Bhala (1989) *Risk-Based Capital: A Guide to the New Risk-Based Capital Adequacy Rules*, Bank Administration Institute, Rolling Meadow, IL.

Bhattacharya S. and Thakor A.V. (1993) Contemporary banking theory, *Journal of Financial Intermediation*, 3(1), October, 2–50.

Bierwag, Kaufman, Schwitzer and Toevs (1981) The art of risk management, *Journal of Portfolio Management*, Spring, 27–36.

Bierwag G. (1987) *Duration Analysis—Managing Interest Rate Risk*, Ballinger Publishing, Cambridge, MA.

Birkes D. and Dodge Y. (1993) *Alternative Methods of Regression*, Wiley, New York.

Bisksler J. and Chen A.H. (1986) An economic analysis of interest rate swaps, *Journal of Finance*, 41, July, 645–655.

Bitner J. (1992) *Successful Bank Asset–Liability Management*, Wiley, Chichester.

Black F. and Scholes M. (1973) The pricing of options and corporate liabilities, *Journal of Political Economy*, 81, 637–659.

Black F. (1976) The pricing of commodity contracts, *Journal of Financial Economics*, 3, March, 167–179.

Black F. and Cox J.C. (1976) Valuing corporate securities: some effects of bond indenture provisions, *Journal of Finance*, 31, 351–368.

Black F., Derman E. and Toy W. (1990) A one-factor model of interest rates and its application to Treasury bond options, *Financial Analysts Journal*, 46(1), January/February, 33–39.

Black F. (1992) The holes in Black–Scholes, in *From Black–Scholes to Black Holes*, Risk Books, London.

Blejer M. and Schumacher L. (1999) Central bank vulnerability and the credibility of its commitments: a value-at-risk approach, *Journal of Risk*, 2, Fall, 37–55.

Bliss R. and Smith D. (1998) The elasticity of interest rate volatility, *Journal of Risk*, 1, Fall, 21–46.

Block S.B. and Gallagher T.J. (1986) The use of interest rate futures and options by corporate financial managers, *Financial Management*, Autumn, 73–78.

Blum M. (1974) Failing company discriminant analysis, *Journal of Accounting Research*, Spring.

Blume M. and Keim D. (1991) Realized returns and defaults on low-grade bonds: the cohort of 1977 and 1978, *Financial Analysts Journal*, 47, 63–72.

Blume M.E., Keim D.B. and Patel S.A. (1991a) Returns and volatility of low-grade bonds 1977–1989, *The Journal of Finance*, XLVI(1), March, 49–74.

Blume M.E., Butcher III H. and Keim D.B. (1991b) The risk and return of low-grade bonds: an update, *Financial Analysts Journal*, September/October, 85–89.

Blume M., Lim F. and MacKinlay C. (1998) The declining credit quality of US corporate debt: myth or reality?, *Journal of Finance*, August.

Bollerslev T. (1986) Generalized autoregressive conditional heteroskedasticity, *Journal of Econometrics*, 31, 307–327.

Bollerslev T., Chou R. and Kroner K. (1992) ARCH modelling in finance: a review of the theory and empirical evidence, *Journal of Econometrics*, 52, 5–59.

Bollerslev T., Engle R.F. and Nelson D.B. (1994) ARCH models, in Engle R. and McFadden D. (eds), *The Handbook of Econometrics*, Vol. 4, North-Holland, Amsterdam, pp. 2959–3038.

Bondar G.M., Hayt G.S., Marston R.C. and Smithson C.W. (1995) Wharton survey of derivatives usage by US non-financial firms, *Financial Management*, 24(2), Summer, 104–114.

Boness J. (1964) Elements of a theory of stock-option value, *Journal of Political Economy*, 12, 163–175.

Bookstaber R. (1997) Global risk management: are we missing the point?, *Journal of Portfolio Management*, 23, Spring, 102–107.

Boot A. and Thakor A.V. (1991) Off-balance sheet liabilities, deposit insurance and capital regulation, *Journal of Banking and Finance*, 15, 825–846.

Boot A., Thakor A.V. and Udell G.F. (1991) Credible commitments, contract enforcement problems and banks: intermediation as credibility assurance, *Journal of Banking and Finance*, 15, June, 605–632.

Boot A. and Thakor A.V. (1993) Security design, *Journal of Finance*, 48(3), September, 1349–1378.

Boothe and Hutchinson (1989) Distinguishing between failing and growing firms: a note on the use of decomposition measure analysis, *Journal of Business Finance and Accounting*, 267–271.

Boudoukh J., Richardson M. and Whitelaw R. (1995a) Expect the worst, *Risk*, 8(9), 100–101.

Boudoukh J., Richardson M., Stanton R. and Whitelaw R. (1995b) A new strategy for dynamically hedging mortgage-backed securities, *Journal of Derivatives*, 2, Summer, 60–77.

Boudoukh J., Richardson M. and Whitelaw R. (1998) The best of both worlds, *Risk*, 11, May, 64–67.

Boyle P. (1977) Options: a Monte Carlo approach, *Journal of Financial Economics*, 4, 323–338.

Boyle P., Broadie M. and Glasserman P. (1997) Monte Carlo methods for security pricing, *Journal of Economic Dynamics and Control*, 21, 1267–1321.

Brace A., Gatarek D. and Musiela M. (1997) The market model of interest rate dynamics, *Mathematical Finance*, 7(2), 127–155.

Brady Report (1989) Presidential task force on market mechanisms, in *Black Monday and the Future of Financial Markets*, Irwin, Homewood, IL.

Bralver C. and Kuritzkes A. (1993) Risk adjusted performance measurement in the trading room, *Journal of Applied Corporate Finance*, 6, 104–108.

Brealey R. and Myers S. (2000) *Principles of Corporate Finance*, 6th edn, McGraw-Hill, New York.

Brennan M. and Schwartz E. (1979) A continuous time approach to the pricing of bonds, *Journal of Banking and Finance*, 3, 133–155.

Brennan M.J. and Schwarz E.S. (1982) An equilibrium model of bond pricing and a test of market efficiency, *Journal of Financial and Quantitative Analysis*, 17(3), September, 301–329.

Brewer E. (1985) Bank gap management and the use of financial futures, *Economic Perspectives, Federal Reserve Bank of Chicago*, March/April, 12–22.

Brinson G., Singer B. and Beebower G. (1991) Determinants of portfolio performance II: an update, *Financial Analysts Journal*, 47, May, 40–48.

Broadie M. and Glasserman P. (1998) Simulation for option pricing and risk management, in Alexander C. (ed.), *Risk Management and Analysis*, Vol. 1, *Measuring and Modeling Financial Risk*, Wiley, New York.

Brown K.C. and Smiths D.J. (1993) Default risk and innovations in the design of interest rate swaps, *Financial Management*, 22, Summer, 94–105.

Burghardt G. and Hanweck G.A. (1993) Calendar-adjusted volatilities, *Journal of Derivatives*, 1(2), Winter, 23–32.

Buser S., Chen A.H. and Kane E.J. (1981) Federal deposit insurance, regulatory policy, and optimal bank capital, *Journal of Finance*, March, 51–60.

Butler J.S. and Schachter B. (1998) Estimating value at risk with a precision measure by combining kernel estimation with historical simulation, *Review of Derivatives Research*, 1(37), 371–390.

Campa J.M. and Chang K. (1998) The forecasting ability of correlations implied in foreign exchange options, *Journal of International Money and Finance*, 17, 855–880.

Campbell J.Y., Lo A.W. and MacKinlay A.C. (1997) *The Econometrics of Financial Markets*, Princeton University Press, Princeton, NJ.

Cantor R. and Packer F. (1994) The credit rating industry, *Federal Reserve Bank of New York Quarterly Review*, 19(2), 1–26.

Cantor R. and Packer F. (1996) Determinants and impact of sovereign credit ratings, *Economic Policy Review, Federal Reserve Bank of New York*, 2(2), October, 37–53.

Cantor R. and Packer F. (1997) Differences of opinion in the credit rating industry, *Journal of Banking and Finance*, 21(10), 1395–1417.

Caouette J.B., Altman E.I. and Naranayan P. (1998) *Managing Credit Risk: The Next Financial Challenge*, Wiley, New York.

Carty L. and Fons J.S. (1993) Measuring changes in credit quality, Moody's Investors Service, Special Report, November [also in *Journal of Fixed Income*, June (1996), 27–41].

Carty L.V. and Lieberman D. (1996a) Corporate bond defaults and default rates 1938–1995, Moody's Investors Service, Global Credit Research, January.

Carty L.V. and Lieberman D. (1996b) Defaulted bank loan recoveries, Moody's Investors Service, Global Credit Research, Special Report, November.

Casey and Bartczak (1984) Cash flow: it's not the bottom line, *Harvard Business Review*, July/August, 61–66.

Ceske R. and Hernandez J. (1999) Operational risk: where theory meets practice, *Risk*, November, 17–20.

Chance D. (1990) Default risk and the duration of zero coupon bonds, *Journal of Finance*, 45(1), 265–274.

Chen K. and Shimerda T. (1981) An empirical analysis of useful financial ratios, *Financial Management*, Spring.

Chen N., Roll R. and Ross S. (1986) Economic forces and the stock market, *Journal of Business*, 59, 368–403.

Chen Y., Weston J.F. and Altman E.I. (1995) Financial distress and restructuring models, *Financial Management*, 24(2), Summer, 57–75.

Chew L. (1996) *Managing Derivative Risks: The Use and Abuse of Leverage*, Wiley, New York.

Chow G., Jacquier E., Kritzman M. and Lowry K. (1999) Optimal portfolios in good times and bad, *Financial Analysts Journal*, 55, May, 65–73.

Cluck J. (1996) Measuring and controlling the credit risk of derivatives, in Klein R. and Lederman J. (eds), *Derivatives Risk and Responsibility*, Irwin, Chicago, IL.

Coleman T., Fisher L. and Ibbotson R. (1992) Estimating the term structure of interest rates from data that include the prices of coupon bonds, *Journal of Fixed Income*, September, 85–116.

Colub B. and Tilman L. (2000) *Risk Management: Approaches for Fixed-income Markets*, Wiley, New York.

Cook D.O. and Spellman L.J. (1996) Firm and guarantor risk, risk contagion, and the interfirm spread among insured deposits, *Journal of Financial and Quantitative Analysis*, June, 265–281.

Cooper I. and Mello A. (1991) The default risk of swaps, *Journal of Finance*, 46(2), 597–620.

Cooper's & Lybrand (1996) *Generally Accepted Risk Principles*, Cooper's & Lybrand, London.

Cooper's & Lybrand and The British Bankers' Association (1997) Operational Risk Management Survey.

Copeland T. and Weston J.F. (1988) *Financial Theory and Corporate Policy*, Addison-Wesley, Reading, MA.

Counterparty Risk Management Policy Group (1999) Improving Counterparty Risk Management Practices, Counterparty Risk Management Policy Group, New York.

Cox J.C. and Ross S.A. (1976) The valuation of options for alternative stochastic processes, *Journal of Financial Economics*, 3, 145–166.

Cox J.C., Ross S.A. and Rubinstein M. (1979) Option pricing: a simplified approach, *Journal of Financial Economics*, 7, October, 229–263.

Cox J.C., Ingersoll J.E. and Ross S.A. (1981) A re-examination of traditional hypotheses about the term structure of interest rates, *Journal of Finance*, 36, September, 769–799.

Cox J.C. and Rubinstein M. (1985) *Options Markets*, Prentice-Hall, Englewood Cliffs, NJ.

Cox J.C., Ingersoll J.E. and Ross S.A. (1985) A theory of the term structure of interest rates, *Econometrica*, 53, March, 385–408.

Crabbe L. and Post M.A. (1994) The effect of a rating downgrade on outstanding commercial paper, *The Journal of Finance*, XLIX(1), March, 39–56.

Crabbe L. (1995) A framework for corporate bond strategy, *The Journal of Fixed Income*, June, 15–25.

Credit Suisse (1997) *CreditRisk+: A Credit Risk Management Framework*, Credit Suisse Financial Products.

Crouhy M. and Galai D. (1986) An economic assessment of capital requirements in the banking industry, *Journal of Banking and Finance*, 10, 231–241.

Crouhy M., Galai D. and Mark R. (1998) Key steps in building consistent operational risk measurement and management, in *Operational Risk and Financial Institutions*, Risk Books, London.

Crouhy M., Turnbull S. and Wakeman L. (1999) Measuring risk adjusted performance, *Journal of Risk*, 2(1), Fall, 1–31.

Crouhy M., Galai D. and Mark R. (2001) *Risk Management*, McGraw-Hill, New York.

Cruz M., Coleman S. and Salkin G. (1998) Modeling and measuring operational risk, *Journal of Risk*, 1, Fall, 63–72.

Culp C.L. and Miller M.H. (1994) Risk management lessons from Metallgesellschaft, *Journal of Applied Corporate Finance*, 7(4), 62–76.

Culp C.L. and Miller M.H. (1995) Hedging in the theory of corporate finance: a reply to our critics, *Journal of Applied Corporate Finance*, 8, 121–127.

Cumming C. (1987) The economics of securitization, *Federal Reserve Bank of New York Quarterly Review*, 12, Autumn, 11–23.

Curry D.A., Gluck J.A., May W.L. and Eackman A.C. (1995) Evaluating derivative product companies, in *Derivative Credit Risk: Advances in Measurement and Management*, Risk Books, London.

Dambolena K. (1980) Ratio stability and corporate failure, *Journal of Finance*, 1017–1026.

Das S.R. (1995) Credit risk derivatives, *Journal of Derivatives*, 2(3), Spring, 7–23.

Das S. and Tufano P. (1995) Pricing credit sensitive debt when interest rates, credit ratings and credit spreads are stochastic, *Journal of Financial Engineering*, 5(2), 161–198.

Das S. (1998) *Credit Derivatives: Trading and Management of Credit & Default Risk*, Wiley, Singapore.

Dattatreya R.E. et al. (1994) *Interest Rate and Currency Swaps*, Probus, Chicago, IL.

Davanzo L.E. and Nesbitt S. (1987) Performance fees for investment management, *Financial Analysts Journal*, 43, January, 14–20.

Davidson C. (1997) Testing the testers, *Risk*, 10(6), 58–63.

Dawes R. (1979) The robust beauty of improper linear models in decision making, *American Psychologist*, 34, 571–582.

Deakin E. (1972) A discriminant analysis of predictors of business failure, *Journal of Accounting Research*, Spring, 167–179.

Demirgüç K.A. (1989) Deposit-institution failures: a review of empirical literature, *Economic Review, Federal Reserve Bank of Cleveland*, 25, Quarter IV, 2–18.

Derivative Credit Risk, 2nd edn, Risk Books, London, 1999.

Derivatives Policy Group (1995) *A Framework for Voluntary Oversight*, Derivatives Policy Group, New York.

Derman E. (1996) Valuing models and modeling value, *Journal of Portfolio Management*, 22, Spring, 106–114.

Derman E. (1997) Model risk, in *VAR—Understanding and Applying Value-at-Risk*, Risk Books, London.

Dermine J. (1985) The measurement of interest rate risk by financial intermediaries, *Journal of Bank Research*, Summer.

Deshmukh S.D., Greenbaum S.I. and Kamatas G. (1983) Interest rate uncertainty and the financial intermediary's choice of exposure, *Journal of Finance*, 38, March, 141–147.

Diamond D.W. and Dybvig P. (1983) Bank runs, deposit insurance, and liquidity, *Journal of Political Economy*, 91, June, 401–419.

Dimson E. and Marsh P. (1995) Capital requirements for securities firms, *Journal of Finance*, 50, 821–851.

Dolde W. (1993) The trajectory of corporate financial risk management, *Journal of Applied Corporate Finance*, 6, 33–41.

Dowd K. (1998) *Beyond Value at Risk: The New Science of Risk Management*, Wiley, New York.

Duan J.C. (1995) The GARCH option pricing model, *Mathematical Finance*, 5, 13–32.

Duffee C.R. and Zhou C. (1997) Credit derivatives in banking: useful tools for loan risk management, Working Paper, Federal Reserve Board, Washington, DC.

Duffie D. (1989) *Futures Markets*, Prentice-Hall, Englewood Cliffs, NJ.

Duffie D. (1992) *Dynamic Asset Pricing Theory*, Princeton University Press, Princeton, NJ.

Duffie D. and Huang M. (1996) Swap rates and credit quality, *Journal of Finance*, 51, 921–949.

Duffie D. and Pan J. (1997) An overview of value at risk, *Journal of Derivatives*, 4(3), Spring, 7–49.

Duffie D. and Singleton V.K. (1999) Modeling term structures of defaultable bonds, *Review of Financial Studies*, 12(4), 687–720.

Dunbar N. (1999) The new emperors of Wall Street, *Risk*, 12, March, 26–33.

Dutta S. and Shekhar S. (1988) Bond rating: a non-conservative application of neural networks, IEEE International Conference on Neural Networks, July, pp. 443–458.

Eagle R., Lilien D. and Robins R. (1987) Estimating time-varying risk premia in the term structure: the ARCH-M model, *Econometrica*, 55, 391–407.

Eberhart A.C. and Sweeney R.J. (1992) Does the bond market predict bankruptcy settlements?, *The Journal of Finance*, XLVII(3), July, 943–980.

Edmister (1997) An empirical test of financial ratio analysis for small business failure prediction, *Journal of Financial and Quantitative Analysis*, 1477–1493.

Elderfield M. (1995) Capital countdown, *Risk*, 8(2), 18–21.

El Hennawy M. (1983) The significance of base year in developing failure prediction models, *Journal of Business Finance and Accounting*, 209–223.

Elton E.J. and Gruber M.J. (1995) *Modern Portfolio Theory and Investment Analysis*, Wiley, New York.

Embrechts P., Klupperlberg C. and Mikosch T. (1997) *Modelling Extremal Events for Insurance and Finance*, Springer, Berlin.

Engle R.F. (1982) Autoregressive conditional heteroskedasticity with estimates of the variance of United Kingdom inflation, *Econometrica*, 50, 987–1007.

Engle R.F. (1993) Measuring and testing the impact of news on volatility, *Journal of Finance*, 48(1), 749–778.

Ernst & Young (1994) *Performance Measurement for Financial Institutions*, Probus, Chicago, IL.

Ernst & Young (1995) Survey of Investment Concerns.

Estrella A., Hendricks D., Kambhu J., Shin S. and Walter S. (1994) The price risk of options positions: measurement and capital requirements, *Federal Reserve Bank of New York Quarterly Review*, 19, 27–43.

European Union (1989) Council Directive 89/647/EEC of 18 December 1989 on a Solvency Ratio for Credit Institutions, European Union, Brussels.

European Union (1993) Council Directive 93/6/EEC of 15 March 1993 on the Capital Adequacy of Investment Firms and Credit Institutions, European Union, Brussels.

Fabozzi F. and Konishi A. (1991) *Asset–Liability Management*, Probus, Chicago, IL.

Fabozzi F.J. (1993) *Fixed Income Mathematics*, Probus, Chicago, IL.

Fabozzi F.J. (1997) *The Handbook of Fixed Income Securities*, 5th edn, McGraw-Hill, New York.

Falkenstein F. (1997) Value-at-risk and derivatives risk, *Derivatives Quarterly*, 4(1), Fall, 42–50.

Fama E.F. (1965) The behavior of stock prices, *Journal of Business*, 38, January, 34–105.

Fama E. and Miller M. (1974) *The Theory of Finance*, Holt, Rinehart and Winston, New York.

Fama E. and French K. (1992) The cross-section of expected stock returns, *Journal of Finance*, 47(2), June.

Figlewski S. (1986) *Hedging with Financial Futures for Institutional Investors—From Theory to Practice*, Ballinger Publishing, Cambridge, MA.

Figlewski S. (1994) The birth of the AAA derivatives subsidiary, *Journal of Derivatives*, 1(4), 80–84.

Financial Accounting Standards Board (1998) Statement No. 133: Accounting for Derivative Instruments and Hedging Activities, Financial Accounting Standards Board, Norwalk, CT.

Finnerty J. (1988) Financial engineering in corporate finance: an overview, *Financial Management*, 17, 14–33.

Fishman G. (1997) *Monte Carlo: Concepts, Algorithms, and Applications*, Springer Series in Operations Research, Springer, New York.

Fite D. and Pfleiderer P. (1995) Should firms use derivatives to manage risk?, in Beaver W.H. and Parker G. (eds), *Risk Management, Problems and Solutions*, McGraw-Hill, New York.

Fitzpatrick A. (1932) Comparison of ratios of successful industrial enterprises with those of failed firms, *Certified Public Accountant*, 598–605, 656–662, 727–731.

Fons J.S. and Carty L.V. (1995) Probability of default: a derivatives perspective, in *Derivative Credit Risk—Advances in Measurements and Management*, Risk Books, London.

Foss G.W. (1995) Quantifying risk in the corporate bond markets, *Financial Analysts Journal*, March/April, 29–34.

Foulke R.A. (1968) *Practical Financial Statement Analysis*, McGraw-Hill, New York.

Francis J.C., Frost J.A. and Whittaker J.G. (1999) *Handbook of Credit Derivatives*, McGraw-Hill, New York.

Franks J.R. and Torous W.N. (1989) An empirical investigation of US firms in reorganization, *The Journal of Finance*, July, 747–769.

French K. (1983) A comparison of futures and forward prices, *Journal of Financial Economics*, 12, November, 311–342.

French K., Schwett W. and Starnhaugh R. (1987) Expected stock returns and volatility, *Journal of Financial Economics*, 19, 3–29.

Fridson M.S. and Gao Y. (1996) Primary versus secondary pricing of high-yield bonds, *Financial Analysts Journal*, May/June, 20–27.

Froot K.A. (1989) New hope for the expectations hypothesis of the term structure of interest rates, *Journal of Finance*, 44, June, 283–305.

Froot K.A., Scharfstein D. and Stein I. (1993a) A framework for risk management, *Harvard Business Review*, November/December, 1–94.

Froot K.A., Scharfstein D. and Stein J. (1993b) Risk management: coordinating investment and financing policies, *Journal of Finance*, 48, 1629–1658.

Froot K. and Stein J. (1998) Risk management, capital budgeting and capital structure policy for financial institutions: an integrated approach, *Journal of Financial Economics*, 47, 55–82.

Frye J. (1997) Principals of risk: finding VaR through factor-based interest rate scenarios, in *VaR: Understanding and Applying Value at Risk*, Risk Publications, London, pp. 275–288.

Galai D. and Masulis R.W. (1976) The option pricing model and the risk factor of stocks, *Journal of Financial Economics*, 3, January/March, 53–82.

Galai D. (1977) Characterization of options, *Journal of Banking and Finance*, 11, 373–385.

Galai D. (1978) On the Boness and Black–Scholes models for valuation of call options, *Journal of Financial and Quantitative Analysis*, 13, 15–27.

Gannan M. (1997) Taking VAR to pieces, *Risk*, 10, October, 70–71.

Gardner M.J. and Mills D.L. (1994) *Managing Financial Institutions*, The Dryden Press, Orlando, FL.

Garman M.B. (1996) Improving on VaR, *Risk*, 9(5), 61–63.

General Accounting Office (1994) Financial Derivatives: Actions Needed to Protect Financial Systems, US General Accounting Office, Washington, DC.

General Accounting Office (1996) Financial Derivatives: Actions Taken or Proposed Since May 1994, US General Accounting Office, Washington, DC.

General Accounting Office (1998) Risk-Based Capital: Regulatory and Industry Approaches to Capital and Risk, US General Accounting Office, Washington, DC.

Geske R. (1977) The valuation of corporate liabilities as compound options, *Journal of Financial and Quantitative Analysis*, 12, 541–552.

Giovannini A. and Jorion P. (1989) The time-variation of risk and return in the foreign exchange and stock markets, *Journal of Finance*, 44, 307–325.

Gollinger T.L. and Morgan J.B. (1993) Calculation of an efficient frontier for a commercial loan portfolio, *Journal of Portfolio Management*, Winter, 39–46.

Golubchin L. (1994) The ARCH structure of the sovereign debt risk spread, Working Paper, Preliminary Draft, 29-Dec-94, City University of New York.

Gombola M.J. and Ketz J.E. (1983) A note on cash flow and classification patterns of financial ratios, *Accounting Review*, 105–114.

Gordy M.B. (2000) A comparative anatomy of credit risk models, *Journal of Banking and Finance*, 24, 119–149.

Grinold R. and Rudd A. (1987) Incentive fees: who wins? who loses?, *Financial Analysts Journal*, 43, January, 27–38.

Group of Thirty (1993) Derivatives: Practices and Principles, Global Derivatives Study Group, Washington, DC.

Group of Twelve (1999) Improving Counterparty Risk Management Practices, Counterparty Risk Management Policy Group, June.

Guldiman T., Zangari P., Longerstaey J., Mateo J. and Howard I. (1995) *RiskMetrics, Technical Document*, 3rd edn, Morgan Guaranty Trust Company, New York.

Gumerlock R. (1996) Lacking commitment, *Risk*, 9(6), June, 36–39.

Gup B. and Brooks R. (1993) *Interest Rate Risk Management*, Bankers' Publishing Company/Probus, Chicago, IL.

Hamer M. (1983) Failure prediction: sensitivity of classification accuracy to alternative statistical methods and variable sets, *Journal of Accounting and Public Policy*, 289–307.

Hardle W. (1990) *Applied Nonparametric Regression*, Cambridge University Press, Cambridge.

Harlow W. (1991) Asset allocation in a downside risk framework, *Financial Analysts Journal*, 47, September, 28–40.

Hayt G. and Song S. (1995) Handle with sensitivity, *Risk*, 9, September, 94–99.

Heath D., Jarrow R. and Morton A. (1990) Bond pricing and the term structure of interest rates: a discrete time approximation, *Journal of Financial and Quantitative Analysis*, 25(4), December, 419–440.

Heath D., Jarrow R. and Morton A. (1992) Bond pricing and the term structure of interest rates: a new methodology for contingent claims valuation, *Econometrica*, 60, 77–106.

Hempel G.H. and Simonson D.G. (1992) The case for comprehensive market values reporting, *Bank Accounting and Finance*, Spring.

Herrity J., Keenan S.C., Sobehart J.R., Carty L.V. and Falkenstein E. (1999) Measuring private firm default risk, Moody's Investors Service, Special Comment, June.

Hertsen E. and Fields P. (eds) (1993) *Derivative Credit Risk*, Risk Publications, London.

Ho T. and Singer R.F. (1982) Bond indenture provisions and the risk of corporate debt, *Journal of Financial Economics*, 10, 375–406.

Ho T. and Lee S.B. (1986) Term structure movements and pricing interest rate contingent claims, *Journal of Finance*, 41, December, 1011–1029.

Ho T. (1992) Key rate durations: measures of interest rate risks, *Journal of Fixed Income*, 2(2), 29–44.

Hoffman D. and Johnson M. (1996) Operating procedures, *Risk*, 9(10), October, 60–63.

Howe D.M. (1992) *A Guide to Managing Interest-Rate Risk*, New York Institute of Finance, New York.

Hradsky G.T. and Long R.D. (1989) High-yield default losses and the return performance of bankrupt debt, *Financial Analysts Journal*, July/August, 38–49.

Hughston L.R. (1997) Pricing models for credit derivatives, Mimeo, AIC Conference on Credit Derivatives, London, April.

Hull J. (1992) Assessing credit risk in a financial institution's off-balance sheet commitments, *Journal of Financial and Quantitative Analysis*, 24, 489–501.

Hull I. and White A. (1992) The price of default, *Risk*, September, 101–103.

Hull J.C. and White A. (1994) Numerical procedures for implementing term structure models I: single factor models, *Journal of Derivatives*, 2(1), 7–16.

Hull J. and White A. (1995) The impact of default risk on the prices of options and other derivative securities, *Journal of Banking and Finance*, 19(2), May, 299–322.

Hull J.C. and White A. (1996) Using Hull–White interest rate trees, *Journal of Derivatives*, Spring, 26–36.

Hull J.C. and White A. (1998a) Value at risk when daily changes in market variables are not normally distributed, *Journal of Derivatives*, 5(3), Spring, 9–19.

Hull J. and White A. (1998b) Incorporating volatility updating into the historical simulation method for value-at-risk, *Journal of Risk*, 1, Fall, 5–19.

Hull J. (2000) *Options, Futures, and Other Derivatives*, Prentice-Hall, Englewood Cliffs, NJ.

Hurley W.J. and Johnson L.D. (1996) On the pricing of bond default risk, *Journal of Portfolio Management*, Winter, 66–70.

Hyndman C. (1994/1995) Are bank regulators ready for credit scoring of commercial loans?, *Commercial Lending Review*, Winter, 92–95.

International Swap and Derivatives Association (1995) Public Disclosure and Risk Management Activities Including Derivatives, International Swap and Derivatives Association, New York.

International Swap and Derivatives Association (1998) Credit Risk and Regulator, Capital, International Swap and Derivatives Association, New York.

J. P. Morgan (1995) *Risk Metrics Technical Manual*, J. P. Morgan Bank, New York.

J. P. Morgan (1997) *CreditMetrics Technical Document*, April.

Jackson P., Maude D. and Perraudin W. (1997) Bank capital and value-at-risk, *Journal of Derivatives*, 4, Spring, 73–90.

Jacobs R.L. (1983) Fixed-rate lending and interest rate futures hedging, *Journal of Bank Research*, 13, Autumn, 193–202.

Jameson R. (ed.) (1998) *Operational Risk and Financial Institutions*, Risk Books, London.

Jamshidian F. and Zhu Y. (1997) Scenario simulation: theory and methodology, *Finance and Stochastics*, 1, January, 43–68.

Jarrow R.A. and Turnbull S.M. (1995a) Pricing derivatives on financial securities subject to credit risk, *The Journal of Finance*, 1, March, 53–85.

Jarrow R.A. and Turnbull S.M. (1995b) Pricing options on derivative securities subject to credit risk, *Journal of Finance*, 50, 53–85.

Jarrow R., Lando D. and Turnbull S. (1997) A Markov model for the term structure of credit spreads, *Review of Financial Studies*, 10, 481–523.

Jarrow R. and Turnbull S. (2000) *Derivatives Securities*, 2nd edn, South-Western College Publishing, Cincinnati, OH.

Johnson H. and Stulz R. (1987) The pricing of options with default risk, *Journal of Finance*, 42(2), 267–280.

Johnson H.J. (1994) *Bank Asset–Liability Management*, Probus, Chicago, IL.

Johnson J. (1993) *The Bank Valuation Handbook*, Bankers' Publishing Company/Probus, Chicago, IL.

Johnson N.L. and Kotz S. (1972) *Distribution in Statistics: Continuous Univariate Distributions*, Vol. 1, Wiley, New York.

Johnson N., Kotz S. and Balakrishan N. (1995) *Distribution in Statistics: Continuous Univariate Distributions*, Vol. 2, 2nd edn, Wiley, New York.

Jones D. and King K.K. (1995) The implementation of prompt corrective action: an assessment, *Journal of Banking and Finance*, 19, 491–510.

Jones E.P., Mason S.P. and Rosenfeld E. (1984) Contingent claims analysis of corporate capital structures: an empirical analysis, *Journal of Finance*, 39, 611–625.

Jónsson J.G. and Fridson M.S. (1996) Forecasting default rates on high-yield bonds, *The Journal of Fixed Income*, June, 69–77.

Jordan I. and Morgan G. (1990) Default risk in futures markets: the customer–broker relationship, *Journal of Finance*, 45, 909–933.

Jorion P. (1989) Asset allocation with hedged and unhedged foreign stocks and bonds, *Journal of Portfolio Management*, 15, Summer, 49–54.

Jorion P. (1995) Predicting volatility in the foreign exchange market, *Journal of Finance*, 50, 507–528.

Jorion P. (1996) Risk: measuring the risk in value-at-risk, *Financial Analysts Journal*, 52, November, 47–56.

Jorion P. (2001) *Value at Risk—The New Benchmark for Managing Financial Risk*, 2nd edn, McGraw-Hill, New York.

Ju X. and Pearson N. (1999) Using value-at-risk to control risk taking: how wrong can you be?, *Journal of Risk*, 1, Winter, 5–36.

Kahane Y. (1977) Capital adequacy and the regulation of financial intermediaries, *Journal of Banking and Finance*, 1, June, 207–218.

Kahn R.N. (1995) Fixed-income risk modeling in the 1990s, *Journal of Portfolio Management*, Fall, 94–101.

Kahneman D., Paul S. and Tversky A. (1982) *Judgment Under Uncertainty*, University of Cambridge, New York, 1997.

Katz S., Linien S. and Nelson B. (1985) Stock market behavior around bankruptcy model distress and recovery predictions, *Financial Analysts Journal*, January/February, 70–73.

Kaufman G. (1984) Measuring and managing interest rate risk: a primer, *Economic Perspectives, Federal Reserve Bank of Chicago*, 8, January/February, 16–29.

Kealhofer S. (1995) Managing default risk in portfolios of derivatives, in *Derivative Credit Risk*, Risk Books, London.

Keasey K. and McGuiness P. (1976) The failure of UK industrial firms for the period 1976–84, logistic analysis and entropy measures, *Journal of Business Finance and Accounting*, 119–135.

Keenan S. and Sobehart J. (1999) Performance measures for credit risk models, Moody's Research Report.

Kim D. and Santomero A.M. (1988) Risk in banking and capital regulation, *Journal of Finance*, 43, 1218–1233.

Kim I.J., Ramaswamy K. and Sundaresan S.M. (1993) Valuation of corporate fixed-income securities, *Financial Management*, 22(3), 60–78.

Klein R. and Lederman J. (1996) *Derivatives Risk and Responsibility*, Irwin, Chicago, IL.

Koch T. (1988) *Bank Management*, The Dryden Press, Orlando, FL.

Koehn M. and Santomero A.M. (1980) Regulation of bank capital and portfolio risk, *Journal of Finance*, 35, 1235–1244.

Kolb R.W., Timme S.G. and Gay G.D. (1984) Macro versus micro futures hedges at commercial banks, *Journal of the Futures Markets*, 4, 47–54.

Koppenhaver G.D. (1986) Futures options and their use by financial intermediaries, *Economic Perspectives, Federal Reserve Bank of Chicago*, 10, January/February, 18–31.

Koppenhaver G.D. (1987) Standby letters of credit, *Economic Review, Federal Reserve Bank of San Francisco*, Fall, 5–19.

Koyluoglu H.U. and Hickman A. (1999) Reconcilable differences, in *Credit Risk: Models and Management*, Risk Books, London.

Kritzrnan M. (1987) Incentive fees: some problems and some solutions, *Financial Analysts Journal*, 43, January, 21–26.

Kupiec P. (1995) Techniques for verifying the accuracy of risk measurement models, *Journal of Derivatives*, 3, 73–84.

Kupiec P. and O'Brien J. (1995d) Model alternative, *Risk*, 8(6), 37–40.

Kupiec P. and O'Brien J. (1996) Commitment is the key, *Risk*, 9(9), 60–63.

Kupiec P. and O'Brien J. (1997) The pre-commitment approach: using incentives to set market risk capital requirements, Report 1997-14, Board of Governors of the Federal System, Washington, DC.

Kupiec P. (1998) Stress testing in a value at risk framework, *Journal of Derivatives*, 6, Fall, 7–24.

Kupiec P. (1999) Risk capital and VAR, *Journal of Derivatives*, 7(4), Winter, 1–52.

Lando D. (1997) Modeling bonds and derivatives with default risk, in Dempster M. and Pliska S. (eds), *Mathematics of Derivatives Securities*, Cambridge University Press, Cambridge.

Lando D. (1998) On Cox process and credit risky securities, *Review of Derivatives Research*, 2(2/3), 99–120.

Lau A.H.L. (1987) A five-state financial distress prediction model, *Journal of Accounting Research*, 18, 109–131.

Lawrence C. and Robinson G. (1997) Liquidity, dynamic hedging and value at risk, in *Risk Management for Financial Institutions*, Risk Publications, London, pp. 63–72.

Lee C.J. (1981) The pricing of corporate debt: a note, *Journal of Finance*, 36, 1187–1189.

Leeson N. (1996) *Rogue Trader*, Little, Brown & Co., New York.

Leibowitz M.L. (1986) Total portfolio duration: a new perspective on asset allocation, *Financial Analysts Journal*, 42, September/October, 18–29.

Leibowitz M. et al. (1989) A total differential approach to equity duration, *Financial Analysts Journal*, 45, September/October, 30–37.

Leibowitz M.L., Kogelman S. and Bader L.R. (1995), The spread curve and the risk/return decision, *The Journal of Fixed Income*, June, 43–50.

Leland H. (1994) Corporate debt value, bond covenants and optimal capital structure, *Journal of Finance*, 49, 1213–1252.

Leland H.E. and Toft K.B. (1996) Optimal capital structure, endogenous bankruptcy, and the term structure of credit spreads, *Journal of Finance*, 51, July, 987–1019.

Lennox C. (1999a) Identifying failing companies: a re-evaluation of the logit–probit and MDA approaches, *Journal of Economics and Business*, 51(4), 347–364.

Lennox C. (1999b) The accuracy and incremental information content of audit reports in predicting bankruptcy, *Journal of Business, Finance and Accounting*, 26(5&6), 757–778.

Leong K. (1992) Exorcising the demon, in *From Black–Scholes to Black Holes*, Risk Books, London.

Levy H. (1971) *Financial Statement Analysis: A New Approach*, Prentice-Hall, Englewood Cliffs, NJ.

Libby R. (1975) Accounting ratios and the prediction of failure: some behavioral evidence, *Journal of Accounting Research*, 150–161.

Linsmeier I.J. and Pearson N.D. (1996) Risk measurement: an introduction to value-at-risk, Mimeo, University of Illinois at Urbana Champaign.

Lintner J. (1965) Security prices, risk and maximal gains from diversification, *Journal of Finance*, 20, December, 587–615.

Litterman R. and Scheinkman J. (1988) Common factors affecting bond returns, *Journal of Fixed Income*, 1, 54–61.

Litterman R. and Iben I. (1991) Corporate bond valuation and the term structure of credit spreads, *Financial Analysts Journal*, 47, Spring, 52–64.

Litterman R. (1996) Hot spots and hedges, *Journal of Portfolio Management*, Special Issue, December, 52–75.

Litzenberger R.H. (1992) Swaps: plain and fanciful, *Journal of Finance*, 47(3), 831–850.

Longin F. (1996) The asymptotic distribution of extreme stock market returns, *Journal of Business*, 69, 383–408.

Longin F. (2000) From value at risk to stress testing: the extreme value approach, *The Journal of Banking and Finance*, 24, 1097–1130.

Longstaff F.A. and Schwarz E.S. (1992) Interest rate volatility and the term structure: a two-factor general equilibrium model, *Journal of Finance*, 47(4), September, 1259–1282.

Longstaff F.A. and Schwartz E. (1995a) Valuing credit derivatives, *Journal of Fixed Income*, 5(1), June, 6–12.

Longstaff F.A. and Schwartz E. (1995b) A simple approach to valuing risky fixed and floating rate debt, *Journal of Finance*, 50, 789–819.

Lopez J. (1999) Regulatory evaluation of value-at-risk models, *Journal of Risk*, I, Winter, 37–63.

Lucas D.J. (1995a) Default correlation and credit analysis, *Journal of Fixed Income*, 4(4), March, 76–87.

Lucas D.J. (1995b) The effectiveness of downgrade provisions in reducing counterparty credit risk, *The Journal of Fixed Income*, June, 32–41.

Machauer A. and Weber M. (1998) Bank behavior based on internal credit ratings of borrowers, *Journal of Banking and Finance*, 22, 1355–1383.

Margrabe W. (1978) The value of an option to exchange one asset for another, *Journal of Finance*, 33, 177–186.

Mark R. (1997) Risk oversight for the senior manager: controlling risk in dealers, in *Derivatives Handbook*, Wiley Financial Engineering Series, Wiley, London.

Mark R. (1999) Integrated credit risk management, in *Derivative Credit Risk*, 2nd edn, Risk Books, London.

Markowitz H.M. (1952) Portfolio selection, *Journal of Finance*, 7, 77–91.

Markowitz H.M. (1959) *Portfolio Selection: Efficient Diversification of Investments*, Wiley, New York.

Marshall C. and Siegel M. (1997) Value at risk: implementing a risk measurement standard, *Journal of Derivatives*, 4(3), 91–111.

Marshall C.L. (2001a) *Measuring and Managing Operational Risk in Financial Institutions*, Wiley, Asia.

Marshall C. (2001b) *Operational Risks*, Wiley, New York.

Marshall J.F. and Kapner K.R. (1993) *Understanding Swaps*, Wiley, New York.

Martin D. (1977) Early warning of bank failure: a logit regression approach, *Journal of Banking and Finance*, 1, 249–276.

Marvin S. (1995) Capital Allocation: A Study of Current and Evolving Practices in Selected Banks, Office of the Comptroller of the Currency.

Matten C. (2000) *Managing Bank Capital: Capital Allocation and Performance Measurement*, 2nd edn, Wiley, New York.

Matz L.M. (1986) *Bank Solvency. A Banker's Guide to Practical Liquidity Management*, Bank Administration Institute, Rolling Meadows, IL.

May D.O. (1995) Do managerial motives influence firm risk reduction strategies?, *Journal of Finance*, 50, 1275–1290.

McAllister P.H. and Mingo J.J. (1994) Commercial loan risk management, credit-scoring, and pricing: the need for a new shared database, *The Journal of Commercial Lending*, 76(9), 6–22.

McDonough W.J. (1998) Issues for the Basle Accord, Speech delivered before the Conference on Credit Risk Modeling and Regulatory Implications, Bank of England, September [also in the 1998 Annual Report of the Federal Reserve Bank of New York].

McNees S. (1995) An assessment of the official economic forecasts, *New England Economic Review*, July/August, 17–32.

McNeil A. (1999) Extreme value theory for risk managers, in *Internal Modelling and CAD II*, Risk Publications, London, pp. 93–113.

McNew L. (1996) So near, so VAR, *Risk*, 9(10), 54–56.

Meiselman D. (1962) *The Term Structure of Interest Rates*, Prentice-Hall, Englewood Cliffs, NJ.

Mengle D.L. and Walter J.R. (1991) How market value accounting would affect banks, in *Proceedings of the Conference on Bank Structure and Competition*, Federal Reserve Bank of Chicago, Chicago, IL, pp. 511–533.

Merton R.C. (1972) An inter-temporal capital asset pricing model, *Econometrica*, 41(5), 867–888.

Merton R.C. (1973) Theory of rational option pricing, *Bell Journal of Economics and Management Science*, 4(1), 141–183.

Merton R. (1974) On the pricing of corporate debt: the risky structure of interest rates, *Journal of Finance*, 29, 449–470.

Merton R. and Samuelson P. (1974) Fallacy of the log-normal approximation to portfolio decision-making over many periods, *Journal of Financial Economics*, 1, 67–94.

Merton R.C. (1977a) On the pricing of contingent claims and the Modigliani–Miller theorem, *Journal of Financial Economics*, 5, 241–249.

Merton R.C. (1977b) An analytic derivation of the cost of deposit insurance and loan guarantees: an application of modern option pricing theory, *Journal of Banking and Finance*, 1, June, 3–11.

Merton R.C. (1990) *Continuous-Time Finance*, Blackwell, Cambridge, MA.

Merton R.C. and Perold A. (1993) Theory of risk capital for financial firms, *Journal of Applied Corporate Finance*, 6(3), 16–32.

Meyer D.W. (1995/1996) Using quantitative methods to support credit-risk management, *Commercial Lending Review*, 11(1), Winter, 54–70.

Meyer P. and Pfifer H. (1970) Prediction of bank failures, *Journal of Finance*, September.

Mian S. (1996) Evidence on corporate hedging policy, *Journal of Financial and Quantitative Analysis*, 31, 419–439.

Miher M. (1986) Financial innovations: the last twenty years and the next, *Journal of Financial and Quantitative Analysis*, 21, 459–471.

Miller M.H. (1977) Debt and taxes, *Journal of Finance*, 32, 261–275.

Miller M.H. (1991) *Financial Innovation and Market Volatility*, Blackwell, Cambridge, MA.

Miller R. (1998) Refining risk, *Risk Magazine*, August.

Modigliani F. and Miller M.H. (1958) The cost of capital, corporation finance, and the theory of investment, *American Economic Review*, 48, 261–297.

Moody's Investors Service (1996) Corporation Default Rates, 1970–1995, Moody's Investors Service, New York.

Moody's Investors Service (2000a) Historical Default Rates, 1920–1999, Moody's Investors Service, New York.

Moody's Investors Service (2000b) RiskCalc Private Model, Moody's Investors Service, New York, May.

Moro B. (1995) The full monty, *Risk*, 8, February, 57–58.

Moyer (1984) Forecasting financial failure: a re-examination, *Financial Management*, 11–15.

Muralidar A. and Van Der Wouden R. (2000) Optimal ALM strategies for defined benefit pension plans, *Journal of Risk*, 2, Winter, 47–69.

Mussman M. (1995/1996) In praise of RAROC, *Balance Sheet*, Winter.

Nance D.R., Smith C.W. and Smithson C.W. (1993) On the determinants of corporate hedging, *Journal of Finance*, 48(1), 267–284.

Napoli J.A. (1992) Derivative markets and competitiveness, *Economic Perspectives*, *Federal Reserve Bank of Chicago*, 16, July/August, 13–24.

Neftci S. (1996) *Introduction to Mathematics of Financial Derivatives*, Academic Press, New York.

Nelken I. (1999) *Implementing Credit Derivatives*, McGraw-Hill, New York.

Nelson C.R. (1972) *The Term Structure of Interest Rates*, Basic Books, New York.

Nelson C. and Siegel A. (1987) Parsimonious modelling of yield curves, *Journal of Business*, 60, 473–490.

Nelson D. (1990a) ARCH models as diffusion approximations, *Journal of Econometrics*, 45, 7–38.

Nelson D. (1990b) Conditional heteroscedasticity and asset returns: a new approach, *Econometrica*, 59.

Ohlson J.S. (1980) Financial ratios and the probabilistic prediction of bankruptcy, *Journal of Accounting Research*.

Olson R.L. and Schneckenburger K. (1993) New regulation would include interest rate risk in measures of capital adequacy, *Bank Accounting and Finance*, Spring.

Ong M. (1999) *Internal Credit Risk Models*, Risk Books, London.

Papageorgiou A. and Paskov S. (1999) Deterministic simulation for risk management, *Journal of Portfolio Management*, May, 122–127.

Parkinson M. (1980) The extreme value method for estimating the variance of the rate of return, *Journal of Business*, 53, 61–65.

Paskow S. and Taub J. (1995) Faster valuation of financial derivatives, *Journal of Portfolio Management*, 22, 113–120.

Pavel C.A. (1989) *Securitization*, Probus, Chicago, IL.

Pedrosa M. and Roll R. (1998) Systematic risk in corporate bond credit spreads, *Journal of Fixed Income*, 8(3), December, 7–26.

Pérold A. and Schulman E. (1988) The free lunch in currency hedging: implications for investment policy and performance standards, *Financial Analysts Journal*, 44, May, 45–50.

Perold A.F. (1999) Long-Term Capital Management, Case Study, Harvard Business School, N9-200-007.

Picoult E. (1997) Calculating value at risk with Monte Carlo simulation, in *Risk Management for Financial Institutions*, Risk Publications, London, pp. 73–92.

Pinches G., Mingo K. and Caruthers J. (1973) The stability of financial patterns in industrial organizations, *Journal of Finance*, May.

Pindyck R.S. and Rubinfeld D.L. (1991) *Econometric Models and Economic Forecasts*, McGraw-Hill, New York.

Platt H.D. and Platt M.B. (1991) A note on the use of industry-relative ratios of bankruptcy prediction, *Journal of Banking and Finance*, 15(6), 1183–1194.

Platt R. (ed.) (1986) *Controlling Interest Rate Risk*, Wiley, New York.

President's Working Group on Financial Markets (1999) Hedge Funds, Leverage, and the Lessons of Long-Term Capital Management, Washington, DC, April.

Press W.H., Teulosky S.A., Vetterling W.T. and Flannery B.P. (1992) *Numerical Recipes: The Art of Scientific Computing*, Cambridge University Press, Cambridge.

Price Waterhouse (1991) Bank Capital Adequacy and Capital Convergence, Price Waterhouse, London.

Pridgen T. and Verna M.F. (1995) CBO–CLO Rating Criteria, Fitch Research, Fitch Investors Service, March.

Principle J.C., Euliano N.R. and Lefebvre W.C. (2000) *Neural and Adaptive Systems*, Wiley, New York.

Pritsker M. (1997) Evaluating value-at-risk methodologies: accuracy versus computational time, *Journal of Financial Services Research*, 12(2/3), 201–242.

Pyle D. (1986) Capital regulation and deposit insurance, *Journal of Banking and Finance*, 10(2), 189–201.

Queen M. and Roll R. (1987) Firm mortality: using market indicators to predict survival, *Financial Analysts Journal*, May/June, 9–26.

Rafle J. (1996) Reasons to be hedging—1, 2, 3, *Risk*, 9(7), 20–21.

Rawnsley J. (1995b) *Total Risk: Nick Leeson and the Fall of Barings Bank*, Harper, New York.

Ray C. (1993) *The Bond Market: Trading and Risk Management*, Business One Irwin, Homewood, IL.

Rebonato R. (1998) *Interest Rate Option Models*, 2nd edn, Wiley, Chichester.

Rebonato R. and P. Jackel (2000) The most general methodology to create a valid correlation matrix for risk management and option pricing purposes, *Journal of Risk*, 2, Winter, 17–27.

Redington F.M. (1952) Review of the principles of life-office valuations, *Journal of the Institute of Actuaries*, 78, 286–340.

Reed N. (1994) Explosive consolidation, *Risk*, 7(4), 26–32.

Rendleman R. and Bartter B. (1980) The pricing of options on debt securities, *Journal of Financial and Quantitative Analysis*, 15, March, 11–24.

Risk Publications (1995) *Derivative Credit Risk: Advances in Measurement and Management*, Risk Publications, London.

Risk Publications (1996) *Value at Risk*, RISK Supplement, June.

Rodriguez R.J. (1988) Default risk, yield spreads, and time to maturity, *Journal of Financial and Quantitative Analysis*, 23, 111–117.

Rodriguez R.M. (1981) Corporate exchange risk management: theme and aberrations, *Journal of Finance*, 36(2), May, 427–438.

Roley V. (1981) The determinants of the Treasury yield curve, *Journal of Finance*, 36, December, 1103–1126.

Ronn E.I. and Verma A.K. (1986) Pricing risk-adjusted deposit insurance: an option-based model, *Journal of Finance*, 41, September, 871–895.

Rosenberg B. (1974) Extra market components of covariances in security returns, *Journal of Financial and Quantitative Analysis*, 9(2), 263–274.

Ross S.A. (1976) The arbitrage theory of capital asset pricing, *Journal of Economic Theory*, 13, December, 343–362.

Ross S.A., Westerfield R.W. and Jaffe J.F. (1993) *Corporate Finance*, Irwin, Chicago, IL.

Roy A.D. (1952) Safety first and the holding of assets, *Econometrica*, 20, 431–449.

Rubinstein M. and Leland H.E. (1981) Replicating options with positions in stock and cash, *Financial Analyst Journal*, 37, July/August, 63–72.

Rubinstein M. and Cox J.C. (1985) *Options Markets*, Prentice-Hall, Englewood Cliffs, NJ.

Rubinstein M. (1994) Implied binomial trees, *Journal of Finance*, 69, 771–818.

Ryan T.P. (1997) *Modern Regression Methods*, Wiley, New York.

Sang O. and Warga A. (1995) The risk structure of interest rates, *Journal of Finance*, 44, 1351–1360.

Santomero A. and Vinso J. (1977) Estimating the probability of failure for firms in the banking system, *Journal of Banking and Finance*, 185–215.

Santomero A.M. (1995) Financial risk management: the why and hows, *Financial Markets, Institutions and Instruments*, 4(5), 1–14.

Sarig O. and Warga A. (1989) The risk structure of interest rates, *Journal of Finance*, 44, 1351–1360.

Saunders A. (1999) *Credit Risk Measurement*, Wiley, New York.

Schaefer S. (1986) Immunization and duration: a review of theory, performance and applications, in Stern J.M. and Chew Jr D.H. (eds), *The Revolution in Corporate Finance*, Blackwell, Oxford.

Scherr F.C. (1996) Optimal trade credit limits, *Financial Management*, 25(1), Spring, 71–85.

Schwartz R.J. and Clifford W.S. (1993) *Advanced Strategies in Financial Risk Management*, New York Institute of Finance, New York.

Scott D. (1992) *Multivariate Density Estimation: Theory, Practice and Visualization*, Wiley, New York.

Scott J. (1981) The probability of bankruptcy: a comparison of empirical predictions and theoretical models, *Journal of Banking and Finance*, 317–344.

Securities and Exchange Commission (1997) Disclosure of Accounting Policies for Derivative Financial Instruments and Derivative Commodity Instruments and Disclosure of Quantitative and Qualitative Information about Market Risk Inherent in Derivative Financial Instruments, Other Financial Instruments, and Derivative Commodity Instruments, SEC, Washington, DC.

Securities and Exchange Commission (1998) Review of the First Phase of Filings of Disclosures of Quantitative and Qualitative Information about Market Risks Inherent in Derivative Instruments and Other Financial Instruments, SEC, Washington, DC.

Shane H. (1994) Co-movements of low-grade debt and equity returns of highly leveraged firms, *The Journal of Fixed Income*, March, 79–89.

Sharpe W.F. (1964) Capital asset prices: a theory of market equilibrium under conditions of risk, *Journal of Finance*, 19, 425–442.

Sharpe W.F. (1966) Evaluating mutual fund performance, *Journal of Business*, 39, 119–138.

Sharpe W. and Alexander C.J. (1990) *Investments*, Prentice-Hall, Englewood Cliffs, NJ.

Sherdan W.A. (1999) *The Fortune Sellers: The Big Business of Buying and Selling Predictions*, Wiley, New York.

Shimko D., Tejima N. and Van Deventer D. (1993) The pricing of risky debt when interest rates are stochastic, *Journal of Fixed Income*, 3, 58–65.

Shimko D. (1996) VAR for corporates, *Risk*, 9(6), 28–29.

Shimko D. (1997) Accentuate the positive, *Risk*, VAR for End-Users Supplement, March, 10–15.

Shimko D. (ed.) (1999) *Credit Risk, Models and Management*, Risk Books, London.

Shleifer A. and Vishny R.W. (1992) Liquidation values and debt capacity: a market equilibrium approach, *The Journal of Finance*, 4, September, 1343–1366.

Silber W. (1981) Innovation, competition and new contract design in futures markets, *Journal of Futures Markets*, 1, 123–156.

Silverman B.W. (1986) *Density Estimation for Statistics and Data Analysis*, Chapman & Hall, London.

Sinkey J.F. (1978) Identifying problem banks: how do the banking authorities measure a bank's risk exposure?, *Journal of Money, Credit and Banking*, May.

Sinkey J.F. (1985) Regulatory attitudes toward risk, in Aspinwall R.C. and Eisenbeis R.A. (eds), *Handbook for Banking Strategy*, Wiley, New York.

Sinkey J.F. (1992) *Commercial Bank Financial Management*, 4th edn, MacMillan, London.

Skinner F.S. (1994) A trinomial model of bonds with default risk, *Financial Analysts Journal*, March/April, 73–78.

Smith C.W. (1976) Option pricing: a review, *Journal of Financial Economics*, 9, June, 3–54.

Smith C.W. and Stulz R. (1985) The determinants of firms' hedging policies, *Journal of Financial and Qualitative Analysis*, 18, 391–405.

Smith C.W., Smithson C.W. and Wakeman L.M. (1988) The market for interest rate swap, *Financial Management*, 18, Winter, 34–44.

Smith C.W. and Smithson C. (1990) *The Handbook of Financial Engineering*, Harper and Row, New York.

Smith C.W., Smithson C. and Wilford D. (1990) *Strategic Risk Management*, Institutional Investor Series in Finance, Harper and Row, New York.

Smith L.D. and Lawrence E.C. (1995) Forecasting losses on a liquidating long-term loan portfolio, *Journal of Banking and Finance*, 19, 959–985.

Smithson C.W. (1995) A financial risk-management framework for non-financial corporations, *Financial Derivatives and Risk Management*, 4, 3–11.

Smithson C.W. (1996) Credit derivatives, 2, *Risk*, 9(6), 47–48.

Smithson C.W. (1997) Firm-wide risk, *Risk*, 10(3), 25–26.

Smithson C. and Smith C. (1998) *Managing Financial Risk: A Guide to Derivative Products, Financial Engineering, and Value Maximization*, McGraw-Hill, New York.

Sobehart J.R. and Keenan S.C. (1999) An introduction to market-based credit analysis, Moody's Research Report.

Sobehart J.R., Keenan S.C. and Stein R. (2000) Benchmarking Quantitative Default Risk Models: A Validation Methodology, Risk Management Services, Moody's, Rating Methodology, March.

Sorensen E.H. and Bollier T.F. (1994) Pricing swap default risk, *Financial Analysts Journal*, May/June, 23–33.

Spahr R.W., Sunderman M.A. and Amalu C. (1991) Corporate bond insurance: feasibility and insurer risk assessment, *Journal of Risk and Insurance*, 58(3), 418–437.

Stahl G. (1997) Three cheers, *Risk*, 10, October, 67–69.

Standard & Poor's (2000a) *Ratings Performance 1999: Stability and Transition*, Standard & Poor's, New York, February.

Standard & Poor's (2000b) *Credit Model*, Standard & Poor's, New York.

Steiinherr A. (1998) *Derivatives: The Wild Beast of Finance*, Wiley, New York.

Stevenson B.G. and Fadil M.W. (1995) Modern portfolio theory: can it work for commercial loans?, *Commercial Lending Review*, 10(2), Spring, 4–12.

Stoll H. (1969) The relationship between put and call option prices, *Journal of Finance*, 24(5), 801–824.

Stone C. and Zissu A. (ed.) *Risk Based Capital Regulations: Asset Management and Funding Strategies*, Vol. I, *Capital Adequacy*, Vol. II, *Management and Funding Strategies*, Business One Irwin, Chicago, IL.

Studer G. (1999) Market risk computation for nonlinear portfolios, *Journal of Risk*, 1, Summer, 33–53.

Stulz R.M. (1984) Optimal hedging policies, *Journal of Financial and Quantitative Analysis*, 19(2), 127–140.

Stulz R.M. (1996) Rethinking risk management, *Journal of Applied Corporate Finance*, 9(2), 8–24.

Swank T.A. and Root T.H. (1995) Bonds in default: is patience a virtue?, *The Journal of Fixed Income*, June, 26–31.

Taffler H. and Tisshaw J. (1977) Going, going, gone—four factors which predict, *Accountancy*, March, 50–54.

Taffler H. (1984) Empirical models for the monitoring of UK corporations, *Journal of Banking and Finance*, 199–227.

Toevs A.L. and Haney W.C. (1986) Measuring and managing interest rate risk: a guide to asset/liability models used in banks and thrifts, in Platt R.B. (ed.), *Controlling Interest Rate Risk. New Techniques and Applications for Money Management*, Wiley, New York.

Treynor J.L. (1965) How to rate management investment funds, *Harvard Business Review*, 43, 63–75.

Troughton G.H. (ed.) (1986) *Asset–Liability Management*, Irwin, Chicago, IL.

Tuckman B. (1995) *Fixed Income Securities: Tools for Today's Markets*, Wiley, New York.

Turner C. (1996) VAR as an industrial tool, *Risk*, 9, March, 38–40.

Uyemura D.G. and Van Deventer D.R. (1993) *Financial Risk Management in Banking*, Bankers' Publishing Company/Probus, Chicago, IL.

Van Horne J. (1965) Interest rate risk and the term structure of interest rate, *Journal of Political Economy*, 73, August, 344–351.

Van Horne J.C. (1994) *Financial Market Rates & Flows*, 4th edn, Prentice-Hall, Englewood Cliffs, NJ

VaR: Understanding and Applying Value-at-Risk, Risk Books, London, 1997.

Vasicek O. (1977) An equilibrium characterization of the term structure, *Journal of Financial Economics*, 5, 177–188.

Vasicek O. and Fong G. (1982) Term structure modeling using exponential splines, *Journal of Finance*, 37, 339–348.

Vinso J.D. (1979) A determination of the risk of ruin, *Journal of Financial and Quantitative Analysis*, 77–100.

Wagner III H.S. (1996) The pricing of bonds in bankruptcy and financial restructuring, *The Journal of Fixed Income*, June, 40–47.

Wakeman L. (1996) Credit enhancement, in Alexander C. (ed.), *The Handbook of Risk Management and Analysis*, Wiley, New York.

Walwyn H. and Byres W. (1997) Price check, *Risk*, 10(11), 18–24.

Ward D.J. and Griepentrog G.L. (1993) Risk and return in defaulted bonds, *Financial Analysts Journal*, May/June, 61–65.

Warner J. (1997) Bankruptcy costs: some evidence, *Journal of Finance*, 52, May.

Watt R.C. (1985) A factor-analytic approach to bank conditions, *Journal of Banking and Finance*, 9(2), 253–266.

Wee L. and Lee J. (1999) Integrating stress testing with risk management, *Bank Accounting and Finance*, Spring, 7–19.

Weiss L. (1990) Bankruptcy resolution: direct costs and violation of priority claims, *Journal of Finance and Economics*, 27(2), 285–314.

Weston J.F. and Copeland T.E. (1989) *Managerial Finance*, The Dryden Press, Orlando, FL.

Whittaker J.G. (1987) Interest rate swaps: risk and regulation, *Economic Review, Federal Reserve Bank of Kansas City*, 72, March, 3–13.

Wilcox A. (1971) Simple theory of financial ratios as predictors of failure, *Journal of Accounting Research*, 389–395.

Wilcox A. (1973) Prediction of business failure using accounting data, *Journal of Accounting Research*, Supplement on Empirical Research in Accounting, 163–190.

Wilcox A. (1977) Gambler's ruin: prediction of business failure using accounting data, *Sloan Management Review*, 12, September.

Williams D. (2000) Selecting and implementing enterprise risk management technologies, in Lore M. and Borodovsky L. (eds), *The Professional Handbook of Risk Management*, Butterworth, London.

Wilson D. (1995) VAR in operation, *Risk*, 8, December, 24–25.

Wilson J.S.G. (ed.) (1988) *Managing Banks Assets and Liabilities*, Euromoney Publications, London.

Wilson T. (1994) Debunking the myths, *Risk*, 7, April, 67–72.

Wilson T. (1997a) Portfolio credit risk I, *Risk*, 10(9), 111–117.

Wilson T. (1997b) Portfolio credit risk II, *Risk*, 10(10), 56–61.

Wyderko L. (1989) *A Practical Guide to Duration Analysis*, Probus, Chicago, IL.

Zaik E.T., Walter J., Kelling C. and James C. (1996) RAROC at Bank of America: from theory to practice, *Journal of Applied Corporate Finance*, 9(2), 83–92.

Zangari P. (1996) A VAR methodology for portfolios that include options, *Risk Metrics Monitor*, First Quarter, 4–12.

Zarnowitz V. (1979) An analysis of annual and multiperiod quarterly forecast of aggregate income, output and price level, *Journal of Business*, 52(1), 1–32.

Zavgren C. (1983) The prediction of corporate failure: the state of the art, *Journal of Accounting Literature*, 2, 1–37.

Zavgren C.Y. (1985) Assessing the vulnerability to failure of American industrial firms: a logistic analysis, *Journal of Business Finance and Accounting*.

Ziemba W. and Mulvey J. (1998) *Worldwide Asset and Liability Modeling*, Cambridge University Press, Cambridge.

Zmijewski M.E. (1984) Methodological issues related to the estimation of financial distress prediction models, *Journal of Accounting Research*, Supplement on Current Econometric Issues in Accounting Research, 59–82.

Index

Note: Pages in *italics* refer to Figures; those in **bold** refer to Tables